Russian Grammar

Second Edition

James S. Levine, Ph.D.

Associate Professor of Russian
and Director of Russian Studies
George Mason University

Schaum's Outline Series

New York Chicago San Francisco
Lisbon London Madrid Mexico City
Milan New Dehli San Juan
Seoul Singapore Sydney Toronto

The McGraw·Hill Companies

To Jody, Sasha, and Erica

JAMES S. LEVINE received his B.A. in History and Russian from the State University of New York at Buffalo, and his M.A. and Ph.D. in Slavic Linguistics from the University of Illinois at Urbana-Champaign. Dr. Levine also studied Russian language, literature, and culture at Moscow University and St. Petersburg University, Russia. He has taught Russian for the past thirty-five years at several universities, including the University of Illinois, the University of Maryland at College Park, and George Mason University in Fairfax, Virginia. He is currently Associate Professor of Russian at George Mason University, where he is also Director of Russian Studies. He has served as a consultant on foreign language education projects for the American Council on Education, and as a specialist reviewer and panelist for the National Endowment for the Humanities, the National Security Education Program, the Institute of International Education, and the American Council of Teachers of Russian. He is cotranslator of the *Black Book* (Holocaust Library), coeditor of *Case in Slavic* (Slavica Publishers, Inc.), and author of numerous articles on Russian language and linguistics.

Schaum's Outline of
RUSSIAN GRAMMAR

6 7 8 9 0 CUS CUS 0 1 4 3

ISBN 978-0-07-161169-5
MHID 0-07-161169-X

Sponsoring Editor: Anya Kozorez
Production Supervisor: Tama L. Harris
Editing Supervisor: Maureen B. Dennehy
Project Supervision: Village Bookworks, Inc.

Library of Congress Cataloging-in-Publication Data

Levine, James S., 1949–
Schaum's outline of Russian grammar. — 2nd ed.
p. cm. — (Schaum's outlines)
Includes index.
ISBN-13: 978-0-07-161169-5
ISBN-10: 0-07-161169-X
1. Russian language—Grammar. I. Title. II. Title: Russian grammar.
PG2112.L394 2009
491.782′421—dc22 2009007885

Preface to the Second Edition

The second edition of *Schaum's Outline of Russian Grammar* contains a number of amendments and improvements. The section on vowel reduction in Chapter 1 has been revised, and the information on the pronunciation of unstressed vowels now conforms more precisely to current norms. The section on money and prices in Chapter 6 has been amended and updated to reflect the current value of Russian currency. New illustrative examples have been added, and stylistic improvements made, throughout the book. The most significant improvement in the second edition, however, is a new comprehensive Index of Russian Words and Affixes, which will now provide the user with easier access to information about almost any Russian word, or grammatical form, mentioned in the book.

I wish to express my sincere appreciation to several people who helped me with this new edition. Two colleagues, Marianna Ryshina-Pankova (Georgetown University) and Tatiana M. Vasilyeva (George Mason University), both graciously agreed to read the book, and each of them offered many valuable suggestions for improvement.

My thanks also go to my friend Victor Zabolotnyi, who, over the years, has answered my many questions about subtleties, style, and changes in Russian language usage. I am also grateful to my friend and former professor William S. Hamilton (Wake Forest University) for sharing his observations and insightful comments on my revisions in Chapter 1. My gratitude goes as well to the *Schaum's Outlines* editorial staff at McGraw-Hill Professional, who invited me to prepare this new edition. In particular, I am grateful to Anya Kozorev (Sponsoring Editor), Tama L. Harris (Production Supervisor), and Kimberly-Ann Eaton (Associate Editor). I am likewise indebted to Daniel Franklin and Terry Yokota of Village Bookworks, who transformed the manuscript into the finished book and whose meticulous copyediting and perceptive queries helped me to clarify several points. Naturally, any errors or infelicities that remain in the second edition are my responsibility alone.

Last, but not least, I would like to thank my students at George Mason University. Their enthusiastic response to the first edition leaves me with the hope that future students will also benefit from this new and improved edition of *Schaum's Outline of Russian Grammar.*

JAMES S. LEVINE

Preface to the First Edition

Schaum's Outline of Russian Grammar is intended as a study aid to assist English speakers in their acquisition of contemporary Russian. It is designed for students from the beginning to advanced levels: beginning students can use this book as a companion to any basic Russian language textbook, while intermediate-advanced students will find the book useful as a review text and reference for grammar. For individuals learning the language outside of an academic setting, the numerous practice exercises and answer key make it possible to use the Outline as a text for independent study.

The book consists of eight chapters: The Sounds of Russian; Nouns; Prepositions; Pronouns; Adjectives and Adverbs; Numbers, Dates, and Time; Verbs; and Conjunctions.

The first chapter, "The Sounds of Russian," introduces the Cyrillic alphabet and presents a guide to the pronunciation of Russian consonants and vowels. This chapter also presents aspects of the Russian writing system, e.g., spelling rules, peculiarities of capitalization, transliteration from English to Russian, as well as a brief section on different Russian letter styles.

Chapters 2–8 present all the essentials for a solid foundation in Russian grammar. Grammatical terms, including the basic parts of speech and associated grammatical concepts (e.g., gender, number, and case in the noun; tense, aspect, mood, and voice in the verb), are clearly explained and illustrated with numerous examples. Comparisons between English and Russian—their similarities and differences with respect to particular grammatical features—are made throughout the book. In the author's view, such comparisons will provide native speakers of English with greater insight into the structure of their own language, which in turn will enhance their understanding and ultimate mastery of the grammatical structure of Russian.

One of the most challenging tasks for English speakers is mastering the variable forms of Russian words, for example, the declensional endings of nouns, pronouns, adjectives, and numbers, as well as the changes undergone by verbs in conjugation. In *Schaum's Outline of Russian Grammar* the task of learning grammatical endings is made easier by highlighting them in declension tables throughout the text. The presentation of verb conjugation addresses the dual audience of Russian learners: those who have learned verbs the traditional way, and others who have been exposed to the "single-stem system." Verbs are classified according to their suffixed or nonsuffixed "basic (single) stem," an approach which has become increasingly common in American textbooks at the first- and second-year levels. In addition, a representative example of each verb class is fully conjugated in a special box, and is then followed by a description of its stress and consonant alternation properties. All students will benefit from the thorough coverage of verbal aspect, and of the other major topics in the Russian verb, e.g., the conditional and subjunctive, verbs in **-ся**, verbs of motion, participles, and verbal adverbs.

The development of grammatical accuracy requires a good deal of practice in manipulating the structures of the language. In this book numerous drills and exercises follow the explanations of each grammatical point and provide practice and reinforcement of the covered material. Together with the answer key, the practice exercises enable students to gauge their own understanding and progress. Finally, the comprehensive index provides quick and easy access to information.

JAMES S. LEVINE

Acknowledgments to the First Edition

I am indebted to the many Russian language specialists whose work I consulted, and benefited from, in writing various portions of this book. In particular, I would like to acknowledge my debt to the following: G. G. Timofeeva's *Новые английские заимствования в русском языке* in the discussion of English-to-Russian transliteration (Chapter 1); Johanna Nichols' *Predicate Nominals: A Partial Surface Syntax of Russian* in the description of predicate nominatives and predicate instrumentals after forms of **быть** (Chapter 2) and in the description of the two types of **это** sentences (Chapter 4); Derek Offord's *Using Russian: A Guide to Contemporary Usage* in the presentation of prepositions (Chapter 3); Genevra Gerhart's *The Russian's World* in the presentation of numbers and fractions (Chapter 6); Alexander Nakhimovsky's *Overview of Russian Conjugation* in the description of the single-stem verb system (Chapter 7); and O. P. Rassudova's *Aspectual Usage in Modern Russian* in the discussion of the meaning and uses of the aspects (Chapter 7). A valuable source of information on topics throughout the book was Terrence Wade's *A Comprehensive Russian Grammar.* Complete references for these works, and for other sources consulted, are given in the Bibliography.

I would like to thank the following friends, colleagues, and students who helped in various ways in the preparation of this book. Particular thanks must go to William S. Hamilton (Wake Forest University), whose teaching first inspired me to learn Russian, and who has been a mentor and friend throughout my career. His advice and comments on an earlier draft of this book resulted in several improvements. I am also grateful to Thomas R. Beyer, Jr. (Middlebury College), who reviewed the manuscript and wrote a detailed report with many helpful recommendations. To Marybeth Spain go my sincere thanks for her help in the preparation of Chapter 8; certain formulations on the use of conjunctions originated with her, as did many of this chapter's illustrative examples. The book has fewer errors thanks to careful proofreading by Mikhail Feldman, who read an early draft, and by Tatiana Vasilyeva, who read the page proofs for Chapter 3. I am also deeply grateful to Viktor Zabolotnyi, with whom I frequently consulted on questions of style and usage. He gave most generously of his time, sharing his native intuitions and judgments on my examples, often suggesting adjustments or replacing my examples with his own.

I would like to express my appreciation to the editorial staff of Schaum Publications of McGraw-Hill: Barbara Gilson (Editorial Director), who initiated the process of having a Russian volume added to the foreign-language grammars in the Schaum's Outline Series; Mary Loebig Giles (Associate Editor), who handled correspondence and coordinated the initial review of the manuscript; Maureen Walker (Editing Supervisor); and Meaghan McGovern (Editorial Assistant), who coordinated the final review of the manuscript, and was always helpful in responding to my questions and concerns. I am also grateful to the staff at Keyword Publishing Services Ltd, London: Alan Hunt, who expertly managed the copy-editing and typesetting of the manuscript, and Olga Abbott, who read the final proofs and helped eliminate a number of errors that I had missed. This book is certainly a better one for the efforts of all those mentioned, but any inaccuracies and mistakes that remain are mine alone.

On a more personal note, I would like to thank my wife, Jody, and my daughters, Sasha and Erica, for generously tolerating my frequent absences and my near monopoly of the computer over the past year and a half. Their love and enthusiasm make everything possible. This book is dedicated to them.

Contents

The Sounds of Russian

The Russian (Cyrillic) Alphabet

The Russian alphabet is also known as the Cyrillic alphabet, named in honor of St. Cyril, the Greek monk and scholar who is credited with devising an early version of it. The Russian alphabet contains 33 letters, most of which represent sounds similar to those of English.

Alphabet

CYRILLIC LETTER	NAME OF LETTER	ENGLISH EQUIVALENT (APPROXIMATE)	CYRILLIC LETTER	NAME OF LETTER	ENGLISH EQUIVALENT (APPROXIMATE)
А а	a	*a* as in *father*	Р р	er	*r* as in *better*
Б б	be	*b* as in *bet*	С с	es	*s* as in *sun*
В в	ve	*v* as in *very*	Т т	te	*t* as in *Tanya*
Г г	ge	*g* as in *get*	У у	u	*u* as in *flu*
Д д	de	*d* as in *dog*	Ф ф	ef	*f* as in *fun*
Е е	ye	*ye* as in *yes*	Х х	kha	*ch* as in *Bach*
Ё ё	yo	*yo* as in *York*	Ц ц	tse	*ts* as in *cats*
Ж ж	zhe	*z* as in *azure*	Ч ч	che	*ch* as in *cheese*
З з	ze	*z* as in *zoo*	Ш ш	sha	*sh* as in *shoe*
И и	i	*i* as in *visa*	Щ щ	shcha	*shsh* as in *fresh sheen*
Й й	i kratkoye (short i)	y as in *boy*	ъ	tvyordiy znak (hard sign)	no sound value
К к	ka	*k* as in *skate*	ы	yeri	*i* as in *vigor*
Л л	el	*l* as in *lot*	ь	myagkiy znak (soft sign)	no sound value
М м	em	*m* as in *Mike*			
Н н	en	*n* as in *net*	Э э	e oborotnoye (reversed e)	*e* as in *echo*
О о	o	*o* as in *ought*			
П п	pe	*p* as in *span*	Ю ю	yu	*yu* as in *Yukon*
			Я я	ya	*ya* as in *yacht*

The alphabet chart above lists approximate English equivalents for the sound values of the Cyrillic letters as well as the *Russian names* of the letters in the Cyrillic alphabet. It is important to learn the pronunciation of the letter names, as well as the order in which they occur, for several reasons. First, in order to pronounce the many acronyms that occur in Russian, one must know the names of the Cyrillic letters, since many acronyms are pronounced as a succession of individual letters, e.g., **МБ** is pronounced "em-be" and stands for **Миров́ой б́анк** *World Bank,* **ЦБР** is pronounced "tse-be-er" for **Центр́альный б́анк Росс́ии** *Central Bank of Russia,* and **РФ** is pronounced "er-ef" for **Росс́ийская Федер́ация** *Russian*

Federation. Second, knowing the names of the letters is important for those situations when it is necessary to spell words such as names and addresses, for example, when traveling in Russia or when speaking to Russians on the telephone. Finally, when looking up words in a dictionary, knowing the correct sequence of the letters will make the search for words easier and faster.

Shapes and Sounds

Several Cyrillic letters are immediately recognizable from their similarity to English letters, and some of these are also pronounced close to their English counterparts. However, rarely are there exact sound equivalents between languages, and so the comparisons between Russian and English sounds given in this pronunciation key should be viewed only as a guide to correct pronunciation in Russian. In order to acquire native-like pronunciation it is important not only to study the differences between English and Russian sounds, but also to *practice* the correct Russian pronunciation with CDs and DVDs, and, of course, to take every opportunity to listen to, and talk with, native speakers of Russian.

In illustrating the sounds of Russian consonants and vowels, we use a *phonetic transcription,* which is shown in square brackets [ ]. The transcription used in this book employs the Latin letters of English and, when needed, a few diacritical marks, e.g., the sounds associated with the letter combinations *sh* and *ch* in English *shop* and *cheese* are represented as [š] and [č], respectively, with the "haček" symbol ˇ above the letter. Also, Russian stressed vowels (discussed below) are represented by an acute accent mark [´]. It should be noted that the English equivalents of the Russian vowels in the alphabet chart are for the pronunciation of these vowels when they are stressed. If they are not stressed, they may shift to less distinct values, as we shall see below.

Letters Similar to English Letters in Form and Pronunciation

LETTER	SOUND	RUSSIAN EXAMPLE	ENGLISH TRANSLATION	APPROXIMATE PRONUNCIATION
А а	[á]	áкт	*act*	like *a* in English *father,* but with the mouth open a bit wider
О о	[ó]	кóт	*cat*	like *o* in English *ought,* but with the lips more rounded and protruded
Е е	[é]	тéма	*theme*	like *e* in English *tempo*
М м	[m]	мáма	*mom*	just like English *m*
К к	[k]	кóмик	*comic*	like English *k,* but without the puff of air following it; like English *skate*
Т т	[t]	тóм	*tome*	like English *t,* but a pure dental, with the tip of the tongue touching the upper teeth, not the teeth ridge as in English

Letters Similar to English Letters in Form, But Not in Pronunciation

Other Cyrillic letters correspond in shape to letters in English, but they correspond in pronunciation to *different* English letters. These are examples of *faux amis,* or "false friends," in the alphabet.

LETTER	SOUND	RUSSIAN EXAMPLE	ENGLISH TRANSLATION	APPROXIMATE PRONUNCIATION
У у	[ú]	у́тка	*duck*	like *u* in English *flu,* but shorter and with the lips more rounded and protruded
В в	[v]	во́дка	*vodka*	just like English *v*
Н н	[n]	нéт	*no*	like *n* in English, but a pure dental, with the tip of the tongue touching the upper teeth (like Russian **т**)
Р р	[r]	ка́рта	*map*	like *r* in English *better* or *ladder,* i.e., a flapped [r], produced by the tip of the tongue tapping against the teeth ridge
С с	[s]	нóс	*nose*	like the *s* and *c* in English *sauce,* but a pure dental, with the tongue touching the upper teeth; never like the *c* in English *cat* or *contact*

Letters Corresponding to Letters in Greek

In addition to the letters that are shaped like those in English, a few Cyrillic letters resemble letters in the Greek alphabet, on which they were modeled. The following letters were fashioned after the Greek letters *gamma, delta, lambda, pi, phi,* and *chi,* respectively (also, Greek *rho* served as a model for Cyrillic **Р**, listed in the previous group due to its misleading similarity to English *p*).

LETTER	SOUND	RUSSIAN EXAMPLE	ENGLISH TRANSLATION	APPROXIMATE PRONUNCIATION
Г г	[g]	га́з	*gas*	like *g* in English *get*; never like the first or second *g* in *George*
Д д	[d]	дóм	*house*	like *d* in English, but a pure dental, with the tip of the tongue touching the upper teeth (like Russian **т** and **н**)
Л л	[l]	Ла́ра	*Lara*	like *l* in English *pill,* but with the tongue farther back in the mouth
П п	[p]	па́спорт	*passport*	like *p* in English *span*; not like the "aspirated" *p* in English *pan*
Ф ф	[f]	кафé	*café*	like *f* in English
Х х	[x]	са́хар	*sugar*	like *ch* in German *Bach*

Remaining Letters

The remaining Cyrillic letters do not resemble letters in English or Greek. At least one letter, **ш** [š], is modeled after the Hebrew letter *shin*. Three others look like the reverse of English letters: Cyrillic **я** [ya] has the shape of a backward English **R**. Cyrillic **и** [i] is the reverse of English **N**. And Cyrillic **э** [e] is shaped like a reverse, but more rounded, English **E**.

LETTER	SOUND	RUSSIAN EXAMPLE	ENGLISH TRANSLATION	APPROXIMATE PRONUNCIATION
Б б	[b]	бана́н	*banana*	like *b* in English, but not aspirated (like Russian **п**)
З з	[z]	ва́за	*vase*	like *z* in English, but with the tip of the tongue touching the upper teeth (like Russian **с**)
Ё ё	[yo]	ёлка	*fir tree*	like *yo* in English *York* and *yore*
Ж ж	[ž]	журна́л	*magazine*	like *z* in English *azure,* but with the tongue farther back and the lips rounded
И и	[i]	ди́ск	*disk*	like *i* in English *visa*
Й й	[y]	ма́й	*May*	a "glide," like *y* in English *toy, boy*
Ц ц	[c]	ца́рь	*tsar*	similar to the *ts* in English *nuts,* but pronounced together as one sound
Ч ч	[č']	ча́й	*tea*	like *ch* in English *cheese* but softer, with the tongue raised higher
Ш ш	[š]	шо́к	*shock*	like *sh* in English, but with the tongue farther back in the mouth
Щ щ	[šš']	бо́рщ	*borsch*	similar to *shsh* in English *fresh sheen,* but softer, with the tongue higher and more forward in the mouth
ы	[ɨ]	сы́н	*son*	no close English equivalent; similar to *i* in English *sin, vigor,* but with the tongue drawn farther back and the lips spread
Э э	[e]	э́ра	*era*	similar to *e* in English *echo,* but with the mouth open wider
Ю ю	[yu]	ю́мор	*humor*	similar to English *yu* in *Yukon,* and *u* in *use*
Я я	[ya]	Я́лта	*Yalta*	similar to English *ya* in *Yalta* or *yacht*

The Two "Signs"

Finally, Russian has two "signs" that, by themselves, have no sound value, but serve important functions, especially the "soft sign":

ь soft sign — indicates that a preceding consonant is "soft" or "palatalized," which in transcription is represented by an apostrophe after the consonant, e.g., **со́ль** *salt* [sól'] (see the section Paired Consonants: Hard and Soft below). Between a soft consonant (C) and a vowel (V) the letter **ь** indicates the sequence C + [y] + V, e.g., **Татья́на** is pronounced **Та** [t' + y + á] **на**.

ъ hard sign — occurs only after a prefix ending in a consonant before a root beginning with a vowel, e.g., **въе́зд** *entrance* **в** + **ъ** + **езд** where **в** is a prefix meaning "in" and **езд** is a root meaning "drive"; **ъ** also indicates the presence of [y] before a vowel, e.g., **въ** [ye] **зд**.

To summarize, of the 33 letters in the Cyrillic alphabet, 10 are vowels, 20 are consonants, one is a "glide" (**й** [y]), and two are "signs," the "soft sign" (**ь**) and the "hard sign" (**ъ**).

The Vowels

There are five vowel *sounds* represented by 10 vowel *letters,* two letters for each sound. The vowel letters can be divided into two series: the "hard series" and the "soft series."

Hard Series	а [a]	э [e]	о [o]	у [u]	ы [ɨ]
Soft Series	я [ya]	е [ye]	ё [yo]	ю [yu]	и [i]
	['a]	['e]	['o]	['u]	['i]

The terms "hard" and "soft" do not refer to the vowels themselves, but to the consonants that precede them. A hard consonant is the basic articulation of the consonant, just as it is described above in this pronunciation key. A *soft,* or *palatalized,* consonant is identical except for one important modification—in pronouncing a soft consonant the tongue is simultaneously raised toward the palate, or roof of the mouth. Most Russian consonants have these two forms of pronunciation. When a consonant is capable of occurring either hard or soft, it will be hard before the letters **а э о у ы**, and soft before the letters **я е ё ю и**. The soft series vowels with a preceding soft consonant are indicated in transcription by ['a] ['e] ['o] ['u] ['i], the apostrophe indicating the soft pronunciation of the consonant. In addition, the soft series vowels **я е ё ю** (but not **и**) are pronounced with a preceding [y] (as [ya] [ye] [yo] [yu]) in the following positions.

Word-Initial	Я́лта	[yá]	Е́льцин	[yé]	ёлка	[yó]	ю́мор	[yú]
After a Vowel	моя́	[yá]	поéл	[yé]	моё	[yó]	мою́	[yú]
After ь and ъ	друзья́	[yá]	въéзд	[yé]	бельё	[yó]	мáтерью	[yu]

Stressed Vowels

Russian, like English, is characterized by a heavy *stress* within a word. A stressed vowel is one that is emphasized by pronouncing it with greater force, or louder, than unstressed vowels. The stressed vowels are also tense and a bit longer than unstressed vowels in the word. However, even when stressed, Russian vowels are shorter than the long vowels in English, which may begin as one sound and *glide* into another sound, producing a diphthong. In pronouncing Russian vowels it is important to avoid pronouncing them like English diphthongs. Compare, for example, the vowel sound [uw] in English *boots* with Russian [u] in **бýтсы** *soccer boots*; the sound [oə] in English *cork* with [o] in Russian **кóрка** *crust*; and the sound [iy] in English *mere, feel,* and *fear* with [i] in Russian **ми́р** *peace,* **филé** *fillet,* and **фи́рма** *firm.* The Russian vowels in these examples, and in Russian words generally, are monophthongs, that is, they begin and end with the same sound.

Stress in Russian, as in English, is "free," that is, it can fall on any vowel in the word: first (**дóктор** *doctor*), second (**профéссор** *professor*), third (**ресторáн** *restaurant*), fourth (**америкáнец** *American*), etc. Russian stress is also "mobile," i.e., the stress may shift from one syllable to another within the grammatical forms of the same word, for example, within the singular and plural forms of a noun: **áдрес** *address* and **адресá** *addresses.* Also, stress can determine the meaning and/or the part of speech of certain words that are spelled alike, e.g., **мукá** *flour* and **мýка** *torture,* the adverb **дóма** *at home* and the plural noun **домá** *houses.* (The same phenomenon occurs in English: Only the stress differentiates the noun *pérmit* and the verb *permít.*) For these reasons, it is very important when learning new words to learn the stress of the word as well. Stressed vowels are not normally marked in a Russian text, but they are marked in dictionaries and textbooks of Russian. Note also that the vowel letter **ё** [yo]/['o] always indicates a stressed vowel, so it is the only vowel whose stress is not indicated by the acute accent ´.

Unstressed Vowels

The stressed vowel in a word is emphasized at the expense of the other, unstressed vowels. Thus, in relation to the stressed vowel, unstressed vowels are usually shorter and lax, i.e., pronounced in a more "relaxed" way. These changes are referred to as *vowel reduction.* Not all vowels in Russian are reduced. For example, the vowels **ю/у** and **и/ы** when unstressed remain essentially the same. Nor can the vowel **ё** ever be reduced, since this vowel is *always* stressed. Therefore, the only vowels that may have a reduced pronunciation are **а о э я е**. The first two vowels, **а** and **о**, are reduced to varying degrees, depending on their location in relation to the stressed syllable. The least amount of reduction occurs in the syllable immediately preceding the stressed syllable—called the "pretonic" syllable—and in word-initial position. In any other syllable before or after the stress, the vowels **а** and **о** undergo a further reduction. It is important to keep in mind that a preposition and its object are pronounced as if they were a *single* phonetic unit, i.e., as one word. As a result, unstressed vowels in prepositions are reduced according to their position in relation to the stressed vowel of the following word. Examples are given below.

Vowel Reduction Rules

1. *Reduction of the Vowels* **а** *and* **о**

   (a) **а** [a] and **о** [o] → [ʌ]
   (b) **а** [a] and **о** [o] → [ə]

   (a) In pretonic (i.e., the syllable immediately preceding the stressed syllable) and/or word-initial position both **а** and **о** are pronounced as a slightly shorter and more lax *a* sound. In phonetic transcription it is customary to represent this sound with the symbol [ʌ].

   Pretonic

   бана́н [bʌnán] *banana*
   Москва́ [mʌskvá] *Moscow*
   доска́ [dʌská] *blackboard*
   вопро́с [vʌprós] *question*
   над до́мом [nʌddóməm] *above the house*
   до за́втра [dʌzáftrə] *until tomorrow*
   под но́сом [pʌdnósəm] *under the nose*

   Word-Initial

   она́ [ʌná] *she*
   окно́ [ʌknó] *window*
   отве́т [ʌtv'ét] *answer*
   оборо́т [ʌbʌrót] *turn*
   анана́с [ʌnʌnás] *pineapple*
   об э́том [ʌbétəm] *about this*

   (b) In any position other than pretonic or word-initial, Russian **а** and **о** are pronounced even shorter and more lax, similar to the sound of the first and last vowel, respectively, of English ***about*** and *sof****a***. This sound is represented with the symbol [ə].

   ма́ма [mámə] *mom*
   соба́ка [sʌbákə] *dog*
   молоко́ [məlʌkó] *milk*
   ко́мната [kómnətə] *room*
   под водо́й [pədvʌdóy] *under water*
   до́ктор [dóktər] *doctor*
   хорошо́ [xərʌšó] *good*
   городо́к [gərʌdók] *town*
   панора́ма [pənʌrámə] *panorama*
   на мосту́ [nəmʌstú] *on the bridge*

   NOTE: When preceded by the consonant **ч**, unstressed **а** is pronounced [ɩ], a sound midway between [i] and [e], e.g., in **часы́** [č'ɩsí] *watch,* **части́ца** [č'ɩst'ícə] *particle,* **частота́** [č'ɩstʌtá] *frequency.*

   NOTE: When preceded by the consonant **ж**, unstressed **а** is pronounced [ɨ], e.g., in the words **жале́ть** [žɨl'ét'] *to regret* and **к сожале́нию** [ksəžɨl'én'iyu] *unfortunately.*

2. *Reduction of the Vowel* **э** [e]

   э [e] → [ɩ]

   In many words the vowel **э** [e] when unstressed is pronounced [ɩ]. This vowel letter occurs primarily in words of foreign origin, and almost always at the beginning of the word.

эква́тор [ɩkvátər] *equator*	эмба́рго [ɩmbárgə] *embargo*
эпо́ха [ɩpóxə] *epoch*	эконо́мика [ɩkʌnóm'ikə] *economics*

3. *Reduction of the Vowels* **я** [ya] *and* **е** [ye]

   (a) **я** [ya] and **е** [ye] → [yɩ]/[ɩ]
   (b) **я** [ya] → [yə]/[ə]
   е [ye] → [yɩ]/[ɩ]

   (a) Except in grammatical endings, unstressed **я** [ya] and **е** [ye] are both pronounced [yɩ] in word-initial position or after a vowel; after a soft consonant, these vowels are pronounced [ɩ], without the initial [y].

   Word-Initial

язы́к [yɩzɨ́k] *language*	езда́ [yɩzdá] *ride*
яйцо́ [yɩycó] *egg*	еда́ [yɩdá] *food*

   After a Vowel

по́яс [póyɩs] *belt*	поеди́м [pəyɩd'ím] *let's eat*

   After a Soft Consonant

телефо́н [t'ɩl'ɩfón] *telephone*	ветерина́р [v'ɩt'ɩr'inár] *veterinarian*
мясни́к [m'ɩsn'ík] *butcher*	де́сять [d'és'ɩt'] *ten*

   (b) In grammatical endings, the pronunciation of unstressed **я** is usually distinguished from unstressed **е**, as indicated in the following general rules.

   (i) **я** [ya] → [yə]/[ə]

но́вая [nóvəyə] *new*	си́няя [s'ín'əyə] *dark blue*
ба́ня [bán'ə] *bathhouse*	галере́я [gəl'ɩr'éyə] *gallery*

   (ii) **е** [ye] → [yɩ]/[ɩ]

в ба́не [vbán'ɩ] *in the bathhouse*	к Та́не [ktán'ɩ] *to Tanya*
мо́ре [mór'ɩ] *sea*	извини́те [izv'in'ít'ɩ] *excuse (me)*
чита́ет [č'itáyɩt] *(s)he reads*	краси́вее [krʌs'ív'ɩyɩ] *prettier*

   NOTE: In certain endings, an alternative, old Moscow pronunciation of unstressed **е** [ye] as [yə]/[ə] is also acceptable, e.g., in the neuter nouns **мо́ре** [mór'ə] *sea* and **по́ле** [pól'ə] *field.* This pronunciation also occurs in the neuter singular adjective endings **-ое**/**-ее**, where the final **-е** is pronounced [yə], just like the final **-я** in the feminine ending **-ая**/**-яя**, e.g., both **но́вое** and **но́вая** are pronounced [nóvəyə].

   NOTE: After the consonants **ш**, **ж**, and **ц** in posttonic syllables, unstressed **е** is typically pronounced [ə], e.g., in **хоро́шее** [xʌróšəyə] *good,* **с му́жем** [smúžəm] *with (her) husband,* **вы́шел** [vɨ́šəl] *walked out.* However, in certain endings after these same consonants, unstressed **е** is pronounced like the vowel **ы** [ɨ], such as in the suffix of comparatives, e.g., in **ра́ньше** [rán'šɨ] *earlier,* **бли́же** [bl'ížɨ] *closer.* This pronunciation also occurs in pretonic position, e.g., in the words **жена́** [žɨná] *wife,* **шесто́й** [šɨstóy] *sixth,* **цена́** [cɨná] *price.*

The Consonants

There are 20 consonants in Russian, 15 of which are paired, that is, they occur in pairs of hard and soft (palatalized) versions.

Paired Consonants: Hard and Soft

б	[b]–[b']	д	[d]–[d']	л	[l]–[l']	п	[p]–[p']	т	[t]–[t']
в	[v]–[v']	з	[z]–[z']	м	[m]–[m']	р	[r]–[r']	ф	[f]–[f']
г	[g]–[g']	к	[k]–[k']	н	[n]–[n']	с	[s]–[s']	х	[x]–[x']

A soft consonant is pronounced the same way as its hard counterpart, except for one important additional feature—the consonant is pronounced with the middle of the tongue raised toward the roof of the mouth, as in the pronunciation of the vowel **и**. As a result, the soft consonant has an [i]-like quality superimposed on it. Soft consonants are represented in transcription as the consonant letter followed by an apostrophe, e.g., a soft **т** is [t']. Also, it is important to remember that a soft consonant is *one* sound, not two. Be careful to avoid pronouncing a soft consonant as a hard consonant with a following [y] sound, that is, avoid pronouncing [t + y], e.g., the Russian word for "aunt," **тётя**, is pronounced [t'ót'ə], NOT *[tyótyə].

Since the same consonant letter is used for both the hard and soft versions of the consonant, it is only possible to determine which ones are hard and which are soft by what *follows* the consonant in spelling. Remember that hard consonants are those that are followed by one of the hard series vowels **а э о у ы**, or they occur with no vowel following. Soft consonants are those followed by one of the soft series vowels **я е ё ю и**, or they are followed by the soft sign **ь**. Examples follow.

гуля́ть	**г** is hard; **л**, **т** are soft
телефо́н	**т**, **л** are soft; **ф**, **н** are hard
весёлый	**в**, **с** are soft; **л** is hard
изю́м	**з** is soft; **м** is hard
изумру́д	**з**, **м**, **р**, **д** are hard
зде́сь	**з**, **д**, **с** are soft

NOTE: In the last example, **зде́сь**, not only the **д** but also the preceding **з** is soft. This "double softening" affects the consonants **д**, **т**, **н**, **с**, and **з** when they precede a consonant that is softened by a soft series vowel, or a consonant that is *always* soft: **ч** and **щ**, e.g., **ко́нчик** [kón'č'ik] *tip, point,* **же́нщина** [žén'šš'inə] *woman* (see the section Unpaired Consonants below).

The rules for identifying hard and soft consonants are as follows.

1. Hard consonants precede **а**, **э**, **о**, **у**, or **ы**.
2. Soft consonants precede **я**, **е**, **ё**, **ю**, **и**, or **ь**.

Unpaired Consonants

The remaining five consonants do not form pairs of hard and soft counterparts. Two consonants are always soft: **ч** and **щ**. Three consonants are always hard: **ш**, **ж**, **ц**.

Consonants That Are Always Soft	ч	щ	
Consonants That Are Always Hard	ж	ш	ц

The consonants **ш**, **ж**, and **ц** remain hard even when they are followed by soft series vowels. In fact, when following these consonants, the stressed soft series vowels **е и ё** are pronounced like their hard series counterparts: **э ы о**. Recall, however, that when unstressed and pretonic, the combinations **же**, **ше**, and **це** are pronounced [žɨ], [šɨ], and [cɨ].

шéст [šést] *pole*
маши́на [mʌšɨnə] *car*
шедéвр [šɨd'évr] *masterpiece*
жестóкий [žɨstókiy] *cruel*
живóт [žɨvót] *stomach*
цéнтр [céntr] *center*
шестóй [šɨstóy] *sixth*
шёлк [šólk] *silk*
жéст [žést] *gesture*
жёлтый [žóltɨy] *yellow*
ци́рк [cɨrk] *circus*
центрáльный [cɨntrál'nɨy] *central*

Clusters of Unpaired Consonants

The Clusters *жч, сч,* and *зч*

In the consonant cluster **жч**, the unpaired hard consonant **ж** assimilates to the following unpaired soft consonant **ч**, resulting in the pronunciation of the cluster as a long soft [šš'], e.g., **мужчи́на** [mušš'ínə] *man.* In certain words, the clusters **сч** and **зч** are also pronounced [šš'], e.g., **сча́стье** [šš'ás't'yɩ] *happiness,* **сча́стливо** [šš'ástl'ivə] *happily,* **счёт** [šš'ót] *bill,* **зака́зчик** [zʌkášš'ik] *client, customer.*

The Clusters *жж* and *зж*

The clusters of unpaired hard consonants **жж** and **зж** are pronounced as a long soft [žž'] in the words **дрóжжи** [dróžž'i] *yeast,* **жжёт** [žž'ót] *burns,* **éзжу** [yéžž'u] *I travel,* **поезжáй** [pəyɩžž'áy] *go!,* **пóзже** [póžž'ɩ] *later.*

Voiced and Voiceless Consonants

There are six pairs of voiced and voiceless consonants.

Voiced Consonants	б [b]	в [v]	г [g]	д [d]	ж [ž]	з [z]
Voiceless Consonants	п [p]	ф [f]	к [k]	т [t]	ш [š]	с [s]

The remaining consonants are unpaired as to voice: **л**, **р**, **м**, and **н** are voiced; **ц**, **х**, **ч**, and **щ** are voiceless.

Voiced consonants are pronounced with the vocal cords vibrating, whereas voiceless consonants are pronounced without the vibration of the vocal cords. As in English, the opposition of voiced and voiceless consonants can distinguish the meaning of words, e.g., English ***bin*** and ***pin.*** Note the following Russian words whose meaning is distinguished solely by the *voiced* or *voiceless member* of a consonant pair.

бáр *bar* — **пáр** *steam*
дóм *house* — **тóм** *tome*
игрá *game* — **икрá** *caviar*
зýб *tooth* — **сýп** *soup*

Voicing Rules

Paired consonants may change in pronunciation from their voiced to voiceless counterpart and vice versa, depending on their position in a word. Following are the rules governing the voicing and devoicing of the paired consonants.

1. In word-final position, voiced consonants are pronounced voiceless.

б [b] → [p] — зý**б** [zúp] *tooth*
в [v] → [f] — лé**в** [l'éf] *lion*
г [g] → [k] — дó**г** [dók] *Great Dane*
д [d] → [t] — гó**д** [gót] *year*
ж [ž] → [š] — нó**ж** [nóš] *knife*
з [z] → [s] — гá**з** [gás] *gas*

2. In a cluster of two consonants within a word, or at a boundary between two words pronounced rapidly together, the second consonant causes the first consonant to assimilate to it. This rule has two parts.

   (a) A voiceless consonant is pronounced voiced when followed by a voiced consonant.

   тб → [db] фу**тб**óл [fudból] *soccer*
   сб → [zb] бей**сб**óл [beyzból] *baseball*
   кд → [gd] ка**к д**елá [kagd'ɩlá] *how are you?*
   кж → [gž] тá**кж**е [tágžɨ] *also*

   (b) A voiced consonant is pronounced voiceless when followed by a voiceless consonant.

   дк → [tk] лó**дк**а [lótkə] *boat*
   вт → [ft] **в т**еáтр [ft'ɩátr] *to the theater*
   жк → [šk] лó**жк**а [lóškə] *spoon*
   бк → [pk] прó**бк**а [própkə] *cork*
   вч → [fč] **вч**ерá [fčɩrá] *yesterday*
   гт → [kt] ля**гт**е [l'ákt'ɩ] *lie down*

   NOTE: There is one exception to rule 2(a): The voiced consonant **в** [v] does not cause a preceding voiceless consonant to be pronounced voiced, e.g., the **т** in the cluster **тв** is not pronounced [d], e.g., **твóй** [tvóy] *your.*

Syllabification

Words are more easily pronounced when they are divided up into rhythmic parts, called *syllables.* Each syllable in Russian consists of a vowel and, usually, one or more surrounding consonants, e.g., the two syllables in **кнú-га** *book.* Essentially, there is one basic principle to follow in pronouncing Russian words consisting of more than one syllable: wherever possible, *make the syllable break at a vowel.*

при-вéт [pr'i-v'ét] *hi*
спа-сú-бо [spʌ-s'í-bə] *thank you*
га-зé-та [gʌ-z'é-tə] *newspaper*
пи-сьмó [p'i-s'mó] *letter*
хо-ро-шó [xə-rʌ-šó] *good*

The only exception to this pattern involves words that contain consonant clusters beginning with **р**, **л**, **м**, **н**, or **й**. In these words, make the syllable break *after* these consonants.

жур-нáл [žur-nál] *magazine*
пóл-ка [pól-kə] *shelf*
сýм-ка [súm-kə] *handbag*
бан-кéт [bʌn-két] *banquet*
трóй-ка [tróy-kə] *three*

The same general rules that apply for pronouncing words in syllables also apply for hyphenating words that must be divided at the end of a written line. For example, words with various consonant clusters, including clusters of identical consonants, are normally hyphenated between the consonants: **кáс-са** *cashier window,* **вáн-на** *bathtub.*

Spelling Rules

Russian, like English, has a few spelling rules. Students learning English, for example, memorize the rule "write *i* before *e* except after *c*" to help them remember to spell correctly words like *relieve, believe* vs. *deceive, receive, conceive,* etc. Russian has three spelling rules that, like this English rule, remind us that certain combinations of letters are not permitted. The Russian rules are important for choosing the correct spelling of endings on nouns, adjectives, and verbs.

Rule 1: Write **и**, NEVER **ы**, after **к г х** or **ж ч ш щ**

(a) in forming plurals of nouns.

рубáшка ~ рубáшк**и** *shirt ~ shirts*
кни́га ~ кни́г**и** *book ~ books*

(b) in adjective endings (masculine singular/nominative plural forms).

ру́сск(**ий**)/ру́сск(**ие**) *Russian*
хорóш(**ий**)/хорóш(**ие**) *good*

Rule 2: Write **а** and **у**, NEVER **я** and **ю**, after **г к х ж ч ш щ ц** in the conjugation of verbs (first-person singular and third-person plural).

я́ молч**у́** / они́ молч**á**т *I am silent / they are silent*
я́ леж**у́** / они́ леж**á**т *I am lying / they are lying*
я́ пиш**у́** / они́ пи́ш**у**т *I write / they write*

Rule 3: Write unstressed **е**, but stressed **ó**, after **ж ч ш щ ц**.

хорóш**е**е *good*
больш**ó**е *big*
танц**е**вáть *to dance*
танц**е**вáльный *dancing* (adj.)
BUT танц**ó**вщик *(ballet) dancer*

Capitalization

Russian is similar to English in that it capitalizes proper nouns (**Би́лл**, **Вашингтóн**, **Амéрика**, **Бори́с**, **Москвá**, **Росси́я**), and the first word of a sentence. Russian differs from English in NOT capitalizing the following words.

(a) The first-person singular pronoun "I" (**я́**), unless it is the first word of a sentence

(b) Nouns (and adjectives) denoting nationalities (**америкáнец** *American,* **япóнец** *Japanese,* **ру́сский** *Russian*), as well as cities from which one originates (**москви́ч** *Muscovite,* **петербу́ржец** *Petersburger*)

(c) Words that follow the first word of a title (**«Войнá и ми́р»** *War and Peace*), the name of a holiday (**Нóвый гóд** *New Year*), or the name of an organization (**Акадéмия нау́к** *Academy of Sciences*)

(d) Days of the week (**понедéльник** *Monday,* **втóрник** *Tuesday*)

(e) Months of the year (**янвáрь** *January,* **феврáль** *February,* **мáрт** *March*)

Transliteration: English to Russian

Often it is necessary to represent a word originating in one alphabet with the corresponding letters of another alphabet. This is called *transliteration.* Words commonly transliterated include the names of people and places, as well as loanwords, i.e., those words of foreign origin that are "borrowed" and become part of the vocabulary of the borrowing language. Examples of Russian words transliterated into English are the names Yeltsin, Gorbachev, Chekhov, Tolstoy, Volga, and Vladivostok. English also has a handful of loanwords from Russian, such as sputnik, dacha, borsch, samovar, and more recently, glasnost and perestroika. Russian, in contrast to English, has literally thousands of words that have been borrowed directly, or indirectly, from English, and the influx of English words into Russian has greatly accelerated since the 1990s. In some of these loanwords the English *spelling* of the word determines the way the word is transliterated in Russian, each English letter being replaced by its counterpart in the Cyrillic alphabet, e.g., *Robert* > **Ро́берт**. In other words, the *phonetics* of the English word dictate the choice of Cyrillic letters that most accurately capture the English *pronunciation,* e.g., *Michael* > **Ма́йкл**. Often, a combination of the spelling and the pronunciation of an English word influences the way the word is transliterated. Though there is no one agreed-upon system for transliterating from English to Russian (which may result in variant forms, e.g., *David* > **Дави́д/Дэ́йвид**, *Pamela* > **Па́мела/Пэ́мела**), it is very important to be able to pair English letters with their closest phonetic counterparts in the Cyrillic alphabet. In particular, knowing the phonetic correspondences between English and Russian *consonants* will make it much easier to recognize, and make use of, the numerous English words that have been borrowed and assimilated into Russian.

English Consonants and Their Cyrillic Counterparts

Most English consonants have one-to-one phonetic counterparts in the Cyrillic alphabet and, consequently, present little difficulty for transliteration.

English Consonants	b	c	d	f	g	k	l	m	n	p	r	s	t	v	z
Cyrillic Consonants	б	к	д	ф	г	к	л	м	н	п	р	с	т	в	з

NOTE: English *c* is sometimes transliterated in Cyrillic as **ц** (e.g., *Cincinnati* > **Цинцинна́ти**) and rarely as **с** (*city* > **си́ти**, as in **Дже́рси-си́ти** *Jersey City*).

English Consonant Letters Lacking One-to-One Phonetic Equivalents

There are five English consonants that have no one-to-one phonetic counterparts in the Cyrillic alphabet. These are *h, j, q, w,* and *x.* The sounds of English *h* and English *w* do not occur in Russian, and the sounds of English *j, q,* and *x* can be approximated in Russian only by Cyrillic letter combinations. It is important to know how these consonants are transliterated, since these letters commonly occur in English loanwords.

1. English *h* is transliterated as Cyrillic **г** or, as in many recent borrowings, **х**.

Harvard	>	Га́рвард	Hamburg	>	Га́мбург
Henry	>	Ге́нри/Хе́нри	Hong Kong	>	Гонко́нг
Houston	>	Хью́стон	Hillary	>	Хи́ллари
hacker	>	ха́кер	hot dog	>	хот-до́г

2. English *j* is transliterated as the Cyrillic letter combination **дж**.

Jeff	>	Дже́ф(ф)	jazz	>	джа́з
Jessica	>	Дже́с(с)ика	jeans	>	джи́нсы

English *g*, when equivalent to *j* in pronunciation, is also transliterated as **дж**.

George > Джóрдж
manager > мéнеджер
image > и́мидж
pager > пéйджер

3. English *q* is normally transliterated as the Cyrillic letter combination **кв**.

aquarium > аквáриум
aquamarine > аквамари́н
quartet > квартéт
quart > квáрта

4. English *w* is usually transliterated as Cyrillic **у**, occasionally (in earlier loanwords) as **в**. Some words may have variants.

William > Уи́льям/Ви́льям
weekend > уик-э́нд
Washington > Вашингтóн
walkman > уóкмен/вóкмен
show > шóу
whisky > ви́ски

5. English *x* is usually transliterated in Cyrillic as the letter combination **кс** (rarely as **х**).

Maxine > Макси́н
Mexico > Мéксика
fax > фáкс
taxi > такси́

But note the following.

Texas > Техáс

English Letter Combinations Transliterated by Single Letters in Cyrillic

Finally, there are a few English letter combinations that are transliterated into Russian by single letters in Cyrillic.

1. English *ch* with the sound value [č] is usually transliterated by Cyrillic **ч**; *ch* with the sound value [š] is transliterated by Cyrillic **ш**.

Charles > Чáрльз
Charlotte > Шарлóтт

But note the following.

chocolate > шоколáд

2. English *sh* [š] is transliterated in Cyrillic as **ш**.

Sharon > Шáрон

3. English *ph* [f] is transliterated in Cyrillic as **ф**.

Sophie > Сóфи

4. English *th* [θ] does not occur in Russian; therefore, *th* is normally transliterated in English loanwords as Cyrillic **т**.

Cynthia > Си́нтия
Theodore > Тéодор

But in this last example, and in a few other words originally from Greek, English *th* may also correspond to **ф**, based on the biblical Greek form of the word.

Theodore > Фёдор
Thaddeus > Фаддéй

Russian Letter Styles

Italic Letters

The Russian letters introduced above in the alphabet chart are given in the ordinary printed block style found in books and other printed texts. These letters can also occur in an italicized form, which in most instances is quite similar to the regular printed style. However, a few of the small italicized letters have a different shape from their printed block style counterparts and therefore must be specially noted. These letters are given in the table below.

PRINTED LETTERS	*ITALICIZED* LETTERS
В в	*В в*
Г г	*Г г*
Д д	*Д д*
И и	*И и*
П п	*П п*
Т т	*Т т*

Cursive Letters

In general, when Russians write by hand, they do not print, but use a cursive script. Like italic, some letters in Cyrillic cursive differ in various ways from their printed block style counterparts. One letter in particular, the small Cyrillic block letter **д**, has the italicized form ***д*** (as noted above), but is written in cursive script as *д*. Fortunately, most cursive letters do not differ so dramatically from the printed block or italic styles. The three letter styles are listed below for comparison, and the most important features of the cursive letters are noted for reference.

PRINTED	ITALICS	CURSIVE SCRIPT	NOTES ON FORMING CURSIVE
А а	*А а*	*А а*	
Б б	*Б б*	*Б б*	
В в	*В в*	*В в*	The small letter is as tall as the capital.
Г г	*Г г*	*Г г*	The small letter is rounded on top.
Д д	*Д д*	*Д д*	The small *д* looks like English script *g*.
Е е	*Е е*	*Е е*	
Ё ё	*Ё ё*	*Ё ё*	The two dots are often omitted.
Ж ж	*Ж ж*	*Ж ж*	
З з	*З з*	*З з*	Capital *З* looks like the number 3.
И и	*И и*	*И и*	
Й й	*Й й*	*Й й*	Note the half circle above the letters.
К к	*К к*	*К к*	The small letter is half as tall as the capital.
Л л	*Л л*	*Л л*	Both letters must begin with a hook.
М м	*М м*	*М м*	Both letters must begin with a hook.
Н н	*Н н*	*Н н*	
О о	*О о*	*О о*	
П п	*П п*	*П п*	
Р р	*Р р*	*Р р*	The small letter is not closed on the right.
С с	*С с*	*С с*	
Т т	*Т т*	*Т т*	

PRINTED	ITALICS	CURSIVE SCRIPT	NOTES ON FORMING CURSIVE
У у	*У у*	У у	Capital У does not extend below the baseline.
Ф ф	*Ф ф*	Ф ф	
Х х	*Х х*	Х х	
Ц ц	*Ц ц*	Ц ц	Both letters have a short tail.
Ч ч	*Ч ч*	Ч ч	
Ш ш	*Ш ш*	Ш ш	The small ш often has a line underneath.
Щ щ	*Щ щ*	Щ щ	Both letters have a short tail.
ъ	*ъ*	ъ	
ы	*ы*	ы	
ь	*ь*	ь	
Э э	*Э э*	Э э	Both letters have a rounded back.
Ю ю	*Ю ю*	Ю ю	
Я я	*Я я*	Я я	Both letters must begin with a hook, like Л л and М м.

1. Using the Cyrillic equivalents of the English letters, write the Russian name for each of the following states of the U.S. Review the section Shapes and Sounds.

1. Alabama __________
2. Arizona __________
3. Vermont __________
4. Indiana __________
5. Colorado __________
6. Illinois __________
7. Minnesota __________
8. Montana __________
9. Nebraska __________
10. Nevada __________
11. Oregon __________
12. Florida __________

2. Substituting Cyrillic letters for their English counterparts, write the Russian name for each of the following cities and countries.

1. America __________
2. Canada __________
3. Pakistan __________
4. Toronto __________
5. Boston __________
6. London __________
7. Berlin __________
8. Erevan __________
9. Madrid __________
10. Panama __________

3. The following words were borrowed into Russian from English. Identify each word, and give its original English spelling.

1. студе́нт __________
2. профе́ссор __________
3. ка́мпус __________
4. колле́дж __________
5. га́мбургер __________
6. ке́тчуп __________
7. хот-до́г __________
8. компа́кт-ди́ск __________
9. компью́тер __________
10. при́нтер __________

4. In each of the following words, identify the soft consonant(s), then write the word, underlining the relevant consonant(s). Review the sections The Vowels and Paired Consonants: Hard and Soft.

MODELS перerýв про́рубь

1. приве́т ________________
2. спаси́бо ________________
3. па́мять ________________
4. письмо́ ________________
5. телеви́зор ________________
6. сёрфинг ________________
7. рюкза́к ________________
8. го́сть ________________
9. рэ́ппер ________________
10. де́сять ________________

5. Study the list of words below. In order of appearance, write each word that contains the sound [y], and underline the relevant letters. Review the alphabet chart and the sections The Two "Signs," The Vowels, and Paired Consonants: Hard and Soft.

MODELS моя́ статья́

прямо́й, по́яс, де́нь, еда́, сёмга, съёмка, Ка́тя, пла́тье, Та́ня, Татья́на, я́блоко, мя́со, май, мой, мю́зикл, ю́мор, Ива́н, заём

1. ________________
2. ________________
3. ________________
4. ________________
5. ________________
6. ________________
7. ________________
8. ________________
9. ________________
10. ________________

6. Study the list of words and phrases below. In order of appearance, write each word that contains the short, lax sound [ʌ], and underline the relevant vowels. Review the section Vowel Reduction Rules.

MODELS окно́ хорошо́

до́ктор, астроно́м, парадо́кс, о́блоко, тарака́н, ко́мната, голова́, мото́р, над до́мом, молоко́, у́лица, газе́та, тала́нт, о кла́ссе

1. ________________
2. ________________
3. ________________
4. ________________
5. ________________
6. ________________
7. ________________
8. ________________
9. ________________
10. ________________

7. In each of the following words, identify the vowel(s) with the sound [ə], then write the word, underlining the relevant vowel(s). Review the section Vowel Reduction Rules.

MODELS ла́мпа разгово́р

1. о́рган ________________
2. ко́локол ________________
3. панора́ма ________________
4. ба́ня ________________
5. ю́мор ________________
6. ме́сто ________________
7. но́вое ________________
8. дя́дя ________________
9. потоло́к ________________
10. кварти́ра ________________

8. In each of the following words, identify the vowel(s) with the sound [ɪ], then write the word, underlining the relevant vowel(s). Review the section Vowel Reduction Rules.

MODELS свитер тянуть

1. телефóн	________	6. пáмятник	________
2. мяснóй	________	7. ветеринáр	________
3. вéчер	________	8. рекá	________
4. ресторáн	________	9. этáж	________
5. экóлог	________	10. сейчáс	________

9. Study the list of words below. In order of appearance, write each word that contains the sound [ɨ], and underline the relevant vowels. Review the section Unpaired Consonants.

MODELS ши́на жени́ть

бы́стро, цéнтр, цемéнт, жи́вопись, цыплёнок, ци́рк, жéнщина, женá, жёны, мешóк, шикáрный, шéсть, шестóй, решётка, шербéт

1. ________	6. ________
2. ________	7. ________
3. ________	8. ________
4. ________	9. ________
5. ________	10. ________

10. Study the list of words below. In order of appearance, write each word that contains the sound [šš'], and underline the relevant consonant(s) or consonant cluster(s).

MODELS счёт щенóк

щи, ужé, ещё, éшь, сши́ть, считáешь, щекá, мужчи́на, расскáзчик, подпи́счик, исчезáть, искáть, и́щут, шёл, щёлк

1. ________	6. ________
2. ________	7. ________
3. ________	8. ________
4. ________	9. ________
5. ________	10. ________

11. Study the list of words and phrases below. In order of appearance, write each word that contains consonants that, due to one of the *voicing* rules, are pronounced differently from the way they are spelled, and underline the relevant consonants.

MODELS сáд в кинó

глазóк, глáс, глáз, сбóр, спáть, оттéнок, отдéл, кру́жка, круи́з, дрóбь, твёрдо, творóг, вéчер, вчерá, аптéка, абсу́рд, к дóму

1. ________	6. ________
2. ________	7. ________
3. ________	8. ________
4. ________	9. ________
5. ________	10. ________

12. Rewrite each word below, dividing it into syllables. Review the section Syllabification.

MODELS пи́-во спа-си́-бо

1. скажи́те	__________	6. слова́рь	__________
2. понима́йте	__________	7. ко́мната	__________
3. лаборато́рия	__________	8. ру́чка	__________
4. дире́ктор	__________	9. каранда́ш	__________
5. нача́льник	__________	10. университе́т	__________

13. The following words were borrowed into Russian from English. Identify each word, and give its original English spelling.

1. ксе́рокс	__________	6. ноу-ха́у	__________
2. ко́микс	__________	7. диск-пле́йер	__________
3. сэ́ндвич	__________	8. фа́кс	__________
4. ма́ркетинг	__________	9. компью́тер	__________
5. ме́неджер	__________	10. хэппи-э́нд	__________

14. Give the English equivalent of each of the following names of famous people.

1. Ага́та Кри́сти __________
2. Дже́к Ло́ндон __________
3. Эрне́ст Хе́мингуэй __________
4. Ча́рльз Ди́ккенс __________
5. Уо́лт Дисне́й __________
6. Ри́чард Ни́ксон __________
7. Джо́н Кви́нси А́дамс __________
8. Уи́нстон Че́рчилль __________

Nouns

A noun is a word that names a person (Sasha, sister, girl), a place (Washington, Russia), a thing (desk, table, lamp), a quality (joy, happiness, sadness), or act (request, rebellion, voting). Nouns are classified into *proper* and *common* nouns. Proper nouns are those that indicate a specific person, place, or thing. For example, the noun "Moscow" is the name of a specific, unique place, whereas "city" is a common noun, i.e., one that refers to a whole class of things. Proper nouns in Russian, as in English, are capitalized. (On differences between Russian and English capitalization, see Chapter 1.)

Articles

Russian, unlike English, has no articles. The meaning of "definite" and "indefinite" conveyed by the English definite article *the* and the indefinite article *a,* respectively, is expressed in Russian through context, by word order, or by other means.

Noun Structure

Russian nouns (as well as adjectives, pronouns, and verbs) consist of a *stem* followed by an *ending.* The stem always includes a *root,* where the lexical meaning resides. The root may be preceded by a *prefix* and/or followed by a *suffix,* structural elements that contribute additional meanings to a word. Consider, for example, the structure of the Russian noun **сотру́дники** *coworkers.*

STEM			+ ENDING
(prefix)	+ root	+ (suffix)	
со	+ **труд**	+ **ник**	+ **и**
co	+ *work*	+ *er*	+ *s*

Many nouns in English have a similar structure. For example, the English equivalent of the Russian **сотру́дники**, *coworkers,* has a stem consisting of the root *work,* the prefix *co-* ("together"), and the suffix *-er* ("one who"), followed by the ending *-s* (plural). While many English words share the same *stem + ending* structure of Russian words, *endings* in Russian are far more extensive and play a far greater role than in English. In particular, the ending on a Russian noun can give information about its **gender**, **number**, and **case**.

Gender

All nouns in Russian belong to one of three genders: *masculine, feminine,* or *neuter.* There are two types of gender: grammatical gender and natural gender. The first type, as its name suggests, has to do with the grammatical form of the noun. Grammatical gender is the assignment of gender according to the noun's ending; the meaning of the noun plays no role. For example, the noun **кни́га** *book* is feminine even though it has no relation to female persons; it is grammatically feminine simply because it ends in the vowel **-а**. The vast majority of nouns in Russian are assigned gender in this way. The second type of gender, natural gender, is meaning-based: It is the assignment of masculine or feminine gender based on the *sex* of the person (or animal) denoted by the noun. In most instances, grammatical gender and natural gender coincide, e.g., the noun **ма́ма** *mom* is both grammatically feminine (since it has the ending **-а**), and "naturally" feminine, because its meaning is that of a female person. In a relatively small number of instances, however, grammatical and natural gender do not coincide, e.g., the noun **па́па** *dad* has the *form* of a feminine noun (the ending **-а**), but the *meaning* of a masculine noun. In all such instances, the meaning of the noun, not its form, determines gender.

Grammatical Gender

In most instances, the grammatical gender of a Russian noun is easily determined by its ending in the nominative singular (the form in which a noun is cited in dictionaries). The following table illustrates grammatical gender.

	MASCULINE -∅	FEMININE -а/-я	NEUTER -о/-е (ё)
Hard Stem	дива́н	ла́мпа	кре́сло
Soft Stem	музе́й	ку́хня	зда́ние

Masculine Nouns

In the nominative singular most masculine nouns have *no ending* (or a "zero ending," symbolized by -∅, e.g., **дива́н-∅** *sofa*). Masculine nouns, then, consist only of a stem ending in a consonant, which may be hard or soft. Nouns ending in a hard consonant are characterized as having a *hard stem,* those ending in a soft consonant, a *soft stem.* Specifically, a masculine noun is one whose stem ends in

(a) a hard paired consonant.

дива́н *sofa*
сто́л *table*
до́м *house*
институ́т *institute*
магази́н *store*

(b) one of the unpaired consonants: hard **ж**, **ш**, or soft **ч**, **щ**.

но́ж *knife*
каранда́ш *pencil*
вра́ч *doctor*
пла́щ *raincoat*
бо́рщ *borsch*

(c) the soft (semi-consonantal) glide **-й**.

музе́й *museum*
трамва́й *trolley car*
ча́й *tea*
кра́й *edge*
хокке́й *hockey*

(d) a soft consonant, which is indicated by a following soft sign **-ь**.

портфе́ль *briefcase*
слова́рь *dictionary*
ру́бль *ruble*
де́нь *day*
Кре́мль *Kremlin*

Feminine Nouns

Feminine nouns have either a hard stem or a soft stem, and this difference correlates with the hard type or soft type of vowel ending. Specifically,

(a) feminine nouns with a hard stem end in the hard-series vowel **-а**.

ла́мпа *lamp*	ру́чка *pen*
кни́га *book*	гости́ница *hotel*
газе́та *newspaper*	

(b) most feminine nouns with a soft stem end in the soft-series vowel **-я**.

ку́хня *kitchen*	земля́ *earth*
дере́вня *village*	тётя *aunt*
ле́кция *lecture*	

(c) some feminine nouns, just like some masculine nouns, end in the soft sign **-ь**.

пло́щадь *square*	крова́ть *bed*
тетра́дь *notebook*	ро́ль *role*
две́рь *door*	

Neuter Nouns

Neuter nouns, like feminine nouns, occur with a hard or soft stem, and it is, again, this difference that accounts for the different endings. Specifically,

(a) neuter nouns with a hard stem end in the hard-series vowel **-о**.

кре́сло *armchair*	сло́во *word*
окно́ *window*	ме́сто *place*
письмо́ *letter*	

(b) neuter nouns with a soft stem end in the soft-series vowel **-е**, or if the ending is stressed, **-ё**.

зда́ние *building*	бельё *linen*
мо́ре *sea*	ружьё *gun*
пла́тье *dress*	

NOTE: Exceptions to the regular neuter endings **-о**, **-е** (**-ё**) are the few neuter nouns that end in **-мя**. These nouns should be memorized to avoid mistaking them for feminine nouns in **-я**. The most common are the following.

и́мя *name*	зна́мя *banner*
вре́мя *time*	пла́мя *flame*
бре́мя *burden*	се́мя *seed*

1. Give the gender of each of the following nouns, and indicate whether the noun stem is hard or soft.

1. письмо́ ________________	6. зда́ние ________________
2. газе́та ________________	7. ру́бль ________________
3. трамва́й ________________	8. сто́л ________________
4. магази́н ________________	9. и́мя ________________
5. ле́кция ________________	10. пло́щадь ________________

Why Gender Is Important

The gender of a noun is important because it determines the endings of pronouns, adjectives, and the past-tense forms of verbs that must *agree* with, i.e., express the same gender as, the noun they modify or refer to. Following are examples of gender agreement.

Pronoun (Possessive and Third-Person) Agreement

The gender of the noun determines both the ending of the modifying possessive pronoun, as well as the form of the third-person pronoun that can replace it.

Гдé **мóй стóл**? Вóт **óн**.	*Where is my table? Here it is.*
Гдé **моё окнó**? Вóт **онó**.	*Where is my window? Here it is.*
Гдé **моя́ ла́мпа**? Вóт **она́**.	*Where is my lamp? Here it is.*

Adjective Agreement

An adjective must express the same gender as the noun it modifies.

Э́то **нóвый** стóл.	*This is a new table.*
Э́то **нóвое** окнó.	*This is a new window.*
Э́то **нóвая** ла́мпа.	*This is a new lamp.*

A predicate adjective must express the same gender as its subject noun.

Сту́л **за́нят**.	*The chair is occupied.*
Мéсто **за́нято**.	*The seat is occupied.*
Кóмната **занята́**.	*The room is occupied.*

Past Tense of Verbs

A predicate verb in the past tense must agree with the subject noun it refers to.

Стóл **бы́л** та́м.	*The table was there.*
Окнó **бы́ло** та́м.	*The window was there.*
Ла́мпа **была́** та́м.	*The lamp was there.*

2. Write the form of the personal pronoun **óн**, **онó**, **она́** that replaces each of the following nouns.

1. гóрод __________	6. рóль __________
2. дерéвня __________	7. журна́л __________
3. пятнó __________	8. врéмя __________
4. каранда́ш __________	9. река́ __________
5. ча́й __________	10. зада́ние __________

3. Write the form of the possessive pronoun "my" (**мóй**, **моё**, or **моя́**) that modifies each of the following nouns.

1. __________ дóм	5. __________ сту́л
2. __________ мéсто	6. __________ кóмната
3. __________ ва́за	7. __________ крова́ть
4. __________ слова́рь	8. __________ фотогра́фия

Gender Identification by Noun Groups

Masculine Nouns of Natural Gender in *-а* and *-я*

A small number of masculine nouns have an ending in **-а** or **-я**. These are all nouns that denote male persons. There are three subgroups of these "naturally" masculine nouns.

(a) Nouns that are masculine by virtue of their real-world referents

мужчи́на *man*
па́па *dad*
дя́дя *uncle*
де́душка *grandfather*
ю́ноша *youth*

(b) The full first name of males (very few)

Илья́
Ники́та
Фома́

(c) The diminutive forms of male first names (The full name is given in parentheses below.)

Са́ша (Алекса́ндр)
Алёша (Алексе́й)
То́ля (Анато́лий)
Бо́ря (Бори́с)
Ва́ся (Васи́лий)
Ви́тя (Ви́ктор)
Же́ня (Евге́ний)
Ко́ля (Никола́й)
Лёня (Леони́д)
Ми́ша (Михаи́л)
Па́ша (Па́вел)
Пе́тя (Пётр)

Masculine Nouns with a Stem Ending in the Soft Sign

A relatively small number of nouns ending in the soft sign **-ь** are masculine. Identifying these nouns as masculine is less straightforward, since the stem of both masculine *and* feminine nouns may end in **-ь**. However, there are some generalizations that help determine the gender of certain groups of these nouns as masculine.

Months of the Year

янва́рь *January*
февра́ль *February*
апре́ль *April*
ию́нь *June*
ию́ль *July*
сентя́брь *September*
октя́брь *October*
ноя́брь *November*
дека́брь *December*

Nouns Denoting Male Persons

кня́зь *prince*
коро́ль *king*
ца́рь *tsar*
па́рень *lad*
зя́ть *son-in-law, brother-in-law*
те́сть *father-in-law (wife's father)*

Nouns Ending in the Suffix *-тель* (cf. the English suffix *-er, -or*) **or *-арь***

Many denote a person, usually a male (BUT: **слова́рь** *dictionary,* **фона́рь** *lantern, light*).

писа́тель *writer*
чита́тель *reader*
води́тель *driver*
учи́тель *(school) teacher*
преподава́тель *(university) teacher*
покупа́тель *shopper*
зри́тель *spectator*

библиоте́карь *librarian*
пе́карь *baker*
апте́карь *pharmacist*
врата́рь *goalkeeper*

Feminine Nouns with a Stem Ending in the Soft Sign

A large majority of nouns with a stem ending in the soft sign **-ь** are feminine. As in the case of masculine soft-sign nouns, there are a few generalizations that help to identify groups of soft-sign nouns that are feminine.

Nouns Denoting Females (Nouns of Natural Gender)

ма́ть *mother*
до́чь *daughter*
свекро́вь *mother-in-law* (*husband's mother*)

Nouns Ending in the Soft Sign Preceded by an Unpaired Consonant: -*жь*, -*чь*, -*шь*, or -*щь*

молодёжь *young people*
ло́жь *lie*
пе́чь *stove*
но́чь *night*
бро́шь *brooch*
чу́шь *nonsense*
мы́шь *mouse*
ве́щь *thing*
мо́щь *power, might*
по́мощь *help*

Abstract Nouns Formed with the Suffix -*ость* or -*есть*

мо́лодость *youth*
гру́бость *rudeness*
ве́жливость *politeness*
но́вость *news*
ра́дость *joy*
сме́лость *boldness*
зре́лость *maturity*
гла́сность *openness*
све́жесть *freshness*
тя́жесть *gravity*
неуклю́жесть *clumsiness*

4. Write the form of the third-person pronoun that replaces each of the following nouns.

1. дя́дя ________
2. до́чь ________
3. коро́ль ________
4. Ми́ша ________
5. бро́шь ________
6. свекро́вь ________
7. писа́тель ________
8. но́вость ________
9. янва́рь ________
10. апте́карь ________

Nouns of Common Gender

A relatively small number of nouns ending in **-а** or **-я** that denote people are of "common gender," i.e., they may be either masculine or feminine depending on whether, in a particular context, they refer to a male or a female, e.g., **О́н *большо́й* у́мница** *He is a very clever person,* **Она́ *больша́я* у́мница** *She is a very clever person.*

у́мница *clever person*
колле́га *colleague*
сирота́ *orphan*
пья́ница *drunkard*
бродя́га *tramp*
неве́жда *ignoramus*
пла́кса *crybaby*
рази́ня *scatterbrain*
неря́ха *slob, slovenly person*
обжо́ра *glutton*
малю́тка *baby, little one*
одино́чка *lone person*

Gender of Nouns Denoting Professions

Nouns denoting professions or occupations that were once largely dominated by men are generally of masculine gender. Nevertheless, these nouns are used to refer not only to men, but also to women who have entered these professions, e.g., **Михаи́л био́лог и Мари́на био́лог** *Michael is a biologist and Marina is a biologist.*

хиру́рг *surgeon*
вра́ч *doctor*
ветерина́р *veterinarian*
профе́ссор *professor*
доце́нт *university lecturer*
адвока́т *lawyer*
педаго́г *teacher*
био́лог *biologist*
гео́лог *geologist*
гео́граф *geographer*
карто́граф *cartographer*
архите́ктор *architect*
космона́вт *cosmonaut*
инжене́р *engineer*
парикма́хер *hairdresser*
строи́тель *builder*
секрета́рь *secretary*

Regarding such nouns, there are two facts to remember about *gender agreement.*

1. Regardless of whether these nouns denote a male or female, a modifying adjective normally agrees with the *masculine* gender of the noun.

   Она́ **хоро́ший** вра́ч. — *She is a good doctor.*
   Моя́ сестра́—**изве́стный** педаго́г. — *My sister is a well-known teacher.*

2. When these nouns are used with a predicate adjective, or with a verb in the past tense, the gender form of the adjective or verb is normally determined by the *sex reference* of the noun.

   With a Predicate Adjective

   Экскурсово́д **бо́лен**. — *The (male) guide is sick.*
   Экскурсово́д **больна́**. — *The (female) guide is sick.*

   With a Verb in the Past Tense

   Профе́ссор Ивано́в **чита́л** ле́кцию. — *Professor Ivanov read a lecture.*
   Профе́ссор Ивано́ва **чита́ла** ле́кцию. — *Professor Ivanova read a lecture.*

NOTE: The noun **судья́** *judge,* though feminine in form, is masculine in gender. Like the other nouns of profession listed above, it may be used to denote women, but it requires a modifying adjective to have masculine agreement, e.g., **Она́ уважа́емый судья́** *She is a respected judge.*

NOTE: The noun **челове́к** *person* may refer to either a male or female, but always requires masculine agreement, e.g., **Ле́на—о́чень *ми́лый* челове́к** *Lena is a very nice girl.*

5. Choose the form of the adjective in parentheses that agrees in gender with the noun it modifies.

1. Влади́мир Ива́нович—_______________ колле́га. (но́вый/но́вая)
2. Но́вый учéбник _______________ профе́ссор Серге́ева. (написа́л/написа́ла)
3. Э́та же́нщина _______________ судья́. (изве́стный/изве́стная)
4. Ири́на Петро́вна _______________ инжене́р. (о́пытный/о́пытная)
5. Тво́й бра́т _______________ неря́ха. (большо́й/больша́я)
6. Вра́ч _______________. Она́ консульти́рует с больны́м. (за́нят/занята́)

Gender Differentiation by Suffix

Nouns Denoting People

A number of masculine nouns denoting profession or occupation have a corresponding feminine form with a suffix indicating the female member of the profession (cf. English *poet/poetess, actor/actress*). In fact, males and females may be differentiated by a suffix not only in nouns of occupation, but also in nouns denoting various functions, as well as in those denoting nationality. Below is a representative list of the different suffixes used to distinguish females from males, with examples of commonly used nouns denoting professions, occupations, functions, nationalities, etc. Wherever appropriate, the suffix denoting the female is paired with a suffix denoting the male.

Male	**Female** ***-ка***	
журнали́ст	журнали́ст**ка**	*journalist*
арти́ст	арти́ст**ка**	*performing artist*
программи́ст	программи́ст**ка**	*computer programmer*
официа́нт	официа́нт**ка**	*waiter/waitress*

Male	**Female** ***-иса/-есса***	
актёр	актр**и́са**	*actor/actress*
поэ́т	поэт**е́сса**	*poet/poetess*
при́нц	принц**е́сса**	*prince/princess*

Male	**Female** ***-и́ха***	
по́вар	повар**и́ха**	*cook*
сто́рож	сторож**и́ха**	*guard*
портно́й	портн**и́ха**	*tailor/dressmaker*

Male ***-ец***	**Female** ***-ка***	
вегетариа́н**ец**	вегетариа́н**ка**	*vegetarian*
америка́н**ец**	америка́н**ка**	*American*
кана́д**ец**	кана́д**ка**	*Canadian*
не́м**ец**	не́м**ка**	*German*

Male ***-анин/-янин***	**Female** ***-анка/-янка***	
англич**а́нин**	англич**а́нка**	*Englishman/Englishwoman*
христи**ани́н**	христи**а́нка**	*Christian*
кресть**я́нин**	кресть**я́нка**	*peasant*
слав**яни́н**	слав**я́нка**	*Slav*

Male ***-ин***	**Female** ***-ка***	
армян**и́н**	армя́н**ка**	*Armenian*
болга́р**ин**	болга́р**ка**	*Bulgarian*
груз**и́н**	грузи́н**ка**	*Georgian*
россия́н**ин**	россия́н**ка**	*Russian (citizen)*
тата́р**ин**	тата́р**ка**	*Tatar*

Male ***-ец***	**Female** ***-щица***	
продав**е́ц**	продав**щи́ца**	*salesperson*

Male ***-щик***	**Female** ***-щица***	
танцо́в**щик**	танцо́в**щица**	*ballet dancer*
мехов**щи́к**	мехов**щи́ца**	*furrier*
гардеро́б**щик**	гардеро́б**щица**	*cloakroom attendant*

Male -*чик*	**Female -*чица***	
перевóд**чик**	перевóд**чица**	*translator*
лёт**чик**	лёт**чица**	*pilot*
буфéт**чик**	буфéт**чица**	*snack bar attendant*
Male -*ец*	**Female -*ица***	
пев**éц**	пев**и́ца**	*singer*
красá**вец**	красá**вица**	*attractive person*
счастли́**вец**	счастли́**вица**	*lucky person*
Male -*ник*	**Female -*ница***	
худóж**ник**	худóж**ница**	*artist*
рабóт**ник**	рабóт**ница**	*helper*
уче**ни́к**	уче**ни́ца**	*pupil*
Male -*тель*	**Female -*ница***	
учи́**тель**	учи́тель**ница**	*(school) teacher*
преподавá**тель**	преподавáтель**ница**	*(university) instructor*
писá**тель**	писáтель**ница**	*writer*

6. For each of the following nouns, write its missing male or female counterpart.

MODELS студéнт <u>студéнтка</u> <u>учени́к</u> учени́ца

1.	певéц	________	8.	худóжник	________
2.	________	счастли́вица	9.	________	перевóдчица
3.	америкáнец	________	10.	танцóвщик	________
4.	канáдец	________	11.	англичáнин	________
5.	________	испáнка	12.	________	грузи́нка
6.	писáтель	________	13.	портнóй	________
7.	________	учи́тельница	14.	________	продавщи́ца

Gender of Indeclinable Nouns of Foreign Origin

Thousands of words have been borrowed into Russian from English and other languages. Among these foreign borrowings is a fairly large number of nouns that are indeclinable, that is, their endings do not change for number or case. Nearly all of these nouns end in a vowel, but for this group of nouns the vowel ending is often not a reliable indicator of gender. Rather, the gender of indeclinable loanwords is determined by certain categories.

(a) Indeclinable loanwords denoting inanimate objects are generally neuter.

Москóвское метрó *Moscow metro*	дли́нное резюмé *long résumé*
удóбное купé *comfortable compartment*	разнообрáзное меню́ *varied menu*
нóвое кинó *new cinema*	ую́тное кафé *cozy café*
свобóдное такси́ *available taxi*	интерéсное интервью́ *interesting interview*

NOTE: But the noun **кóфе** *coffee* is masculine (**чёрный кóфе** *black coffee*).

NOTE: The gender of a few indeclinable loanwords denoting inanimate objects is determined by the gender of the native Russian word that denotes the relevant generic class, e.g., **торнáдо** *tornado* is masculine (cf. **вéтер** *wind*), **саля́ми** *salami* is feminine (cf. **колбасá** *sausage*), as is **авеню́** *avenue* (cf. **у́лица** *street*) and **цунáми** *tsunami* (cf. **волнá** *wave*).

(b) Indeclinable loanwords denoting people are "naturally" masculine or feminine.

знамени́тый маэ́стро *famous maestro*
настоя́щая ле́ди *a real lady*
но́вый рефери́ *new referee*
краси́вая инженю́ *pretty ingénue*

(c) Indeclinable loanwords denoting animals and birds are normally masculine.

большо́й кенгуру́ *big kangaroo*
симпати́чный по́ни *nice pony*
ро́зовый флами́нго *pink flamingo*
у́мный шимпанзе́ *intelligent chimpanzee*
краси́вый какаду́ *beautiful cockatoo*

Indeclinable loanwords denoting *place names* generally have the same gender as the native Russian generic noun that denotes the relevant class. Note the following classes.

(a) Indeclinable loanwords denoting cities are masculine (cf. **го́род** *city*).

Хе́льсинки *Helsinki*
То́кио *Tokyo*
Гонолу́лу *Honolulu*
Ка́лгари *Calgary*
Тбили́си *Tbilisi*
О́сло *Oslo*
Сан-Франци́ско *San Francisco*
Торо́нто *Toronto*

(b) Indeclinable loanwords denoting islands are masculine (cf. **о́стров** *island*).

краси́вый Кюраса́о *beautiful Curaçao*
живопи́сный Анти́гуа *picturesque Antigua*
со́лнечный Ко́рфу *sunny Corfu*
го́рный Ка́при *mountainous Capri*

(c) Nouns denoting rivers are generally feminine (cf. **река́** *river*).

Янцзы́ *Yangtze*
Ога́йо *Ohio*
Ко́нго *Congo*
Миссиси́пи *Mississippi*

The nouns that denote both the river and state of the U.S. are masculine when they refer to the state (cf. **шта́т** *state*), but feminine when they denote the river.

споко́йная Миссиси́пи *the calm Mississippi*
дли́нная Миссу́ри *the long Missouri*
бы́страя Колора́до *the rapid Colorado*

(d) Indeclinable loanwords denoting lakes are neuter (cf. **о́зеро** lake).

пресново́дное Э́ри *freshwater Erie*
просто́рное Гуро́н *expansive (Lake) Huron*

7. Identify the gender of each of the following loanwords by writing **о́н**, **оно́**, or **она́**.

1. такси́ ________
2. рефери́ ________
3. меню́ ________
4. авеню́ ________
5. инженю́ ________
6. Сан-Франци́ско ________
7. Ко́нго ________
8. ко́фе ________
9. по́ни ________
10. Анти́гуа ________
11. Гонолу́лу ________
12. Э́ри ________

Number

Most nouns in Russian, as in English, distinguish singular and plural number. English nouns normally form their plural by adding an ending to the singular form, usually *-s* or *-es,* as in *book, books*; *box, boxes.* In Russian too, nouns are made plural either by *adding* an ending (to the stem of masculine nouns that have no singular ending) or by *changing* the ending of the singular (feminine and neuter nouns). In changing from singular to plural, the (singular) ending that may have indicated the noun's gender is removed; consequently, gender is not expressed in the plural of nouns.

Nominative Plural of Nouns

The nominative plural ending of Russian nouns is normally determined by the gender of the noun in the singular and by whether the noun has a hard or soft stem. Specifically, the nominative plural ending for the majority of masculine and feminine nouns with a hard stem is **-ы**, and with a soft stem, **-и**. The nominative plural ending for neuter nouns with a hard stem is **-а**, and with a soft stem, **-я**. The following table illustrates the way stems and endings combine to form the nominative plural of most nouns.

GENDER	SINGULAR	PLURAL	ENDING
Masculine			
Hard Stem	дива́н	дива́ны	-ы
Soft Stem	музе́й	музе́и	-и
	портфе́ль	портфе́ли	
Feminine			
Hard Stem	газе́та	газе́ты	-ы
Soft Stem	ку́хня	ку́хни	-и
	пло́щадь	пло́щади	
Neuter			
Hard Stem	кре́сло	кре́сла	-а
Soft Stem	зда́ние	зда́ния	-я

NOTE: Some words of foreign origin are indeclinable, that is, they never change their ending, and so they do not form a plural, e.g., **метро́**, **кафе́**, **такси́**, **кино́**. However, such clues as a plural ending on a modifying adjective (**-ые**, **-ие**) or a plural verb ending, can indicate when an indeclinable noun is being used to denote more than one object, e.g. **но́вые такси́** *new taxis,* **В це́нтре бы́ли ую́тные кафе́** *In the center there were cozy cafés.*

Spelling Rule 1 and Nominative Plurals

Russian has a spelling rule that applies, among other places, in forming the nominative plural of certain nouns. This spelling rule (Rule 1, page 11) states that the vowel **-ы** cannot occur after the letters **к г х** or **ж ш ч щ**; whenever an "i" vowel is required after one of these letters, it must be spelled **-и**. Therefore, masculine and feminine nouns whose stem ends in one of these consonants must spell their nominative plural ending as **-и**.

SINGULAR	PLURAL	SINGULAR	PLURAL
учёбник *textbook*	учёбники	пля́ж *beach*	пля́жи
кни́га *book*	кни́ги	ро́ща *grove*	ро́щи
стару́ха *old lady*	стару́хи	но́чь *night*	но́чи

8. Rewrite each of the following sentences, changing the noun to the plural and marking its stressed vowel.

MODEL Э́то журна́л. (*This is a magazine.*) > Э́то журна́лы. (*These are magazines.*)

1. Э́то газе́та. ____________
2. Э́то уче́бник. ____________
3. Э́то кни́га. ____________
4. Э́то кре́сло. ____________
5. Э́то ру́чка. ____________
6. Э́то тетра́дь. ____________
7. Э́то пла́тье. ____________
8. Э́то телефо́н. ____________
9. Э́то портфе́ль. ____________
10. Э́то музе́й. ____________
11. Э́то ла́мпа. ____________
12. Э́то студе́нт. ____________
13. Э́то студе́нтка. ____________
14. Э́то институ́т. ____________
15. Э́то пля́ж. ____________
16. Э́то пло́щадь. ____________

Stress Shifts in Nominative Plurals

In some nouns the change from singular to plural is accompanied by a shift of the stress to a different syllable. Some commonly used nouns undergo a stress shift. Below are examples of such nouns from each gender.

Masculine

In masculine nouns the stress shifts from the final syllable of the stem in the singular to the ending of the plural.

SINGULAR	PLURAL	SINGULAR	PLURAL
каранда́ш *pencil*	карандаши́	вра́ч *doctor*	врачи́
слова́рь *dictionary*	словари́	но́ж *knife*	ножи́
сто́л *table*	столы́	клю́ч *key*	ключи́

Neuter

In neuter nouns there is a regular pattern of stress shift that is observed in many two-syllable nouns: The syllable that is unstressed in the singular, gets the stress in the plural.

SINGULAR	PLURAL	SINGULAR	PLURAL
сло́во *word*	слова́	письмо́ *letter*	пи́сьма
ме́сто *place*	места́	окно́ *window*	о́кна
мо́ре *sea*	моря́	лицо́ *face*	ли́ца

Feminine

The stress shifts in some feminine nouns from the ending to the stem.

SINGULAR	PLURAL	SINGULAR	PLURAL
сестра́ *sister*	сёстры	рука́ *hand*	ру́ки
жена́ *wife*	жёны	нога́ *leg*	но́ги
звезда́ *star*	звёзды	голова́ *head*	го́ловы
страна́ *country*	стра́ны	гора́ *mountain*	го́ры

Fleeting Vowels in the Nominative Plural

Some masculine nouns that have the vowel **о**, **е**, or **ё** in the final syllable of the singular, drop this vowel when the nominative plural (or any other) ending is added. The omission of these "fleeting vowels" occurs in a number of nouns, especially in those that end in the suffixes **-ок**, **-ёк**, and **-ец**.

SINGULAR	PLURAL	SINGULAR	PLURAL
значо́к *badge*	значки́	оте́ц *father*	отцы́
кусо́к *piece*	куски́	коне́ц *end*	концы́
кружо́к *small circle*	кружки́	кана́дец *Canadian*	кана́дцы
огонёк *small light*	огоньки́	америка́нец *American*	америка́нцы

9. Rewrite each of the following sentences, changing the noun to the plural and marking its stressed vowel.

MODEL Где́ письмо́? (*Where is the letter?*) > Где́ пи́сьма? (*Where are the letters?*)

1. Где́ значо́к? ____________
2. Где́ но́ж? ____________
3. Где́ плато́к? ____________
4. Где́ слова́рь? ____________
5. Где́ сестра́? ____________
6. Где́ оте́ц? ____________
7. Где́ звезда́? ____________
8. Где́ клю́ч? ____________
9. Где́ окно́? ____________
10. Где́ жена́? ____________

Nominative Plurals in *-á* (*-я́*)

A small number of masculine nouns form their nominative plural with the stressed ending **-á** (**-я́**). The following examples occur frequently and should be memorized.

SINGULAR	PLURAL	SINGULAR	PLURAL
гла́з *eye*	глаза́	но́мер *number*	номера́
го́род *city*	города́	по́езд *train*	поезда́
а́дрес *address*	адреса́	па́спорт *passport*	паспорта́
до́м *house*	дома́	ве́чер *evening*	вечера́
го́лос *voice*	голоса́	кра́й *edge*	края́
профе́ссор *professor*	профессора́	учи́тель *teacher*	учителя́

Irregular Plurals

Irregular Nominative Plurals in *-ья*

A few masculine and neuter nouns form their nominative plural irregularly with the ending **-ья**. These nouns should be memorized.

MASCULINE		NEUTER	
SINGULAR	PLURAL	SINGULAR	PLURAL
бра́т *brother*	бра́тья	де́рево *tree*	дере́вья
сту́л *chair*	сту́лья	перо́ *feather*	пе́рья
му́ж *husband*	мужья́	крыло́ *wing*	кры́лья

A few nouns from this group undergo a stem change in the plural.

SINGULAR	PLURAL
дру́г *friend*	друзья́
сы́н *son*	сыновья́

NOTE: Two nouns augment their stem in the plural by adding the element **-ер-** (as in English *mother* and *daughter*) before the ending **-и**.

SINGULAR	PLURAL
ма́ть *mother*	ма́тери *mothers*
до́чь *daughter*	до́чери *daughters*

Irregular Plurals from Different Words

Two nouns use a completely different word for the plural.

SINGULAR	PLURAL
ребёнок *child*	де́ти *children*
челове́к *person*	лю́ди *people*

Plurals of Neuter Nouns in *-мя*

The small group of neuter nouns in **-мя** undergo a stem change in the plural.

SINGULAR	PLURAL	SINGULAR	PLURAL
вре́мя *time*	времена́	пле́мя *tribe*	племена́
и́мя *name*	имена́	бре́мя *burden*	бремена́
се́мя *seed*	семена́	зна́мя *banner*	знамёна

10. Rewrite each of the following sentences, changing all words to the plural and marking all stressed vowels.

MODEL Мо́й дру́г профе́ссор. (*My friend is a professor.*) >
Мои́ друзья́ профессора́. (*My friends are professors.*)

1. Мо́й сы́н учи́тель. ____________________
2. Моя́ до́чь учи́тельница. ____________________
3. Мо́й бра́т вра́ч. ____________________
4. Моя́ сестра́ студе́нтка. ____________________
5. Мо́й дру́г америка́нец. ____________________

11. Rewrite each of the following sentences, changing the pronoun and noun to the plural and marking all stressed vowels.

MODEL Во́т на́ш клю́ч. (*Here is our key.*) > Во́т на́ши ключи́. (*Here are our keys.*)

1. Во́т на́ш ребёнок. ____________________
2. Во́т на́ш па́спорт. ____________________
3. Во́т на́ш сту́л. ____________________
4. Во́т на́ше и́мя. ____________________
5. Во́т на́ше де́рево. ____________________

Nouns Used Only in the Singular

Some nouns in Russian, as in English, have only a singular form. These include the names of various materials and substances (e.g. English *gold, straw*), abstract nouns denoting various qualities and properties (e.g., English *courage, devotion*), as well as *collective* nouns, i.e., those that, while singular in form, denote a collection of people or things viewed as a whole (e.g., English *youth, mankind, furniture*). In many instances, the same nouns are treated as "singular only" in both English and Russian. There are some nouns, however, that in English are often used in the plural, but whose equivalents in Russian are collective nouns, e.g., English *clothes, dishes,* and various nouns denoting fruits and vegetables, e.g., *strawberries, potatoes, peas.* Below are examples of Russian nouns from various categories used only in the singular. Special note should be taken of those collective nouns that are used with the plural form in English, but in Russian are used only in the singular.

Materials and Substances

де́рево *wood*	молоко́ *milk*
зо́лото *gold*	шокола́д *chocolate*
соло́ма *straw*	ма́сло *butter*
желе́зо *iron*	са́хар *sugar*
ста́ль *steel*	ри́с *rice*

Abstract Nouns Denoting Qualities, Conditions, Sensations, etc.

че́стность *honesty*	све́тлость *brightness*
ло́жь *falsehood*	темнота́ *darkness*
доброта́ *goodness*	гру́сть *sadness*
го́ре *grief*	жара́ *heat, hot weather*

Collective Nouns Denoting People and Objects

молодёжь *young people*	оде́жда *clothes*
студе́нчество *the students*	о́бувь *shoes, footwear*
профессу́ра *the professors*	посу́да *dishes*
детвора́ *children*	бельё *linen(s)*
родня́ *relatives*	листва́ *leaves, foliage*

Collective Nouns Denoting Fruits and Vegetables

изю́м *raisins*	морко́вь *carrots*
виногра́д *grapes*	горо́х *peas*
клубни́ка *strawberries*	капу́ста *cabbage*
мали́на *raspberries*	лу́к *onions*
ежеви́ка *blackberries*	карто́фель *potatoes*
ви́шня *cherries*	крупа́ *groats*

Note that for some of these nouns denoting fruits and vegetables the suffix **-ина** can be added to the noun to express "a raisin," "a grape," etc.: **изю́мина** *a raisin,* **виногра́дина** *a grape,* **горо́шина** *a pea,* **карто́фелина** (or the colloquial noun **карто́шка**) *a potato.* Note also the suffix **-ка** in **морко́вка** *a carrot* (and similarly, **шокола́дка** *a chocolate*). Along with the noun **лу́к** *onions,* there is the related word **лу́ковица** *an onion.* To denote "a strawberry," "a raspberry," one can use the word **я́года** *berry,* e.g., **я́года клубни́ки** *a strawberry*; alternatively, the word **шту́ка** *item* may be used to express one or more individual pieces, e.g., **Да́йте лу́ку, три́ шту́ки, пожа́луйста** *Give me some onions, three (pieces) please.*

Note also that a collective noun requires singular agreement. For example, a modifying adjective must agree in singular number and in gender (masculine, feminine, and neuter adjective endings are, respectively, **-ый**, **-ая**, and **-ое**).

Э́то вку́сный виногра́д.	*These are tasty grapes.*
Э́то све́жая клубни́ка.	*These are fresh strawberries.*
Э́то чи́стое бельё.	*These are clean linens.*

Also, a predicate verb must agree in the singular.

Оде́жда лежи́т на крова́ти.	*The clothes are lying on the bed.*

(The form **лежи́т** is the third-person singular, present tense form of the verb **лежа́ть** *to lie.*)

Nouns Used Only in the Plural

Some nouns denote objects or processes comprised of at least two essential parts or participants. Often, language reflects this real-world fact grammatically by allowing such nouns to occur generally in the plural, e.g., English *jeans, scissors, the races, negotiations,* etc. The Russian equivalents of these particular nouns also occur only in the plural. In a few instances, however, Russian and English differ in this regard, e.g., the English noun *watch* is a plural-only noun in Russian: **часы́**. Below is a representative list of commonly used nouns that normally occur only in the plural. Take special note of the nouns in the column on the right, which in English are used in the singular, but are plural-only nouns in Russian.

(a) *Plural-only nouns ending in* **-ы**, **-и**

часы́ *watch, clock*	де́ньги *money*
очки́ *eyeglasses*	сли́вки *cream*
но́жницы *scissors*	счёты *abacus*
брю́ки *trousers*	духи́ *perfume*
джи́нсы *jeans*	каче́ли *swing*
шо́рты *shorts*	са́ни *sleigh*
трусы́ *underpants*	ша́хматы *chess*
пла́вки *swimming trunks*	кани́кулы *vacation, holidays*
перегово́ры *negotiations*	ро́ды *childbirth*
вы́боры *elections*	по́хороны *funeral*

(b) *Plural-only nouns ending in* **-a**

бега́ *harness races*	пери́ла *railings*
черни́ла *ink*	воро́та *gate*
дрова́ *firewood*	письмена́ *alphabet characters*

12. For each noun below, write a noun phrase, using the correct form of the adjective in parentheses.

MODEL (посте́льный *bed*) бельё > посте́льное бельё (*bed linen*)
(но́вый *new*) часы́ > но́вые часы́ (*new watch*)

1. (ру́сский *Russian*) молодёжь ______________________
2. (мо́дный *stylish*) оде́жда ______________________
3. (кра́сный *red*) черни́ла ______________________
4. (све́жий *fresh*) мали́на ______________________
5. (желе́зный *iron*) пери́ла ______________________
6. (чи́стый *clean*) посу́да ______________________
7. (прия́тный *pleasant*) духи́ ______________________
8. (сухо́й *dry*) дрова́ ______________________
9. (но́вый *new*) де́ньги ______________________
10. (весёлый *cheerful*) детвора́ ______________________

Declension of Nouns

All nouns in Russian (except some of foreign origin, e.g., **ра́дио** *radio,* **меню́** *menu,* **кафе́** *café*) *decline,* that is, change their endings to express a particular *case* in the singular or plural (see the section Case below). Every declinable noun belongs to one of three declension classes: *first declension, second declension,* or *third declension.* The particular declension class a noun belongs to is based on its gender and form in the nominative singular.

First Declension

Masculine nouns with a stem ending in a consonant or **-й**
Masculine nouns with a stem ending in **-ь**
Neuter nouns ending in **-о**, **-е**, **-ё**

Second Declension

Feminine nouns ending in **-а**, **-я**
Masculine nouns ending in **-а**, **-я**

Third Declension

Feminine nouns with a stem ending in **-ь**

The following table illustrates the distribution of nouns into the three declension classes.

CASE	FIRST DECLENSION	SECOND DECLENSION	THIRD DECLENSION
Nominative	**Masculine**	**Feminine**	**Feminine**
	сто́л	маши́на	пло́щадь
	портфе́ль	ку́хня	
	музе́й	**Masculine**	
	Neuter	па́па	
	кре́сло	дя́дя	
	зда́ние		
	бельё		

Most nouns are easily assigned to one of the three declensions. The only nouns whose declension is difficult to determine are those ending in the soft sign (**-ь**). Remember that masculine soft-sign nouns belong to the first declension, while feminine soft-sign nouns are the *only* nouns in the third declension. It is important to know the declension class to which a noun belongs because each declension class has its own set of endings that correspond to the different cases in Russian.

Case

The term *case* refers to the function, or type of relation, a noun (or pronoun) has with respect to the other words in a sentence. For example, in the sentence *Mary gave the book to John* the noun *Mary* is the "subject" of the sentence, *book* functions as "direct object" of the verb, and *John* has the function of "indirect object." These three functions normally are fulfilled by nouns in the **nominative**, **accusative**, and **dative** cases, respectively. Similarly, in the phrase *Tanya's brother* the noun *Tanya* functions as the "possessor" in relation to the noun *brother* (what is "possessed"), a relation indicated in English by the ending *-'s.* This "possessor" relation is typically expressed by the **genitive** case. In English these grammatical functions, or relation types, are indicated formally by word order (e.g., the subject is to the left of the verb, the direct object to the verb's right), by prepositions (e.g., the preposition *to* in *to John* signals indirect object), or by an ending on the noun (e.g., the possessive ending *-'s* added to the noun *Tanya*). In Russian, certain types of relations, like the English possessive, are indicated by a case ending on the noun. Others, as we shall see in Chapter 3, are expressed by both a preposition and a case ending.

Animacy

Some nouns denote living beings, such as people and animals (**оте́ц** *father,* **бра́т** *brother,* **ко́т** *tomcat*), while others denote various nonliving objects and abstract things (**сто́л** *table,* **сту́л** *chair,* **ра́дость** *joy*). The grammatical terms for these two classes of nouns are *animate* and *inanimate,* respectively. The distinction between animate and inanimate nouns is important in determining which nouns are functioning as "subject" or "object" in Russian. In English, grammatical relations like "subject" and "object" are determined by a fixed subject-verb-object word order, but in Russian, where word order is "free," an animate direct object can precede a verb and potentially be mistaken for the subject. This potential ambiguity is generally avoided in Russian by marking masculine animate, but not inanimate, nouns with a special ending when they function as a direct object of the verb in the accusative case. For example, the inanimate masculine noun **сто́л** *table* has the same form whether it functions as subject (**Сто́л та́м** *The table is there*), or object (**Я́ ви́жу сто́л** *I see the table*). But the animate masculine noun **сы́н** *son* adds the ending **-а** when it functions as a direct object in the accusative case (**Я́ ви́дел сы́на** *I saw my son*). Therefore, in the sentence **Оте́ц лю́бит сы́на** *The father loves his son* the direct object is formally distinguished from the subject **оте́ц** *father,* and these roles remain the same even when, for reasons of emphasis, the object precedes the subject (**Сы́на лю́бит оте́ц** *It is the father who loves his son*).

Animate nouns functioning as direct objects in the accusative case have a special ending not only in the singular of first-declension masculines; the plurals of animate nouns in all three declensions have an ending that differentiates them from inanimate nouns.

The Cases of Russian

Russian has six cases.

Nominative
Accusative
Genitive
Prepositional
Dative
Instrumental

Nominative Case

Singular and Plural Endings

The following table summarizes nominative case endings in both singular and plural.

GENDER	SINGULAR	ENDING	PLURAL	ENDING
Masculine				
Hard Stem	дива́н	-∅	дива́ны	-ы
Soft Stem	музе́й		музе́и	-и
	портфе́ль		портфе́ли	
Feminine				
Hard Stem	газе́та	-а	газе́ты	-ы
Soft Stem	ку́хня	-я	ку́хни	-и
	пло́щадь	-∅	пло́щади	
Neuter				
Hard Stem	кре́сло	-о	кре́сла	-а
Soft Stem	зда́ние	-е	зда́ния	-я

The nominative case can be viewed as the basic form of the noun. As previously mentioned, it is the nominative case form in which words are cited in dictionaries, or when they are in other ways removed from context. The nominative case in Russian has several uses.

Uses of the Nominative Case

Nominative as Subject

The nominative case is used for the grammatical subject of the sentence. The noun in the nominative case controls agreement on its predicate: A predicate verb in the present tense must agree with the subject in person and number; in the past tense, a verb in the singular agrees in gender as well. A predicate adjective must also agree with its nominative-case subject in both gender and number.

Профе́ссор чита́ет ле́кцию.	*The professor is reading a lecture.*
Студе́нты слу́шают ле́кцию.	*The students listen to the lecture.*
Учени́к за́дал вопро́с.	*The pupil asked a question.*
Студе́нтка задала́ вопро́с.	*The coed asked a question.*
Письмо́ лежи́т на столе́.	*The letter is (lying) on the table.*
Маши́ны стоя́т на у́лице.	*Cars are parked on the street.*
За́л свобо́ден.	*The hall is free* (*available*).
Ме́сто свобо́дно.	*The seat is free.*
Ко́мната свобо́дна.	*The room is free.*
Места́ свобо́дны.	*The seats are free.*

As a Predicate Nominative

A predicate nominative is a noun (or pronoun or adjective) that follows a linking verb (stated or implied) and is *equated* with the subject in some way. For example, in the sentence *John is a student* the predicate nominative denotes a class or status—that of "student"—that is attributed to the subject. In Russian, the equivalent of the English linking verb *to be,* **бы́ть**, generally is not used in the present tense, but its meaning is always implied in sentences with predicate nominatives. The implicit "am/is/are" meaning is sometimes indicated in punctuation by a dash.

Ива́н—**студе́нт**.	*Ivan is a student.*
Пу́шкин и Че́хов—**писа́тели**.	*Pushkin and Chekhov are writers.*
Москва́—**столи́ца Росси́и**.	*Moscow is the capital of Russia.*
Э́то **моя́ сестра́**.	*This is my sister.*
Э́то **мои́ роди́тели**.	*These are my parents.*

Nouns following a past-tense form of the verb **бы́ть** (**бы́л**, **была́**, **бы́ли**) may occur as predicates in the nominative case when they denote a permanent property, or one felt to be a defining characteristic of the subject. These include nouns denoting nationalities, kinship terms (e.g., **бра́т** *brother,* **сестра́** *sister*), as well as nouns with evaluative meaning (e.g., **добря́к** *good guy,* **краса́вица** *a beauty,* **у́мница** *smart person*).

Мо́й де́душка **бы́л америка́нец**.	*My grandfather was American.*
Моя́ ба́бушка **была́ ру́сская**.	*My grandmother was Russian.*
Ва́ня **бы́л добря́к**.	*Vanya was a good guy.*
Ле́на **была́ у́мница**.	*Lena was a smart person.*

NOTE: When they occur after the past tense (or other forms) of **бы́ть**, unmodified nouns of occupation, and other nouns denoting function or status, are normally in the instrumental case. See the section Uses of the Instrumental Case.

Nominative as a Form of Direct Address

The nominative case can be used as a vocative, that is, a form used to call or address someone directly.

Ю́рий Серге́евич! Мо́жно ва́с?	*Yuri Sergeevich! Can I speak with you?*
Са́ша! Тебя́ к телефо́ну.	*Sasha! You're wanted on the phone.*
Ва́ня! Познако́мься с моей жено́й.	*Vanya! I'd like you to meet my wife.*

NOTE: In colloquial style the informal nouns used as vocatives may lose their final vowel, thus taking on a form different from the nominative: **Са́ш!** *Sash!,* **Ма́м!** *Mom!,* **Ва́нь!** *Vanya!*

As a Noun Title in Apposition

A noun denoting the name or title of something in apposition to the noun denoting its generic class is in the nominative case.

Мы́ чита́ем рома́н **«Война́ и ми́р»**.	*We are reading the novel "War and Peace."*
О́н слу́шал о́перу **«Евге́ний Оне́гин»**.	*He listened to the opera "Evgenij Onegin."*
Она́ рабо́тает в газе́те **«Пра́вда»**.	*She works for the newspaper "Pravda."*

Accusative Case

Singular and Plural Endings

The accusative case endings of first-declension *inanimate* masculine nouns, as well as neuter nouns, are identical to the nominative case endings, in both singular and plural.

First Declension

Masculine Inanimate Nouns

	SINGULAR		PLURAL	
CASE	HARD STEM	SOFT STEM	HARD STEM	SOFT STEM
Nom.	сто́л	портфе́ль	столы́	портфе́ли
Acc. = Nom.	сто́л	портфе́ль	столы́	портфе́ли

Neuter Nouns

	SINGULAR		PLURAL	
CASE	HARD STEM	SOFT STEM	HARD STEM	SOFT STEM
Nom.	окно́	зда́ние	о́кна	зда́ния
Acc. = Nom.	окно́	зда́ние	о́кна	зда́ния

The accusative case endings of first-declension *animate* masculine nouns in both singular and plural are identical to the genitive case endings (see the section Animacy).

Animate Masculine Nouns

	SINGULAR		PLURAL	
CASE	HARD STEM	SOFT STEM	HARD STEM	SOFT STEM
Nom.	студе́нт	писа́тель	студе́нты	писа́тели
Acc. = Gen.	студе́нта	писа́теля	студе́нтов	писа́телей

Second Declension

Second-declension feminine nouns ending in **-а/-я**, as well as masculine nouns ending in **-а/-я**, take the ending **-у/-ю** in the accusative singular. Both masculine and feminine *animate* nouns in the plural have an ending in the accusative identical to the genitive plural.

Feminine and Masculine Nouns in *-а*

	SINGULAR			PLURAL		
CASE	FEMININE INANIMATE	ANIMATE	MASCULINE ANIMATE	FEMININE INANIMATE	ANIMATE	MASCULINE ANIMATE
Nom.	спáльня	бáбушка	дéдушка	кóмнаты	бáбушки	дéдушки
Acc.	спáльню	бáбушку	дéдушку	кóмнаты	бáбушек	дéдушек

Third Declension

Third-declension *inanimate* nouns in the singular and plural have an ending identical to the nominative. Third-declension *animate* nouns, of which there are few (e.g., **свекрóвь** *mother-in-law*), have an ending in the accusative plural identical to the genitive plural.

Feminine Nouns in -ь

	SINGULAR		PLURAL	
CASE	INANIMATE	ANIMATE	INANIMATE	ANIMATE
Nom.	тетрáдь	свекрóвь	тетрáди	свекрóви
Acc.	тетрáдь	свекрóвь	тетрáди	свекрóвей

Uses of the Accusative Case

As the Direct Object of a Transitive Verb

The direct object of a verb is the noun (or pronoun) that often is understood to be the goal of the action, the object affected (or effected) by the action of the verb.

Áвтор пи́шет **ромáн**. — *The author is writing a novel.*
Óн пи́шет **интерéсные ромáны**. — *He writes interesting novels.*
Учи́тель откры́л **окнó**. — *The teacher opened the window.*
Профéссор спрáшивал **студéнта**. — *The professor was questioning the student.*
Óн чáсто спрáшивает **студéнтов**. — *He often questions students.*
Мáльчик читáет **кни́гу**. — *The boy is reading a book.*
Рýсские лю́бят читáть **кни́ги**. — *Russians love to read books.*
Дéвочка лю́бит **бáбушку и дéдушку**. — *The girl loves her grandma and grandpa.*
Нáдо уважáть **бáбушек и дéдушек**. — *One must respect grandmas and grandpas.*

To Express Duration and Repetition of Time

Онá говори́ла по телефóну **цéлый чáс**. — *She spoke on the phone a whole hour.*
Бáбушка болéла **всю́ зи́му**. — *Grandma was sick all winter.*
Мы́ бы́ли в Москвé **мéсяц**. — *We were in Moscow a month.*
Ви́ка пи́шет пи́сьма **кáждую недéлю**. — *Vika writes letters every week.*

To Express Extent of Distance, Cost, or Weight

Кáждое ýтро óн бéгает **пя́ть киломéтров**. — *Every morning he runs five kilometers.*
Всю́ дорóгу они́ игрáли в кáрты. — *They played cards the whole way.*
Кольцó стóит **ты́сячу** дóлларов. — *The ring costs a thousand dollars.*
Э́та маши́на вéсит **тóнну**. — *This car weighs a ton.*

As the Object of Prepositions

Prepositions that require the accusative case are presented in Chapter 3.

13. For each of the following sentences, identify the case of the underlined word.

	Nominative	Accusative
1. Профе́ссор чита́л ле́кцию.	☐	☐
2. Ле́кцию чита́л профе́ссор.	☐	☐
3. Профе́ссора лю́бят студе́нты.	☐	☐
4. Э́то моя́ жена́.	☐	☐
5. Моя́ жена́—программи́ст.	☐	☐
6. Де́вочка убира́ет ко́мнату.	☐	☐
7. Мы́ чита́ем журна́л «Та́йм».	☐	☐
8. Она́ была́ в Росси́и ме́сяц.	☐	☐
9. Па́па бе́гает ка́ждый де́нь.	☐	☐
10. Мы́ ви́дели но́вый фи́льм.	☐	☐
11. Фи́льм шёл в кинотеа́тре «Росси́я».	☐	☐
12. Како́й интере́сный фи́льм!	☐	☐
13. Шокола́д сто́ит оди́н до́ллар.	☐	☐
14. Моя́ сестра́ у́мница.	☐	☐

14. For each of the following sentences, write the plural form of the underlined noun.

1. Па́па чита́ет журна́л. ____________________
2. Са́ша лю́бит компью́тер. ____________________
3. Ма́ма пи́шет письмо́. ____________________
4. Профе́ссор спра́шивает студе́нта. ____________________
5. Шко́льники покупа́ют тетра́дь. ____________________
6. Ма́льчик купи́л слова́рь. ____________________
7. Де́вочка ча́сто но́сит пла́тье. ____________________
8. Мы́ зна́ем свекро́вь. ____________________

15. Complete each of the following sentences by giving the correct case form of the noun on the left.

MODEL му́зыка Она́ слу́шает <u>му́зыку</u>.

1. литерату́ра Мы́ изуча́ем ____________________.
2. исто́рия О́н лю́бит ____________________.
3. бра́т Я́ зна́ю ____________________.
4. соба́ка Мы́ ви́дели ____________________.
5. преподава́тель Студе́нт слу́шает ____________________.
6. зада́ние Мы́ де́лаем ____________________.
7. ра́дио Ле́на слу́шает ____________________.
8. матема́тика Са́ша пло́хо зна́ет ____________________.
9. ма́ть Сы́н лю́бит ____________________.
10. оте́ц О́н не зна́ет ____________________.

Genitive Case

Genitive Singular

The endings of the genitive singular for masculine and neuter nouns are as follows.

-а for nouns with a hard stem
-я for nouns with a soft stem

NOMINATIVE SINGULAR	GENITIVE SINGULAR
сто́л *table*	стола́
портфе́ль *briefcase*	портфе́ля
бра́т *brother*	бра́та
го́сть *guest*	го́стя

The endings of the genitive singular for feminine nouns are as follows.

-ы for nouns with a hard stem
-и for nouns with a soft stem

NOMINATIVE SINGULAR	GENITIVE SINGULAR
ко́мната *room*	ко́мнаты
сестра́ *sister*	сестры́
ку́хня *kitchen*	ку́хни

NOTE: The only exceptions to the generalizations above are those nouns subject to either Spelling Rule 1 or Spelling Rule 2 (see page 11). For example, due to Spelling Rule 1, the genitive singular of feminine nouns whose stem ends in a hard **г**, **к**, **х**, or **ж/ш** takes the ending **-и** (rather than **-ы**): **кни́га** *book* > **кни́ги**, **ко́шка** *cat* > **ко́шки**, **ко́жа** *leather* > **ко́жи**. Due to Spelling Rule 2, masculine nouns whose stem ends in the soft consonant **ч** or **щ** take the ending **-а** (rather than **-я**): **вра́ч** *doctor* > **врача́**, **пла́щ** *raincoat* > **плаща́**.

NOTE: Masculine nouns that end in **-а** or **-я** in the nominative singular (**па́па**, **дя́дя**) take the same ending in the genitive case as feminine nouns ending in **-а** or **-я**: **Ру́чка *ма́мы*** *Mom's pen* ~ **Ру́чка *па́пы*** *Dad's pen*. Such nouns referring to male persons decline like feminine nouns in all the cases.

Genitive Plural

There are three possible endings in the genitive plural: (1) **-ов** (**-ев**), (2) **-ей**, and (3) **-∅**. The distribution of these endings is as follows.

The Genitive Plural Ending *-ов*

(a) Masculine nouns whose stem ends in a hard paired consonant

NOMINATIVE SINGULAR	GENITIVE PLURAL
сто́л *table*	столо́в
до́м *house*	домо́в
студе́нт *student*	студе́нтов

(b) Masculine nouns with the stressed suffix **-éц**

NOMINATIVE SINGULAR	GENITIVE PLURAL
отéц *father*	отцóв
певéц *singer*	певцóв

NOTE: The suffix **-ец** contains a "fleeting vowel" that is omitted when any ending follows this suffix. This is also true of the suffix **-ок**: **платóк** *shawl* > **платкóв**.

The Genitive Plural Ending *-ев*

(a) Masculine nouns with the unstressed suffix **-ец**

NOMINATIVE SINGULAR	GENITIVE PLURAL
америкáнец *American*	америкáнцев
мéсяц *month*	мéсяцев

NOTE: The spelling of this suffix as **-ев** is due to Spelling Rule 3 (see page 11).

(b) Masculine nouns with a stem ending in **-й**

NOMINATIVE SINGULAR	GENITIVE PLURAL
музéй *museum*	музéев
герóй *hero*	герóев
кафетéрий *cafeteria*	кафетéриев

(c) Nouns whose nominative plural is stem-stressed and ends in **-ья**

NOMINATIVE SINGULAR	NOMINATIVE PLURAL	GENITIVE PLURAL
брáт *brother*	брáтья	брáтьев
стýл *chair*	стýлья	стýльев
лúст *leaf*	лúстья	лúстьев
дéрево *tree*	дерéвья	дерéвьев

The Genitive Plural Ending *-ей*

(a) All masculine and feminine nouns whose stem ends in the soft sign **-ь**

NOMINATIVE SINGULAR	GENITIVE PLURAL
словáрь *dictionary*	словарéй
тетрáдь *notebook*	тетрáдей
писáтель *writer*	писáтелей

NOTE: The nouns **мáть** *mother* and **дóчь** *daughter* take the genitive plural in **-ей**, but the ending is preceded by the element **-ер-**: **матерéй**, **дочерéй**.

(b) All masculine nouns ending in the unpaired consonants **ж ч ш щ**

NOMINATIVE SINGULAR	GENITIVE PLURAL
вра́ч *doctor*	враче́й
но́ж *knife*	ноже́й
каранда́ш *pencil*	карандаше́й
пла́щ *raincoat*	плаще́й

(c) Nouns whose nominative plural ends in stressed **-ья́**

NOMINATIVE SINGULAR	NOMINATIVE PLURAL	GENITIVE PLURAL
дру́г *friend*	друзья́	друзе́й
сы́н *son*	сыновья́	сынове́й
му́ж *husband*	мужья́	муже́й

(d) A few nouns form their genitive plural from a different word.

NOMINATIVE SINGULAR	NOMINATIVE PLURAL	GENITIVE PLURAL
ребёнок *child*	де́ти	дете́й
челове́к *person*	лю́ди	люде́й
го́д *year*	го́ды	ле́т

NOTE: After certain words denoting quantity, e.g., **ско́лько** *how many,* **не́сколько** *several,* and the numerals **пя́ть** *five,* **ше́сть** *six,* and higher, the noun **челове́к** has a genitive plural form that is identical to its nominative singular: **Ско́лько челове́к? Пя́ть челове́к.**

NOTE: The genitive plural of the noun **го́д** *year* is formed from the noun **ле́то** *summer,* e.g., **Ско́лько ле́т?** *How many years?*

The Genitive Plural Zero Ending -∅

(a) Most feminine nouns in **-а**, **-я** and neuter nouns in **-о**, **-е** drop this vowel in the genitive plural, leaving only the noun stem (= zero ending).

NOMINATIVE SINGULAR	GENITIVE PLURAL
кни́га *book*	кни́г
газе́та *newspaper*	газе́т
де́ло *affair, business*	де́л
фами́лия *surname*	фами́лий
зда́ние *building*	зда́ний
галере́я *gallery*	галере́й

NOTE: Nouns whose nominative singular ends in **-ие**, **-ия**, or **-ея** have a stem ending in **-й**, i.e., **ие**, **ия**, and **ея** are structurally [ий-е], [ий-а], and [ей-а], respectively. Therefore, dropping the final vowel to form the genitive plural results only in a stem in **-й**, i.e., a form with a zero ending.

NOTE: Three nouns, **тётя** *aunt,* **дя́дя** *uncle,* and **ю́ноша** *youth,* do not take the expected zero ending; instead they form the genitive plural irregularly with the ending **-ей**: **тётей**, **дя́дей**, **ю́ношей**.

NOTE: Two neuter nouns, **мо́ре** *sea* and **по́ле** *field,* do not have the expected zero ending, but instead irregularly form the genitive plural in **-ей**: **море́й**, **поле́й**. Similarly, the neuter noun **о́блако** *cloud* forms its genitive plural irregularly in **-ов**: **облако́в**.

(b) Certain nouns with the zero ending in the genitive plural also "insert" the vowel **-о-** or **-е-** in order to break up a consonant cluster at the end of the word.

NOMINATIVE SINGULAR	GENITIVE PLURAL
студе́нтка *coed*	студе́нток
ку́хня *kitchen*	ку́хонь
дере́вня *village*	дереве́нь
балала́йка *balalaika*	балала́ек
сестра́ *sister*	сестёр
окно́ *window*	о́кон
письмо́ *letter*	пи́сем

NOTE: The noun **яйцо́** *egg* has the inserted vowel **-и-** in the genitive plural **яи́ц**.

(c) Nouns whose nominative singular ends in stressed **-ья́** have an inserted vowel **-е-** before a zero ending.

NOMINATIVE SINGULAR	GENITIVE PLURAL
семья́ *family*	семе́й
статья́ *article*	стате́й
судья́ *judge*	суде́й

NOTE: These nouns in the singular have a stem ending in **-й**, e.g., **статья́** is comprised of the stem [stat'y-] and the ending [-a]. Therefore, dropping the nominative singular [-a] (and replacing the soft sign **-ь-** with **-е-**) leaves a zero ending in the genitive plural.

(d) A few nouns have a genitive plural that is identical to the nominative singular.

NOMINATIVE SINGULAR	GENITIVE PLURAL
гла́з *eye*	гла́з
ра́з *time*	ра́з
чуло́к *stocking*	чуло́к
солда́т *soldier*	солда́т
челове́к *person*	челове́к

NOTE: The noun **челове́к** has two genitive plural forms: **челове́к** (only after certain words expressing quantity, as noted above) and **люде́й**.

The following table summarizes the regular genitive-case endings of nouns in both singular and plural.

Table of Regular Genitive Singular and Plural Noun Endings

GENDER	NOMINATIVE SINGULAR	GENITIVE SINGULAR	ENDING	GENITIVE PLURAL	ENDING
Masculine					
Hard Stem	стóл	столá	-а	столóв	-ов
	студéнт	студéнта		студéнтов	
Soft Stem	музéй	музéя	-я	музéев	-ев
	портфéль	портфéля		портфéлей	-ей
	писáтель	писáтеля		писáтелей	
Neuter					
Hard Stem	окнó	окнá	-а	óкон	-∅
Soft Stem	здáние	здáния	-я	здáний	
Feminine					
Hard Stem	газéта	газéты	-ы	газéт	-∅
Soft Stem	недéля	недéли	-и	недéль	
	истóрия	истóрии		истóрий	
	тетрáдь	тетрáди		тетрáдей	-ей

Uses of the Genitive Case

Genitive After a Noun

The genitive case is used to express various kinds of relationships between two nouns.

To Denote the Possessor of Something

This use of the genitive case in Russian corresponds to the English possessive construction with *'s*: *the professor's briefcase.* Note, however, that in Russian the possessor follows, rather than precedes, the possessed object.

Э́то портфéль **профéссора**.	*This is the professor's briefcase.*
Маши́на **отцá** стои́т в гаражé.	*My father's car is parked in the garage.*
Гдé словáрь **сестры́**?	*Where is the sister's dictionary?*
Дóм **роди́телей** на э́той у́лице.	*The parents' house is on this street.*

To Denote the Person After Whom Something Is Named

у́лица **Чéхова**	*Chekhov Street*
плóщадь **Гагáрина**	*Gagarin Square*
дом-музéй **Пу́шкина**	*Pushkin Museum*

To Denote the Whole in Relation to the Part

This use of the genitive, and those that follow it, is often expressed in English by the preposition *of.*

переплёт **кни́ги**	*cover of a book*
ру́чка **чемодáна**	*handle of a suitcase*
кры́ша **дóма**	*roof of a house*
колесó **маши́ны**	*wheel of a car*

To Denote the Agent of an Action

выступлéние **арти́стов**	*performance of the artists*
смéх **детéй**	*laughter of children*
объяснéние **преподавáтеля**	*explanation of the teacher*

To Denote the Object of an Action

изуче́ние **языко́в**	*study of languages*
чте́ние **те́кста**	*reading of the text*
откры́тие **вы́ставки**	*opening of the exhibit*

To Denote an Entity to Which a Property or Quality Is Attributed

красота́ **Кавка́за**	*the beauty of the Caucasus*
теплота́ **со́лнца**	*the warmth of the sun*
доброта́ **челове́ка**	*the goodness of Man*

To Denote a Container or Specific Quantity of an Object

коро́бка **конфе́т**	*a box of candy*
буты́лка **вина́**	*a bottle of wine*
па́чка **сигаре́т**	*a pack of cigarettes*
паке́т **молока́**	*a carton of milk*
пол-ли́тра **во́дки**	*a half-liter of vodka*

Genitive After Numerals

The previous use of the genitive case after nouns denoting specific quantity is only one example of a more general use of the genitive case to express quantity.

The numerical expression **о́ба/о́бе** *both,* the cardinal numbers **два́/две́** *two,* **три́** *three,* **четы́ре** *four,* and compounds ending in these numbers (e.g., **два́дцать два́** *twenty-two,* **два́дцать три́** *twenty-three,* **три́дцать четы́ре** *thirty-four),* all require the genitive singular of the following noun, when the numerals themselves are in the nominative or (inanimate) accusative case.

два́ **карандаша́**	*two pencils*
три́ **словаря́**	*three dictionaries*
две́ **ру́чки**	*two pens*
четы́ре **студе́нта**	*four students*

The cardinal numbers **пя́ть** *five,* **ше́сть** *six,* **се́мь** *seven,* **во́семь** *eight,* **де́вять** *nine,* **де́сять** *ten,* and higher up to "twenty-one," require the genitive plural on the following noun, when these numbers themselves are in the nominative or accusative case.

пя́ть **студе́нтов**	*five students*
ше́сть **сто́лов**	*six tables*
се́мь **ру́чек**	*seven pens*
во́семь **маши́н**	*eight cars*
де́вять **словаре́й**	*nine dictionaries*
де́сять **карандаше́й**	*ten pencils*

Genitive After Adverbial Expressions of Quantity

The genitive case is used after words denoting indefinite quantity, e.g., **ско́лько** *how many / how much,* **сто́лько** *so many / so much,* **мно́го** *many/much,* **немно́го** *not many / not much,* **ма́ло** *few/little,* **не́сколько** *a few.* With nouns denoting objects that can be counted, the genitive plural is used; with abstract nouns or those denoting substances, the genitive singular occurs.

Ско́лько **столо́в**?	*How many tables?*	Ско́лько **су́па**?	*How much soup?*
сто́лько **дете́й**	*so many children*	сто́лько **шу́ма**	*so much noise*
мно́го **друзе́й**	*many friends*	мно́го **вина́**	*a lot of wine*
ма́ло **госте́й**	*few guests*	ма́ло **во́дки**	*little vodka*

NOTE: These adverbial quantifiers require a verb in the past tense to be in the neuter singular: **Та́м *бы́ло* мно́го кни́г** *There were many books there.* Also, when used with the noun **челове́к** *person,* **ско́лько** and

не́сколько take the genitive plural **челове́к**, but **мно́го** and **ма́ло** take the genitive plural **люде́й**: **—Ско́лько та́м бы́ло *челове́к*? —Та́м бы́ло мно́го *люде́й*.** *"How many people were there?" "There were many people there."*

Genitive After Verbs

After Transitive Verbs to Express a "Partitive" Meaning

The genitive case may be used for the object of certain transitive verbs to express a "partitive" sense, that is, to denote a part of the whole, "some" of something.

Да́й, пожа́луйста, **хле́ба**.	*Please give me some bread.*
Она́ вы́пила **вина́**.	*She drank some wine.*
Го́сти пое́ли **пирожко́в**.	*The guests ate some pirozhki.*
Ма́льчик нарва́л **цвето́в**.	*The boy picked some flowers.*

NOTE: The same object in the accusative case would imply "the whole" of what is referred to, and is often expressed in English by the use of the definite article: **Переда́й, пожа́луйста, *хле́б*** *Please pass the bread.*

A small number of masculine nouns have two genitive case endings in the singular: the regular genitive ending **-а/-я** and a second "partitive genitive" ending **-у/-ю**, which may be used to convey the partitive meaning. This partitive genitive **-у** ending is losing ground to the regular genitive case ending, but is still encountered in colloquial Russian: **Она́ попила́ *ча́ю*** *She drank some tea,* **Ма́льчик пое́л *су́пу*** *The boy ate some soup.* Some common examples of these nouns, many of which denote substances to eat or drink, are given below.

NOMINATIVE	GENITIVE	PARTITIVE GENITIVE
су́п *soup*	су́па	су́пу
са́хар *sugar*	са́хара	са́хару
лу́к *onion*	лу́ка	лу́ку
мёд *honey*	мёда	мёду
пе́рец *pepper*	пе́рца	пе́рцу
сы́р *cheese*	сы́ра	сы́ру
ча́й *tea*	ча́я	ча́ю
ри́с *rice*	ри́са	ри́су
коньяк *cognac*	коньяка́	коньяку́
шокола́д *chocolate*	шокола́да	шокола́ду

The partitive genitive also occurs after nouns denoting a specific quantity of something, e.g., **буты́лка *коньяку́*** *bottle of cognac,* **ча́шка *ча́ю*** *cup of tea,* **таре́лка *су́пу*** *plate of soup,* **ба́нка *мёду*** *jar of honey,* **па́чка *са́хару*** *package of sugar.* When the meaning is one other than quantity, or when these nouns are modified by an adjective, they take the regular genitive ending in **-а**, **-я**: **цена́ *ча́я*** *price of tea,* **стака́н армя́нского *коньяка́*** *glass of Armenian cognac.*

After Negated Transitive Verbs

When used affirmatively, a transitive verb takes a direct object in the accusative case, or, when a partitive meaning is intended, in the genitive case. Similarly, when transitive verbs are negated, the direct object may be in the accusative or the genitive case: **Де́вочка не чита́ла *расска́з/расска́за*** *The girl didn't read the story.* Though it is sometimes possible to use either the genitive or accusative case for the direct object of a negated transitive verb, the genitive is strongly preferred when

1. the object is an abstract noun.

Вы́ не име́ете **пра́ва** та́к говори́ть.	*You don't have the right to talk that way.*
Не обраща́й **внима́ния** на э́то.	*Don't pay any attention to that.*

2. the object is the abstract pronoun **э́то**.

Я́ **э́того** не понима́ю.	*I don't understand that.*
Мы́ **э́того** не зна́ли.	*We didn't know that.*

3. the object is indefinite or nonspecific.

Мы́ не е́ли **мя́са** це́лый ме́сяц.	*We didn't eat (any) meat for a whole month.*
Она́ не чита́ла **детекти́вов**.	*She didn't read detective stories.*

4. the object is preceded by an emphatic negative expression with **ни**.

О́н не сказа́л ни **сло́ва**.	*He didn't say a word.*
Она́ не чита́ла ни одно́й **страни́цы**.	*She didn't read a single page.*

5. the object follows a negated verb of perception.

Она́ не слы́шала **вопро́са**.	*She didn't hear the question.*
Са́ша не по́нял **объясне́ния**.	*Sasha didn't understand the explanation.*
Мы́ не ви́дели **таксофо́нов**.	*We didn't see any pay telephones.*

After Negated Forms of the Verb *бы́ть*

The genitive case is used to express the "absence" or "nonexistence" of something in locational and possessive sentences with **не́т** *there is no,* **не́ было** *there was/were no,* **не бу́дет** *there will be no.*

Зде́сь не́т **телефо́на**.	*There is no telephone here.*
Та́м не́ было **словаря́**.	*There was no dictionary there.*
До́ма не́т **компью́тера**.	*There is no computer at home.*
У меня́ не́т **соба́ки**.	*I don't have a dog.*
У нас не́ было **вре́мени**.	*We didn't have time.*
У бра́та не бу́дет **биле́та**.	*The brother will not have a ticket.*

After Verbs That Govern the Genitive

There are certain verbs that govern, that is, require the genitive case on their object. The following are common examples.

жела́ть *to wish*
добива́ться *to strive for*
достига́ть *to achieve*
боя́ться *to be afraid of*
пуга́ться *to be frightened of*
избега́ть *to avoid*

Genitive After Adjectives

After Adjectives That Govern the Genitive

A few adjectives, in both long and short form, govern the genitive case.

по́лный *full (of)*

Та́м бы́л кувши́н, по́лный **воды́**.	*There was a pitcher full of water.*

досто́йный *worthy (of)*

Его́ тру́д, досто́йный **награ́ды**.	*His work is worthy of an award.*

лишённый *devoid (of)*

Э́тот челове́к лишён **чу́вства ю́мора**.	*This person lacks a sense of humor.*

After the Comparative of an Adjective

In a comparative construction, the second term of the comparison may be a noun in the genitive case.

Москва́ бо́льше **Петербу́рга**.	*Moscow is bigger than St. Petersburg.*
Во́лга длинне́е **Днепра́**.	*The Volga is longer than the Dnieper.*
Ма́ть моло́же **отца́**.	*The mother is younger than the father.*

Genitive After Prepositions

The genitive case is used for the object of certain prepositions, which are presented in Chapter 3.

16. For each of the following sentences, identify the case of each underlined word by writing it in the appropriate column.

	Nominative	Accusative	Genitive
1. Она́ записа́ла но́мер телефо́на.	______	______	______
2. Во́т фотогра́фия жены́.	______	______	______
3. Где́ у́лица Королёва?	______	______	______
4. О́н съе́л ещё ло́мтик хле́ба.	______	______	______
5. До́чь профе́ссора—студе́нтка.	______	______	______
6. Я́ зна́ю бра́та студе́нта.	______	______	______
7. Ма́ма купи́ла паке́т молока́.	______	______	______
8. Вопро́с учи́теля бы́л тру́дный.	______	______	______
9. Я́ откры́л две́рь кварти́ры.	______	______	______
10. Откры́тие вы́ставки бы́ло интере́сное.	______	______	______
11. Мы́ слы́шали сме́х дете́й.	______	______	______
12. На столе́ была́ буты́лка во́дки.	______	______	______
13. У меня́ оди́н бра́т и две́ сестры́.	______	______	______
14. О́н съе́л таре́лку су́па.	______	______	______
15. Студе́нт не слы́шал вопро́са.	______	______	______
16. Зде́сь е́сть сто́л, но не́т сту́ла.	______	______	______
17. Та́м была́ во́дка, но не́ было вина́.	______	______	______
18. Она́ лю́бит ко́шек, но бо́ится соба́к.	______	______	______
19. Ко́мната была́ полна́ дете́й.	______	______	______
20. Ма́ма моло́же па́пы.	______	______	______

17. Rewrite each of the following pairs of sentences as one sentence, using the genitive of possession.

MODEL Э́то Бори́с. А э́то его́ кни́га. (*This is Boris. And this is his book.*) >
Э́то кни́га Бори́са. (*This is Boris's book.*)

1. Э́то профе́ссор. А э́то его́ портфе́ль. ______________________
2. Э́то ма́ма. А э́то её су́мка. ______________________
3. Э́то па́па. А э́то его́ кабине́т. ______________________
4. Э́то го́сть. А э́то его́ пода́рок. ______________________
5. Э́то сестра́. А э́то её пла́тье. ______________________
6. Э́то де́ти. А э́то и́х игру́шки. ______________________
7. Э́то оте́ц. А э́то его́ маши́на. ______________________
8. Э́то студе́нты. А э́то и́х учё́бники. ______________________
9. Э́то бра́тья. А э́то и́х кварти́ра. ______________________
10. Э́то друзья́. А э́то и́х жёны. ______________________
11. Э́то студе́нтка. А э́то её бра́т. ______________________

12. Э́то писа́тель. А э́то его́ рома́н. ______________
13. Э́то дя́дя. А э́то его́ да́ча. ______________
14. Э́то ба́бушка. А э́то её плато́к. ______________
15. Э́то ребёнок. А э́то его́ крова́ть. ______________

18. Name each of the following places, using the correct form of the name of the person in parentheses.

MODEL университе́т (Ломоно́сов) > университе́т Ломоно́сова (*Lomonosov University*)

1. пло́щадь (Пу́шкин) ______________
2. у́лица (Королёв) ______________
3. бульва́р (Го́голь) ______________
4. теа́тр (Мейерхо́льд) ______________
5. библиоте́ка (Ге́рцен) ______________

19. Each of the following sentences contains an agent performing an action. After the deverbal noun on the right, write the genitive singular or plural form, as appropriate, of the noun denoting the agent.

MODEL Профе́ссор объясни́л пра́вило. (*The professor explained the rule.*) > объясне́ние профе́ссора (*explanation of the professor*)

1. Арти́стка выступа́ла по телеви́зору. выступле́ние ______________
2. Пев́ец пе́л эмоциона́льно. пе́ние ______________
3. Де́ти игра́ли во дворе́. игра́ ______________
4. Ученики́ проси́ли вы́йти из кла́сса. про́сьба ______________
5. Врачи́ до́лго его́ диагности́ровали. диа́гноз ______________

20. Each of the following sentences contains an agent performing an action. After the action noun on the right, write the genitive form of the noun denoting the object of the action.

MODEL Аспира́нт защити́л диссерта́цию. (*The graduate student defended his dissertation.*) > защи́та диссерта́ции (*the defense of the dissertation*)

1. Оте́ц купи́л маши́ну. поку́пка ______________
2. Ма́ма пригото́вила обе́д. приготовле́ние ______________
3. Учи́тель прове́рил зада́ние. прове́рка ______________
4. Тури́сты посети́ли музе́й. посеще́ние ______________
5. Студе́нт изуча́ет литерату́ру. изуче́ние ______________

21. Each of the following noun phrases contains an object or person to which a property or quality is ascribed. After the property/quality noun on the right, write the genitive singular or plural form, as appropriate, of the noun denoting the object or person.

MODEL тёплый кли́мат (*warm climate*) > теплота́ кли́мата (*warmth of the climate*)

1. тёмная но́чь темнота́ ______________
2. у́мная студе́нтка у́м ______________
3. краси́вое мо́ре красота́ ______________
4. до́брая ма́ть доброта́ ______________
5. бога́тые лю́ди бога́тство ______________
6. све́тлый о́браз све́тлость ______________
7. ще́дрые друзья́ ще́дрость ______________
8. изве́стные писа́тели изве́стность ______________

9. ую́тные гости́ницы   ую́т ____________
10. серьёзные оши́бки   серьёзность ____________

22. Each of the following sentences asserts the existence or availability of some object or person. Rewrite the sentence in the negative, so that it denies the existence/availability of the object or person. Make all necessary changes.

MODEL Зде́сь е́сть телефо́н. (*There is a telephone here.*) >
Зде́сь не́т телефо́на. (*There is no telephone here.*)

1. Зде́сь бу́дет гости́ница. ____________
2. Сего́дня семина́р. ____________
3. Вчера́ в клу́бе бы́л конце́рт. ____________
4. У меня́ сейча́с е́сть вре́мя. ____________
5. У на́с вчера́ была́ ле́кция. ____________
6. Сего́дня в кла́ссе Ви́ктор. ____________
7. Вчера́ Серге́й бы́л до́ма. ____________
8. За́втра бу́дут роди́тели. ____________
9. Сего́дня бу́дет до́ждь. ____________
10. В ка́ссе теа́тра бы́ли биле́ты. ____________

23. Complete the answer to each of the following questions, giving the genitive singular or plural form, as appropriate, of the underlined noun.

MODEL —Та́м е́сть рестора́н? (*Is there a restaurant there?*) >
—Да́, та́м мно́го рестора́нов. (*Yes, there are many restaurants there.*)

1. —Та́м е́сть теа́тр? —Да́, та́м мно́го ____________.
2. —Зде́сь е́сть музе́й? —Да́, зде́сь не́сколько ____________.
3. —Зде́сь е́сть библиоте́ка? —Да́, зде́сь две́ ____________.
4. —Та́м бы́ли де́вушки? —Да́, та́м бы́ло мно́го ____________.
5. —Та́м одна́ спа́льня? —Не́т, та́м две́ ____________.
6. —Зде́сь то́лько одно́ письмо́? —Не́т, зде́сь пя́ть ____________.
7. —Та́м то́лько одна́ лаборато́рия? —Не́т, та́м не́сколько ____________.
8. —Зде́сь то́лько оди́н каранда́ш? —Не́т, зде́сь ше́сть ____________.
9. —Та́м одна́ ру́чка? —Не́т, та́м де́сять ____________.
10. —Та́м оди́н челове́к? —Не́т, та́м се́мь ____________.

24. Change the underlined direct object(s) in each of the following sentences from the accusative to the genitive case, thereby giving the sentence a partitive meaning.

MODEL Она́ купи́ла цветы́. (*She bought flowers.*) >
Она́ купи́ла цвето́в. (*She bought some flowers.*)

1. О́н взя́л са́хар. ____________
2. Она́ купи́ла мёд и я́блоки. ____________
3. Переда́й, пожа́луйста, пирожки́. ____________
4. Мы́ съе́ли су́п. ____________
5. Хозя́йка налила́ коньяк. ____________
6. Сы́н проси́л де́ньги. ____________
7. Го́сти съе́ли ри́с и о́вощи. ____________
8. Де́ти попроси́ли фру́кты. ____________
9. Она́ купи́ла грибы́. ____________
10. Мы́ принесли́ сы́р и хле́б. ____________

25. Rewrite each of the following sentences, negating the verb and making the necessary change to the verb's object.

MODEL Я́ зна́л э́то. (*I knew that.*) >
Я́ не зна́л э́того. (*I did not know that.*)

1. Же́нщины име́ли пра́во го́лоса. ______
2. Фи́льм произвёл впечатле́ние. ______
3. Она́ ви́дела авто́бус. ______
4. О́н пи́л спи́рт. ______
5. Студе́нт по́нял отве́т. ______

Prepositional Case

Singular and Plural Endings

The endings of the prepositional singular are as follows.

-е for most nouns (except those that follow)
-и for third-declension feminine nouns in **-ь**
for nouns whose nominative singular ends in **-ие**, **-ия**, or **-ий**

The endings of the prepositional plural are as follows.

-ах for all nouns ending in a hard stem
-ях for all nouns ending in a soft stem

The following table illustrates the endings of the prepositional case.

GENDER	NOMINATIVE SINGULAR	PREPOSITIONAL SINGULAR	ENDING	PREPOSITIONAL PLURAL	ENDING
Masculine					
Hard Stem	сто́л	столе́	-е	стола́х	-ах
Soft Stem	музе́й	музе́е		музе́ях	-ях
	портфе́ль	портфе́ле		портфе́лях	
Stem in *-ий*	кафете́рий	кафете́рии	-и	кафете́риях	
Neuter					
Hard Stem	окно́	окне́	-е	о́кнах	-ах
Soft Stem	мо́ре	мо́ре		моря́х	-ях
Stem in *-ие*	зда́ние	зда́нии	-и	зда́ниях	
Feminine					
Hard Stem	газе́та	газе́те	-е	газе́тах	-ах
Soft Stem	неде́ля	неде́ле		неде́лях	-ях
Stem in *-ия*	аудито́рия	аудито́рии	-и	аудито́риях	
Stem in *-ь*	тетра́дь	тетра́ди	-и	тетра́дях	
	ма́ть	ма́тери		матеря́х	

Use of the Prepositional Case

The prepositional case, as its name might suggest, occurs exclusively with prepositions. All the prepositions that take the prepositional case, and the meanings expressed by these prepositions, are presented in Chapter 3.

It is appropriate to note here, however, that after only two prepositions, **в** *in, at* and **на** *on, at, in,* a small number of masculine nouns take a special prepositional singular case ending in stressed **-ý**, which is sometimes called the "locative," since it is used to denote location, but not other meanings conveyed by other prepositions. Therefore, these nouns may take two prepositional case endings: the regular prepositional case ending for masculine nouns **-е**, and a second prepositional, or "locative," case ending; cf. **о ле́се** *about the forest* and **в лесý** *in the forest.* The list below contains the most commonly used nouns that take the locative ending in stressed **-ý** after **в** and **на**. The preposition **о/об** governs the prepositional case in the meaning *about, concerning.*

NOMINATIVE	PREPOSITIONAL	LOCATIVE
аэропо́рт *airport*	об аэропо́рте	в аэропортý
бе́рег *shore*	о бе́реге	на берегý
гла́з *eye*	о гла́зе	в глазý
До́н *the Don*	о До́не	на Донý
Кры́м *the Crimea*	о Кры́ме	в Крымý
лёд *ice*	о льде́	на льдý
ле́с *forest*	о ле́се	в лесý
мо́ст *bridge*	о мо́сте	на мостý
но́с *nose*	о но́се	на носý
по́л *floor*	о по́ле	на полý
по́рт *port*	о по́рте	в портý
ро́т *mouth*	о рте́	во ртý
са́д *garden*	о са́де	в садý
сне́г *snow*	о сне́ге	в снегý
ýгол *corner*	об угле́	в углý, на углý
шка́ф *cupboard*	о шка́фе	в шкафý

Dative Case

Singular and Plural Endings

The dative singular endings of masculine and neuter nouns are as follows.

-у for nouns with a hard stem
-ю for nouns with a soft stem

The dative singular endings of feminine nouns are as follows.

-е for all nouns in **-а** and **-я**
-и for all nouns ending in **-ия**
for all third-declension feminine nouns in **-ь**

The dative plural endings are as follows.

-ам for all nouns with a hard stem
-ям for all nouns with a soft stem

The following table illustrates the dative case endings of nouns.

GENDER	NOMINATIVE SINGULAR	DATIVE SINGULAR	ENDING	DATIVE PLURAL	ENDING
Masculine					
Hard Stem	сто́л	столу́	-у	стола́м	-ам
	студе́нт	студе́нту		студе́нтам	
Soft Stem	музе́й	музе́ю	-ю	музе́ям	-ям
	писа́тель	писа́телю		писа́телям	
Neuter					
Hard Stem	окно́	окну́	-у	о́кнам	-ам
Soft Stem	зда́ние	зда́нию	-ю	зда́ниям	-ям
Feminine					
Hard Stem	газе́та	газе́те	-е	газе́там	-ам
Soft Stem	тётя	тёте		тётям	-ям
Stem in *-ия*	аудито́рия	аудито́рии	-и	аудито́риям	
Stem in *-ь*	ма́ть	ма́тери		матеря́м	

Uses of the Dative Case

As the Indirect Object of a Verb

The indirect object is normally an animate noun denoting the person *to whom* or *for whom* an action is performed. The indirect object is often understood to be the "addressee," "recipient," or "beneficiary" of an action. Transitive verbs, like those listed below, may take not only a direct object in the accusative case, but also an indirect object in the dative case.

дава́ть *to give*
Ма́ша даёт биле́т **Бори́су**. — *Masha is giving the ticket to Boris.*

дари́ть *to give a gift*
Оте́ц ча́сто да́рит **де́тям** пода́рки. — *Father often gives gifts to the children.*

покупа́ть *to buy*
Мы́ покупа́ем сувени́ры **друзья́м**. — *We are buying souvenirs for friends.*

посыла́ть *to send*
Она́ посыла́ет письмо́ **подру́ге**. — *She is sending a letter to a friend.*

писа́ть *to write*
Сы́н ча́сто пи́шет **отцу́ и ма́тери**. — *The son often writes to his father and mother.*

чита́ть *to read*
Ба́бушка чита́ла ска́зку **вну́ку**. — *Grandma read a fairy tale to her grandson.*

говори́ть *to say, speak*
О́н не говори́л пра́вду **роди́телям**. — *He did not tell the truth to his parents.*

объясня́ть *to explain*
Па́па объя́сняет зада́чу **до́чери**. — *Dad explains the problem to his daughter.*

After Verbs That Govern the Dative

A number of other verbs require their complements to be in the dative case. Several of them can be organized into different groups based on shared elements of meaning. Below are frequently used examples from each group.

1. *Verbs denoting assistance or service*

помога́ть *to help*
сове́товать *to advise*
служи́ть *to serve*

2. *Verbs denoting harm or annoyance*

   вреди́ть *to harm*
   меша́ть *to bother; to prevent*
   изменя́ть *to betray*

3. *Verbs meaning "to permit" someone to do something or "to forbid" someone from doing something*

   позволя́ть *to allow, permit*
   разреша́ть *to allow, permit*
   запреща́ть *to forbid*

4. *Verbs denoting various emotions*

   удивля́ться *to be surprised at*
   зави́довать *to envy*
   нра́виться *to appeal to*

5. *Verbs meaning "to teach" or "to learn"*

   The verb **учи́ть** in the meaning *to teach,* and the verb **учи́ться** *to study,* govern the dative case on the noun denoting the subject taught or studied.

   учи́ть *to teach*
   Оте́ц у́чит дочере́й **ру́сскому языку́**. — *The father is teaching his daughters Russian.*
   учи́ться *to study*
   Студе́нты у́чатся **ру́сской интона́ции**. — *The students are studying Russian intonation.*

   NOTE: The verb **учи́ть (вы́учить)** can be used in the meaning *to study* (*learn*); in this meaning the noun denoting the subject studied is a direct object in the accusative case.

   Она́ у́чит **ру́сский язы́к**. — *She is studying the Russian language.*

6. *Verbs with other meanings*

   звони́ть *to call on the phone*
   Бра́т звони́т **сестре́**. — *The brother is calling his sister.*

   The verb **отвеча́ть** *to answer* is used with the dative when the complement is a person. When the complement is an inanimate object, this verb takes the preposition **на** and the accusative case.

   Профе́ссор отве́тил **студе́нту**. — *The professor answered the student.*
   Профе́ссор отве́тил **на вопро́с**. — *The professor answered the question.*

   The verb **ве́рить** in the meaning *to believe someone* is used with the dative, but in the meaning *to believe in someone/something* this verb requires the preposition **в** and the accusative case.

   Оте́ц ве́рит **сы́ну**. — *The father believes his son.*
   Оте́ц ве́рит **в Бо́га**. — *The father believes in God.*

After Adjectives

A few adjectives, in both the long and short form, require the dative case.

благода́рный *grateful (to)*
Сы́н благода́рен **роди́телям**. — *The son is grateful to his parents.*
ве́рный *true, faithful (to)*
О́н ве́рен **свои́м при́нципам**. — *He is true to his principles.*

подóбный *similar (to)*
Нáш дóм подóбен **э́тому дóму**. *Our house is similar to this house.*

The following adjective, which occurs only in the predicate short form, requires the dative.

рáд, рáда, рáды *glad*
Мы́ óчень рáды **твоемý успéху**. *We are very glad about your success.*

In Impersonal Constructions

Impersonal constructions, by definition, lack a grammatical subject in the nominative case. However, an impersonal construction may contain a logical (semantic) subject, which is often a noun (or pronoun) in the dative case. When a logical subject is present, it is often interpreted as the "experiencer," that is, the person who experiences some emotional or physical state. The following are different groups of states or conditions that are expressed in impersonal constructions with a dative experiencer.

1. *Expressions of necessity*

   Below are commonly used expressions of necessity. What the subject needs to do is expressed by the infinitive form of the verb.

   нáдо *need, must, have to*
   Студéнтам нáдо занимáться. *The students need to study.*

   нýжно *need, must, have to*
   Дéтям нýжно убирáть свою́ кóмнату. *The children need to clean up their room.*

   необходи́мо *it is essential, must*
   А́втору необходи́мо кóнчить кни́гу. *The author must finish the book.*

2. *Expressions of permission/prohibition*

   мóжно *it is permitted*
   Бори́су мóжно сдáть задáние зáвтра. *Boris may turn in the assignment tomorrow.*

   нельзя́ *it is not permitted*
   Дéтям нельзя́ открывáть окнó. *Children are not allowed to open the window.*

   The word **нельзя́** has the meaning *is not permitted* only when it is used with an infinitive of the imperfective aspect (**открывáть**). When used with an infinitive of the perfective aspect (**откры́ть**), **нельзя́** means *it is not possible.* (See the discussion of verbal aspect in Chapter 7.)

   нельзя́ *it is not possible*
   Нельзя́ откры́ть окнó. *It is impossible to open the window.*

   NOTE: The word **мóжно** may be used in the meaning *it is possible,* but in this meaning it does not normally occur with a logical subject in the dative, e.g., **Гдé здéсь мóжно купи́ть газéту?** *Where can one buy a newspaper here?* The words **возмóжно/невозмóжно** are synonymous with **мóжно/нельзя́** only in the meanings *it is possible / it is impossible* (not in the meanings *it is permitted / it is not permitted*).

3. *Feelings and physical states*

   These are in the neuter short form of the adjective. Some common expressions in this group include the following.

   вéсело *cheerful*
   Ви́ктору вéсело. *Victor feels cheerful.*

   грýстно *sad*
   Сы́ну грýстно. *The son feels sad.*

оби́дно *hurt*	
Сестре́ оби́дно.	*The sister feels hurt.*
жа́лко/жа́ль *sorry*	
Ле́не жа́лко ма́му.	*Lena is sorry for her mom.*
интере́сно *interesting*	
Бра́ту интере́сно.	*It's interesting for the brother.*
ску́чно *boring*	
До́чери ску́чно.	*The daughter is bored.*
тру́дно *difficult*	
Студе́нту тру́дно.	*It's difficult for the student.*
легко́ *easy*	
Де́вушке легко́.	*It's easy for the girl.*
хо́лодно *cold*	
Ба́бушке хо́лодно.	*Grandma feels cold.*
тепло́ *warm*	
Де́душке тепло́.	*Grandpa feels warm.*

4. *Impersonal verbs in* **-ся**

In many of the examples with verbs in **-ся** the logical subject is understood to feel either inclined or disinclined for some reason to perform the action denoted by the verb. The subject's disposition toward performing the action is felt to be beyond his control. The verb is in the third-person singular present tense, or neuter singular past tense.

Са́ше хо́чется е́сть.	*Sasha feels like eating.*
Ва́се сего́дня пи́шется легко́.	*Writing is coming easily for Vasya today.*
Серге́ю сего́дня не чита́ется.	*Sergey doesn't feel like reading today.*
Ири́не что́-то не спало́сь.	*Irina for some reason couldn't sleep.*

Expressing Age

The dative case is used to express the age of the person or object denoted by the logical subject.

Ско́лько лет **ва́шим роди́телям**!	*How old are your parents?*
Отцу́ со́рок ле́т.	*Father is forty years old.*
Ма́тери три́дцать три́ го́да.	*Mother is thirty-three.*
Э́тому де́реву бо́льше ста́ ле́т.	*This tree is more than a hundred years old.*

26. For each of the following sentences, identify the case of the underlined word.

	Accusative	Dative
1. Сы́н пи́шет письмо́ ма́тери.	☐	☐
2. Мы́ даём пода́рок сестре́.	☐	☐
3. Ма́ма говори́т до́чери: «Здра́вствуй!»	☐	☐
4. Ири́на пока́зывает фотоальбо́м подру́ге.	☐	☐
5. Сестра́ чита́ет бра́ту.	☐	☐
6. Сестра́ чита́ет бра́ту ска́зку.	☐	☐
7. Ученики́ покупа́ют учи́тельнице цветы́.	☐	☐
8. Оте́ц обеща́л сы́ну соба́ку.	☐	☐
9. Профе́ссор помога́ет студе́нтам.	☐	☐
10. Ки́ра да́рит роди́телям ди́ск.	☐	☐

27. Each of the following sentences contains an underlined noun in the dative singular. Write the noun in the dative plural.

1. Бо́ря покупа́ет пода́рок сестре́. ______
2. Ле́на пи́шет письмо́ дру́гу. ______
3. Библиоте́карь даёт кни́ги чита́телю. ______
4. Хозя́йка пока́зывала го́стю кварти́ру. ______
5. Вра́ч вы́писал реце́пт пацие́нту. ______
6. Ната́ша звони́ла бра́ту. ______
7. Де́ти покупа́ли пода́рки ма́тери. ______
8. Ма́ть не разреша́ет до́чери кури́ть. ______
9. Ба́бушка печёт пироги́ вну́ку. ______
10. Студе́нт отвеча́ет профе́ссору. ______

28. Complete each of the following sentences by giving the dative form of the underlined noun.

MODEL Э́то бра́т. Я́ помога́ю бра́ту. (*This is the brother. I help the brother.*)

1. Э́то сестра́. Мы́ пи́шем ______.
2. Э́то учи́тель. Учени́к отвеча́ет ______.
3. Э́то до́чь. Ма́ма ве́рит ______.
4. Э́то вну́чка. Ба́бушка чита́ет ______.
5. Э́то вра́ч. Андре́й звони́т ______.
6. Э́то дя́дя. Племя́нник благода́рен ______.
7. Э́то го́сть. Го́род нра́вится ______.
8. Э́то де́ти. Игру́шки нра́вятся ______.

29. Rewrite each of the following sentences as an impersonal sentence, replacing the adjective **до́лжен, должна́, должны́** *should/must* with the word **на́до**, or replacing the verb **мо́жет** *can* with the word **мо́жно** or **нельзя́**.

MODELS Па́ша до́лжен занима́ться. (*Pasha should study.*) >
Па́ше на́до занима́ться. (*Pasha needs to study.*)

Ива́н мо́жет слу́шать му́зыку. (*Ivan can listen to music.*) >
Ива́ну мо́жно слу́шать му́зыку. (*Ivan is allowed to listen to music.*)

Га́ля не мо́жет кури́ть. (*Galya cannot smoke.*) >
Га́ле нельзя́ кури́ть. (*Galya is not allowed to smoke.*)

1. Де́ти должны́ убира́ть ко́мнату. ______
2. Сестра́ мо́жет отдыха́ть. ______
3. Серёжа не мо́жет гуля́ть сего́дня. ______
4. Пожилы́е лю́ди мо́гут входи́ть без о́череди. ______
5. Вра́ч до́лжен прописа́ть лека́рство. ______

30. Rewrite each of the following sentences as an impersonal sentence, using a verb in **-ся** and making all necessary changes.

MODEL Оте́ц не рабо́тает. (*Father isn't working.*) >
Отцу́ не рабо́тается. (*Father doesn't feel like working.*)

1. Ма́льчик не чита́ет. ______
2. До́чка не е́ла. ______
3. Певи́ца не поёт. ______
4. Сы́н сего́дня не игра́л. ______
5. Тётя вчера́ не спала́. ______

Instrumental Case

Singular and Plural Endings

The instrumental singular endings of masculine and neuter nouns are as follows.

-ом for nouns with a hard stem
-ем for nouns with a soft stem when the ending is not stressed
for nouns with a stem in **-ж**, **-ч**, **-ш**, **-щ**, **-ц** that undergo Spelling Rule 3 (page 11)
-ём for nouns with a soft stem when the ending is stressed

The instrumental singular endings of feminine nouns are as follows.

-ой for nouns with a hard stem
-ей for nouns with a soft stem when the ending is not stressed
for nouns with a stem in **-ж**, **-ч**, **-ш**, **-щ**, **-ц** that undergo Spelling Rule 3
-ёй for nouns with a soft stem when the ending is stressed
-ью for third-declension feminine nouns in **-ь**

The instrumental plural endings are as follows.

-ами for all nouns with a hard stem
-ями for all nouns with a soft stem

The singular and plural endings of nouns in the instrumental case are illustrated in the following table.

GENDER	NOMINATIVE SINGULAR	INSTRUMENTAL SINGULAR	ENDING	INSTRUMENTAL PLURAL	ENDING
Masculine					
Hard Stem	авто́бус	авто́бусом	-ом	авто́бусами	-ами
Soft Stem	трамва́й	трамва́ем	-ем	трамва́ями	-ями
End-stress	секрета́рь	секретарём	-ём	секретаря́ми	
Neuter					
Hard Stem	окно́	окно́м	-ом	о́кнами	-ами
Soft Stem	по́ле	по́лем	-ем	поля́ми	-ями
Feminine					
Hard Stem	газе́та	газе́той	-ой	газе́тами	-ами
Soft Stem	тётя	тётей	-ей	тётями	-ями
End-stress	семья́	семьёй	-ёй	се́мьями	
Stem in -ь	ма́ть	ма́терью	-ью	матеря́ми	

NOTE: A few nouns have the irregular instrumental plural ending **-ьми́**. For example, the nouns **де́ти** *children* and **лю́ди** *people* have the instrumental plurals **детьми́** and **людьми́**. Also, the nouns **до́чь** *daughter,* **две́рь** *door,* and **ло́шадь** *horse* may form the instrumental plural with the regular ending **-ями**, as well as with the exceptional ending **-ьми́**: **дочеря́ми/дочерьми́**, **дверя́ми/дверьми́**, **лошадя́ми/лошадьми́**.

Uses of the Instrumental Case

To Express the Instrument or Means by Which an Action Is Performed

Учени́к пи́шет **карандашо́м**.	*The student writes with a pencil.*
Оте́ц ре́жет хле́б **ножо́м**.	*Father cuts bread with a knife.*
Мы́ еди́м су́п **ло́жкой**.	*We eat soup with a spoon.*
Кита́йцы едя́т **па́лочками**.	*Chinese eat with chopsticks.*
О́н ле́чит себя́ **тра́вами**.	*He is treating himself with herbs.*

To Denote the Agent of the Action in Passive Sentences

Кни́га была́ надпи́сана **а́втором**. *The book was inscribed by the author.*
Тетра́ди бы́ли прове́рены **учи́телем**. *The notebooks were corrected by the teacher.*
Вопро́с обсужда́ется **студе́нтами**. *The question is being discussed by the students.*
Сме́та составля́ется **строи́телем**. *An estimate is being prepared by the builder.*

To Denote the Force Responsible for an Action in Impersonal Sentences

Кры́шу сорва́ло **ве́тром**. *The roof was torn off by the wind.*
Доро́гу занесло́ **сне́гом**. *The road was covered over by the snow.*
Де́рево уда́рило **мо́лнией**. *The tree was struck by lightning.*

To Express the Manner or Way an Action Is Performed

Она́ говори́ла **шёпотом**. *She spoke in a whisper.*
Ребёнок спа́л **кре́пким сно́м**. *The baby slept soundly.*
Ма́льчик шёл **бы́стрым ша́гом**. *The boy walked at a brisk pace.*
Они́ приходи́ли **то́лпами**. *They came in droves.*
В Росси́и я́йца продаю́т **деся́тками**, а не **дю́жинами**. *In Russia eggs are sold by the tens, and not by the dozen.*

To Denote Similarity

Она́ поёт **соловьём**. *She sings like a nightingale.*
По́езд лете́л **стрело́й**. *The train flew like an arrow.*
По́езд ползёт **черепа́хой**. *The train is moving like a turtle.*

To Express the Means of Travel

Де́ти е́здят в шко́лу **авто́бусом**. *The children go to school by bus.*
Студе́нты е́хали в Москву́ **по́ездом**. *The students went to Moscow by train.*
Мы́ лете́ли **самолётом**. *We went by airplane.*

NOTE: To express the means of travel, the preposition **на** + prepositional case is used more often, e.g., **е́хать на по́езде**, **лете́ть на самолёте**.

To Denote the Route Taken

Они́ шли́ **ле́сом**. *They went by way of the woods.*
Маши́на е́хала **бе́регом**. *The car drove along the shore.*
Мы́ шли́ **переу́лками**. *We went by way of side streets.*
О́н шёл **друго́й доро́гой**. *He went a different way.*

To Denote the Time When Something Occurs

This use of the instrumental occurs in time expressions that denote the following.

(a) *Parts of the day*

Я́ тебе́ расскажу́ **у́тром**. *I'll tell you in the morning.*
Сего́дня я рабо́таю **днём**. *Today I'm working in the daytime.*
Мы́ занима́лись **це́лыми дня́ми**. *We studied for days on end.*
Они́ встреча́ются **вечера́ми**. *They meet in the evenings.*
Она́ отказа́лась е́хать **но́чью**. *She refused to go at night.*

(b) *Seasons of the year*

Мы́ отдыха́ем **ле́том**, а они́ **зимо́й**. *We vacation in summer, but they in winter.*
Учёбный го́д начина́ется **о́сенью**. *The school year begins in the fall.*
Они́ е́дут в о́тпуск **весно́й**. *They are going on vacation in spring.*

After Adjectives

A small number of adjectives, in both the short and long form, govern the instrumental case.

дово́льный *pleased, satisfied with*	
Оте́ц дово́лен **но́вой рабо́той.**	*Father is pleased with his new job.*
бога́тый *rich (in)*	
Э́то страна́, бога́тая **не́фтью.**	*This is a country rich in oil.*
изве́стный *(well) known for*	
О́н изве́стен **своей щедростью.**	*He is known for his generosity.*
за́нятый *busy, occupied with*	
Па́па за́нят **составле́нием** докла́да.	*Dad is busy compiling a report.*
бере́менная *pregnant (with)*	
Она́ бере́менна **пе́рвым ребёнком.**	*She's pregnant with her first child.*
больно́й *sick (with)*	
Ма́льчик бо́лен **гри́ппом.**	*The boy is sick with the flu.*

After Verbs That Govern the Instrumental

Several verbs require their complement to be in the instrumental case. A number of these verbs can be grouped together according to shared elements of meaning.

(a) *Verbs denoting the interests or attitudes of the subject*

интересова́ться *to be interested in*
увлека́ться *to be fascinated with*
занима́ться *to be engaged in; to study*
наслажда́ться *to enjoy*
любова́ться *to enjoy looking at*
горди́ться *to be proud of*
хва́статься *to boast of*
дорожи́ть *to value*

(b) *Verbs denoting some type of control, direction, or use*

руководи́ть *to be in charge of, direct*
владе́ть *to control, command, own*
управля́ть *to govern, rule; to drive*
пра́вить *to govern; to drive*
заве́довать *to manage*
по́льзоваться *to use*
злоупотребля́ть *to misuse, abuse*

As a Predicate Instrumental

In the English sentence *Viktor was a translator,* the phrase *was a translator* is a compound predicate consisting of the linking verb *was* and the predicate noun *translator.* In Russian, the verb **бы́ть** *to be* may serve as a linking verb, i.e., one that connects a subject with a predicate noun or adjective. When the predicate is a noun it is normally in the instrumental case, especially when the linking verb *to be* is in the infinitive form (**бы́ть**), future tense (**бу́ду**, **бу́дешь**, **бу́дет**, etc.), conditional with **бы** (e.g., **бы́л бы**, **е́сли бы бы́л**), imperative (**бу́дь**, **бу́дьте**), or gerund (**бу́дучи**).

Она́ хо́чет бы́ть **перево́дчицей.**	*She wants to be a translator.*
О́н бу́дет **профе́ссором.**	*He will be a professor.*
Не бу́дь **дурако́м.**	*Don't be a fool.*

Бýдучи **инвали́дом**, óн не мóг рабóтать. — *Being handicapped, he wasn't able to work.*
На твоём мéсте, я́ былá бы **актри́сой**. — *If I were you, I would have been an actress.*
Áх! Éсли бы я́ бы́л **поэ́том**! — *Oh! If only I were a poet!*

The past-tense forms of the verb *to be* (**бы́л, бы́ло, былá, бы́ли**) may be followed by a predicate either in the nominative (see the section Uses of the Nominative Case above) or instrumental case. The instrumental case of a predicate noun is strongly favored under the following conditions.

1. The noun denotes an occupation, function, or status.

Моя́ бáбушка былá **портни́хой**. — *My grandmother was a dressmaker.*
Мóй дéдушка бы́л **купцóм**. — *My grandfather was a merchant.*
Бори́с бы́л **председáтелем** клýба. — *Boris was the chairman of the club.*
Óн бы́л **секретарём** институ́та. — *He was the secretary of the institute.*

NOTE: Even in the present tense, when the verb *to be* is not normally used, the predicate noun denoting an occupation or function may be in the instrumental case, e.g., **Óн здéсь свидéтелем** *He is here as a witness.*

2. The noun is abstract or deverbal.

Ми́ша бы́л **очеви́дцем** происшéствия. — *Misha was a witness to the accident.*
Э́то бы́ло **причи́ной** егó успéха. — *This was the reason for his success.*
Её **люби́мым заня́тием** бы́ло вязáние. — *Her favorite pastime was knitting.*
Мýзыка былá **выражéнием** егó чу́вств. — *Music was an expression of his feelings.*

A number of near-synonyms of **бы́ть** function as linking verbs, and take a predicate noun (or adjective) in the instrumental case.

явля́ться *to be*
Украина явля́ется **рóдиной** Булгáкова. — *Ukraine is the birthplace of Bulgakov.*

станови́ться *to become*
Сы́н станóвится хорóшим **музыкáнтом**. — *The son is becoming a good musician.*

казáться *to seem to be*
Онá мнé казáлась **у́мницей**. — *She seemed to me to be a clever person.*

окáзываться *to turn out to be*
Óн всегдá окáзывается **победи́телем**. — *He always turns out to be the winner.*

считáться *to be considered*
Онá считáется **лу́чшей учи́тельницей**. — *She is considered to be the best teacher.*

оставáться *to remain as*
Э́то для нáс остаётся **загáдкой**. — *For us this remains a mystery.*

A few verbs are commonly used instead of **бы́ть** in the sense *to work as, serve as, function as,* e.g., **Óн рабóтал (бы́л) учи́телем** *He worked as (was) a teacher.* When used in this sense, these verbs take a predicate noun denoting an occupation, function, or status.

рабóтать *to work*
Онá рабóтает **биóлогом**. — *She works as (is) a biologist.*

служи́ть *to serve*
Óн слу́жит **арби́тром**. — *He serves as (is) the arbitrator.*

выступáть *appear (publicly)*
Онá выступáла **доклáдчиком**. — *She appeared as (was) a speaker.*

As the Second Object of a Transitive Verb

Several verbs, when used transitively, take a direct object in the accusative and a second object in the instrumental case. Below are common examples of such verbs.

называ́ть *to name, call*
Роди́тели назва́ли ребёнка **Ми́шей**. *The parents named the child Misha.*

счита́ть *to consider*
Учителя́ счита́ют ма́льчика **ге́нием**. *The teachers consider the boy a genius.*

выбира́ть *to elect*
Наро́д вы́брал его́ **президе́нтом**. *The people elected him president.*

нанима́ть *to hire*
Мы́ нанима́ем её **преподава́телем**. *We're hiring her as an instructor.*

31. Complete each of the following sentences by placing the noun in parentheses in the instrumental case.

1. Учи́тель пи́шет на доске́ ______________ (ме́л).
2. Студе́нты пи́шут на экза́мене ______________ (ру́чки).
3. Ма́льчик рису́ет ______________ (каранда́ш).
4. О́н открыва́ет две́рь ______________ (клю́ч).
5. Она́ вытира́ет слёзы ______________ (плато́к).
6. Она́ сде́лала же́ст ______________ (рука́).
7. Пока́зывать ______________ (па́лец) неве́жливо.
8. Мы́ э́то ви́дели свои́ми ______________ (глаза́).
9. Мы́ э́то слы́шали свои́ми ______________ (у́ши).
10. Она́ э́то сде́лала свои́ми ______________ (ру́ки).

32. Complete each of the following sentences by placing the noun in parentheses in the instrumental case.

1. Ми́мо нас маши́на пролете́ла ______________ (стрела́).
2. Де́ти говори́ли ______________ (хо́р).
3. Они́ е́хали ______________ (гру́ппа).
4. Сне́г па́дал больши́ми ______________ (хло́пья).
5. Таки́е сувени́ры продаю́тся ______________ (ты́сячи).
6. Спортсме́ны лете́ли ______________ (самолёт).
7. О́н говори́л серьёзным ______________ (то́н).
8. Мы́ шли́ к це́нтру ______________ (у́лица) Го́рького.
9. Ли́я е́хала домо́й ______________ (трамва́й).
10. Ребя́та бежа́ли ______________ (бе́рег).

33. Complete each of the following sentences, stating when the action occurs by placing the time expression in parentheses in the instrumental case.

1. Мы́ отдыха́ем ______________ (зима́).
2. О́н рабо́тает то́лько ______________ (вечера́).
3. Она́ верну́лась по́здней ______________ (но́чь).
4. Они́ е́здят в о́тпуск ______________ (весна́).
5. Оте́ц вста́л ра́но ______________ (у́тро).
6. Уче́бный го́д начина́ется ______________ (о́сень).
7. Вра́ч принима́ет ______________ (де́нь), до пяти́ часо́в.

34. Complete the change from the active sentence on the left to the passive sentence on the right by placing the underlined noun, which denotes the agent of the action, in the instrumental case.

MODEL Студе́нтка реша́ет зада́чу. (*The student is solving the problem.*) >
Зада́ча реша́ется студе́нткой. (*The problem is being solved by the student.*)

1. Журнали́ст пи́шет статью́.	Статья́ пи́шется ________.
2. Студе́нты изуча́ют эконо́мику.	Эконо́мика изуча́ется ________.
3. Ма́ть мо́ет посу́ду.	Посу́да мо́ется ________.
4. Секрета́рь гото́вит докуме́нты.	Докуме́нты гото́вятся ________.
5. Тётя посыла́ет пода́рки.	Пода́рки посыла́ются ________.

35. Complete the change from the personal sentence on the left to the impersonal sentence on the right by placing the underlined noun, which denotes the inanimate "force" responsible for the action, in the instrumental case.

MODEL Его́ ослепи́ла мо́лния. (*The lightning blinded him.*) >
Его́ ослепи́ло мо́лнией. (*The lightning blinded him.*)

1. Ло́дку опроки́нула волна́.	Ло́дку опроки́нуло ________.
2. Его́ ра́нила грана́та.	Его́ ра́нило ________.
3. Ве́тер сорва́л кры́шу.	Кры́шу сорва́ло ________.
4. Све́т зали́л ко́мнату.	Ко́мнату зали́ло ________.
5. Маши́на задави́ла соба́ку.	Соба́ку задави́ло ________.

36. Complete each of the following sentences by placing the predicate noun in parentheses in the instrumental case.

1. Ра́ньше То́ля бы́л ________ (учи́тель).
2. Ви́ка тогда́ была́ ________ (студе́нтка).
3. Моя́ до́чка бу́дет ________ (ветерина́р).
4. На́ш сы́н хо́чет бы́ть ________ (вра́ч).
5. Оте́ц рабо́тает ________ (программи́ст).
6. Она́ подраба́тывала ________ (перево́дчица).
7. Пу́шкин бы́л вели́ким ________ (поэ́т).
8. Де́вочка мечта́ет бы́ть ________ (балери́на).
9. Ми́ша слу́жит ________ (председа́тель) клу́ба.
10. Та́ня рабо́тает ________ (секрета́рша).
11. Вашингто́н явля́ется ________ (столи́ца) США.
12. Когда́ он пьёт, он стано́вится ________ (дура́к).
13. Она́ мне́ ка́жется хоро́шей ________ (ма́ть).
14. Ма́льчик счита́ется ________ (ге́ний).
15. Для на́с о́н остаётся ________ (геро́й).

37. Complete each of the following sentences by placing the second object in parentheses in the instrumental case.

1. Мы́ счита́ем её ________ (специали́ст).
2. Рабо́чие вы́брали его́ ________ (ме́неджер).
3. Роди́тели назва́ли де́вочку ________ (Со́ня).
4. Друзья́ устро́или его́ ________ (преподава́тель).
5. Его́ назна́чили ________ (судья́).

38. Complete each of the following sentences by placing the verb complement in parentheses in the instrumental case.

1. Де́вочки интересу́ются ________________ (бале́т).
2. Са́ша увлека́ется ________________ (футбо́л).
3. Ири́на занима́ется ________________ (гимна́стика).
4. О́н не мо́г не любова́ться её ________________ (красота́).
5. Роди́тели горди́тся ________________ (до́чь).
6. Она́ дорожи́т его́ ________________ (и́скренность).
7. Ма́ша руководи́т ________________ (кружо́к).
8. Они́ владе́ют ________________ (кварти́ра).
9. Президе́нт управля́ет ________________ (госуда́рство).
10. Сы́н не всегда́ по́льзуется ________________ (сове́ты) отца́.

39. Complete each of the following sentences by placing the adjective complement(s) in parentheses in the instrumental case.

1. Профе́ссор дово́лен ________________ (студе́нты).
2. Ма́ша больна́ ________________ (анги́на).
3. Они́ бы́ли недово́льны ________________ (еда́) в рестора́не.
4. Сиби́рь бога́та ________________ (леса́) и ________________ (озёра).
5. Петербу́рг изве́стен своей ________________ (красота́).
6. Ба́бушка занята́ ________________ (шитьё) пла́тья.

Personal Names (Part I)

First Names and Patronymics

Russians have three names: a first name (**и́мя**), a middle name, called the patronymic (**о́тчество**), and a family name (**фами́лия**). The patronymic is formed by adding a suffix to the stem of the father's first name: For sons, this suffix is **-ович**, for daughters **-овна**. If the father's first name ends in **-й** (or **-ь**), then these suffixes are spelled **-евич** and **-евна**. The formation of patronymics is illustrated in the following table.

FATHER'S FIRST NAME	PATRONYMIC (SON OF)	PATRONYMIC (DAUGHTER OF)
Ива́н	Ива́нович	Ива́новна
Серге́й	Серге́евич	Серге́евна
И́горь	И́горьевич	И́горьевна

The combined *first name and patronymic* (e.g., **Михаи́л Серге́евич**) is a polite form of address roughly corresponding to the use of English titles, such as Mr., Mrs., Dr., etc., and a surname (e.g., *Mr. Jones, Dr. Smith*). Russian adults use the first name and patronymic in formal situations, such as when first making an acquaintance, and generally when addressing people with whom they are not well acquainted. Students in Russia use this form of address when speaking to their teachers. Foreigners should use the first name and patronymic when addressing Russians in official situations.

Russian first names and patronymics are declined like nouns, as shown below.

	MASCULINE	FEMININE
Nom.	Ви́ктор Степа́нович	Татья́на Степа́новна
Acc.	Ви́ктора Степа́новича	Татья́ну Степа́новну
Gen.	Ви́ктора Степа́новича	Татья́ны Степа́новны
Dat.	Ви́ктору Степа́новичу	Татья́не Степа́новне
Prep.	о Ви́кторе Степа́новиче	о Татья́не Степа́новне
Instr.	Ви́ктором Степа́новичем	Татья́ной Степа́новной

Foreign first names follow a different declensional pattern. Foreign first names ending in a consonant are declined as nouns if they denote males, but are indeclinable if they denote females, e.g., **Мы́ слы́шали о Джо́не и о Дже́йн** *We heard about John and Jane.* However, foreign names of females that end in **-а/-я** decline like second-declension feminine nouns, e.g., **Я ви́дел Ли́нду и Си́нтию** *I saw Linda and Cynthia.*

Russian family names either have a mixed noun/adjective declension, or decline completely like adjectives. Family names are discussed in Chapter 5 (page 159).

Summary Table of Case Endings of Nouns in the Singular

	MASCULINE			NEUTER			FEMININE		
CASE	HARD STEM/SOFT STEM			HARD STEM/SOFT STEM			HARD STEM/SOFT STEM		
Nominative	-∅/-∅ (-ь) (-й)		(-ий)	-о/-ё -е	-ие	-мя	-а/-я	-ия	-∅ (-ь)
Accusative									
Inanimate	*= Nominative*			*= Nominative*			-у/-ю	-ю	-ь
Animate	*= Genitive*								
Genitive	-а/-я		-я	-а/-я	-я	-и	-ы/-и	-и	-и
Prepositional	-е		-и	-е	-и	-и	-е	-и	-и
Dative	-у/-ю		-ю	-у/-ю	-ю	-и	-е	-и	-и
Instrumental	-ом/-ём	-ем	-ем	-ом/-ём	-ем	-ем	-ой/-ей -ёй	-ей	-ью

Summary Table of Case Endings of Nouns in the Plural

	MASCULINE	NEUTER	FEMININE
CASE	HARD STEM/SOFT STEM	HARD STEM/SOFT STEM	HARD STEM/SOFT STEM
Nominative	-ы/-и	-а/-я	-ы/-и
Accusative			
Inanimate	*= Nominative*	*= Nominative*	*= Nominative*
Animate	*= Genitive*	*= Genitive*	*= Genitive*
Genitive	-ов/-ев -ей	-∅ -ей	-∅ -ей
Prepositional	-ах/-ях	-ах/-ях	-ах/-ях
Dative	-ам/-ям	-ам/-ям	-ам/-ям
Instrumental	-ами/-ями	-ами/-ями	-ами/-ями

Prepositions

Prepositions are words that indicate the relation of a noun (or pronoun) to other words in the sentence. Prepositions can indicate various types of relations between words. For example, they may indicate location (*in* the room), direction (*to* the store), time (*before* dinner), cause (*from* fear), manner (*by* bus), purpose (*for* reading), and many other relations. In general, the meaning of a preposition, and the type of relation it indicates, is dependent on the context. For example, in the sentence *He returned* ***from his trip,*** the preposition *from* indicates a directional relation, while in the sentence *He is tired* ***from his trip,*** the same preposition indicates a causal relation, this difference being determined by the lexical meaning of the predicates used. Similarly, changing the object of a preposition may change the type of relation expressed, e.g., *He lived in* ***Boston*** (location), *He lived in* ***luxury*** (manner), *He lived in* ***the Stalin era*** (time).

In English, where case is reflected only in a few personal pronouns, and variation is limited to the choice between the nominative and the accusative cases, all prepositions require their object to be in the accusative case (e.g., nominative *she,* but following a preposition, accusative *her*: at *her,* by *her,* for *her,* in *her,* near *her,* with *her,* etc.). In Russian, by contrast, the noun or pronoun following a preposition can occur in whichever of the six cases is required by the preposition (though the nominative is rare). Therefore, it is important for the student of Russian to learn the case(s) that a given preposition governs. Some prepositions govern only one case, while others may govern two or more cases—and express correspondingly different meanings.

It is also important to keep in mind that close correspondences between English and Russian prepositions are rare. On the one hand, the same preposition in English may be used in several different meanings, which in Russian are each expressed by a different preposition. For example, the English preposition *for* is rendered by six different Russian prepositions in the following phrases: *a gift* ***for*** *Dad* (**пода́рок *для* па́пы**), *closed* ***for*** *repairs* (**закры́то *на* ремо́нт**), ***for*** *the first time* (***в*** **пе́рвый ра́з**), *thanks* ***for*** *everything* (**спаси́бо *за* всё**), *respect* ***for*** *parents* (**уваже́ние *к* роди́телям**), ***for*** *this reason* (***по*** **э́той причи́не**). On the other hand, some meanings of English prepositions are not expressed in Russian by a preposition at all, but, as shown in Chapter 2, may be expressed by a Russian case form alone.

Prepositions Governing the Nominative Case

The nominative case is highly restricted in its use after a preposition. The nominative case occurs only after the following two prepositions.

в
за

в

The nominative plural of animate nouns denoting members of a profession, class, or other group may be used after the preposition **в** in idiomatic expressions, the general meaning of which is *join the ranks of, become a member of* the group indicated.

О́н пошёл **в** солда́ты.	*He became a soldier.*
О́н не годи́тся **в** офице́ры.	*He is not cut out to be an officer.*
Она́ пошла́ **в** ня́ньки.	*She went to work as a nanny.*
Она́ пошла́ **в** го́сти.	*She went visiting (as a guest).*

за

The preposition **за** is followed by the nominative case in two expressions: (i) the interrogative **Что́ э́то *за* ...?** *What sort/kind of ... is...?* and (ii) the exclamatory expression **Что́ *за* ...!** *What (a) ...!*

Что́ э́то **за** кни́га?	*What kind of book is that?*
Что́ о́н **за** челове́к?	*What sort of person is he?*
Что́ **за** пого́да!	*What (terrible/wonderful) weather!*
Что́ **за** ерунда́!	*What nonsense!*

Prepositions Governing the Accusative Case

The following three prepositions are always followed by the accusative case.

про
че́рез
сквозь

про

(a) *about* (NOTE: This preposition is characteristic of colloquial Russian.)

О́н рассказа́л **про** тебя́ всё.	*He told everything about you.*
Ска́зки обы́чно **про** звере́й.	*Fairy tales are usually about animals.*
Фи́льм бы́л **про** войну́.	*The film was about the war.*

(b) *to* (NOTE: When **про** is followed by **себя́**, the phrase means *to oneself.*)

Де́ти чита́ли **про** себя́.	*The children read to themselves.*
Она́ ду́мала **про** себя́.	*She thought to herself.*

че́рез

(a) *across, over, through* a place

Мы́ перешли́ **че́рез** у́лицу.	*We walked across the street.*
Она́ перепры́гнула **че́рез** лу́жу.	*She jumped over a puddle.*
Они́ вошли́ **че́рез** окно́.	*They came in through the window.*

(b) *through* some means or intermediary

О́н нашёл рабо́ту **че́рез** газе́ту.	*He found a job through the newspaper.*
Они́ познако́мились **че́рез** дру́га.	*They met through a friend.*
Мы́ говори́ли **че́рез** перево́дчика.	*We spoke through an interpreter.*

(c) *in* a certain amount of time or space before some action occurs

Онá приéдет **чéрез** недéлю.	*She will arrive in a week.*
Я́ выхожý **чéрез** однý останóвку.	*I'm getting off in one stop.*

(d) *every* unit of time or space, at the intervals indicated (NOTE: In this meaning, **чéрез** is followed by the plural form of the pronoun **кáждый**.)

О́н звони́т **чéрез** кáждые двé недéли.	*He calls every two weeks.*
Чéрез кáждые три́ строки́ éсть оши́бка.	*Every three lines there is a mistake.*

(e) *every other* unit of time or space

Онá занимáется аэрóбикой **чéрез** дéнь.	*She does aerobics every other day.*
Шкóльники писáли **чéрез** стрóчку.	*The students wrote every other line.*
О́н печáтает статью́ **чéрез** строкý.	*He is typing the article double-spaced.*

сквóзь

through (NOTE: **Сквóзь** often implies passing *through* some sort of obstruction.)

Они́ пробирáлись **сквóзь** толпý.	*They pushed through the crowd.*
Водá протекáла **сквóзь** кры́шу.	*Water was leaking through the roof.*
Трýдно уви́деть бéрег **сквóзь** тумáн.	*It is difficult to see the shore through the fog.*

1. Complete each of the following sentences with the correct preposition: **в**, **за**, **про**, **чéрез**, or **сквóзь**.

1. Чтó ____________ мýзыка!
2. Они́ нашли́ квартиру ____________ газéту.
3. Мы́ пошли́ ____________ гóсти.
4. Мáльчик пры́гнул ____________ забóр.
5. Ученики́ читáли не вслýх, а ____________ себя́.
6. Пáпа вернётся ____________ мéсяц.
7. А́втор печáтает рýкопись ____________ стрóчку.
8. Они́ расскáзывали ____________ поéздку.
9. Они́ разгляде́ли человéка ____________ ды́м.
10. Егó вы́брали ____________ начáльники.

The following three prepositions govern the accusative case when used in the meanings indicated.

о
по
с

о (об)

against in the physical sense of *bump, knock, smash against* something

О́н разби́л буты́лку **о** стóлб.	*He smashed a bottle against the pole.*
Лóдка разби́лась **о** скáлы.	*The boat broke up against the rocks.*
Онá удáрилась ногóй **о** стóл.	*She bumped her leg against the table.*
О́н стýкнулся головóй **о** бáлку.	*He knocked his head against a beam.*
Я́ удáрился пáльцем ноги́ **о** кáмень.	*I stubbed my toe on a rock.*

по

(a) *up to* and including a certain point in time or space

У меня́ о́тпуск **по** пя́тое января́.	*I am on vacation up to (and including) the fifth of January.*
Биле́т действи́телен **по** суббо́ту.	*The ticket is valid through Saturday.*
О́н стоя́л **по** по́яс в воде́.	*He stood up to his waist in water.*
Они́ в долга́х **по́** уши.	*They are in debt up to their ears.*
Я́ сы́т **по** го́рло.	*I'm stuffed to the gills.* (lit., *I'm full up to the throat.*)

(b) *each*, i.e., indicates a distributive meaning when followed by the numerals **два́/две́**, **три́**, **четы́ре** (and higher) and a noun in the genitive case: *two … each, three … each, four … each* (NOTE: The preposition **по** governs the dative case when followed by a form of the numeral **оди́н**, i.e., when something is distributed singly to each of multiple recipients: **На́м да́ли *по* одному́ жето́ну** *We were given one token each.*)

Мы́ вы́пили **по** два́ стака́на.	*We drank two glasses each.*
Они́ купи́ли **по** три́ ру́чки.	*They bought three pens each.*
Мы́ получи́ли **по** четы́ре жето́на.	*We received four tokens each.*

с

about, approximately with respect to measurement of weight, time, distance, or size

Паке́т ве́сит **с** килогра́мм.	*The package weighs about a kilo.*
Я́ поду́мал **с** мину́ту.	*I thought for about a minute.*
Мы́ провели́ та́м **с** неде́лю.	*We spent about a week there.*
О́н пробежа́л **с** киломе́тр.	*He ran about a kilometer.*
Она́ уже́ ро́стом **с** ма́ть.	*She's already about as tall as her mother.*

2. Complete each of the following sentences with the correct accusative preposition: **о**, **по**, or **с**.

1. Ученики́ получи́ли ____________ две́ тетра́ди.
2. Вода́ в де́тском бассе́йне ____________ коле́но.
3. О́н уже́ ро́стом ____________ отца́.
4. Ви́за действи́тельна ____________ деся́тое а́вгуста.
5. Она́ уда́рилась ____________ две́рцу маши́ны.
6. Мы́ та́м про́жили ____________ ме́сяц.

Prepositions Governing Either the Accusative or the Prepositional Case

When used to indicate a *spatial* relation, the following two prepositions can be used with either the accusative or the prepositional case.

в
на

Whether these prepositions govern the accusative or the prepositional case is determined by the nature of the verb that occurs with the preposition.

The accusative case is used when the co-occurring verb expresses *direction, motion,* or *change in position.* In this context these prepositions answer the question **Куда́?** *Where to?*

The prepositional case is used when the co-occurring verb expresses *location, position,* or *motion within a particular location* (e.g., **Óн гуля́л *в* па́рке** *He walked in the park*). In this context these prepositions answer the question **Где́?** *Where?* or *In what place?*

в (accusative)

to, into, in

Она́ идёт **в** шко́лу. — *She is walking to school.*
Она́ вошла́ **в** ко́мнату. — *She walked into the room.*
Óн положи́л письмо́ **в** я́щик. — *He put the letter in(to) the drawer.*

в (prepositional)

in, at

Она́ была́ **в** шко́ле. — *She was in/at school.*
Она́ сиде́ла **в** ко́мнате. — *She sat in the room.*
Письмо́ лежи́т **в** я́щике. — *The letter is in the drawer.*

на (accusative)

to, into, on(to)

Са́ша идёт **на** рабо́ту. — *Sasha is going to work.*
Она́ пошла́ **на** по́чту. — *She went to the post office.*
Па́па положи́л ру́чку **на** сто́л. — *Dad put the pen on(to) the table.*

на (prepositional)

at, in, on

Са́ша бы́л **на** рабо́те. — *Sasha was at work.*
Она́ была́ **на** по́чте. — *She was in/at the post office.*
Ру́чка лежи́т **на** сто́ле. — *The pen is lying on the table.*

NOTE: The choice of the preposition **в** or **на** to express location with a given noun is determined in part by the meaning of that noun. (See below, pages 89–92.)

3. Complete each of the following sentences by placing the object of the preposition in parentheses in the accusative or prepositional case, whichever is required by the context.

1. Она́ положи́ла де́ньги в ______________ (су́мка).
2. Óн сиде́л на ______________ (дива́н).
3. Они́ пошли́ на ______________ (ры́нок).
4. На́ши друзья́ побыва́ли в ______________ (музе́й).
5. Дава́й ся́дем на ______________ (скаме́йка).
6. Газе́ты лежа́т на ______________ (сто́л).
7. Ма́ма поста́вила ча́шки в ______________ (шка́ф).
8. За́втра мы́ е́дем на ______________ (да́ча).
9. Кни́ги стоя́т на ______________ (по́лка).
10. Го́сти сидя́т на ______________ (вера́нда).

The prepositions **в** and **на** govern the accusative case in several other meanings.

в

(a) *at* a given hour (NOTE: In telling time, the numeral following the preposition **в** is in the accusative case, but the noun following the numeral is in the genitive case, which is the case governed by the numeral.)

Она́ легла́ спа́ть **в** два́ часа́.	*She went to sleep at two o'clock.*
Она́ встаёт **в** се́мь часо́в.	*She gets up at seven o'clock.*
Нача́ло фи́льма **в** по́лдень.	*The film begins at noon.*

(b) *at* a given age

Де́ти иду́т в шко́лу **в** пя́ть ле́т.	*Kids begin school at five years of age.*
Она́ вы́шла за́муж **в** два́дцать ле́т.	*She got married at the age of twenty.*

(c) *on* a day or a part of the day (NOTE: The preposition **на** is used in the expressions ***на* сле́дующий де́нь** *on the following day* and ***на* друго́й де́нь** *on the next day*, but the preposition **в** is used in ***в* друго́й де́нь** *(on) another day.*)

У меня́ семина́р **в** сре́ду.	*I have a seminar on Wednesday.*
В пя́тницу я́ е́ду к врачу́.	*On Friday I'm going to the doctor.*
В э́то у́тро я́ узна́л пра́вду.	*On that morning I learned the truth.*
В ту́ но́чь мне́ сни́лся стра́шный со́н.	*That night I had a frightening dream.*

(d) *per* unit of time

О́н звони́т два́ ра́за **в** де́нь.	*He calls two times a day.*
У на́с исто́рия три́ ра́за **в** неде́лю.	*We have history three times per week.*
Ско́лько о́н зараба́тывает **в** ме́сяц?	*How much does he earn per month?*

Verbs Followed by the Preposition *в* + Accusative Case

Below are verbs that require the preposition **в** followed by the accusative case, when used in the meanings given.

ве́рить в *to believe in*

Она́ **ве́рит в** чудеса́.	*She believes in miracles.*

вме́шиваться в *to interfere in*

Не **вме́шивайся в** мои́ дела́.	*Do not interfere in my affairs.*

вступа́ть в *to enter (into), join*

Нельзя́ с ни́м **вступа́ть в** разгово́р.	*You shouldn't get into a conversation with him.*
О́н **вступа́ет в** ша́хматный клу́б.	*He is joining the chess club.*

игра́ть в *to play (a sport or game)*

Они́ **игра́ют в** те́ннис.	*They play tennis.*
Де́ти **игра́ли в** каку́ю-то игру́.	*The children were playing some game.*

превраща́ть(ся) в *to turn into*

О́н всё **превраща́ет в** шу́тку.	*He turns everything into a joke.*

на

(a) *for* a length of time (NOTE: The preposition **на** + accusative of time is used only with a verb of motion, or one involving a change in position, to indicate how long an action will last, or lasted. When a verb of location occurs, the time expression is in the accusative case, but with no preposition: **Она́ была́ в Москве́ ме́сяц** *She was in Moscow a month.*)

Они́ поéдут в Москву́ **на** ме́сяц.	*They will go to Moscow for a month.*
Она́ вы́шла **на** пя́ть мину́т.	*She stepped out for five minutes.*
Ма́ша дала́ мне́ кни́гу **на** неде́лю.	*Masha gave me the book for a week.*
Ба́бушка се́ла **на** мину́тку.	*Grandma sat down for a minute.*

(b) *for* a purpose, intended *for,* or (when followed by a numeral) sufficient *for*

Музе́й закры́ли **на** ремо́нт.	*They closed the museum for repairs.*
Па́па ко́пит де́ньги **на** маши́ну.	*Dad is saving money for a car.*
Мы́ заброни́ровали но́мер **на** двои́х.	*We reserved a room for two.*
Она́ гото́вит обе́д **на** де́сять челове́к.	*She is making dinner for ten people.*

(c) *by* a certain amount

Мо́й бра́т ста́рше меня́ **на** го́д.	*My brother is older than me by a year.*
Она́ похуде́ла **на** три́ килогра́мма.	*She lost (got thinner by) three kilos.*
Мы́ опозда́ли **на** ча́с.	*We were an hour late / late by an hour.*

Verbs Followed by the Preposition *на* + Accusative Case

The following verbs require the preposition **на** followed by the accusative case, when they are used in the meanings given.

влия́ть на *to influence, have an effect on*
Приро́да хорошо́ **влия́ет на** на́с. — *Nature has a positive effect on us.*

жа́ловаться на *to complain about*
Она́ **жа́ловалась** мне́ **на** шу́м. — *She complained to me about the noise.*

крича́ть на *to shout at*
Сосе́дка **крича́ла на** дете́й. — *The neighbor was shouting at the kids.*

наде́яться на *to hope for; to rely on*
Она́ **наде́ется на** по́мощь роди́телей. — *She relies on help from her parents.*

рассчи́тывать на *to count on, depend on*
Мы́ **рассчи́тываем на** тебя́. — *We are counting on you.*

серди́ться на *to be angry at*
О́н **се́рдится на** дру́га. — *He is angry at his friend.*

смотре́ть на *to look at*
Она́ **смотре́ла на** фотогра́фию. — *She was looking at the photograph.*

NOTE: The verb **смотре́ть** may be used without a preposition, e.g., **смотре́ть телеви́зор** *to watch television,* **смотре́ть фотоальбо́м** *to look through a photo album.*

4. Complete each of the following sentences with the correct preposition: **в** or **на**.

1. Музе́й закры́т __________ ремо́нт.
2. Она́ принима́ет табле́тки три́ ра́за __________ де́нь.
3. Мы́ е́дем в Пари́ж __________ неде́лю.
4. Я́ заказа́л сто́лик __________ трои́х.
5. О́н суеве́рный челове́к и ве́рит __________ приме́ты.
6. Хозя́йка пове́сила пальто́ __________ ве́шалку.
7. Друзья́ приезжа́ют к на́м __________ суббо́ту.
8. О́н научи́лся води́ть маши́ну __________ шестна́дцать ле́т.
9. Я́ моло́же бра́та __________ четы́ре го́да.
10. Моя́ до́чка лю́бит игра́ть __________ ша́хматы.
11. Мы́ обы́чно у́жинаем __________ се́мь часо́в.
12. Она́ о́чень наде́ется __________ ва́шу по́мощь.
13. Вода́ при́ кипе́нии превраща́ется __________ па́р.
14. Мы́ жа́ловались официа́нту __________ еду́.
15. О́н сли́шком любопы́тный и лю́бит вме́шиваться __________ чужи́е дела́.

Prepositions Governing Either the Accusative or the Instrumental Case

When used to indicate a *spatial* relation, the following two prepositions can be followed either by the accusative or the instrumental case.

за
под

Whether these prepositions are followed by the accusative or by the instrumental case depends on the nature of the verb used in the sentence. The same factors that determine the choice of accusative or prepositional case after the prepositions **в** and **на**, also determine the choice of accusative or instrumental case after the prepositions **за** and **под**.

The accusative case is used when the co-occurring verb expresses *motion, direction,* or a *change in position.* These prepositions answer the question **Куда́?** *Where to?*

The instrumental case is used when the co-occurring verb expresses *location* or *position.* These prepositions answer the question **Где́?** *Where?* or *In what location?*

за (accusative)

behind, beyond

Ма́льчик забежа́л **за** де́рево.	*The boy ran behind the tree.*
Она́ поста́вила ла́мпу **за** компью́тер.	*She put the lamp behind the computer.*
О́н се́л **за** сто́л.	*He sat down at* (lit., *behind*) *the table.*
Они́ пое́хали **за** гра́ницу.	*They went abroad* (lit., *beyond the border*).

за (instrumental)

behind, beyond

Ма́льчик пря́чется **за** де́ревом.	*The boy is hiding behind the tree.*
Ла́мпа стои́т **за** компью́тером.	*The lamp is behind the computer.*
О́н сиди́т **за** столо́м.	*He is sitting at* (lit., *behind*) *the table.*
Они́ жи́ли **за** грани́цей.	*They lived abroad* (lit., *beyond the border*).

под (accusative)

under

Ру́чка упа́ла **под** сто́л.	*The pen fell under the table.*
Мы́ се́ли **под** берёзу.	*We sat down under a birch tree.*
О́н положи́л чемода́н **под** крова́ть.	*He put the suitcase under the bed.*

под (instrumental)

under

Ру́чка лежи́т **под** столо́м.	*The pen is lying under the table.*
Мы́ сиде́ли **под** берёзой.	*We were sitting under a birch tree.*
Чемода́н лежи́т **под** крова́тью.	*The suitcase is lying under the bed.*

5. Complete each of the following sentences by placing the object of the preposition in parentheses in the accusative or instrumental case, whichever is required by the context.

1. Маши́на поверну́ла за́ ________________ (угол).
2. На́ши друзья́ живу́т за ________________ (у́гол).
3. Кни́га упа́ла за ________________ (по́лка).
4. Ребёнок забра́лся под ________________ (скаме́йка).
5. Письмо́ лежи́т под ________________ (кни́га).
6. Ла́мпа стои́т за ________________ (кре́сло).
7. Со́лнце зашло́ за ________________ (ту́ча).
8. Э́то лежи́т пря́мо у него́ под ________________ (но́с).
9. О́н лю́бит пла́вать под ________________ (вода́).
10. Ко́шка зале́зла под ________________ (вера́нда).

The prepositions **за** and **под** govern the accusative case in several other meanings.

за

(a) *for* (i.e., *in exchange for*)

О́н получи́л ава́нс **за** кни́гу.	*He received an advance for his book.*
Ско́лько ты́ заплати́ла **за** ку́клу?	*How much did you pay for the doll?*
Они́ купи́ли биле́т **за** 10 до́лларов.	*They bought a ticket for 10 dollars.*
Большо́е спаси́бо **за** по́мощь.	*Thank you very much for your help.*

Several verbs occur with the preposition **за** in the meaning *in exchange for.*

благодари́ть за *to thank* (*someone*) *for*

Мы́ **благодари́ли** его́ **за** по́мощь.	*We thanked him for his help.*

хвали́ть за *to praise, compliment* (*someone*) *for*

О́н **хва́лит** на́с **за** хоро́шую рабо́ту.	*He praises us for good work.*

руга́ть за *to scold, criticize* (*someone*) *for*

Оте́ц **руга́л** сы́на **за** гру́бость.	*The father scolded his son for being rude.*

нака́зывать за *to punish* (*someone*) *for*

Его́ не ра́з **нака́зывали за** враньё.	*He has often been punished for lying.*

(b) *for* someone (i.e., do something on behalf of or in place of someone else)

Сы́н расписа́лся **за** отца́.	*The son signed for his father.*
О́н при́нял пре́мию **за** а́втора.	*He accepted the prize for the author.*
Ми́ша сде́лал э́то **за** дру́га.	*Misha did it in place of his friend.*
Она́ сего́дня рабо́тает **за** колле́гу.	*She is working today for a colleague.*

(c) *for* someone (i.e., feel something for someone, due to their circumstances)

Мы́ пережива́ем **за** тебя́.	*We feel badly for you.*
Она́ беспоко́ится **за** му́жа.	*She is worried for her husband.*
Ма́ть бои́тся **за** сы́на.	*The mother is afraid for her son.*
Мы́ о́чень ра́ды **за** ва́с.	*We are very glad for you.*

(d) *for* someone or something (i.e., do something in support of or in favor of)

Наро́д голосова́л **за** Пу́тина.	*The people voted for Putin.*
Дава́йте вы́пьем **за** дру́жбу.	*Let's drink to our friendship.*
О́н вступи́лся **за** дру́га.	*He stood up for his friend.*
Я́ боле́ю **за** тебя́.	*I am rooting for you.*

(e) *in (the space of)* (NOTE: The preposition **за** is used here with a verb of the perfective aspect to express the period of time within which an action is *completed.* Compare this meaning with the prepositionless accusative of time and a verb of the imperfective aspect to denote the *duration* of the action: **Письмо́ шло́ две́ неде́ли** *The letter was en route for two weeks.*)

Письмо́ дошло́ до на́с **за** две́ неде́ли.	*The letter reached us in two weeks.*
О́н прочита́л ве́сь рома́н **за** три́ дня́.	*He read the entire novel in three days.*
Она́ написа́ла докла́д **за** неде́лю.	*She finished the report in a week.*
О́н сде́лал всю́ рабо́ту **за** пя́тницу.	*He did all the work on Friday.*

(f) *after* a certain time, *over* a certain age

Она́ звони́ла уже́ **за** по́лночь.	*She called well after midnight.*
Ему́ уже́ **за** пятьдеся́т.	*He is already over fifty.*

(g) *before* an event (NOTE: The preposition **за** + accusative case is used in combination with the preposition **до** + genitive case to express the amount of time that one event precedes another.)

Мы́ прие́хали в аэропо́рт **за** ча́с **до** вы́лета.	*We arrived at the airport an hour before departure.*
О́н вы́шел **за** мину́ту **до** оконча́ния фи́льма.	*He walked out a minute before the end of the movie.*

(h) *at* the distance indicated (NOTE: The preposition **за** + accusative is used in combination with the preposition **от** + genitive case to denote the distance from a place that something occurs; the preposition **в** + prepositional case can also be used in this meaning, e.g., **в дву́х кварта́лах отсю́да** *two blocks from here.*)

Маши́на слома́лась **за** ми́лю **от** его́ до́ма.	*His car broke down a mile from his house.*
За два́ кварта́ла **отсю́да** стро́ят бассе́йн.	*Two blocks from here they are building a pool.*

(i) *by* with verbs meaning *to lead, take, hold, seize, pull by*

Она́ вела́ ребёнка **за́** руку.	*She led the child by the hand.*
Она́ схвати́ла его́ **за** рука́в.	*She seized him by the sleeve.*
О́н схвати́л ко́шку **за** шки́рку.	*He seized the cat by the scruff of the neck.*

под

(a) *toward, approaching* a certain time or age

Мы́ встре́тились **под** Но́вый го́д.	*We met on New Year's Eve.*
Она́ пришла́ **под** ве́чер.	*She arrived toward evening.*
Ему́ **под** пятьдеся́т.	*He is approaching fifty.*

(b) *to* the accompaniment of

Они́ танцева́ли **под** ро́к-му́зыку.	*They danced to rock music.*
Она́ пе́ла **под** гита́ру.	*She sang to (the accompaniment of) the guitar.*

6. Complete each of the following sentences with the correct preposition: **за** or **под**.

1. Она́ чита́ла докла́д __________ колле́гу.
2. Оте́ц хвали́л сы́на __________ хоро́шую учёбу.
3. Мы́ просну́лись __________ пе́ние пти́ц.
4. О́н зако́нчил рабо́ту __________ у́тро.
5. Они́ купи́ли видеомагнитофо́н __________ бесце́нок.
6. Мы́ беспоко́имся __________ дру́га.
7. Бра́т боле́ет __________ сестру́.
8. Я́ засну́л __________ зву́ки ле́са.
9. О́н напеча́тал курсову́ю рабо́ту __________ неде́лю.
10. До́мик нахо́дится __________ два́ кварта́ла от бе́рега мо́ря.
11. Сы́н взя́л отца́ __________ руку.
12. Мы́ пришли́ __________ пя́ть мину́т до нача́ла спекта́кля.

Prepositions Governing the Genitive Case

Prepositions governing the genitive case are the most numerous. The core prepositions, those most commonly used, are presented below with their principal meanings. All of the prepositions in the following list, except for **с**, are followed only by the genitive case.

Core Prepositions Governing the Genitive Case

без	ми́мо
для	о́коло
до	от
из	по́сле
из-за	про́тив
из-под	с
кро́ме	у

без

(a) *without*

Она́ говори́т по-ру́сски **без** акце́нта.	*She speaks Russian without a (foreign) accent.*
Нельзя́ выходи́ть зимо́й **без** ша́пки.	*One shouldn't go out in winter without a hat.*
О́н да́л отве́т **без** колеба́ния.	*He answered without hesitation.*

(b) in telling time, to indicate the number of minutes until the hour

Сейча́с **без** пяти́ во́семь.	*It is now five minutes to eight.*
Было **без** че́тверти де́сять.	*It was a quarter to ten.*

для

(a) *for* the benefit of (NOTE: In the meaning *for the benefit of* the preposition **для** + genitive case has a near-synonym in the prepositionless dative case construction, e.g., **Она́ купи́ла пода́рок *бра́ту*** *She bought a present for her brother.*)

Она́ купи́ла пода́рок **для** бра́та.	*She bought a present for her brother.*
Э́тот а́втор пи́шет кни́ги **для** дете́й.	*This author writes books for children.*

(b) *for* the purpose of

О́н собира́ет материа́л **для** докла́да.	*He is collecting material for a report.*
О́н пьёт то́лько **для** удово́льствия.	*He drinks only for pleasure.*

до

(a) *before* or *until* a certain time

До войны́ они́ жи́ли в Москве́.	*Before the war they lived in Moscow.*
Мы́ рабо́таем **до** пяти́ часо́в.	*We work until five o'clock.*

(b) *up to, as far as* a certain place (NOTE: When the preposition **до** is used in this meaning, the co-occurring verb often has the prefix **до-**.)

Она́ досмотре́ла фи́льм **до** конца́.	*She watched the film to the end.*
Мы́ дочита́ли **до** страни́цы 65.	*We read up to page 65.*
Они́ дошли́ **до** Кра́сной пло́щади.	*They walked as far as Red Square.*

из

(a) *from, out of* when motion or movement is indicated (NOTE: The preposition **из** is used in this meaning only with nouns that require the preposition **в** + accusative case to express motion or movement *in, to,* or *into,* e.g., **Мы́ е́дем *в* Москву́** *We are going to Moscow,* **О́н положи́л биле́т *в* карма́н** *He put the ticket into his pocket.*)

Моя́ подру́га прие́хала **из** Москвы́.	*My girlfriend arrived from Moscow.*
Вра́ч вы́шел **из** кабине́та.	*The doctor stepped out of his office.*
Па́па вы́нул биле́т **из** карма́на.	*Dad took the ticket out of his pocket.*

(b) *from* indicating source of information, place of origin, or material from/of which something is made

О́н узна́л **из** газе́т.	*He found out from the newspapers.*
Э́то цита́та **из** рома́на Толсто́го.	*This is a quotation from a novel by Tolstoy.*
О́н **из** хоро́шей семьи́.	*He is from a good family.*
Моя́ ба́бушка **из** Ми́нска.	*My grandmother is from Minsk.*
Бензи́н де́лают **из** не́фти.	*Gasoline is made from oil.*

(c) *of,* i.e., one or more *out of* a larger group

Оди́н **из** студе́нтов вы́рос в Ки́еве.	*One of the students grew up in Kiev.*
Мно́гие **из** ни́х учи́лись в Росси́и.	*Many of them have studied in Russia.*
Не́сколько **из** ни́х говоря́т по-ру́сски.	*Several of them speak Russian.*

(d) *consisting of, comprised of*

Э́то семья́ **из** пяти́ челове́к.	*This is a family of five people.*
Э́то кварти́ра **из** четырёх ко́мнат.	*This is an apartment with four rooms.*
Комите́т состои́т **из** десяти́ чле́нов.	*The committee is composed of ten members.*

(e) *from, out of* indicating cause or reason

Óн сде́лал всё **из** любви́ к не́й.	*He did everything out of love for her.*
Она́ э́то сказа́ла **из** ре́вности.	*She said it out of jealousy.*
Они́ пришли́ **из** любопы́тства.	*They came out of curiosity.*
Мы́ слу́шали его́ **из** ве́жливости.	*We listened to him out of politeness.*

из-за

(a) *from behind/beyond*

Ма́льчик вы́шел **из-за** де́рева.	*The boy came out from behind a tree.*
Óн вста́л **из-за** стола́.	*He got up from (behind) the table.*
Они́ верну́лись **из-за** грани́цы.	*They returned from abroad* (lit., *from beyond the border*).

(b) *because of* referring to the cause of something undesirable

Из-за дождя́ мы́ не пошли́ в па́рк.	*Because of the rain, we didn't go to the park.*
Мы́ опозда́ли **из-за** ава́рии.	*We were late because of an accident.*

из-под

(a) *from under*

Из-под дива́на вы́лезла ко́шка.	*A cat crawled out from under the sofa.*
Маши́на вы́шла **из-под** контро́ля.	*The car went out of control.*

(b) to indicate the purpose of a container

ба́нка **из-под** варе́нья	*a jam jar*
буты́лка **из-под** молока́	*a milk bottle*
карто́нка **из-под** шля́пы	*a hatbox*
коро́бка **из-под** ту́фель	*a shoe box*

кро́ме

except, besides, apart from

Она́ съе́ла всё, **кро́ме** колбасы́.	*She ate everything except the sausage.*
Кро́ме меня́, бы́ло ещё тро́е госте́й.	*There were three guests besides me.*
Кро́ме того́, е́сть и други́е причи́ны.	*Apart from that, there are other reasons.*

ми́мо

past (NOTE: The preposition **ми́мо** often occurs after a motion verb with the prefix **про-**.)

Авто́бус прохо́дит **ми́мо** э́того моста́.	*The bus goes past this bridge.*
Óн ча́сто хо́дит **ми́мо** на́шего до́ма.	*He often walks past our house.*

о́коло

(a) *near*

Они́ живу́т **о́коло** институ́та.	*They live near the institute.*
Она́ сиде́ла **о́коло** на́с.	*She sat near us.*

(b) *around, about* (*approximately*)

Óн пробежа́л **о́коло** пяти́ киломе́тров.	*He ran about five kilometers.*
Мы́ бы́ли та́м **о́коло** трёх часо́в.	*We were there around three hours.*

от

(a) *from* indicating the point of origin of motion, or source of something (NOTE: The preposition **от** + genitive must be used to express motion or movement *from a person.*)

Она́ идёт **от** подру́ги.	*She is coming from her girlfriend.*
Они́ получи́ли письмо́ **от** сы́на.	*They received a letter from their son.*
Мы́ узна́ли но́вость **от** друзе́й.	*We learned the news from friends.*

(b) *away from* used with a noun denoting the starting point of motion (NOTE: When used in this meaning, the preposition **от** often occurs with a verb of motion that has the prefix **от-**.)

По́езд отошёл **от** ста́нции.	*The train pulled away from the station.*
Кора́бль отплы́л **от** бе́рега.	*The ship sailed away from the shore.*

Verbs Followed by the Preposition *от* + Genitive Case

Several commonly used verbs are followed by the preposition **от** and the genitive case. Many of them convey figuratively the sense of movement *away from* something.

защища́ть(ся) от *to defend, protect (oneself) from*

Дере́вья **защища́ли** до́м **от** ве́тра.	*The trees protected the house from the wind.*
Она́ **защища́лась от** со́лнца зо́нтиком.	*She protected herself from the sun with an umbrella.*

избавля́ть(ся) от *to rid (oneself) of*

То́лько э́то лека́рство **избавля́ет** меня́ **от** головно́й бо́ли.	*Only this medicine can rid me of a headache.*
О́н **избавля́ется от** дурно́й привы́чки.	*He is getting rid of a bad habit.*

освобожда́ть(ся) от *to free (oneself) of/from*

Сла́бое здоро́вье **освобожда́ет** челове́ка **от** вое́нной слу́жбы.	*Poor health exempts a person from military service.*
Я́ сегодня́ **освобожу́сь от** рабо́ты в ча́с.	*I will get off work today at one o'clock.* (lit., *I will free myself from work ...*)

отка́зываться от *to refuse, decline, turn down*

Она́ всегда́ **отка́зывается от** мои́х приглаше́ний.	*She always turns down my invitations.*

отключа́ться от *to turn off, escape from*

Му́зыка помога́ет мне́ **отключа́ться от** э́той пробле́мы.	*Music helps me escape from this problem.*

отлича́ться от *to differ from*

Мы́ си́льно **отлича́емся** дру́г **от** дру́га.	*We are very different from one another.*

пря́таться от *to hide from*

Бра́т **пря́чется от** сестры́.	*The brother is hiding from his sister.*

(c) *from* one place to another (NOTE: In this meaning the preposition **от** + genitive case usually combines with the preposition **до** + genitive case.)

Она́ зна́ет поэ́му **от** нача́ла **до** конца́.	*She knows the poem from beginning to end.*
В я́слях де́ти **от** го́да **до** трёх ле́т.	*In the nursery there are children from one to three years of age.*
Мно́гие лю́ди живу́т **от** зарпла́ты **до** зарпла́ты.	*Many people live from paycheck to paycheck.*

(d) *from,* i.e., the distance from a point (NOTE: The distance may be expressed either by **за** + accusative case or **в** + prepositional case, as shown in the first two examples below.)

Аэропо́рт нахо́дится за де́сять киломе́тров **от** го́рода.	*The airport is located 10 kilometers from the city.*
О́н жи́л в дву́х кварта́лах **от** Кремля́.	*He lived two blocks from the Kremlin.*
Их да́ча располо́жена далеко́ **от** го́рода.	*Their dacha is located far from the city.*

(e) to indicate the purpose for which an object is intended

клю́ч **от** маши́ны	*the key to the car*
кры́шка **от** ба́нки	*the lid to the jar*
пу́говица **от** руба́шки	*a shirt button*

(f) to indicate something to counter or protect against (NOTE: This meaning is sometimes expressed by the preposition **про́тив** + genitive case, as indicated below.)

страхова́ние **от** пожа́ра и кра́ж	*insurance against fire and theft*
лека́рство **от** ка́шля	*cough medicine*
табле́тки **от** бо́ли	*pain pills*

(g) to indicate the cause of some physical or emotional state (NOTE: In colloquial style this meaning is often expressed by the preposition **с** + genitive case, as shown below.)

Не́которые пью́т **от** ску́ки.	*Some people drink from boredom.*
Она́ дрожи́т **от** хо́лода.	*She is shivering from the cold.*
Де́ти закрича́ли **от** испу́га.	*The children screamed with fright.*
Они́ запла́кали **от** ра́дости.	*They cried with joy.*

по́сле

after

Мы́ встре́тились **по́сле** заня́тий.	*We met after class.*
По́сле дождя́ вы́глянуло со́лнце.	*After the rain the sun came out.*

про́тив

(a) *against*

О́н голосова́л **про́тив** нало́гов.	*He voted against taxes.*
Мы́ шли́ **про́тив** ве́тра.	*We were walking against the wind.*
Я́ ничего́ не име́ю **про́тив** э́того.	*I have nothing against this.*
Ему́ сде́лали уко́л **про́тив** ти́фа.	*He was inoculated against typhus.*

(b) *opposite*

О́н поста́вил га́лочку **про́тив** её фами́лии.	*He put a checkmark opposite her name.*
Мы́ сиде́ли дру́г **про́тив** дру́га.	*We sat opposite each other.*

с (со)

(a) *from* a place (NOTE: The preposition **с** + genitive case is used to indicate place of origin or motion from a place, when the noun denoting the place requires the preposition **на** + accusative case to express motion *to, in(to), on(to)* and **на** + prepositional case to express location *in, on,* or *at.*)

Она́ **с** Кавка́за.	*She is from the Caucasus.*
Ма́ма верну́лась **с** рабо́ты.	*Mom has returned from work.*
Мы́ шли́ пешко́м **с** по́чты.	*We walked from the post office.*

(b) *off* the surface of, *down from* something

Кни́га упа́ла **с** по́лки.	*The book fell off the shelf.*
О́н сня́л часы́ **со** стены́.	*He took the clock down from the wall.*
Официа́нтка убрала́ посу́ду **со** стола́.	*The waitress cleared the dishes off the table.*
Маши́на сверну́ла **с** доро́ги.	*The car turned off the road.*

(c) *from, out of, with* in a causal sense (NOTE: The preposition **с** + genitive case to express the cause of an action is a colloquial synonym of **от** + genitive case. Note the prepositional object in the first two examples has the genitive case ending **-у**, also characteristic of colloquial style.)

Она́ закрича́ла **с** испу́гу.	*She cried with fright.*
Ма́льчик убежа́л **со** стра́ху.	*The boy ran away out of fear.*
О́н позвони́л е́й **с** отча́яния.	*He called her out of despair.*
Она́ запла́кала **с** го́ря.	*She began to cry from grief.*

(d) *since, from* in a temporal sense (NOTE: To express time *from ... to ...* the preposition **с** + genitive case is used with **до** + genitive case.)

Мы́ живём зде́сь **с** а́вгуста.	*We've been living here since August.*
О́н говори́л по-ру́сски **с** де́тства.	*He spoke Russian from childhood.*
У на́с заня́тия **с** девяти́ часо́в.	*We have classes from nine o'clock.*
Переры́в на обе́д **с** ча́са **до** дву́х.	*Lunch break is from one to two.*

у

(a) *by, at* a place

Мы́ жи́ли на да́че **у** реки́.	*We lived in a dacha by the river.*
Учи́тель стоя́л **у** доски́.	*The teacher stood at the blackboard.*

(b) *at* someone's place (NOTE: The preposition **у** + genitive case of a noun denoting a person may function like French *chez.*)

Она́ была́ **у** подру́ги.	*She was at her girlfriend's (place).*
Вчера́ о́н бы́л **у** врача́.	*Yesterday he was at the doctor's.*
Мы́ останови́лись **у** дру́га.	*We stayed with a friend (at a friend's).*
У на́с пого́да всегда́ жа́ркая.	*In our area the weather is always hot.*

(c) used with a noun or personal pronoun to express a relation of possession (NOTE: The preposition **у** + genitive case normally expresses possession by a person or animal, and corresponds to the English verb *to have.*)

У бра́та е́сть но́вый компью́тер.	*My brother has a new computer.*
У его́ сестры́ краси́вые глаза́.	*His sister has pretty eyes.*
У меня́ к ва́м вопро́с.	*I have a question for you.*

Verbs Followed by the Preposition *у* + Genitive Case

Several verbs in combination with the preposition **у** and an animate noun indicate the source of something, especially the person from whom something is obtained.

бра́ть у *to take, borrow from*

Я́ **бра́л** кни́гу **у** колле́ги.	*I borrowed the book from a colleague.*

занима́ть у *to borrow from*

О́н **занима́ет** де́ньги **у** друзе́й.	*He borrows money from friends.*

отнима́ть у *to take away*
Э́то **отнима́ет у** меня́ часа́ два́. *This takes me about two hours.*

спра́шивать у *to ask (information)*
О́н **спра́шивал у** на́с доро́гу. *He asked us the way.*

проси́ть у *to ask, request*
О́н **проси́л у** меня́ де́ньги. *He asked me for money.*

покупа́ть у *to buy from*
Мы́ **покупа́ем у** него́ о́вощи. *We buy vegetables from him.*

7. Complete each of the following sentences with the most appropriate preposition: **без**, **для**, **из-за**, **из-под**, **кро́ме**, **ми́мо**, **о́коло**, **по́сле**, or **про́тив**.

1. ______________ ле́кции профе́ссор отвеча́л на вопро́сы слу́шателей.
2. На́ш до́м нахо́дится пря́мо ______________ па́рка.
3. Авто́бус проезжа́ет ______________ на́шего до́ма.
4. Мы́ жи́ли в Москве́ ______________ шести́ ме́сяцев.
5. О́н пьёт ко́фе чёрный ______________ са́хара.
6. О́н вста́л ______________ стола́ и предложи́л то́ст.
7. На ку́хне е́сть насте́нный шка́ф ______________ посу́ды.
8. Ребёнок съе́л всё, что бы́ло на таре́лке, ______________ зелёного горо́шка.
9. На столе́ стоя́ла буты́лка ______________ молока́.
10. Ко́шка вы́лезла ______________ дива́на.
11. Уо́лт Дисне́й со́здал прекра́сные фи́льмы ______________ дете́й.
12. Но́вые дома́ расту́т бы́стро, как грибы́ ______________ дождя́.
13. Э́та доро́га прохо́дит где́-то ______________ о́зера.
14. Самолёты не могли́ вы́лететь ______________ тума́на.
15. Делега́ты выступа́ли ______________ предложе́ния президе́нта.

8. Complete each of the following sentences with the most appropriate preposition(s): **до**, **из**, **от**, **с**, or **у**.

1. В я́сли принима́ют дете́й __________ пяти́ ле́т.
2. Она́ вы́нула па́спорт __________ су́мки.
3. О́н взя́л кни́гу __________ ве́рхней по́лки.
4. Мы́ получи́ли письмо́ __________ дру́га.
5. О́н проси́л де́ньги __________ роди́телей.
6. Мы́ узна́ли об э́том __________ газе́ты.
7. Ло́дка отплыла́ __________ бе́рега.
8. Э́ти ло́жки сде́ланы __________ серебра́.
9. О́н до́лго стоя́л на моро́зе и дрожа́л __________ хо́лода.
10. Она́ устро́ила сканда́л __________ ре́вности.
11. О́н бы́л __________ врача́, ему́ сде́лали уко́л __________ гри́ппа.
12. Ма́ма __________ Росси́и, а па́па __________ Украи́ны.
13. Сего́дня я́ доéхал __________ университе́та за 30 мину́т.
14. Мы́ занима́емся __________ девяти́ __________ дву́х часо́в.
15. Где́ клю́ч __________ кварти́ры?
16. Дава́й смотре́ть фи́льм, __________ на́с е́сть но́вый ви́дик.
17. О́н не мо́г изба́виться __________ мы́сли, что она́ встреча́ется с други́м па́рнем.
18. Не покупа́й матрёшки __________ у́личных торго́вцев, э́ти матрёшки ни́зкого ка́чества.

Other Prepositions Governing the Genitive Case

A number of other prepositions govern the genitive case. Many are structurally more complex than those presented in the first group. Some of them are derived from nouns, e.g., **вме́сто** *instead of, in place of* is an amalgam of the more basic preposition **в** *in* and the noun **ме́сто** *place.* Others, formed from adverbs, may function both as adverbs and prepositions, e.g., **позади́** is used as an adverb in **Они́ оста́вили всё *позади́*** *They left everything behind,* but as a preposition in **Де́ти игра́ют *позади́* на́шего до́ма** *The children play behind our house.* Since many of the prepositions in this next group are more characteristic of written style, familiarity with these prepositions will contribute to greater proficiency in reading Russian.

бли́з	внутри́	ме́жду	ра́ди
вблизи́	вну́трь	напро́тив	све́рх
ввиду́	во́зле	пове́рх	сза́ди
вдо́ль	вокру́г	позади́	среди́
вме́сто	впереди́	посреди́	
вне́	вро́де	путём	

бли́з

near, close to (NOTE: The preposition **бли́з** is characteristic of poetic style.)

До́м стоя́л **бли́з** мо́ря.	*The house stood near the sea.*

вблизи́ (от)

near, close to, not far from (NOTE: The preposition **вблизи́**, a synonym of **бли́з**, is stylistically neutral. **Вблизи́** may be followed by the preposition **от**, as in the example below.)

До́м находи́лся **вблизи́ от** мо́ря.	*The house was located close to the sea.*

ввиду́

in view of

Ввиду́ э́тих обстоя́тельств, мы́ реши́ли отложи́ть заседа́ние.	*In view of these circumstances, we decided to postpone the meeting.*

вдо́ль

along a line or the length of something

Посади́ли дере́вья **вдо́ль** доро́ги.	*They planted trees along the road.*
Дельфи́ны плы́ли **вдо́ль** бе́рега.	*Dolphins swam along the shore.*
Мы́ шли́ **вдо́ль** на́бережной.	*We walked along the embankment.*
Вдо́ль у́лицы стоя́ли ма́шины.	*Cars were parked along the street.*

вме́сто

instead of, in place of

Вме́сто во́дки лу́чше пи́ть вино́.	*Instead of vodka, it is better to drink wine.*
Она́ пошла́ туда́ **вме́сто** му́жа.	*She went there in place of her husband.*

вне́

outside, out of, beyond

Кури́ть мо́жно, но то́лько **вне** до́ма.	*You may smoke, but only outside the house.*
На́м нельзя́ де́йствовать **вне** зако́на.	*We cannot act outside the law.*
Ребёнок роди́лся **вне** бра́ка.	*The child was born out of wedlock.*
Э́то **вне** вся́кого сомне́ния.	*This is beyond any doubt.*

внутри́

inside indicating the position or location in which something is found

Мы́ не́ были **внутри́** дворца́.	*We haven't been inside the palace.*
Медве́дь бы́л **внутри́** пеще́ры.	*The bear was inside the cave.*

вну́трь

inside indicating motion or direction inward (NOTE: This preposition also occurs in the form **вовну́трь**, which is used in colloquial style.)

Тури́сты вошли́ **вну́трь** дворца́.	*The tourists went inside the palace.*
Де́ти загляну́ли **вовну́трь** пеще́ры.	*The kids glanced inside the cave.*

во́зле

near, very close to (NOTE: In comparison with **вблизи́**, **бли́з**, and **о́коло**, the preposition **во́зле** denotes closer proximity to something.)

Они́ живу́т **во́зле** на́с.	*They live very close to us.*
На́ш до́м **во́зле** са́мой реки́.	*Our house is right near the river.*

вокру́г

around, surrounding

Земля́ враща́ется **вокру́г** со́лнца.	*The earth revolves around the sun.*
Вокру́г него́ собрала́сь толпа́.	*A crowd gathered around him.*
Ситуа́ция **вокру́г** Ира́ка обостри́лась.	*The situation surrounding Iraq has worsened.*

впереди́

in front of, ahead of

Ги́д шёл **впереди́** гру́ппы тури́стов.	*The guide walked in front of the tourist group.*
Мили́ция е́хала **впереди́** автоколо́нны.	*The police rode ahead of the motorcade.*

вро́де

like

У ни́х е́сть дива́н **вро́де** на́шего.	*They have a sofa like ours.*
О́н что́-то **вро́де** консульта́нта.	*He's something like a consultant.* (*He's a consultant of sorts.*)

ме́жду

between (NOTE: The preposition **ме́жду** + genitive case occurs quite rarely. It is found in a few idiomatic expressions, and always when the objects involved are of the same type. More often, **ме́жду** is followed by the instrumental case.)

О́н оказа́лся **ме́жду** дву́х огне́й.	*He found himself between two fires.* (i.e., *between two unpleasant alternatives*)
О́н сиди́т **ме́жду** дву́х сту́льев.	*He is sitting between two chairs.* (i.e., *trying to please both sides in a dispute*)
На́до чита́ть **ме́жду** стро́к.	*One must read between the lines.*

напро́тив
opposite, across from

Они́ живу́т **напро́тив** па́рка.	*They live opposite the park.*
Напро́тив на́шего до́ма е́сть кафе́.	*Across from our house is a café.*

пове́рх
over, above, on top of a physical surface

Она́ постели́ла про́стыню **пове́рх** матра́ца.	*She lay the sheet over the mattress.*
О́н смотре́л **пове́рх** очко́в.	*He looked over the top of his glasses.*

позади́
behind

Позади́ на́шего до́ма е́сть огоро́д.	*Behind our house there is a vegetable garden.*

посреди́
in the middle of (in a spatial sense only)

Посреди́ пло́щади стоя́л кио́ск.	*In the middle of the square was a kiosk.*

путём
by means of

Вопро́с реши́ли **путём** перегово́ров.	*The question was decided by means of negotiations.*

ра́ди
for the sake of someone or something

Они́ помири́лись **ра́ди** дете́й.	*They reconciled for the sake of the children.*
О́н де́лал всё **ра́ди** на́шей дру́жбы.	*He did everything for the sake of our friendship.*

све́рх
on top of, in excess of, beyond (in an abstract sense)

О́н получи́л пре́мию **све́рх** зарпла́ты.	*He received a bonus on top of his salary.*
Его́ реше́ние бы́ло **све́рх** мои́х ожида́ний.	*His decision was beyond my expectations.*

сза́ди
behind

Сза́ди до́ма была́ ре́чка.	*Behind the house was a stream.*
Сза́ди на́с разда́лся кри́к.	*A shout was heard behind us.*

среди́
(a) *in the middle of* (in a spatial or temporal sense)

Село́ затеря́лось **среди́** лесо́в.	*The village was lost in the middle of the woods.*
Она́ просну́лась **среди́** но́чи.	*She woke up in the middle of the night.*
Его́ огра́били **среди́** бе́ла дня́.	*He was robbed in broad daylight.*

(b) *among*

О́н выделя́лся умо́м **среди́** все́х.	*He stood out among everyone for his intelligence.*
Мы́ нашли́ письмо́ **среди́** ста́рых бума́г.	*We found the letter among the old papers.*
Да́ча стоя́ла **среди́** дере́вьев.	*The dacha stood among the trees.*

9. Complete each of the following sentences with the most appropriate preposition: **ввиду́**, **вме́сто**, **вне́**, **вро́де**, **путём**, **ра́ди**, or **све́рх**.

1. О́н э́того доби́лся ____________ больши́х уси́лий.
2. О́н поменя́л рабо́ту ____________ семьи́.
3. Ему́ предложи́ли зарпла́ту ____________ его́ ожида́ний.
4. Мы́ реши́ли заказа́ть ры́бу ____________ мя́са.
5. ____________ вспы́шки холе́ры в э́той стране́ мы́ не поéхали туда́.
6. Его́ спосо́бности к языка́м ____________ спо́ра.
7. О́н купи́л костю́м ____________ моего́.

10. Complete each of the following sentences with the most appropriate preposition: **вблизи́**, **вдо́ль**, **внутри́**, **вну́трь**, **во́зле**, **вокру́г**, **впереди́**, **ме́жду**, **напро́тив**, **пове́рх**, **посреди́**, **сза́ди**, or **среди́**.

1. О́н живёт в до́ме ______________ са́мого вокза́ла.
2. Они́ путеше́ствовали ______________ све́та.
3. Мы́ шли́ ______________ бе́рега, собира́я раку́шки.
4. И́х до́м нахо́дится ______________ мо́ря.
5. О́н загляну́л ______________ шкафа́.
6. Соба́ка бежа́ла ______________ хозя́ина.
7. Мы́ не́ были ______________ э́того музе́я, его́ закры́ли на ремо́нт.
8. ______________ домо́в ду́л си́льный ве́тер.
9. ______________ руба́шки, о́н наде́л ку́ртку.
10. Она́ сиде́ла ______________ него́ и массажи́ровала ему́ пле́чи.
11. ______________ рове́сников, о́н выделя́лся больши́м ро́стом.
12. ______________ па́рка, в са́мом его́ це́нтре, бы́л фонта́н.
13. Как ра́з ______________ на́шего до́ма была́ це́рковь.

Prepositions Governing the Prepositional or Locative Case

The following preposition is followed only by the prepositional case.

при

при

(a) *under/during (the reign of), in the time of*

Санкт-Петербу́рг бы́л осно́ван **при** Петре́ Пе́рвом.	*St. Petersburg was founded during the reign of Peter the First.*
Проце́сс демократиза́ции в Росси́и начался́ **при** Горбачёве.	*The process of democratization in Russia began under Gorbachev.*

(b) *affiliated with, attached to* (NOTE: In this use the preposition **при** indicates that something is closely connected with, or is administered by, an institution. In this meaning the preposition itself may not be translated.)

Она́ обе́дает в столо́вой **при** университе́те.	*She has lunch at the university cafeteria.*
При заво́де е́сть я́сли.	*The factory has a day care center.*
При до́ме е́сть небольшо́й огоро́д.	*The house has a small vegetable garden on the grounds.*

(c) *in the presence of*

Мы́ не говори́м об э́том **при** де́тях.	*We don't talk about that in front of the children.*
Э́ти докуме́нты на́до подпи́сать **при** свиде́телях.	*These documents must be signed in the presence of witnesses.*

(d) *given, with* indicating a certain condition or property

При жела́нии о́н мо́г бы всего́ доби́ться.	*Given the desire, he could accomplish anything.*
При таки́х тала́нтах о́н непреме́нно найдёт хоро́шую рабо́ту.	*With such talent, he will surely find a good job.*

The following prepositions govern the prepositional case when used in the meanings indicated.

в
на
о
по

в

(a) *in, at* indicating position or location (NOTE: The preposition **в** governs the accusative case when motion or directionality is expressed or implied.)

Они́ живу́т **в** дере́вне.	*They live in the country.*
Мы́ бы́ли **в** теа́тре.	*We were at the theater.*

(b) *in* certain articles of clothing, i.e., indicating what someone is/was wearing

Я́ бу́ду **в** джи́нсах и кроссо́вках.	*I'll be in jeans and tennis shoes.*
Она́ была́ **в** бе́лом сви́тере.	*She was wearing a white sweater.*

(c) *in* certain periods of time, i.e., indicating the time when an event occurred, when the unit of time is a month, semester, year, century, various life periods, or ages.

Она́ родила́сь **в** ма́рте.	*She was born in March.*
Они́ поже́нятся **в** бу́дущем году́.	*They will get married next year.*
Она́ умерла́ **в** девятна́дцатом ве́ке.	*She died in the nineteenth century.*
В мо́лодости она́ мечта́ла ста́ть балери́ной.	*In her youth she dreamed of becoming a ballerina.*

(d) *at* half past the hour, when telling time (NOTE: This is an exception to the rule that, when telling time, the preposition **в** is used with the accusative case; see above.)

Она́ встаёт **в** полови́не седьмо́го.	*She gets up at half past seven.*

(e) to indicate the distance *at* which something is located from another point (expressed by the preposition **от** + genitive case)

Метро́ нахо́дится **в** киломе́тре **от** на́шего до́ма.	*The metro is located a kilometer from our house.*
О́н жи́л **в** пяти́ мину́тах ходьбы́ **от** на́с.	*He lived a five-minute walk from us.*

Verbs Followed by the Preposition *в* + Prepositional Case

A number of verbs require the preposition **в** and the prepositional case. Some of the most commonly used among these verbs are given below.

нужда́ться в *to be in need of*
О́н **нужда́ется в** на́шей по́мощи. — *He needs our help.*

обвиня́ть в *to accuse (someone) of*
Его́ не ра́з **обвиня́ли в** кра́же. — *More than once he's been accused of theft.*

отка́зывать в *to refuse, deny (someone something)*
Она́ **отка́зывала** на́м **в** про́сьбах. — *She has refused our requests.*

подозрева́ть в *to suspect (someone) of*
Его́ **подозрева́ют в** преступле́нии. — *He is suspected of a crime.*

разбира́ться в *to be proficient in, have an understanding of*
Она́ пло́хо **разбира́ется в** му́зыке. — *She doesn't understand music.*

сомнева́ться в *to doubt*
Я́ не **сомнева́юсь в** её и́скренности. — *I don't doubt her sincerity.*

убежда́ть(ся) в *to convince, be convinced of*
Мы́ **убежда́ли** его́ **в** пра́вде. — *We tried to convince him of the truth.*

уверя́ть в *to assure of*
О́н **уверя́л** её **в** свое́й ве́рности. — *He tried to assure her of his faithfulness.*

уча́ствовать в *to participate in*
Она́ **уча́ствует в** конце́рте. — *She is participating in the concert.*

на

(a) *on* the surface of a physical object, i.e., indicating the position or location where something or someone is found (NOTE: The preposition **на** governs the accusative case when motion or direction *to* a place is expressed.)

Кни́ги стоя́т **на** по́лке.	*The books are (standing) on the shelf.*
Журна́лы лежа́т **на** столе́.	*The magazines are (lying) on the table.*
Мы́ сиде́ли **на** дива́не.	*We sat on the sofa.*

(b) *in, at, on* indicating location in a place that typically has an activity or event associated with it. Since learning the particular types of nouns that must be used with the preposition **на** typically presents some difficulty for the student, a special section is devoted to this problem.

Nouns That Require the Preposition *на* to Express Location

The preposition **на**, not the preposition **в**, must be used with a number of nouns to express location. Many of the nouns that require **на** denote places that involve an open area, and/or one where people tend to gather for various activities, e.g., **на де́тской площа́дке** *on the playground,* **на ко́ртах** *on the tennis courts.* Some of these nouns in combination with **на** refer to buildings, but the reference may also be to the surrounding grounds, e.g., **на вокза́ле** *at the railroad station* (i.e., the terminal building, along with the tracks and platforms outside). Other nouns may not seem to fit this general description and must simply be memorized. Below are some commonly used nouns that require **на**, grouped into a few broad categories.

Places Associated with Activities of Students and Teachers

заня́тие *university class*	**на** заня́тии
ка́федра *(university) department*	**на** ка́федре
ку́рс *course*	**на** ку́рсе
ле́кция *lecture*	**на** ле́кции
пра́ктика *practical training*	**на** пра́ктике
семина́р *seminar*	**на** семина́ре
уро́к *lesson*	**на** уро́ке
факульте́т *faculty, department*	**на** факульте́те
экза́мен *examination*	**на** экза́мене

Places for Social Gatherings, Relaxation, and Various Types of Entertainment

бале́т *ballet*	**на** бале́те
ве́чер *party* (*formal*)	**на** ве́чере
вечери́нка *evening get-together*	**на** вечери́нке
вы́ставка *exhibition*	**на** вы́ставке
да́ча *summer cottage*	**на** да́че
конце́рт *concert*	**на** конце́рте
ко́рты *(tennis) courts*	**на** ко́ртах
куро́рт *resort*	**на** куро́рте
ку́хня *kitchen*	**на** ку́хне
ма́тч *match* (*sports*)	**на** ма́тче
о́пера *opera*	**на** о́пере
пье́са *play*	**на** пье́се
приём *reception*	**на** приёме
сва́дьба *wedding*	**на** сва́дьбе
спекта́кль *performance*	**на** спекта́кле
стадио́н *stadium*	**на** стадио́не

NOTE: The nouns **бале́т**, **о́пера**, **пье́са**, **спекта́кль** occur with the preposition **на** when reference is made to attendance at an event: **Вчера́ мы́ бы́ли *на* бале́те** *Yesterday we were at the ballet.* These same nouns, however, may occur with the preposition **в** when reference is made to an artist's participation in a particular performance, or to the content of the ballet, opera, etc.: ***В*** **э́том бале́те танцева́л Бары́шников** *Baryshnikov danced in this ballet,* ***В*** **э́том бале́те прекра́сная му́зыка** *There is wonderful music in this ballet.*

Places Associated with the Conduct of Work, Trade, and Types of Meetings

база́р *market, bazaar*	**на** база́ре
би́ржа *stock exchange*	**на** би́рже
вокза́л *railway station*	**на** вокза́ле
заво́д *factory*	**на** заво́де
заседа́ние *meeting (of key personnel)*	**на** заседа́нии
конфере́нция *conference*	**на** конфере́нции

по́чта *post office*	**на** по́чте
предприя́тие *enterprise*	**на** предприя́тии
рабо́та *work*	**на** рабо́те
ры́нок *market*	**на** ры́нке
собра́ние *meeting*	**на** собра́нии
ста́нция *station*	**на** ста́нции
съе́зд *congress*	**на** съе́зде
фа́брика *factory*	**на** фа́брике
фе́рма *farm*	**на** фе́рме
я́рмарка *fair*	**на** я́рмарке

Geographic Places

(i) *Points of the compass*

восто́к *east*	**на** восто́ке
за́пад *west*	**на** за́паде
се́вер *north*	**на** се́вере
ю́г *south*	**на** ю́ге

(ii) *Natural formations*

бе́рег *shore*	**на** берегу́
лу́г *meadow*	**на** лугу́
мо́ре *sea*	**на** мо́ре
о́зеро *lake*	**на** о́зере
океа́н *ocean*	**на** океа́не
о́стров *island*	**на** о́строве
пля́ж *beach*	**на** пля́же
побере́жье *coast*	**на** побере́жье
полуо́стров *peninsula*	**на** полуо́строве
равни́на *plain*	**на** равни́не
река́ *river*	**на** реке́

NOTE: The nouns denoting bodies of water occur with the preposition **на** when the intended meaning is location "on the surface of" or "on the shores of": **Мы́ провели́ де́нь *на* о́зере, купа́лись, загора́ли *на* пля́же** *We spent the day at the lake, we swam, we sunbathed on the beach.* However, the same nouns may occur with the preposition **в** when the intended meaning is location "beneath the surface of": ***В* э́том о́зере о́чень чи́стая вода́** *The water in this lake is very pure.*

(iii) *Place names (of specific islands, lakes, mountain ranges, peninsulas, etc.)*

Аля́ска *Alaska*	**на** Аля́ске
Байка́л *(Lake) Baikal*	**на** Байка́ле
Балка́ны *the Balkans*	**на** Балка́нах
Бли́жний Восто́к *Middle East*	**на** Бли́жнем Восто́ке
Да́льний Восто́к *Far East*	**на** Да́льнем Восто́ке
Гава́йи *Hawaii*	**на** Гава́йях, **на** Гава́йских острова́х
Кавка́з *Caucasus*	**на** Кавка́зе
Ку́ба *Cuba*	**на** Ку́бе
Украи́на *Ukraine*	**на/в** Украи́не
Ура́л *Urals*	**на** Ура́ле

NOTE: Recently, **в Украи́не** *in Ukraine* has been gaining acceptance among some speakers, and **в За́падной Украи́не** *in Western Ukraine* is standard usage.

(iv) *Cityscape: streets, roads, squares, etc.*

бульва́р *avenue, boulevard*	**на** бульва́ре
дво́р *yard*	**на** дворе́
доро́га *road*	**на** доро́ге
мо́ст *bridge*	**на** мосту́
окра́ина *outskirts*	**на** окра́ине
пло́щадь *square*	**на** пло́щади
проспе́кт *avenue*	**на** проспе́кте
стоя́нка *parking lot*	**на** стоя́нке
у́гол *(street) corner*	**на** углу́
у́лица *street*	**на** у́лице

NOTE: A few nouns in the group above may occur with the preposition **в**, but the resulting phrase will have a different meaning, e.g., **у́гол**: ***на* углу́** *on the corner (of the street)* / ***в* углу́** *in the corner (of something)*, and **дво́р**: ***на* дворе́** *outside* / ***в* дворе́** *in a yard (enclosed by a fence or surrounded by buildings)*.

Conditions of Nature, Weather

во́здух *air*	**на** све́жем/откры́том во́здухе *in the fresh/open air*
восхо́д (со́лнца) *sunrise*	**на** восхо́де со́лнца
зака́т *sunset*	**на** зака́те
моро́з *frost, intense cold*	**на** моро́зе
рассве́т *dawn*	**на** рассве́те
со́лнце *sun*	**на** со́лнце

(c) used with nouns denoting vehicles and other forms of transportation to indicate the means by which one travels. This construction is synonymous with the use of the instrumental case of the noun to express "the means of travel" (see Chapter 2, page 60).

Мы́ е́хали на рабо́ту **на** авто́бусе.	*We went to work by bus.*
До́чка лю́бит е́здить **на** велосипе́де.	*The daughter likes to ride her bicycle.*
Они́ прие́хали к на́м **на** трамва́е.	*They came to our place by tram.*

NOTE: The preposition **в** is used with nouns denoting types of transportation when reference is made to an activity that takes place inside the vehicle, e.g., **Она́ сиде́ла и чита́ла *в* авто́бусе** *She sat and read in the bus.*

(d) to indicate time when the unit of time is weeks

На про́шлой неде́ле она́ была́ больна́.	*Last week she was sick.*
На э́той неде́ле о́н идёт к врачу́.	*This week he is going to the doctor.*
На бу́дущей неде́ле мы́ е́дем в о́тпуск.	*Next week we are going on vacation.*

Verbs Followed by the Preposition *на* + Prepositional Case

A few common verbs are followed by the preposition **на** and the prepositional case.

жени́ться на *to marry (of men)*

Бори́с **жени́лся на** Та́не.	*Boris married Tanya.*

игра́ть на *to play (instrument)*

Са́ша хорошо́ **игра́ет на** гита́ре.	*Sasha plays the guitar well.*

ката́ться на *to go for a ride on*	
Ле́на **ката́ется на** велосипе́де.	*Lena is out riding her bicycle.*
наста́ивать на *to insist on*	
О́н **наста́ивает на** то́чности.	*He insists on accuracy.*
осно́вываться на *to be based on*	
Э́ти вы́воды **осно́вываются на** фа́ктах.	*These conclusions are based on facts.*

о (об, обо)

about, concerning (NOTE: The preposition **о** + prepositional case is synonymous with the colloquial preposition **про** + accusative case. It is written **об** when the following noun begins with the vowel **а**, **э**, **и**, **о**, or **у**: ***об*** **А́нне** *about Anna,* ***об*** **э́том** *about that,* ***об*** **Ива́не** *about Ivan,* ***об*** **окне́** *about the window,* ***об*** **уро́ке** *about the lesson.* The form **обо** occurs only with pronoun objects in the expressions ***обо*** **мне́** *about me,* ***обо*** **всём** *about everything,* ***обо*** **всéх** *about everyone.*)

Мы́ ду́маем **о** де́тях.	*We think about the children.*
О́н ча́сто говори́т **о** рабо́те.	*He often talks about work.*
Она́ мечта́ет **о** любви́.	*She dreams about love.*

по

after, on, upon (NOTE: The preposition **по** + prepositional case is characteristic of formal, written Russian and is used primarily with deverbal nouns.)

По оконча́нии университе́та о́н реши́л, что пора́ жени́ться.	*Upon graduating from the university, he decided it was time to get married.*
По прие́зде домо́й она́ позвони́ла му́жу.	*Upon her arrival home, she called her husband.*

11. Complete each of the following sentences with the most appropriate preposition(s): **при**, **в**, **на**, **о**, or **по**. Each preposition is followed by the prepositional case.

1. Она́ была́ ________ ле́кции ________ Кита́е.
2. ________ де́тстве о́н игра́л ________ балала́йке.
3. ________ капитали́зме це́ны зави́сят от спро́са и предложе́ния.
4. ________ оконча́нии шко́лы о́н поступи́л на вое́нную слу́жбу.
5. ________ жела́нии всего́ мо́жно доби́ться.
6. Ка́к меня́ узна́ть? Я́ бу́ду ________ джи́нсах и пуло́вере.
7. О́н е́здит ________ рабо́ту ________ метро́.
8. О́н роди́лся ________ ма́е.
9. Я́ ча́сто ду́маю ________ на́шей встре́че в Петербу́рге.
10. Го́сти сиде́ли ________ дива́не.
11. О́н жени́лся ________ во́зрасте тридцати́ ле́т.
12. Нельзя́ руга́ться ________ де́тях.
13. Институ́т нахо́дится ________ двадцати́ мину́тах езды́ отсю́да.
14. ________ заво́де е́сть де́тский ла́герь.
15. Америка́нские пиани́сты уча́ствовали ________ э́том ко́нкурсе.
16. Я́ пло́хо разбира́юсь ________ матема́тике.
17. ________ её красоте́ она́ могла́ бы ста́ть и манеке́нщицей.
18. Зде́сь зимо́й все́ де́ти ката́ются ________ конька́х.
19. ________ про́шлой неде́ле мы́ бы́ли ________ Москве́.
20. Мы́ не сомнева́емся ________ его́ спосо́бностях.

Prepositions Governing the Dative Case

The following prepositions are followed only by the dative case.

благодаря́
вопреки́
к
навстре́чу
согла́сно

благодаря́

thanks to indicating the cause of an action that usually has a desirable result

Они́ вы́жили то́лько **благодаря́** твое́й по́мощи. — *They survived only thanks to your help.*

вопреки́

contrary to, despite

Вопреки́ сове́ту врача́, о́н ещё ку́рит. — *Contrary to the advice of his doctor, he still smokes.*

к

(a) *toward, up to* a point (in a spatial sense)

Де́ти бегу́т **к** о́зеру. — *The children are running toward the lake.*
Маши́на подъе́хала **к** до́му. — *The car drove up to the house.*

(b) *toward, by* a point in time

Она́ пришла́ домо́й **к** ве́черу. — *She arrived home toward evening.*
Я́ зако́нчу докла́д **к** пя́тнице. — *I will finish the report by Friday.*
Мы́ придём домо́й **к** ча́су. — *We will be home by one o'clock.*

(c) *to* a person (NOTE: After a verb of motion, the preposition **к** + dative case must be used when the destination is a person. The general sense is going *to someone's place, home, office,* etc. The translation may be going *to see* someone.)

Сего́дня мы́ идём **к** врачу́. — *Today we are going to the doctor's.*
Вчера́ мы́ е́здили **к** роди́телям. — *Yesterday we went to our parents'.*
Она́ за́шла **к** подру́ге. — *She dropped by to see a friend.*

(d) after certain nouns to indicate feelings or an attitude *toward* something or someone

дове́рие к *trust/faith in*
У меня́ нет **дове́рия к** нему́. — *I have no faith in him.*

интере́с к *interest in*
У него́ большо́й **интере́с к** му́зыке. — *He has a strong interest in music.*

любо́вь к *love for*
О́н э́то сде́лал из **любви́ к** де́тям. — *He did it out of love for his children.*

сла́бость к *weakness for*
У меня́ **сла́бость к** шокола́ду. — *I have a weakness for chocolate.*

стра́сть к *passion for*
Она́ име́ет **стра́сть к** чте́нию. — *She has a passion for reading.*

уваже́ние к *respect for*
О́н поéхал туда́ из **уваже́ния к** отцу́. — *He went there out of respect for his father.*

(e) with noun objects denoting certain emotions

к сожале́нию *unfortunately*
к сча́стью *fortunately*
к моему́ удивле́нию *to my surprise*

Verbs Followed by the Preposition *к* + Dative Case

A number of verbs require the preposition **к** and the dative case. Several have the prefix **при-** and denote approach or attachment to something.

гото́виться к *to prepare for*
Студе́нты **гото́вятся к** экза́мену. — *The students are preparing for an examination.*

обраща́ться к *to turn to*
Когда́ ему́ нужны́ де́ньги, о́н **обраща́ется к** отцу́. — *When he needs money, he turns to his father.*

относи́ться к *to relate to*
Э́тот профе́ссор хорошо́ **отно́сится к** студе́нтам. — *This professor relates well to students.*

подходи́ть к *to approach*
По́езд **подхо́дит к** ста́нции. — *The train is approaching the station.*

приближа́ться к *to approach, draw near to*
Мы́ **приближа́емся к** Эрмита́жу. — *We are approaching the Hermitage.*

привыка́ть к *to get used to, grow accustomed to*
Она́ ещё **привыка́ет к** кли́мату. — *She is still getting used to the climate.*

прикле́ивать к *to glue/paste to, affix to*
О́н **прикле́ивает** ма́рки **к** конве́ртам. — *He is gluing the stamps onto the envelopes.*

прилипа́ть к *to stick/adhere to* (*intransitive*)
Иногда́ таре́лки **прилипа́ют к** столу́. — *Sometimes plates stick to the table.*

принадлежа́ть к *to belong to, be a member of*
О́н **принадлежи́т к** ша́хматному клу́бу. — *He belongs to the chess club.*

пришива́ть к *to sew on*
Она́ **пришива́ет** пу́говицу **к** руба́шке. — *She is sewing a button on the shirt.*

навстре́чу

toward, to meet

Я́ вы́шел **навстре́чу** гостя́м. — *I came out to meet the guests.*
Я́ пошёл ему́ **навстре́чу**. — *I met him halfway* (figurative).

согла́сно
in accordance with

Мы́ поступи́ли **согла́сно** реше́нию комите́та.	*We acted in accordance with the decision of the committee.*

The following preposition is followed by the dative case when used in the meanings indicated.

по

по

(a) *along, down* a line (NOTE: This use of **по** + dative case is synonymous with the use of the instrumental case to express the route taken, cf. **Де́ти бежа́ли бе́регом.**)

Де́ти бежа́ли **по** бе́регу.	*The children ran along the shore.*
Мы́ шли́ **по** у́лице Че́хова.	*We walked down Chekhov Street.*

(b) *around, throughout* indicating movement in various directions

Чита́я ле́кцию, профе́ссор ходи́л **по** ко́мнате.	*While lecturing, the professor walked around the room.*
Но́вость бы́стро разнесла́сь **по** всему́ го́роду.	*The news quickly spread throughout the whole city.*
Они́ бе́гали **по** всё́м магази́нам.	*They ran around to all the stores.*

(c) *on* the surface (NOTE: This meaning occurs with verbs meaning *to hit, strike, bang,* etc.)

До́ждь стуча́л **по** о́кнам.	*The rain was pattering on the windows.*
О́н уда́рил кулако́м **по́** столу.	*He banged on the table with his fist.*
О́н хло́пнул дру́га **по** спине́.	*He slapped his friend on the back.*

(d) *according to, by*

Поезда́ хо́дят то́чно **по** расписа́нию.	*The trains run precisely according to schedule.*
О́н де́лает всё **по** пра́вилам.	*He does everything by the rules.*
Кни́ги расста́влены **по** те́мам.	*The books are arranged by subject.*

(e) *by* a certain means of communication

Они́ познако́мились **по** Интерне́ту.	*They met over the Internet.*
Они́ посла́ли посы́лку **по** по́чте.	*They sent the package by mail.*
Мы́ говори́ли **по** телефо́ну.	*We spoke by telephone.*
Она́ слы́шала но́вость **по** ра́дио.	*She heard the news over the radio.*

(f) *in (the field of), on (the subject of), by (= with respect to)*

О́н специали́ст **по** компью́терам.	*He is a specialist in computers.*
О́н чита́л ле́кцию **по** фина́нсам.	*He gave a lecture on finance.*
По профе́ссии она́ бухга́лтер.	*She is an accountant by profession.*
О́н гре́к **по** происхожде́нию.	*He is Greek by descent.*

(g) *on, in* indicating days and other time periods when an action recurs

О́н посеща́ет ку́рсы води́телей **по** сре́дам.	*He has driver education classes on Wednesdays.*
Ба́нки закрыва́ют **по** пра́здникам.	*The banks are closed on holidays.*
Она́ рабо́тает **по** вечера́м.	*She works in the evenings.*

(h) *one (thousand, million) each* indicating distribution of objects by ones (NOTE: With the numerals two, three, and four, the preposition **по** takes the accusative case: **Они́ получи́ли *по* два́/три́ я́блока** *They received two/three apples each.* With other numerals, the dative or the accusative may be used.)

Они́ получи́ли **по** одному́ я́блоку.	*They received one apple each.*
Она́ дала́ де́тям **по** биле́ту.	*She gave the children one ticket each.*
Ма́льчикам да́ли **по** ты́сяче рубле́й.	*The boys were given one thousand rubles each.*

(i) *for, out of, due to* indicating the cause of an action

По како́й причи́не?	*For what reason?*
О́н э́то сде́лал **по** глу́пости.	*He did it out of stupidity.*
О́н ра́но вы́шел на пе́нсию **по** боле́зни.	*He retired early due to illness.*
Она́ сде́лала оши́бку **по** нео́пытности.	*She made the mistake out of inexperience.*

12. Complete each of the following sentences with the most appropriate dative preposition: **благодаря́**, **вопреки́**, **к**, **навстре́чу**, **по**, or **согла́сно**.

1. Ру́ки прилипа́ют ______________ кра́ске.
2. На́м да́ли ______________ одному́ жето́ну.
3. Вчера́ в институ́те была́ ле́кция ______________ маркетингу.
4. О́н прие́хал сюда́ неда́вно и ещё с трудо́м привыка́ет ______________ э́той культу́ре.
5. ______________ ва́шей подде́ржке, мы́ доби́лись на́шей це́ли.
6. ______________ предупрежде́ниям, о́н реши́л пое́хать в э́ту страну́.
7. У неё сла́бость ______________ сла́достям.
8. ______________ постановле́нию президе́нта ограни́чилась прода́жа спи́рта.
9. Соба́ка побежа́ла на́м ______________.
10. О́н ча́сто бе́гает ______________ э́тому па́рку.
11. За́втра мы́ идём ______________ на́шим друзья́м.
12. Ма́льчик разби́л ва́зу ______________ неосторо́жности.
13. Ле́том молоды́е па́ры лю́бят гуля́ть ______________ на́бережной.

Prepositions Governing the Instrumental Case

The following prepositions are followed only by the instrumental case.

над
пе́ред

над

(a) *over, above*

Ла́мпа виси́т **над** столо́м.	*The lamp is hanging over the table.*
Самолёт лете́л **над** облака́ми.	*The airplane flew above the clouds.*

(b) used figuratively after certain verbs

ду́мать над *to think over*

Мне́ на́до **поду́мать над** э́тим.	*I need to think this over.*

издева́ться над *to tease*

Де́ти **издева́лись над** то́лстым ма́льчиком.	*The children teased the fat boy.*

рабóтать над *to work on*
Онá **рабóтает над** доклáдом. — *She is working on a report.*

смеяться над *to laugh at*
Всé **смеялись над** егó нелóвкостью. — *Everyone laughed at his clumsiness.*

пéред

(a) *in front of, before* in a spatial sense

Автóбус стоит **пéред** музéем.	*The bus is parked in front of the museum.*
Онá стояла **пéред** зéркалом.	*She stood in front of the mirror.*
Óн предстáл **пéред** судóм.	*He appeared before the court.*

(b) *before* in a temporal sense (NOTE: In contrast to the preposition **до** + genitive case, which may also denote time *before,* **пéред** + instrumental case usually denotes time *immediately or shortly before.*)

Онá всегдá читáет **пéред** снóм.	*She always reads before going to bed.*
Óн погасил свéт **пéред** ухóдом.	*He turned out the light before leaving.*
Мы́ вы́шли **пéред** сáмым концóм спектáкля.	*We walked out just before the end of the performance.*

The following prepositions are followed by the instrumental case when used in the meanings indicated.

за
мéжду
под
с

за

(a) *behind, beyond* when location is indicated (NOTE: When the preposition **за** follows a verb expressing motion or direction, this preposition governs the accusative case.)

За нáшим дóмом—лéс.	*Behind our house are woods.*
За лéсом—дорóга.	*Beyond the woods is a road.*

(b) *during, at, over*

За зáвтраком пáпа читáет газéту.	*During breakfast Dad reads the newspaper.*
За обéдом мы́ бýдем говорить обо всём.	*At lunch we'll talk about everything.*

(c) after a verb of motion to indicate the object that is the goal of the motion

Óн пошёл в библиотéку **за** книгой.	*He went to the library for a book.*
Онá побежáла в магазин **за** хлébом.	*She ran to the store for bread.*

Verbs Followed by the Preposition *за* + Instrumental Case

A few common verbs are followed by the preposition **за** + instrumental case.

наблюдáть за *to keep an eye on, observe*
Врачи **наблюдáют за** новорождёнными. — *The doctors are observing the newborn babies.*

слéдовать за *to follow*
Туристы **слéдуют за** гидом. — *The tourists are following the guide.*

следи́ть за *to keep up with; to look after*

О́н **следи́т за** теку́щими собы́тиями.	*He keeps up with current events.*
Ба́бушка **следи́т за** свои́м здоро́вьем.	*Grandma looks after her health.*

ме́жду

between, among (NOTE: Though a few idiomatic expressions show an older use of **ме́жду** followed by the genitive case, in contemporary Russian the preposition **ме́жду** is normally followed by the instrumental case.)

Ме́жду сто́ло́м и стено́й стои́т ла́мпа.	*Between the table and the wall is a lamp.*
Ме́жду до́мом и ле́сом течёт ре́чка.	*Between the house and the woods is a stream.*
Пу́сть э́то бу́дет **ме́жду** на́ми.	*Let's keep that (just) between us.*

под

(a) *below, beneath, under* indicating literal or figurative location (NOTE: When motion or direction is expressed, the preposition **под** is followed by the accusative case.)

Гео́логов интересу́ет, что́ лежи́т **подо** льдо́м Антаркти́ды.	*Geologists are interested in what lies beneath the ice of the Antarctic.*
О́н пря́чется **под** крова́тью.	*He is hiding under the bed.*
Она́ нашла́ серёжку **под** поду́шкой.	*She found an earring under the pillow.*
О́н нахо́дится **под** её влия́нием.	*He is under her influence.*
О́н пи́шет **под** псевдони́мом.	*He writes under a pseudonym.*
Го́род **под** угро́зой сне́жной бу́ри.	*The city is under threat of a snowstorm.*

(b) *with* indicating foods prepared with (i.e., under) a dressing or sauce

Она́ заказа́ла ры́бу **под** бе́лым со́усом.	*She ordered fish with white sauce.*

(c) *in the environs of, near*

О́н живёт **под** Москво́й.	*He lives in the environs of Moscow.*

с

(a) *with* in the sense of *together with, along with, accompanied by*

Она́ ча́сто говори́т **с** подру́гой.	*She often talks with her girlfriend.*
О́н пошёл на вы́ставку **с** жено́й.	*He went to the exhibit with his wife.*
Мы́ пьём ча́й **с** лимо́ном и са́харом.	*We drink tea with lemon and sugar.*

(b) to indicate an accompanying characteristic or attribute of someone or something

Э́то де́вушка **с** краси́выми глаза́ми.	*This is a girl with beautiful eyes.*
О́н челове́к **с** вы́сшим образова́нием.	*He is a person with a higher education.*
Мы́ сня́ли кварти́ру **с** балко́ном.	*We rented a flat with a balcony.*

(c) to indicate manner

О́н говори́т по-ру́сски **с** акце́нтом.	*He speaks Russian with an accent.*
Я́ слу́шал его́ **с** больши́м интере́сом.	*I listened to him with great interest.*
Мы́ **с** удово́льствием при́няли и́х приглаше́ние.	*We accepted their invitation with pleasure.*

(d) used in expressions of congratulations after the verb **поздравля́ть** *to congratulate,* which is often omitted

Поздравля́ем ва́с **с** пра́здником!	*Happy Holidays!*
С Но́вым го́дом!	*Happy New Year!*
Поздравля́ем с рожде́нием ребёнка!	*Congratulations on the birth of your child.*

Verbs Followed by the Preposition *c* + Instrumental Case

Several verbs are followed by the preposition **c** + instrumental case. Following is a partial list of these verbs.

встреча́ться с *to meet with*
Она́ ча́сто **встреча́ется с** дру́гом. — *She often meets with her friend.*

знако́миться с *to become acquainted with*
Ему́ легко́ **знако́миться с** людьми́. — *It is easy for him to meet people.*

расстава́ться с *to part with, leave*
Жа́лко, что ты́ **расстаёшься с** не́й. — *It's a pity you are parting with her.*

сове́товаться с *to consult with*
О́н ча́сто **сове́туется с** ме́неджером. — *He often consults with the manager.*

13. Complete each of the following sentences with the most appropriate instrumental preposition: **над**, **пе́ред**, **за**, **ме́жду**, **под**, or **c**.

1. Она́ пошла́ на по́чту __________ ма́рками и конве́ртами.
2. На́до мы́ть ру́ки __________ едо́й.
3. О́н __________ ра́достью согласи́лся на́м помо́чь.
4. Доро́га идёт __________ ци́рком и университе́том.
5. Пти́цы лете́ли __________ ле́сом.
6. Зри́тели входи́ли в кинотеа́тр дру́г __________ дру́гом.
7. Вы́ в э́том де́ле игра́ете __________ огнём.
8. Такси́ останови́лось __________ на́шим до́мом.
9. Конце́рт бы́л в па́рке __________ откры́тым не́бом.
10. Мы́ ещё ду́маем __________ э́тим вопро́сом.
11. Де́ти жда́ли кани́кул __________ нетерпе́нием.
12. Ма́ма пошла́ в де́тский са́д __________ до́чкой.
13. __________ бе́регом реки́ и доро́гой шла́ у́зкая тропи́нка.
14. О́н челове́к высо́кого ро́ста и __________ бородо́й.
15. Она́ рабо́тает __________ статьёй.
16. Па́русная ло́дка шла́ __________ мосто́м.
17. Посети́тели рестора́на сле́довали __________ официа́нтом к столу́.
18. Она́ челове́к __________ твёрдыми убежде́ниями.

Pronouns

A pronoun is a word used in place of a noun or another pronoun. Pronouns are classified according to their function.

Personal Pronouns

Nominative Case

PERSON	SINGULAR		PLURAL	
First	я́	*I*	мы́	*we*
Second	ты́	*you*	вы́	*you*
Third	о́н	*he/it*	они́	*they*
	оно́	*it*		
	она́	*she/it*		

First Person

The first person (**я́, мы́**) is used to indicate the speaker or writer.

Second Person

The second person (**ты́, вы́**) is used to indicate the addressee, i.e., the person or persons to whom one is speaking. The two second-person pronouns not only distinguish singular and plural, but also may convey different degrees of formality.

The singular pronoun **ты́** is the "familiar" *you.* Within a family the pronoun **ты́** is used by all family members, regardless of age. Outside the family context, the pronoun **ты́** is normally used between friends, between professional peers of similar age, by an adult addressing a child, by a child to another child, or when addressing a pet.

The pronoun **вы́** must be used when addressing two or more people, but when addressing one person, it also serves as the "formal" *you.* The second-person **вы́** is used when addressing a person in authority (e.g., student to teacher, employee to supervisor) or a person higher in status or years (e.g., child to non-related adult). It is also customary for adults to use the formal form of address when they first meet. It is important that foreigners, in particular, address adult Russians using the formal **вы́**; use of the informal **ты́** should normally be initiated by the Russian. Generally speaking, **вы́** is the appropriate form of address to use when the speaker wishes to show respect. In letter writing, this pronoun is often capitalized.

The informal/formal difference signaled by the two second-person pronouns **ты́/вы́** in the singular is also conveyed by two different forms of the word for "Hello": informal **Здра́вствуй!** and formal (with added **-те**) **Здра́вствуйте!**

Здра́вствуй, Са́ша. Ка́к **ты** живёшь?	*Hello, Sasha. How are you doing?*
Здра́вствуйте! **Вы́** профе́ссор Во́лков?	*Hello! Are you Professor Volkov?*

Third Person

The third person (**о́н, оно́, она́, они́**) indicates the person(s) or object(s) spoken about. In the singular, a third-person pronoun must reflect the gender of its antecedent, i.e., the noun mentioned earlier to which the pronoun refers. When the antecedent is a male or female person, the pronouns **о́н** and **она́** mean *he* and *she,* respectively. When these same pronouns refer to an inanimate object, they, like the neuter pronoun **оно́**, are translated into English as *it.*

The third-person plural pronoun **они́** *they* may refer both to people and to things. The plural pronoun, like the plural form of the noun in Russian, does not distinguish between masculine, neuter, and feminine gender.

—Где́ Бори́с?	*Where is Boris?*
—**О́н** до́ма.	*He is at home.*
—Где́ каранда́ш?	*Where is the pencil?*
—**О́н** на столе́.	*It is on the table.*
—Где́ ма́ма?	*Where is Mom?*
—**Она́** на ку́хне.	*She is in the kitchen.*
—Где́ ру́чка?	*Where is the pen?*
—**Она́** на по́лке.	*It is on the shelf.*
—Где́ бра́т и сестра́?	*Where are the brother and sister?*
—**Они́** в шко́ле.	*They are in school.*

1. Complete each of the following sentences with the correct personal pronoun in the nominative case.

1. —Ма́ма, _________ не зна́ешь, где́ моя́ тетра́дь?
   —Да́, зна́ю. _________ ту́т на столе́.
2. —Здра́вствуйте! _________ профе́ссор Смирно́в?
   —Да́, _________ Смирно́в.
3. —Я́ до́ма и Ле́на то́же.
   —Что́ _________ де́лаете?
   —_________ слу́шаем му́зыку.
4. —Где́ ма́ма и па́па?
   —_________ на рабо́те.
5. —Ма́м, где́ мои́ но́вые джи́нсы?
   —_________ лежа́т на сту́ле.
6. —Ле́на, посмотри́ на но́вое кольцо́.
   —О́й, _________ тако́е краси́вое!
7. —Зна́ешь, Серге́й провёл це́лый семе́стр в Аме́рике.
   —Интере́сно. _________, наве́рное, говори́т хорошо́ по-англи́йски.

Accusative Case

PERSON	SINGULAR		PLURAL	
First	меня́	*me*	на́с	*us*
Second	тебя́	*you*	ва́с	*you*
Third	его́ (на него́)	*him/it*	и́х (на ни́х)	*them*
	его́ (на него́)	*it*		
	её (на неё)	*her/it*		

NOTE: In the masculine and neuter third-person accusative pronoun **его́**, the consonant **г** is pronounced [v], e.g., **его́** is pronounced [yɪvó]. The preposition **на** is only one of several prepositions that may take the accusative case.

The accusative case of the personal pronouns is used when they occur as the direct object of the verb or as the object of a preposition that governs the accusative case. When the third-person pronouns **о́н, оно́, она́** are the object of a preposition, they must occur in the accusative case with an initial **н**, as shown in the table above. The third-person pronouns take this initial **н** not only in the accusative case after a preposition, but after most prepositions governing any of the cases (except the nominative).

The accusative case of the personal pronouns can be illustrated with the verb **зва́ть** *to call* and the construction used in Russian to ask and give someone's name. The question **Ка́к зову́т ...?** literally means *How do they call ...?* and the person referred to is grammatically the direct object of the verb in the accusative case. So, ***Меня́*** **зову́т Джи́м** literally means "Me they call Jim," but in English is translated as *My name is Jim.*

NOTE: The direct object pronoun in this construction occurs before the verb, whereas the direct object noun follows the verb. This is due to a general principle of Russian word order according to which "old information" (i.e., previously mentioned or present in the context) normally precedes "new information" (i.e., newly introduced into the discourse). For example, the direct object pronoun in the second sentence below is "old information," since its antecedent is mentioned in the previous sentence: **Э́то мо́й бра́т. *Его́*** **зову́т Серёжа** *This is my brother. His name is Seryozha.*

—Ка́к **тебя́** зову́т? *What is your name?*
—**Меня́** зову́т Са́ша. А **тебя́**? *My name is Sasha. And yours?*
—Ле́на. *Lena.*

—Ка́к **ва́с** зову́т? *What is your name?*
—**Меня́** зову́т Никола́й. А **ва́с**? *My name is Nikolaj. And yours?*
—Татья́на. *Tatyana.*
—О́чень прия́тно. *Pleased to meet you.*

—Ка́к зову́т ва́шего бра́та? *What is your brother's name?*
—**Его́** зову́т Па́вел. *His name is Pavel.*

—Ка́к зову́т ва́шу сестру́? *What is your sister's name?*
—**Её** зову́т Та́ня. *Her name is Tanya.*

—Ка́к зову́т ва́ших друзе́й? *What are the names of your friends?*
—**И́х** зову́т Ди́ма и Пе́тя. *Their names are Dima and Petya.*

Below are examples of the accusative case of the personal pronouns functioning as objects of a preposition.

—О́н хоро́ший дру́г. *He is a good friend.*
—Да́, на **него́** мо́жно положи́ться. *Yes, we can count on him.*

—Они́ хоро́шие друзья́. *They are good friends.*
—Да́, на **ни́х** мо́жно наде́яться. *Yes, we can count on them.*

—Э́тот слова́рь мне́ о́чень ну́жен. *I really need this dictionary.*
—Спаси́бо за **него́**. *Thank you for it.*
—Пожа́луйста. *You're welcome.*

2. Complete each of the following sentences with the correct personal pronoun in the accusative case.

1. —Бори́с пи́шет докла́д?
   —Да́, о́н ________ пи́шет.
2. Сы́н пло́хо у́чится в шко́ле. Ма́ть беспоко́ится за ________.
3. —Ири́на отве́тила на письмо́?
   —Да́, она́ на ________ отве́тила.
4. —Ты́ ви́дела ма́му?
   —Не́т, я ________ не ви́дела.
5. —Зна́ешь, Га́ля получи́ла при́з!
   —Да́, мы́ ра́ды за ________.
6. —Вы́ зна́ете Све́ту и Бо́рю?
   —Да́, мы́ ________ зна́ем.
7. —Вы́ смотре́ли на мо́й рису́нки?
   —Да́, мы́ на ________ смотре́ли.
8. —Ка́к зову́т твоего́ брата́?
   —________ зову́т Ди́ма.
9. —Ка́к зову́т твою́ подру́гу?
   —________ зову́т Ма́ша.
10. Э́та кни́га мне́ о́чень нужна́. Большо́е спаси́бо за ________.
11. Учи́тель за́дал вопро́с, но учени́к не мо́г отве́тить на ________.
12. Мы́ ви́дели на́ших друзе́й, но они́ не ви́дели ________.
13. Я́ говори́л по-ру́сски, но ________ не понима́ли.
14. Ми́ша, мы́ вчера́ ви́дели ________, когда́ ты́ шёл домо́й.
15. —Мы́ вы́играли в лотере́ю!
    —Ка́к здо́рово! Я́ ра́д за ________.

Genitive Case

PERSON	SINGULAR		PLURAL	
First	меня́	*me*	на́с	*us*
Second	тебя́	*you*	ва́с	*you*
Third	его́ (у него́)	*him/it*	и́х (у ни́х)	*them*
	его́ (у него́)	*it*		
	её (у неё)	*her/it*		

NOTE: The third-person personal pronouns in the genitive case **его́**, **её**, **и́х** also serve as possessive pronouns with the meaning *his, her, their.* When used as possessives, these forms do not have the initial **н** that is added to the object forms after most prepositions. Compare the genitive case object in the first sentence with the possessive pronoun in the second: **У него́ е́сть сестра́** *He has a sister* (literally, "By him is a sister"), but **У его́ сестры́ краси́вые глаза́** *His sister has pretty eyes* (literally, "By his sister [are] pretty eyes").

The personal pronouns in the genitive case are identical in form to those in the accusative case. The genitive case of the personal pronouns is used after verbs that govern the genitive (e.g., **боя́ться** *to be afraid of,* **избега́ть** *to avoid*) and after prepositions that govern the genitive case (e.g., **у** *by,* **для** *for the benefit of,* **от** *from*).

Я́ давно́ тебя́ не ви́дел. Ты́ что́, избега́ешь **меня́**!	*I haven't seen you for a long time. What are you doing, avoiding me?*
Ты́ мне́ та́к помо́г, я хочу́ купи́ть для **тебя́** пода́рок.	*You helped me so much, I want to buy a present for you.*
О́н тако́й зло́бный челове́к. Де́ти **его́** боя́тся.	*He is such a mean person. The children are afraid of him.*
О́н ре́дко пи́шет, но то́лько сего́дня я получи́л от **него́** письмо́.	*He rarely writes, but just today I received a letter from him.*
Она́ зло́бная же́нщина. Мы́ **её** избега́ем.	*She is a mean woman. We avoid her.*
Она́ на́м о́чень нужна́, без **неё** про́сто нельзя́ обойти́сь.	*She is really important to us, it's simply impossible to manage without her.*
Мы́ купи́ли но́вые ди́ски. У **на́с** больша́я колле́кция ди́сков.	*We bought new compact discs. We have a big collection of CDs.*
Они́ зде́сь бы́ли го́д наза́д, но́ с те́х по́р мы́ не слы́шали от **ни́х**.	*They were here a year ago, but since then we haven't heard from them.*

3. Complete each of the following sentences with the genitive form of the underlined personal pronoun.

1. Я́ иду́ в университе́т. У __________ заня́тия.
2. Я слы́шал, ты́ сего́дня бы́л в институ́те. У __________ что́, экза́мен бы́л?
3. О́н о́чень стро́гий учи́тель, ученики́ __________ боя́тся.
4. О́н бы́л на рабо́те. У __________ бы́ло собра́ние.
5. Она́ давно́ не писа́ла, мы́ не получа́ли от __________ ни одного́ письма́.
6. Мы́ идём в университе́т. У __________ сего́дня ле́кция.
7. Когда́ вы та́к кричи́те на дете́й, они́ __________ боя́тся.
8. Заче́м они́ купи́ли ещё ру́чки, у __________ уже́ мно́го ру́чек.

Prepositional Case

PERSON	SINGULAR		PLURAL	
First	обо мне́	*about me*	о на́с	*about us*
Second	о тебе́	*about you*	о ва́с	*about you*
Third	о нём	*about him/it*	о ни́х	*about them*
	о нём	*about it*		
	о не́й	*about her/it*		

The prepositional case of the personal pronouns is used only after prepositions that govern the prepositional case (e.g., **в** *in,* **на** *on,* **о/об/обо** *about*).

—Во́т институ́т фи́зики. —В **нём** у́чится моя́ сестра́.	*Here is the physics institute.* *My sister studies in it.*
—Во́т но́вая шко́ла би́знеса. —В **не́й** гото́вят ме́неджеров.	*Here is the new school of business.* *Managers are trained in it.*
—Ты́ ду́мал о Бори́се? —Да́, я ду́мал о **нём**.	*Were you thinking about Boris?* *Yes, I was thinking about him.*

—Ты́ писа́ла об Ири́не?	*Did you write about Irina?*
—Да́, я писа́ла о **не́й**.	*Yes, I wrote about her.*
—Вы́ беспоко́итесь об экза́менах?	*Are you anxious about the exams?*
—Не́т, мы́ не беспоко́имся о **ни́х**.	*No, we're not anxious about them.*
—А, вот и ты́!	*Oh, here you are!*
—Мы́ ка́к ра́з спра́шивали о **тебе́**.	*We were just asking about you.*
—Обо **мне́**?	*About me?*
—Да́, о **тебе́**.	*Yes, about you.*

4. Complete each of the following sentences with the prepositional form of the underlined personal pronoun.

1. О́н неда́вно зде́сь. Я́ ма́ло зна́ю о ________.
2. Я́ неда́вно прие́хал. Вы́ наве́рно не слы́шали обо ________.
3. Она́ отли́чная студе́нтка. О ________ говори́л на́ш профе́ссор.
4. Вы́ зде́сь но́вый, и о ________ ма́ло зна́ют.
5. Они́ победи́ли в соревнова́ниях. Все́ о ________ говоря́т.
6. Э́то ты́ вы́играл в лотере́ю? О ________ говори́т ве́сь го́род!

5. Rewrite each of the following sentences, replacing the underlined noun phrase with the correct form of the appropriate personal pronoun.

1. Мы́ мно́го слы́шали о но́вом преподава́теле. ____________________
2. Де́ти говори́ли о роди́телях. ____________________
3. О́н ча́сто ду́мает о жене́. ____________________
4. Она́ не забы́ла о дя́де. ____________________
5. Они́ спра́шивали о на́ших де́тях. ____________________

Dative Case

PERSON	SINGULAR		PLURAL	
First	мне́	*to/for me*	на́м	*to/for us*
Second	тебе́	*to/for you*	ва́м	*to/for you*
Third	ему́ (к нему́)	*to/for him*		
	ему́ (к нему́)	*to/for it*	и́м (к ни́м)	*to/for them*
	е́й (к не́й)	*to/for her*		

The dative forms of the personal pronouns are used when they are the indirect object of a verb, the object of a verb that governs the dative case (e.g., **звони́ть** *to call,* **помога́ть** *to help,* **меша́ть** *to bother, prevent,* **сове́товать** *to advise*), or the object of a preposition that governs the dative (e.g., **к** *to, toward,* **по** *along*).

—Ма́ма, что́ ты́ купи́ла **мне́**?	*Mom, what did you buy for me?*
—Я́ купи́ла **тебе́** игру́шку.	*I bought a toy for you.*
—Ты́ всё рассказа́ла па́пе?	*Did you tell Dad everything?*
—Да́, я́ **ему́** всё рассказа́ла.	*Yes, I told him everything.*
—Ты́ посла́л Све́те письмо́?	*Did you send the letter to Sveta?*
—Да́, я посла́л **е́й** письмо́.	*Yes, I sent her the letter.*
—Вы́ помогли́ сосе́дям?	*Did you help the neighbors?*
—Да́, мы́ **и́м** помогли́.	*Yes, we helped them.*

—Дéти вáм мешáют? —Нéт, онѝ **нáм** не мешáют.	*Are the children bothering you?* *No, they are not bothering us.*
—Ты́ звонѝла сестрé? —Дá, я **éй** звонѝла.	*Did you call your sister?* *Yes, I called her.*
—Ты́ éздила к родѝтелям? —Дá, я́ к **нѝм** éздила.	*Did you go to (see) your parents?* *Yes, I went to (see) them.*
—А ты́ вчерá ходѝл к сестрé? —Дá, я́ к **нéй** ходѝл.	*Did you go to your sister's yesterday?* *Yes, I went to her (place).*
—Кудá ты́ идёшь? —К брáту, я́ к **нему́** давнó не ходѝл.	*Where are you going?* *To my brother's, I haven't been to see him in a long time.*

6. Complete each of the following sentences with the dative form of the underlined personal pronoun.

1. Óн нáш хорóший дру́г. Мы́ покупáем ________ подáрок.
2. Онѝ дóлго не писáли. Я́ ________ позвоню́.
3. Онá просѝла у нáс пóмощь, и мы́ ________ помоглѝ.
4. Ты́ собирáешь мáрки, поэ́тому я́ дáм ________ э́ту красѝвую мáрку.
5. Я́ хотéл пѝть, и онѝ дáли ________ воды́.

7. Rewrite each of the following sentences, replacing the underlined noun phrase with the dative form of the appropriate personal pronoun.

1. Мы́ купѝли сы́ну велосипéд. ________________
2. Онá подарѝла мáме шáрф. ________________
3. Óн пошёл к начáльнику. ________________
4. Мы́ чáсто ходѝли в гóсти к друзья́м. ________________
5. Óн придёт к сестрé. ________________
6. Мы́ чáсто ходѝли по Нéвскому проспéкту. ________________

Instrumental Case

PERSON	SINGULAR		PLURAL	
First	мнóй	*with me*	нáми	*with us*
Second	тобóй	*with you*	вáми	*with you*
Third	и́м (с нѝм)	*with him/it*		
	и́м (с нѝм)	*with it*	и́ми (с нѝми)	*with them*
	éй (с нéй)	*with her/it*		

NOTE: The forms **мнóй**, **тобóй**, **éй** have the alternative forms **мнóю**, **тобóю**, **éю**, which may occur in poetic as well as in colloquial style.

NOTE: The meaning *with* given in the table above is appropriate for several uses of the instrumental case, including its most basic use as "instrument" of the action, as well as in combination with the preposition **с** in the meaning *along with, together with.* However, the instrumental case has several other uses following verbs and other prepositions where this meaning does not apply, as shown below.

The instrumental personal pronouns are used when they are the object of a verb that governs the instrumental case (e.g., **занимáться** *to involve oneself with,* **увлекáться** *to be fascinated with,* **любовáться** *to admire,* **пóльзоваться** *to use*), an adjective that governs the instrumental case (e.g., **довóлен** *pleased with,* **недовóлен** *displeased with*), or the object of a preposition (e.g., **за** *behind,* **мéжду** *between,* **нáд** *above,* **пéред** *in front of,* **под** *below,* **с** *with*), or a verb followed by a preposition that governs the instrumental case (e.g., **знакóмиться с** *to become acquainted with,* **встречáться с** *to meet with,* **рабóтать над** *to work on,* **следи́ть за** *to look after*).

The instrumental forms of the personal pronouns may occur after the preposition **с** in an idiomatic construction involving a plural subject. The following are common examples.

(Я́ и ты́)	Мы́ с **тобóй**	*You* (fam.) *and I*
(Я́ и вы́)	Мы́ с **вáми**	*You* (formal) *and I*
(Я́ и óн)	Мы́ с **ни́м**	*He and I*
(Я́ и онá)	Мы́ с **нéй**	*She and I*
(Я́ и они́)	Мы́ с **ни́ми**	*They and I*
(Вы́ и óн)	Вы́ с **ни́м**	*You and he*
(Вы́ и онá)	Вы́ с **нéй**	*You and she*

NOTE: This instrumental case construction is also used when the subject consists of a personal pronoun and a noun (e.g., **Мы́ с женóй** *My wife and I,* **Мы́ с друзья́ми** *My friends and I,* **Вы́ с брáтом** *You and your brother*), or when two nouns are conjoined (e.g., **Сáша с Натáшей** *Sasha and Natasha*).

—Óн увлекáется спóртом?	*Is he taken with sports?*
—Дá, он **и́м** óчень увлекáется.	*Yes, he is really fascinated with them.*
—Онá ужé пóльзуется космéтикой?	*Does she already use makeup?*
—Нéт, онá покá **éю** не пóльзуется.	*No, she doesn't use it yet.*
—Каки́е краси́вые гóры!	*What beautiful mountains!*
—Дá, я сáм чáсто любýюсь **и́ми**.	*Yes, I often admire them myself.*
—Ты́ давнó встречáешься с Ми́шей?	*Have you been dating Misha long?*
—Дá, я с **ни́м** встречáюсь ужé гóд.	*Yes, I've been dating him for a year already.*
—Ты́ написáл отли́чный доклáд!	*You wrote an excellent report!*
—Спаси́бо, я сáм довóлен **и́м**.	*Thanks, I am pleased with it myself.*
—Вы́ знáете Мáшу Волóдину?	*Do you know Masha Volodina?*
—Дá, мы́ с **нéй** знáкомы.	*Yes, we are acquainted with her.*
—Знáешь, Пéтя бы́л на лéкции.	*You know, Petya went to the lecture.*
—Знáю, мы́ сидéли прямо за **ни́м**.	*I know, we sat right behind him.*

8. Complete each of the following sentences with the appropriate personal pronoun in the instrumental case.

1. Ты́ хорошó ýчишься. Мы́ óчень довóльны ________.
2. Я́ былá в кинотеáтре и пéредо ________ сидéл Бóря Петрóв!
3. Мы́ ви́дели большóе дéрево и реши́ли отдыхáть под ________.
4. Мы́ шли́ по пóлю и вдрýг над ________ пролетéл самолёт.
5. Дéтям нельзя́ оставáться одни́м. Ктó-то дóлжен следи́ть за ________.
6. Доклáд ещё не готóв. Нáдо порабóтать ещё немнóго над ________.
7. Ты́ знáешь Лéну Смирнóву? Я́ вчерá ходи́л с ________ в кинó.
8. Э́то хорóший учéбник. Мы́ ________ пóльзовались на кýрсах.
9. В пáрке растýт больши́е берёзы. Мéжду ________ стои́т скамéйка.
10. И́ра получи́ла плохýю отмéтку. Учи́тель недовóлен ________.

The Reflexive Personal Pronoun *себя́*

The reflexive personal pronoun **себя́** *oneself* refers to the subject of the clause in which it is located. This pronoun occurs in five of the six cases, each indicating different ways the action of the subject is reflected back to it. Since this pronoun reflects the action of the subject, it cannot *itself* occur as subject in the nominative case. The reflexive personal pronoun has the same form for all persons, i.e., it does not change for gender or number.

Nom.	—
Acc./Gen.	себя́
Prep./Dat.	себе́
Instr.	собо́й

Accusative Case

Я́ смотре́л на **себя́** в зе́ркало. — *I looked at myself in the mirror.*
Ты́ представля́ешь **себя́** отцо́м? — *Do you imagine yourself as a father?*
Она́ счита́ет **себя́** актри́сой. — *She considers herself an actress.*
Ва́м на́до ве́рить в **себя́**. — *You must believe in yourself.*

NOTE: The direct object pronoun **себя́** gives reflexive meaning to transitive verbs that are not normally used as reflexives. True reflexive verbs, which typically involve a subject performing an action that directly affects himself, normally do not occur with direct object **себя́**, but instead are used intransitively with post-verbal **-ся**, e.g., **Она́ одева́ется** *She is dressing (herself)*, **О́н мо́ется** *He is washing (himself)*. See the section Verbs with the Particle **-ся (-сь)** in Chapter 7.

Genitive Case

Я́ посмотре́л вокру́г **себя́**. — *I looked around myself.*
Ты́ купи́л пода́рок для **себя́**! — *Did you buy a present for yourself?*
О́н бы́л вне́ **себя́** от гне́ва. — *He was beside himself with rage.*

Prepositional Case

Ты́ ду́маешь то́лько о **себе́**. — *You think only of yourself.*
О́н всегда́ име́ет при **себе́** де́ньги. — *He always has money on him.*
Она́ уве́рена в **себе́**. — *She has confidence in herself.*

Dative Case

Я́ купи́л **себе́** кни́гу. — *I bought a book for myself.*
Ты́ о́чень тре́бователен к **себе́**. — *You are very demanding of yourself.*

Instrumental Case

Мы́ разложи́ли пе́ред **собо́й** пла́н го́рода. — *We spread the city map before us (ourselves).*
О́н не мо́г владе́ть **собо́й**. — *He could not control himself.*
Она́ дово́льна **собо́й**. — *She is pleased with herself.*
Они́ спо́рили ме́жду **собо́й**. — *They argued among themselves.*

Idiomatic Uses of *себя́*

Several verbs combine with a form of the reflexive personal pronoun in fixed expressions, where the reflexive meaning of **себя́** is more abstract, or may not be felt at all.

бра́ть с собо́й *to take along* (lit., *with oneself*)
О́н всегда́ **берёт с собо́й** портфе́ль. — *He always takes his briefcase along.*

вести́ себя́ *to behave* (*conduct oneself*)
Ты́ **ведёшь себя́** ка́к ребёнок. — *You are behaving like a child.*

представля́ть себе́ *to imagine* (*represent to oneself*)
Ра́ньше о́н **представля́л себе́** Аме́рику ра́ем. — *Earlier he imagined America as paradise.*

чу́вствовать себя́ *to feel*
Я́ чу́вствую себя́ хорошо́. — *I feel well.*

The pronoun **себя́** is used in a number of other idiomatic expressions.

Я́ поду́мал про себя́.	*I thought to myself.*
Она́ о́чень **хороша́ собо́ю**.	*She is very good-looking.*
О́н **вы́шел из себя́**.	*He lost his temper.*
Ему́ ка́к-то **не по себе́**.	*He is somehow not himself.*
Э́то **само́ собо́й разуме́ется**.	*That goes without saying.*
Профе́ссор Орло́в **у себя́**?	*Is Professor Orlov in (his office)?*
Она́ **пошла́ к себе́** домо́й.	*She went home (to her own place).*

9. Complete each of the following sentences with the correct form of the reflexive personal pronoun **себя́**.

1. О́н тако́й эгои́ст, о́н всегда́ ду́мает то́лько о ________.
2. Она́ провали́лась на экза́мене и о́чень недово́льна ________.
3. О́н уве́ренный в ________ челове́к, о́н всегда́ наде́ется на ________.
4. У него́ ро́вный хара́ктер, о́н никогда́ не выхо́дит из ________.
5. Я́ купи́л пода́рки не то́лько для жены́ и дете́й, но и для ________.
6. Она́ положи́ла пе́ред ________ меню́ и ста́ла ду́мать, что́ заказа́ть на обе́д.
7. О́н вошёл в ко́мнату и закры́л за ________ две́рь.
8. О́н сде́ржанный челове́к, о́н ре́дко говори́т о ________.
9. Она́ скро́мная де́вушка, она́ не лю́бит привлека́ть к ________ внима́ние.
10. У него́ хоро́шее чу́вство ю́мора, о́н мо́жет смея́ться и на́д ________.
11. Прочита́й письмо́ вслу́х, а не про ________.
12. Ма́льчик не ходи́л вчера́ в шко́лу, о́н пло́хо чу́вствовал ________.
13. Сы́н попроси́л па́пу: —Возьми́ меня́ с ________.
14. Мы́ пригласи́ли к ________ в го́сти но́вую колле́гу.
15. Ма́ма так ра́да, что де́ти веду́т ________ хорошо́.

The Reciprocal Pronoun *дру́г дру́га*

The reciprocal pronoun **дру́г дру́га** *each other* is comprised of two parts, the first of which is not declined, while the second part declines like an animate masculine noun (i.e., Acc. = Gen.). The declined form takes the case required by the governing verb, adjective, or preposition. When a preposition occurs, it is placed between undeclined **дру́г** and the declined form. Like the reflexive personal pronoun **себя́**, the reciprocal pronoun **дру́г дру́га** *each other* does not occur in the nominative case. The declension of the reciprocal pronoun is presented in the table below.

Nom.	—
Acc.	дру́г дру́га
	дру́г на дру́га
Gen.	дру́г дру́га
	дру́г у дру́га
Prep.	дру́г о дру́ге
Dat.	дру́г дру́гу
	дру́г к дру́гу
Instr.	дру́г дру́гом
	дру́г с дру́гом

NOTE: The pronoun **дру́г дру́га** adds reciprocal meaning to verbs that are not typically understood to express a reciprocal action. Verbs that do have an inherently reciprocal meaning, such as *embrace, kiss, meet,* etc., normally do not occur with the pronoun **дру́г дру́га**; instead, they incorporate the post-verbal particle **-ся**, e.g., **При встре́че, они́ всегда́ обнима́ются и целу́ются** *Upon meeting, they always embrace and kiss (each other).* On verbs with reciprocal meaning, see Chapter 7.

Accusative Case

Ми́ша и Та́ня лю́бят **дру́г дру́га**.	*Misha and Tanya love each other.*
Они́ полага́ются **дру́г** на **дру́га**.	*They rely on each other.*
Мы́ ве́рим **дру́г** в **дру́га**.	*We believe in each other.*

Genitive Case

Они́ боя́тся **дру́г дру́га**.	*They are afraid of each other.*
Мы́ ча́сто быва́ем **дру́г** у **дру́га**.	*We often visit each other.*
Они́ не мо́гут жи́ть **дру́г** без **дру́га**.	*They can't live without each other.*

Prepositional Case

Они́ ду́мают **дру́г** о **дру́ге**.	*They think about each other.*
Мы́ забо́тимся **дру́г** о **дру́ге**.	*We take care of each other.*

Dative Case

Они́ посыла́ют пи́сьма **дру́г дру́гу**.	*They send letters to each other.*
Они́ помога́ют **дру́г дру́гу**.	*They help each other.*
Они́ верны́ **дру́г дру́гу**.	*They are faithful to each other.*
Мы́ привыка́ем **дру́г** к **дру́гу**.	*We are getting used to each other.*

Instrumental Case

Они́ интересу́ются **дру́г дру́гом**.	*They are interested in each other.*
Мы́ ча́сто спо́рим **дру́г** с **дру́гом**.	*We often argue with each other.*
Они́ посмея́лись **дру́г** над **дру́гом**.	*They played a joke on each other.*

10. Complete each of the following sentences with the correct form of the reciprocal pronoun (with a preposition, if required).

1. Э́ти де́вушки ча́сто говоря́т по телефо́ну _______________ (with each other).
2. Са́ша и Та́ня поздра́вили _______________ (each other) с Но́вым го́дом.
3. Они́ всегда́ покупа́ют пода́рки _______________ (for each other).
4. Они́ не мо́гут обойти́сь _______________ (without each other).
5. Они́ молодожёны, и ещё привыка́ют _______________ (to each other).
6. Они́ хоро́шие друзья́, они́ всегда́ наде́ются _______________ (on each other).
7. На́с критикова́ли, но мы́ заступа́лись _______________ (for each other).
8. Му́ж и жена́ не всегда́ живу́т в ладу́, иногда́ они́ се́рдятся _______________ (at each other).
9. Хотя́ они́ похо́жи по вне́шности, по хара́ктеру э́ти близнецы́ си́льно отлича́ются _______________ (from each other).
10. Когда́ мои́ сыновья́ бы́ли детьми́, они́ ча́сто спо́рили, но тепе́рь, ста́в взро́слыми, они́ хорошо́ отно́сятся _______________ (toward each other).

Interrogative Pronouns: *кто́, что́*

Nom.	кто́	что́
Acc.	кого́	что́
Gen.	кого́	чего́
Prep.	о ко́м	о чём
Dat.	кому́	чему́
Instr.	ке́м	че́м

The Pronoun *кто́*

The pronoun **кто́** *who* requires its predicate to agree in the singular.

Кто́ идёт в кино́?	*Who is going to the movies?*
Кто́ говори́т по-ру́сски?	*Who speaks Russian?*

Кто́ requires its predicate to agree in the masculine gender.

Кто́ вы́шел?	*Who stepped out?*
Кто́ гото́в?	*Who is ready?*

Masculine agreement is required by **кто́** even in instances when reference is clearly made to females; for example, the subject of the phrase **вы́йти за́муж** *to get married* can only be a woman.

Кто́ из твои́х подру́г вы́шел за́муж?	*Who of your girlfriends got married?*
Кто́ гото́в вы́йти за́муж?	*Who is ready to get married?*

Кто́ *who* is used in Russian to refer to people, even in certain instances where native speakers of English would use the pronoun *what.*

Кто́ у ни́х роди́лся, ма́льчик?	*What did they have, a boy?*
Кто́ она́ по профе́ссии?	*What is she by profession?*
Ке́м о́н рабо́тает, инжене́ром?	*What does he work as, an engineer?*
Кто́ о́н по происхожде́нию, шве́д?	*What is he by descent, a Swede?*

When asking about someone whose name s/he does not know, the speaker may ask the question **Кто́ э́то?** *Who is that?* The pronoun **кто́** also has a wider application than its English equivalent, in that it may be used to refer to animals as well as people.

—**Кто́** э́то?	*Who is that?*
—Э́то мо́й бра́т, Ми́ша.	*That's my brother, Misha.*
—А **кто́** э́то?	*And who is that?*
—Э́то моя́ ко́шка.	*That is my cat.*

When the speaker already knows someone's name, but wishes to learn more about the person's identity, the appropriate question is **Кто́ о́н?** *Who is he?* **Кто́ она́?** *Who is she?* Alternatively, one may ask **Кто́ о́н тако́й?** or **Кто́ тако́й ...** followed by the person's name (for a female **Кто́ она́ така́я?** or **Кто́ така́я ...?**).

—Ребя́та, **кто́** э́то?	*Guys, who is that?*
—Э́то Мари́я Во́лкова.	*That's Maria Volkova.*
—**Кто́** она́ (така́я)?	*Who is she?*
—Она́ но́вая аспира́нтка.	*She is a new graduate student.*
—**Кто́** э́то?	*Who is that?*
—Э́то Васи́лий Аксёнов.	*That is Vasilij Aksyonov.*
—**Кто́ тако́й** Васи́лий Аксёнов?	*Who is Vasilij Aksyonov?*
—Аксёнов—э́то ру́сский писа́тель.	*Aksyonov is a Russian writer.*

The pronoun **кто́** occurs in both direct questions (***Кто́*** **э́та де́вушка?** *Who is that girl?*) and indirect questions (**О́н меня́ спроси́л, *кто́* э́та де́вушка?** *He asked me who that girl was*). This pronoun may occur in any of the six Russian cases.

Кто́ сказа́л тебе́ об э́том?	*Who told you about this?*
Кого́ ты́ ви́дел на ле́кции?	*Whom did you see at the lecture?*
У **кого́** ты́ взя́л э́ту кни́гу?	*From whom did you get this book?*
О **ко́м** вы́ говори́те?	*Whom are you talking about?*
Кому́ ты́ да́л мо́й а́дрес?	*To whom did you give my address?*
С **ке́м** она́ идёт в кино́?	*With whom is she going to the movie?*

11. Complete each of the following sentences with the correct form of the interrogative personal pronoun **кто́**.

1. Я́ не зна́ю, о _________ ты́ говори́шь.
2. Она́ меня́ спроси́ла, с _________ я́ встреча́юсь.
3. На _________ ты́ наде́ешься?
4. _________ вы́ там ви́дели?
5. Они́ на́с спроси́ли, _________ мы́ бои́мся.
6. _________ ты́ покупа́ешь пода́рки?
7. Учи́тель спроси́л, _________ в кла́ссе не́т.
8. _________ па́па недово́лен, мно́й, или тобо́й?
9. За _________ ты́ беспоко́ишься, за сы́на?
10. Мы́ её спроси́ли, у _________ она́ была́.

The Pronoun *что́*

The interrogative pronoun **что́** *what* requires its predicate to agree in the neuter gender and singular number.

Что́ случи́лось?	*What happened?*
Что́ бы́ло на семина́ре?	*What went on at the seminar?*

Что́ is used to ask about the identity of an inanimate object or abstract notion, or about a verbal action. When asking about the identity of some object, the speaker normally asks **Что́ э́то?** *What is that?* or **Что́ э́то тако́е?** *What is that?* If the name of something is known, but more information is desired, one may ask **Что́ тако́е ...** followed by the name of the thing in question.

—**Что́** э́то?	*What is that?*
—Э́то пле́йер.	*That is a CD player.*
—А **что́** э́то тако́е?	*And what is that?*
—Э́то компа́кт-ди́ск.	*That is a compact disc.*
—**Что́** тако́е «хот-до́г»?	*What is a "hot dog"?*
—«Хот-до́г»—э́то соси́ска.	*A hot dog is a sausage.*

The interrogative pronoun **что́** may occur in any of the six cases, in both independent clauses (**Что́ э́то?** *What is that?*), as well as dependent clauses (**Я́ зна́ю, *что́* э́то** *I know what that is*).

Что́ с тобо́й?	*What is (the matter) with you?*
Что́ ты́ зна́ешь об э́том?	*What do you know about this?*
Чего́ вы́ бои́тесь?	*What are you afraid of?*
О **чём** ты́ говори́шь?	*What are you talking about?*
К **чему́** она́ гото́вится?	*What is she preparing for?*
Я́ зна́ю, с **чём** она́ знако́ма.	*I know with what she is acquainted.*

12. Complete each of the following sentences with the correct form of the interrogative pronoun **что́**.

1. Над ________ ты́ рабо́таешь?
2. На ________ он смо́трит?
3. Для ________ э́тот футля́р?
4. ________ вы́ об э́том ду́маете?
5. От ________ э́тот ключ?
6. Во ________ ты́ ве́ришь? В астроло́гию?
7. За ________ мы́ вы́пьем? За твоё здоро́вье!
8. ________ она́ бои́тся, экза́мена?
9. ________ ты́ пи́шешь, ру́чкой или карандашо́м?
10. С ________ ты́ пьёшь ча́й, с са́харом или с мёдом?

Possessive Pronouns

Russian has a possessive pronoun corresponding to each of the personal pronouns, and an interrogative possessive pronoun corresponding to the interrogative pronoun **кто́**.

PERSON	кто́? *who?*	че́й? *whose?*
Singular		
First	я́	мо́й
Second	ты́	тво́й
Third	о́н, оно́	его́
	она́	её
Plural		
First	мы́	на́ш
Second	вы́	ва́ш
Third	они́	и́х

The Possessive Pronouns *че́й?, мо́й, тво́й, на́ш, ва́ш*

The interrogative possessive **че́й** *whose* and the possessive pronouns **мо́й** *my/mine,* **тво́й** *your/yours,* **на́ш** *our/ours,* **ва́ш** *your/yours* must agree in gender, number, and case with the noun they modify. The tables below give the complete declensions for these pronouns.

CASE	MASCULINE,	NEUTER	FEMININE	PLURAL
Nom.	че́й	чьё	чья́	чьи́
Acc.	че́й/чьего́	чьё	чью́	чьи́/чьи́х
Gen.	чьего́		чье́й	чьи́х
Prep.	о чьём		о чье́й	о чьи́х
Dat.	чьему́		чье́й	чьи́м
Instr.	чьи́м		чье́й	чьи́ми

NOTE: In the declension of **че́й**, and that of all the other possessive pronouns that change for agreement, when the noun modified is singular masculine *inanimate,* the accusative case is identical to the nominative; when the noun modified is singular masculine *animate,* the accusative case is identical to the genitive. The rule "inanimate accusative = nominative / animate accusative = genitive," which affects only masculine nouns and their modifiers in the singular, applies to all three genders in the plural.

CASE	MASCULINE,	NEUTER	FEMININE	PLURAL
Nom.	мо́й	моё	моя́	мои́
Acc.	мо́й/моего́	моё	мою́	мои́/мои́х
Gen.	моего́		мое́й	мои́х
Prep.	о моём		о мое́й	о мои́х
Dat.	моему́		мое́й	мои́м
Instr.	мои́м		мое́й	мои́ми

CASE	MASCULINE,	NEUTER	FEMININE	PLURAL
Nom.	на́ш	на́ше	на́ша	на́ши
Acc.	на́ш/на́шего	на́ше	на́шу	на́ши/на́ших
Gen.	на́шего		на́шей	на́ших
Prep.	о на́шем		о на́шей	о на́ших
Dat.	на́шему		на́шей	на́шим
Instr.	на́шим		на́шей	на́шими

NOTE: The declension of **тво́й** is identical to that of **мо́й**, and the declension of **ва́ш** is identical to that of **на́ш**.

—**Чéй** э́то словáрь, **твóй**?	*Whose dictionary is this, yours?*
—Дá, э́то **мóй** словáрь.	*Yes, this is my dictionary.*
—**Чья́** э́то кни́га, **твоя́**?	*Whose book is this, yours?*
—Дá, **моя́**.	*Yes, mine.*
—**Чéй** чемодáн взя́л швейцáр?	*Whose suitcase did the porter take?*
—Óн взя́л **вáш** чемодáн.	*He took your suitcase.*
—**Чьегó** ребёнка вы́ ви́дели?	*Whose child did you see?*
—Мы́ ви́дели **вáшего** ребёнка.	*We saw your child.*
—**Чью́** кни́гу вы́ читáете?	*Whose book are you reading?*
—Я́ читáю **вáшу** кни́гу.	*I'm reading your book.*
—О **чьéй** подрýге óн спрáшивал?	*About whose girlfriend did he ask?*
—О **вáшей** подрýге.	*About yours.*
—Вóт **нáш** сы́н и **нáша** дóчь.	*Here is our son and our daughter.*
—Я́ ужé знакóм с **вáшим** сы́ном и **вáшей** дóчерью.	*I'm already acquainted with your son and your daughter.*
—Познакóмьтесь, э́то **нáши** друзья́.	*I'd like you to meet our friends.*
—Мы́ с **вáшими** друзья́ми ужé знакóмы.	*We are already acquainted with your friends.*

13. Complete each of the following sentences with the correct form of the pronoun **чéй**, **мóй**, **твóй**, **нáш**, or **вáш**.

1. Вóт идёт мóй брáт. Ты́ знáешь ____________ брáта?
2. Вóт нáши сосéди. Вы́ знакóмы с ____________ сосéдями?
3. Ты́ недáвно бы́л за грани́цей. Расскажи́ нáм о ____________ поéздке!
4. Вы́ мнóго сдéлали для нáс. Мы́ óчень благодáрны за ____________ пóмощь.
5. ____________ э́то кни́га? Мóжет бы́ть, э́то кни́га Ви́ктора?
6. Вы́ не знáете, ____________ э́то письмó? Э́то не Сáшино письмó?
7. Вóн тáм стои́т моя́ сестрá. По-мóему, ты́ не знакóм с ____________ сестрóй.
8. Óн расскáзывал мнé о статья́х мнóгих áвторов. Но я́ не пóмню, о ____________ статьé óн расскáзывал с бóльшим интерéсом.
9. Я́ остáвил ключи́ у когó-то дóма, но я забы́л в ____________ дóме э́то бы́ло.
10. Мы́ хотéли тебé позвони́ть, но мы́ не знáли нóмер ____________ телефóна.
11. У нáс в университéте éсть теáтр. В ____________ теáтре бывáют хорóшие концéрты.
12. В ____________ кóмнате пóлный беспоря́док. Тебé нáдо её убрáть.

The Possessive Pronouns *егó, её, úх*

The third-person possessive pronouns **егó** *his*, **её** *her/hers*, **и́х** *their/theirs* are invariable, that is, they do not change according to the gender, number, or case of the noun they qualify.

Вóт **егó** брáт и **егó** сестрá.	*Here is his brother and his sister.*
Я́ знáю **егó** брáта и **егó** сестрý.	*I know his brother and his sister.*
Я́ слы́шал о **егó** брáте и о **егó** сестрé.	*I heard about his brother and his sister.*
Мы́ знакóмы с **егó** роди́телями.	*We are acquainted with his parents.*
Вóт **её** мáма и **её** пáпа.	*Here are her mom and her dad.*
Мы́ ужé ви́дели **её** мáму и **её** пáпу.	*We already saw her mom and her dad.*
И́х дóм ря́дом с нáшим.	*Their house is next to ours.*
Мы́ чáсто бывáем в **и́х** дóме.	*We often visit in their house.*

The pronouns **егó**, **её**, and **и́х** never refer to the subject of the clause in which they occur; the noun or pronoun they refer to must be outside of their clause.

Ми́ша нé сказáл Антóну, но óн сказáл **егó** дрýгу.	*Misha didn't tell Anton, but he told his (Anton's) friend.*

NOTE: The third-person possessive pronouns are identical in form to the genitive case of the third-person personal pronouns **óн** *he,* **онá** *she,* **они́** *they.* Unlike the personal pronouns, however, the third-person possessive pronouns never have an initial **н-** affixed when they follow a preposition; cf. **подáрок для негó** (personal pronoun) *a gift for him* and **подáрок для *егó* жены́** (possessive pronoun) *a gift for his wife.*

The Reflexive Possessive Pronoun *свóй*

Russian has a reflexive possessive pronoun **свóй** *one's own,* which declines exactly like **мóй** (and **твóй**). Unlike **мóй**, however, **свóй** normally does not modify the nominative subject of the clause, but refers back to, and gets its meaning from, the subject.

Я́ урони́л **свóй** карандáш.	*I dropped my pencil.*
Ты́ урони́л **свóй** карандáш.	*You dropped your pencil.*
Онá урони́ла **свóй** карандáш.	*She dropped her pencil.*

In clauses with a subject in the first or second person, **свóй** may be used as an *optional alternative* to the corresponding first- and second-person possessive pronouns **мóй**, **твóй**, **нáш**, and **вáш**.

Я́ забы́л **мóй/свóй** зóнтик.	*I forgot my umbrella.*
Ты́ забы́л **твóй/свóй** зóнтик.	*You forgot your umbrella.*
Мы́ забы́ли **нáш/свóй** зóнтик.	*We forgot our umbrella.*
Вы́ забы́ли **вáш/свóй** зóнтик.	*You forgot your umbrella.*

In clauses where the subject is a noun or a third-person pronoun, however, the reflexive **свóй** is *obligatory* when the subject and possessor are the same. Replacing **свóй** with one of the third-person possessive pronouns **егó**, **её**, and **и́х** changes the meaning of the sentence, such that the possessor is someone other than the subject.

Ми́ша ви́дел **свою́** сестрý.	*Misha saw his (own) sister.*
Ми́ша ви́дел **егó** сестрý.	*Misha saw his (someone else's) sister.*
Онá звони́ла **своемý** дрýгу.	*She called her (own) friend.*
Онá звони́ла **её** дрýгу.	*She called her (someone else's) friend.*
Они́ рассказáли о **своéй** поéздке.	*They told about their (own) trip.*
Они́ рассказáли об **и́х** поéздке.	*They told about their (others') trip.*

NOTE: When the subject and the possessor are conjoined in a noun phrase, and therefore are both in the same case, **свóй** is not allowed: **Óн и егó** [****свóй***] **дрýг бы́ли у нáс** *He and his friend were at our place.*

The reflexive possessive **свóй** can only be used when the possessor and subject are in the same clause. Thus, in a complex sentence where the possessor in the subordinate clause refers to the subject in the main clause, **свóй** is not allowed, as indicated below by the asterisk *.

Пéтя сказáл, что **егó** брáт ушёл.	*Pete said that his brother left.*
Пéтя сказáл, что ***свóй** …	
Лéна дýмает, что **её** подрýга больнá.	*Lena thinks that her friend is sick.*
Лéна дýмает, что ***своя́** …	
Они́ говоря́т, что **и́х** дéти ýмные.	*They say that their children are smart.*
Они́ говоря́т, что ***свои́** …	

When **свой** does occur in a subordinate clause, it must refer back to the subject of that clause.

Бо́ря сказа́л, что **его́** дру́г потеря́л **свою́** кни́гу.	*Borya said that his friend lost his book.*

Note that while the English translation of this sentence is ambiguous with regard to whether it was Borya's or his friend's book that was lost, use of **сво́й** in the Russian sentence eliminates any ambiguity: The book can only be understood to belong to the friend.

In impersonal sentences that have no overt subject, only **сво́й** can be used to express possession.

Ва́жно зна́ть ко́рни **свое́й** семьи́.	*It is important to know the roots of one's family.*

Finally, as noted above, **сво́й** does not normally occur in the nominative case. However, in a few Russian proverbs, and in a small number of other idiomatic expressions, **сво́й** can be found in the nominative case.

Сво́й своя́ка ви́дит издалека́.	*Birds of a feather flock together.*
Сво́й дура́к доро́же чужо́го у́мника.	*Blood is thicker than water.*
Своя́ руба́шка бли́же к те́лу.	*Charity begins at home.*
У на́с **своя́** маши́на.	*We have our own car.*
О́н бы́л са́м не **сво́й**.	*He was not himself.*
Она́ сама́ не **своя́**.	*She is not herself.*

14. Complete each of the following sentences with the correct form of the pronoun **его́**, **её**, **и́х**, or **сво́й**.

1. У Да́ши оди́н бра́т и одна́ сестра́. Она́ ча́сто говори́т о ______________ (her) бра́те и о ______________ (her) сестре́. ______________ (her) бра́т и сестра́ живу́т далеко́ от Да́ши.
2. Пе́тя пошёл в го́сти к ______________ (his) дру́гу. ______________ (his) дру́г живёт в це́нтре.
3. Ка́тя лю́бит ______________ (her) му́жа. Она́ ча́сто говори́т о ______________ (her) му́же.
4. Ру́сские лю́бят ______________ (their) да́чи. ______________ (their) да́чи—э́то возмо́жность уедини́ться.
5. Ле́на неда́вно е́здила в Пари́ж. Она́ рассказа́ла всём о ______________ (her) пое́здке.
6. Э́то до́чь Серге́я. ______________ (his) до́чь прие́хала вчера́ из Москвы́. Серге́й о́чень ра́д ви́деть ______________ (his) до́чь.
7. Петербу́рг родно́й го́род моего́ де́душки. Де́душка хорошо́ по́мнит ______________ (his) родно́й го́род. ______________ (his) го́род нахо́дится на реке́ Неве́. О́н мно́го зна́ет об исто́рии ______________ (his) родно́го го́рода.
8. У ба́бушки о́чень симпати́чная сосе́дка. Ба́бушка ча́сто хо́дит к ______________ (her) сосе́дке.
9. Мо́й знако́мый пьёт, ку́рит, и не занима́ется спо́ртом. О́н пло́хо забо́тится о ______________ (his) здоро́вье.
10. На́ши друзья́ живу́т хорошо́. У ни́х уже́ ______________ (their own) маши́на.
11. У Све́ты родила́сь де́вочка. Све́та лю́бит ______________ (her) де́вочку. Она́ ду́мает, что ______________ (her) де́вочка о́чень у́мная и краси́вая.
12. Когда́ ко́нчился уро́к, все́ ученики́ взя́ли ______________ (their) ве́щи и ушли́ домо́й.
13. ______________ (her) друзья́ купи́ли да́чу. Она́ ра́да за ______________ (her) друзе́й.
14. О́чень ва́жно зна́ть исто́рию ______________ (one's own) страны́. Ведь э́то при́знак образо́ванного челове́ка.

Demonstrative Pronouns

The Demonstrative Pronouns *э́тот* and *тóт*

The demonstrative pronouns **э́тот** *this* (or *that*) and **тóт** *that* are used to point out a particular object or person. These pronouns are modifiers, and agree in gender, number, and case with the modified noun. The complete declensions of these pronouns are given in the tables below.

CASE	MASCULINE,	NEUTER	FEMININE	PLURAL
Nom.	э́тот	э́то	э́та	э́ти
Acc.	э́тот/э́того	э́то	э́ту	э́ти/э́тих
Gen.	э́того		э́той	э́тих
Prep.	об э́том		э́той	э́тих
Dat.	э́тому		э́той	э́тим
Instr.	э́тим		э́той	э́тими

CASE	MASCULINE,	NEUTER	FEMININE	PLURAL
Nom.	тóт	тó	тá	тé
Acc.	тóт/тогó	тó	тý	тé/тéх
Gen.	тогó		тóй	тéх
Prep.	о тóм		тóй	тéх
Dat.	томý		тóй	тéм
Instr.	тéм		тóй	тéми

NOTE: Observe in the tables above that the stem-final **т** in both pronouns changes from hard to soft in the masculine and neuter of the instrumental singular, and throughout the plural.

Of the two pronouns **э́тот** and **тóт**, the former is more general in meaning. For example, the singular forms of **э́тот** may be translated into English as either *this* or *that*, the plural forms as either *these* or *those*, depending on the context.

Э́тот ресторáн дорогóй.	*This/That restaurant is expensive.*
Э́то окнó бы́ло откры́то.	*This/That window was open.*
Э́та кни́га интерéсная.	*This/That book is interesting.*
Э́ти ключи́ не мои́.	*These/Those keys are not mine.*

The forms of **тóт** are normally translated as *that* (and plural *those*) and are frequently used to contrast with forms of **э́тот**. When contrasted in this way, **э́тот** may be understood to refer to that which is nearer to the speaker, and **тóт** to that which is more remote from the speaker.

Э́тот гáлстук мóдный, а **тóт** нéт.	*This tie is stylish, but that one isn't.*
Э́та кни́га моя́, а **тá** егó.	*This book is mine, and that one his.*
Я́ возьмý **э́ту** блýзку, а не **тý**.	*I'll take this blouse, but not that one.*
Я́ куплю́ **э́ти** джи́нсы, а не **тé**.	*I'll buy these jeans, but not those.*
Óн живёт в **э́том** дóме, а онá живёт в **тóм** дóме.	*He lives in this house, and she lives in that house.*
Я́ довóлен **э́тим** результáтом, но не **тéм**.	*I'm satisfied with this result, but not with that one.*

The pronoun **то́т** may also be used when no explicit contrast is made with a form of **э́тот**, although such a contrast is implied. Note that in the following examples, **то́т** conveys the sense of a more remote *that,* in contrast to an implied, nearer *this.*

На́ш до́м на **то́й** стороне́ у́лицы. — *Our house is on that side of the street.*
О́н рабо́тает во́н та́м, в **то́м** большо́м но́вом зда́нии. — *He works over there, in that big new building.*

There are several other important uses of **то́т**, all of which imply a contrast of some kind. Below are some common expressions with this important pronoun.

(a) **не то́т** *the wrong (one)*

Negated forms of **то́т** (**не то́т**, **не то́**, **не та́**, **не те́**) may express the idea "the wrong one," in contrast to an implied "right one."

Я́ набра́л **не то́т** но́мер. — *I dialed the wrong telephone number.*
Официа́нт принёс на́м **не то́** блю́до. — *The waiter brought us the wrong dish.*
О́н взя́л с по́лки **не ту́** кни́гу. — *He took the wrong book off the shelf.*
На́м да́ли **не те́** биле́ты. — *We were given the wrong tickets.*

(b) **то́т же (са́мый)** *the (very) same*

Forms of **то́т** followed by the emphatic particle **же (са́мый)** express the idea "the (very) same." The pronoun **то́т (же)** may occur in the main clause of a complex sentence as a modifier of the antecedent to the relative pronoun **кото́рый** *that/who* in the subordinate clause, e.g., **то́т же ..., кото́рый** *the same ... that.*

О́н наде́л **то́т же са́мый** костю́м, в кото́ром о́н бы́л на ве́чере. — *He put on the very same suit that he was wearing at the party.*
Мы́ жи́ли в **то́й же** гости́нице, в кото́рой и вы́ жи́ли. — *We lived in the same hotel that you lived in.*
О́н говори́л с **те́м же** челове́ком, с кото́рым о́н говори́л вчера́. — *He spoke with the same person with whom he spoke yesterday.*

(c) **и то́т и друго́й** *both*

Forms of **то́т** conjoined with forms of **друго́й** *other* have the meaning *both,* i.e., *that one and the other.* This phrase is used when the two entities referred to differ in some way. When the two things differ in gender or number, the neuter form **и то́ и друго́е** must be used, as in the first example below.

—Что́ ты́ возьмёшь с собо́й, пла́щ и́ли ку́ртку? — *What will you take with you, a raincoat or a jacket?*
—Я́ возьму́ **и то́, и друго́е**. — *I'll take both.*

—Како́й га́лстук тебе́ нра́вится, э́тот кра́сный, и́ли то́т зелёный? — *Which tie do you like, this red one or that green one?*
—Мне́ нра́вятся **и то́т, и друго́й**. — *I like both.*

—Каки́е брю́ки мне́ купи́ть, чёрные в поло́ску, и́ли се́рые в клётку? — *Which pants should I buy, the black striped or the gray plaid?*
—Купи́ **и те́, и други́е**. — *Buy both.*

15. Complete each of the following sentences with the correct form of the pronoun **э́тот** or **то́т**.

1. Она́ жила́ не на ______________ у́лице, а на ______________ у́лице.
2. На́ша гру́ппа чита́ла ______________ расска́зы, а ______________ мы́ не чита́ли.
3. Иностра́нцы живу́т в ______________ общежи́тии, а ру́сские живу́т в ______________.
4. Мы́ заказа́ли ______________ блю́до, а не ______________.
5. ______________ кварти́ра больша́я, а ______________ кварти́ра ещё бо́льше.
6. Мы́ посла́ли приглаше́ния ______________ лю́дям, а ______________ не посла́ли.
7. ______________ си́ний костю́м мне́ нра́вится, а ______________ се́рый мне́ не нра́вится.
8. Я́ знако́м с ______________ студе́нтами, а с ______________ я не знако́м.
9. Мы́ да́ли на́ш зака́з ______________ официа́нту, а не ______________.
10. Да́й мне́, пожа́луйста, ______________ меню́, а ______________ возьми́ себе́.

16. Complete each of the following sentences with the correct form of the pronoun **то́т**.

1. Я́ не могу́ откры́ть две́рь. Мо́жет бы́ть, у меня́ не __________ клю́ч.
2. Э́то __________ же кроссо́вки, в кото́рых я вы́играл соревнова́ние.
3. Она́ не могла́ реши́ть, каки́е ту́фли купи́ть. Поэ́тому, она́ купи́ла и __________ и други́е.
4. Э́ти брю́ки мне́ не подхо́дят. Мне́ ка́жется, э́то не __________ разме́р.
5. На э́то интервью́ я наде́л __________ же га́лстук, кото́рый мне́ всегда́ приноси́л уда́чу.
6. Э́то __________ же маши́на, кото́рая была́ у меня́ 5 ле́т наза́д.

The Indeclinable Pronoun *э́то*

The "Identifying" *э́то*

Russian has an invariable pronoun **э́то** *this/that is, these/those are,* which may be used both to question and give the identify of an object or person (**Что́ *э́то*? *Э́то* часы́.** *What's that? That's a watch*). It is identical to the neuter singular form of the demonstrative pronoun **э́тот**, but unlike the latter, "identifying" **э́то** does not modify the following noun; rather, it serves as the sentence subject, and the following noun is the predicate in the nominative case.

—Что́ та́м лежи́т?	*What is that lying there?*
—**Э́то** пе́йджер.	*That is a pager.*
—Кто́ э́ти молоды́е лю́ди?	*Who are those young people?*
—**Э́то** мои́ студе́нты.	*Those are my students.*

In sentences with identifying **э́то**, an accompanying verb agrees with the predicate nominative, not with **э́то**.

—Кто́ приходи́л?	*Who came by?*
—**Э́то** бы́л мо́й бра́т.	*That was my brother.*
—Кто́ звони́л?	*Who called?*
—**Э́то** была́ моя́ жена́.	*That was my wife.*
—Кто́ бы́л у ва́с ве́чером?	*Who was at your place last night?*
—**Э́то** бы́ли мои́ друзья́.	*Those were my friends.*

The "Characterizing" *э́то*

The pronoun **э́то** can also be used as the subject of a sentence that refers to, and characterizes, a *situation* described in a preceding statement.

—Ка́тя Воло́дина вы́шла за́муж.	*Katya Volodina got married.*
—**Э́то** интере́сно.	*That's interesting.*
—Са́ша обеща́л мне́ помо́чь.	*Sasha promised to help me.*
—**Э́то** хорошо́.	*That's good.*

When a verb occurs with **э́то** in this characterizing function, it agrees in the neuter singular past tense with **э́то**, the subject; if a predicate noun follows, it is normally (if abstract) in the instrumental case.

В про́шлом году́ у Та́ни родила́сь де́вочка. **Э́то** бы́ло большо́й ра́достью для на́с.	*Last year Tanya gave birth to a girl. This was a great joy for us.*
Вчера́ зашла́ ко мне́ Ви́ка. **Э́то** бы́ло по́лной неожи́данностью для меня́.	*Yesterday Vika dropped by my place. This was a complete surprise for me.*

17. Determine whether each of the following sentences involves "identifying" or "characterizing" **э́то**, then complete the second sentence with the correct past-tense form of the verb **бы́ть**: **бы́л**, **бы́ло**, **была́**, or **бы́ли**.

1. Вчера́ на у́лице ла́яла кака́я-то жёлтая соба́ка. По-мо́ему, э́то __________ англи́йский лабрадо́р.
2. Она́ пришла́ на рабо́ту в ми́ни-ю́бке. Э́то __________ для всéх шо́ком.
3. Мы́ расста́лись. О́н мне́ позвони́л го́д спустя́. Э́то __________ для меня́ большо́й неожи́данностью.
4. —Кто́ заходи́л?
   —Э́то __________ подру́га до́чери.
5. Мы́ уви́дели впереди́ све́т. Э́то __________ огни́ го́рода.
6. Когда́ ты́ позвони́л, э́то __________ тако́й сюрпри́з.

The Demonstrative Pronoun *тако́й*

The demonstrative pronoun **тако́й** *such a / like that* declines like a hard-stem adjective (see page 141, Chapter 5), and in the plural is subject to Spelling Rule 1 (page 11). The declension of **тако́й** is given in the following table.

CASE	MASCULINE,	NEUTER	FEMININE	PLURAL
Nom.	тако́й	тако́е	така́я	таки́е
Acc.	тако́й/тако́го	тако́е	таку́ю	таки́е/таки́х
Gen.	тако́го		тако́й	таки́х
Prep.	о тако́м		о тако́й	о таки́х
Dat.	тако́му		тако́й	таки́м
Instr.	таки́м		тако́й	таки́ми

In the examples below, **тако́й** points to a property or quality of the noun it modifies.

Э́то споко́йная, ла́сковая соба́ка.	*This is a calm, affectionate dog.*
Мне́ нужна́ **така́я** соба́ка.	*I need a dog like that.*
Ми́ша надёжный, ве́рный дру́г.	*Misha is a reliable, loyal friend.*
Тако́го дру́га тру́дно найти́.	*Such a friend is difficult to find.*

О́н извéстный и уважáемый профéссор. Я́ бы хотéл учи́ться у **такóго** профéссора.	*He is a famous and respected professor. I would like to study with such a professor.*
О́н высокомéрный и догмáтик. Тру́дно рабóтать с **таки́м** человéком.	*He is arrogant and dogmatic. It's difficult to work with such a man.*

When an adjective follows, the pronoun **такóй** functions as an intensifier, and may be rendered into English as *such a* or *so*.

Онá **такáя** у́мная дéвочка.	*She is such a clever little girl.*
Онá **такáя** ми́лая.	*She is so nice.*
О́н **такóй** серьёзный человéк.	*He is such a serious person.*
Э́ти цветы́ **таки́е** краси́вые.	*These flowers are so beautiful.*

The demonstrative pronoun **такóй** can modify the noun antecedent of the relative pronoun **какóй**, e.g., **О́н купи́л *такóй* (же) костю́м, *какóй* и я́ купи́л** *He bought the (same) kind of suit that I bought.* This construction is illustrated in greater detail in the section on relative pronouns.

18. Complete each of the following sentences with the correct form of the pronoun **такóй**.

1. Едá в э́том ресторáне ______________ вку́сная.
2. Экзáмен бы́л ______________ тру́дный, что мнóгие студéнты провали́лись на нём.
3. У ни́х большáя, свéтлая кварти́ра. Мы́ хоти́м сня́ть ______________ кварти́ру.
4. И́х дóм похóж на дворéц. Мы́ никогдá не ви́дели ______________ большóго дóма.
5. Э́то не моя́ су́мка. Э́та су́мка бéлая, мáленькая. Моя́ су́мка не ______________. Онá чёрная, большáя, и чéрез плечó.
6. Вéтер бы́л ______________ си́льный, что мы́ не могли́ идти́.

Determinative Pronouns

The Emphatic Pronoun *сáм*

The pronoun **сáм** adds emphasis to a particular noun or pronoun in the sentence. It corresponds to the English "intensive" pronoun ending in *-self,* as in "He *himself* is to blame," "She said so *herself,*" "We solved the problem *ourselves.*" The Russian emphatic pronoun must agree in gender, number, and case with the noun it modifies. This pronoun declines like the demonstrative pronoun **э́тот**; note, however, that except for the nominative and accusative (inanimate) plural, the pronoun **сáм** is *stressed on the ending* throughout.

The declension of the emphatic pronoun **сáм** is presented in the following table.

CASE	MASCULINE,	NEUTER	FEMININE	PLURAL
Nom.	сáм	самó	самá	сáми
Acc.	сáм/самогó	самó	саму́	сáми/сами́х
Gen.	самогó		самóй	сами́х
Prep.	о самóм		о самóй	о сами́х
Dat.	самому́		самóй	сами́м
Instr.	сами́м		самóй	сами́ми

The pronoun **са́м** may refer to a noun functioning as subject or object. When it refers to an animate subject, it emphasizes that the subject performs the action independently, with no help from others.

Е́й никто́ не помога́ет, она́ де́лает всё **сама́**.	*No one helps her; she does everything herself.*
Не объясня́й ему́. Пу́сть о́н **са́м** поймёт.	*Don't explain it to him. Let him figure it out himself.*

Similarly, when the subject is inanimate, the pronoun **са́м** may be used to emphasize that the action of the subject-referent occurs by itself, without the assistance of a human agent.

Никто́ не откры́л две́рь, она́ откры́лась **сама́**.	*No one opened the door; it opened by itself.*
Я́ не вы́ключил компью́тер, о́н **са́м** отключи́лся.	*I didn't turn off the computer; it shut off by itself.*

The pronoun **са́м** may also be used to emphasize that a particular person, and not some other, is involved in the action.

Она́ **сама́** винова́та.	*She herself is to blame.*
За э́то предложе́ние вы́ступил **са́м** президе́нт.	*The president himself came out in favor of this proposal.*

The pronoun **са́м** is also used to lend emphasis to the reflexive pronoun **себя́**.

Я́ виню́ то́лько **самого́ себя́**.	*I blame only myself.*
Вчера́ во сне́ ты́ разгова́ривал **са́м** с **собо́й**.	*Last night in your sleep you were talking to yourself.*

19. Complete each of the following sentences with the correct form of the emphatic pronoun **са́м**.

1. Ма́льчик у́меет всё де́лать ______________.
2. Окно́ ______________ откры́лось.
3. Мы́ ______________ удиви́лись э́тому.
4. На́м на́до ви́деть её ______________, а не её подру́гу.
5. У него́ ______________ не́т вре́мени.
6. Я́ не чита́л ______________ статьи́, но я слы́шал о не́й.
7. У на́с не́т ______________ докуме́нтов; у на́с е́сть то́лько ксероко́пии.
8. Она́ передала́ докла́д ______________ нача́льнику.
9. Скажи́ об э́том не её сестре́, а е́й ______________.
10. Они́ встре́тились не на у́лице, а в ______________ теа́тре.
11. Мы́ не говори́ли с ______________ дека́ном, мы́ говори́ли с его́ ассисте́нтом.
12. Они́ живу́т не под Москво́й, а в ______________ Москве́.
13. На́ша кварти́ра нахо́дится не в при́городе, а в ______________ це́нтре го́рода.
14. Ва́м на́до спроси́ть об э́том не на́с, а ______________ себя́.

The Pronoun *са́мый*

The pronoun **са́мый** *the very* expresses a precise point in space or time. It is sometimes easy to confuse this pronoun with the emphatic pronoun **са́м**, as shown in the following pair of sentences.

Она́ живёт в **са́мом** це́нтре го́рода.	*She lives in the very center of the city.*
Она́ живёт в **само́м** це́нтре го́рода.	*She lives in the city center itself.*

Although similar in form and meaning, the pronouns **са́мый** and **са́м** differ in their declensions: **Са́м**, as discussed above, declines like a pronoun with the stress falling largely on the endings, while **са́мый** declines like a hard-stem adjective (see Chapter 5, page 141) with *the stress on the stem.*

The following sentences further illustrate this use of **са́мый**.

Она́ живёт на **са́мом** конце́ у́лицы.	*She lives at the very end of the street.*
Дава́йте начнём с **са́мого** нача́ла.	*Let's start from the very beginning.*
Э́тот авто́бус идёт до **са́мой** Я́лты.	*This bus goes all the way to Yalta.*
Мя́ч попа́л ему́ в **са́мый** гла́з.	*The ball hit him right in the eye.*
Проходи́те в **са́мый** коне́ц трамва́я.	*Go to the very back of the trolley.*

The pronoun **са́мый**, as discussed above in the section on demonstrative pronouns, may be used after the pronoun **то́т (же)**, e.g., **то́т (же) са́мый**, **то́ са́мое**, **та́ са́мая**, in the meaning *the (very) same:* **Э́то то́т са́мый челове́к, кото́рый бы́л зде́сь ра́ньше** *This is the same person who was here before.*

The pronoun **са́мый** is also used to form the compound superlative of adjectives. This use of **са́мый** will be presented in Chapter 5.

20. Complete each of the following sentences with the correct form of the pronoun **са́мый**.

1. Сне́г шёл с ______________ утра́.
2. Не на́до жда́ть до ______________ зимы́, на́до загота́вливать дрова́ ле́том.
3. О́н стоя́л на ______________ краю́ про́пасти.
4. Мы́ дошли́ до ______________ конца́ доро́ги.
5. Они́ шли́ по ______________ кра́ю обры́ва.

The Pronoun *ве́сь*

The English translation of the pronoun **ве́сь** differs, depending on whether it is used as a modifier or whether it stands alone as a subject or object. When it is used to modify a noun, in the singular it normally translates as *the whole* (**ве́сь го́род** *the whole city*), while in the plural it means *all* (**все́ студе́нты** *all (the) students*). When it stands alone as a subject or object of the sentence, the neuter singular form means *everything* (**Всё решено́** *Everything is decided*; **О́н ду́мает, что́ всё зна́ет** *He thinks he knows everything*), while the plural means *everyone/everybody.* Note that unlike the English pronoun *everyone,* which is grammatically singular, Russian **все́** is plural and requires plural agreement: **Все́ зна́ют об э́том** *Everyone knows about this.*

The declension of the pronoun **вéсь** is given in the following table.

CASE	MASCULINE,	NEUTER	FEMININE	PLURAL
Nom.	вéсь	всё	вся́	всé
Acc.	вéсь/всегó	всё	всю́	всé/всéх
Gen.	всегó		всéй	всéх
Prep.	обо всём		обо всéй	обо всéх
Dat.	всемý		всéй	всéм
Instr.	всéм		всéй	всéми

NOTE: The preposition **о** *about* takes the form **обо** with the prepositional case forms of this pronoun.

Following are examples of the pronoun **вéсь**, first in its use as a modifier, then as a noun-like subject or object of the sentence.

The Pronoun *вéсь* as Modifier

Всё студéнчество волнýется о стóимости обучéния. — *The whole student body is concerned about the cost of tuition.*
Вся́ странá ждёт разрешéния кри́зиса. — *The whole country is waiting for a resolution to the crisis.*
Всé рабóтники получáют óтпуск по болéзни. — *All workers are given sick leave.*
Óн рассказáл нáм **всю́** истóрию. — *He told us the whole story.*
Óн достáл билéты для **всéй** грýппы. — *She got tickets for the whole group.*
Мы́ говори́ли обо **всём** плáне. — *We talked about the whole plan.*
Онá одинáково забóтится о **всéх** свои́х дéтях. — *She cares equally for all of her children.*
Нóвость разнеслáсь по **всемý** гóроду. — *The news spread throughout the whole city.*
Óн éздил по **всéй** странé. — *He has traveled throughout the whole country.*
Óн знакóм со **всéми** гостя́ми. — *He is acquainted with all the guests.*

The Pronoun *вéсь* as Subject

Всё в поря́дке. — *Everything is okay* (lit., *in order*).
Всé здéсь имéют прáво гóлоса. — *Everyone here has the right to vote.*

The Pronoun *вéсь* as Object

Мы́ благодáрны вáм за **всё**. — *We are grateful to you for everything.*
Загрязнéния вóздуха волнýет **всéх**. — *Air pollution concerns everyone.*
Óн рассказáл нáм **обо всём**. — *He told us about everything.*
Óн вы́болтал её секрéт при **всéх**. — *He blurted out her secret in front of everyone.*
Ко **всемý** мóжно привы́кнуть. — *One can get used to anything.*
Онá всегдá помогáет **всéм**. — *She is always helping everyone.*
Онá довóльна **всéм**. — *She is satisfied with everything.*
Óн ужé познакóмился со **всéми**. — *He has already met everyone.*

21. Complete each of the following sentences with the correct form of the determinative pronoun **вéсь**.

1. ______________ лю́ди хотя́т сча́стья.
2. ______________ меня́ется в э́том ми́ре.
3. О́н побыва́л во ______________ уголка́х земно́го ша́ра.
4. Когда́ оте́ц спроси́л до́чь, почему́ она́ но́сит три́ серёжки, она́ отве́тила «______________ та́к де́лают».
5. О́н справедли́вый челове́к, о́н отно́сится ко ______________ одина́ково.
6. Ка́к сказа́ли в кни́ге «Три́ Мушкетёра», оди́н за ______________, ______________ за́ одного́.
7. Во ______________ ми́ре зна́ют и́мя ру́сского космона́вта Ю́рия Гага́рина.
8. О́н э́того добьётся ______________ пра́вдами и непра́вдами.
9. Тури́сты спра́шивали ги́да обо ______________ карти́нах в галере́е.
10. О́н большо́й э́ксперт и зна́ет ______________ то́нкости пробле́мы.

Relative Pronouns

The Relative Pronoun *кото́рый*

A relative pronoun refers back to a noun or pronoun in the main clause of a complex sentence—its antecedent—and it introduces a subordinate clause that *relates* to that antecedent. Relative pronouns in English include *who* ("The girl *who* called was Russian"), *which* ("The books, *which* he gave me, are interesting"), and *that* ("The food *that* they served was delicious"). The most commonly used relative pronoun in Russian is **кото́рый**, and this one pronoun, depending on whether its antecedent is animate or inanimate, may be rendered by English *who, that,* or *which.*

The relative pronoun **кото́рый** is used with a noun antecedent. **Кото́рый** must have the same gender and number as its antecedent, but its case is determined by its function within the relative clause. Thus, if this pronoun is the grammatical subject of the relative clause, it will be in the nominative case; if it is the direct object of a verb within the relative clause, it will be in the accusative case; and if it is the object of a preposition or the complement of a case-assigning verb, it must be in whichever case is governed by the preposition or verb.

The pronoun **кото́рый** declines like a hard-stem adjective. The complete declension of this pronoun is given in the table below.

CASE	MASCULINE,	NEUTER	FEMININE	PLURAL
Nom.	кото́рый	кото́рое	кото́рая	кото́рые
Acc.	кото́рый/ кото́рого	кото́рое	кото́рую	кото́рые/ кото́рых
Gen.	кото́рого		кото́рой	кото́рых
Prep.	о кото́ром		о кото́рой	о кото́рых
Dat.	кото́рому		кото́рой	кото́рым
Instr.	кото́рым		кото́рой	кото́рыми

Unlike the English relative pronouns, which may be "dropped" in relaxed speech, the Russian relative pronoun **кото́рый** may not be omitted, e.g., *The movie (that) I saw was interesting* **Фи́льм, кото́рый я ви́дел, бы́л интере́сный**. Note, also, that in Russian the relative clause is always set off by commas. Following are examples of **кото́рый** in each of the cases.

Nominative Case

The relative pronoun in each of the following examples is in the nominative case because it functions as the subject of the relative clause.

Э́то мо́й дру́г, **кото́рый** учи́лся в Ки́еве.	*This is my friend who studied in Kiev.*
Где́ письмо́, **кото́рое** пришло́ сего́дня?	*Where is the letter that came today?*
Э́то моя́ сестра́, **кото́рая** вы́шла за́муж.	*This is my sister who got married.*
Во́т джи́нсы, **кото́рые** мне́ нра́вятся.	*Here are the jeans that I like.*

22. Combine each of the following pairs of sentences into a complex sentence with a relative clause introduced by **кото́рый**. Note that **кото́рый** will be in the same *case* as the word it *replaces*.

MODEL Э́то мо́й дру́г Ви́ктор. Ви́ктор ра́ньше жи́л в Москве́. >
Э́то мо́й дру́г Ви́ктор, кото́рый ра́ньше жи́л в Москве́.

1. Как зову́т э́ту де́вушку? Де́вушка прие́хала неда́вно из Новосиби́рска.
____
2. О́н живёт в до́ме. До́м нахо́дится в це́нтре го́рода.
____
3. Во́т иду́т ма́льчики. Ма́льчики у́чатся в шко́ле вме́сте с на́шим сы́ном.
____

Accusative Case

The relative pronoun in each of the following examples is in the accusative case because it is either the direct object of the verb or the object of a preposition that governs the accusative case. When it functions as direct object, the relative pronoun is identical to the nominative case when the noun it refers to is masculine inanimate singular, or inanimate plural; when the noun it refers to is masculine animate singular, or animate plural, the form of the relative pronoun in the accusative is identical to the genitive.

Э́то фи́льм, **кото́рый** я́ ви́дел вчера́.	*This is the movie that I saw yesterday.*
Э́то дру́г, **кото́рого** я́ встре́тил вчера́.	*This is the friend whom I met yesterday.*
Где́ статья́, **кото́рую** ты́ прочита́л?	*Where is the article that you read?*
Э́то усло́вия, на **кото́рые** вы́ согласи́лись.	*These are the conditions to which you agreed.*
Во́т но́вые ту́фли, **кото́рые** я купи́л.	*Here are the new shoes that I bought.*
Э́то лю́ди, **кото́рых** мы́ уважа́ем.	*These are people whom we respect.*

23. Combine each of the following pairs of sentences into a complex sentence with a relative clause introduced by **кото́рый** in the accusative case.

MODEL Я́ уже́ получи́л письмо́. Ты́ посла́л мне́ э́то письмо́ вчера́. >
Я́ уже́ получи́л письмо́, кото́рое ты́ мне́ посла́л вчера́.

1. Я́ чита́л статью́. Профе́ссор рекомендова́л э́ту статью́.
____
2. Ка́к называ́ется университе́т? Ты́ око́нчил э́тот университе́т.
____
3. Я́ зна́ю одного́ бизнесме́на. Бизнесме́на зову́т Влади́мир Соро́кин.
____
4. На́ши сосе́ди нашли́ де́ньги. Ты́ потеря́л э́ти де́ньги.
____
5. Вчера́ к на́м прие́хали друзья́. Мы́ давно́ не ви́дели э́тих друзе́й.
____

Genitive Case

As shown in the first three examples below, the English meaning *whose* is expressed by the relative pronoun in the genitive case. The genitive case of the pronoun immediately follows the noun denoting the possessed object or person. As always, the pronoun **котóрый** takes its gender and number from the noun it refers to, which in these examples is the noun denoting the possessor.

As the last two examples show, the relative pronoun is also in the genitive case when it is the object of a preposition or verb that governs the genitive.

Э́то дру́г, маши́ну **котóрого** укра́ли.	*This is my friend whose car was stolen.*
Э́то де́вушка, оте́ц **котóрой** откры́л сво́й би́знес.	*This is the girl whose father opened his own business.*
Э́то друзья́, до́чь **котóрых** неда́вно вы́шла за́муж.	*These are the friends whose daughter recently got married.*
Э́то та́ де́вушка, для **котóрой** мы́ купи́ли пода́рок.	*That's the girl for whom we bought the gift.*
То́т ма́льчик, **котóрого** боя́лся на́ш сы́н, бы́л аресто́ван за дра́ку.	*That boy whom our son was afraid of was arrested for fighting.*

24. Combine each of the following pairs of sentences into a complex sentence with a relative clause introduced by **котóрый** in the genitive case.

MODEL У меня́ хоро́шая подру́га. У подру́ги неда́вно роди́лся ребёнок. >
У меня́ хоро́шая подру́га, у которой неда́вно роди́лся ребёнок.

1. Я́ позвони́л дру́гу. От дру́га я́ давно́ не получа́л письма́.
___
2. На́с помести́ли в све́тлую ко́мнату. О́кна ко́мнаты смо́трят на пля́ж.
___
3. О́н рабо́тает в институ́те. О́коло институ́та стро́ят гости́ницу.
___
4. Ка́к фами́лия студе́нтки? Роди́тели студе́нтки живу́т в Росто́ве.
___
5. О́н подари́л е́й духи́. За́пах духо́в е́й о́чень понра́вился.
___

Prepositional Case

The relative pronoun is in the prepositional case when it is the object of a preposition that governs this case. Note that whenever it is the object of a preposition, **котóрый** immediately follows that preposition, which must be at the *beginning of the clause.* This is an important difference between Russian and English: English allows prepositions to "dangle" at the end of a sentence (see the English translations below), but Russian does not permit a preposition to be moved out of the phrase it heads.

Э́то до́м, в **котóром** мы́ жи́ли ра́ньше.	*This is the house that we used to live in.*
Во́т де́вушка, о **котóрой** я́ тебе́ говори́л.	*Here is the girl whom I told you about.*
Э́то фотогра́фии гости́ниц, в **котóрых** мы́ остана́вливались.	*These are photographs of the hotels that we stayed in.*

25. Combine each of the following pairs of sentences into a complex sentence with a relative clause introduced by **кото́рый** in the prepositional case.

MODEL Óн написа́л письмо́. В письме́ о́н на́м всё объясни́л. >
Óн написа́л письмо́, в кото́ром о́н на́м всё объясни́л.

1. Ты́ чита́л кни́гу? Я́ тебе́ говори́л о кни́ге.

____

2. Мы́ бы́ли на спекта́кле. В спекта́кле уча́ствовала на́ша до́чь.

____

3. Сего́дня ко мне́ прие́дет дру́г. Я́ расска́зывал тебе́ о дру́ге.

____

4. Че́рез воро́та Кремля́ прое́хал лимузи́н. В лимузи́не е́хал президе́нт.

____

5. Та́м стро́ят общежи́тия. В общежи́тиях бу́дут жи́ть студе́нты.

____

Dative Case

The relative pronoun is in the dative case when it functions as an indirect object, or when it is the complement of a preposition, adjective, or verb that governs the dative case.

Э́то сы́н, **кото́рому** я́ посла́л письмо́.	*This is the son to whom I sent a letter.*
Э́то на́ш ста́рый дру́г, **кото́рому** мы́ всегда́ бу́дем благода́рны.	*This is our old friend to whom we will always be grateful.*
Э́то сосе́дка, **кото́рой** мы́ помогли́.	*This is the neighbor whom we helped.*
Э́то друзья́, к **кото́рым** мы́ е́здили.	*These are the friends we went to see.*
Она́ ведёт то́т о́браз жи́зни, к **кото́рому** она́ привы́кла.	*She is living the lifestyle to which she has become accustomed.*

26. Combine each of the following pairs of sentences into a complex sentence with a relative clause introduced by **кото́рый** in the dative case.

MODEL На́с поблагодари́л дру́г. Мы́ помогли́ дру́гу. >
На́с поблагодари́л дру́г, кото́рому мы́ помогли́.

1. Они́ вы́шли из ле́са и уви́дели о́зеро. Они́ направля́лись к о́зеру.

____

2. Ка́к зову́т де́вушку? Я́ до́лжен переда́ть письмо́ де́вушке.

____

3. Во́т бе́рег. Мы́ бе́гаем по бе́регу ка́ждое у́тро.

____

4. Вчера́ я́ сдава́ла экза́мен. Я́ до́лго гото́вилась к экза́мену.

____

5. За́втра к на́м прие́дут друзья́. Мы́ е́здим к друзья́м ча́сто.

____

Instrumental Case

The relative pronoun is in the instrumental case when it is the object of a preposition, adjective, or verb that governs the instrumental case, or when it expresses one of the many uses of this case: "the instrument or means of the action," "the route taken," etc.

Э́то же́нщина, с **кото́рой** я рабо́таю.	*This is a woman with whom I work.*
Э́то де́ти, за **кото́рыми** она́ следи́т.	*These are the children she looks after.*
Та́м лежи́т ру́чка, **кото́рой** о́н подписа́л докуме́нты.	*There is the pen with which he signed the documents.*
Докла́дчик освети́л вопро́сы, **кото́рыми** интересова́лись слу́шатели.	*The speaker shed light on questions in which the audience was interested.*
Э́то доро́жка, **кото́рой** я́ хожу́ домо́й.	*This is the path that I take to go home.*

27. Combine each of the following pairs of sentences into a complex sentence with a relative clause introduced by **кото́рый** in the instrumental case.

MODEL Профе́ссор зако́нчил уче́бник. О́н до́лго рабо́тал на́д уче́бником. >
Профе́ссор зако́нчил уче́бник, на́д кото́рым о́н до́лго рабо́тал.

1. Я́ хочу́ познако́мить тебя́ с де́вушкой. Я́ рабо́таю с де́вушкой в институ́те.
____
2. Вдали́ мы́ уви́дели го́ры. Ме́жду гора́ми вила́сь доро́га.
____
3. Студе́нт подошёл к столу́. За столо́м сиде́л экзамена́тор.
____
4. Мы́ подошли́ к теа́тру. Пе́ред теа́тром тяну́лась дли́нная о́чередь.
____
5. Она́ вчера́ узна́ла результа́ты экспериме́нта. Она́ о́чень дово́льна результа́тами.
____

The Relative Pronoun *како́й*

The pronoun **како́й**, declined like **тако́й** (see page 122), may be used both as an interrogative and as a relative pronoun. When used as a relative pronoun, **како́й** has a noun antecedent that, for emphasis, may be modified by the demonstrative pronoun **тако́й**. Like **кото́рый**, the pronoun **како́й** takes its gender and number from its antecedent, but its case is determined by its function in its own clause.

The construction **тако́й (же) ..., како́й** may be rendered into English as *the (same) kind of ... that.* Following are several examples of this construction.

Э́то **така́я** маши́на, **кака́я** е́сть у Пе́ти.	*This is the kind of car that Petya has.*
Э́то то́чно **така́я же** зада́ча, **кака́я** была́ у на́с на экза́мене.	*This is exactly the same kind of problem we had in the exam.*
О́н слу́шает **таку́ю** му́зыку, **каку́ю** слу́шают мно́гие лю́ди его́ во́зраста.	*He listens to the kind of music that many people his age listen to.*
Мы́ жи́ли в **тако́й** кварти́ре, в **како́й** и вы́ жи́ли.	*We lived in an apartment like the one that you lived in.*
Таки́х де́вушек, на **како́й** ты́ жени́лся, нечáсто встреча́ешь.	*Girls of the kind that you married don't come along very often.*
Ю́ра совсе́м не измени́лся, о́н оста́лся **таки́м**, **каки́м** и бы́л.	*Yura has not changed at all, he has stayed just as he was.*

28. Complete each of the following sentences with the correct form of the relative pronoun **како́й**.

1. Мне́ ну́жен тако́й слова́рь, ______________ у тебя́ е́сть.
2. Я́ да́же никогда́ не слы́шал о тако́м о́вощe, о ______________ ты́ говори́шь.
3. Таки́х специали́стов, ______________ вы́ и́щете, тру́дно найти́.
4. Я́ хочу́ то́чно тако́й же мотоци́кл, ______________ у него́ е́сть.
5. А́х, е́сли бы у меня́ была́ така́я фигу́ра, ______________ у тебя́!

6. Óн живёт в тако́м до́ме, в ______________ живу́т то́лько бога́тые лю́ди.
7. Óн уже́ не получа́ет таки́е больши́е де́ньги, к ______________ óн привы́к.
8. Продаве́ц показа́л ему́ таки́е кроссо́вки, ______________ óн и иска́л.

The Relative Pronouns *кто́* and *что́*

The words **кто́** and **что́** may be used not only as interrogative pronouns, but also as relative pronouns. Unlike **кото́рый** and **како́й**, which take a noun antecedent, **кто́** and **что́** normally take a pronoun antecedent. Typical antecedents include forms of the demonstrative pronoun **то́т** (**то́т, кто́** *he who,* **те́, кто́** *those who,* **то́, что́** *that which),* forms of the pronoun **ве́сь** *all* (**все́, кто́** *all/everyone who,* **всё, что́** *everything that*), and the pronouns **ка́ждый** *each (one)* and **любо́й** *any (one)* (**ка́ждый, кто́** *each one who,* **любо́й, кто́** *anyone who*).

When its antecedent is plural, as in **те́, кто́** *those who* and **все́, кто́** *everyone who,* the pronoun **кто́** may take either singular (masculine) or plural agreement. This option is indicated by the parentheses in two examples below.

Те́, кто́ чита́л(и) докла́д, бы́ли дово́льны и́м.	*Those who read the report were pleased with it.*
Все́, кто́ бы́л(и) на ве́чере, пото́м собрали́сь на дискоте́ке.	*Everyone who was at the party, gathered afterwards at the dance club.*
Ка́ждый, кто́ подходи́л к нему́, поздравля́л его́.	*Each person who approached, congratulated him.*
Любо́й, кто́ хоте́л, мо́г задава́ть вопро́сы.	*Anyone who wanted to, was able to ask questions.*

The construction **то́т, кто́** *he who / one who* is usually used in general statements such as those characteristic of proverbs. The two pronouns in these constructions may be contiguous, or they may be separated, as shown in the following two Russian proverbs.

Хорошо́ смеётся **то́т, кто́** смеётся после́дним.	*He laughs best who laughs last.*
Кто́ мно́го грози́т, **то́т** ма́ло вреди́т.	*He who has a loud bark, seldom has a sharp bite.*

In constructions containing the relative pronouns **кто́** and **что́**, as in other relative clause constructions, the case of the relative pronoun, as well as the case of its pronoun antecedent, is determined by the function of each pronoun within its own clause.

The following examples demonstrate how the case of the relative pronoun **что́** changes according to its grammatical function within the relative clause.

Произошло́ то́,	**что́** на́с о́чень обра́довало.
Something occurred	*that* (Nom.) *made us very happy.*
	что́ мы́ давно́ ожида́ли.
	that (Acc.) *we had long expected.*
	чего́ мы́ все́ боя́лись.
	that (Gen.) *we had all been afraid of.*
	о чём мы́ бу́дем вспомина́ть до́лго.
	that (Prep.) *we will think about a long time.*
	чему́ удиви́лись все́.
	that (Dat.) *everyone was surprised at.*
	че́м мы́ до си́х по́р восхища́емся.
	that (Instr.) *we are delighted with to this day.*

The following examples illustrate how the case of the demonstrative pronoun **то́т** is determined by its grammatical function within the main clause. Note that while Russian grammar requires that the various case forms of the word **то́т** occur (except for the accusative direct object **то́**, which may be omitted), this word is not translated into English.

На́с обра́довало **то́**,	что́ он сде́лал.
We were gladdened by (Nom.)	*what he did.*
Мы́ понима́ем **(то́)**,	
We understand (Acc.)	
Мы́ испуга́лись **того́**,	
We were frightened by (Gen.)	
Мы́ беспоко́имся о **то́м**,	
We are worried about (Prep.)	
Мы́ не́ были гото́вы к **тому́**,	
We were not prepared for (Dat.)	
Мы́ о́чень дово́льны **те́м**,	
We are very pleased with (Instr.)	

29. Complete each of the following sentences with the correct form of the missing pronoun in the construction **то́, что́**.

1. ________, что́ о́н сде́лал, на́м о́чень помогло́.
2. Она́ расска́зывала о ________, че́м она́ занима́ется.
3. Мы́ о́чень дово́льны ________, чего́ ты́ доби́лся.
4. Она́ бои́тся того́, на́д ________ о́н рабо́тает.
5. Роди́тели удиви́лись тому́, ________ увлека́ется сы́н.
6. Она́ не согла́сна с ________, что́ он де́лает.
7. У меня́ сомне́ния в ________, что́ они́ предлага́ют.
8. Я́ о́чень интересу́юсь ________, на́д че́м вы́ рабо́таете.
9. На́м ну́жно и́менно то́, к ________ они́ стремя́тся.
10. Она́ не пове́рила ________, что́ ей рассказа́ли.

30. Complete each of the following sentences with the correct form of the missing pronoun in the construction **то́т, кто́**.

1. Сча́стлив то́т, у ________ мно́го друзе́й.
2. Хорошо́ тому́, ________ занима́ется интере́сной рабо́той.
3. Для э́той рабо́ты на́м ну́жен ________, кто́ име́ет большо́й о́пыт.
4. Кто́ ра́но встаёт, ________ уда́ча ждёт.
5. Кому́ везёт в ка́ртах, ________ не везёт в любви́.

Indefinite Pronouns

The Pronouns *ктó-то/ктó-нибудь, чтó-то/чтó-нибудь, какóй-то/какóй-нибудь, чéй-то/чéй-нибудь*

The unstressed particles **-то** and **-нибудь** can be attached to the interrogative pronouns **ктó**, **чтó**, **какóй**, and **чéй** (and to certain adverbs—see Chapter 5) to create indefinite pronouns with the meaning *someone, anyone,* etc. However, as the table below indicates, the particles **-то** and **-нибудь** do not directly correspond to English *some* and *any,* respectively: While the forms with the particle **-то** are normally rendered by English pronouns beginning with *some,* it must be noted that indefinite pronouns with **-нибудь** can be translated into English by either *any-* or *some-*.

ктó *who*	ктó-то *someone*	ктó-нибудь *anyone, someone*
чтó *what*	чтó-то *something*	чтó-нибудь *anything, something*
какóй *what (sort of)*	какóй-то *some (sort of)*	какóй-нибудь *any (sort of), some (sort of)*
чéй *whose*	чéй-то *someone's, somebody else's*	чéй-нибудь *anyone's, someone else's*

The indefinite pronouns in **-то** and **-нибудь** decline just like the interrogative pronouns (**ктó-то, когó-то, комý-то** ...; **чтó-нибудь, о чём-нибудь, чéм-нибудь** ...).

Meaning and Uses of the Particle *-то*

A form with **-то** is used when the speaker has a definite person or thing in mind, but one that s/he does not mention by name, either because (a) s/he does not know it (s/he may have known, but has forgotten), or (b) s/he may know it, but simply chooses for some reason not to mention it. Forms with the particle **-то** are limited primarily to *statements* expressed in the *past tense* or the *present tense,* unless the action or state denoted by the verb is repeated or habitual.

NOTE: In the *future tense,* forms with **-то** are possible, but occur more rarely: They are used only when the speaker refers to a particular person or thing that s/he does not wish to identify, e.g., **Я́ приведý *когó-то* на вéчер, но я́ не скажý тебé, ктó э́то. Э́то бýдет мóй сюрпри́з для тебя́** *I'm going to bring someone to the party, but I won't tell you who. This will be my surprise for you.*

Past Tense

Ктó-то звони́л, но я́ забы́л, ктó.	*Someone called, but I forget who.*
Óн **чтó-то** сказáл, но я́ не пóнял.	*He said something, but I didn't understand.*
К тебé заходи́ла **какáя-то** дéвушка, но онá не сказáла своё и́мя.	*Some girl came by to see you, but she didn't say what her name was.*
Я́ по оши́бке взя́л **чéй-то** зóнтик.	*I took somebody's umbrella by mistake.*

Present Tense

Ктó-то стучи́т в двéрь.	*Someone is knocking at the door.*
Мóй бóсс в плохóм настроéнии, óн я́вно **чéм-то** недовóлен.	*My boss is in a bad mood, he is obviously unhappy about something.*
Сегóдня идёт **какóй-то** нóвый фи́льм, не пóмню, кáк назывáется.	*Some new movie is playing today, I don't remember what it is called.*
Здéсь лежи́т **чья́-то** сýмка, но не знáю, чья́.	*Somebody's handbag is lying here, but I don't know whose.*

Meaning and Uses of the Particle *-нибудь*

Unlike **-то**, the particle **-нибудь** is used when the speaker has no particular person or object in mind, but refers instead to someone or something indefinite, and whose very identity is still unknown. As a general rule, pronouns with **-нибудь** are used in *questions*, after *commands*, in statements expressed in the *future tense*, as well as with *repeated actions in the present tense*.

Questions

Ктó-нибудь звони́л?	*Did anyone call?*
Ты́ **чтó-нибудь** зна́ешь об э́том?	*Do you know anything about this?*
Ты́ с **кéм-нибудь** говори́л об э́том?	*Did you talk with anyone about this?*
Та́м продаю́т **каки́е-нибудь** сувени́ры?	*Do they sell any souvenirs there?*
Вы́ ви́дели та́м **чью́-нибудь** маши́ну?	*Did you see anyone's car there?*

Commands

Спроси́те **когó-нибудь** из его́ друзе́й.	*Ask one of his friends.*
Возьми́ **чтó-нибудь** почита́ть.	*Take something to read.*
Спо́й на́м **каку́ю-нибудь** пе́сню.	*Sing us a song (any one at all).*
Не покупа́йте но́вый рюкза́к для своего́ пе́рвого похо́да. Попроси́те **чéй-нибудь** на вре́мя.	*Don't buy a new backpack for your first hike. Ask (to borrow) someone else's for a time.*

Future Tense

Я́ спрошу́ **когó-нибудь** об э́том.	*I'll ask someone (or other) about this.*
Ма́ма пригото́вит **чтó-нибудь** на обе́д.	*Mom will make something for lunch.*
Я́ куплю́ себе́ **каки́е-нибудь** санда́лии, когда́ прие́ду на мо́ре.	*I will buy myself some sandals when I get to the seashore.*
Когда́ авто́буса не́т, я́ е́ду на по́чту на **чьём-нибудь** велосипе́де.	*When there is no bus, I go to the post office on somebody's bicycle.*

Present Tense (Repeated Actions)

Когда́ ему́ тру́дно, о́н всегда́ про́сит **когó-нибудь** по́мочь.	*When he is having trouble, he always asks someone to help.*
Она́ ча́сто покупа́ет **чтó-нибудь** на э́том ры́нке.	*She often buys something at this market.*
О́н всегда́ чита́ет **какóй-нибудь** детекти́в.	*He is always reading some detective story.*
По́сле ле́кции в большо́й аудито́рии, всегда́ остаю́тся **чьи́-нибудь** ве́щи.	*After a lecture in a large classroom, someone's things are always left (behind).*

It is important to note that in contrast to the English pronouns *anything, anyone,* etc., which can occur in both positive and negative sentences, the Russian indefinite pronouns with the particles **-то** and **-нибудь** cannot be used in negative sentences; in a negative sentence the English pronouns beginning in *any-* are expressed in Russian by forms of the negative pronouns in **ни-** (**никтó**, **ничтó**), as shown in the following examples.

—Ты́ **чтó-нибудь** купи́л?	*Did you buy anything?*
—Не́т, я́ **ничегó** не купи́л.	*No, I didn't buy anything.*
—Вы́ **когó-нибудь** та́м ви́дели?	*Did you see anyone there?*
—Не́т, я́ **никогó** не ви́дел.	*No, I didn't see anyone.*

31. Complete each of the following sentences with the correct form of the appropriate indefinite pronoun.

1. —Мне́ ________________ звони́л?
   —Да́. ________________ звони́л, но не сказа́л своё и́мя.
2. —Что́ же мне́ тепе́рь де́лать с э́тими биле́тами?!
   —Отда́й и́х ________________ студе́нтам.
3. —Где́ вчера́ бы́л Па́ша?
   —О́н ходи́л к ________________ из свои́х друзе́й, но я́ не зна́ю, к кому́.
4. —Ко мне́ ________________ приходи́л?
   —Да́. Приходи́ла Ната́ша и ещё ________________ па́рень, но о́н не предста́вился.
5. —Вы́ чита́ли ________________ книги э́того писа́теля?
   —Да́, я давно́ чита́ла ________________ его́ кни́гу, но не по́мню её назва́ние.
6. —Ка́к узна́ть, бу́дет ли за́втра экза́мен?
   —Позвони́ ________________ из на́шей гру́ппы.
7. —Отку́да ты́ зна́ешь но́мер её телефо́на?
   —Я́ ________________ спроси́л.
8. —Пе́тя, когда́ сего́дня футбо́льный ма́тч?
   —Я́ не зна́ю, я́ ________________ спрошу́.
9. —Сего́дня де́нь рожде́ния Та́ни. Что́ е́й подари́ть?
   —Подари́ е́й ________________ прия́тное для неё, ... цветы́, духи́.
10. —Что́ чита́ет Ма́ша?
    —Она́ чита́ет ________________ из Бу́нина, ка́жется ________________ расска́з.
11. —За́втра я е́ду в командиро́вку, но у меня́ не́т ма́ленького чемода́на.
    —Ну́, возьми́ ________________.
12. —О́й, э́то не моя́ ру́чка. Ка́жется, я́ по оши́бке взя́л ________________ ру́чку.

Negative Pronouns

Negative Pronouns in *ни-*: *никто́, ничто́, никако́й, ниче́й*

Russian has a series of negative pronouns (and adverbs—see Chapter 5) that are formed from the pronouns **кто́**, **что́**, **како́й**, and **че́й** by means of the prefix **ни-**. These negative pronouns are declined like **кто́**, **что́**, etc., except that **ничто́** in the accusative case always takes the form of the genitive: **ничего́**. When a preposition occurs, it is placed between the **ни-** and the pronoun, which takes the case governed by the preposition, e.g., **ни о ко́м** *not about anyone,* **ни с че́м** *not with anything,* **ни для́ кого́** *not for anyone.*

кто́ *who*	никто́ (ни ... кто́) *no one*
что́ *what*	ничто́ (ни ... что́) *nothing, not anything*
како́й *what kind*	никако́й (ни ... како́й) *no (kind), not any (kind)*
че́й *whose*	ниче́й (ни ... че́й) *no one's, not anyone's*

The predicate of this type of negative pronoun must always be negated with **не**, which results in a "double negative" (**ни- ... не ...**), e.g., ***Никто́ не* звони́л** *No one called.* Note that in these negative sentences the pronouns in **ни-** are the Russian equivalent of English pronouns in *any-* (*anyone, anything,* etc.). However, in positive sentences, as noted in the preceding section, English *any-* is expressed in Russian by the indefinite pronouns in **-нибудь**.

—Ты́ кому́-нибудь звони́л?	*Did you call anyone?*
—Не́т, я **никому́** не звони́л.	*No, I didn't call anyone.*

The following examples further illustrate the use of the negative pronouns in **ни-**.

—Ктó пришёл? —**Никтó** не пришёл.	*Who came?* *No one came.*
—Вы́ когó-нибудь тáм ви́дели? —Нéт, мы́ **никогó** тáм не ви́дели.	*Did you see anyone there?* *No, we didn't see anyone there.*
—У когó éсть словáрь? —**Ни** у **когó** нéт словаря́.	*Who has a dictionary?* *No one has a dictionary.*
—О кóм ты дýмаешь? —Я́ **ни** о **кóм** не дýмаю.	*Who are you thinking about?* *I'm not thinking about anyone.*
—Комý нрáвится э́та мýзыка? —**Никомý** не нрáвится.	*Who likes this music?* *No one likes it.*
—Óн с кéм-нибудь говори́л об э́том? —Нéт, óн **ни** с **кéм** не говори́л.	*Did he speak with anyone about this?* *No, he did not speak with anyone.*
—Каки́е у вáс éсть вопрóсы? —У нáс нéт **никаки́х** вопрóсов.	*What questions do you have?* *We do not have any questions.*
—О какóй кни́ге óн спрáшивал? —Óн не спрáшивал **ни** о **какóй** кни́ге.	*What book was he asking about?* *He wasn't asking about any book.*
—Чтó тебя́ беспокóит? —**Ничтó** меня́ не беспокóит.	*What is bothering you?* *Nothing is bothering me.*
—Óн чéм-нибудь зáнят? —Нéт, óн **ничéм** не зáнят.	*Is he busy with something?* *No, he is not busy with anything.*
—Чéй рисýнок тебé понрáвился? —Мнé **ничéй** рисýнок не понрáвился.	*Whose drawing did you like?* *I didn't like anybody's drawing.*

32. Answer each of the following questions in the negative, using a negative pronoun.

1. Ктó тебé нрáвится? ____________________
2. Чтó егó интересýет? ____________________
3. Чтó ты́ дéлаешь? ____________________
4. К комý ты́ идёшь? ____________________
5. О кóм ты́ мечтáешь? ____________________
6. Чéм онá занимáется? ____________________
7. С кéм óн встрéтился? ____________________
8. У когó ты́ былá? ____________________
9. Чегó óн бои́тся? ____________________
10. К чемý ты́ готóвишься? ____________________
11. На каки́е устýпки они́ согласи́лись? ____________________
12. Чьи́ совéты онá слýшала? ____________________
13. Каки́е вопрóсы вáс интересýют? ____________________
14. Чью маши́ну ты́ води́л? ____________________
15. На когó ты́ надéешься? ____________________

Negative Pronouns in *не́-*: *не́кого, не́чего*

The negative pronouns **не́кого** *there is no one* and **не́чего** *there is nothing* are formed from the interrogative pronouns **кто́** and **что́** by means of the stressed negative prefix **не́-**. These pronouns are declined like **кто́** and **что́**, except that (a) they do not occur in the nominative case and (b) the prepositionless accusative of the pronoun based on **что́** has the same form as the genitive: **не́чего**. When a preposition occurs, it is placed between **не́** and the pronoun. The declension of these pronouns is given in the following table.

	не́кого *there is no one*	**не́чего** *there is nothing*
Nom.	—	—
Acc.	не́кого (не́ ... кого)	не́чего (не́ ... что)
Gen.	не́кого (не́ ... кого)	не́чего (не́ ... чего)
Prep.	не́ ... ком	не́ ... чем
Dat.	не́кому (не́ ... кому)	не́чему (не́ ... чему)
Instr.	не́кем (не́ ... кем)	не́чем (не́ ... чем)

NOTE: Nominative-case forms with the prefix **не́-** do occur, but in a different meaning: **не́кто** *someone, a certain* (**Не́кто Смирно́в** *a certain Smirnov*), **не́что** *something* (**не́что невероя́тное** *something unbelievable*).

NOTE: When a preposition occurs, the three elements of the negative pronoun are written separately, but they are pronounced as one word, and with only one stress, on **не́**: **не́ у кого** [n'éukəvə], **не́ за что** [n'ézəštə].

The negative pronouns in **не́-** are typically used in impersonal (subjectless) constructions with the infinitive form of the verb. The case of the pronoun is determined either by the infinitive or by a co-occurring preposition.

Не́кого спроси́ть.	*There is no one to ask.*
Не́ с **кем** говори́ть.	*There is no one to talk with.*
Не́чего боя́ться.	*There is nothing to be afraid of.*
Не́ о **чем** беспоко́иться.	*There is nothing to worry about.*

A noun or pronoun denoting the performer of the action must be in the dative case.

Бра́ту **не́** к **кому́** обрати́ться.	*My brother has no one to turn to.*
Мне́ **не́кого** боя́ться.	*I have no one to fear.*
Не́кому пойти́ за вино́м.	*There is no one to go for the wine.*

The past and future tenses are expressed by **бы́ло** *was* and **бу́дет** *will be.*

Мне́ **не́кому** бы́ло звони́ть.	*There was no one for me to call.*
Тебе́ **не́** с **кем** бу́дет говори́ть.	*There will be no one for you to talk to.*

33. Complete each of the following sentences with the correct form of **нéкого** or **нéчего** (with a preposition, if required).

1. —Когó тýт мóжно спросúть?
   —Тýт ____________ спросúть.
2. —На чтó óн бýдет жáловаться?
   —Емý ____________ жáловаться.
3. —Чтó бы нáм сдéлать?
   —Нáм ____________ дéлать.
4. —Чéм ты́ бýдешь писáть?
   —Мнé ____________ писáть.
5. —Комý онá бýдет звонúть?
   —Éй звонúть бýдет ____________.
6. —С кéм вы́ бýдете говорúть?
   —Мнé бýдет ____________ говорúть.
7. —К комý он пойдёт?
   —Емý ____________ пойтú.
8. —Ктó пойдёт за хлéбом?
   —____________ пойтú за хлéбом.
9. —О чём вы́ бýдете говорúть?
   —Нáм ____________ говорúть.
10. —За чтó егó благодарúть?
    —Егó благодарúть ____________.

CHAPTER 5

Adjectives and Adverbs

Adjectives

Qualitative and Relational Adjectives

Most adjectives in Russian are *qualitative,* i.e., they denote a quality or property of the noun or pronoun they modify. A qualitative adjective may denote size (*big, small, tall*), color (*red, green, blue*), taste (*sweet, sour, salty*), temperature (*hot, cold, warm*), and various other qualities of people and things (*intelligent, happy, sad, interesting*). Russian qualitative adjectives have a number of important grammatical properties.

(a) They may be used in both a *long* form (expressing gender, number, and case) and a *short* (caseless) form.

(b) The long form may be used *attributively,* usually preceding the noun it modifies (*The* ***new*** *teacher arrived*), or *predicatively,* usually after a form of the linking verb *be* (*This teacher is* ***new***). The short form, however, is used *only* predicatively.

(c) They form comparatives (*quicker, more interesting*) and superlatives (*quickest, most interesting*).

(d) They form derived adverbs (*quickly, interestingly*).

A smaller number of adjectives in Russian are *relational,* i.e., they express a relationship, indicating that the noun modified is of, from, or connected in some way with something or someone else. For example, a relational adjective may denote a property of the modified noun that relates to people (***де́тские*** **кни́ги** *children's books*), to animals (***ко́нский*** **база́р** *horse market*), to an inanimate object (***мото́рная*** **ло́дка** *motorboat*), to the material from which it is made (***деревя́нный*** **до́м** *wooden house*), to a place (***городска́я*** **библиоте́ка** *city library*), to time (***ле́тние*** **кани́кулы** *summer vacation*), and to various other categories. Compared with qualitative adjectives, relational adjectives are more restricted in usage.

(a) They have only an attributive long form.

(b) They do not have comparatives or superlatives.

(c) They do not form derived adverbs.

The Long Form of Adjectives

Attributive and Predicative Adjectives

In Russian, as in English, an attributive adjective normally precedes, but may immediately follow, the noun it modifies.

Э́то **надёжная** маши́на.	*This is a reliable car.*
Маши́ну **надёжную**, ка́к э́та, легко́ содержа́ть.	*A car reliable like this (one), is easy to maintain.*

Qualitative adjectives may also occur predicatively, as a "predicate adjective," usually after the verb **бы́ть** *to be,* which in the present tense is not stated, but is implied.

Э́та маши́на **надёжная**.	*This car is reliable.*
Э́ти маши́ны **надёжные**.	*These cars are reliable.*

Adjective Structure

As the different endings on the adjective above demonstrate, the long form of the adjective, in both its attributive and predicative use, must agree with the noun it modifies in gender, number, and case. Like nouns and pronouns, adjectives consist of a stem followed by an ending. Taking the adjective above as an example, the stem of the adjective **надёжн-** is constant, but the ending changes to reflect the change in case from nominative to accusative, and in number from singular to plural.

STEM	+	ENDING	
надёжн	+	**ая**	(feminine, singular, nominative)
надёжн	+	**ую**	(feminine, singular, accusative)
надёжн	+	**ые**	(plural, nominative)

Declension of Adjectives

The spelling of the adjective's declensional endings is influenced by the phonetic nature of its stem-final consonant. Adjectives with the following types of stems occur.

- Stem ending in a hard consonant (**но́вый** *new,* **молодо́й** *young*)
- Stem ending in a soft consonant (**си́ний** *blue,* **ле́тний** *summer,* **пти́чий** *bird*)
- Stem ending in the consonants **-г**, **-к**, **-х** (**до́лгий** *long,* **ру́сский** *Russian,* **ти́хий** *quiet*)
- Stem ending in the unpaired consonants **-ж**, **-ш**, **-ч**, **-щ** (**хоро́ший** *good,* **све́жий** *fresh*)

Adjectives Whose Stems End in a Hard Consonant

Adjectives with a stem ending in a hard consonant take endings that begin with a hard-series vowel (**ы**, **о**, **а**, or **у**). Hard-stem adjectives may have the stress on the stem (**но́в-ый** *new*) or on the ending (**молод-о́й** *young*). The declensional endings are the same for both stem-stressed and end-stressed adjectives, except in the nominative and accusative inanimate masculine singular (**-ый** vs. **-о́й**). The following table shows the declension of the hard-stem adjective **но́вый** *new.*

	MASCULINE,	NEUTER	FEMININE	PLURAL
Nom.	но́вый	но́вое	но́вая	но́вые
Acc. Inan.	но́вый	но́вое	но́вую	но́вые
Anim.	но́вого			но́вых
Gen.	но́вого		но́вой	но́вых
Prep.	о но́вом		о но́вой	о но́вых
Dat.	но́вому		но́вой	но́вым
Instr.	но́вым		но́вой	но́выми

NOTE: The **г** is pronounced [v] in the genitive case of the adjective ending **-ого**: [əvə].

NOTE: It is important to remember the "animate accusative rule": The accusative singular of an *animate masculine* noun—and its modifying adjective or pronoun—is identical to the genitive: **Óн ви́дел *но́вого студе́нта*** *He saw the new student.* In the plural, the animate accusative rule applies to *animate nouns of all genders*: **Óн ви́дел *но́вых студе́нтов и студе́нток*** *He saw the new male and female students.* In the masculine singular and the plural of all genders, *inanimate* nouns in the accusative are identical to the nominative: **Óн купи́л *но́вый* сто́л и *но́вые* сту́лья** *He bought a new table and new chairs.*

NOTE: An adjective (or pronoun) modifying a "naturally masculine" second-declension noun (**де́душка** *grandfather,* **мужчи́на** *man,* **дя́дя** *uncle*) must show *masculine* agreement, but the noun declines like a feminine noun in **-а**, **-я**: **Она́ встре́тила *симпати́чного* мужчи́ну** *She met a nice-looking man.*

Following are some common adjectives with a stem ending in a hard consonant.

аккура́тный *neat*
бе́лый *white*
бы́стрый *fast*
ве́жливый *polite*
весёлый *cheerful*
глу́пый *stupid*
гру́бый *rude*
гру́стный *sad*
гря́зный *dirty*
до́брый *kind*
зло́бный *mean*
интере́сный *interesting*
краси́вый *pretty*
лени́вый *lazy*
ме́дленный *slow*
молодо́й *young*
молчали́вый *taciturn*
некраси́вый *ugly*
неопря́тный *sloppy*
но́вый *new*
разгово́рчивый *talkative*
све́тлый *light*
серьёзный *serious*
ску́чный *boring*
смешно́й *funny*
ста́рый *old*
тёмный *dark*
трудолюби́вый *industrious*
у́мный *smart*
чи́стый *clean*
чёрный *black*

1. Complete each of the following sentences with the correct form of the antonym of the underlined adjective. Choose the antonym from the list above.

1. Та́ня трудолюби́вая де́вушка, а её подру́га Ле́на ________________.
2. Мы́ живём в но́вой кварти́ре, а они́ живу́т в ________________ кварти́ре.
3. Хотя́ о́н у́мный челове́к, о́н за́дал ________________ вопро́с.
4. О́н лю́бит носи́ть чёрную ша́пку, а она́ обы́чно но́сит ________________ ша́пку.
5. Ты́ обы́чно тако́й весёлый, почему́ у тебя́ сего́дня тако́й ________________ ви́д?
6. В го́роде движе́ние ме́дленное, а за́ городом движе́ние ________________.
7. Ма́льчик ве́жливый с прия́телями, но ________________ с ро́дственниками.
8. Она́ до́брый челове́к, но её му́ж челове́к ________________.
9. О́н интере́сный челове́к, но ________________ собесе́дник.
10. Э́ти бра́тья о́чень отлича́ются: оди́н разгово́рчивый, а друго́й ________________.
11. Она́ лю́бит смешны́е фи́льмы, а о́н бо́льше лю́бит ________________ фи́льмы.
12. Она́ со све́тлыми волоса́ми, а её сестра́ с ________________ волоса́ми.
13. У э́той молодо́й де́вушки ________________ му́ж.
14. У неё краси́вая причёска, а у её подру́ги причёска ________________.
15. Э́тот шка́ф для чи́стой оде́жды, а э́тот для ________________ оде́жды.
16. У него́ на рабо́те аккура́тный ви́д, а до́ма ви́д у него́ ________________.

Adjectives Whose Stems End in a Soft *-н*

A small number of adjectives have a stem ending in a soft **-н**. These soft-stem adjectives take endings beginning with a soft-series vowel (**и**, **е**, **я**, or **ю**). The declension of the soft-stem adjective **синий** *blue* is given in the following table.

	MASCULINE,	NEUTER	FEMININE	PLURAL
Nom.	си́ний	си́нее	си́няя	си́ние
Acc. Inan.	си́ний		си́нюю	си́ние
Anim.	си́него			си́них
Gen.	си́него		си́ней	си́них
Prep.	о си́нем		о си́ней	о си́них
Dat.	си́нему		си́ней	си́ним
Instr.	си́ним		си́ней	си́ними

Following are some common adjectives with a stem ending in a soft **-н**. The majority of these adjectives denote either "time" or "place."

Time

весе́нний *spring*
зи́мний *winter*
ле́тний *summer*
осе́нний *autumn*
вчера́шний *yesterday's*
за́втрашний *tomorrow's*
сего́дняшний *today's*
ра́нний *early*
по́здний *late*
вече́рний *evening*
у́тренний *morning*
ны́нешний *present-day*
тепе́решний *present-day*
тогда́шний *of that time*
неда́вний *recent*
да́вний *old, long-standing*
дре́вний *ancient*
пре́жний *former*

Place

ве́рхний *upper, top*
ни́жний *lower, bottom*
пере́дний *front*
сре́дний *middle*
за́дний *back, rear*
зде́шний *local*
бли́жний *near*
да́льний *far*
вну́тренний *internal*
вне́шний *external*
дома́шний *home, domestic*
сосе́дний *neighboring*

Miscellaneous

и́скренний *sincere*
си́ний *blue*
после́дний *last*
ли́шний *spare, unnecessary*
посторо́нний *outside, extraneous*

2. Complete each of the following sentences with the correct form of the soft-stem adjective in parentheses.

1. О́н рабо́тал над докла́дом с ________________ (ра́нний) утра́ до ________________ (по́здний) ве́чера.
2. Ко мне́ подошли́ и спроси́ли: «У ва́с не́т ________________ (ли́шний) биле́та?»
3. В ________________ (сосе́дний) кварти́ре живёт америка́нский бизнесме́н.
4. Студе́нты гото́вятся к ________________ (после́дний) экза́мену.
5. Мо́й оте́ц чита́ет «Пра́вду» и «________________ (Вече́рняя) Москву́».
6. Она́ сама́, без по́мощи му́жа, занима́ется все́ми ________________ (дома́шний) дела́ми.

7. Мы́ бы́ли с детьми́ в ку́кольном теа́тре на ________________ (у́тренний) спекта́кле.
8. Я́ узна́л э́ту но́вость из ________________ (сего́дняшний) газе́ты.
9. Пассажи́р положи́л свои́ ве́щи на ________________ (ве́рхний) по́лку.
10. У ________________ (зде́шний) людей надо́лго оста́нется в па́мяти э́то землетрясе́ние.

Adjectives Whose Stems End in *-г, -к,* or *-х*

Adjectives with a stem ending in the consonants **-г**, **-к**, or **-х** undergo Spelling Rule 1 (after **г**, **к**, **х** write **-и**, never **-ы**) in the plural of all the cases, and in certain forms of the singular. Adjectives with a stem in one of these consonants usually have stress on the stem (**ру́сский** *Russian*), but may also occur with stress on the ending (**дорого́й** *expensive*). The declension of stem-stressed **ру́сский** is presented in the following table.

	MASCULINE,	NEUTER	FEMININE	PLURAL
Nom.	ру́сский	ру́сское	ру́сская	ру́сские
Acc. Inan.	ру́сский		ру́сскую	ру́сские
Anim.	ру́сского			ру́сских
Gen.	ру́сского		ру́сской	ру́сских
Prep.	о ру́сском		о ру́сской	о ру́сских
Dat.	ру́сскому		ру́сской	ру́сским
Instr.	ру́сским		ру́сской	ру́сскими

NOTE: The interrogative pronoun **како́й?** *what sort of, which?* and the demonstrative pronoun **тако́й** *such a* decline like the end-stressed adjective **дорого́й**.

Following are some commonly used adjectives with a stem in **г**, **к**, or **х**.

Stem-stressed

бли́зкий *close*	лёгкий *easy*
высо́кий *tall*	мя́гкий *soft*
вели́кий *great*	сла́дкий *sweet*
ги́бкий *flexible*	стро́гий *severe*
гро́мкий *loud*	ти́хий *quiet*
жа́ркий *hot*	то́нкий *thin*
далёкий *distant*	у́зкий *narrow*
до́лгий *long*	широ́кий *wide*
жа́ркий *hot*	я́ркий *bright*

End-stressed

дорого́й *dear, expensive*	плохо́й *bad*
городско́й *city*	глухо́й *deaf*
мужско́й *masculine, male*	сухо́й *dry*

3. Complete each of the following sentences with the correct form of the adjective in parentheses.

1. В ________________ (жа́ркий) дни́ лю́ди ча́сто приезжа́ют на э́то го́рное о́зеро.
2. Са́мым ________________ (вели́кий) поэ́том в Росси́и счита́ется Алекса́ндр Пу́шкин.
3. Всё бо́льше и бо́льше автомоби́лей е́здят по ________________ (широ́кий) у́лицам Москвы́.

4. В ________________ (такóй) ________________ (дорогóй) ресторáнах обéдают тóлько богáтые лю́ди.
5. Смотрéть без тёмных очкóв на ________________ (я́ркий) сóлнце врéдно для глáз.
6. Нью-Йорк извéстен свои́ми óчень ________________ (высóкий) домáми.
7. Отéц ругáл сы́на за ________________ (плохóй) отмéтки.
8. Дéти лю́бят ________________ (слáдкий) пи́щу.
9. Óн об э́том говори́л тóлько с ________________ (бли́зкий) друзья́ми.
10. Всé тури́сты устáли пóсле ________________ (дóлгий) экскýрсии.

Adjectives Whose Stems End in *-ж, -ч, -ш,* or *-щ*

Like adjectives with a stem in **-г**, **-к**, **-х**, adjectives whose stem ends in one of the unpaired consonants **-ж**, **-ч**, **-ш**, **-щ** undergo Spelling Rule 1 and therefore have several endings beginning with **-и** (e.g., the plural endings **-ие**, **-их**, **-им**, **-ими**). In addition, adjectives in one of these unpaired consonants undergo Spelling Rule 3 (page 11): After the unpaired consonants write unstressed **е**, but stressed **ó**. The declension of both stem-stressed **хорóший** *good* and end-stressed **большóй** *big* is presented in the table below.

	MASCULINE,	NEUTER	FEMININE	PLURAL
Nom.	хорóший большóй	хорóшее большóе	хорóшая большáя	хорóшие больши́е
Acc.	*Inan. = Nom.* *Anim. = Gen.*		хорóшую большýю	*Inan. = Nom.* *Anim. = Gen.*
Gen.	хорóшего большóго		хорóшей большóй	хорóших больши́х
Prep.	о хорóшем о большóм		о хорóшей о большóй	о хорóших о больши́х
Dat.	хорóшему большóму		хорóшей большóй	хорóшим больши́м
Instr.	хорóшим больши́м		хорóшей большóй	хорóшими больши́ми

Following are some common adjectives with a stem ending in **-ж**, **-ч**, **-ш**, or **-щ**.

бýдущий *future*
бы́вший *former*
везýчий *lucky*
горя́чий *hot*
млáдший *younger*
неуклю́жий *clumsy*
настоя́щий *real, genuine*
óбщий *common*
ры́жий *red-haired*
рабóчий *working*
свéжий *fresh*
стáрший *older*
хорóший *good*
чужóй *someone else's*

4. Complete each of the following sentences with the correct form of the adjective in parentheses.

1. Не сýйте свóй нóс в ________________ (чужóй) делá.
2. Земля́ покры́лась ________________ (свéжий) снéгом.
3. Осторóжно! Не трóгай блю́до, онó ________________ (горя́чий).
4. Нáм повезлó с ________________ (хорóший) погóдой.
5. У неё с мýжем мнóго ________________ (óбщий) интерéсов.
6. Автóбус останови́лся пéред ________________ (большóй) здáнием.

7. Роди́тели осо́бенно забо́тятся о ______________ (мла́дший) сы́не.
8. Я́ всегда́ легко́ узнаю́ свою́ до́чь по её ______________ (ры́жий) голове́.
9. Она́ мечта́ет о ______________ (настоя́щий) любви́.
10. По ______________ (рабо́чий) дня́м магази́ны откры́ты до девяти́.
11. Она́ уже́ сейча́с гото́вится к своему́ ______________ (бу́дущий) ребёнку.
12. Преподава́тель получи́л письмо́ от ______________ (бы́вший) студе́нта.

The Short Form of Adjectives

Most qualitative adjectives can occur in a short form, used only predicatively. Relational adjectives, including all adjectives with the suffix **-ск-** (e.g., **де́тский** *children's*) and **-ян-** (e.g., **деревя́нный** *wooden*) do not have short forms.

The short form of the adjective is derived from the long form. The masculine short form is equal to the adjective stem minus the long-form ending. The feminine, neuter, and plural forms are comprised of the stem plus the first vowel of the long-form ending: feminine **-а**, neuter **-о**, and plural **-ы** (or **-и**). Compare the long and short forms of the adjectives **краси́вый** *pretty* and **высо́кий** *tall.*

	LONG FORM	SHORT FORM	LONG FORM	SHORT FORM
Masculine	краси́в-**ый**	краси́в	высо́к-**ий**	высо́к
Feminine	краси́в-**ая**	краси́в-**а**	высо́к-**ая**	высок-**а́**
Neuter	краси́в-**ое**	краси́в-**о**	высо́к-**ое**	высок-**о́**
Plural	краси́в-**ые**	краси́в-**ы**	высо́к-**ие**	высок-**и́**

An adjective whose stem ends in a cluster of two or more consonants normally has a vowel inserted between the final two consonants in the *masculine* form. For adjectives that have a consonant cluster with a final **-н**, the inserted vowel is usually **-е-**; for clusters with a final **-к**, the inserted vowel is usually **-о-**.

Following are some common adjectives that have a consonant cluster ending in **-н** with an inserted **-е-** in the masculine short form.

STEMS WITH A CLUSTER IN *-н-*	SHORT FORMS
бе́дный *poor*	бе́ден (бедна́, бе́дно, бедны́)
ва́жный *important*	ва́жен (важна́, ва́жно, важны́)
голо́дный *hungry*	го́лоден (голодна́, голодно́, голодны́)
гря́зный *dirty*	гря́зен (грязна́, гря́зно, грязны́)
дли́нный *long*	дли́нен (длинна́, дли́нно, длинны́)
дру́жный *amicable*	дру́жен (дружна́, дру́жно, дружны́)
жела́тельный *desirable*	жела́телен (жела́тельна, жела́тельно, жела́тельны)
заба́вный *amusing*	заба́вен (заба́вна, заба́вно, заба́вны)
интере́сный *interesting*	интере́сен (интере́сна, интере́сно, интере́сны)
кра́сный *red*	кра́сен (красна́, красно́, красны́)
ло́жный *false*	ло́жен (ло́жна, ло́жно, ло́жны)
мо́дный *fashionable*	мо́ден (модна́, мо́дно, мо́дны)
ну́жный *necessary*	ну́жен (нужна́, нужно́, нужны́)
поле́зный *useful, helpful*	поле́зен (поле́зна, поле́зно, поле́зны)
ра́вный *equal*	ра́вен (равна́, равно́, равны́)
серьёзный *serious*	серьёзен (серьёзна, серьёзно, серьёзны)
тру́дный *difficult*	тру́ден (трудна́, тру́дно, трудны́)
у́мный *smart*	умён (умна́, умно́, умны́)
я́сный *clear*	я́сен (ясна́, я́сно, ясны́)

NOTE: Two adjectives with a consonant cluster ending in **-н** have an inserted **-о-** in the masculine short form: **по́лный** *full* (**по́лон**) and **смешно́й** *funny* (**смешо́н**).

Following are a few common adjectives with a consonant cluster ending in **-к** that have an inserted **-о-** in the masculine short form.

STEMS WITH A CLUSTER IN *-К-*	SHORT FORMS
бли́зкий *near*	бли́зок (близка́, бли́зко, близки́)
коро́ткий *short, brief*	коро́ток (коротка́, ко́ротко, коротки́)
кре́пкий *strong*	кре́пок (крепка́, кре́пко, крепки́)
лёгкий *easy, light*	лёгок (легка́, легко́, легки́)
ни́зкий *low*	ни́зок (низка́, ни́зко, низки́)
сла́дкий *sweet*	сла́док (сладка́, сла́дко, сладки́)
у́зкий *narrow*	у́зок (узка́, у́зко, узки́)

The following two adjectives have special short forms.

большо́й *big*	вели́к (велика́, велико́, велики́)
ма́ленький *small*	ма́л (мала́, мало́, малы́)

NOTE: Alongside the short-form adjective **вели́к** *(too) big* is a long-form adjective with the same root, but with a different meaning: **вели́кий** *great,* e.g., **Пётр Вели́кий** *Peter the Great,* **Екатери́на Вели́кая** *Catherine the Great.*

Use of Short-Form Adjectives

Short-form adjectives can only be used predicatively after a linking verb, usually **бы́ть** *to be.* Short-form adjectives agree in gender and number with the subject, but they are not inflected for case.

In the present tense the linking verb **бы́ть** is omitted before a predicate adjective.

Фи́льм **интере́сен**.	*The movie is interesting.*
Кни́га **интере́сна**.	*The book is interesting.*
Письмо́ **интере́сно**.	*The letter is interesting.*
Заня́тия **интере́сны**.	*The classes are interesting.*

In the past tense one of the forms **бы́л**, **была́**, **бы́ло**, **бы́ли** is used, whichever agrees with the gender and number of the subject.

Ча́й бы́л **кре́пок**.	*The tea was strong.*
Во́дка была́ **крепка́**.	*The vodka was strong.*
Вино́ бы́ло **вку́сно**.	*The wine was tasty.*
Блины́ бы́ли **вкусны́**.	*The pancakes were tasty.*

In the future tense either **бу́дет** or **бу́дут** is used, depending on whether the subject is singular or plural.

Зада́ча бу́дет **трудна́**.	*The problem will be difficult.*
Экза́мены бу́дут **трудны́**.	*The exams will be difficult.*

5. Rewrite each of the following sentences, replacing the attributive long form of the adjective with its predicative short form.

MODEL Э́то тру́дный вопро́с. (*This is a difficult question.*) >
Вопро́с тру́ден. (*The question is difficult.*)

1. Э́то кре́пкий ча́й. ____________________
2. Э́то поле́зный сове́т. ____________________
3. Э́то серьёзная пробле́ма. ____________________
4. Э́то прекра́сный де́нь. ____________________
5. Э́то коро́ткий пиджа́к. ____________________
6. Э́то бе́дный стари́к. ____________________
7. Э́то ну́жный слова́рь. ____________________
8. Э́то ни́зкий за́работок. ____________________
9. Э́то лёгкий зачёт. ____________________
10. Э́то сла́дкий апельси́н. ____________________
11. Э́то у́мный ребёнок. ____________________
12. Э́то по́лный за́л. ____________________
13. Э́то ра́вные по́рции. ____________________
14. Э́то свобо́дные места́. ____________________
15. Э́то лёгкая су́мка. ____________________

Choosing the Short Form or Long Form in the Predicate

Many adjectives have both a long form and a short form that can occur predicatively.

Э́та кни́га **интере́сная**. — *This book is interesting.*
Э́та кни́га **интере́сна**. — *This book is interesting.*

Вода́ была́ **тёплая**. — *The water was warm.*
Вода́ была́ **тепла́**. — *The water was warm.*

Ча́й бу́дет **кре́пкий**. — *The tea will be strong.*
Ча́й бу́дет **кре́пок**. — *The tea will be strong.*

The choice between the short and long (nominative case) forms of the adjective in predicative position is determined by several factors. Following are some often-noted distinctions between the short and long forms.

(i) For many adjectives, the choice between the predicative short form and long form is essentially one of style. The short form indicates a more formal style characteristic of written Russian; the long form indicates a more informal style typical of spoken Russian.

Она́ **у́мная**. — *She is smart.* (informal)
Она́ **умна́**. — *She is smart.* (formal)

О́н **лени́вый**. — *He is lazy.* (informal)
О́н **лени́в**. — *He is lazy.* (formal)

(ii) For some adjectives, the predicative short form in certain contexts may denote a temporary property or state of the subject; the long form, by contrast, indicates a property that is permanently or inherently associated with the subject. Following are a few common adjectives that may show this distinction.

больно́й *ill* (chronically)	бо́лен *ill, sick* (at a particular time)
занято́й *(a) busy (person)*	за́нят *busy* (at a particular time)

здоро́вый *healthy* (in general) здоро́в *healthy* (not now ill)
споко́йный *calm* (by nature) споко́ен *calm* (at the moment)

Де́душка **больно́й**.	*Grandfather is (chronically) ill.*
Де́душка сего́дня **бо́лен**.	*Grandfather is ill today.*
О́н **занято́й**.	*He is (a) busy (man).*
О́н сейча́с **за́нят**.	*He is busy now.*
О́н тако́й **здоро́вый**.	*He is so healthy (strong).*
О́н бы́л бо́лен, но тепе́рь о́н **здоро́в**.	*He was sick, but now he is well.*
Э́та река́ **споко́йная**.	*This river is (a) calm (one).*
Река́ сего́дня **споко́йна**.	*The river today is calm.*

6. Complete each of the following sentences with the correct long or short form(s) of the adjective in parentheses.

(здоро́вый/здоро́в)
1. Она́ спортсме́нка. Она́ всегда́ така́я ________________. Но сего́дня она́ не ________________. Она́ простуди́лась.

(занято́й/за́нят)
2. Мо́й му́ж дире́ктор иностра́нной компа́нии. О́н тако́й ________________. Но сего́дня он не ________________, потому́ что в стране́ его́ компа́нии пра́здник.

(больно́й/бо́лен)
3. Ба́бушка ________________. Она́ до́лго страда́ет а́стмой.
4. Моя́ до́чь не пошла́ сего́дня в шко́лу. Она́ ________________.

(споко́йный/споко́ен)
5. Чёрное мо́ре ________________. Но сейча́с оно́ не ________________ из-за се́верных ветро́в.

(iii) A small number of adjectives that denote certain quantifiable properties like size and age (e.g., "big," "small," "young," "old") have a predicative short form indicating that the given property is excessive ("too …") with respect to the needs of a particular person or circumstance. The predicative long form of the same adjective, by contrast, wholly identifies this property with the subject. Following are common adjectives that may show this distinction.

большо́й *big*	вели́к *too big*
ма́ленький *small*	ма́л *too small*
дли́нный *long*	дли́нен *too long*
коро́ткий *short*	коро́ток *too short*
у́зкий *narrow*	у́зок *too narrow*
широ́кий *wide*	широ́к *too wide*
молодо́й *young*	мо́лод *too young*
ста́рый *old*	ста́р *too old*

Э́та шля́па **больша́я**.	*This hat is big (compared to others).*
Э́та шля́па **велика́**.	*This hat is too big (for someone).*
Э́ти де́тские ту́фли таки́е **ма́ленькие**.	*These children's shoes are so small.*
Э́ти ту́фли мне́ **малы́**.	*These shoes are too small for me.*

Её ю́бки всегда́ **дли́нные**. Э́та ю́бка е́й **длинна́**.	*Her skirts are always long (ones).* *This skirt is too long for her.*
Я́ уже́ **ста́рый**. **Я́ ста́р** для неё.	*I'm already (an) old (man).* *I am too old for her.*
О́н **молодо́й**. О́н **мо́лод** для э́той рабо́ты.	*He is (a) young (man).* *He is too young for this work.*

7. Complete each of the following sentences with the correct long or short form(s) of the adjective in parentheses.

(ма́ленький/ма́л)
1. Э́та кварти́ра ________________ для на́шей семьи́.
2. На́ша кварти́ра ________________, но ую́тная.

(ста́рый/ста́р)
3. Дома́ в э́том райо́не ________________, но больши́е.
4. Хотя́ э́тот мужчи́на не ________________, но он ________________ для э́той рабо́ты.

(широ́кий/широ́к)
5. По-мо́ему, э́ти мо́дные брю́ки тебе́ не иду́т, они́ ________________ тебе́.
6. Брю́ки у него́ всегда́ дли́нные и ________________, как у кло́уна в ци́рке.

(у́зкий/у́зок)
7. Э́та ю́бка о́чень ________________. Та́ ю́бка е́й то́же о́чень ________________.

(дли́нный/дли́нен)
8. Э́ти чёрные брю́ки не ________________, но ему́ они́ ________________.

(молодо́й/мо́лод)
9. Она́ не ________________ выходи́ть за́муж, но име́ть дете́й она́ ещё ________________.

(большо́й/вели́к)
10. Э́то пальто́ не ________________, но оно́ ________________ для меня́.

(iv) The short and long forms of some adjectives may differ in meaning; that is, in certain adjectives that have more than one sense, one of those senses may predominate in the short form of the adjective. Following are a few examples of adjectives of this type.

живо́й *lively* (*full of energy*)	жи́в *alive*
пра́вый *right* (*just*)	пра́в *right* (*correct*)
смешно́й *funny*	смешо́н *ridiculous*
ужа́сный *horrible* (*very bad*)	ужа́сен *horrifying* (*evoking horror*)

Ребёнок о́чень **живо́й**. Ры́ба ещё **жива́**.	*The child is very lively.* *The fish is still alive.*
На́ше де́ло **пра́вое**. Вы́ соверше́нно **пра́вы**.	*Our cause is just.* *You are absolutely right.*
Его́ анекдо́ты о́чень **смешны́е**. О́н **смешо́н**.	*His jokes are very funny.* *He is (being) ridiculous.*
Пого́да была́ **ужа́сная**. Его́ ви́д бы́л **ужа́сен**.	*The weather was horrible.* *His appearance was horrifying.*

8. Complete each of the following sentences with the correct long or short form of the adjective in parentheses.

(живо́й/жи́в)
1. И́х до́чка така́я ________________. Она́ всегда́ бе́гает и весели́тся.
2. Мо́й дру́г попа́л в большу́ю ава́рию, но о́н оста́лся ________________.

(непра́вый/непра́в)
3. Э́то реше́ние бы́ло ________________. На́до пода́ть на апелля́цию.
4. На э́тот раз она́ была́ ________________.

(смешно́й/смешо́н)
5. О́н тако́й ________________. Он всегда́ заставля́ет на́с смея́ться на уро́ке.
6. Э́то утвержде́ние ________________. Никто́ не пове́рит э́тому.

(ужа́сный/ужа́сен)
7. Когда́ он посмотре́л на меня́, его́ глаза́ бы́ли ________________.
8. Де́нь у меня́ бы́л ________________. Я́ не сда́л экза́мен и опозда́л на по́езд.

(v) If the grammatical subject is one of a small number of pronouns, e.g., **э́то** *this/that, it,* **всё** *everything,* or **что́** *what,* a predicate adjective must be in the neuter short form.

Всё **хорошо́**.	*Everything is good.*
Всё **норма́льно**.	*Everything is okay* (lit., *normal*).
Э́то очень **интере́сно**.	*That is very interesting.*
Э́то бы́ло про́сто **смешно́**.	*That was simply ridiculous.*
Э́то бу́дет **тру́дно**.	*It will be difficult.*
Что́ **непоня́тно**?	*What is not understood?*
Всё **я́сно**.	*Everything is clear* (*understood*).

(vi) A predicate adjective followed by a complement must be in the short form. Below are several adjectives commonly found in the predicative short form followed by various complements.

NOTE: All of the short forms below, except **до́лжен** *supposed to* and **ра́д** *glad (to),* have a corresponding long form.

Followed by an Infinitive

гото́в *ready to*

Мы́ **гото́вы** е́хать в аэропо́рт.	*We are ready to go to the airport.*

до́лжен *supposed to, must*

Она́ **должна́** позвони́ть на́м.	*She is supposed to call us.*

наме́рен *intend to*

Я́ **наме́рен** голосова́ть за него́.	*I intend to vote for him.*

ра́д *glad to*

Мы́ очень **ра́ды** ви́деть тебя́.	*We are very glad to see you.*

свобо́ден *free to*

Ты́ **свобо́дна** де́лать, что́ хо́чешь.	*You are free to do as you wish.*

спосо́бен *capable of*

О́н не **спосо́бен** поня́ть э́то.	*He is incapable of understanding that.*

скло́нен *inclined to*

Я́ **скло́нен** согласи́ться с ва́ми.	*I am inclined to agree with you.*

Followed by a Prepositional Phrase

бли́зок с (+ Instr.) *close to; intimate with*

О́н о́чень **бли́зок с** отцо́м.	*He is very close to his father.*
Она́ была́ **близка́ с** ни́м.	*She was intimate with him.*

винова́т в (+ Prep.); пе́ред (+ Instr.) *at fault, to blame for; guilty before*

Я́ винова́т во всём.	*I'm to blame for everything.*
О́н **винова́т в** то́м, что она́ ушла́.	*It is his fault that she left.*
О́н **винова́т пе́ред** жено́й.	*He did his wife wrong.*

гото́в к (+ Dat.); на (+ Acc.) *prepared/ready for*

Она́ **гото́ва к** экза́мену.	*She is prepared for the exam.*
О́н **гото́в на** всё.	*He is ready for anything* (i.e., *ready to resort to any measure*).

знако́м с (+ Instr.) *acquainted with*

Я́ хорошо́ **знако́м с** его́ рабо́той.	*I am well acquainted with his work.*

похо́ж на (+ Acc.) *similar to*

Она́ о́чень **похо́жа на** ма́му.	*She is very much like her mom.*

равноду́шен к (+ Dat.) *indifferent to*

О́н **равноду́шен к** поли́тике.	*He is indifferent to politics.*

серди́т на (+ Acc.) *angry at*

Она́ **серди́та на** меня́.	*She is angry at me.*

силён в (+ Prep.) *strong in, good at*

О́н **силён в** иностра́нных языка́х.	*He is good at foreign languages.*

согла́сен с (+ Instr.); на (+ Acc.) *agree with; agree to*

Я́ согла́сен с э́той иде́ей.	*I agree with this idea.*
Я́ не **согла́сен на** э́то.	*I do not agree to that.*

Followed by a Noun/Pronoun in an Oblique Case

благода́рен (+ Dat.) *grateful to*

Мы́ о́чень **благода́рны** ва́м.	*We are very grateful to you.*

бога́т (+ Instr.) *rich in*

Росси́я **бога́та** ре́ками и озёрами.	*Russia is rich in rivers and lakes.*

дово́лен (+ Instr.) *satisfied/pleased with*

Дире́ктор **дово́лен** на́шей рабо́той.	*The director is pleased with our work.*

досто́ин (+ Gen.) *worthy/deserving of*

Она́ **досто́йна** награ́ды.	*She deserves an award.*

по́лон (+ Gen.) *full of*

У́лицы бы́ли **полны́** наро́ду.	*The streets were full of people.*

пре́дан (+ Dat.) *devoted to*

О́н **пре́дан** свои́м де́тям.	*He is devoted to his children.*

9. Complete each of the following sentences with the correct long or short form(s) of the adjective in parentheses.

(тру́дный/тру́ден)
1. Э́то не ________________ зада́ча, но для него́ она́ бу́дет ________________.

(бога́тый/бога́т)
2. У него́ не́т мно́го де́нег, но о́н ________________ душо́й.

(дово́льный/дово́лен)
3. Мо́й дя́дя ве́чно не ________________, но моя́ тётя всегда́ ________________ всем.

(досто́йный/досто́ин)
4. О́н ________________ похвалы́.
5. Она́ ________________ же́нщина.

(пре́данный/пре́дан)
6. О́н доби́лся мно́гого в жи́зни, потому́ что бы́л ________________ своему́ де́лу.
7. Она́ лю́бящая ма́ть и ________________ жена́.

(по́лный/по́лон)
8. У на́с сейча́с ________________ до́м. Прие́хали все́ ро́дственники на пра́здник.
9. У меня́ до́м ________________ госте́й.

(свобо́дный/свобо́ден)
10. Она́ не ________________ пойти́ на конце́рт сейча́с.
11. Мы́ живём в ________________ стране́.

(бли́зкий/бли́зок)
12. Мои́ де́ти о́чень ________________ друг с дру́гом.
13. Они́ ________________ друзья́ и хорошо́ подде́рживают друг дру́га.

(винова́тый/винова́т)
14. О́н созна́лся, что ________________ в э́том.
15. Соба́ка смотре́ла на меня́ ________________ глаза́ми.

(спосо́бный/спосо́бен)
16. Я́ ________________ программи́ст, но я не ________________ реши́ть э́ту зада́чу.

(скло́нный/скло́нен)
17. Я́ ________________ пове́рить ему́.
18. Лю́дям, ________________ к депре́ссии, не рекоменду́ется смотре́ть э́тот фи́льм.

(гото́вый/гото́в)
19. Строи́тели сдаю́т де́сять ________________ домо́в в конце́ ме́сяца, и жи́тели ________________ въе́хать уже́ сейча́с.

(знако́мый/знако́м)
20. Я́ шёл по о́чень ________________ у́лице, но лю́ди мне́ бы́ли уже́ не ________________.

(похо́жий/похо́ж)
21. Э́ти де́вочки двойня́шки, но они́ не о́чень ________________ друг на дру́га.
22. У Ле́ны с ма́мой о́чень ________________ голоса́, и и́х ча́сто пу́тают по телефо́ну.

(си́льный/силён)
23. Она́ отли́чная пловчи́ха, и она́ та́кже ________________ в гимна́стике.
24. В э́той кома́нде е́сть и ________________, и сла́бые игроки́.

(равноду́шный/равноду́шен)
25. О́н пресле́дует её, но она́ ________________ к нему́.
26. Они́ ________________ лю́ди, и поэ́тому у ни́х не́т друзе́й.

(норма́льный/норма́лен)
27. Ка́к дела́? Всё ________________?
28. У ни́х ________________, стаби́льные отноше́ния.

(непоня́тный/непоня́тен)
29. Мо́жет бы́ть, э́то совреме́нно и аванга́рдно, но мне́ э́то ________________.
30. Для меня́ э́то тако́й ________________ предме́т.

Use of *какóй* vs. *какóв* and *такóй* vs. *такóв*

Corresponding to the long and short forms of adjectives are two different interrogative pronouns, **какóй** and **какóв** (**каковá**, **каковó**, **каковы́**) *what (sort of)*. The pronoun **какóй** agrees in gender, number, and case with the noun it modifies; the pronoun **какóв** is a short (caseless) form used only predicatively.

—**Какóй** óн студéнт?	*What kind of student is he?*
—Óн **у́мный** студéнт.	*He is a smart student.*
—**Какóв** óн?	*What is he like?*
—Óн **умён**.	*He is smart.*
—**Какóе** у вáс впечатлéние?	*What impression do you have?*
—У меня́ **хорóшее** впечатлéние.	*I have a good impression.*
—**Каковó** вáше мнéние о нём?	*What is your opinion of him?*
—По-мóему, óн спосóбный человéк.	*I think he is a capable person.*
Какáя сегóдня погóда?	*What is the weather like today?*
Каковá цéль э́того плáна?	*What is the goal of this plan?*
Каки́е у вáс плáны?	*What plans do you have?*
Каковы́ вáши плáны?	*What are your plans?*

NOTE: Both **какóй** and **какóв** function not only as interrogatives but also as relative pronouns (see Chapter 4); they also occur in exclamations, e.g., ***Какóй*** **у неё гóлос!** *What a voice she has!* ***Каковá*** **тáм прирóда!** *What (beautiful) nature there is there!*

Similarly, there are two different demonstrative pronouns, **такóй** and **такóв** (**таковá**, **таковó**, **таковы́**) *so, such*, corresponding to the long and short forms of adjectives. The pronoun **такóй**, like the long-form adjective it qualifies, can be used both attributively and predicatively. The short demonstrative **такóв**, however, is used only predicatively, and may precede the noun.

Óн **такóй** человéк, какóй нáм ну́жен.	*He is just the kind of person we need.*
Такáя шáпка мнé и нужнá.	*I need a hat just like that.*
Я́ хочу́ прожи́ть **таку́ю** жи́знь.	*I want to live such a life.*
Моё пальтó не **такóе**.	*My coat is not like that one.*
Óн **такóв**, кáк ты́ егó и опи́сывал.	*He is just as you described him.*
Таковá жи́знь.	*Such is life.*
Таковó моё мнéние.	*Such is my opinion.*
Таковы́ нáши впечатлéния.	*Such are our impressions.*

Use of *такóй* vs. *тáк* and *какóй* vs. *кáк*

The pronoun **такóй** may also be used to intensify the property or state denoted by the long form of the adjective, with which it agrees in gender, number, and case. The same intensifying function with the short form of adjectives (and adverbs) is carried by the adverb **тáк**.

Вáша дóчь **такáя** краси́вая.	*Your daughter is such a pretty girl.*
Онá **тáк** краси́ва в э́том плáтье.	*She is so pretty in that dress.*
Ты́ **такóй** дóбрый.	*You are such a kind man.*
Ты́ **тáк** дóбр к нáм.	*You are so kind to us.*
Расскáзы **таки́е** интерéсные.	*The stories are such interesting ones.*
Расскáзы **тáк** интерéсны.	*The stories are so interesting.*
Óн **тáк** интерéсно расскáзывает.	*He tells stories so interestingly.*

In exclamatory sentences the pronoun **како́й** *what* modifies the long form of the adjective, while the adverb **ка́к** *how* modifies the short form.

Кака́я она́ у́мная! *What a smart girl she is!*
Ка́к она́ умна́! *How smart she is!*

Како́й о́н молодо́й! *What a young man he is!*
Ка́к о́н мо́лод! *How young he is!*

Каки́е они́ глу́пые! *How foolish they are!*
Ка́к они́ глупы́! *How stupid they are!*

Ка́к э́то до́рого! *How expensive this is!*
Ка́к э́то хорошо́! *How good this is!*

10. Complete each of the following sentences with the correct form of the appropriate Russian pronoun or adverb: **како́й**, **тако́й**, **та́к**, **ка́к**, **како́в**, or **тако́в**.

1. ____________ (What) ва́ши наме́рения?
2. ____________ (What) у ва́с пла́ны на бу́дущее?
3. ____________ (Such) челове́ка на́до уважа́ть.
4. О́н ____________ (so) умён.
5. ____________ (What) же о́н идио́т!
6. О́н ника́к не спра́вится с э́тим. ____________ (Such) моё мне́ние.
7. Сего́дня бы́ло голосова́ние. ____________ (What) результа́т?
8. О́н ____________ (such) любе́зный челове́к.
9. ____________ (What) она́ краси́ва!

Adjectives Used as Nouns

Russian has a number of adjectives that can also function as nouns, e.g., **ру́сский** *a Russian.* Typically, such an "adjectival noun" arises from the omission of a "modified" noun, which, though absent, still determines its gender and number, e.g., **ру́сский** (**челове́к** *person*). Though they function as nouns, these words decline like any long-form adjective, e.g., **Она́ вы́шла за́муж за *ру́сского*** (Acc. Anim.) *She married a Russian.*

Following are some commonly used adjectival nouns grouped according to their omitted, but understood, nouns. Among the adjectives that refer to people, some have both a masculine and feminine form, while others occur only in the masculine; all adjectives referring to people can occur in the plural (e.g., **ру́сские** *Russians*).

NOTE: Some adjectival nouns can be used as an adjective or a noun (**Зде́сь живёт *ру́сская* семья́** *A Russian family lives here*; **Зде́сь живёт *ру́сская*** *A Russian* (f.) *lives here*); others have lost the ability to function as an adjective, and are used only as a noun (**портно́й** *tailor*).

NOTE: A large number of participles, which decline like adjectives, may also be used as nouns denoting people and things, e.g., **куря́щий** *a smoker,* **люби́мый** *loved one,* **ископа́емые** *minerals,* **отдыха́ющий** *vacationer.*

(мужчи́на *man* / же́нщина *woman*)
больно́й/больна́я *ill person* (m./f.)
взро́слый/взро́слая *grown-up, adult* (m./f.)
знако́мый/знако́мая *acquaintance* (m./f.)
ру́сский/ру́сская *Russian* (m./f.)

(челове́к *person*)
вое́нный *soldier*
портно́й *tailor*
рабо́чий *worker*
учёный *scientist*

(ко́мната *room*)
ва́нная *bathroom*
гости́ная *living room*
де́тская *nursery, children's room*
операцио́нная *operating room*
приёмная *reception room*
прихо́жая *entrance hall*
убо́рная *half bath*
столо́вая *dining room*

(ла́вка *shop*)
бу́лочная *bread store*
бутербро́дная *sandwich shop*
заку́сочная *snack bar*
конди́терская *candy store*
моло́чная *dairy shop*
парикма́херская *hair salon*
пивна́я *alehouse, pub*
шашлы́чная *shish kebab house*

(существо́ *being*)
живо́тное *(domestic) animal*
насеко́мое *insect*

(блю́до *dish*)
пе́рвое *first course*
второ́е *second course, entrée*
тре́тье *third course, dessert*
жарко́е *roasted meat dish*
сла́дкое *dessert*

(вино́ *wine*)
шампа́нское *champagne*

(молоко́ *milk*)
моро́женое *ice cream*

(вре́мя *time*)
настоя́щее *the present*
про́шлое *the past*
бу́дущее *the future*

(де́ньги *money*)
нали́чные *cash*
сверхуро́чные *overtime*
чаевы́е *gratuities, tip*

11. Complete each of the following sentences with the correct form of the adjectival noun in parentheses.

1. На́м ну́жен хле́б. Я́ сбе́гаю в ________________ (бу́лочная).
2. Мы́ встре́тились с дру́гом в ________________ (пивна́я).
3. Всё э́то тепе́рь в ________________ (про́шлое).
4. Мо́й дру́г до́лго жи́л в Росси́и и жени́лся на ________________ (ру́сская).
5. Э́тот вра́ч всегда́ забо́тится о свои́х ________________ (больно́й).
6. В Росси́и за поку́пки не пла́тят че́ками, а то́лько ________________ (нали́чные).
7. Я́ уважа́ю рабо́ты э́того ________________ (учёный).
8. Мои́ де́ти лю́бят ча́й с ________________ (моро́женое).
9. На столе́ стоя́ла буты́лка ________________ (шампа́нское).
10. У э́той де́вочки е́сть и ко́шка, и соба́ка. Она́ лю́бит ________________ (живо́тные).
11. Э́ти общежи́тия то́лько для ________________ (вое́нный).
12. В э́тот па́рк с аттракцио́нами дете́й впуска́ют то́лько со ________________ (взро́слый).

Neuter Singular Adjectives Used as Nouns

A number of Russian adjectives can be used as nouns with abstract meaning. Unlike the adjectival nouns discussed above, these are not related to some deleted, but still implicit, noun; rather, these occur in the neuter singular long form of the adjective with a very general, abstract meaning (**но́вое** *the new,* **ста́рое** *the old,* **мо́дное** *the stylish,* **совреме́нное** *the contemporary*): **Она́ лю́бит всё** ***мо́дное и совреме́нное*** *She loves everything stylish and contemporary.*

These neuter adjectival nouns often occur in the genitive case after words expressing quantity, such as **мно́го** *much,* **ма́ло** *little,* **ничего́** *nothing,* and others, when used in a "partitive" sense, e.g., **что́** *what (of),* **что́-нибудь** *something (of).*

Что́ **но́вого**?	*What's new?*
Ничего́ **но́вого**.	*Nothing's new.*
О́н сде́лал мно́го **хоро́шего**.	*He has done much good.*
Та́м бы́ло ма́ло **интере́сного**.	*There was little of interest.*
Хо́чется съе́сть что́-нибудь **сла́денького**.	*I feel like eating something sweet.*

NOTE: These abstract neuter adjectival nouns can also be of participle origin, e.g., the verb **забы́ть** *to forget* > **забы́тый** *forgotten* (passive participle and adjective) > **забы́тое** *what is forgotten* (adjectival noun), as in **Мне́ ну́жно вспо́мнить** ***забы́тое*** *I need to remember what I have forgotten.* Some other examples of departicipial adjectival nouns in **-ое** are **зарабо́танное** *what is earned,* **поте́рянное** *what is lost,* **укра́денное** *what is stolen* (cf. **кра́деное** *stolen goods,* which functions only as a noun).

12. Complete each of the following sentences with the correct form of the abstract adjectival noun based on the adjective in parentheses.

1. В Москве́ мно́го ________________ (ста́рый) и ________________ (но́вый).
2. Все́ де́ти лю́бят ________________ (сла́дкий).
3. О́н но́сит всё ________________ (дорого́й).
4. Мне́ ________________ (ста́рый) надое́ло.
5. О́н пропи́л всё ________________ (зарабо́танный).
6. В э́том не́т ничего́ ________________ (смешно́й).
7. Хо́чется чего́-нибудь съе́сть ________________ (о́стренький).
8. У меня́ от ________________ (о́стрый) живо́т боли́т.
9. Мне́ ну́жно вы́пить чего́-нибудь ________________ (горя́чий).
10. Альпини́сты взя́ли с собо́й то́лько ________________ (необходи́мый).

Possessive Adjectives

Possessive Adjectives of the Type *пти́чий*

A number of adjectives derived from nouns denoting animals, birds, and other living things have a possessive-relational meaning: **во́лк** *wolf* / **во́лчий** *wolf's,* **коро́ва** *cow* / **коро́вий** *cow's,* **лиса́** *fox* / **ли́сий** *fox's,* **медве́дь** *bear* / **медве́жий** *bear's,* **пти́ца** *bird* / **пти́чий** *bird's,* **соба́ка** *dog* / **соба́чий** *dog's.* Several of these possessive adjectives occur in idiomatic colloquial phrases, e.g., ***во́лчий*** **аппети́т** *voracious appetite,* ***медве́жий*** **у́гол** *godforsaken place,* ***соба́чий*** **хо́лод** *intense cold.* Possessive adjectives of this type follow the declensional pattern of **пти́чий** given in the table below.

	MASCULINE,	NEUTER	FEMININE	PLURAL
Nom.	пти́чий	пти́чье	пти́чья	пти́чьи
Acc. Inan. = Nom.	пти́чий	пти́чье	пти́чью	пти́чьи/
Anim. = Gen.	пти́чьего			пти́чьих
Gen.	пти́чьего		пти́чьей	пти́чьих
Prep.	о пти́чьем		о пти́чьей	о пти́чьих
Dat.	пти́чьему		пти́чьей	пти́чьим
Instr.	пти́чьим		пти́чьей	пти́чьими

NOTE: The ordinal adjective **тре́тий** *third* declines like **пти́чий** (see Chapter 6, page 193).

Possessive Adjectives with the Suffix *-ин*

Russian has a possessive adjective used in informal, colloquial style that is formed by adding the suffix **-ин** to the stem of nouns ending in **-а/-я**, most of which fall into two groups.

(a) *Family kinship terms*

ма́ма *mom*	ма́мин *mom's*	ба́бушка *grandma*	ба́бушкин *grandma's*
па́па *dad*	па́пин *dad's*	де́душка *grandpa*	де́душкин *grandpa's*
дя́дя *uncle*	дя́дин *uncle's*	тётя *aunt*	тётин *aunt's*

(b) *Familiar first names*

Алёша	Алёшин *Alyosha's*	Ми́ша	Ми́шин *Misha's*
Ва́ля	Ва́лин *Valya's*	Ната́ша	Ната́шин *Natasha's*
Ко́ля	Ко́лин *Kolya's*	Са́ша	Са́шин *Sasha's*
Ма́ша	Ма́шин *Masha's*	Та́ня	Та́нин *Tanya's*

NOTE: This familiar possessive adjective may also be based on nouns denoting pets and other animals, e.g., **ко́шка** *cat,* **соба́ка** *dog* (cf. also the pejorative **су́кин сы́н** *son of a bitch* from the possessive adjective based on the noun **су́ка** *bitch*).

The possessives in **-ин** agree in gender, number, and case with the modified noun. In the nominative case they have the endings of the short-form adjective.

MASCULINE -Ø	NEUTER -о	FEMININE -а	PLURAL -ы
Са́шин до́м *Sasha's house*	Са́шино письмо́ *Sasha's letter*	Са́шина кни́га *Sasha's book*	Са́шины ту́фли *Sasha's shoes*

However, the endings in the other cases reflect a mixed noun/adjective declension. The complete declension of the possessive adjective **Са́шин** is presented in the following table.

	MASCULINE,	NEUTER	FEMININE	PLURAL
Nom.	Са́шин	Са́шино	Са́шина	Са́шины
Acc. Inan. = Nom.	Са́шин	Са́шино	Са́шину	Са́шины
Anim. = Gen.	Са́шиного			Са́шиных
Gen.	Са́шиного		Са́шиной	Са́шиных
Prep.	о Са́шином		о Са́шиной	о Са́шиных
Dat.	Са́шиному		Са́шиной	Са́шиным
Instr.	Са́шиным		Са́шиной	Са́шиными

NOTE: A few of these possessive adjectives denoting animals have acquired the endings of the long-form adjective in all forms, e.g., **лéбедь** *swan* > **лебеди́ный** *swan's* (**«Лебеди́ное о́зеро»** *Swan Lake*).

Я́ ви́дел **ма́мину** подру́гу.	*I saw Mom's girlfriend.*
Портфе́ль лежи́т в **па́пином** кабине́те.	*The briefcase is in Dad's study.*
Мы́ лю́бим **ба́бушкины** пирожки́.	*We love Grandma's pirozhki.*
Она́ ушла́ бе́з **дя́диного** а́дреса.	*She left without her uncle's address.*
Я́ да́л письмо́ **тётиной** сосе́дке.	*I gave the letter to my aunt's neighbor.*

13. Complete each of the following sentences with the correct possessive form of the noun in parentheses.

1. Я́ взя́л э́ти де́ньги и́з ________________ (ма́ма) су́мки.
2. Письмо́ лежи́т на ________________ (па́па) столе́.
3. Я́ не могу́ найти́ ________________ (соба́ка) игру́шку.
4. Сего́дня мы́ встре́тили ________________ (Та́ня) дру́га.

Personal Names (Part II)

Family Names in *-ин* and *-ов, -ев/-ёв*

Russian family names in **-ин**, **-ов**, **-ев/-ёв** (**Пу́шкин**, **Че́хов**, **Турге́нев**) originally had a possessive meaning similar to that of the possessive adjectives of the type **Са́шин** described above. Family names formed with one of these suffixes, like the possessive adjectives in **-ин**, have a mixed declension: Some case forms are noun endings, while others are adjective endings. The following table gives the complete declension of the family name **Аксёнов**.

	MASCULINE	FEMININE	PLURAL
Nom.	Аксёнов	Аксёнова	Аксёновы
Acc. (Anim.)	Аксёнова	Аксёнову	Аксёновых
Gen.	Аксёнова	Аксёновой	Аксёновых
Prep.	об Аксёнове	об Аксёновой	об Аксёновых
Dat.	Аксёнову	Аксёновой	Аксёновым
Instr.	Аксёновым	Аксёновой	Аксёновыми

Family Names in *-ий* and *-о́й*

Russian family names in **-ий** and **-о́й** (**Го́рький**, **Чайко́вский**, **Толсто́й**) are declined like regular adjectives, e.g., **Я́ люблю́ му́зыку *Чайко́вского*** *I love Tchaikovsky's music*; **Э́та кни́га о *Чайко́вском*** *This book is about Tchaikovsky.*

Foreign family names follow the same pattern as foreign first names (page 66): Family names ending in a consonant decline like first-declension nouns if they denote males (e.g., **стихи́ *Ба́льмонта*** *Balmont's poetry*), but do not decline if they denote females (e.g., **биогра́фия Э́леонор *Ру́звельт*** *biography of Eleanor Roosevelt*). Foreign family names of both males and females that end in unstressed **-а**, **-я** normally do decline, especially if they are well known (**автопортре́т *Го́йи*** *self-portrait of Goya,* **пе́сни *Фра́нка Сина́тры*** *songs by Frank Sinatra*).

Comparison of Adjectives and Adverbs

The Degrees of Comparison

Adjectives can be used to compare the qualities of the nouns or pronouns they modify. Similarly, adverbs can be used to compare the manner in which verbal actions occur. Russian, like English, has three degrees of comparison: positive, comparative, and superlative.

The positive degree denotes the basic (uncompared) quality of a person or thing. Adjectives and adverbs are cited in the dictionary in the positive degree (*new, old, smart, quickly, slowly, interestingly*).

The comparative degree *compares* the qualities of two persons, things, or actions. In English, comparatives are formed in one of two ways: (i) by adding to the positive degree the ending *-er* (e.g., *newer, smarter, faster, slower*), or (ii) by combining the word *more* with the adjective or adverb (e.g., *more interesting, more interestingly*).

The superlative is used to indicate that, compared to several others, one person or thing possesses a quality to the *highest* degree or to a very great degree. The English superlative, like the comparative, is formed either by adding an ending (*-est*) to the positive degree (*newest, smartest, fastest, slowest*), or by combining the word *most* with the adjective or adverb (*most interesting, most interestingly*).

The methods of forming comparatives and superlatives in Russian are similar to those in English: They can be formed either by adding an ending to the adjective/adverb stem, producing a "simple comparative" and "simple superlative," or they can be formed with the Russian equivalent of English *more* and *most,* combined with the positive degree of the adjective. This method results in the "compound comparative" and "compound superlative," respectively.

Formation of the Compound Comparative

The compound comparative consists of two words, the indeclinable adverb **бóлее** *more* (or **мéнее** *less*) and the long form of the adjective, which agrees with the modified noun.

POSITIVE DEGREE	COMPOUND COMPARATIVE
нóвый *new*	бóлее нóвый дóм *newer house*
	бóлее нóвое здáние *newer building*
	бóлее нóвая машúна *newer car*
	бóлее нóвые райóны *newer neighborhoods*
дорогóй *expensive*	мéнее дорогóй костю́м *less expensive suit*
	мéнее дорогóе кольцó *less expensive ring*
	мéнее дорогáя кни́га *less expensive book*
	мéнее дороги́е джи́нсы *less expensive jeans*

The compound comparative can be formed from almost any adjective. A few adjectives, however, do not form a comparative with **бóлее**. The following four adjectives, for example, do not form a compound comparative, but they do have a related adjective with comparative meaning.

большóй *big*	бóльший *bigger*
мáленький *small*	мéньший *smaller*
плохóй *bad*	хýдший *worse* (OR *worst*)
хорóший *good*	лýчший *better* (OR *best*)

Они́ живýт в **бóльшем** дóме.	*They live in a bigger house.*
Мы́ сня́ли **мéньшую** квартиру.	*We rented a smaller apartment.*
Ктó из ни́х **лýчший** писáтель?	*Which of them is the better/best writer?*

A few other adjectives form a regular compound comparative with **бóлее**, and in addition have a special comparative (or superlative) adjective with a different sense.

POSITIVE DEGREE	COMPOUND/SPECIAL COMPARATIVES
молодо́й *young*	бо́лее молодо́й *younger* (in age) мла́дший *junior* (in rank) / *younger/youngest* (in one's family)
ста́рый *old*	бо́лее ста́рый *older* (in age) ста́рший *senior* (in rank) / *older/eldest* (in one's family)

О́н влюби́лся в **бо́лее молоду́ю** же́нщину. — *He fell in love with a younger woman.*

О́н **мла́дший** нау́чный сотру́дник. — *He is a junior research associate.*
Э́то моя́ **мла́дшая** сестра́. — *This is my younger/youngest sister.*

О́н купи́л **бо́лее ста́рый**, но наворо́ченный автомоби́ль. — *He bought an older automobile, but one that was "loaded" (with all the extras).*

Она́ **ста́рший** преподава́тель. — *She is a senior instructor.*
Э́то мо́й **ста́рший** бра́т. — *This is my older/eldest brother.*

высо́кий *high, tall*	бо́лее высо́кий *higher, taller* (in size) вы́сший *higher* (in status)
ни́зкий *low*	бо́лее ни́зкий *lower* (in size) ни́зший *lower* (in status)

Э́то **бо́лее высо́кая** гора́. — *This is a higher mountain.*
Институ́т—э́то **вы́сшее** уче́бное заведе́ние. — *An institute is a higher educational institution.*

Для дро́в испо́льзуйте **ни́зшие** сорта́ де́рева. — *For firewood use inferior kinds of wood.*

Use of the Compound Comparative

The compound comparative with **бо́лее** is used primarily in *attributive* position, that is, preceding the noun, with which it agrees in gender, number, and case.

Для мое́й спины́ ну́жен **бо́лее тве́рдый** матра́ц. — *For my back I need a firmer mattress.*
Я́ предпочита́ю **бо́лее мя́гкий** кли́мат. — *I prefer a milder climate.*
Э́тот костю́м сши́т для **бо́лее кру́пного** мужчи́ны. — *This suit is tailored for a larger man.*
Мы́ живём в **бо́лее но́вом** райо́не. — *We live in a newer area.*
Она́ зави́дует **бо́лее молоды́м** же́нщинам. — *She envies younger women.*
Она́ занима́ется с **бо́лее о́пытным** тре́нером. — *She practices with a more experienced trainer.*

14. Complete each of the following sentences with the correct form of the Russian comparative.

1. На э́тот ра́з преподава́тель да́л на́м ______________ (less difficult) зада́чу.
2. Я́ никогда́ не встреча́л ______________ (a more interesting) челове́ка.
3. Мы́ останови́лись в ______________ (more expensive) гости́нице.
4. Моя́ сестра́ лю́бит ______________ (higher) матема́тику.
5. Э́то оди́н из ______________ (newer) микрорайо́нов.
6. Мы́ говори́м о ______________ (more serious) дела́х.

7. Я́ познако́млю тебя́ с мои́м ______________________ (older) бра́том.
8. О́н предпочита́ет ______________________ (older) ви́на.
9. Тру́дно сказа́ть, кто́ из ни́х ______________________ (better) гитари́ст, они́ оба́ та́к хорошо́ игра́ют.
10. Чтóбы уви́деть мо́ре, на́м на́до взойти́ на ______________________ (higher) го́ру.
11. Ра́ньше мы́ жи́ли в ______________________ (smaller) кварти́ре.
12. Для э́той рабо́ты нужны́ ______________________ (younger) и си́льные ру́ки.

Formation of the Simple Comparative

The simple comparative consists of only one word, to which a comparative ending is added. The comparative forms of most Russian adjectives and adverbs have the ending **-ee** (**-ей** in poetic or colloquial style). For adjectives whose stem in the positive degree consists of two or more syllables, the stress normally remains on the same syllable in the comparative.

ADJECTIVE	ADVERB	COMPARATIVE
интере́сн-ый *interesting*	интере́сн-о	интере́сн-ее
краси́в-ый *beautiful*	краси́в-о	краси́в-ее
ме́дленн-ый *slow*	ме́дленн-о	ме́дленн-ее
осторо́жн-ый *careful*	осторо́жн-о	осторо́жн-ее
поле́зн-ый *useful, of benefit*	поле́зн-о	поле́зн-ее
серьёзн-ый *serious*	серьёзн-о	серьёзн-ее
споко́йн-ый *calm*	споко́йн-о	споко́йн-ее
удо́бн-ый *convenient*	удо́бн-о	удо́бн-ее

Adverbs of manner are derived from qualitative adjectives by adding to their stems the ending **-o** (**-e** to a few soft stems): **серьёзн-ый** *serious* / **серьёзн-о** *seriously,* **и́скренн-ий** *sincere* / **и́скренн-е** *sincerely.* These adverbs are usually identical to the neuter short form of the adjective.

If the stem of the adjective has only one syllable, or if the feminine short form is stressed, then the comparative ending is stressed **-е́е**, as shown in the following table.

LONG-FORM ADJECTIVE	ADVERB	SHORT-FORM FEMININE	COMPARATIVE
бы́стр-ый *fast*	бы́стр-о	быстр-а́	быстр-е́е
весёл-ый *cheerful*	ве́сел-о	весел-а́	весел-е́е
дли́нн-ый *long*	дли́нн-о	длинн-а́	длинн-е́е
мо́дн-ый *stylish*	мо́дн-о	модн-а́	модн-е́е
но́в-ый *new*	но́в-о	нов-а́	нов-е́е
тёпл-ый *warm*	тепл-о́	тепл-а́	тепл-е́е
тру́дн-ый *hard*	тру́дн-о	трудн-а́	трудн-е́е
у́мн-ый *smart*	умн-о́	умн-а́	умн-е́е
холо́дн-ый *cold*	хо́лодн-о	холодн-а́	холодн-е́е

A small number of adjectives form their comparatives using the ending **-e**, with the stress invariably on the syllable preceding this ending. All of these undergo some modification in the final consonant of the adjective/adverb stem. Certain changes to the stem-final consonant are regular and predictable. Among these regular changes are the following.

- Stems ending in **-г**, **-к**, **-х** change these consonants to **-ж**, **-ч**, **-ш**, respectively.

LONG-FORM ADJECTIVE	ADVERB	COMPARATIVE
дорог-ой *dear, expensive*	дорог-о	дорож-е
жарк-ий *hot*	жарк-о	жарч-е
строг-ий *strict*	строг-о	строж-е
громк-ий *loud*	громк-о	громч-е
мягк-ий *soft*	мягк-о	мягч-е
тих-ий *quiet*	тих-о	тиш-е

- Stems ending in the cluster **-ст** change the cluster to **-щ**.

LONG-FORM ADJECTIVE	ADVERB	COMPARATIVE
прост-ой *simple*	прост-о	прощ-е
толст-ый *thick*	толст-о	толщ-е
част-ый *frequent*	част-о	чащ-е
чист-ый *clean*	чист-о	чищ-е

The formation of some comparatives in **-е** entails other changes to the adjective/adverb stem that are irregular. These comparatives must be memorized.

близк-ий *close*	близк-о	ближ-е
высок-ий *tall*	высок-о	выш-е
глубок-ий *deep*	глубок-о	глубж-е
далёк-ий *far*	далек-о	дальш-е
дешёв-ый *inexpensive*	дёшев-о	дешевл-е
долг-ий *long*	долг-о	дольш-е
коротк-ий *short*	коротк-о	короч-е
лёгк-ий *easy*	легк-о	легч-е
молод-ой *young*	молод-о	молож-е (OR младше)
поздн-ий *late*	поздн-о	позж-е (OR позднее)
ранн-ий *early*	ран-о	раньш-е
редк-ий *rare*	редк-о	реж-е
сладк-ий *sweet*	сладк-о	слащ-е
стар-ый *old*	—	старше (comparing people) старее (comparing things)
широк-ий *wide*	широк-о	шир-е

Finally, a few adjectives have a simple comparative in **-е** that is a different word from the positive degree or the associated adverb.

хорош-ий *good*	хорош-о	лучш-е
плох-ой *bad*	плох-о	хуж-е
больш-ой *big*	много	больш-е
маленьк-ий *small*	мал-о	меньш-е

Use of the Simple Comparative

The simple comparative is almost always used predicatively after a linking verb. Simple comparatives are invariable, i.e., their form is constant regardless of the gender or number of the subject.

О́н вы́глядит **моло́же.**	*He looks younger.*
Она́ вы́глядит **моло́же.**	*She looks younger.*
Они́ вы́глядят **моло́же.**	*They look younger.*
Бы́ло жа́рко, но ста́ло **жа́рче.**	*It was hot, but it became hotter.*
Дни́ стано́вятся **длинне́е.**	*The days are getting longer.*
Э́тот ча́й **кре́пче.**	*This tea is stronger.*
О́н чу́вствует себя́ **лу́чше.**	*He feels better.*
Поезда́ тепе́рь хо́дят **ча́ще.**	*The trains now run more often.*

NOTE: In conversational Russian the simple comparative can also be used with attributive meaning. In this usage the comparative invariably follows the noun, and it generally occurs with the prefix **по-**, which adds the meaning "a little, slightly": **Покажи́те мне́ брю́ки *подеше́вле*** *Show me some slightly cheaper pants.*

Adverbs Used with Comparatives

Comparatives are often preceded by one of the following adverbs.

(a) **ещё** *still* (*even more*)

Она́ у́мная, но её подру́га **ещё умне́е.**	*She is smart, but her friend is even smarter.*

(b) **гора́здо, намно́го** *much*

На э́той рабо́те вы́ бу́дете получа́ть **гора́здо бо́льше.**	*In this job you will receive much more (money).*
Вчера́ бы́ло жа́рко, но сего́дня **намно́го жа́рче.**	*Yesterday it was hot, but today it is much hotter.*

(c) **Всё** preceding a comparative means "more and more." For greater emphasis the comparative may be repeated (as in the English translation).

Дни́ стано́вятся **всё коро́че.**	*The days are becoming shorter and shorter.*
На́ш сы́н пи́шет на́м **всё ре́же и ре́же.**	*Our son writes to us more and more rarely.*

15. Complete each of the following sentences with the correct form of the comparative of the underlined adjective or adverb.

1. В магази́не це́ны на фру́кты высо́кие, а на ры́нке они́ ещё ________________.
2. О́н зараба́тывает мно́го, а его́ дру́г гора́здо ________________.
3. Проду́кты уже́ и та́к бы́ли дороги́е, а сейча́с ста́ли ещё ________________.
4. О́н ча́сто е́здит в Петербу́рг, а в Москву́ ________________.
5. И́горь симпати́чный, а Вади́м ещё ________________.
6. Ра́ньше ты́ хорошо́ говори́л по-ру́сски, а тепе́рь ты́ говори́шь ещё ________________.
7. Э́тот до́м высо́кий, а то́т намно́го ________________.
8. Пе́рвая зада́ча лёгкая, а втора́я зада́ча гора́здо ________________.
9. О́н е́здит бы́стро, а его́ бра́т е́здит ещё ________________.
10. У меня́ действи́тельно по́черк плохо́й, но́ у моего́ отца́ ещё ________________.

Expressing the Second Term of a Comparison

In comparisons where the two terms being compared are explicitly stated, such as in *Viktor is smarter than Vadim, He speaks Russian better than he speaks German, It's warmer in Moscow than in St. Petersburg,* the Russian equivalent of English *than* is rendered in one of two ways.

1. In most instances, the conjunction **чём** is used (preceded by a comma). A construction with **чём** is *obligatory* when

   (a) the compound comparative is used.

Та́ня бо́лее серьёзная студе́нтка, **чём** Ма́ша.	*Tanya is a more serious student than Masha.*
Э́то бо́лее мо́дный га́лстук, **чём** то́т.	*This is a more stylish tie than that (tie).*

   NOTE: When, as in the two examples above, what follows **чём** is a noun or pronoun, the word must be in the *nominative* case.

   (b) the second term of the comparison is an indeclinable expression, such as an adverb, an infinitive, a prepositional phrase, or a clause.

   Adverb

Мне́ прия́тнее ходи́ть в кино́ вдвоём, **чём одному́**.	*It's more enjoyable to go to the movies with someone than alone.*

   Infinitive

Я́ люблю́ бо́льше ходи́ть, **чём бе́гать**.	*I like to walk more than to run.*

   Prepositional Phrase

Мне́ прия́тнее на мо́ре, **чём в гора́х**.	*It is more pleasant for me at the seashore than in the mountains.*

   Clause

Э́то доро́же, **чём я ду́мал**.	*This is more expensive than I thought.*

2. If the second term of the comparison is a declinable noun or pronoun, it may *optionally* be followed by **чём**; otherwise, it must be in the *genitive* case.

   (a) When **чём** is used, the nouns or pronouns being compared must be in the same case.

О́н зараба́тывает бо́льше, чём **я́**.	*He earns more than I do.*
Тебе́ даю́т бо́льше, чём **мне́**.	*They give more to you than to me.*
У **него́** бо́лее тёмные во́лосы, чём у **неё**.	*He has darker hair than she has.*

   (b) The *genitive* case can be used only after a simple predicative comparative, and only when the first term of the comparison is in the *nominative* case.

Ви́ктор умне́е **Вади́ма**.	*Viktor is smarter than Vadim.*
Ле́на вы́ше **Та́ни**.	*Lena is taller than Tanya.*
Тво́й костю́м модне́е **моего́**.	*Your suit is more stylish than mine.*
Му́ж ста́рше **жены́**.	*The husband is older than the wife.*
Э́та маши́на старе́е **то́й**.	*This car is older than that one.*

16. Answer each of the following questions, using the genitive of comparison where possible; otherwise use a construction with **че́м**.

MODEL Что́ бо́льше: деся́ток и́ли дю́жина? > Дю́жина бо́льше деся́тка.

1. Кака́я страна́ бо́льше: Росси́я и́ли Кита́й? ________________
2. Где́ холодне́е: в Торо́нто и́ли в Новосиби́рске? ________________
3. Како́й ме́сяц коро́че: октя́брь и́ли ноя́брь? ________________
4. Когда́ зде́сь тепле́е: в декабре́ и́ли в ма́е? ________________
5. Кто́ вы́ше: кенгуру́ и́ли жира́ф? ________________
6. Что́ да́льше от США: Пари́ж и́ли Ки́ев? ________________
7. Како́й шта́т ме́ньше: Нью-Йо́рк и́ли Теха́с? ________________
8. Како́й го́род старе́е: Санкт-Петербу́рг и́ли Москва́?
____
9. Кака́я маши́на доро́же: «Мерседе́с» и́ли «Москви́ч»?
____
10. Како́е о́зеро глу́бже: Мичига́н и́ли Байка́л? ________________
11. Что́ сла́ще: мёд и́ли со́к? ________________
12. Что́ кре́пче: конья́к и́ли шампа́нское? ________________
13. Что́ удо́бнее: печа́тать на компью́тере и́ли на пи́шущей маши́нке?
____
14. Что́ поле́знее: пи́ть ко́ка-ко́лу и́ли е́сть фру́кты?
____
15. Кака́я река́ длинне́е: Дне́пр и́ли Во́лга? ________________
16. Что́ ва́м ле́гче: говори́ть по-ру́сски и́ли чита́ть по-ру́сски?
____
17. Где́ веселе́е: на ле́кции и́ли на дискоте́ке? ________________
18. На чём е́здить быстре́е: на трамва́е и́ли на авто́бусе?
____

Other Expressions with Comparatives

Following are three common expressions containing comparatives.

1. **ка́к мо́жно ...** *as ... as possible*

Я́ приду́ домо́й **ка́к мо́жно скоре́е**.	*I will come home as soon as possible.*
О́н бежа́л **ка́к мо́жно быстре́е**.	*He ran as fast as possible.*
Сде́лай э́то **ка́к мо́жно лу́чше**.	*Do it as well as possible.*

2. **че́м ..., те́м ...** *the ...er, the ...er*

Че́м бо́льше ты́ занима́ешься, **те́м лу́чше** твои́ успе́хи.	*The more you study, the better your progress.*
Че́м скоре́е ты́ уберёшь ко́мнату, **те́м скоре́е** ты́ пойдёшь гуля́ть.	*The sooner you clean up your room, the sooner you can go have a good time.*
Че́м ста́рше мы́ стано́вимся, **те́м лу́чше** мы́ понима́ем дру́г дру́га.	*The older we become, the better we understand each other.*

3. **бóльше всегó** *most of all* (*more than anything else*)
   бóльше всéх *most of all* (*more than anyone else*)

These phrases are used as superlative adverbs. Similarly used are **лýчше всегó** *best of all* (*better than all other things*), **лýчше всéх** *best of all* (*better than all other people*).

Мóй сы́н лю́бит всé жáнры мýзыки: джáз, кáнтри, блю́з, но **бóльше всегó** он лю́бит рок-мýзыку.	*My son likes all types of music: jazz, country, blues, but most of all he likes rock music.*
Мнóгие ребя́та хорошó игрáют на гитáре, но Сáша игрáет **лýчше всéх**.	*Many of the guys play guitar well, but Sasha plays best of all.*

The Compound Superlative: Form and Use

The compound superlative consists of two words, the adjective **сáмый** *most* and the long form of the adjective that is being compared. Both adjectives decline, agreeing in gender, number, and case with the modified noun.

POSITIVE DEGREE	COMPOUND SUPERLATIVE
краси́вый	**сáмый** краси́вый гóрод *the most beautiful city*
	сáмое краси́вое óзеро *the most beautiful lake*
	сáмая краси́вая маши́на *the most beautiful car*
	сáмые краси́вые гóры *the most beautiful mountains*

Росси́я—**сáмая большáя** странá в ми́ре.	*Russia is the biggest country in the world.*
Кавкáзские гóры—э́то **сáмые высóкие** гóры в Росси́и.	*The Caucasus Mountains are the highest mountains in Russia.*
Сан Ди́его—оди́н из **сáмых краси́вых** городóв в США.	*San Diego is one of the most beautiful cities in the U.S.A.*

Note that sentences with the compound superlative often contain a phrase that defines the context within which someone or something, compared to others, is *the most* ..., e.g., in the sentences above: **в ми́ре** *in the world*, **в Росси́и** *in Russia*, **в США** *in the U.S.A.*

Another phrase, **из всéх (...)** *of all* ..., indicates the group of people or things out of which someone or something is distinguished as *the most....*

Из всéх нóвых гости́ниц, э́то **сáмая роскóшная**.	*Of all the new hotels, this is the most luxurious.*
Рóллс Рóйс—э́то **сáмая дорогáя маши́на** из всéх.	*Rolls-Royce is the most expensive car of all.*

17. Complete each of the following sentences with the correct form of the compound superlative in Russian.

1. Óзеро Байкáл—э́то ________________ (deepest) óзеро ми́ра.
2. Рекá Миссýри—э́то ________________ (the longest) рекá в США.
3. Сели́н Диóн—однá из ________________ (most popular) певи́ц в нáшей странé.
4. Учи́тель расскáзывал об Аля́ске, ________________ (the biggest) штáте США.
5. Я́ считáю егó моим ________________ (closest) дрýгом.

The Simple Superlative: Form and Use

The simple superlative is sometimes called the superlative of "high degree," since it often is used in the meaning "a most" (e.g., *a most important matter*). It is formed by adding the suffix **-ейш-** (and the soft ending **-ий**) to the stem of the long adjective.

POSITIVE DEGREE	SIMPLE SUPERLATIVE
ва́жн-ый *important*	важн-е́йший
вку́сн-ый *tasty*	вкусн-е́йший
глу́п-ый *stupid*	глуп-е́йший
но́в-ый *new*	нов-е́йший
у́мн-ый *smart*	умн-е́йший
интере́сн-ый *interesting*	интере́сн-ейший
тру́дн-ый *difficult*	трудн-е́йший

The suffix **-айш-** (and the ending **-ий**) is added to adjectives whose stem ends in the consonants **г**, **к**, **х**, and **ст**, which then change to **ж**, **ч**, **ш**, and **щ**, respectively.

стро́г-ий *strict*	строж-а́йший
вели́к-ий *great*	велич-а́йший
высо́к-ий *tall*	высоч-а́йший
кре́пк-ий *strong*	крепч-а́йший
ти́х-ий *quiet*	тиш-а́йший

The simple superlative is common in scientific and literary Russian; however, the same form is also used in colloquial Russian to express the speaker's personal impressions (***интере́снейшая*** **кни́га** *a most interesting book*, ***вкусне́йший*** **бо́рщ** *a very tasty borsch*).

The following two sentences illustrate the difference in meaning between the compound superlative (*the most …*) and the simple superlative, when the latter has the force of "high degree."

Би́лл Ге́йтс—**са́мый бога́тый** челове́к в ми́ре. — *Bill Gates is the richest man in the world.*

О́н **богате́йший** челове́к. — *He is an extremely rich man.*

A few other examples of the simple comparative follow.

«Преступле́ние и наказа́ние»—**серьёзнейший** рома́н. — *"Crime and Punishment" is a most serious novel.*

Пу́шкин—**велича́йший** ру́сский писа́тель. — *Pushkin is a very great Russian writer.*

Во́дка—**крепча́йший** напи́ток. — *Vodka is a very strong drink.*

18. Rewrite each of the following sentences, replacing the underlined compound superlative with a simple superlative.

MODEL У Вади́ма бы́л <u>са́мый интере́сный</u> докла́д. >
У Вади́ма бы́л интере́снейший докла́д.

1. Нью-Йорк—э́то <u>са́мый кру́пный</u> морско́й по́рт.

   ____

2. В э́том рестора́не подаю́т <u>са́мые вку́сные</u> пельме́ни.

   ____

3. Сибиряки́ счита́ются <u>са́мыми здоро́выми</u> людьми́.

   ____

4. Гора́ Эвере́ст—э́то <u>са́мая высо́кая</u> гора́.

____

5. Влади́мир Петро́в—<u>са́мый стро́гий</u> учи́тель.

____

Adverbs

Adverbs are indeclinable words that can modify a verb, adjective, noun, or another adverb. Note the following examples.

Modifying a Verb

писа́ть **хорошо́** *to write well*
чита́ть **вслу́х** *to read aloud*
рабо́тать **вме́сте** *to work together*
говори́ть **шёпотом** *to speak in a whisper*
идти́ **пешко́м** *to go on foot*

Modifying an Adjective

удиви́тельно хоро́ший *surprisingly good*
невероя́тно у́мный *incredibly smart*

Modifying a Noun

ша́г **вперёд** *a step forward*
езда́ **верхо́м** *riding horseback*

Modifying Another Adverb

о́чень хорошо́ *very well*
соверше́нно ве́рно *quite right*
кра́йне интере́сно *extremely interesting*

Adverbs can be classified according to their meaning. For example, the primary semantic groups of Russian adverbs are those referring to manner, time, place, and measure or degree.

Adverbs of Manner

Adverbs of manner answer the question **ка́к?** *how?* They are formed from adjectives of various types, as well as from nouns.

(a) One type of manner adverb is identical to the neuter short form of a qualitative adjective (some of these originated as past passive participles, e.g., **взволно́ванно** *excitedly*); most of these manner adverbs have the ending **-o**.

аккура́тно *neatly*
интере́сно *interestingly*
ме́дленно *slowly*
мо́дно *stylishly*
осторо́жно *carefully*
серьёзно *seriously*
хорошо́ *well*
умно́ *intelligently*

(b) Adverbs of manner are also formed from present active participles, or the adjectives derived from them, by adding the ending **-e** to the participle/adjective stem, e.g., **понима́ющ-ий** *understanding* > **понима́ющ-е** *understandingly.* These adverbs often correspond to English manner adverbs ending in *-ingly.*

бодря́ще *invigoratingly*
одобря́юще *approvingly*
осужда́юще *in a condemning way*
раздража́юще *irritatingly*
угрожа́юще *threateningly*
умоля́юще *imploringly*

(c) Adjectives with the suffix **-ск-** and **-цк-**, which do not have short forms, can derive adverbs by adding **-и** to the adjective stem, e.g., **дру́жеск-ий** *amicable* > **дру́жеск-и** *amicably.* Sometimes these adverbs occur with the hyphenated prefix **по-** in virtually the same meaning: **по-дру́жески** *like a friend.*

бра́тски, по-бра́тски *brotherly, like a brother*
де́тски, по-де́тски *childishly, like a child*
дура́цки, по-дура́цки *foolishly, like a fool*
челове́чески, по-челове́чески *humanly, like a human being*

(d) Adverbs prefixed in **по-** and ending in **-и** are derived from adjectives with the suffix **-ск-** that denote nationality, e.g., **ру́сск-ий** > **по-ру́сски** *in Russian* or *in the Russian style.*

по-англи́йски *in English*
по-кита́йски *in Chinese*
по-францу́зски *in French*

(e) Adverbs of manner are formed from the dative case of the masculine/neuter form of certain adjectives prefixed in **по-**, e.g., **но́вый** *new* > **по-но́вому** *in a new way.*

по-друго́му *in a different way, otherwise*
по-пре́жнему *as before*
по-ра́зному *in various ways*

(f) Following are a few examples of manner adverbs derived from nouns.

верхо́м *on horseback*
босико́м *barefoot*
пешко́м *on foot*
вслу́х *aloud*

19. Complete each of the following sentences with the Russian equivalent of the manner adverb on the right.

1. Она́ всегда́ о́чень ____________ одева́ется. *fashionably*
2. О́н выполня́ет рабо́ту ____________. *neatly*
3. Моя́ до́чь у́чится е́здить ____________. *on horseback*
4. О́н обня́л меня́ ____________. *like a brother*
5. Я́ бы отве́тил на э́тот вопро́с ____________. *in a different way*
6. Ка́ждый и́з на́с прореаги́ровал ____________. *in different ways*
7. О́н кивну́л ____________. *understandingly*
8. Па́па ____________ смотре́л на сы́на. *approvingly*
9. О́н е́л своё блю́до па́лочками, ____________. *in the Chinese style*
10. Учени́к чита́л поэ́му ____________. *aloud*
11. Вы́ ко мне́ всегда́ относи́лись ____________. *like a human being*
12. О́н ____________ помаха́л мне́ кулако́м. *threateningly*
13. Ничего́ не измени́лось, мы́ живём ____________. *as before*
14. На у́лице ско́льзко, на́до идти́ ____________. *carefully*
15. О́н о́чень ____________ расска́зывал о поéздке. *interestingly*
16. Ребёнок ____________ смотре́л на ма́му. *imploringly*
17. Де́ти бе́гали ____________ по двору́. *barefoot*

18. О́н вёл себя́ ________________. *like a fool*
19. Му́зыка звуча́ла ________________ гро́мко. *irritatingly*
20. Э́тот моро́з тако́й ________________-освежа́ющий. *invigoratingly*

Adverbs of Time

Adverbs of time answer questions such as **когда́?** *when?*, **ско́лько вре́мени? / на ско́лько вре́мени?** *how long?*, and **как ча́сто?** *how often?* Some of the most common adverbs of time are listed below.

Adverbs Answering the Question *когда?*

сего́дня *today*	неда́вно *recently*
за́втра *tomorrow*	ско́ро *soon*
послеза́втра *day after tomorrow*	наконе́ц *finally*
вчера́ *yesterday*	сра́зу *immediately*
позавчера́ *day before yesterday*	сейча́с *now, at the moment*
снача́ла *(at) first*	тепе́рь *now, nowadays*
пото́м *then (afterwards)*	ра́но *early*
тогда́ *then (at that time)*	по́здно *late*
давно́ *a long time ago*	во́время *on time*

The following adverbs referring to periods of the day, and the seasons, are all formed from the instrumental case of a noun, e.g., **у́тро** *morning* > **у́тром** *in the morning*, **весна́** *spring* > **весно́й** *in the spring*.

у́тром *in the morning*	весно́й *in the spring*
днём *during the day*	ле́том *in the summer*
ве́чером *in the evening*	о́сенью *in the fall*
но́чью *in the night*	зимо́й *in the winter*

20. Complete each of the following sentences with the Russian equivalent of the adverb(s) of time on the right.

1. Я́ обы́чно пью́ ко́фе то́лько ________________. *in the morning*
2. Моя́ ба́бушка ________________ иммигри́ровала в Аме́рику. *a long time ago*
3. Она́ ________________ рабо́тала портни́хой. *at that time*
4. Мы́ уезжа́ем в о́тпуск ________________. *day after tomorrow*
5. Па́па прие́хал из командиро́вки ________________. *day before yesterday*
6. ________________ мы́ пошли́ в кино́, а ________________ в кафе́. *first, afterwards*
7. В Аме́рике ________________ почти́ у ка́ждого е́сть моби́льник. *now*
8. Ма́ма ________________ на ку́хне, бесе́дует с подру́гой. *now*
9. Мы́ отдыха́ем ________________, когда́ пого́да тёплая. *in the summer*
10. А́втор три го́да писа́л кни́гу, и ________________ зако́нчил её. *finally*
11. ________________ на́ша до́чь хо́дит в де́тский са́д. *during the day*
12. На́м о́чень нужна́ твоя́ по́мощь, ты́ ________________ придёшь? *soon*
13. Приро́да у на́с ________________ про́сто прекра́сная. *in the spring*
14. Лу́чше ________________, чём никогда́. *late*
15. Па́па та́к уста́л, что лёг на дива́н и ________________ засну́л. *immediately*
16. О́н не опа́здывает на рабо́ту, о́н всегда́ прихо́дит ________________. *on time*
17. Кто́ ________________ ложи́тся и ________________ встаёт, здоро́вье, бога́тство и у́м наживёт. *early, early*

Adverbs Answering the Question *ско́лько вре́мени?*

до́лго *(for) a long time*
давно́ *for a long time* (*and continuing up to a defined point*)

Adverbs Answering the Question *на ско́лько вре́мени?*

надо́лго *for a long time* (*following the completion of an action*)
навсегда́ *forever*

21. Complete each of the following sentences with the Russian equivalent of the adverb of time on the right.

1. Она́ влюби́лась ______________________. *forever*
2. Мы́ ______________________ его́ жда́ли, и, наконе́ц-то, о́н пришёл. *a long time*
3. Моя́ до́чка лю́бит ______________________ мы́ться в ва́нне. *a long time*
4. Мы́ уже́ ______________________ живём в Вашингто́не. *a long time*
5. О́н к на́м прие́хал ______________________, наве́рное, на го́д. *for a long time*

Adverbs Answering the Question *ка́к ча́сто?*

всегда́ *always*
иногда́ *sometimes*
обы́чно *usually*
ре́дко *rarely*

22. Complete each of the following sentences with the Russian equivalent of the adverb of time on the right.

1. Мы́ ______________________ ра́ды тебя́ ви́деть. *always*
2. Мы́ ______________________ обе́даем в рестора́не, сли́шком до́рого. *rarely*
3. Я́ ______________________ бе́гаю в спортза́ле. *usually*
4. О́н лю́бит джа́з, но ______________________ о́н слу́шает и рок-му́зыку. *sometimes*

Other Important Temporal Adverbs

уже́ *already, as early as*
уже́ не, бо́льше не *no longer*
ещё (всё ещё) *still*
ещё не *not yet*

23. Complete each of the following sentences with the Russian equivalent of the adverb of time on the right.

1. Мо́жете меня́ поздра́вить, я́ ______________________ курю́. *no longer*
2. К сожале́нию, мо́й му́ж ______________________ бо́лен. *still*
3. Е́й всего́ 18 ле́т, а она́ ______________________ выхо́дит за́муж. *already*
4. О́н до́лго реша́ет зада́чу, но́ ______________________ реши́л. *not yet*
5. Она́ ______________________ вчера́ зако́нчила писа́ть письмо́. *as early as*

Adverbs of Place

Adverbs of place are divided into those that indicate location and answer the question **где́?** *where?* and those that indicate direction and answer the question **куда́?** *where to?* or **отку́да?** *from where?* The choice of adverb, therefore, normally depends on whether a sentence contains a verb of location or a verb of motion/direction.

The following list contains many of the most commonly used adverbs of place expressing either location or direction.

LOCATION	DIRECTION (TO)	DIRECTION (FROM)
где́? *where?*	куда́? *where to?*	отку́да? *from where?*
зде́сь *here*	сюда́ *here*	отсю́да *from here*
та́м *there*	туда́ *there*	отту́да *from there*
везде́, всю́ду *everywhere*	—	отовсю́ду *from everywhere*
до́ма *at home*	домо́й *home*	—
сле́ва *on the left*	нале́во *to the left*	—
спра́ва *on the right*	напра́во *to the right*	—
впереди́ *in front, ahead*	вперёд *forward, ahead*	—
позади́, сза́ди *behind*	наза́д *back(ward)*	—
наверху́ *above*	наве́рх *up(ward)*	све́рху *from above*
внизу́ *below*	вни́з *down(ward)*	сни́зу *from below*
внутри́ *inside*	вну́трь *inside*	изнутри́ *from inside*
снару́жи *outside*	нару́жу *outside*	снару́жи *from outside*

24. Complete each of the following sentences with the Russian equivalent of the adverb(s) of location or direction on the right.

1. Вчера́ я бы́л бо́лен и оста́лся ________. *at home*
2. Води́тель повора́чивал маши́ну ________ и ________. *to the left, to the right*
3. Я́ спроси́л де́вушку, ________ она́. *where from*
4. Мы́ подошли́ к кра́ю скалы́ и посмотре́ли ________. *down*
5. Пришла́ весна́, и ________ зацвели́ цветы́. *everywhere*
6. Э́то окно́ открыва́ется ________. *to the outside*
7. ________ на́ша да́ча окра́шена в си́ний цве́т. *on the outside*
8. На съе́зд прие́хали учёные ________. *from everywhere*
9. Мы́ подняли́сь ________ по ле́стнице. *up*
10. Ма́льчик за́пер две́рь ________. *from inside*
11. О́н спусти́лся на ли́фте ________ на пе́рвый эта́ж. *down*
12. Нельзя́ смотре́ть ________, на́до смотре́ть ________. *back, forward*
13. Мы́ подняли́сь на́ гору и ________ уви́дели о́зеро. *from above*
14. Охо́тники нашли́ пещéру и заглянýли ________. *inside*
15. Я́ положи́л журна́лы ________ на по́лку. *here*
16. О́н рабо́тает ________, ________ я́ рабо́тал ра́ньше. *there, where*
17. Когда́ о́н е́здит в маши́не, он во́зит дете́й ________. *behind*
18. У меня́ ________ ещё мно́го рабо́ты. *ahead*
19. По́сле рабо́ты я пошёл пря́мо ________. *home*
20. У э́той маши́ны зеркала́ за́днего ви́да ________ и ________. *on the left, on the right*

Adverbs of Measure or Degree

Adverbs of measure or degree answer questions such as **ско́лько?** *how much/many?* and **в како́й сте́пени?** *to what degree?* Some of the most common of these adverbs are listed below.

о́чень *very, very much*	слегка́ *slightly*
та́к *so*	достато́чно *sufficiently*
мно́го *a lot, very much*	совсе́м *quite*
ма́ло *little*	соверше́нно *absolutely*
немно́го *a little*	сли́шком *too*
чу́ть (чуть-чу́ть) *a tiny bit*	почти́ *almost, nearly*

NOTE: One must be careful in choosing the correct adverb to express English *much, a lot,* or *very much,* which can be rendered in Russian both by **очень** and by **много**. These two adverbs, however, are not interchangeable: When used to modify a verb, **очень** refers to the intensity of an action (answering the question **в како́й сте́пени?**), whereas **мно́го** refers to quantity (answering the question **ско́лько?**).

Он **о́чень** лю́бит её и **мно́го** де́лает для неё.	*He loves her very much and does (very) much for her.*

25. Complete each of the following sentences with the Russian equivalent of the adverb of measure or degree on the right.

1. Я́ бы́л ________ за́нят, что не успе́л пообе́дать. *so*
2. Э́та студе́нтка пи́шет по-ру́сски ________ аккура́тно. *very*
3. Мо́й оте́ц дире́ктор компа́нии и ________ рабо́тает. *a lot*
4. Ты́ ________ гото́ва? На́м пора́ идти́ в теа́тр. *almost*
5. Я́ удиви́лся, что за все́ э́ти го́ды о́н та́к ________ измени́лся. *little*
6. Я́ ________ бою́сь, что Са́ше не понра́вится но́вая шко́ла. *a little*
7. Я́ согла́сен с ва́ми, вы́ ________ пра́вы! *absolutely*
8. Пиро́г тако́й вку́сный! Да́й мне́ ________ побо́льше. *a tiny bit*
9. Вчера́ о́н бы́л бо́лен, а сего́дня о́н ________ здоро́в. *quite*
10. Она́ ________ умна́, что́бы э́то поня́ть. *sufficiently*
11. Не покупа́й э́тот костю́м, о́н ________ до́рого сто́ит. *too*
12. Жа́лко! Э́то мя́со ________ пережа́рено. *slightly*

Indefinite Adverbs

Adverbs of place, time, and manner, as well as other adverbs, can occur with the particles **-то** and **-нибудь** to form indefinite adverbs.

Place			
Location	где́? *where?*	где́-то *somewhere*	где́-нибудь *somewhere*
Direction	куда́? *where?*	куда́-то *somewhere*	куда́-нибудь *somewhere*
Time	когда́? *when?*	когда́-то *once, at one time*	когда́-нибудь *ever, at any time*
Manner	ка́к? *how?*	ка́к-то *somehow*	ка́к-нибудь *somehow (or other)*
Cause	почему́? *why?*	почему́-то *for some reason*	почему́-нибудь *for any reason*

The meanings that the particles **-то** and **-нибудь** give to adverbs are the same as those given to indefinite pronouns (**кто́-то** *someone,* **кто́-нибудь** *someone/anyone,* etc.) described in Chapter 4 (page 134). Also, the contexts for use of adverbs and pronouns in **-то** and **-нибудь** are the same. To review those contexts briefly, forms in **-то** are used primarily in statements in the past tense and in sentences with nonrepeated actions in the present tense; forms in **-нибудь** are used in many more sentence types: in questions, after imperatives, in sentences expressed in the future tense, as well as in those expressing repeated actions in the present tense.

—Они́ **где́-нибудь** отдыха́ли про́шлым ле́том?	*Did they vacation anywhere last summer?*
—Да́, они́ **где́-то** отдыха́ли, но я́ не по́мню где́.	*They vacationed somewhere, but I don't remember where.*
—Ле́на **куда́-нибудь** е́дет на кани́кулы?	*Is Lena going anywhere for the holidays?*
—Я́ не зна́ю, е́дет ли она́ **куда́-нибудь**.	*I don't know if she is going anywhere.*
—Вы́ **когда́-нибудь** бы́ли в Нью-Йо́рке?	*Have you ever been to New York?*
—Да́, я́ **когда́-то** бы́л в Нью-Йо́рке с роди́телями.	*Yes, I was once in New York with my parents.*

26. Complete each of the following sentences with the Russian equivalent of the indefinite adverb on the right.

1. Ты́ до́лжен за́втра ________________ е́хать? *somewhere*
2. В де́тстве ба́бушка жила́ ________________ на Украи́не. *somewhere*
3. На́м ________________ уда́стся э́то сде́лать. *somehow*
4. Е́сли ты́ ________________ не смо́жешь прийти́, то позвони́. *for any reason*
5. Положи́ свои́ ве́щи ________________. *anywhere*
6. Пойдём ________________ погуля́ем. *somewhere*
7. О́н приезжа́л к на́м ________________ давно́. *once*
8. Она́ ________________ не пришла́ на рабо́ту. *for some reason*
9. О́н ________________ спра́вился с тру́дной ситуа́цией. *somehow*
10. Мы́ э́то ку́пим ________________ в сле́дующем году́. *sometime*

Negative Adverbs

There are two types of negative adverbs, those with the prefix **ни-** (e.g., **никогда́** *never*) and those with the stressed prefix **не́-** (e.g., **не́когда** *there is no time*).

1. Negative adverbs may be formed by prefixing **ни-** to certain interrogative adverbs, as shown below.

ADVERB	NEGATIVE ADVERB
где́? *where?*	нигде́ *nowhere*
куда́? *where (to)?*	никуда́ *(to) nowhere*
когда́? *when?*	никогда́ *never*
ка́к? *how?*	ника́к *in no way*
ско́лько? *how much?*	ниско́лько *not at all*

Negative adverbs in **ни-** are used in personal sentences, that is, with a subject in the nominative case. A sentence with a negative adverb of this type requires a finite verb form preceded by the negative particle **не**, which results in a construction with a "double negative" (see negative pronouns **никто́**, **ничто́** in Chapter 4, page 136).

О́н **нигде́ не** рабо́тает.	*He doesn't work anywhere.*
Мы́ **никуда́ не** ходи́ли.	*We didn't go anywhere.*
Она́ та́м **никогда́ не** была́.	*She has never been there.*
Я́ ниско́лько не уста́л.	*I'm not at all tired.*

2. Negative adverbs with the prefix **не́-** are formed from some of the same adverbs, as shown below.

ADVERB	NEGATIVE ADVERB
где́? *where?*	не́где *there is no place*
куда́? *where?*	не́куда *there is no place (to go)*
когда́? *when?*	не́когда *there is no time*
заче́м? *what for?*	не́зачем *there is no point*

Adverbs in **не́-** are used just like pronouns in **не́-** (e.g., **не́кого** *there is no one*; see page 138): They occur in impersonal sentences that either have no subject or have a logical subject in the dative case; the verb is in the infinitive form, and past and future tenses are expressed by **бы́ло** and **бу́дет**, respectively.

Не́где бу́дет спа́ть.	*There will be no place to sleep.*
Не́куда бы́ло се́сть.	*There was no place to sit down.*
Мне́ **не́когда** писа́ть.	*There is no time for me to write.*
Тебе́ **не́зачем** идти́ туда́.	*There is no need for you to go there.*

27. Answer each of the following questions, using a sentence with the appropriate negative adverb.

MODELS —Когда́ ты́ чита́л э́тот рома́н? > —Я́ никогда́ не чита́л э́тот рома́н.

—Когда́ на́м встре́титься с ни́м? > —Ва́м не́когда встре́титься с ни́м.

1. —Куда́ мне́ пойти́ сего́дня ве́чером? ____________________
2. —Куда́ ты́ пойдёшь по́сле semина́ра? ____________________
3. —Где́ же на́м рабо́тать? ____________________
4. —Где́ мы́ бу́дем рабо́тать? ____________________
5. —Заче́м ему́ чита́ть э́ту кни́гу? ____________________
6. —Ка́к о́н спра́вится с э́тим? ____________________

CHAPTER 6

Numbers, Dates, Time

Numbers

There are three classes of numbers in Russian: cardinal, collective, and ordinal. All three classes decline.

Cardinal Numbers

Cardinal numbers, such as 1, 20, and 500, are used in counting, and in general are used to indicate quantity. The nominative-case forms of the cardinal numbers are as follows.

0	но́ль/ну́ль	16	шестна́дцать	300	три́ста
1	оди́н, одно́, одна́, одни́	17	семна́дцать	400	четы́реста
2	два́/две́	18	восемна́дцать	500	пятьсо́т
3	три́	19	девятна́дцать	600	шестьсо́т
4	четы́ре	20	два́дцать	700	семьсо́т
5	пя́ть	21	два́дцать оди́н	800	восемьсо́т
6	ше́сть	30	три́дцать	900	девятьсо́т
7	се́мь	40	со́рок	1 000	ты́сяча
8	во́семь	50	пятьдеся́т	1 001	ты́сяча оди́н
9	де́вять	60	шестьдеся́т	2 000	две́ ты́сячи
10	де́сять	70	се́мьдесят	5 000	пя́ть ты́сяч
11	оди́ннадцать	80	во́семьдесят	1 000 000	миллио́н
12	двена́дцать	90	девяно́сто	2 000 000	два́ миллио́на
13	трина́дцать	100	сто́	5 000 000	пя́ть миллио́нов
14	четы́рнадцать	101	сто́ оди́н	1 000 000 000	миллиа́рд/биллио́н
15	пятна́дцать	200	две́сти	2 000 000 000	два́ миллиа́рда

NOTE: Several numbers are an amalgam of two or more individual elements. The numbers 11–19 are derived forms that consist of three elements: a number 1–9 (e.g., **оди́н-** *one*), **-на-** *on,* and **-дцать** (a contraction of **де́сять** *ten*): **оди́н-на-дцать** *eleven,* literally, "one-on-ten." The numbers 20 and 30 are derived from the two elements **два́-дцать**, **три́-дцать**, that is, "two tens," "three tens." And the numbers 300 and 400 are an amalgam of **три́** *three* or **четы́ре** *four* and **ста** (the genitive singular of **сто́** *hundred*): **три́ста**, **четы́реста**; similarly formed are 500, 600, 700, 800, and 900, e.g., **пятьсо́т** (**пя́ть** + **сот**, the genitive plural of **сто́**).

NOTE: The numbers 5–20 and 30 all end in the soft sign **-ь** (**пя́ть**, **ше́сть**, **два́дцать**, **три́дцать**). The numbers 50, 60, 70, 80, and 500, 600, 700, 800, 900 all have the soft sign in the middle of the word, separating its component parts (**пятьдеся́т**, **шестьдеся́т**, **пятьсо́т**, **шестьсо́т** … **девятьсо́т**).

NOTE: Any numbers higher than 20 that end in 1–9 (e.g., 21, 33, 45, 101, 542) are compounds formed by two or more words written separately: **двáдцать оди́н** *twenty-one,* **три́дцать три́** *thirty-three,* **сóрок пя́ть** *forty-five,* **стó оди́н** *hundred and one,* **пятьсóт сóрок двá** *five hundred and forty-two.*

Use of *нóль/нýль* (*0*)

The masculine nouns **нóль** and **нýль** *nought, nil, zero* are end-stressed (e.g., **Нáм пришлóсь начáть с *нуля́*** *We had to start from zero/scratch*), and are followed by the genitive case (e.g., **В э́той óбласти у негó *нóль* знáний** *He has zero knowledge in this field*). Though synonymous, these nouns tend to have their own spheres of use: **Нýль** is used, for example, to express temperature at *zero* degrees, while **нóль** is used to indicate *zero* in telephone numbers, in game scores, and in expressing the time of an event at a precise hour using the 24-hour clock.

Температýра упáла ни́же **нуля́**.	*The temperature fell below zero.*
Мóй телефóн: 251-03-05 (двéсти пятьдеся́т оди́н **нóль** три́ **нóль** пя́ть).	*My telephone number is 251-03-05.*
Игрá окóнчилась со счётом 7:0 (сéмь: **нóль**).	*The game ended with a score of seven to nothing.*
Пóезд отхóдит в пятнáдцать **нóль-нóль**.	*The train departs at fifteen hundred (15:00).*

Declension and Use of 1

The number **оди́н** *one* takes the same endings as the demonstrative pronoun **э́тот** (page 119). The complete declension of **оди́н** is presented in the following table.

	MASCULINE,	NEUTER	FEMININE	PLURAL
Nom.	оди́н	однó	однá	одни́
Acc. Inan.	оди́н	однó	однý	одни́
Anim.	одногó			одни́х
Gen.	одногó		однóй	одни́х
Prep.	об однóм		об однóй	об одни́х
Dat.	одномý		однóй	одни́м
Instr.	одни́м		однóй	одни́ми

NOTE: The medial vowel **-и-** that occurs in the masculine nominative and accusative inanimate singular (**оди́н**) is omitted in all other forms.

NOTE: When counting up from one, Russians use the word **рáз** instead of **оди́н**, e.g., **рáз, двá, три́ ...** *one, two, three....*

The number "one" is a modifier, which changes its form to agree with the masculine, feminine, or neuter gender, as well as number and case, of the modified noun.

У нáс в семьé **оди́н сы́н**, **однá дóчка** и **однó домáшнее живóтное**.	*In our family we have one son, one daughter, and one pet.*
В киóске óн купи́л **оди́н конвéрт** и **однý мáрку**.	*At the kiosk he bought one envelope and one stamp.*
Дéти ýчатся считáть от **одногó** до двадцати́.	*The children learn to count from one to twenty.*

In compound numbers ending in *one* (e.g., 21, 31, 41), agreement is normally in the singular (but see below on uses of *one* in the plural).

В э́той гру́ппе два́дцать **оди́н** студе́нт.	*There are twenty-one students in this group.*
Я́ заказа́л для студе́нтов два́дцать **одну́** кни́гу.	*I ordered twenty-one books for the students.*

Other Meanings of *оди́н*

In addition to its basic meaning "one," **оди́н** may also be used in the following meanings.

(a) *a, a certain*

У меня́ е́сть **оди́н** знако́мый, кото́рый ра́ньше жи́л в Сиби́ри.	*I have a friend who used to live in Siberia.*

(b) *alone, by oneself*

Она́ живёт **одна́**.	*She lives alone.*
Ему́ тру́дно жи́ть **одному́**.	*It is difficult for him to live alone.*
Нельзя́ оставля́ть младе́нца **одного́**.	*One can't leave a baby alone.*

(c) *the same*

Мы́ учи́лись в **одно́й** шко́ле.	*We studied in the same school.*
Мы́ сиде́ли за **одни́м** столо́м.	*We sat at the same table.*

(d) *only*

Оди́н Бо́г зна́ет!	*God only knows!*

Use of *оди́н* in the Plural

It is important to note that in all of its meanings, **оди́н** may be used in the plural. For example, when used to modify a noun that occurs only in the plural (e.g., **часы́** *watch*), the plural form of "one" is required.

У меня́ то́лько **одни́** часы́.	*I have only one watch.*
На столе́ бы́ли **одни́** но́жницы.	*There was one pair of scissors on the table.*

Note the following example of the plural of **оди́н** in the meaning "only (nothing but)."

На таре́лке оста́лись **одни́** кро́шки.	*Nothing but crumbs remained on the plate.*

Also, **оди́н** occurs in the expression **оди́н … друго́й …** *one … the other …*, and in the plural form of this expression: **одни́ … други́е …** *some … others…*

У ни́х два́ сы́на: **оди́н** журнали́ст, а **друго́й** бизнесме́н.	*They have two sons; one is a journalist, and the other is a businessman.*
Одни́ студе́нты живу́т в общежи́тиях, а **други́е** живу́т до́ма у роди́телей.	*Some students live in dormitories, while others live at home with their parents.*

1. Complete each of the following sentences with the correct form of **оди́н**.

1. То́лько о́н _______________ мо́жет реши́ть, что́ де́лать.
2. Ко дню́ рожде́ния до́чери ма́ма купи́ла то́рт и два́дцать _______________ свечу́.
3. Мы́ заказа́ли ра́зные блю́да: _______________ мясны́е, а други́е вегетариа́нские.
4. Мы́ бы́ли в Москве́ то́лько _______________ неде́лю.
5. Ты́ молоде́ц! В дикта́нте ты́ не сде́лал ни _______________ оши́бки.
6. Бы́ло те́сно, но мы́ все́ помести́лись в _______________ маши́не.
7. У меня́ две́ сестры́: _______________ рабо́тает врачо́м, а друга́я учи́тельницей.
8. У него́ в ко́мнате бы́ли _______________ кни́ги: они́ бы́ли везде́, да́же на полу́.
9. Я́ слы́шал об _______________ челове́ке, кото́рый излечи́лся от э́той боле́зни.
10. Мы́ с Вади́мом из _______________ го́рода.

Declension and Use of 2, 3, and 4

The number *two* has two gender forms: **два́** when followed by a masculine or neuter noun, and **две́** when followed by a feminine noun. The numbers *three* **три́** and *four* **четы́ре** (and higher) have only one form for all genders. The full declensions for *two, three,* and *four* are given in the following table.

	2		3	4
Nom.	два́ (m./n.)	две́ (f.)	три́	четы́ре
Acc. Inan. = Nom.	два́, две́		три́	четы́ре
Anim. = Gen.	двух		трёх	четырёх
Gen.	дву́х		трёх	четырёх
Prep.	о двух		о трёх	о четырёх
Dat.	дву́м		трём	четырём
Instr.	двумя́		тремя́	четырьмя́

Use of the Numbers 2, 3, and 4 Followed by a Noun

(a) In the nominative and inanimate accusative

The numbers **два́/две́**, **три́**, and **четы́ре** (including compounds ending in these numbers) take the genitive singular of the following noun, *when the numbers themselves are either in the nominative or inanimate accusative.*

У меня́ **два́ бра́та** и **две́ сестры́**.	*I have two brothers and two sisters.*
В э́той гру́ппе **два́дцать два́ челове́ка**.	*In this group there are twenty-two people.*
В э́том авто́бусе помеща́ется **три́дцать три́ пассажи́ра**.	*This bus holds thirty-three passengers.*
Мы́ ви́дели **три́ авто́буса** и **четы́ре маши́ны**.	*We saw three buses and four cars.*

(b) In the animate accusative

When **два́/две́**, **три́**, or **четы́ре** modifies an *animate* noun in the accusative case, the "animate accusative" rule applies, i.e., the accusative of both the number and the noun takes the form of the genitive, with the modified noun in the *plural.*

Мы́ ви́дели **дву́х ма́льчиков** и **трёх де́вочек**.	*We saw two boys and three girls.*

However, in compound numbers ending in **два́/две́**, **три́**, or **четы́ре** the "animate accusative" rule does *not* apply: The number is in the form of the accusative that is identical to the nominative, and the animate noun following the number is in the *genitive singular.*

На де́нь рожде́ния мы́ пригласи́ли **два́дцать два́ малыша́**.	*We invited twenty-two kids to the birthday party.*

(c) In the oblique cases

When the number 2, 3, or 4 modifies a noun phrase in an "oblique" case (i.e., genitive, prepositional, dative, or instrumental), the number must be in the same case as the modified noun, which is in the *plural.*

Genitive

Она́ прожила́ в Москве́ о́коло **четырёх ме́сяцев**.	*She lived in Moscow about four months.*

Prepositional

Я́ говорю́ об э́тих **дву́х но́вых студе́нтах**.	*I'm talking about these two new students.*

Dative

Они́ подошли́ к **трём де́вушкам**.	*They walked up to the three girls.*

Instrumental

Она́ владе́ет **тремя́ языка́ми**.	*She has command of three languages.*

2. Complete each of the following sentences with the correct forms of the number and noun in parentheses.

MODEL Она́ живёт с ____________ (2, подру́га). > Она́ живёт с <u>двумя́ подру́гами</u>.

1. Мы́ ча́сто звони́м на́шим ____________ (2, сы́н).
2. Когда́ мы́ бы́ли в Росси́и, мы́ побыва́ли в ____________ (3, го́род).
3. В аудито́рии бы́ло ____________ (34, студе́нт), но то́лько ____________ (32, ме́сто).
4. На рабо́ту в рестора́н взя́ли ____________ (2, мужчи́на) и ____________ (3, же́нщина).
5. На э́тот ку́рс преподава́тель принима́ет то́лько ____________ (22, студе́нт).
6. У на́с в университе́те ____________ (2, библиоте́ка).
7. И́х маши́на слома́лась в ____________ (4, киломе́тр) от на́шего до́ма.
8. У э́тих ____________ (3, де́вушка) не́т биле́тов.
9. Оте́ц о́чень горди́тся свои́ми ____________ (3, до́чка).
10. Я́ написа́л пи́сьма ____________ (3, дру́г).

Use of the Numbers 2, 3, and 4 Followed by an Adjective + Noun

(a) In the nominative and inanimate accusative

When the number **два́/две́**, **три́**, or **четы́ре** is itself in the nominative or inanimate accusative case, it takes the *genitive plural* of a following adjective that is modifying a masculine or neuter noun, and usually the *nominative plural* of an adjective modifying a feminine noun; the noun, however, is in the genitive singular.

На по́лке бы́ло **два́ ру́сских словаря́**. — *There were two Russian dictionaries on the shelf.*
В э́той ко́мнате **три́ больши́х окна́**. — *There are three big windows in this room.*
О́н купи́л **две́ но́вые кни́ги**. — *He bought two new books.*

NOTE: An adjectival noun (page 155) after 2, 3, or 4, like a regular adjective, is in the genitive plural (due to an implicit masculine head noun) or nominative plural (with an implicit feminine head noun): **два́ *учёных*** *two scientists,* **четы́ре *взро́слых*** *four adults,* **две́ *бу́лочные*** *two bakeries,* **три́ *столо́вые*** *three cafeterias.* In fractions (page 195), however, an ordinal adjective after 2, 3, or 4 is in the *genitive plural,* even though it is modifying the implied feminine noun **часть** *part*: ⅖ is read as **две́ *пя́тых (ча́сти)*.**

NOTE: An adjective (or pronoun) that precedes a number is normally in the nominative or accusative plural: ***Э́ти пе́рвые* два́ дня́ прошли́ бы́стро** *These first two days passed quickly*; **В часы́ пи́к поезда́ хо́дят *ка́ждые* три́ мину́ты** *During rush hour, trains run every three minutes.*

3. Complete each of the following sentences with the correct form of the adjective + noun phrase in parentheses.

MODEL Студе́нт реши́л 3 __________ (тру́дная зада́ча). >
Студе́нт реши́л 3 тру́дные зада́чи.

1. На э́той у́лице откры́ли 2 ____________________ (но́вый рестора́н).
2. К на́м на обме́н прие́хали 3 ____________________ (ру́сский учёный).
3. В Москве́ неда́вно постро́или 3 ____________________ (больша́я гости́ница).
4. В пе́рвом ряду́ бы́ло 2 ____________________ (свобо́дное ме́сто).
5. У на́с в общежи́тии живёт 4 ____________________ (иностра́нный студе́нт).
6. В на́шем университе́те 2 ____________________ (студе́нческая столова́я).

(b) In the animate accusative and the oblique cases

In the animate accusative, as well as in the oblique cases, **два́/две́**, **три́**, or **четы́ре** and the following adjective are in the same case as the modified noun, and the adjective and noun are in the *plural.*

Animate Accusative

Мы́ встре́тили **дву́х но́вых студе́нтов**. — *We met the two new students.*

Genitive

Мы́ купи́ли пода́рки для **дву́х ма́леньких де́вочек**. — *We bought presents for two little girls.*

Prepositional

Ле́кции прохо́дят в **трёх больши́х аудито́риях**. — *Lectures are held in three large lecture halls.*

Dative

Мы́ да́ли тало́ны на пита́ние **дву́м иностра́нным студе́нтам**. — *We gave meal tickets to the two foreign students.*

Instrumental

Они́ о́чень дово́льны э́тими **четырьмя́ но́выми компью́терами**. — *They are very pleased with these four new computers.*

4. Complete each of the following sentences with the correct form of the number and adjective + noun phrase in parentheses.

MODEL Профе́ссор говори́л с ____________ (3, но́вый студе́нт). >
Профе́ссор говори́л с ___тремя́ но́выми студе́нтами___.

1. В боло́те мы́ ви́дели ______________________ (2, живо́й крокоди́л).
2. Мы́ позвони́ли ______________________ (2, но́вая студе́нтка).
3. На́м не хвата́ет ______________________ (3, ча́йная ло́жка).
4. На́ш сы́н игра́ет с ______________________ (2, ру́сский ма́льчик).
5. Уча́стники конфере́нции жи́ли в ______________________ (4, университе́тское общежи́тие).

Declension of 5–20 and 30

The numbers 5–20 and 30 end in the soft sign **-ь**, and they decline exactly like feminine nouns of the third declension (e.g., **две́рь** *door*). The following table shows the declension of the numbers 5–10, 20, and 30, all of which have the stress shifting from the stem in the nominative/accusative to the ending in the other cases.

	5	6	7	8	9	10	20	30
Nom. **Acc.**	пя́ть	ше́сть	се́мь	во́семь	де́вять	де́сять	два́дцать	три́дцать
Gen. **Prep.** **Dat.**	пяти́	шести́	семи́	восьми́	девяти́	десяти́	двадцати́	тридцати́
Instr.	пятью́	шестью́	семью́	восьмью́	девятью́	десятью́	двадцатью́	тридцатью́

NOTE: The vowel **-е-** in the nominative/accusative of **во́семь** is replaced by **-ь-** in the oblique cases. However, the instrumental case **восьмью** has a variant form, **восемью́**, sometimes found in more formal, written styles.

NOTE: The numbers 11–19 have the same endings as those in the table above, but have the stress fixed on the same syllable of the stem: Nom./Acc. **оди́ннадцать**, Gen./Prep./Dat. **оди́ннадцати**, Instr. **оди́ннадцатью**.

Declension of 50, 60, 70, and 80

The numbers **пятьдеся́т**, **шестьдеся́т**, **се́мьдесят**, and **во́семьдесят** consist of two parts, both of which decline like third-declension nouns, except that the nominative/accusative does not end in the soft sign.

	50	60	70	80
Nom. **Acc.**	пятьдеся́т	шестьдеся́т	се́мьдесят	во́семьдесят
Gen. **Prep.** **Dat.**	пяти́десяти	шести́десяти	семи́десяти	восьми́десяти
Instr.	пятью́десятью	шестью́десятью	семью́десятью	восьмью́десятью

Declension of 40, 90, and 100

The numbers **со́рок**, **девяно́сто**, and **сто́** have a very simple declension, with only one oblique case ending: **-a**.

	40	90	100
Nom./Acc.	со́рок	девяно́сто	сто́
Gen./Prep./Dat./Instr.	сорока́	девяно́ста	ста́

Declension of 200, 300, and 400

There are two parts to the numbers **две́сти**, **три́ста**, and **четы́реста**, and both parts decline: The first part declines just like **две́**, **три́**, and **четы́ре**, and the second part, **сто́**, declines like a noun following the numbers 2, 3, and 4, i.e., it either has the form of the genitive singular **-ста** (except for **-сти** in **две́сти**, an old "dual" form), or it is in the genitive, prepositional, dative, or instrumental plural (**-со́т**, **-ста́х**, **-ста́м**, **-ста́ми**).

	200	300	400
Nom./Acc.	две́сти	три́ста	четы́реста
Gen.	двухсо́т	трёхсо́т	четырёхсо́т
Prep.	двухста́х	трёхста́х	четырёхста́х
Dat.	двумста́м	трёмста́м	четырёмста́м
Instr.	двумяста́ми	тремяста́ми	четырьмяста́ми

Declension of 500, 600, 700, 800, and 900

Like the numbers 200, 300, and 400, the numbers **пятьсо́т**, **шестьсо́т**, **семьсо́т**, **восемьсо́т**, and **девятьсо́т** consist of two declined parts: The first part declines like the numbers **пя́ть–де́вять**, and the second part, **сто́**, declines like a noun in the plural of the oblique cases.

	500	600	700	800	900
Nom./Acc.	пятьсо́т	шестьсо́т	семьсо́т	восемьсо́т	девятьсо́т
Gen.	пятисо́т	шестисо́т	семисо́т	восьмисо́т	девятисо́т
Prep.	пятиста́х	шестиста́х	семиста́х	восьмиста́х	девятиста́х
Dat.	пятиста́м	шестиста́м	семиста́м	восьмиста́м	девятиста́м
Instr.	пятьюста́ми	шестьюста́ми	семьюста́ми	восьмьюста́ми	девятьюста́ми

Use of Cardinal Numbers 5–999

(a) In the nominative and accusative

When the numbers 5–999 are themselves in the nominative or accusative case, both adjectives and nouns follow in the *genitive plural.*

К на́м по обме́ну приезжа́ют **пя́ть ру́сских студе́нтов**.	*Five Russian students are coming to us on an exchange.*
На э́той у́лице стро́ят **ше́сть больши́х домо́в**.	*They are building five big houses on this street.*
Мы́ посмотре́ли **де́сять иностра́нных фи́льмов**.	*We saw ten foreign films.*
В э́той гости́нице **двести два́дцать во́семь просто́рных номеро́в**.	*There are two hundred and twenty-eight spacious rooms in this hotel.*

The numbers 5 and above do not undergo the "animate accusative" rule, i.e., the accusative-case form of the number is identical to the nominative, whether the modified noun is animate or inanimate.

В зоопа́рке мы́ ви́дели **пя́ть ти́гров и ше́сть льво́в**.	*At the zoo we saw five tigers and six lions.*
Э́тот конце́ртный за́л вмеща́ет **восемьсо́т пятьдеся́т зри́телей**.	*This concert hall holds eight hundred and fifty spectators.*

NOTE: Compound numbers higher than 5 whose last component is 1 follow the pattern of agreement discussed above for **оди́н** (e.g., **два́дцать *оди́н конве́рт*** *twenty-one envelopes,* **три́дцать *одна́ ма́рка*** *twenty-one stamps*). Compounds ending in 2, 3, or 4 (e.g., 22, 33, 54), when in the nominative/accusative case, follow the rules given above for these numbers: They take the genitive singular of the following noun: **два́дцать *два́ карандаша́*** *twenty-two pencils,* **три́дцать *четы́ре биле́та*** *thirty-four tickets.*

(b) In the oblique cases

In the oblique cases the numbers 5 and higher function as modifiers, agreeing in case with the modified noun (and any modifying adjective) in the *plural.*

Мы́ побыва́ли в **пяти́ изве́стных музе́ях**.	*We visited five famous museums.*
Я́ посла́л откры́тки **семи́ хоро́шим друзья́м**.	*I sent postcards to seven good friends.*
Что́ де́лать с **десятью́ рубля́ми**?	*What can one do with ten rubles?*

In the oblique cases each part of a compound number declines.

На конфере́нцию прие́хали учёные из **девяно́ста дву́х стра́н**.	*Scholars from ninety-two countries came to the conference.*
Спортсме́нов размести́ли в **тридцати́ трёх номера́х**.	*The athletes were placed in thirty-three rooms.*
В его́ колле́кции бо́льше **двухсо́т шести́десяти пяти́ ру́сских ма́рок**.	*In his collection there are more than two hundred and sixty-five Russian stamps.*

5. Complete each of the following sentences with the correct forms of the number, adjective, and noun in parentheses.

MODEL У на́ших сосе́дей ________ (5, ма́ленький ребёнок). >
У на́ших сосе́дей пя́ть ма́леньких дете́й.

1. Мы́ познако́мились с ________ (6, ру́сский тури́ст).
2. Студе́нт реши́л ________ (7, тру́дная зада́ча).
3. Учи́тельница дала́ карандаши́ ________ (10, но́вый учени́к).
4. В Вашингто́не ________ (5, ча́стный университе́т).
5. Э́та стару́ха живёт с ________ (20, ста́рая ко́шка).
6. Мы́ посла́ли приглаше́ния ________ (35, хоро́ший дру́г).
7. Санкт-Петербу́рг бы́л постро́ен на ________ (100, небольшо́й о́стров).
8. В э́том университе́те преподаю́т бо́льше ________ (350, о́пытный профе́ссор).
9. Говоря́т, что в Петербу́рге о́коло ________ (215, дождли́вый де́нь) в году́.
10. В э́том ма́леньком городке́ ме́ньше ________ (540, постоя́нный жи́тель).

Declension and Use of *тысяча*

The word **ты́сяча** *thousand* is declined like the second-declension noun **встре́ча** *meeting,* except that in the instrumental singular it has the form **ты́сячью**, which in most contexts has replaced the expected **ты́сячей** (the latter form, however, is still used when preceded by **одно́й**: **с одно́й ты́сячей** *with one thousand*).

	SINGULAR	PLURAL
Nom.	ты́сяча	ты́сячи
Acc.	ты́сячу	ты́сячи
Gen.	ты́сячи	ты́сяч
Prep.	ты́сяче	ты́сячах
Dat.	ты́сяче	ты́сячам
Instr.	ты́сячью/ты́сячей	ты́сячами

As a noun, **ты́сяча** can itself be quantified like any other noun. For example, when preceded by **две́**, **три́**, or **четы́ре** in the nominative or inanimate accusative, **ты́сяча** is in the genitive singular (**две́ ты́сячи** *two thousand,* **три́ ты́сячи** *three thousand,* **четы́ре ты́сячи** *four thousand*). Similarly, when preceded by the nominative or accusative of the numbers **пя́ть**, **ше́сть**, and higher, **ты́сяча** is in the genitive plural (**пя́ть ты́сяч** *five thousand,* **два́дцать ты́сяч** *twenty thousand*).

The noun **ты́сяча** is normally followed by the genitive plural, regardless of its own case in a given context.

На съе́зд собрала́сь **одна́ ты́сяча делега́тов**.	*One thousand delegates gathered at the congress.*
Ка́ждый ме́сяц о́н прино́сит домо́й **одну́ ты́сячу до́лларов**.	*Each month he brings home one thousand dollars.*

В забасто́вке уча́ствовали бо́лее **пяти́десяти ты́сяч шахтёров.** — *More than fifty thousand coal miners participated in the strike.*

На́до почини́ть брако́ванный водопрово́д в **одно́й ты́сяче но́вых домо́в.** — *Faulty water pipes have to be repaired in one thousand new homes.*

Прави́тельство пошло́ на усту́пки **пятиста́м ты́сячам забасто́вщиков.** — *The government made concessions to fifty thousand strikers.*

Мы́ не смо́жем обойти́сь **пятью́ ты́сячами рубле́й.** — *We cannot manage with five thousand rubles.*

NOTE: When unmodified in an oblique case, **ты́сяча** may also be treated as a number. It then behaves just like the numbers **пя́ть** and above, i.e., it is followed by a plural noun in the same oblique case (e.g., **Он уе́хал с *ты́сячью рубля́ми*** *He left with a thousand rubles*). This usage is characteristic of colloquial style.

Declension and Use of *миллио́н* and *миллиа́рд/биллио́н*

The numbers **миллио́н** *million* and **миллиа́рд/биллио́н** *billion* are declined as regular hard-stem masculine nouns. Like **ты́сяча**, these nouns can themselves be quantified (**два́ миллио́на** *two million,* **се́мь миллио́нов** *seven million,* **три́ миллиа́рда** *three billion,* **де́сять миллиа́рдов** *ten billion*), and they govern the genitive plural of following nouns and adjectives.

Населе́ние Росси́и—**сто́ пятьдеся́т миллио́нов челове́к.** — *The population of Russia is one hundred and fifty million people.*

Би́лл Ге́йтс—миллиарде́р. У него́ бо́льше **пятидесяти́ семи́ миллиа́рдов до́лларов.** — *Bill Gates is a billionaire. He is worth more than fifty-seven billion dollars.*

Representing Thousands and Millions in Figures

When using figures to write numbers in the thousands and higher, Russian requires either a period or a space where English has a comma, e.g., **ты́сяча** 1.000 / 1 000 (= English 1,000), **сто́ ты́сяч** 100.000 / 100 000 (= English 100,000), **два́ миллио́на** 2.000.000 / 2 000 000 (= English 2,000,000).

6. Complete each of the following sentences with the correct forms of the number and noun in parentheses.

1. На́м придётся ограни́читься ____________________ (10 000, ру́бль).
2. На вы́ставку прие́хали о́коло ____________________ (15 000, посети́тель).
3. В на́шем университе́те у́чатся ____________________ (24 000, студе́нт).
4. Студе́нты и аспира́нты живу́т в ____________________ (10 000, ко́мната) университе́тских общежи́тий.
5. Граби́тели ба́нка скры́лись, прихвати́в с собо́й бо́льше ____________________ (150 000, до́ллар).
6. Во Второ́й мирово́й войне́ поги́бло бо́льше ____________________ (20 000 000, сове́тский гражда́нин).
7. Специали́сты предска́зывают дефици́т в ____________________ (900.000.000.000, до́ллар) в госбюдже́те США.

Money and Prices

The two monetary units in Russia are the **ру́бль** *ruble* and the **копе́йка** *kopeck* (1/100 ruble). Over the past decade, the Central Bank of Russia has kept the ruble fairly stable in relation to both the euro and the U.S. dollar. As of January 1, 2009, the exchange rate was $1 = 29.4 rubles. At the same time, due to rising inflation, Russian kopecks have little value, and the one-kopeck and five-kopeck coins, in particular, are rarely used in transactions.

The following table illustrates the case forms of the nouns **ру́бль** and **копе́йка** after numbers.

1 (оди́н) ру́бль	2 (два́), 3, 4 рубля́	5, 6, 7, … рубле́й
1 (одна́) копе́йка	2 (две́), 3, 4 копе́йки	5, 6, 7, … копе́ек

—Ско́лько де́нег вы́ зараба́тываете в ме́сяц?	*How much money do you earn in a month?*
—Я́ зараба́тываю 12 ты́сяч рубле́й в ме́сяц.	*I earn twelve thousand rubles a month.*
—Ско́лько де́нег у де́вочки в копи́лке?	*How much money does the little girl have in her piggy bank?*
—У неё 200 рубле́й 23 копе́йки.	*She has two hundred rubles, twenty-three kopecks.*

7. The prices of the food items listed below in parentheses were advertised in August 2008 on **Ле́нта** (*www.lenta.com*), an online discount store similar to America's Costco. Write out the numbers in words, and use the correct forms for the nouns *rubles* and *kopecks.*

1. Кра́сное вино́ 0,75 л (69 р 33 к) ______________________
2. Попко́рн 100 г (17 р 6 к) ______________________
3. Ке́тчуп 1 шту́ка (70 р 49 к) ______________________
4. Пе́пси 2 л (33 р 85 к) ______________________
5. У́ксус 0,95 л (18 р 79 к) ______________________

Telephone Numbers

In large Russian cities such as Moscow and St. Petersburg, telephone numbers, like those in America, consist of 7 digits. However, unlike in America, where telephone numbers are normally read and spoken one digit at a time, telephone numbers in Russia are divided into three separate units: an initial three-digit number in the "hundreds," followed by two two-digit numbers in the "tens," e.g., 350-21-44 is read as **три́ста пятьдеся́т – два́дцать оди́н – со́рок четы́ре**). A true zero (0), one that is not part of a larger number, is rendered by **но́ль**, e.g., -10- is **де́сять**, but -01- is **но́ль оди́н** and -00- is **но́ль но́ль** (or **два́ ноля́**).

8. Write out the following telephone numbers as they would be read and spoken in Russian.

1. 742-00-66 ______________________
2. 239-12-10 ______________________
3. 444-87-09 ______________________
4. 993-03-30 ______________________
5. 521-55-77 ______________________

Numerical Nouns Formed from Cardinal Numbers

The following nouns with numerical meaning are derived from the cardinal numbers.

едини́ца *one*	шестёрка *six*
дво́йка *two*	семёрка *seven*
тро́йка *three*	восьмёрка *eight*
четвёрка *four*	девя́тка *nine*
пятёрка *five*	деся́тка *ten*

In addition to being the names of the corresponding figures (e.g., **семёрка** *the figure 7*), these nouns have several special uses.

University and School Grades

In the Russian educational system, the first five nouns in the list above refer to grades given for academic work: **едини́ца** (**пло́хо** *bad/F*), **дво́йка** (**неудовлетвори́тельно** *unsatisfactory/D*), **тро́йка** (**удовлетвори́тельно** *satisfactory/C*), **четвёрка** (**хорошо́** *good/B*), and **пятёрка** (**отли́чно** *excellent/A*).

Бо́ря мно́го занима́лся и получи́л **пятёрку** на экза́мене.	*Borya studied hard and got an A on the exam.*
Пе́тя пло́хо написа́л экза́мен и получи́л **дво́йку**.	*Pete wrote poorly on the exam and got a D.*

Numbered Playing Cards

The nouns **дво́йка** through **деся́тка** also denote the numbered playing cards of a suit.

дво́йка бубён *two of diamonds*
пятёрка пи́к *five of spades*
восьмёрка черве́й *eight of hearts*
деся́тка тре́ф *ten of clubs*

О́н сда́л мне́ **семёрку** тре́ф.	*He dealt me the seven of clubs.*

Numbers of Buses and Trolleys

In colloquial Russian, nouns in the list above (and a few others, e.g., **двадца́тка** *20*, **тридца́тка** *30*) can be used to refer to the numbers of buses and trolleys.

Мо́жно доеха́ть до университе́та на **восьмёрке**.	*You can get to the university on (bus or trolley) No. 8.*
Я́ прие́хал домо́й на **пятёрке**.	*I came home on (bus or trolley) No. 5.*

Groups of People and Objects Comprised of Several Units

Several of the nouns in the list above are used to refer to groups of people or objects consisting of several units; examples follow.

тро́йка *three-person commission; team of three horses; three-piece suit;* etc.
четвёрка *team of four horses; four-oar boat*
пятёрка *five-ruble note*
семёрка *group of seven people*
деся́тка *ten-ruble note*

О́н пришёл на рабо́ту в **тро́йке**.	*He came to work in a three-piece (suit).*

Similarly, the nouns **пято́к** and **деся́ток** are used colloquially to refer, respectively, to groups of five and ten (usually similar) objects, e.g., **пято́к огурцо́в** *five cucumbers,* **деся́ток я́иц** *a ten of eggs.*

В Росси́и я́йца продаю́тся **деся́тками**, а не дю́жинами.	*In Russia eggs are sold in tens, not in dozens.*

NOTE: The noun **со́тня** *a hundred* is used in a similar way, typically when money is implied.

О́н проси́л у меня́ **со́тню**.	*He asked me for a hundred (rubles).*

9. Complete each of the following sentences with the correct form of the numerical noun in parentheses.

1. За хоро́шее сочине́ние учи́тель поста́вил е́й _______________ (5).
2. У меня́ при себе́ не́т де́нег. Ты́ не да́шь мне́ _______________ (10-ruble note)?
3. Ле́на была́ на ры́нке и купи́ла _______________ (а 10) све́жих яи́ц.
4. Что́бы дое́хать до гости́ницы «Ми́р», на́до се́сть на _______________ ((bus) No. 6).
5. Что́бы вы́играть па́ртию, мне́ нужна́ была́ _______________ (7) бубён.
6. О́н вообще́ не занима́лся и получи́л _______________ (2) на экза́мене.

Collective Numbers

Collective numbers indicate the number of people, animals, or things in a group, and present them as a *single unit.* The collective numbers include **о́ба/о́бе** *both,* along with the series **дво́е** *two* to **де́сятеро** *ten.*

о́ба/о́бе *both*	ше́стеро *six*
дво́е *two*	се́меро *seven*
тро́е *three*	во́сьмеро *eight*
че́тверо *four*	де́вятеро *nine*
пя́теро *five*	де́сятеро *ten*

The Collective Number *о́ба/о́бе*

Like the cardinal number **два́/две́** *two,* the collective number **о́ба/о́бе** *both* has two gender forms: one for masculine and neuter nouns, the other for feminine nouns. However, unlike **два́/две́**, which distinguishes gender only in the nominative/accusative case, the collective **о́ба/о́бе** distinguishes gender (via the stem vowel **-о-** vs. **-е-**) throughout the entire declension. **О́ба/о́бе** in the oblique cases takes soft-stem plural adjective endings.

	MASCULINE AND NEUTER	FEMININE
Nom.	о́ба	о́бе
Acc. Inan. = Nom.	о́ба	о́бе
Anim. = Gen.	обо́их	обе́их
Gen.	обо́их	обе́их
Prep.	об обо́их	об обе́их
Dat.	обо́им	обе́им
Instr.	обо́ими	обе́ими

The case of nouns and adjectives after **óба/óбе** follows the same pattern as the case after **двá/двé**: When the number itself is in the nominative or inanimate accusative, the following noun is in the *genitive singular*, and the adjective is in the *genitive plural* (for masculine and neuter adjectives) or the *nominative plural* (for feminine adjectives). **Óба/óбе** is used when *both* of the things referred to are of the same kind.

Óба нóвых ресторáна нахóдятся на Нéвском проспéкте.	*Both new restaurants are located on Nevsky Prospekt.*
Óбе нóвые гостúницы открылись веснóй.	*Both new hotels opened in the spring.*

In an oblique case, **óба/óбе** agrees in case with the following *plural* noun and adjective.

Нáши друзья́ останови́лись в **обéих гости́ницах**.	*Our friends have stayed in both hotels.*
Держи́сь за ру́ль **обéими рукáми**.	*Hold the steering wheel with both hands.*

The Collective Number Series *двóе, трóе, ...*

The declension of the collective numbers **двóе** and **чéтверо** is presented in the table below. The declension of **трóе** is like that of **двóе**, and **пя́теро**, **шéстеро**, **сéмеро**, etc., are declined like **чéтверо**.

Nom.	двóе	чéтверо
Acc. Inan. = Nom.	двóе	чéтверо
Anim. = Gen.	двои́х	четверы́х
Gen.	двои́х	четверы́х
Prep.	о двои́х	о четверы́х
Dat.	двои́м	четверы́м
Instr.	двои́ми	четверы́ми

When a collective number itself is in the nominative or inanimate accusative, the number is followed by the genitive plural of adjectives, nouns, and pronouns. In all other cases, the number is followed by the required plural case form of the (usually animate) noun.

Онá мáть **двои́х** краси́вых детéй.	*She is the mother of two beautiful children.*

Collective numbers have the following uses.

(i) Collective numbers must be used with nouns that have only a plural form (see page 34).

двóе нóвых джи́нсов *two new pairs of jeans*
трóе швейцáрских часóв *three Swiss watches*
чéтверо су́ток *four days*

Collective numbers may also be used with nouns denoting things that come in "pairs," e.g., socks, gloves, shoes, skis. However, with such nouns the same meaning can also be expressed by a cardinal number combined with the noun **пáра** *pair.*

двóе носкóв / двé пáры носкóв *two pairs of socks*
трóе лы́ж / три́ пáры лы́ж *three pairs of skis*

(ii) Collective nouns are used with nouns denoting male persons.

дво́е ма́льчиков *two boys*	пя́теро холостяко́в *five bachelors*
тро́е мужчи́н *three men*	ше́стеро женихо́в *six bridegrooms*
че́тверо ю́ношей *four youths*	се́меро студе́нтов *seven students*

Cardinal numbers are also possible with nouns denoting males (**два́ ма́льчика** *two boys,* **три́ мужчи́ны** *three men,* **четы́ре студе́нта** *four students*). The cardinal presents the people in a group as *individuals,* whereas the collective presents a group of people as *a whole.* With nouns denoting female persons, only a cardinal number is possible (**две́ де́вушки** *two girls,* but NOT ***дво́е де́вушек**).

(iii) Collective nouns are used with pronouns denoting a group of males or females, or a group of mixed gender.

На́с **тро́е**.	*There are three of us.*
На́м **трои́м** нужны́ биле́ты.	*The three of us need tickets.*
Их бы́ло **че́тверо**: две́ же́нщины и дво́е мужчи́н.	*There were four of them: two women and two men.*

(iv) Collective nouns are used independently, without an accompanying noun or pronoun.

Пришло́ **дво́е**.	*Two people came.*
О́н е́ст за **тро́их**.	*He eats (enough) for three people.*
Я́ заказа́л сто́лик на **четверы́х**.	*I ordered a table for four.*

(v) Collective nouns are used with the plural nouns **лю́ди** *people,* **де́ти** *children,* **близнецы́** *twins,* and **ребя́та** *kids.*

За столо́м сиде́ло **тро́е люде́й**.	*Three people sat at the table.*
У на́с **дво́е дете́й**.	*We have two children.*
У неё родило́сь **че́тверо близнецо́в**.	*She gave birth to quadruplets.*

(vi) Collective nouns are used with nouns denoting young animals.

У неё **дво́е котя́т**.	*She has two kittens.*
В зоомагази́не мы́ ви́дели **трои́х щеня́т**.	*We saw three puppies at the pet store.*

10. Complete each of the following sentences with the correct form of the collective number(s) in parentheses.

1. ________________ (Both) сестры́ вы́шли за́муж.
2. Я́ зна́ю ________________ (both) бра́тьев и ________________ (both) сестёр.
3. Мы́ провели́ на да́че ________________ (3) су́ток.
4. Она́ купи́ла ________________ (2) но́жниц.
5. Мы́ заброни́ровали но́мер на ________________ (4).
6. У него́ большо́й аппети́т. Он мо́жет е́сть за ________________ (2).
7. На углу́ стоя́ло ________________ (3) ма́льчиков.
8. Они́ все́ ________________ (4) ушли́ ра́но с ле́кции.
9. Неда́вно в США у одно́й же́нщины родило́сь ________________ (7) близнецо́в.
10. Ка́к же она́ бу́дет расти́ть ________________ (7) дете́й?

Ordinal Numbers

An ordinal number indicates relative position, or rank, in a series, e.g., *first, third, fifth.* Ordinal numbers, with the exception of **пе́рвый** *first* and **второ́й** *second,* are derived from their corresponding cardinal numbers, e.g., **пя́тый** (< **пя́ть**), **шесто́й** (< **ше́сть**).

1st	пе́рвый	40th	сороково́й
2nd	второ́й	50th	пятидеся́тый
3rd	тре́тий	60th	шестидеся́тый
4th	четвёртый	70th	семидеся́тый
5th	пя́тый	80th	восьмидеся́тый
6th	шесто́й	90th	девяно́стый
7th	седьмо́й	100th	со́тый
8th	восьмо́й	200th	двухсо́тый
9th	девя́тый	300th	трёхсо́тый
10th	деся́тый	400th	четырёхсо́тый
11th	оди́ннадцатый	500th	пятисо́тый
12th	двена́дцатый	600th	шестисо́тый
13th	трина́дцатый	700th	семисо́тый
14th	четы́рнадцатый	800th	восьмисо́тый
15th	пятна́дцатый	900th	девятисо́тый
16th	шестна́дцатый	1000th	ты́сячный
17th	семна́дцатый	1001st	ты́сяча пе́рвый
18th	восемна́дцатый	2000th	двухты́сячный
19th	девятна́дцатый	3000th	трёхты́сячный
20th	двадца́тый	5000th	пятиты́сячный
21st	два́дцать пе́рвый	1 000 000th	миллио́нный
30th	тридца́тый	1 000 000 000th	миллиа́рдный

NOTE: The final soft sign **-ь** of a cardinal number is omitted before the adjective ending of the ordinal: **де́сять** > **деся́т-ый**. Also, the **-ь-** in the middle of the cardinal numbers 50, 60, 70, 80 and 500, 600, 700, 800, 900 is replaced by **-и-** in the corresponding ordinal: **пятьдеся́т** 50 > **пят*и*деся́тый** *50th,* **семьсо́т** *700* > **сем*и*со́тый** *700th.*

NOTE: In compounds the initial element is an undeclined *cardinal* number and the final element is a declined *ordinal,* e.g., **три́дцать *восьмо́й* авто́бус** *bus thirty-eight* (lit., *thirty-eighth bus*).

Ordinal numbers decline like hard-stem adjectives (see page 141), except for **тре́тий** *third,* which has the special declension shown in the following table.

	MASCULINE,	NEUTER	FEMININE	PLURAL
Nom.	тре́тий	тре́тье	тре́тья	тре́тьи
Acc. Inan. = Nom.	тре́тий	тре́тье	тре́тью	тре́тьи
Anim. = Gen.	тре́тьего			тре́тьих
Gen.	тре́тьего		тре́тьей	тре́тьих
Prep.	тре́тьем		тре́тьей	тре́тьих
Dat.	тре́тьему		тре́тьей	тре́тьим
Instr.	тре́тьим		тре́тьей	тре́тьими

Since an ordinal number is an adjective, it agrees in gender, number, and case with the noun it modifies.

Мы́ живём в **два́дцать пе́рвом** ве́ке.	*We are living in the twenty-first century.*
Мо́й о́фис нахо́дится на **второ́м** этаже́.	*My office is located on the second floor.*
О́н за́нял **тре́тье** ме́сто.	*He took third place.*
Они́ сиде́ли в **тре́тьем** ряду́.	*They sat in the third row.*

11. Complete each of the following sentences with the correct form of the ordinal number in parentheses.

1. Моя́ до́чка у́чится в ________________ (1st) кла́ссе.
2. Э́тот студе́нт на ________________ (2nd) ку́рсе.
3. Мы́ выхо́дим на ________________ (3rd) остано́вке.
4. Мы́ останови́лись у ________________ (5th) подъе́зда.
5. Она́ была́ на ________________ (7th) не́бе.
6. Я́ люблю́ ________________ (9th) симфо́нию Бетхо́вена.

Use of Russian Ordinals for English Cardinals

Ordinal numbers are often used in Russian where English typically uses a cardinal, for example, to indicate hotel rooms, buses and trolleys, seat numbers, TV and radio channels, and pages, chapters, and volumes of books. Note the English translations of the following Russian examples.

Мы́ жи́ли в **три́ста шесто́м** но́мере.	*We stayed in Room 306.*
Она́ ждёт **со́рок пе́рвый** авто́бус.	*She is waiting for bus No. 41.*
О́н сиде́л на **два́дцать второ́м** ме́сте.	*He was sitting in seat 22.*
Что́ по **тре́тьей** програ́мме?	*What is on Channel 3?*
Я́ дочита́л до **пятьдеся́т пя́той** страни́цы.	*I read up to page 55.*
Я́ тепе́рь пишу́ **шесту́ю** главу́.	*I am now writing Chapter 6.*

12. Write the Russian equivalent of each of the following phrases.

1. Chapter 32 ________________________
2. Volume 17 ________________________
3. Row 56 ________________________
4. Channel 3 ________________________
5. Bus No. 67 ________________________
6. Seat 125 ________________________

Fractions

A fraction denotes part of a whole number. It is comprised of both a cardinal and an ordinal number. The numerator of a fraction is denoted by the cardinal number in the *nominative* case. The denominator is denoted by an ordinal number, which is in one of the following two forms.

1. If the numerator of the fraction is the number 1 (**одна́**), the denominator is in the nominative case, and (like the numerator) takes the feminine form (to agree with the understood feminine noun **ча́сть** *part*).

1/5	одна́ пя́тая	*one fifth*
1/6	одна́ шеста́я	*one sixth*
1/7	одна́ седьма́я	*one seventh*
1/8	одна́ восьма́я	*one eighth*
1/9	одна́ девя́тая	*one ninth*
1/10	одна́ деся́тая	*one tenth*
1/100	одна́ со́тая	*one one-hundredth*
1/1000	одна́ ты́сячная	*one one-thousandth*

2. If the numerator of the fraction is 2 (**две́**), 3, 4, or a higher number, the ordinal denoting the denominator is in the *genitive plural* (not the nominative plural usually found after 2, 3, and 4 when the modified noun is feminine; see page 182).

2/5	две́ пя́тых	*two fifths*
3/10	три́ деся́тых	*three tenths*
5/8	пя́ть восьмы́х	*five eighths*

Both the numerator and denominator of a fraction decline, as shown in the following table.

	1/10	**2/5**
Nom.	одна́ деся́тая	две́ пя́тых
Acc.	одну́ деся́тую	две́ пя́тых
Gen.	одно́й деся́той	дву́х пя́тых
Prep.	одно́й деся́той	дву́х пя́тых
Dat.	одно́й деся́той	дву́м пя́тым
Instr.	одно́й деся́той	двумя́ пя́тыми

Regardless of the case of the fraction itself, a noun following a fraction is always in the *genitive* case.

У него́ температу́ра подняла́сь всего́ на **одну́ деся́тую гра́дуса**.	*His temperature went up by only one tenth of a degree.*
В го́нке о́н бы́л быстре́е на **две́ со́тых секу́нды**.	*He was faster in the race by two hundredths of a second.*
О́коло **дву́х пя́тых жи́телей го́рода** име́ют маши́ны.	*About two fifths of the residents of the city have cars.*

If a fraction follows a whole number, the adjective **це́лый** *whole* is sometimes used after the cardinal denoting the whole number. Note how such fractions are read or spoken.

1 3/6	одна́ це́лая и три́ шесты́х	*one and three sixths*
2 5/8	две́ це́лых и пя́ть восьмы́х	*two and five eighths*
7 1/5	се́мь це́лых и одна́ пя́тая	*seven and one fifth*

Colloquial Forms of "Quarter," "Third," and "Half"

In colloquial Russian, fractions involving *quarters* (¼, ¾), *thirds* (⅓, ⅔), and a *half* (½) are normally expressed by special nouns that are used instead of the regular form of the denominator.

FRACTION	FORMAL	INFORMAL/COLLOQUIAL
¼	однá четвёртая	(однá) чéтверть
⅓	однá трéтья	(однá) трéть
½	однá вторáя	полови́на, пол

These special nouns, like regular fractions, take the genitive case of a following noun.

двé трéти дорóги *two thirds of the way*
трú чéтверти гóрода *three quarters of the city*

The noun **полови́на** *half is* normally followed by a noun that denotes something other than a unit of measure.

О́н ужé истрáтил **полови́ну** дéнег. *He already spent half of the money.*
О́н подписáл **полови́ну** докумéнтов. *He signed half the documents.*

The truncated form **пол** (**ови́на**) is often combined with nouns denoting measurement. When the compound form with **пол** is used in the nominative or accusative case, the noun denoting measure takes a genitive ending.

Полмéсяца прошлó бы́стро. *Half a month passed quickly.*
Мы́ говори́ли **полчасá**. *We spoke for half an hour.*
О́н прожи́л в Москвé **полгóда**. *He lived in Moscow half a year.*
Онá вы́пила **полстакáна**. *She drank half a glass.*

In the oblique cases, both parts of the compound normally decline: **Пол** changes to **полу**, and the noun denoting measurement takes the oblique-case ending required by the context.

Мы́ ждáли óколо **получáса**. *We waited about half an hour.*
О́н живёт в **получáсе** езды́ отсю́да. *He lives a half hour's drive from here.*

NOTE: In informal, colloquial speech **пол** may not change to **полу** in some nouns, e.g., **О́н вы́пил бóлее *полстакáна*** *He drank more than half a glass.* **Пол** remains constant in certain phrases, e.g., **на полстáвки** *at half-pay / part-time*: **О́н рабóтает на *полстáвки*** *He works part-time (and receives half-pay).*

The Expression *полторá/полторы́* (1½)

Russian has a special number to express *one and a half*; its simple declension is presented in the following table.

	MASCULINE AND NEUTER	FEMININE
Nom./Acc.	полторá	полторы́
Gen./Prep./Dat./Instr.	полу́тора	

The choice of the nominative/accusative-case form **полторá** or **полторы́** is determined by the gender of the following noun: The former is used with masculine and neuter nouns, the latter with feminine nouns. The forms **полторá/полторы́** govern the genitive singular of the following noun.

На столé лежáло **полторá батóна** хлéба.	*One and a half loaves of (white) bread lay on the table.*
Онá вы́пила **полторы́ чáшки** чáя.	*She drank one and a half cups of tea.*

A third form, **полу́тора**, is used for each of the remaining cases. The noun following **полу́тора** is in the *plural* of the case required by the context.

Нáм нáдо ограни́читься **полу́тора ты́сячами** дóлларов.	*We have to limit ourselves to one and a half thousand dollars.*

Other Numbers with "Half"

To express *one half* with other numbers, the phrase **с полови́ной** *with a half* can be used after the number, e.g., **двá с полови́ной** *2½*, **три́ с полови́ной** *3½*. This is an informal way of expressing **три́ цéлых и пя́ть деся́тых** *three wholes and five tenths.*

13. Complete each of the following sentences with the correct forms of the number and noun in parentheses.

1. Óн съéл ________________ (1½ пирожóк).
2. Мы́ поговори́ли тóлько ________________ (1½ мину́та).
3. Онá не смóжет обойти́сь бéз ________________ (1½ ты́сяча).
4. Óн не мóг не ду́мать о ________________ (1½ миллиóн).
5. Онá вернётся чéрез ________________ (1½ чáс).

Decimal Fractions

In expressing percentages, weight, volume, and other forms of measurement, a comma is used in Russian where English uses a decimal point. The following table gives examples of how decimal fractions are read aloud in Russian.

RUSSIAN		ENGLISH
0,1	нóль цéлых и однá деся́тая	0.1 OR 1/10
1,75	однá цéлая и сéмьдесят пя́ть сóтых	1.75
2,4	двé цéлых и четы́ре деся́тых	2.4
3,5	три́ цéлых и пя́ть деся́тых	3.5

NOTE: The word **цéлая/цéлых** may be omitted, leaving the "whole" expressed by the cardinal number itself (see the following section). In this case, the masculine or feminine form of the numbers 1 and 2 is determined by the gender of the noun of measurement, e.g., the masculine noun **килогрáмм** and the feminine noun **тóнна**.

Оди́н и четы́ре деся́тых килогрáмма	*1.4 kilograms*
Двé и сéмь деся́тых тóнны	*2.7 tons*

14. Write out each of the following fractions in words, as it would be read aloud in Russian.

1. 3/8 ________________
2. 0,7 ________________
3. 2 3/5 ________________
4. 4 1/8 ________________
5. 1/4 ________________
6. 2/3 ________________
7. 4,05 ________________

Decimal Fractions in Colloquial Style

In informal conversation Russians often simplify decimal fractions, omitting both the words **це́лый** and **и**, as well as the declined forms of **деся́тый** *tenth* and **со́тый** *hundredth.*

О́н вы́пил небольшу́ю буты́лку пи́ва ёмкостью но́ль три́дцать три́ (0,33).	*He drank a small, .33 (liter) size, bottle of beer.*

The metric system of measurement is used in Russia. The following examples present a few approximate equivalents between the units of measure in the different systems used in America and Russia. Note the simplification of the decimal fractions.

—Ско́лько оди́н фу́нт в килогра́ммах?	*How much is one pound in kilograms?*
—Оди́н фу́нт—но́ль со́рок пя́ть (0,45) килогра́мма.	*One pound is .45 kilograms.*
—Ско́лько одна́ пи́нта в ли́трах?	*How much is one pint in liters?*
—Одна́ пи́нта—но́ль пя́ть (0,5) ли́тра / пол-ли́тра.	*One pint is point five liters (half a liter).*
—Ско́лько одна́ ми́ля в киломе́трах?	*How much is one mile in kilometers?*
—Одна́ ми́ля—оди́н и ше́сть деся́тых (1,6) киломе́тра.	*One mile is one point six kilometers.*

NOTE: Nouns following a decimal fraction, like those in the examples above, are in the genitive singular: **два́ и пя́ть деся́тых *проце́нта*** *2,5%.*

15. The following items are beverages and fruit in quantities that one might typically find on a menu in a Russian restaurant. Write out the decimal fraction in words, as it would be read or spoken informally.

1. Минера́льная вода́ 0,25 л ____________________
2. Ко́ка-Ко́ла 0,33 л ____________________
3. Во́дка 0,5 л ____________________
4. Шампа́нское 0,75 л ____________________
5. Со́к 1,0 л ____________________
6. Апельси́ны 0,5 кг ____________________

Dates

Days of the Week

The days of the week in Russian are not capitalized.

понеде́льник	*Monday*
вто́рник	*Tuesday*
среда́	*Wednesday*
четве́рг	*Thursday*
пя́тница	*Friday*
суббо́та	*Saturday*
воскресе́нье	*Sunday*

NOTE: The names for Tuesday, Thursday, and Friday are formed from ordinal numbers: **вто́рник** (< **второ́й**) is the "second" day, **четве́рг** (< **четвёртый**) is the "fourth" day, and **пя́тница** (< **пя́тый**) is the "fifth" day of the week.

To indicate what day it *is, was,* or *will be,* the noun denoting the day is in the *nominative* case.

—Како́й сего́дня де́нь?	*What day is today?*
—Сего́дня **пя́тница**.	*Today is Friday.*
—Како́й вчера́ бы́л де́нь?	*What day was yesterday?*
—Вчера́ был **четве́рг**.	*Yesterday was Thursday.*
—Како́й за́втра бу́дет де́нь?	*What day will it be tomorrow?*
—За́втра бу́дет **суббо́та**.	*Tomorrow it will be Saturday.*

To express time *on* a particular day (e.g., *on Wednesday, on next Tuesday, on that day*), use the preposition **в** followed by the name of the day in the *accusative* case.

в понеде́льник	*on Monday*
во вто́рник	*on Tuesday*
в сре́ду	*on Wednesday*
в четве́рг	*on Thursday*
в пя́тницу	*on Friday*
в суббо́ту	*on Saturday*
в воскресе́нье	*on Sunday*

—Когда́ у тебя́ экза́мен?	*When do you have an exam?*
—У меня́ экза́мен **в сре́ду**.	*I have an exam on Wednesday.*
—В како́й де́нь вы́ прие́дете домо́й?	*On what day will you come home?*
—Мы́ прие́дем **в суббо́ту**.	*We'll arrive on Saturday.*
—В каки́е дни́ о́н рабо́тает?	*On what days does he work?*
—О́н рабо́тает **во вто́рник** и **в четве́рг**.	*He works on Tuesday and Thursday.*
В э́тот де́нь мы́ перее́хали в Москву́.	*On that day we moved to Moscow.*

To express *this, last,* and *next* referring to days (as well as to weeks, months, seasons, years, and centuries), the noun is preceded by the modifiers **э́тот**, **про́шлый**, and **бу́дущий** (or **сле́дующий**), respectively.

в э́тот понеде́льник *this Monday*
в про́шлую сре́ду *last Wednesday*
в бу́дущий/сле́дующий вто́рник *next Tuesday*

To express repeated occurrence *on* a day of the week (e.g., *on Mondays, on Fridays*), use the preposition **по** followed by the name of the day in the *dative plural.*

Она́ рабо́тает до́ма **по сре́дам**.	*She works at home on Wednesdays.*
По пя́тницам она́ покупа́ет проду́кты.	*On Fridays she buys groceries.*
По суббо́там мы́ е́здим на да́чу.	*On Saturdays we go to the dacha.*

Expressing Parts of a Day

Parts of a day (**у́тро** *morning,* **ве́чер** *evening,* **но́чь** *night*) preceded by a demonstrative pronoun (e.g., *that morning, that evening*) are expressed by the preposition **в** followed by the *accusative* case.

В э́то у́тро мы́ ра́но вста́ли.	*On that morning we got up early.*
В ту́ но́чь мне́ не спало́сь.	*That night I couldn't sleep.*

Otherwise, the *instrumental* case of the noun is used *with no preceding preposition.*

у́тром *in the morning*
днём *in the daytime*
ве́чером *in the evening*
но́чью *in the night*

NOTE: English *in the afternoon* can be rendered in Russian either as **днём** or as **во второ́й полови́не дня́** (lit., *in the second half of the day*).

NOTE: English *this* referring to parts of the day (e.g., *this morning*) is expressed by the adverb **сего́дня** *today*: **сего́дня у́тром** *this morning,* **сего́дня днём** *this afternoon,* **сего́дня ве́чером** *this evening* (*tonight*). With other units of time, *this* is normally expressed by a form of the demonstrative pronoun **э́тот**.

Weeks

To express time with weeks, use the preposition **на** followed by the *prepositional* case of the noun **неде́ля**. Note the following common expressions.

на э́той неде́ле *this week*
на про́шлой неде́ле *last week*
на бу́дущей/сле́дующей неде́ле *next week*

Months

The names of months in Russian are masculine and, unlike in English, they are not capitalized.

янва́рь	*January*	ию́ль	*July*
февра́ль	*February*	а́вгуст	*August*
ма́рт	*March*	сентя́брь	*September*
апре́ль	*April*	октя́брь	*October*
ма́й	*May*	ноя́брь	*November*
ию́нь	*June*	дека́брь	*December*

To express *in* a particular month, use the preposition **в** followed by the name of the month, or the noun **ме́сяц** *month,* in the *prepositional* case. The months from **сентя́брь** through **февра́ль** have stress on the ending, e.g., **в сентябре́** *in September,* **в октябре́** *in October,* **в ноябре́** *in November.* The other months have fixed stress.

Она́ вы́шла за́муж **в а́вгусте**.	*She got married in August.*
О́н око́нчит шко́лу **в ию́не**.	*He will graduate from school in June.*
Она́ ожида́ет ребёнка **в э́том ме́сяце**.	*She is expecting a baby this month.*
О́н бы́л в Ло́ндоне **в про́шлом ме́сяце**.	*He was in London last month.*
Мы́ е́дем в о́тпуск **в бу́дущем ме́сяце**.	*We are going on vacation next month.*

English expressions such as *this June, last August, next September* are rendered in Russian as **в ию́не э́того го́да** *in June of this year,* **в а́вгусте про́шлого го́да** *in August of last year,* **в сентябре́ бу́дущего го́да** *in September of next year.*

Они́ поже́нятся **в ию́ле бу́дущего го́да**.	*They will get married next July.*
О́н вы́шел на пе́нсию **в ма́рте про́шлого го́да**.	*He retired last March.*

Seasons

Following are the nouns denoting the seasons, as well as their *instrumental* case forms, which denote *in* the respective season.

весна́	*spring*	весно́й	*in the spring*
ле́то	*summer*	ле́том	*in the summer*
о́сень	*fall*	о́сенью	*in the fall*
зима́	*winter*	зимо́й	*in the winter*

Мы́ отдыха́ем **ле́том**.	*We vacation in the summer.*
Учё́бный го́д начина́ется **о́сенью**.	*The school year begins in the fall.*
Зде́сь **зимо́й** очень хо́лодно.	*It is very cold here in the winter.*

Expressions with *this/next/last* and the seasons are usually rendered by the *instrumental* case of the modifier + noun phrase, e.g., **э́той весно́й** *this spring,* **бу́дущим ле́том** *next summer,* **про́шлой зимо́й** *last winter.*

Years and Centuries

To express *in* a year or *in* a century, use the preposition **в** followed by the *prepositional* case of the noun **го́д** *year* or **ве́к/столе́тие** *century.* Following are commonly used expressions with years and centuries.

в э́том году́ *this year*	в э́том ве́ке/столе́тии *in this century*
в про́шлом году́ *last year*	в про́шлом ве́ке *in the last century*
в бу́дущем/сле́дующем году́ *next year*	в бу́дущем/сле́дующем ве́ке *in the next century*

16. Write the Russian equivalent of each of the following time expressions.

1. on Friday ____________________
2. next week ____________________
3. last Wednesday ____________________
4. that evening ____________________
5. in the spring ____________________
6. in June ____________________
7. this year ____________________
8. this March ____________________
9. next December ____________________
10. this week ____________________
11. last month ____________________
12. in the afternoon ____________________
13. next Saturday ____________________
14. in the summer ____________________
15. in the last century ____________________
16. last winter ____________________

Dates with Months and Years

To simply state the date (e.g., *today is the seventh of June, yesterday was the sixth),* use the neuter singular *nominative* case form of an ordinal number (the noun **числó** *number* is understood). The name of the month, if mentioned, is in the *genitive* case.

—Какóе сегóдня числó?	*What is the date today?*
—Сегóдня **пéрвое** мáя.	*Today is the first of May.*
—Какóе вчерá бы́ло числó?	*What was the date yesterday?*
—Вчерá бы́ло **тридцáтое** ию́ня.	*Yesterday was the thirtieth of June.*

To express *on* a particular date, the ordinal number (along with the month) is in the *genitive* case, with *no preceding preposition.*

—Какóго числá ты́ уезжáешь?	*On what date are you leaving?*
—Я́ уезжáю **деся́того** áвгуста.	*I'm leaving on the tenth of August.*
—Когдá у тебя́ дéнь рождéния?	*When is your birthday?*
—**Двáдцать вторóго** ию́ня.	*On June twenty-second.*

Unlike in English, where the number expressing the date can either precede or follow the month (*He was born on the fifth of June / on June fifth*), in Russian the ordinal number must *precede* the month.

Use of Prepositions with Dates

To express *from* … (a certain date) or *since* … (a certain time), use the preposition **с** followed by the time expression in the *genitive* case.

Мы́ бу́дем в óтпуске **с седьмóго ию́ля**.	*We'll be on vacation from July seventh on.*
Óн здéсь рабóтает **с пéрвого ию́ня**.	*He's been working here since June first.*

To express *from* … *to* … with dates (or other time expressions), use the prepositions **с … до …**, each of which is followed by the *genitive* case.

Я́ бу́ду в Москвé **с трéтьего до деся́того** января́.	*I'll be in Moscow from the third to the tenth of January.*
Óн занимáлся **с утрá до вéчера**.	*He studied from morning until night.*

The prepositions **с** + *genitive* case and **по** + *accusative* case are used to express inclusive dates: *from … through.…*

Мы́ бу́дем в Пари́же **с вторóго по шестóе** мáрта.	*We will be in Paris from the second through the sixth of March.*

Dates in Years

Dates in years, like months, are expressed by ordinal numbers. For example, unlike in English, where the year 1998 is read or spoken as "nineteen ninety-eight," in Russian one says "the one thousand nine hundred ninety-eighth year." Note that the last number is a declined ordinal number, agreeing with the noun **гóд** *year,* as in the following examples.

Ты́сяча девятьсóт девянóсто **восьмóй** гóд.	*The year 1998.*
Двухты́сячный гóд.	*The year 2000.*
Двé ты́сячи **пéрвый** гóд.	*The year 2001.*

When answering the question **в како́м году́?** *in what year?* (or **когда́?** *when?*), the year date, like the question phrase, is expressed by the preposition **в** followed by the *prepositional* case of the ordinal and the word *year* in the "locative" form, **году́**.

—Когда́ основа́ли го́род Са́нкт-Петербу́рг?	*When was the city of St. Petersburg founded?*
—Са́нкт-Петербу́рг основа́ли **в ты́сяча семьсо́т тре́тьем году́**.	*St. Petersburg was founded in 1703.*
—В како́м году́ роди́лся Бори́с Пастерна́к?	*In what year was Boris Pasternak born?*
—Пастерна́к роди́лся **в ты́сяча восемьсо́т девяно́стом году́**.	*Pasternak was born in 1890.*
—В како́м году́ у́мер Ле́в Толсто́й?	*In what year did Leo Tolstoy die?*
—Толсто́й у́мер **в ты́сяча девятьсо́т деся́том году́**.	*Tolstoy died in 1910.*

To indicate a more specific time of the year (e.g., *in August 1945*; *on September 21, 2009*), the ordinal and the word **го́д** must be in the *genitive* case.

Моя́ до́чь ко́нчит шко́лу в ию́не две́ ты́сячи **восьмо́го го́да**.	*My daughter will graduate from high school in June 2008.*
Они́ пожени́лись два́дцать второ́го ма́я две́ ты́сячи **тре́тьего го́да**.	*They got married on May 22, 2003.*

In Russian, as in English, when the century referred to is obvious from the context, the date may be reduced in conversational style to just the ordinal number and the required form of the word **го́д**.

О́н ко́нчил шко́лу **в шестьдеся́т седьмо́м году́**.	*He graduated from high school in '67.*

To indicate decades (e.g., *the sixties, the nineties*), the preposition **в** is followed by the *accusative* or *prepositional* case of the ordinal number in the plural.

О́н бы́л студе́нтом **в шестидеся́тые го́ды / в шестидеся́тых года́х**.	*He was a student in the sixties.*

NOTE: The Russian equivalents of the abbreviations B.C. and A.D. are, respectively, **до на́шей э́ры (до н.э.)** *before our era* and **на́шей э́ры (н.э.)** *of our era*, e.g., **О́н жи́л в пе́рвом ве́ке *до на́шей э́ры*** *He lived in the first century B.C.*

Order of Numbers in Dates

In Russian, unlike in English, the first number in a date given in figures indicates the day and the second indicates the month (often in Roman numerals), followed by the year. The numbers are separated by either a period or a forward slash: **7.VI.98** or **7/VI/98** (English *6/7/98* or *June 7, 1998*). This is the standard form for dates used in the headings of letters, on Russian visa applications, and in other documents.

Да́та рожде́ния: **22.VI.93**	*Date of Birth: 6/22/93*
Да́та прибы́тия в Росси́ю: **10.III.05**	*Date of Arrival in Russia: 3/10/05*

17. Complete each of the following sentences with the Russian equivalent of the date in parentheses.

1. Сего́дня ________________ (is June 7, 1998).
2. Са́ша родила́сь ________________ (on February 6, 1990).
3. А́нна Ахма́това умерла́ ________________ (in 1966).
4. Ру́сский алфави́т со́здали ________________ (in 860 A.D.).
5. Мы́ бу́дем в о́тпуске ________________ (from the fifth to the twelfth).
6. Вчера́ бы́ло ________________ (twenty-first of April).
7. Да́та прибы́тия в Росси́ю ________________ (5/VII/09).
8. Она́ здесь живёт ________________ (since the fifteenth of September).

Expressing Age

To express age in Russian, the person (or thing) whose age is indicated is in the *dative* case, and the number of years (or months) is typically rendered by a cardinal number and the required case form of the noun *year* (**1, 21, 31, … го́д**; **2, 3, 4, 22, … го́да**; **5, 6, 7, … ле́т**). One may ask **Ско́лько ва́м** (**ему́**, **ей́**, etc.) **ле́т?** *How old are you* (*is he/she,* etc.)*?* or (about an infant) **Ско́лько ему́ (ей́) ме́сяцев?** *How old is he/she*)*?* One may answer in the following ways.

Ребёнку **три́ ме́сяца**.	*The child is three months.*
Де́вочке **го́д и се́мь ме́сяцев**.	*The little girl is a year and seven months.*
Е́й **два́дцать оди́н го́д**.	*She is twenty-one.*
Мне́ **три́дцать два́ го́да**.	*I am thirty-two.*
Отцу́ **со́рок ше́сть ле́т**.	*My father is forty-six.*

To indicate an approaching birthday, the ordinal number may be used with the present or past tense of the verb **идти́**.

Ему́ идёт **восьмо́й го́д**.	*He is going on eight.*
Е́й тогда́ шёл **деся́тый го́д**.	*At that time she was going on ten.*

To ask *at what age* an event takes place, the preposition **в** + the *prepositional* case is used: **в како́м во́зрасте?** This question may be answered either by **в во́зрасте** + the *genitive* case of the number, or simply by **в** + the *accusative* case of the number.

—В како́м во́зрасте она́ вы́шла за́муж?	*At what age did she get married?*
—В **восемна́дцать ле́т**.	*At eighteen.*

18. Translate each of the following sentences into Russian, using words for the numbers.

1. She is twenty-one. ____________________
2. He is forty-five. ____________________
3. How old is the baby? ____________________
4. How old is the mother? ____________________
5. The baby is a year and 3 months. ____________________
6. He is going on sixteen. ____________________
7. At what age did he die? ____________________
8. He died at the age of 71. ____________________

Time

Both cardinal and ordinal numbers are used in answering the questions **Кото́рый ча́с?** or the more colloquial **Ско́лько (сейча́с) вре́мени?** *What time is it (now)?* There are two methods for telling time in Russian: a conversational way of telling time by the clock, and the 24-hour system used for official purposes.

Conversational Clock Time

In the conversational method of telling time by the clock, the time can fall *on the hour,* within *the first half of the hour,* or within *the second half of the hour.* Time on the hour is expressed by a cardinal number and the appropriate case/number form of the noun **ча́с** *o'clock* (lit., *hour*).

On the Hour

RUSSIAN		ENGLISH	
1.00	ча́с	1:00	*one o'clock*
2.00	два́ часа́	2:00	*two o'clock*
3.00	три́ часа́	3:00	*three o'clock*
4.00	четы́ре часа́	4:00	*four o'clock*
5.00	пя́ть часо́в	5:00	*five o'clock*
8.00	во́семь часо́в	8:00	*eight o'clock*
12.00	двена́дцать часо́в	12:00	*twelve o'clock*

NOTE: Russian uses a period instead of a colon to separate hours and minutes.

NOTE: 12:00 *noon* is **по́лдень**, and 12:00 *midnight* is **по́лночь**.

Time that falls during the first half hour is expressed by both a cardinal and an ordinal number: The cardinal is used to state the number of minutes elapsed of the *following* hour, which is expressed by the ordinal number, e.g., 1:10 is understood as "ten minutes (elapsed) of the *second* hour": **де́сять мину́т второ́го**.

In the First Half of the Hour

RUSSIAN		ENGLISH	
12.01	одна́ мину́та пе́рвого	12:01	*one minute after/past twelve*
1.02	две́ мину́ты второ́го	1:02	*two minutes after/past one*
2.05	пя́ть мину́т тре́тьего	2:05	*five minutes after/past two*
3.15	пятна́дцать мину́т четвёртого OR че́тверть четвёртого	3:15	*fifteen minutes after/past three* OR *quarter after/past three*
4.30	полови́на пя́того OR полпя́того	4:30	*thirty minutes after/past four* OR *half past four*

NOTE: In colloquial speech, **че́тверть** *quarter* is used instead of **пятна́дцать мину́т** *fifteen minutes*, and **полови́на** *half* may be shortened to **пол** and prefixed to the ordinal, e.g., **полшесто́го** *half past five.*

The ordinal number denotes the 60-minute period between hours: **пе́рвый ча́с** (the period between 12:00 and 1:00), **второ́й ча́с** (the period between 1:00 and 2:00), **тре́тий ча́с** (the period between 2:00 and 3:00), etc. Thus, when one says in Russian **«в пе́рвом часу́»**, it is comparable to saying in English *"after twelve (o'clock)."*

Сейча́с **шесто́й** ча́с.	*It's now after five.*
Она́ позвони́ла **в восьмо́м часу́**.	*She called after seven.*
О́н прие́хал **в нача́ле деся́того**.	*He arrived shortly after nine.*

In the second half of the hour, the approaching hour is expressed by a cardinal number "less the number of minutes remaining" before the hour strikes, e.g., 2:55, expressed in English as *five minutes until three,* is expressed in Russian as "without five minutes three": **без пяти́ (мину́т) три́**, where the preposition **без** *without* is followed by the genitive case of the cardinal number and (optionally) the genitive case of **мину́та**.

In the Second Half of the Hour

RUSSIAN		ENGLISH	
4.31	без двадцати́ девяти́ (мину́т) пя́ть	4:31	*twenty-nine (minutes) before/until five*
6.40	без двадцати́ (мину́т) се́мь	6:40	*twenty (minutes) before/until seven*
8.45	без че́тверти де́вять	8:45	*fifteen (minutes) before/until nine*
10.57	без трёх (мину́т) оди́ннадцать	10:57	*three (minutes) before/until eleven*
11.59	без одно́й (мину́ты) двена́дцать	11:59	*one (minute) before/until twelve*
12.50	без десяти́ (мину́т) ча́с	12:50	*ten (minutes) before/until one*

One distinguishes A.M. and P.M. (e.g., *7:00 A.M.* and *7:00 P.M., 2:00 A.M.* and *2:00 P.M.*) by using one of the following nouns in the genitive case.

у́тро	(5:00–12:00 A.M.)	се́мь часо́в **утра́** *seven o'clock in the morning*
де́нь	(12:00–5:00 P.M.)	два́ часа́ **дня́** *two o'clock in the afternoon*
ве́чер	(5:00–12:00 P.M.)	се́мь часо́в **ве́чера** *seven o'clock in the evening*
но́чь	(12:00–5:00 A.M.)	два́ часа́ **но́чи** *two o'clock in the morning*

Expressing "At What Time?"

To ask *at what time?* use the phrase **в кото́ром часу́?** or the more colloquial **во ско́лько вре́мени?** The construction used to respond to either of these phrases (or to the question **когда́?** *when?*) depends on the clock time.

(i) On the hour, and up to the first half hour, use the preposition **в** + the *accusative* case.

в ча́с дня́ *at one o'clock in the afternoon*
в одну́ мину́ту второ́го *at one minute past one*
в пя́ть мину́т тре́тьего *at five past two*
в че́тверть восьмо́го *at a quarter past seven*

(ii) In the second half of the hour, **в** is omitted before the preposition **без**.

без че́тверти де́вять *at quarter to nine*
без дву́х мину́т двена́дцать *at two minutes to twelve*

(iii) At the half hour, use the preposition **в** + the *prepositional* case of **полови́на**.

в полови́не второ́го *at one thirty*

Also, to express nonspecific time "between hours," e.g., *after five,* use **в** + *prepositional* case.

в шесто́м часу́ *after five, between five and six*
в нача́ле восьмо́го *shortly after seven*

19. Translate each of the following expressions into Russian, using words for the numbers.

1. It is now 7:00 A.M. ________________
2. It is now after two. ________________
3. 6:00 P.M. ________________
4. 8:15 ________________
5. at 9:30 in the evening ________________
6. at 12:00 midnight ________________
7. at 3:00 in the morning ________________
8. at 12:45 ________________
9. It is now 1:00 in the afternoon. ________________
10. 3:57 ________________
11. at 9:59 ________________
12. 12:00 noon ________________

Official Time: 24-Hour System

Official time in Russia is expressed according to the 24-hour clock. This is the system used for schedules at railroad stations and airports, for newspaper listings of radio and television programming, as well as for movies, concerts, performances, and other official schedules.

In the 24-hour system, the declined forms of the words **ча́с** and **мину́та** may be omitted. A *zero* is usually expressed by **но́ль**. Official time is read as in the table below.

RUSSIAN		ENGLISH
7.30	се́мь (часо́в) три́дцать (мину́т)	7:30 A.M.
8.45	во́семь (часо́в) со́рок пя́ть (мину́т)	8:45 A.M.
11.15	оди́ннадцать (часо́в) пятна́дцать (мину́т)	11:15 A.M.
12.00	двена́дцать но́ль но́ль	Noon
13.05	трина́дцать (часо́в) пя́ть (мину́т) OR трина́дцать но́ль пя́ть	1:05 P.M.
18.00	восемна́дцать но́ль но́ль	6:00 P.M.
21.10	два́дцать оди́н (ча́с) де́сять (мину́т)	9:10 P.M.
0.00	но́ль часо́в (но́ль но́ль мину́т)	Midnight
0.10	но́ль (часо́в) де́сять (мину́т)	12:10 A.M.
1.00	ча́с но́ль но́ль	1:00 A.M.
3.03	три́ (часа́) три́ (мину́ты) OR три́ но́ль три́	3:03 A.M.

To express *at a certain time,* use the preposition **в** + the *accusative* case.

По́езд отправля́ется **в пя́ть со́рок**. *The train departs at 5:40 A.M.*
Самолёт вылета́ет **в во́семь но́ль три́**. *The plane takes off at 8:03 A.M.*

20. Translate each of the following time expressions into Russian according to the 24-hour clock, using words for the numbers.

1. 6:40 A.M. ________________
2. 8:35 A.M. ________________
3. 10:20 A.M. ________________
4. 1:00 P.M. ________________
5. 3:15 P.M. ________________
6. 6:05 P.M. ________________
7. 8:10 P.M. ________________
8. 11:40 P.M. ________________
9. Midnight ________________
10. 12:50 A.M. ________________

Approximation

Approximation with numbers indicating time, quantity, age, distance, weight, etc., can be expressed in the following ways.

(a) By reversing the order of the number and the noun

два́ ме́сяца	*two months*	ме́сяца два́	*about two months*
ему́ со́рок ле́т	*he is 40 years old*	ему́ ле́т со́рок	*he is about 40 years old*

A preposition in a time expression invariably stands before the number.

в два́ часа́	*at two o'clock*	часа́ в два́	*at about two o'clock*
че́рез три́ го́да	*in three years*	го́да че́рез три́	*in about three years*

(b) With **о́коло** *about* followed by the number in the genitive case

о́коло дву́х ме́сяцев	*about two months*
о́коло пяти́ ме́тров	*about five meters*

In colloquial style the indefinite adverb **где́-то** *somewhere* may precede **о́коло** in the meaning *somewhere around.*

где́-то о́коло пяти́ часо́в	*somewhere around five o'clock*

(c) With the adverb **приме́рно** *roughly* or **приблизи́тельно** *approximately*

приме́рно сто́ челове́к	*roughly a hundred people*
приблизи́тельно в ча́с	*at approximately one o'clock*

Verbs

Overview of Verbs

In Russian, as in English, verbs are words that express an action (*run, shout*), a process (*blush, melt*), or a state (*be, know*).

Transitive and Intransitive Verbs

Russian verbs, like English verbs, fall into two fundamental categories—*transitive verbs* and *intransitive verbs.* Transitivity is related to the notion of "direct object." A verb is transitive if it can take a direct object. A direct object is the noun or pronoun that usually follows the verb (with no preceding preposition) and denotes something (or someone) that is directly affected by the action of the verb. In the sentence *He opens the door,* the noun *door* is the direct object of the verb *open.* Similarly, in *She loves him,* the pronoun *him* is the direct object of the verb *love.* In both English and Russian, the direct object answers the question *what?* or *whom?*: ***Что́*** **он открыва́ет?** *What* (Acc.) *does he open?* ***Кого́*** **она́ лю́бит?** *Whom* (Acc.) *does she love?* The direct object in Russian is normally in the accusative case (but a direct object of a negated transitive verb may be in the genitive case; see Chapter 2, page 47).

An intransitive verb is one that cannot (normally) occur with a direct object, for example, the verbs *snore* and *nap.* In the sentences *He snores* and *Grandpa often naps,* a direct object is impossible. A verb that is transitive in English may be intransitive in Russian, e.g., the verb *envy* is transitive in English (*I envy him* (direct object)), but its Russian equivalent, **зави́довать**, is not transitive, since it takes an object in the dative case (**Я́ зави́дую** ***ему́*** (dative object)). Russian verbs that end in the particle **-ся/-сь** are intransitive (see page 212).

Personal Endings

In English one says *I know,* but *s/he knows,* adding an *-s* to the verb when the subject is in the *third person* and is *singular* in *number.* Russian verbs also have endings to indicate the person and number of the verb's subject, but in Russian there are six such *personal endings,* one for each subject in the *first, second,* and *third persons, singular* and *plural.* Changing the personal endings of the verb so that they agree with the subject is called *conjugation.* In Russian there are two conjugation patterns, or sets of verb endings, called the *first conjugation* and the *second conjugation.* All regular verbs belong to one of these two conjugations.

Forms of Address: Informal and Formal

Russian has two forms for the English pronoun *you*—**ты́** and **вы́**. The pronoun **ты́** is a familiar singular form, used when addressing a pet, child, relative, friend, or a colleague who is of similar age or professional status. The pronoun **вы́** has two functions: It is the formal *you,* used both when addressing one or more individuals who are strangers or casual acquaintances; **вы́** also functions simply as the plural *you* when addressing any two or more individuals. Even when it is used to address one person formally, **вы́** requires the verb to agree in the *plural* (see also page 101).

Verb Tenses

In Russian, as in English, verbs have *tense.* Tense relates the time of the action or state denoted by the verb to a particular time, usually to the present moment. Russian verbs distinguish three tenses: the present (now), the past (prior to now), and the future (subsequent to now). English verbs, by contrast, not only distinguish the present, past, and future, but make a number of other distinctions that are described in English grammar as "progressive" and "perfect" tenses, for example, the "present progressive" (*he is writing*), the "present perfect progressive" (*he has been writing*), the "past progressive" (*he was writing*), the "past perfect" (*he had written*), the "future perfect" (*he will have written*), and several others. While Russian lacks equivalents to these English verb forms, the meanings associated with them can be approximated in Russian through a combination of tense and a second temporal property of the verb, that of *aspect.*

Verb Aspects

Nearly all Russian verbs are either *imperfective* or *perfective* in *aspect.* While tense indicates the time *when* an action occurs, aspect refers to different ways of viewing *how* the action occurs in time. For example, *imperfective* verbs are used to describe (a) an action in progress without reference to its completion or result (*she is / was / will be working*); (b) an action that is habitual or repeated (*she works / used to work / will be working every day*); (c) an action viewed in general terms, without reference to its performance on any specific occasion (*she works hard, he speaks Russian well*). *Perfective* verbs are used to describe an action that has been, or will be, carried through to completion, and whose result may be expressed in the context (*He wrote / will write the letter. He will send it tomorrow* (result)).

Verbs of the imperfective aspect have the three tenses: present, past, and future. However, perfective verbs have only the past and future tense, since the meaning of the perfective aspect—"completed action"—is incompatible with the present-tense meaning of an action "in progress at the present moment."

Verb Moods

Verbs in Russian, as in English, have *mood,* that is, a way of indicating the speaker's attitude toward the factuality or likelihood of the stated action. Verbs in Russian distinguish four moods: the *indicative,* the *imperative,* the *conditional,* and the *subjunctive.*

The *indicative* mood is used to make factual statements. This is the most commonly used mood, and the only one that expresses tense (*John* studies *Russian, Sasha* went *to Moscow, Mary* will buy *the wine*).

The *imperative* mood is used to make commands or to give advice (Read *this article!* Don't buy *that book!*).

The *conditional* mood expresses hypothetical and contrary-to-fact statements. These refer to conditional statements that are not likely to be realized (hypothetical) or were not realized (contrary-to-fact). Compare the following statements.

(a) *If you* invite *me, I* will go.
(b) *If you* invited *me, I* would go.
(c) *If you* had invited *me, I* would have gone.

The situation described in (a) *may* in fact occur, and is expressed in the indicative mood. The situation described in (b) is *hypothetical*; statements of this type imply that the situation is doubtful or unlikely (it's unlikely that you will invite me, and unlikely that I will go). The situation in (c) is *contrary-to-fact*; statements of this type imply that the situation described was not realized, i.e., the facts are the opposite (you did not invite me and I did not go). In Russian, statements like those in (b) and (c) are expressed by the particle **бы** + the past tense of the verb in the conditional clause, as well as in the consequence clause (see page 260).

The *subjunctive* mood is used to refer to actions that have yet to be, and may not be, realized, since they are wishes (*I wish you* were *here*), desires (*We asked that he* might bring *some wine*), or even fears (*I am afraid that he* could tell *her*). Like the conditional mood, the subjunctive in Russian is expressed by the particle **бы** or the conjunction **чтобы** (an amalgam of **что́** + **бы**) followed by the past-tense form of the verb (see page 262).

Conjugation

The Infinitive

The infinitive of the verb (e.g., *to read*) is the form used to cite Russian verbs in dictionaries. It is also the form of the verb that often follows another verb (*I love* to read, *He wants* to go). Most Russian verbs have the infinitive ending **-ть** (e.g., **чита́*ть*** *to read);* less common are **-ти** (**нес*ти́*** *to carry)* and **-чь** (**мо́*чь*** *to be able*).

The Past Tense

The past tense of a verb in Russian agrees in gender and number with its subject. The past tense of most verbs can be obtained by removing the infinitive ending and replacing it with **-л** (masc. sing.), **-ло** (neut. sing.), **-ла** (fem. sing.), or **-ли** (plural): **чита́-*ть*: о́н чита́*л*, оно́ чита́*ло*, она́ чита́*ла*, они́ чита́*ли*.**

Russian has only one past tense, formed from both imperfective and perfective verbs. An imperfective verb in the past tense corresponds to several forms of the English past, e.g., English *she read, she was reading,* and *she used to read* can all be rendered by the Russian past-tense imperfective **она́ *чита́ла*,** while English *she read* (to completion) and *she had read* are rendered by the past-tense perfective **она́ *прочита́ла* (журна́л)**.

The Present Tense

Russian has only *one* present-tense form corresponding to numerous forms of the English present; for example, English *she reads, she is reading,* and *she has been reading* can all be rendered, in the appropriate context, by Russian **она́ *чита́ет*.**

First- and Second-Conjugation Endings

The present tense of a verb has six endings, one each to denote the six possible subjects in the first-, second-, and third-person singular (*I, you, he/she/it*) and plural (*we, you, they*). These endings (except in the first-person singular and third-person plural) begin with a vowel that signals present (or future perfective) tense and indicates the verb's conjugation class: **-е-** (or stressed **-ё-**) indicates *first* (I) conjugation, while **-и-** indicates *second* (II) conjugation.

PERSON		CONJUGATION I	CONJUGATION II
Singular			
First	я́	-ю (-у)	-ю (-у)
Second	ты́	-ешь/-ёшь	-ишь
Third	о́н/она́/оно́	-ет/-ёт	-ит
Plural			
First	мы́	-ем/-ём	-им
Second	вы́	-ете/-ёте	-ите
Third	они́	-ют (-ут)	-ят (-ат)

NOTE: In first-conjugation verbs with stressed endings, the vowel **е** is spelled **ё**.

NOTE: The spelling of the first-person singular ending as **-ю** or **-у**, and the third-person plural ending as **-ют** or **-ут** (conjugation I) or as **-ят** or **-ат** (conjugation II), is determined by (1) whether the preceding consonant is soft or hard, respectively, and (2) the spelling rule that requires the unpaired consonants **ж**, **ч**, **ш**, **щ** to be followed only by the vowels **а** and **у**, never **я** and **ю** (see Spelling Rule 2, page 11).

These two sets of endings can be called the *non-past* endings, since "past" is the one tense they do *not* indicate; they indicate the *present* tense of an imperfective verb and the *future* tense of a perfective verb. For example, **прочита́ть** *to read* (perfective), when conjugated, has the meaning of the future tense: **я́ прочита́ю** *I will read,* **ты́ прочита́ешь** *you will read,* etc.

The following table shows the fully conjugated forms of the first-conjugation verbs **чита́ть** *to read,* **писа́ть** *to write,* and **име́ть** *to have,* and the second-conjugation verbs **говори́ть** *to speak* and **ви́деть** *to see.*

	чита́ть *to read*	**писа́ть** *to write*	**име́ть** *to have*	**говори́ть** *to speak*	**ви́деть** *to see*
я́	чита́**ю**	пиш**у́**	име́**ю**	говор**ю́**	ви́ж**у**
ты́	чита́**ешь**	пи́ш**ешь**	име́**ешь**	говор**и́шь**	ви́д**ишь**
о́н/она́	чита́**ет**	пи́ш**ет**	име́**ет**	говор**и́т**	ви́д**ит**
мы́	чита́**ем**	пи́ш**ем**	име́**ем**	говор**и́м**	ви́д**им**
вы́	чита́**ете**	пи́ш**ете**	име́**ете**	говор**и́те**	ви́д**ите**
они́	чита́**ют**	пи́ш**ут**	име́**ют**	говор**я́т**	ви́д**ят**

Verbs can also occur with the particle **-ся/-сь** following the verbal endings. This particle, which signals intransitivity, is spelled **-ся** after a consonant and **-сь** after a vowel, e.g., the verb **занима́ться** *to study.*

NON-PAST				PAST	
я́	занима́ю**сь**	мы́	занима́ем**ся**	о́н	занима́л**ся**
ты́	занима́ешь**ся**	вы́	занима́ете**сь**	она́	занима́ла**сь**
о́н/она́	занима́ет**ся**	они́	занима́ют**ся**	они́	занима́ли**сь**

Stress Patterns in the Non-Past

The verbs presented above illustrate the three regular stress patterns for verbs in the non-past.

1. *Stem stress.* All forms are stressed on the same syllable of the stem, e.g., in **чита́ть**, **име́ть**, and **ви́деть**.

2. *End stress.* All forms are stressed on the same syllable of the ending, e.g., in **говори́ть**.

3. *Shifting stress.* The first-person singular ending is stressed, but the stress shifts back one syllable in all the other forms, e.g., in **писа́ть**.

Consonant Alternations in Conjugation

In a number of verbs the final consonant of the stem alternates with another consonant in certain forms. In first-conjugation verbs that have a consonant alternation, the change takes place in all forms of the non-past, e.g., **с** > **ш** in **писа́ть**: **пи*ш*у́**, **пи́*ш*ешь**, **пи́*ш*ет**, **пи́*ш*ем**, **пи́*ш*ете**, **пи́*ш*ут**. In second-conjugation verbs that have a consonant alternation, the change takes place *only in the first-person singular,* e.g., **д** > **ж** in **ви́деть**: **ви́*ж*у**, **ви́*д*ишь**, **ви́*д*ит**, etc. These consonant alternations are not random; they follow a regular pattern (see below, pages 221 and 225).

In order to conjugate a Russian verb, then, one must know three essential facts.

1. Whether the verb belongs to the first or second conjugation
2. Whether the verb has fixed or shifting stress
3. Whether the stem-final consonant alternates with another consonant in conjugation

However, these facts can*not* be determined from the infinitive form of the verb: While both ***чита́ть*** and ***писа́ть,*** two verbs with an infinitive in **-ать**, belong to the first conjugation, the conjugation patterns of these verbs are very different. Similarly, while both ***име́ть*** and ***ви́деть*** have an infinitive in **-еть**, these verbs differ with respect to two of the above essential facts, namely, (1) and (3).

Since the information needed to conjugate a verb is *not* predictable from the infinitive, one approach to learning the conjugation of verbs is to memorize at least three key forms of each verb: the *infinitive* and the *first- and second-person singular.* The remaining forms of the verb are predictable from these three forms.

Infinitive	писа́ть
First-Person Singular	пишу́
Second-Person Singular	пи́шешь

Knowing the three key forms above, one can correctly conjugate any regular verb. However, a more general approach is possible, one that groups hundreds, even thousands, of verbs into a small number of *types,* based on similar endings, stress patterns, and consonant alternation properties. Obviously, knowing a verb's type will greatly simplify the task of learning the conjugation of Russian verbs. The key to this approach is knowing which verbal *suffix* is found at the end of the verb's *basic stem.* It is the particular suffix (or the shape of a *nonsuffixed* stem) that classifies the verb as belonging to one of the verb types.

Verbal Stem Structure: (Prefix) + Root + (Suffix)

The Basic Stem: Suffixed and Nonsuffixed

Russian verbs, like nouns and adjectives, have the structure *stem + ending.* All verb stems contain a *root,* the segment where the basic meaning resides, e.g., **чит** *read.* In addition, the verb root may be preceded by a *prefix* and/or followed by a *suffix.* A prefix normally adds some element of meaning to the initial verb (and may change its aspect), for example, when added to the verb **чита́ть**, the prefix **пере-** has the meaning *re-* and produces the new (perfective) verb, **перечита́ть** *to re-read.* While prefixes like **пере-** greatly enrich the meanings of verbs, they have no effect on a verb's conjugation.

A suffix, on the other hand, is the element of the stem that specifies the way the verb conjugates. The vast majority of Russian verb stems end in a suffix. However, due to modifications that occur when endings are added to the stem, the suffix may not be visible in all forms of the verb: The suffix may appear in a "truncated" (reduced) form, or if it consists of only a single vowel, it may not appear at all.

Following are the basic stems of the verbs introduced in the table above. Note how the verb's suffix changes in form, or even disappears, in the third-person plural non-past, in the infinitive, and in the past tense.

BASIC STEM	THIRD-PERSON PLURAL	INFINITIVE	PAST
чит-АЙ	чита́ют (читай-ут)	чита́ть	чита́л
пис-А	пи́шут	писа́ть	писа́л
им-ЕЙ	име́ют (имей-ут)	име́ть	име́л
говор-И	говоря́т	говори́ть	говори́л
вид-Е	ви́дят	ви́деть	ви́дел

Rules for Combining Basic Stem + Endings

These changes in the appearance of the verb suffix are governed by two simple rules that apply at the juncture where endings are added to the basic stem. The rules concern what happens to consonants and vowels when they come together. Verb stems may end in a vowel (V) or a consonant (C), and verb endings may begin with a vowel or a consonant. The rules for combining stems and endings are the following.

- When combining "unlikes," i.e., vowel + consonant or consonant + vowel, simply *add* them together.

  V + C = VC
  C + V = CV

- When adding "likes," i.e., vowel + vowel or consonant + consonant, *truncate* (drop) the first element.

  $V^1 + V^2 = V^2$
  $C^1 + C^2 = C^2$

  Let us apply these rules of combination to **чит-ай** and **говор-и**.

C + V	чит-ай-	+ ут	= чита́ют (читай-ут)
$C^1 + C^2$	чит-ай-	+ ть	= чита́ть
	чит-ай-	+ л	= чита́л
$V^1 + V^2$	говор-и-	+ ят	= говоря́т
V + C	говор-и-	+ ть	= говори́ть
	говор-и-	+ л	= говори́л

NOTE: Whenever a stem ending in **й**, such as **чит-ай-** (or **им-ей-**), is combined with vowel endings, the rule C + V applies regularly: The **й** remains at the end of the stem, but is "hidden" by the Cyrillic spelling of the sequence "vowel + soft-series vowel." Recall that when they follow a vowel, the soft-series vowel letters **я**, **е**, **ё**, and **ю** indicate the presence of [y] **й** between the two vowel letters. Therefore, the boundary line between stem and ending runs through these letters, i.e., **чита́ют** has the stem + ending structure **читай-** + **ут** (and **име́ют** has the structure **имей-** + **ут**).

A relatively small number of verbs have a basic stem that does not contain a suffix, e.g., the verb **жи́ть** *to live* has the basic stem **жив-**. All verbs with a nonsuffixed basic stem belong to the first conjugation. The same rules for adding endings to stems apply to nonsuffixed stems.

C + V = CV	жив-	+ ут	= живу́т
$C^1 + C^2 = C^2$	жив-	+ ть	= жи́ть
	жив-	+ л	= жи́л

Stems with a Suffix

Suffixes That Build First-Conjugation Verbs

A small number of suffixes build first-conjugation verbs, and each one of these suffixes distinguishes a verb type or class. These verb classes are either *productive* or *nonproductive*. The productive classes are those on which new verbs entering the language are modeled. The nonproductive classes are remnants from earlier periods, which no longer serve as a model for new verbs.

The following seven suffixes are used to form first-conjugation verbs: (1) **АЙ**, (2) **ЕЙ**, (3) **ОВА/УЙ**, (4) **НУ**, (5) **А**, (6) **А̣-ВАЙ**, and (7) **О**.

(1) Stems in **АЙ**

чита́ть (**чита́**_**й**_-) *to read*

NON-PAST				PAST	
я́	чита́**ю**	мы́	чита́**ем**	о́н	чита́**л**
ты́	чита́**ешь**	вы́	чита́**ете**	она́	чита́**ла**
о́н/она́	чита́**ет**	они́	чита́**ют**	они́	чита́**ли**

Characteristics

Verbs with a stem in **ай** *have fixed stress and no consonant alternations.*

This productive class contains thousands of verbs. In some verbs, such as **гуля́ть** *to take a stroll,* the suffix **ай** is spelled **яй**, to indicate a preceding soft consonant. In other verbs the suffix **ай** occurs within a larger suffix such as **вай** (**наде-*ва́й*-/надева́ть** *to put on*) or **ывай/ивай** (**расска́з-*ывай*-/расска́зывать** *to tell,* **спра́ш*ивай*/спра́шивать** *to ask*), but these verbs conjugate exactly like the verbs with a stem containing the simple suffix **ай**.

Following is a list of some commonly used verbs with a stem in **ай**.

бе́гать *to run, jog*
вспомина́ть *to recall*
встреча́ть *to meet*
выступа́ть *to perform*
гуля́ть *to take a stroll*
де́лать *to do, make*
ду́мать *to think*
за́втракать *to have breakfast*
занима́ться *to study*
зна́ть *to know*
игра́ть *to play*
конча́ть *to finish*
мечта́ть *to dream*
начина́ть *to begin*
обе́дать *to have lunch*
обсужда́ть *to discuss*
объясня́ть *to explain*
опа́здывать *to be late*
отвеча́ть *to answer*
отдыха́ть *to rest, relax*
повторя́ть *to repeat*
покупа́ть *to buy*
помога́ть *to help*
понима́ть *to understand*
посыла́ть *to send*
рабо́тать *to work*
реша́ть *to decide, solve*
слу́шать *to listen*
собира́ть *to collect*
спра́шивать *to ask*
у́жинать *to have dinner*
чита́ть *to read*

1. Complete each of the following sentences with the correct present-tense form of the verb on the right.

1. О́н ча́сто ____________ му́зыку. слу́шать
2. Я́ ____________ ма́рки. собира́ть
3. Она́ ____________ тру́дную зада́чу. реша́ть
4. Мы́ обы́чно ____________ до́ма. за́втракать
5. Что́ ты́ ____________? де́лать
6. О́н ____________ о любви́. мечта́ть
7. Она́ ____________ фру́кты на ры́нке. покупа́ть
8. О́н хорошо́ ____________ на гита́ре. игра́ть
9. Они́ ре́дко ____________ в рестора́не. обе́дать
10. Мы́ ча́сто ____________ э́то вре́мя. вспомина́ть
11. Ка́ждое у́тро о́н ____________ в па́рке. гуля́ть
12. Сего́дня ____________ хоро́ший пиани́ст. выступа́ть
13. Мы́ обы́чно ____________ на мо́ре. отдыха́ть
14. О́н ____________ программи́стом. рабо́тать
15. Та́ня ча́сто ____________ на ле́кции. опа́здывать

16.	Она́ ________________ маркéтингом.	занима́ться
17.	Я́ ________________ интерéсную кни́гу.	чита́ть
18.	Они́ ________________ семéйный бюджéт.	обсужда́ть
19.	Мы́ ча́сто ________________ пи́сьма от сы́на.	получа́ть
20.	Учи́тель ________________ уро́к ученика́м.	объясня́ть
21.	Вы́ ________________ по-ру́сски?	понима́ть
22.	Профéссор ________________ лéкцию в дéвять часо́в.	начина́ть
23.	Ма́ма ________________ рабо́ту в пя́ть часо́в.	конча́ть
24.	Мо́й дру́г ча́сто ________________ анекдо́ты.	расска́зывать
25.	Ребёнок тако́й «почему́чка», всегда́ ________________ «почему́»?	спра́шивать

(2) Stems in **ЕЙ**

имéть (**имéй-**) *to have*

NON-PAST				PAST	
я́	имé**ю**	мы́	имé**ем**	о́н	имé**л**
ты́	имé**ешь**	вы́	имé**ете**	она́	имé**ла**
о́н/она́	имé**ет**	они́	имé**ют**	они́	имé**ли**

Characteristics

Verbs with a stem in **ей** *have fixed stress on the suffix. There are no consonant alternations.*

This productive verb type includes hundreds of verbs, many of which are formed from adjectives in the meaning "to become the property denoted" (e.g., **кра́сный** *red* > **краснéть** *to become red, blush,* **пусто́й** *empty* > **пустéть** *to become empty*). The majority of the verbs in this group are intransitive.

Following is a list of some commonly used verbs with a stem in **ей**.

беднéть *to grow poor*
белéть *to become/show white*
бледнéть *to grow pale*
богатéть *to get rich*
болéть *to be ill*
веселéть *to become cheerful*
владéть *to own*
голубéть *to turn blue*
грéть *to warm*
жалéть *to be sorry, regret*
желтéть *to turn yellow*
здоровéть *to become healthy*
имéть *to have*
краснéть *to turn red, blush*
лысéть *to grow bald*
немéть *to grow numb*
полнéть *to become stout*
пустéть *to become empty*
пьянéть *to get drunk*
редéть *to thin out*
робéть *to be timid*
слабéть *to become weak*
смéть *to dare*
старéть *to grow old, age*
теплéть *to become warm*
умéть *to know how*
успéть *to have time (to do …)*
худéть *to become thin, lose weight*
яснéть *to clear up*

2. Complete each of the following sentences with the correct present-tense form of the verb(s) on the right.

1.	О́н всегда́ ________________, когда́ ему́ дéлают уко́л.	бледнéть
2.	Она́ с дéтства ________________ а́стмой.	болéть
3.	Когда́ о́н сéрдится, лицо́ у него́ ________________.	краснéть
4.	Моя́ нога́ ________________, когда́ я́ сижу́ на нéй.	немéть
5.	Зимо́й со́лнце свéтит, но не ________________.	грéть
6.	О́сенью ли́стья на дерéвьях ________________.	желтéть

7.	О́н вы́глядит ста́рше свои́х ле́т потому́ что ________________.	лысе́ть
8.	Ка́к ты́ ________________ сказа́ть тако́е?	сме́ть
9.	За оди́н де́нь мы́ не ________________ сде́лать всё.	успе́ть
10.	Она́ то́лько неда́вно се́ла на дие́ту и уже́ ________________.	худе́ть
11.	Ба́бушка ________________ от боле́зни.	слабе́ть
12.	Что́ ты́ ________________? Тебе́ не́чего боя́ться.	робе́ть
13.	Во́лосы у меня́ уже́ ________________.	седе́ть
14.	Мно́гие лю́ди в Аме́рике ________________ дома́ми.	владе́ть
15.	Не́бо ________________ по́сле дождя́.	голубе́ть
16.	О́н до́лго боле́л, но тепе́рь он ________________.	здорове́ть
17.	Па́рус ________________ на горизо́нте.	беле́ть
18.	У́лицы ________________ по́сле полу́ночи.	пусте́ть
19.	Она́ ________________ от одно́й рю́мки.	пьяне́ть
20.	Я́ ________________, что не смо́гу прийти́ на ве́чер.	жале́ть
21.	Ма́льчик ________________ от перееда́ния.	полне́ть
22.	Ребёнок всегда́ ________________ при ви́де отца́.	веселе́ть
23.	Вы́ не ________________ пра́ва так к на́м относи́ться.	име́ть
24.	Во́лосы у него́ на голове́ ________________.	реде́ть
25.	В э́той стране́ прави́тели ________________, а наро́д ________________.	богате́ть, бедне́ть

(3) Stems in **ОВА/УЙ**

рискова́ть (риск*ова-*) *to risk*

NON-PAST				PAST	
я́	риску́**ю**	мы́	риску́**ем**	о́н	рискова́**л**
ты́	риску́**ешь**	вы́	риску́**ете**	она́	рискова́**ла**
о́н/она́	риску́**ет**	они́	риску́**ют**	они́	рискова́**ли**

Characteristics

Verbs with a stem in **ова** (*spelled* **ева** *after a soft consonant and the unpaired* **ж**, **ц**, **ч**, **ш**, **щ**) *replace this suffix in the non-past with* **уй**, *to which the personal endings are added* (**риск-у́й-** + **у** is spelled **риску́ю** and **риск-у́й-** + **ешь** is spelled **риску́ешь**, etc.).

The stress is fixed either on the root or on the suffix; if the stress in the infinitive falls on the second vowel of the suffix **ова́**, *in the non-past it will fall on* **у́й**.

There are thousands of verbs with a stem in **ОВА**, most of which contain roots borrowed from English, French, or German. This very productive class is steadily growing. In many verbs **ОВА** is contained within a larger suffix, such as **из-ова-** (**легал-*из-ова́*-ть** *to legalize*) or **(из)-ир-ова-** (**приват-*из-и́р-ова*-ть** *to privatize*, **имит-*и́р-ова*-ть** *to imitate*).

The following list contains some commonly used verbs with a stem in **ОВА**.

анализи́ровать *to analyze*
арестова́ть *to arrest*
волнова́ться *to be nervous*
гаранти́ровать *to guarantee*
горева́ть *to grieve*
де́йствовать *to function, work*
жа́ловаться *to complain*
импорти́ровать *to import*
интересова́ться *to be interested in*
комбини́ровать *to combine*
копи́ровать *to copy*
легализова́ть *to legalize*
организова́ть *to organize*
ночева́ть *to spend the night*
пакова́ть *to pack*
паркова́ть *to park*
практикова́ться *to practice*
приватизи́ровать *to privatize*
про́бовать *to test, try*
путеше́ствовать *to travel*

ра́довать *to gladden*
рекламúровать *to advertise*
рекомендова́ть *to recommend*
ремонтúровать *to repair*
рисова́ть *to draw*
сле́довать *to follow*
танцева́ть *to dance*
тре́бовать *to demand*
уча́ствовать *to take part in*
чу́вствовать *to feel*
фотографúровать *to photograph*
экспортúровать *to export*

3. Complete each of the following sentences with the correct present-tense form of the verb on the right.

1. Студе́нты ________________ ша́хматный клу́б. организова́ть
2. Вы́ ________________ мно́го от ва́ших студе́нтов. тре́бовать
3. Росси́я ________________ пшени́цу из Аме́рики. импорти́ровать
4. Мы́ ________________ маши́ну на э́той стоя́нке. паркова́ть
5. Я́ ________________ ва́м посмотре́ть э́тот фи́льм. сове́товать
6. Э́та де́вушка ________________ в ко́нкурсе красоты́. уча́ствовать
7. Твои́ пи́сьма на́с всегда́ ________________. ра́довать
8. Э́тот худо́жник ________________ карикату́ры. рисова́ть
9. Япо́ния ________________ автомоби́ли в Аме́рику. экспорти́ровать
10. Вы́ ________________ ру́сской литерату́рой? интересова́ться
11. Хотя́ о́н ча́сто боле́ет, о́н никогда́ не ________________. жа́ловаться
12. О́н ка́ждый де́нь ________________ в игре́ на гита́ре. практикова́ться
13. Мы́ ________________ на́шу кварти́ру. ремонти́ровать
14. Прави́тельство ________________ промы́шленность. приватизи́ровать
15. Тури́сты ________________ все́ истори́ческие па́мятники. фотографи́ровать
16. Ли́фт не ________________, поднимемся по ле́стнице. де́йствовать
17. Э́тот худо́жник уника́льно ________________ цвета́. комбини́ровать
18. Э́та фи́рма ча́сто ________________ свои́ това́ры. реклами́ровать
19. Я́ бы́л бо́лен, но я́ ________________ себя́ лу́чше. чу́вствовать
20. Они́ сейча́с в о́тпуске и ________________ по Евро́пе. путеше́ствовать
21. Её му́ж у́мер го́д наза́д, но она́ о нём ещё ________________. горева́ть
22. По суббо́там они́ ча́сто ________________ на дискоте́ке. танцева́ть
23. О́н всегда́ ________________ сове́ту отца́. сле́довать
24. Э́та ксе́рокс-маши́на хорошо́ ________________. копи́ровать
25. Я́ ________________ э́тот рестора́н, у ни́х отли́чное меню́. рекомендова́ть

(4) Stems in **НУ**

Verbs of this type fall into two subgroups: (a) the suffix **ну** remains in the past tense (**кри́кнуть** *to give a shout*, **О́н кри́кнул** *He gave a shout*), and (b) the suffix **(ну)** disappears in the past tense (**исче́знуть** *to disappear*, **О́н исче́з** *He disappeared*).

(a) The suffix **ну** remains in the past tense.

кри́кнуть (**крик*ну*-**) *to give a shout*

NON-PAST				PAST	
я́	кри́кн**у**	мы́	кри́кн**ем**	о́н	кри́кну**л**
ты́	кри́кн**ешь**	вы́	кри́кн**ете**	она́	кри́кну**ла**
о́н/она́	кри́кн**ет**	они́	кри́кн**ут**	они́	кри́кну**ли**

Characteristics

In all but three verbs, the stress is fixed, either on the root or on the suffix/non-past endings. The three verbs with shifting stress are the following.

тону́ть *to drown* (я́ тону́, ты́ то́нешь)
тяну́ть *to pull* (я́ тяну́, ты́ тя́нешь)
помяну́ть *to mention* (я́ помяну́, ты́ помя́нешь)

This is a productive class with hundreds of verbs, most of which are perfective in aspect. Many of the perfective verbs in this group denote an instantaneous action performed once, e.g., **кри́кнуть** *to give a shout,* **пры́гнуть** *to make a jump,* **толкну́ть** *to give a push.* The few imperfective verbs in this group include **гну́ть** *to bend* and the two shifting stress verbs noted above, **тону́ть** and **тяну́ть**.

The following list contains some common verbs with a stem in **ну**.

верну́ться *to return*
взгляну́ть *to cast a glance*
вздохну́ть *to sigh; to take a breath*
вы́кинуть *to throw out*
вы́нуть *to take out*
дёрнуть *to pull*
засну́ть *to fall asleep*
кри́кнуть *to shout*
ло́пнуть *to burst, split*
отдохну́ть *to rest*
просну́ться *to wake up*
пры́гнуть *to jump*
рискну́ть *to risk (once)*
ру́хнуть *to collapse*
улыбну́ться *to smile*
шагну́ть *to step*

(b) The suffix **(ну)** disappears in the past tense.

исче́знуть (исчез*(ну)*-) *to disappear*

NON-PAST				PAST	
я́	исче́зн**у**	мы́	исче́зн**ем**	о́н	исче́з
ты́	исче́зн**ешь**	вы́	исче́зн**ете**	она́	исче́з**ла**
о́н/она́	исче́зн**ет**	они́	исче́зн**ут**	они́	исче́з**ли**

Characteristics

The stress is fixed on the root. The suffix **(ну)** *is normally dropped in the past tense. When the suffix is dropped, the masculine singular form also loses the characteristic past-tense marker* **л**, *though this marker does occur in the other past-tense forms.*

This is a nonproductive group of about 60 verbs, most of which are intransitive. The simple (prefixless) verbs are imperfective, while the prefixed verbs are perfective.

Following are some common verbs that lose the suffix **(ну)** in the past tense.

блёкнуть *to fade; to wither*
га́снуть *to be extinguished*
ги́бнуть *to perish*
гло́хнуть *to go deaf*
дости́гнуть *to reach; to achieve*
замо́лкнуть *to fall silent*
ки́снуть *to turn sour*
кре́пнуть *to grow stronger*
мёрзнуть *to be cold, freeze*
мо́кнуть *to get wet/soaked*
па́хнуть *to smell*
привы́кнуть *to get used to*
сле́пнуть *to go blind*
со́хнуть *to become dry*

4. Complete each of the following sentences with the correct non-past form of the verb on the right.

1. Парово́з ________________ се́мь ваго́нов. тяну́ть
2. На ку́хне ________________ че́м-то вку́сным. па́хнуть
3. Я́ уста́л, дава́йте ________________. отдохну́ть
4. У́личные фонари́ автомати́чески ________________ на рассве́те. га́снуть

5.	В таку́ю жа́ркую пого́ду урожа́й бы́стро ________.	со́хнуть
6.	Ребёнок ско́ро ________ и захо́чет е́сть.	просну́ться
7.	Она́ подойдёт к кра́ю бассе́йна и ________ в во́ду.	пры́гнуть
8.	Жди́ меня́, я ________ че́рез пя́ть мину́т.	верну́ться
9.	Е́сли ты́ не убережёшь свои́ ве́щи, ма́ма и́х ________.	вы́кинуть
10.	Дава́йте ________!	вздохну́ть
11.	Зимо́й така́я труба́ ________ от моро́за.	ло́пнуть
12.	Вода́ в о́зере холо́дная, но вы́ к не́й ________.	привы́кнуть
13.	Молоко́ бы́стро ________ в тепле́.	ки́снуть
14.	Я́ не вы́ношу хо́лода, зимо́й я́ ча́сто ________.	мёрзнуть
15.	О́н занима́ется на тренажёрах и ________ с ка́ждым днём.	кре́пнуть

5. For each of the following sentences, write the past-tense form of the underlined present (or future perfective) verb.

1. Цветы́ поги́бнут от моро́за. ________
2. Цвета́ поблёкнут от со́лнца. ________
3. О́н ско́ро дости́гнет бо́льши́х успе́хов в свое́й рабо́те. ________
4. Де́ти но́вых иммигра́нтов бы́стро привыка́ют к но́вому языку́. ________
5. Ребёнок заснёт и зву́ки из де́тской замо́лкнут. ________, ________
6. Наступи́ла зима́, о́зеро ско́ро замёрзнет. ________
7. Она́ глубоко́ вздохнёт пе́ред прыжко́м в во́ду. ________
8. Костёр га́снет. ________
9. Самолёт ско́ро исче́знет за облака́ми. ________
10. От него́ ча́сто па́хнет табако́м. ________
11. Она́ с ка́ждым днём кре́пнет от лека́рства. ________
12. Секрета́рь вы́шел, но он ско́ро вернётся. ________
13. Кры́ша ру́хнет под тя́жестью сне́га. ________
14. О́н рискнёт на э́тот ра́з. ________

(5) Stems in **А** (**Я**)

Verbs with a basic stem ending in the suffix **a** fall into three subgroups: (a) those that are preceded by a vocalic root and whose root-final consonant alternates (**пис-/пиш-/писа́ть** *to write*); (b) those with a vocalic root ending in **й**, and so the suffix is spelled **я** (**й** + **а**) (**надея-ся/наде́яться** *to hope*); and (c) those that are preceded by a nonvocalic root (**жд-/жда́ть** *to wait*).

(a) Vocalic root followed by **a**

писа́ть (**писа-**) *to write*

NON-PAST				PAST	
я	пиш**у́**	мы́	пи́ш**ем**	о́н	писа́**л**
ты́	пи́ш**ешь**	вы́	пи́ш**ете**	она́	писа́**ла**
о́н/она́	пи́ш**ет**	они́	пи́ш**ут**	они́	писа́**ли**

Characteristics

The suffix **a** *is truncated and the preceding (root-final) consonant undergoes an alternation throughout the non-past.*

If, in the infinitive, the stress falls on the suffix **а**, *then the non-past forms generally will have the shifting stress pattern: stressed on the ending of the first-person singular, and shifting to the stem in all other forms.* (*Two exceptions are* **послáть** to send (**пошлю́, пошлёшь, … пошлю́т**) *and* **колебáться** to shake to and fro, hesitate (**колéблюсь, колéблешься, … колéблются**).)

If the stress in the infinitive falls on the root, it is normally fixed: **рéзать** to cut (**рéжу, рéжешь, … рéжут**).

This is a nonproductive class that contains about 60 verbs. Following are some common verbs of this type. The root-final alternations are shown on the right.

INFINITIVE	NON-PAST	ALTERNATION
писáть *to write*	пишу́, пи́шешь, … пи́шут	с > ш
махáть *to wave*	машу́, мáшешь, … мáшут	х > ш
рéзать *to cut*	рéжу, рéжешь, … рéжут	з > ж
сказáть *to say*	скажу́, скáжешь, … скáжут	з > ж
плáкать *to cry*	плáчу, плáчешь, … плáчут	к > ч
пря́тать *to hide*	пря́чу, пря́чешь, … пря́чут	т > ч
шептáть *to whisper*	шепчу́, шéпчешь, … шéпчут	т > ч
щекотáть *to tickle*	щекочу́, щекóчет, … щекóчут	т > ч
свистáть *to whistle*	свищу́, сви́щешь, … сви́щут	ст > щ
искáть *to look for*	ищу́, и́щешь, … и́щут	ск > щ
сы́пать *to strew*	сы́плю, сы́плешь, … сы́плют	п > пл
колебáть *to shake*	колéблю, колéблешь, … колéблют	б > бл
дремáть *to doze*	дремлю́, дрéмлешь, … дрéмлют	м > мл

NOTE: Other prefixed perfective verbs with the root **-каз-** follow the same pattern as **сказáть**: **рассказáть** *to tell,* **показáть** *to show,* **заказáть** *to order,* etc.

NOTE: All perfective verbs prefixed with **вы-** have fixed stress on this prefix in all forms.

вы́писать *to write out*	вы́пишу, вы́пишешь, … вы́пишут
вы́сказать *to state*	вы́скажу, вы́скажешь, … вы́скажут

6. Complete each of the following sentences with the correct present or future perfective form of the verb on the right.

1. Мáма ________________ письмó сы́ну. — писáть
2. Я́ всегдá ________________ ключ нáд двéрью. — пря́тать
3. О́н кóнчил шкóлу и тепéрь óн ________________ рабóту. — искáть
4. Дéти ________________ бумáгу нóжницами. — рéзать
5. Вы́ не ________________, гдé останóвка автóбуса? — сказáть
6. О́н сиди́т в клáссе и ________________ éй нá ухо. — шептáть
7. Мáльчик ________________, потомý что егó отругáл отéц. — плáкать
8. Вéтер ________________. — свистáть
9. О́н ________________ в своём решéнии. — колебáться
10. У меня́ в гóрле ________________. — щекотáть
11. Дéдушка ________________ в крéсле пóсле обéда. — дремáть
12. Минýточку, я сейчáс ________________ вáм квитáнцию. — вы́писать
13. Онá бои́тся, что начáльник ________________ éй в прóсьбе. — отказáть
14. О́н сиди́т на скамéйке и спокóйно ________________ кóрм голубя́м. — сы́пать

(b) Root-final **й** + **а** (spelled **я**)

надéяться (надея-ся) *to hope for*

NON-PAST				PAST	
я́	надé**юсь**	мы́	надé**емся**	óн	надéя**лся**
ты́	надé**ешься**	вы́	надé**етесь**	онá	надéя**лась**
óн/онá	надé**ется**	они́	надé**ются**	они́	надéя**лись**

Characteristics

The suffix is truncated throughout the present tense, but no alternation occurs.

There are 12 verbs of this type, of which the following are the most common.

INFINITIVE	NON-PAST
сéять *to sow*	сéю, сéешь, … сéют
надéяться *to hope*	надéюсь, надéешься, … надéются
смея́ться *to laugh*	смею́сь, смеёшься, … смею́тся
ла́ять *to bark*	ла́ю, ла́ешь, … ла́ют
та́ять *to melt*	та́ю, та́ешь, … та́ют

7. Complete each of the following sentences with the correct present-tense form of the verb on the right.

1. Соба́ка ____________, когда́ стуча́т в две́рь. ла́ять
2. Сего́дня тепло́, и сне́г ____________. та́ять
3. Я́ всегда́ ____________ на́д его́ шу́тками. смея́ться
4. Мы́ ____________, что тебé уда́стся прие́хать к на́м. надéяться
5. Де́душка ____________ пшени́цу в по́ле. се́ять

(c) Nonvocalic root followed by **а**

жда́ть (жд*а*-) *to wait*

NON-PAST				PAST	
я́	жд**у́**	мы́	жд**ём**	óн	жда́**л**
ты́	жд**ёшь**	вы́	жд**ёте**	онá	жда**ла́**
óн/онá	жд**ёт**	они́	жд**у́т**	они́	жда́**ли**

Characteristics

All verbs with a nonvocalic root and the suffix **а** *have fixed stress on the endings in the non-past. In the past, the stress shifts from the stem in the masculine, neuter, and plural forms to the ending in the feminine.*

There are about 12 verbs of this type, the most common of which appear below.

INFINITIVE	NON-PAST	PAST
вра́ть *to tell lies* (colloquial)	вру́, врёшь, … вру́т	вра́л, врала́, вра́ли
жда́ть *to wait*	жду́, ждёшь, … жду́т	жда́л, ждала́, жда́ли
жра́ть *to guzzle*	жру́, жрёшь, … жру́т	жра́л, жрала́, жра́ли
лга́ть *to lie*	лгу́, лжёшь, … лгу́т	лга́л, лгала́, лга́ли
рва́ть *to tear*	рву́, рвёшь, … рву́т	рва́л, рвала́, рва́ли
ржа́ть *to neigh*	ржу́, ржёшь, … ржу́т	ржа́л, ржала́, ржа́ли

Three verbs in this group have an inserted root vowel in the non past.

INFINITIVE	NON-PAST	PAST
бра́ть *to take*	беру́, берёшь, … беру́т	бра́л, брала́, бра́ли
дра́ть *to tear*	деру́, дерёшь, … деру́т	дра́л, драла́, дра́ли
зва́ть *to call*	зову́, зовёшь, … зову́т	зва́л, звала́, зва́ли

NOTE: Two verbs with a root vowel conjugate like those with no root vowel: **соса́ть** *to suck* (**сосу́**, **сосёшь**, … **сосу́т**) and **стона́ть** *to groan* (**стону́**, **сто́нешь**, … **сто́нут**).

NOTE: Two verbs with a nonvocalic root followed by the suffix **a** belong to the second conjugation: **спа́ть** *to sleep* (**сплю́**, **спи́шь**, … **спя́т**) and **гна́ть** *to chase* (**гоню́**, **го́нишь**, … **го́нят**).

8. Complete each of the following sentences with the correct present-tense form of the verb on the right.

1. Я́ ________________ ча́стные уро́ки ру́сского языка́. бра́ть
2. Ло́шади ________________ при ви́де хозя́ина. ржа́ть
3. О́н ________________ на ка́ждом шагу́ и поэ́тому ему́ никто́ не ве́рит. вра́ть
4. Мы́ ________________ на́ш о́тпуск с больши́м нетерпе́нием. жда́ть
5. Ма́льчик сиди́т на полу́ и ________________ бума́гу на кусо́чки. рва́ть
6. Почему́ ты́ ________________ и не говори́шь пра́вду? лга́ть
7. Пора́ домо́й, ма́ма ________________ на́с на обе́д. зва́ть
8. О́н та́к ________________, ка́к бу́дто о́н це́лый ме́сяц не е́л. жра́ть
9. Они́ ________________ кору́ с пру́тьев и де́лают из пру́тьев корзи́ны. дра́ть

(6) Stems in **А-ВАЙ**

дава́ть (**да-вай-**) *to give*

NON-PAST				PAST	
я́	да**ю́**	мы́	да**ём**	о́н	дава́**л**
ты́	да**ёшь**	вы́	да**ёте**	она́	дава́**ла**
о́н/она́	да**ёт**	они́	да**ю́т**	они́	дава́**ли**

Characteristics

The **ва** *part of the stem is omitted in the non-past, leaving the stem in* **ай**. *The non-past has fixed stress on the endings.*

The verbs in this nonproductive group are formed from one of three roots ending in the vowel **a** (**-да-** *give*, **-зна-** *know*, **-ста-** *stand*) to which the suffix **-вай-** is added. All the verbs in this group are imperfective, and all but **дава́ть** are prefixed.

Some common verbs in this group are listed below according to the underlying root.

(a) Verbs with the root **-да-**

отдава́ть *to give back, return; to give (up), devote*
передава́ть *to pass; to convey; to broadcast*
подава́ть *to serve*
преподава́ть *to teach*
продава́ть *to sell*
раздава́ться *to be heard, resound*

(b) Verbs with the root **-зна-**

признава́ть *to admit, acknowledge*
сознава́ть *to be conscious of, realize*
узнава́ть *to recognize; to find out*

(c) Verbs with the root **-ста-**

вставáть *to get up, stand up*
оставáться *to remain, stay, be left*
отставáть *to fall/lag behind*
переставáть *to stop (something in progress)*
уставáть *to grow tired*

9. Complete each of the following sentences with the correct present-tense form of the verb(s) on the right.

1.	Óн всегдá ________________ нáм от тебя́ привéт.	передавáть
2.	Торгóвцы ________________ вся́кие сувени́ры на ýлице.	продавáть
3.	Óн расстрóен, потомý что ________________ в своéй рабóте.	отставáть
4.	В э́том ресторáне ________________ вкуснéйшие шашлыки́.	подавáть
5.	Мáльчик ________________ свою́ оши́бку.	признавáть
6.	Онá ________________ англи́йский язы́к как инострáнный.	преподавáть
7.	Дá, я ________________ мою́ винý и я прошý прощéния.	сознавáть
8.	Óн всегдá ________________ долги́ вóвремя.	отдавáть
9.	Я́ обы́чно ________________ егó по похóдке.	узнавáть
10.	Óн спи́т днём тóлько, когдá óн óчень ________________.	уставáть
11.	Я́ срáзу ________________, когдá ________________ звонóк буди́льника.	вставáть, раздавáться
12.	Пóсле лéкции óн чáсто ________________ в аудитóрии, чтóбы поговори́ть с преподавáтелем.	оставáться

(7) Stems in **O**

борóться (**бор*о*-**) *to struggle*

NON-PAST				PAST	
я́	бор**ю́сь**	мы́	бó**ремся**	óн	борó**лся**
ты́	бó**решься**	вы́	бó**ретесь**	онá	борó**лась**
óн/онá	бó**рется**	они́	бó**рются**	они́	борó**лись**

Characteristics

The suffix **о** *is truncated before the vowel endings of the non-past, and the root-final* **р** *(or* **л***) becomes soft. These verbs have shifting stress.*

There are only 5 verbs in this group, and each has a stem ending in **оло** or **оро**. In one verb, **молóть** *to grind,* the root vowel **о** becomes **е** in the non-past (**мелю́**, **мéлешь**, ... **мéлют**).

борóться *to struggle*
колóть *to chop, split; to prick*
молóть *to grind*
полóть *to weed*
порóть *to undo, rip at the seams*

10. Complete each of the following sentences with the correct present-tense form of the verb on the right.

1.	Óн ________________ дровá во дворé.	колóть
2.	Мы́ ________________ за охрáну прирóды.	борóться

3. Она́ всегда́ ____________ ко́фе в кофемо́лке. моло́ть
4. Они́ ____________ в огоро́де. поло́ть
5. Портно́й ____________ брю́ки. поро́ть

Suffixes That Build Second-Conjugation Verbs

There are only three suffixes that build second-conjugation verbs, bringing the total number of verb suffixes to ten: (8) **И**, (9) **Е**, and (10) **А** (represented here as **жа**, since it is normally preceded by **ж**, **ч**, **ш**, **щ**, e.g., **лежа́ть/*лежа-*** *to lie* (physical position)).

(8) Stems in **И**

проси́ть (проси-) *to ask, make a request*

NON-PAST				PAST	
я́	прошу́	мы́	про́сим	о́н	проси́л
ты́	про́сишь	вы́	про́сите	она́	проси́ла
о́н/она́	про́сит	они́	про́сят	они́	проси́ли

Characteristics

Root-final **л**, **р**, *and* **и** *are soft throughout, i.e., in the first-person singular and third-person plural non-past they are followed by the endings* **-ю** *and* **-ят**, *respectively* (*e.g.*, **я говорю́, они́ говоря́т**). *Verbs with a root ending in* **д**, **з**, **с**, **т**, **ст**, *or one of the labial consonants* (**б**, **в**, **м**, **п**, **ф**), *undergo a consonant alternation in the first-person singular only.*

Some of these verbs have fixed stress (*e.g.*, **говорю́**, **говори́шь**, ... **говоря́т**), *while others have shifting stress* (*e.g.*, **прошу́**, **про́сишь**, ... **про́сят**).

This class contains thousands of verbs. Following are some common verbs of this type that undergo a consonant alternation in the first-person singular, indicated on the right.

INFINITIVE	NON-PAST	ALTERNATION
ходи́ть *to walk*	хожу́, хо́дишь, ... хо́дят	д > ж
вози́ть *to transport*	вожу́, во́зишь, ... во́зят	з > ж
носи́ть *to carry*	ношу́, но́сишь, ... но́сят	с > ш
плати́ть *to pay*	плачу́, пла́тишь, ... пла́тят	т > ч
чи́стить *to clean*	чи́щу, чи́стишь, ... чи́стят	ст > щ
люби́ть *to like, love*	люблю́, лю́бишь, ... лю́бят	б > бл
гото́вить *to prepare*	гото́влю, гото́вишь, ... гото́вят	в > вл
лови́ть *to catch*	ловлю́, ло́вишь, ... ло́вят	в > вл
ста́вить *to put (upright)*	ста́влю, ста́вишь, ... ста́вят	в > вл
корми́ть *to feed*	кормлю́, ко́рмишь, ... ко́рмят	м > мл
купи́ть *to buy*	куплю́, ку́пишь, ... ку́пят	п > пл

Following are some common verbs whose root-final consonant does not alternate.

вари́ть *to boil*	варю́, ва́ришь, ... ва́рят
говори́ть *to speak*	говорю́, говори́шь, ... говоря́т
жени́ться *to get married*	женю́сь, же́нишься, ... же́нятся
кури́ть *to smoke*	курю́, ку́ришь, ... ку́рят
учи́ть *to teach; to study*	учу́, у́чишь, ... у́чат
хвали́ть *to praise*	хвалю́, хва́лишь, ... хва́лят

11. Complete each of the following sentences with the correct non-past form of the verb(s) on the right.

1.	Э́та учи́тельница всегда́ __________ свои́х ученико́в.	хвали́ть
2.	Меня́ удивля́ет, что ты́ ещё __________.	кури́ть
3.	Ка́ждое у́тро я́ __________ по па́рку.	ходи́ть
4.	Профессора́ ча́сто __________ на заня́тия портфе́ли.	носи́ть
5.	Я́ ча́сто __________ свои́х дете́й в шко́лу.	вози́ть
6.	Э́ти студе́нты хорошо́ __________ по-ру́сски.	говори́ть
7.	Оте́ц __________ свою́ до́чь води́ть маши́ну.	учи́ть
8.	Я́ не __________, когда́ де́ти __________ соба́ку объе́дками.	люби́ть, корми́ть
9.	Мо́й дру́г __________ на о́чень ми́лой и у́мной де́вушке.	жени́ться
10.	Ба́бушка __________ карто́шку.	вари́ть
11.	Я́ всегда́ __________ са́м за себя́.	плати́ть
12.	Му́ж __________ ры́бу, а я её __________.	лови́ть, чи́стить

(9) Stems in **E**

сиде́ть (сиде-) *to sit*

NON-PAST				PAST	
я́	сиж**у́**	мы́	сид**и́м**	о́н	сиде́**л**
ты́	сид**и́шь**	вы́	сид**и́те**	она́	сиде́**ла**
о́н/она́	сид**и́т**	они́	сид**я́т**	они́	сиде́**ли**

Characteristics

Most of the verbs in this class have fixed stress, though the stress in a few common verbs (e.g., **смотре́ть** to watch) *is shifting.*

Like verbs with the suffix **и**, *verbs with the suffix* **е** *undergo an alternation if the root-final consonant is one that alternates; otherwise, the root-final consonant is soft throughout the non-past, as indicated by the spelling of the personal endings (e.g.,* **я́ смотрю́**, **они́ смо́трят**).

This is a nonproductive class containing about 50 verbs. Some commonly used verbs of this type that have an alternation in the first-person singular are listed below.

INFINITIVE	NON-PAST	ALTERNATION
ви́деть *to see*	ви́жу, ви́дишь, … ви́дят	д > ж
висе́ть *to hang* (intr.)	вишу́, виси́шь, … вися́т	с > ш
зави́сеть *to depend*	зави́шу, зави́сишь, … зави́сят	с > ш
лете́ть *to fly*	лечу́, лети́шь, … летя́т	т > ч
свисте́ть *to whistle*	свищу́, свисти́шь, … свистя́т	ст > щ
терпе́ть *to tolerate*	терплю́, те́рпишь, … те́рпят	п > пл
храпе́ть *to snore*	храплю́, храпи́шь, … храпя́т	п > пл
шуме́ть *to make noise*	шумлю́, шуми́шь, … шумя́т	м > мл

Following are a few common verbs in this class whose root-final consonant does not alternate in the first-person singular.

боле́ть *to ache*	(*third-person only*) боли́т, боля́т
горе́ть *to burn*	горю́, гори́шь, … горя́т
смотре́ть *to look, watch*	смотрю́, смо́тришь, … смо́трят

12. Complete each of the following sentences with the correct present-tense form(s) of the verb on the right.

1.	Я́ ________ от твое́й по́мощи.	зави́сеть
2.	Она́ не лю́бит, а то́лько ________ своего́ му́жа.	терпе́ть
3.	Я́ ________ в Москву́, а куда́ ты́ ________?	лете́ть
4.	О́н ________ жела́нием пое́хать в Пари́ж.	горе́ть
5.	Спа́ть с ни́м невозмо́жно: о́н та́к гро́мко ________.	храпе́ть
6.	Я́ гро́мко ________, и соба́ка бежи́т ко мне́.	свисте́ть
7.	Его́ судьба́ ________ на волоске́.	висе́ть
8.	Сосе́ди не лю́бят, когда́ на́ши де́ти ________.	шуме́ть
9.	Я́ пло́хо ________ без очко́в.	ви́деть
10.	Я́ везу́ сы́на к зубно́му врачу́, у него́ ________ зу́б.	боле́ть

(10) Stems in **ЖА**

This class is a historically related subgroup of the verbs in **e**: In an early period the suffix **e** changed to **a** after "palatalizing" a root-final velar consonant, e.g., **к** > **ч** in the verb **крича́ть** *to shout* (***крик-е-ть** > **крич-а-ть**, unlike the perfective **кри́кнуть**, which preserves the original form of the root, **крик**). Since the suffix **a** is almost always preceded by one of the unpaired palatal consonants **ж**, **ч**, **ш**, **щ**, the stem of these verbs is represented as **ЖА**. This representation also serves to differentiate this group from the first-conjugation verbs with a stem in **A** (e.g., **пис*а*-**, but **крич*а*-**).

лежа́ть (**леж*а*-**) *to lie* (physical position)

NON-PAST				PAST	
я́	леж**у́**	мы́	леж**и́м**	о́н	лежа́л
ты́	леж**и́шь**	вы́	леж**и́те**	она́	лежа́**ла**
о́н/она́	леж**и́т**	они́	леж**а́т**	они́	лежа́**ли**

Characteristics

The suffix **а** *in these verbs is normally preceded by* **ж**, **ч**, **ш**, or **щ**, *but in two verbs it is preceded by* **й** (**йа** *spelled* **я**): **стоя́ть** to stand, **боя́ться** to be afraid.

Most verbs in this group have stress fixed on the endings.

Some of the more common verbs in this group are the following.

INFINITIVE	NON-PAST
боя́ться *to be afraid of*	бою́сь, бои́шься, ... боя́тся
держа́ть *to hold, keep*	держу́, де́ржишь, ... де́ржат
дрожа́ть *to tremble*	дрожу́, дрожи́шь, ... дрожа́т
дыша́ть *to breathe*	дышу́, ды́шишь, ... ды́шат
звуча́ть *to sound*	звучу́, звучи́шь, ... звуча́т
крича́ть *to shout*	кричу́, кричи́шь, ... крича́т
молча́ть *to be silent*	молчу́, молчи́шь, ... молча́т
слы́шать *to hear*	слы́шу, слы́шишь, ... слы́шат
стоя́ть *to stand*	стою́, стои́шь, ... стоя́т
стуча́ть *to knock*	стучу́, стучи́шь, ... стуча́т

NOTE: Not every verb whose infinitive ends in **-жать**, **-чать**, **-шать**, or **-щать** is a second-conjugation **лежа́ть**-type verb with a stem in **ЖА**; there are also first-conjugation verbs whose basic stem consists of an unpaired consonant preceding the suffix **-АЙ** (**чита́ть** type), e.g., **сажа́ть** *to seat,* **получа́ть** *to receive,* **слу́шать** *to listen,* **посеща́ть** *to visit.*

13. Complete each of the following sentences with the correct present-tense form of the verb on the right.

1. Ктó-то ________________ в двéрь. стучáть
2. Говори́те грóмче, я́ плóхо ________________. слы́шать
3. О́н ничегó не говори́т, óн ________________. молчáть
4. Переходя́ у́лицу, я́ всегдá ________________ дóчку за рýку. держáть
5. Ты́ ________________ от хóлода, погрéйся у огня́. дрожáть
6. Зачéм ты́ ________________? Мóжно без кри́ка обойти́сь. кричáть
7. На столé ________________ чáшки и блю́дца. стоя́ть
8. Гóлос у неё сегóдня ________________ прекрáсно. звучáть
9. О́н ________________ сóбственной тéни. боя́ться
10. Пóсле у́жина пáпа обы́чно ________________ на диване. лежáть

Irregular Verbs of Mixed Conjugation

There are very few irregular verbs in Russian. The following two irregular verbs are very common and should be memorized: **хотéть** *to want,* **бежáть** *to run.*

хотéть *to want*

PRESENT TENSE				PAST TENSE	
я́	хоч**у́**	мы́	хот**и́м**	óн	хотé**л**
ты́	хóч**ешь**	вы́	хот**и́те**	онá	хотé**ла**
óн/онá	хóч**ет**	они́	хот**я́т**	они́	хотé**ли**

Irregular characteristics

(a) *First-conjugation endings in the singular, second-conjugation endings in the plural*
(b) *Irregular stress pattern*
(c) *Alternation of root-final* **т** > **ч** *in the singular, but not in the plural*

бежáть *to run*

PRESENT TENSE				PAST TENSE	
я́	бег**у́**	мы́	беж**и́м**	óн	бежá**л**
ты́	беж**и́шь**	вы́	беж**и́те**	онá	бежá**ла**
óн/онá	беж**и́т**	они́	бег**у́т**	они́	бежá**ли**

Irregular characteristics
Endings of the second conjugation, except the third-person plural ending **-ут**

14. Complete each of the following sentences, using the correct past or non-past form(s) of the verbs **хотéть** or **бежáть**.

1. Онá ________________ (wants) слу́шать му́зыку, а они́ ________________ (want) пойти́ в кинó.
2. —Чтó вы́ ________________ (want) на обéд, мя́со, и́ли ры́бу?
   —Я́ ________________ (want) ры́бу.
3. Когдá онá былá молодóй, онá ________________ (wanted) бы́ть балери́ной.
4. —Кудá ты́ ________________ (are running)?
   —Я́ ________________ (am running) на заня́тие.
5. Дéти сейчáс ________________ (are running) по бéрегу реки́.
6. Мы́ ________________ (are running) в теáтр, мы́ не ________________ (want) опоздáть.

Summary Table
Conjugation I and II Verbs Classified by Basic Stem with a Suffix

First-Conjugation Verbs

SUFFIX		INFINITIVE	BASIC STEM	THIRD-PERSON PLURAL NON-PAST
(1) АЙ		чита́ть	чит-ай	чита́ют
(2) ЕЙ		име́ть	им-ей	име́ют
(3) ОВА/УЙ		рискова́ть	риск-ова	риску́ют
(4) НУ		кри́кнуть	крик-ну	кри́кнут
(НУ)		исче́знуть	исчез-(ну)-	исче́знут
(5) А	(a)	писа́ть	пис-а	пи́шут
	(b)	наде́яться	наде-я-ся	наде́ются
	(c)	ждать	жд-а-	жду́т
(6) А-ВАЙ		дава́ть	да-вай	даю́т
(7) О		боро́ться	бор-о-ся	бо́рются

Second-Conjugation Verbs

SUFFIX	INFINITIVE	BASIC STEM	THIRD-PERSON PLURAL NON-PAST
(8) И	говори́ть	говор-и	говоря́т
(9) Е	сиде́ть	сид-е	сидя́т
(10) ЖА	лежа́ть	леж-а	лежа́т

Irregular Verbs of Mixed Conjugation

SUFFIX	INFINITIVE	BASIC STEM	THIRD-PERSON PLURAL NON-PAST
	хоте́ть		хотя́т
	бежа́ть		бегу́т

Nonsuffixed Stems

Verbs with nonsuffixed stems all belong to the first conjugation. The stems of these verbs are equal to the root (or prefix + root). Verbs with no suffix are classified according to the final consonant of the stem/root. This consonant will be one of two types.

1. Resonants: **в, й, м, н, р**
2. Obstruents: **б, п, д, т, з, с, г, к, х**

Since all of the nonsuffixed stems end in a consonant, this consonant will be truncated before the consonant endings of the past tense and infinitive, as specified by the rules for combining stems and endings (page 214).

Resonant Stems

(1) Stems in **В**

жи́ть (*жив-*) *to live*

NON-PAST				PAST	
я́	живу́	мы́	**живём**	о́н	**жи́л**
ты́	**живёшь**	вы́	**живёте**	она́	**жила́**
о́н/она́	**живёт**	они́	**живу́т**	они́	**жи́ли**

Characteristics

The consonant **в** *is retained throughout the non-past. The stress shifts to the ending in the feminine past tense.*

There are only three verbs of this type.

INFINITIVE	NON-PAST	PAST
жи́ть *to live*	живу́, живёшь, … живу́т	жи́л, жила́
плы́ть *to swim*	плыву́, плывёшь, … плыву́т	плы́л, плыла́
слы́ть *to be, be reputed*	слыву́, слывёшь, … слыву́т	слы́л, слыла́

15. For each of the following sentences, write the present-tense form of the underlined past-tense verb(s).

1. Мы́ жи́ли в кварти́ре 10, а моя́ тётя жила́ в кварти́ре 15. ______________, ______________
2. Я́ плы́л к ло́дке, а она́ плыла́ к бе́регу. ______________, ______________
3. О́н слы́л знатоко́м в э́той о́бласти. ______________

(2) Stems in **Н**

ста́ть (ста*н*-) *to become; to begin*

NON-PAST				PAST	
я́	ста́ну	мы́	ста́**нем**	о́н	ста́**л**
ты́	ста́**нешь**	вы́	ста́**нете**	она́	ста́**ла**
о́н/она́	ста́**нет**	они́	ста́**нут**	они́	ста́**ли**

Characteristics

The consonant **н** *is retained throughout the non-past. Stress is fixed on the stem.*

There are only a few verbs of this type, mostly prefixed forms of **ста́ть** and **де́ть** *to put.*

INFINITIVE	NON-PAST
вста́ть *to stand up*	вста́ну, вста́нешь, … вста́нут
де́ть *to put, do with*	де́ну, де́нешь, … де́нут
наде́ть *to put on*	наде́ну, наде́нешь, … наде́нут
оде́ться *to get dressed*	оде́нусь, оде́нешься, … оде́нутся
разде́ться *to get undressed*	разде́нусь, разде́нешься, … разде́нутся

16. Complete each of the following sentences with the correct non-past form of the verb on the right.

1. Что́ ты́ сего́дня ____________________: джи́нсы и́ли ю́бку? наде́ть
2. О́н лю́бит живо́тных: наве́рное о́н ____________________ ветерина́ром. ста́ть
3. За́втра у́тром я́ ____________________ в ше́сть часо́в. вста́ть
4. О́н сказа́л, что ____________________ и сра́зу пойдёт спа́ть. разде́ться
5. Сейча́с мы́ ____________________ и бы́стро поза́втракаем. оде́ться

(3) Stems in **ОЙ**

откры́ть (откр*ой*-) *to open*

NON-PAST				PAST	
я́	откро́**ю**	мы́	откро́**ем**	о́н	откры́**л**
ты́	откро́**ешь**	вы́	откро́**ете**	она́	откры́**ла**
о́н/она́	откро́**ет**	они́	откро́**ют**	они́	откры́**ли**

Characteristics

The vowel **о** *is replaced by* **ы** *before consonantal endings. The stress is fixed on the stem.*

There are only a few verbs of this type, the more common of which are the following.

INFINITIVE	NON-PAST	PAST
откры́ть *to open*	откро́ю, откро́ешь, … откро́ют	откры́л, откры́ла
закры́ть *to close*	закро́ю, закро́ешь, … закро́ют	закры́л, закры́ла
мы́ть *to wash*	мо́ю, мо́ешь, … мо́ют	мы́л, мы́ла
ны́ть *to ache*	но́ю, но́ешь, … но́ют	ны́л, ны́ла
ры́ть *to dig*	ро́ю, ро́ешь, … ро́ют	ры́л, ры́ла

17. Complete each of the following sentences with the correct non-past form of the verb on the right.

1. Ма́ма ________________ посу́ду, а па́па вытира́ет. мы́ть
2. Зде́сь ду́шно, я́ ________________ окно́. откры́ть
3. Соба́ка ________________ я́му во дворе́ и пря́чет в не́й еду́. ры́ть
4. Когда́ вы́ сего́дня ________________ магази́н? закры́ть
5. У меня́ мы́шцы ________________ от уста́лости. ны́ть

(4) Stems in **ИЙ**

пи́ть (*пий-*) *to drink*

NON-PAST				PAST	
я́	пь**ю́**	мы́	пь**ём**	о́н	пи́**л**
ты́	пь**ёшь**	вы́	пь**ёте**	она́	пи**ла́**
о́н/она́	пь**ёт**	они́	пь**ю́т**	они́	пи́**ли**

Characteristics

The vowel **и** *is dropped throughout the non-past and is replaced by* **ь**. *The consonant* **й** *is truncated before the consonantal endings of the past tense and infinitive. In three of these verbs the stress shifts to the ending of the feminine past tense.*

There are five unprefixed verbs that conjugate exactly like **пи́ть**.

INFINITIVE	NON-PAST	PAST
би́ть *to beat*	бью, бьёшь, … бьют	би́л, би́ла
ви́ть *to twist*	вью, вьёшь, … вьют	ви́л, вила́
ли́ть *to pour*	лью, льёшь, … льют	ли́л, лила́
пи́ть *to drink*	пью, пьёшь, … пьют	пи́л, пила́
ши́ть *to sew*	шью, шьёшь, … шьют	ши́л, ши́ла

18. Complete each of the following sentences with the correct present-tense form of the verb on the right.

1. Я́ сама́ ________________ свои́ пла́тья. ши́ть
2. Ну и пого́да! До́ждь сего́дня ________________ как из ведра́. ли́ть
3. Она́ из него́ верёвки ________________. ви́ть
4. Вечера́ми мы́ обы́чно ________________ ча́й. пи́ть
5. Когда́ о́н се́рдится, о́н ________________ кулако́м по столу́. би́ть

Miscellaneous Stems in *й*

A few isolated verbs have one or another vowel preceding root-final **й**.

INFINITIVE	NON-PAST	PAST
ду́ть (дуй-) *to blow*	ду́ю, ду́ешь, ... ду́ют	ду́л, ду́ла
гни́ть (гний-) *to rot*	гнию́, гниёшь, ... гнию́т	гни́л, гни́ла

Two very commonly used verbs have one vowel in the infinitive and past tense, and a different vowel in the non-past.

	INFINITIVE	NON-PAST	PAST
(е > о)	пе́ть *to sing*	пою́, поёшь, ... пою́т	пе́л, пе́ла
(и > е)	бри́ть *to shave*	бре́ю, бре́ешь, ... бре́ют	бри́л, бри́ла

19. Complete each of the following sentences with the correct non-past form of the verb on the right.

1. Э́та певи́ца прекра́сно ________________. пе́ть
2. Па́па ________________ на су́п, потому́ что о́н горя́чий. ду́ть
3. Э́тот актёр ча́сто ________________ себе́ го́лову. бри́ть
4. Де́рево ________________ от сы́рости. гни́ть

(5) Stems in **M** or **H**

There are two groups of verbs with a stem in **м** or **н**.

(a) In the verbs of this group root-final **м** or **н** changes to the vowel **а** when followed by the consonantal endings of the infinitive and past tense. The consonant preceding **а** is normally soft (so **а** is spelled **я**, unless preceded by **ч** or **ж**). In two verbs (**взя́ть** *to take,* **нача́ть** *to begin*) the stress shifts from the stem to the ending in the feminine past.

There are six verbs in this group.

ROOT	INFINITIVE	NON-PAST	PAST
-ьм-	взя́ть *to take*	возьму́, возьмёшь, ... возьму́т	взя́л, взяла́
-жм-	жа́ть *to press, squeeze*	жму́, жмёшь, ... жму́т	жа́л, жа́ла
-жн-	жа́ть *to reap*	жну́, жнёшь, ... жну́т	жа́л, жа́ла
-мн-	мя́ть *to crumple*	мну́, мнёшь, ... мну́т	мя́л, мя́ла
-чн-	нача́ть *to begin*	начну́, начнёшь, ... начну́т	на́чал, начала́
-пн-	распя́ть *to crucify*	распну́, распнёшь, ... распну́т	распя́л, распя́ла

(b) The verbs in this group have a non-past stem in **-йм-** or **-ним-**, both of which change to **ня** before the consonantal endings of the infinitive and past tense; the stem **-йм-** follows prefixes ending in a vowel, while **-ним-** follows prefixes ending in a consonant. Verbs in the former group have shifting stress (to the feminine ending) in the past, while those in the latter group have shifting stress in both the non-past and past tenses. All these verbs are prefixed and perfective in aspect.

Following are some common verbs in **-нять** with the non-past in **-йм-**.

INFINITIVE	NON-PAST	PAST
заня́ть *to borrow*	займу́, займёшь, ... займу́т	за́нял, заняла́
наня́ть *to hire*	найму́, наймёшь, ... найму́т	на́нял, наняла́
поня́ть *to understand*	пойму́, поймёшь, ... пойму́т	по́нял, поняла́

Following are some common verbs in **-нять** with the non-past in **-ним-**.

обня́ть *to embrace*	обниму́, обни́мешь, ... обни́мут	о́бнял, обняла́
отня́ть *to take away*	отниму́, отни́мешь, ... отни́мут	о́тнял, отняла́
подня́ть *to raise, lift*	подниму́, подни́мешь, ... подни́мут	по́днял, подняла́
сня́ть *to take off*	сниму́, сни́мешь, ... сни́мут	сня́л, сняла́

One verb, **приня́ть**, has a prefix ending in a vowel, and has **-м-** in the non-past.

приня́ть *to accept*	приму́, при́мешь, ... при́мут	при́нял, приняла́

20. For each of the following sentences, write the non-past form of the underlined past-tense verb.

1. Она́ пра́вильно поняла́ тебя́. __________
2. Я́ взя́л с собо́й схе́му ста́нций метро́. __________
3. Я́ ду́маю, что она́ приняла́ его́ приглаше́ние. __________
4. Э́то де́ло о́тняло у на́с мно́го вре́мени. __________
5. О́н за́нял 5 ты́сяч до́лларов в ба́нке. __________
6. Мы́ на́няли на рабо́ту о́пытного программи́ста. __________
7. Она́ начала́ рабо́тать в 9 часо́в утра́. __________
8. Ма́ма жа́ла со́к из апельси́нов. __________
9. Фе́рмеры жа́ли пшени́цу серпо́м. __________
10. Учени́к бы́стро по́днял ру́ку. __________
11. О́н мя́л цветы́ от волне́ния. __________
12. Я́ сня́л ку́ртку. __________

(6) Stems in **Р**

Stems in **р** are found in a few verbs that contain the roots **мр**, **пр**, and **тр**. The verbs with these roots have the following characteristics.

(a) The **р** changes to **ере** before the infinitive ending **-ть** (**у-мере́-ть** *to die*).

(b) The **р** changes to **ер** before other consonants (**у-мер-ла́** *(she) died*).

(c) The **л** is dropped in the masculine past tense (**о́н у́мер** *he died*).

The verbs with these roots are often prefixed, and therefore are perfective in aspect.

INFINITIVE	NON-PAST	PAST
тере́ть *to rub, grate*	тру́, трёшь, ... тру́т	тёр, тёрла
вы́тереть *to rub (dry)*	вы́тру, вы́трешь, ... вы́трут	вы́тер, вы́терла
стере́ть *to erase*	сотру́, сотрёшь, ... сотру́т	стёр, стёрла
запере́ть *to lock*	запру́, запрёшь, ... запру́т	за́пер, заперла́
отпере́ть *to unlock*	отопру́, отопрёшь, ... отопру́т	о́тпер, отперла́
умере́ть *to die*	умру́, умрёшь, ... умру́т	у́мер, умерла́

21. For each of the following sentences, write the non-past form of the underlined past-tense verb.

1. Э́ти ту́фли тёрли мои́ но́ги. ________________
2. Я́ бы́стро вы́тер ру́ки. ________________
3. Учи́тельница стёрла упражне́ние с доски́. ________________
4. Она́ заперла́ две́рь на замо́к. ________________
5. О́н бы́стро о́тпер се́йф. ________________
6. Ба́бушка умерла́ от ста́рости. ________________

Obstruent Stems

(7) Stems in **З** and **С**

The verbs with a stem ending in **з** or **с** drop the **л** in the masculine past tense. The most common verbs in this group are the following.

INFINITIVE	NON-PAST	PAST
везти́ *to transport*	везу́, везёшь, … везу́т	вёз, везла́
ле́зть *to climb*	ле́зу, ле́зешь, … ле́зут	ле́з, ле́зла
ползти́ *to crawl*	ползу́, ползёшь, … ползу́т	по́лз, ползла́
нести́ *to carry*	несу́, несёшь, … несу́т	нёс, несла́
спасти́ *to save, rescue*	спасу́, спасёшь, … спасу́т	спа́с, спасла́
трясти́ *to shake*	трясу́, трясёшь, … трясу́т	тря́с, трясла́

(8) Stems in **Д** and **Т**

The stem-final **д** and **т** change to **с** before the infinitive ending. The **д** and **т** are dropped before the **л** in each past-tense form.

Following are common verbs with stem-final **д**.

INFINITIVE	NON-PAST	PAST
брести́ *to wander*	бреду́, бредёшь, … бреду́т	брёл, брела́
вести́ *to lead*	веду́, ведёшь, … веду́т	вёл, вела́
кла́сть *to put*	кладу́, кладёшь, … кладу́т	кла́л, кла́ла
кра́сть *to steal*	краду́, крадёшь, … краду́т	кра́л, кра́ла
упа́сть *to fall*	упаду́, упадёшь, … упаду́т	упа́л, упа́ла

In one verb in this group the vowel **е** in the infinitive and past tense changes to **я** in the non-past.

се́сть *to sit down*	ся́ду, ся́дешь, … ся́дут	се́л, се́ла

Following are some common verbs with stem-final **т**.

мести́ *to sweep*	мету́, метёшь, … мету́т	мёл, мела́
плести́ *to weave*	плету́, плетёшь, … плету́т	плёл, плела́
приобрести́ *to acquire*	приобрету́, приобретёшь, … приобрету́т	приобрёл, приобрела́
цвести́ *to bloom*	цвету́, цветёшь, … цвету́т	цвёл, цвела́

The verb **прочéсть** has the nonvocalic root **чт**, which gets the inserted vowel **е** or **ё** before the nonvocalic ending of the infinitive and masculine past tense.

INFINITIVE	NON-PAST	PAST
прочéсть *to read*	прочтý, прочтёшь, ... прочтýт	прочёл, прочлá

(9) Stems in **Б**

The stem-final **б** changes to **с** in the infinitive. The past-tense marker **л** is dropped in the masculine singular. There are only two verbs of this type.

INFINITIVE	NON-PAST	PAST
грести́ *to rake; to row*	гребý, гребёшь, ... гребýт	грёб, греблá, гребли́
скрести́ *to scrape*	скребý, скребёшь, ... скребýт	скрёб, скреблá, скребли́

22. For each of the following sentences, write the non-past form of the underlined past-tense verb or the past-tense form of the underlined non-past verb.

1. Óн сéл на дивáн ря́дом с нéй. ________________
2. Кóшка скреблá крéсло когтя́ми. ________________
3. Óн приобрёл нóвых друзéй. ________________
4. Студéнты несýт на заня́тия словари́. ________________
5. Ты́ всегдá клáл ключ под кóврик? ________________
6. Двóрник метёт тротуáр. ________________
7. Тюльпáны цвели́ в садý. ________________
8. Паýк плетёт паути́ну. ________________
9. Óн гребёт дéньги лопáтой. ________________
10. В часы́ пи́к маши́ны éле ползýт. ________________
11. Кóшка лéзет на дéрево. ________________
12. Мáльчики трясли́ я́блоню. ________________
13. Э́то лекáрство спасёт мнé жи́знь. ________________
14. Мáма везёт ребёнка в katя́ске. ________________
15. Онá велá детéй в шкóлу. ________________
16. Температýра упáла ни́же нуля́. ________________

(10) Stems in **Г** and **К**

Verbs with a stem in **г** and **к** have an infinitive ending in **-чь**. These consonants also alternate in the non-past: **г** > **ж** and **к** > **ч** before the vowel **е/ё** (i.e., in all forms except the first-person singular and third-person plural). The past-tense marker **л** is omitted in the masculine singular only.

Following are some common verbs with stem-final **г**.

INFINITIVE	NON-PAST	PAST
берéчь *to guard*	берегý, бережёшь, ... берегýт	берёг, береглá
стри́чь *to cut (hair)*	стригý, стрижёшь, ... стригýт	стри́г, стри́гла
мóчь *to be able*	могý, мóжешь, ... мóгут	мóг, моглá
помóчь *to help*	помогý, помóжешь, ... помóгут	помóг, помоглá

In one verb from this group the vowel **е/ё** in the infinitive / past tense changes to **я** in the non-past.

INFINITIVE	NON-PAST	PAST
ле́чь *to lie down*	ля́гу, ля́жешь, … ля́гут	лёг, легла́

The verb **же́чь** has the nonvocalic root **жг**, which gets the inserted vowel **е** or **ё** before the nonvocalic endings of the infinitive and masculine past tense.

же́чь *to burn*	жгу́, жгёшь, … жгу́т	жёг, жгла́

Following are some common verbs with stem-final **к**.

пе́чь *to bake*	пеку́, печёшь, … пеку́т	пёк, пекла́
отвле́чь *to distract*	отвлеку́, отвлечёшь, … отвлеку́т	отвлёк, отвлекла́
привле́чь *to attract*	привлеку́, привлечёшь, … привлеку́т	привлёк, привлекла́
те́чь *to flow*	теку́, течёшь, … теку́т	тёк, текла́

23. For each of the following sentences, write the non-past form of the underlined past-tense verb.

1. О́н лёг спа́ть в де́сять часо́в. ________________
2. Она́ не берегла́ своё здоро́вье. ________________
3. О́н мо́г купи́ть биле́ты в теа́тр. ________________
4. Ма́ма ча́сто пекла́ вку́сные пироги́. ________________
5. Мы́ помогли́ ему́ сня́ть кварти́ру. ________________
6. О́тдых на мо́ре отвлёк его́ от забо́т. ________________
7. Парикма́хер стри́г клие́нта. ________________
8. О́н обжёг па́льцы спи́чкой. ________________
9. Вре́мя текло́ бы́стро. ________________
10. Э́тот фи́льм привлёк большо́е внима́ние. ________________

Irregular Verbs with Nonsuffixed Stems

The following verbs depart in various ways from the regular patterns of the verb types presented above. These verbs should be memorized.

INFINITIVE	NON-PAST	PAST
бы́ть *to be*	бу́ду, бу́дешь, … бу́дут	бы́л, была́, бы́ли
да́ть *to give*	да́м, да́шь, да́ст, дади́м, дади́те, даду́т	да́л, дала́, да́ли
е́сть *to eat*	е́м, е́шь, е́ст, еди́м, еди́те, едя́т	е́л, е́ла, е́ли
е́хать *to go by vehicle*	е́ду, е́дешь, … е́дут	е́хал, е́хала, е́хали
идти́ *to go on foot*	иду́, идёшь, … иду́т	шёл, шла́, шли́
расти́ *to grow*	расту́, растёшь, … расту́т	ро́с, росла́, росли́

Summary Table
First-Conjugation Verbs with Nonsuffixed Stems Classified by Stem-Final Consonant

CLASSIFIER	INFINITIVE	BASIC STEM	THIRD-PERSON PLURAL NON-PAST
Resonant Stems			
(1) В	жи́ть	жив-	живу́т
(2) Н	ста́ть	стан-	ста́нут
(3) ОЙ	откры́ть	от-крой-	откро́ют
(4) ИЙ	пи́ть	пий-	пью́т
(5) М OR Н	нача́ть	на-чн-	начну́т
	поня́ть	по-йм-	пойму́т
	сня́ть	с-ним-	сни́мут
(6) Р	умере́ть	у-м/р-	умру́т
Obstruent Stems			
(7) З OR С	везти́	вез-	везу́т
	нести́	нес-	несу́т
(8) Д OR Т	вести́	вед-	веду́т
	мести́	мет-	мету́т
(9) Б	грести́	греб-	гребу́т
(10) Г OR К	мо́чь	мог-	мо́гут
	пе́чь	пек-	пеку́т

Verb Tenses: Formation

Present Tense

The present tense is formed only from imperfective verbs. Conjugating an imperfective verb in the non-past gives the present tense. Numerous examples of the present tense for all types of first- and second-conjugation verbs were presented in the preceding classification of verbs with suffixed and nonsuffixed basic stems.

Past Tense

Russian has but one past-tense form, obtained from both imperfective and perfective verbs. The past tense is obtained by attaching to the verbal stem the ending **-л**, followed by the appropriate gender/number marker to agree with the subject: -∅ (zero ending), **-а**, **-о**, **-и**. In most instances, the rule of "likes" and "unlikes" for combining stems and endings applies as expected.

(a) If a basic stem ends in a vowel, simply add the consonantal ending of the past tense.

VERB STEM		PAST		GENDER/NUMBER		EXAMPLE
				∅	(masc. subject)	о́н писа́л
писа	+	л	+	а	(fem. subject)	она́ писа́ла
				о	(neut. subject)	оно́ писа́ло
				и	(plural)	они́ писа́ли

(b) If the basic stem ends in a consonant, truncate that consonant before the consonant **л**.

VERB STEM		PAST		FORMS
читай	+	л	=	чита́л, чита́ла, чита́ло, чита́ли
жив	+	л	=	жи́л, жила́, жило́, жи́ли
стан	+	л	=	ста́л, ста́ла, ста́ло, ста́ли
вед	+	л	=	вёл, вела́, вело́, вели́
мет	+	л	=	мёл, мела́, мело́, мели́

However, nonsuffixed stems in **з**, **с**, **б**, **р**, **г**, and **к** are exceptions to the rule that the first of two "likes" truncates: Here the stem-final consonant is retained in all past-tense forms, and it is the past-tense marker **л** that is dropped, *but only in the masculine.*

вез	+	л	=	вёз, везла́, везло́, везли́
нес	+	л	=	нёс, несла́, несло́, несли́
греб	+	л	=	грёб, гребла́, гребло́, гребли́
мог	+	л	=	мо́г, могла́, могло́, могли́
пек	+	л	=	пёк, пекла́, пекло́, пекли́
ум/р	+	л	=	у́мер, умерла́, у́мерло, у́мерли

Finally, verbs that lose the suffix **ну** in the past tense, also lose the past-tense marker **л** in the masculine.

дости́г(ну)ть *to achieve*	дости́г, дости́гла, дости́гло, дости́гли
замёрз(ну)ть *to freeze*	замёрз, замёрзла, замёрзло, замёрзли
мо́к(ну)ть *to get wet*	мо́к, мо́кла, мо́кло, мо́кли

Future Tense

The future tense is formed from both imperfective and perfective verbs.

Imperfective Future

The future tense of an imperfective verb is formed from the appropriate conjugated form of the auxiliary verb **бы́ть** *to be* (**я́ бу́ду**, **ты́ бу́дешь**, ... **они́ бу́дут**) followed by the infinitive of the imperfective verb, e.g., the future tense of the imperfective verb **писа́ть** *to write.*

я́	бу́ду писа́ть
ты́	бу́дешь писа́ть
о́н/она́/оно́	бу́дет писа́ть
мы́	бу́дем писа́ть
вы́	бу́дете писа́ть
они́	бу́дут писа́ть
	will write, will be writing

Perfective Future

The future of any perfective verb is obtained simply by conjugating that verb. The endings of the perfective future are identical to those of the imperfective present tense. This is why the first- and second-conjugation endings of any verb are called "non-past": When an imperfective verb is conjugated, these endings indicate the present tense, but when a perfective verb is conjugated, these same endings indicate the perfective future.

The forms and distribution of the present, past, and future tenses are illustrated in the table below with the imperfective/perfective verb pair, **чита́ть/прочита́ть** *to read.*

PAST TENSE		PRESENT TENSE		FUTURE TENSE	
Imperfective читáть					
óн	читáл	я́	читáю	я́	бу́ду читáть
онá	читáла	ты́	читáешь	ты́	бу́дешь читáть
онó	читáло	óн/онá/онó	читáет	óн/онá/онó	бу́дет читáть
они́	читáли	мы́	читáем	мы́	бу́дем читáть
		вы́	читáете	вы́	бу́дете читáть
		они́	читáют	они́	бу́дут читáть
Perfective прочитáть					
óн	прочитáл	——		я́	прочитáю
онá	прочитáла			ты́	прочитáешь
онó	прочитáло			óн/онá/онó	прочитáет
они́	прочитáли			мы́	прочитáем
				вы́	прочитáете
				они́	прочитáют

24. Complete each of the following sentences with the future-tense form of the imperfective verb on the right.

1. Чтó вы́ ______________ зáвтра вéчером? **дéлать**
2. Зáвтра мы́ ______________ фи́льм. **смотрéть**
3. Ты́ сегóдня ______________ упражнéния? **писáть**
4. Сегóдня я́ ______________ на компью́тере. **рабóтать**
5. Онá скóро ______________ ру́сский язы́к. **изучáть**
6. Пóсле лéкции студéнты ______________ задáчи. **решáть**

Verb Aspects: Formation

Most Russian verbs occur in aspectual pairs: an imperfective form and a perfective form. In general, the members of an aspectual pair are similar in appearance, and practically identical in meaning, but are differentiated by (1) prefixation, (2) suffixation, or, rarely, (3) suppletion (which means that the members of the pair are different words, as in **брáть ~ взя́ть** *to take*).

(1) *Prefixation*

The perfective is formed from the imperfective verb by adding a particular prefix. The prefix changes the aspect of the verb, but it does not change its meaning or conjugation. It is important to learn which prefixes perfectivize particular unprefixed imperfective verbs. Following are examples of common imperfective verbs and their prefixed perfective partners.

IMPERFECTIVE	PERFECTIVE	MEANING
	Prefix **вы́-**	
пи́ть (**пий-**)	вы́пить (вы́**пий-**)	*to drink*
учи́ть (уч**и-**)	вы́учить (вы́уч**и-**)	*to learn*
	Prefix **за-**	
плати́ть (плат**и-**)	заплати́ть (заплат**и-**)	*to pay*
хотéть (irreg.)	захотéть (irreg.)	*to want*
	Prefix **ис-**	
пéчь (пе**к-**)	испéчь (испе**к-**)	*to bake*

Continued

IMPERFECTIVE	PERFECTIVE	MEANING
	Prefix **на-**	
печа́тать (печат**ай-**)	напеча́тать (напечат**ай-**)	*to print, type*
писа́ть (пис**а-**)	написа́ть (напис**а-**)	*to write*
рисова́ть (рис**ова-**)	нарисова́ть (нарис**ова-**)	*to draw*
	Prefix **по-**	
звони́ть (звон**и-**)	позвони́ть (позвон**и-**)	*to ring, telephone*
смотре́ть (смотр**е-**)	посмотре́ть (посмотр**е-**)	*to look, watch*
стро́ить (стро**и-**)	постро́ить (постро**и-**)	*to build*
	Prefixes **при-**, **про-**, **раз-**	
гото́вить (готов**и-**)	пригото́вить (приготов**и-**)	*to prepare*
чита́ть (чит**ай-**)	прочита́ть (прочит**ай-**)	*to read*
буди́ть (буд**и-**)	разбуди́ть (разбуд**и-**)	*to awaken*
	Prefix **с-**	
де́лать (дел**ай-**)	сде́лать (сдел**ай-**)	*to do, make*
е́сть (irreg.)	съе́сть (irreg.)	*to eat*
игра́ть (игр**ай-**)	сыгра́ть (сыгр**ай-**)	*to play*
пе́ть (irreg.)	спе́ть (irreg.)	*to sing*
мо́чь (мо**г-**)	смо́чь (смо**г-**)	*to be able*
	Prefix **у-**	
ви́деть (вид**е-**)	уви́деть (увид**е-**)	*to see*
слы́шать (слы**ша-**)	услы́шать (услы**ша-**)	*to hear*

(2) *Suffixation*

(a) The imperfective and perfective partners have different suffixes and, therefore, different conjugation patterns.

IMPERFECTIVE	PERFECTIVE	MEANING
изуча́ть (изуч**ай-**)	изучи́ть (изуч**и-**)	*to study*
конча́ть (конч**ай-**)	ко́нчить (конч**и-**)	*to finish*
покупа́ть (покуп**ай-**)	купи́ть (куп**и-**)	*to finish*
реша́ть (реш**ай-**)	реши́ть (реш**и-**)	*to decide, solve*
крича́ть (крич**-а-**)	кри́кнуть (крик**ну-**)	*to shout*
отдыха́ть (отдых**ай-**)	отдохну́ть (отдох**ну-**)	*to rest*
узнава́ть (узн**авай-**)	узна́ть (узн**ай-**)	*to find out, recognize*
дава́ть (д**авай-**)	да́ть (irreg.)	*to give*
переводи́ть (перевод**и-**)	перевести́ (перевед**-**)	*to translate*

NOTE: The aspectual pair **покупа́ть/купи́ть** *to buy* is the only one where the imperfective is prefixed (**по-**), and not the perfective.

In a few instances, there is also an alternation in the root vowel (**о** > **а**) and/or in the stem-final consonant.

спр**а́ш**ивать (спраш**ивай-**)	спр**о**с**и́**ть (спрос**и-**)	*to ask*
отве**ч**а́ть (отвеч**ай-**)	отве́**т**ить (ответ**и-**)	*to answer*

(b) Certain prefixes added to an imperfective verb change not only the aspect, but also the *meaning* of the verb. The following table shows how the meaning of the imperfective verb **писа́ть** *to write* may be altered by some commonly used prefixes. The meaning given for each prefix, in most instances, is only one of several possible meanings associated with that prefix.

BASIC IMPERFECTIVE		PREFIXED PERFECTIVE (WITH NEW MEANING)	
писа́ть	*to write*	**в**писа́ть	*to write* ***in***
		вы́писать	*to write* ***out***
		дописа́ть	*to* ***finish*** *writing*
		записа́ть	*to write* ***down***
		надписа́ть	*to write* ***on the surface***
		описа́ть	*to describe*
		переписа́ть	*to* ***re****write*
		подписа́ть	*to sign*
		приписа́ть	*to add* (*to something written*)
		прописа́ть	*to prescribe*
		списа́ть	*to copy*

New *derived imperfective* partners for such prefixed perfectives are formed with one of three suffixes: **-ывай-/-ивай-**, **-вай-**, or **-ай-**.

IMPERFECTIVE		PREFIXED PERFECTIVE		DERIVED IMPERFECTIVE	
писа́ть	*to write*	записа́ть	*to write down*	запи́сывать	(-ывай-)
чита́ть	*to read*	дочита́ть	*to finish reading*	дочи́тывать	(-ывай-)
кры́ть	*to cover*	закры́ть	*to close*	закрыва́ть	(-вай-)
мы́ть	*to wash*	умы́ть	*to wash up*	умыва́ть	(-вай-)
де́ть	*to put*	наде́ть	*to put on*	надева́ть	(-вай-)
бра́ть	*to take*	собра́ть	*to collect*	собира́ть	(-ай-)
зва́ть	*to call*	вы́звать	*to summon*	вызыва́ть	(-ай-)

(3) *Suppletion*

Verbs in suppletive pairs are completely different words. There are very few pairs of this type.

IMPERFECTIVE	PERFECTIVE	MEANING
бра́ть	взя́ть	*to take*
говори́ть	сказа́ть	*to speak, say / to tell*
иска́ть	найти́	*to look for / to find*
кла́сть	положи́ть	*to put in a lying position*
лови́ть	пойма́ть	*to try to catch / to catch*

25. For each of the following sentences, replace the underlined present-tense imperfective verb form with the past-tense form of its perfective partner.

MODEL Он <u>пи́шет</u> письмо́. > написа́л

1. Ма́льчик <u>пьёт</u> молоко́. ____________
2. Ма́ма <u>гото́вит</u> обе́д. ____________
3. Студе́нты <u>реша́ют</u> зада́чу. ____________
4. Худо́жник <u>рису́ет</u> портре́т. ____________
5. Актёр <u>у́чит</u> свою́ ро́ль. ____________

6. Мы́ покупа́ем проду́кты. ____________
7. Она́ пла́тит за себя́. ____________
8. О́н отдыха́ет под де́ревом. ____________
9. Студе́нт спра́шивает преподава́теля. ____________
10. Преподава́тель отвеча́ет на вопро́сы студе́нтов. ____________

26. For each of the following sentences, replace the underlined past-tense perfective verb form with the present-tense form of its imperfective partner.

MODEL О́н наде́л джи́нсы. > надева́ет

1. О́н собра́л цветы́. ____________
2. Она́ записа́ла но́мер телефо́на. ____________
3. Мы́ вы́звали врача́. ____________
4. О́н положи́л клю́ч под ко́врик. ____________
5. Она́ взяла́ кни́ги в библиоте́ке. ____________
6. О́н сказа́л пра́вду. ____________
7. Она́ закры́ла окно́. ____________
8. Ма́ма умы́ла ребёнка. ____________
9. О́н нашёл свои́ очки́. ____________
10. Мы́ пойма́ли ры́бу. ____________

Verb Aspects: Meanings and Uses

Of the two aspects, the perfective is the more specific in meaning and limited in use. Available in the past and future (but not in the present) tense, a perfective verb presents the action as a *total event,* one with a beginning and an end. Typically, the perfective focuses on the end of the event, indicating that the action was, or will be, *completed,* often with an attendant *result.*

The imperfective aspect, available in the three tenses—present, past, and future—has a very general, nonspecific meaning: The imperfective merely indicates the occurrence of an action, without referring to its completion or result. The imperfective may be used in a wide range of contexts, and must be used in those contexts that are incompatible with the perfective meaning of "one-time completed action" (e.g., actions in progress, or actions that are indefinitely repeated).

Aspect Choice and Context

Perfective verbs do not occur in the present tense; therefore, any action in the present tense will be expressed by an *imperfective* verb form. However, since both perfective and imperfective verbs occur in the past and future tenses, when describing an action in the past or future, one must choose the correct aspect form of the verb. The choice of perfective or imperfective aspect is very often determined by context. Following are several contexts in the past and future where *only one or the other* aspect is possible.

Aspect in the Past and Future

Contexts for Using Perfective Verbs

(a) *Completion with Attendant Result*

The meaning of result may be expressed in the context by another clause.

Она́ **прочита́ла** письмо́, и тепе́рь она́ всё понима́ет. — *She has read the letter and now she understands everything.*

Она́ **сда́ст** экза́мен и полу́чит стипе́ндию в сле́дующем семе́стре. — *She will pass the exam and receive a stipend for the next semester.*

A resultative nuance is also conveyed when the object of the verb denotes a definite number of items affected by the action of the verb.

О́н **написа́л** де́сять упражне́ний. — *He wrote ten exercises.*
Она́ **реши́т** все́ зада́чи. — *She will solve all the problems.*

The perfective form of the verb tends to co-occur with certain words that imply the completion of the action, e.g., the conjunction **как то́лько** *as soon as,* and with adverbs that signal the completion, suddenness, or immediacy of the action, e.g., **наконе́ц** *finally,* **вдру́г** *suddenly,* **сра́зу/сейча́с же** *immediately,* **сейча́с** *right now.*

Я́ позвони́л тебе́, как то́лько я́ **узна́л** но́вость. — *I called you as soon as I learned the news.*
По́сле конце́рта мы́ сра́зу **пошли́** домо́й. — *After the concert, we immediately started for home.*

(b) *Achievement of Intended Result*

Some verbs fall into aspectual pairs where the imperfective indicates *trying* to do something (a process), while the *perfective* signals that the subject has achieved (or failed to achieve) the *intended result.* These meanings can be clearly illustrated with both verbs occurring in the same sentence.

Я́ всё у́тро **вспомина́л** его́ и́мя и наконе́ц **вспо́мнил**. — *I was trying to recall his name all morning and finally I remembered it.*
О́н **поступа́л** в университе́т, но не **поступи́л**. — *He applied to the university, but didn't get in.*

Some other common imperfective/perfective aspectual pairs that can fit into sentences of this type are the following.

привыка́ть/привы́кнуть	*to try to get used to / to become accustomed*
реша́ть/реши́ть	*to work on, try to solve / to solve*
сдава́ть/сда́ть	*to take / to pass* (*an exam*)
угова́ривать/уговори́ть	*to try to persuade / to talk into*
учи́ть/вы́учить	*to study / to memorize* (+ acc.)
учи́ться/научи́ться	*to study / to learn* (+ infinitive)

(c) *Sequential Actions*

When a single action follows another in sequence, the two actions are expressed by *perfective* verbs.

О́н **вста́л** и **предложи́л** то́ст. — *He stood up and proposed a toast.*
Я́ **откро́ю** буты́лку и **вы́пью** вина́. — *I'll open a bottle and drink some wine.*

(d) *Actions Completed in a Specific Amount of Time* (expressed by **за** + accusative)

A perfective verb must be used with the preposition **за** + *accusative of time* to express the length of time it took to *complete an action.* To elicit this information one asks, **За ско́лько вре́мени ...?**

За ско́лько вре́мени ты́ **реши́л** зада́чу? — *How long did it take you to solve the problem?*
О́н **прочита́л** э́тот рома́н **за неде́лю**. — *He read this novel in a week.*
Э́то зда́ние **постро́или за пя́ть ле́т**. — *This building was built in five years.*

(e) *Actions of Limited Duration*

A perfective verb with the prefix **по-** may be used to express that an action lasted (or will last) a short while. A perfective verb with the prefix **про-** may indicate an action of a comparatively longer duration. The verbs that take these prefixes in the meaning of "limited duration" are intransitive, or they may be transitive verbs that are being used intransitively.

Мы́ **посиде́ли** и **поговори́ли**. — *We sat for a while and had a talk.*
Мы́ **посиди́м** и **поду́маем**. — *We will sit a while and think a bit.*
Я́ **почита́л**, а пото́м **пописа́л**. — *I read a while, and then I wrote a bit.*
О́н немно́го **поспа́л**. — *He took a little nap.*

Мы́ до́лго **простоя́ли** в о́череди. — *We stood in line for a long time.*
Они́ **про́жили** два́ го́да в Москве́. — *They lived in Moscow for two years.*

(f) *Instantaneous Actions*

Instantaneous one-time actions are expressed by *perfective* verbs. Perfectives that denote an action that *begins and ends instantaneously* are formed with the suffix **ну**, e.g., **кри́кнуть** *to give a shout,* **пры́гнуть** *to jump once,* **толкну́ть** *to give a shove.*

О́н **пры́гнул** в во́ду. — *He jumped into the water.*
Она́ **кри́кнула**. — *She gave a shout.*

Another group of perfective verbs denote only the *starting point of the action.* These verbs are typically formed with various prefixes, for example, **за-** (**заболе́ть** *to fall ill,* **засмея́ться** *to begin to laugh,* **заинтересова́ться** *to become interested*), **по-** (**пойти́** *to begin walking,* **полюби́ть** *to fall in love*), **рас-** (**рассерди́ться** *to get angry*), and **у-** (**уви́деть** *to catch sight of,* **услы́шать** *to hear*).

Сы́н **уви́дел** отца́ и **побежа́л** к нему́. — *The son saw his father and started running toward him.*

Она́ прочита́ла письмо́ и **засмея́лась**. — *She read the letter and began to laugh.*

Contexts for Using Imperfective Verbs

(a) *Action in Progress*

The imperfective is obligatory when an action is ongoing or lasts for some time. This durative meaning may be reinforced by temporal adverbs and time expressions such as **до́лго** *a long time,* **недо́лго** *for a short while,* **ве́сь де́нь** *all day,* **всё у́тро** *all morning,* **це́лый ме́сяц** *the whole month.*

Мы́ до́лго **жи́ли** в Москве́. — *We lived in Moscow a long time.*
Она́ ве́сь ве́чер **бу́дет рабо́тать.** — *She will be working all evening.*
О́н це́лый де́нь **смотре́л** телеви́зор. — *He watched television the whole day.*

Note that the durational (prepositionless) accusative contrasts with **за** + accusative, when describing how long an action was *in progress.* To elicit this information one asks, **Ско́лько вре́мени ...?** or **Ка́к до́лго ...?**

—Ско́лько вре́мени о́н **писа́л** кни́гу? — *How long was he writing the book?*
—О́н **писа́л** кни́гу оди́н го́д. — *He was writing the book for a year.*

(b) *Simultaneous Actions*

Two actions occurring at the same time are normally expressed by two *imperfective* verbs.

Мы́ **сиде́ли** и **вспомина́ли** про́шлое. — *We were sitting and recalling the past.*
Ма́ма **гото́вила** обе́д и **слу́шала** ра́дио. — *Mom was preparing dinner while she listened to the radio.*

However, when an action in progress is *interrupted* by another action, the former (background) action is *imperfective,* while the latter (interrupting) action is *perfective.*

Я́ споко́йно **чита́л**, когда́ вдру́г **постуча́ли** в две́рь.	*I was reading quietly when suddenly there was a knock at the door.*

(c) *Repeated (Habitual) Actions*

The imperfective aspect of the verb is used to present an action as recurring on a regular (or irregular) basis. The meaning of repetition is often reinforced by accompanying temporal adverbs and time expressions such as **всегда́** *always,* **ка́ждый де́нь** *every day,* **ча́сто** *often,* **обы́чно** *usually,* **иногда́** *sometimes,* and **ре́дко** *rarely.*

О́н всегда́ **за́втракал** до́ма.	*He always had breakfast at home.*
Они́ ча́сто **звоня́т** дру́г дру́гу.	*They often call each other.*
Я́ бу́ду занима́ться ка́ждый де́нь.	*I will study every day.*

(d) *Annulled (Reversed) Actions*

An *imperfective* verb is used to indicate an action that was carried out and then *reversed,* so that the result of the action is no longer in force at the moment of speaking. This situation can arise only with verbs denoting *reversible* actions, i.e., those that can be done and then undone (or *annulled*). The verbs that can express an annulled action typically involve movement or change in position, e.g., get up / lie down, take/return, open/close, put on / take off, turn on / turn off. The perfective verb in such a pair signals that the result of the action is still in force. Compare the use of the aspects below.

Заче́м ты́ ве́чером **встава́л** с посте́ли? Ты́ бо́лен и до́лжен лежа́ть.	*Why were you out of bed last night? You are sick and should stay in bed.*
Заче́м ты́ **вста́л** с посте́ли? Ложи́сь сейча́с же в посте́ль.	*Why have you gotten out of bed? Get back in bed right now.*
—Где́ ку́ртка, в кото́рой ты́ бы́л вчера́?	*Where's the jacket you were wearing yesterday?*
—Э́то была́ не моя́ ку́ртка, я **бра́л** её у дру́га.	*That was not my jacket, I took (borrowed) it from a friend.*
—Отку́да у тебя́ э́та ку́ртка?	*Where did you get that jacket (from)?*
—**Я́ взя́л** у дру́га. Тебе́ нра́вится?	*I took it from a friend. Do you like it?*

Following are a few verb pairs where the imperfective may indicate an annulled action.

бра́ть/взя́ть *to take*
встава́ть/вста́ть *to get up*
включа́ть/включи́ть *to turn on*
отдава́ть/отда́ть *to give back, return*
открыва́ть/откры́ть *to open*
поднима́ться/подня́ться *to ascend*
приноси́ть/принести́ *to bring*

(e) *Denial of Intent to Perform an Action*

A negated imperfective is used in the past tense to indicate not only that an action did not take place, but that the action was *not intended* or *not expected* to take place.

—Ты́ **взя́л** мою́ расчёску?	*Did you take my comb?*
—Не́т, я́ не **бра́л**.	*No, I didn't take it!*

Compare the two responses below, where the perfective indicates the speaker had expected the letter, while the imperfective indicates the letter was never expected.

	—Вы́ **получи́ли** моё письмо́?	*Did you receive my letter?*
(a)	—Не́т, мы́ ещё не **получи́ли**.	*No, we still haven't received it.*
(b)	—Не́т, мы́ никако́го письма́ не **получа́ли**.	*No, we didn't receive any letter.*

Aspect in Questions

Imperfective Past: Did an Action Take Place? / What Action Took Place?

When a speaker is interested in finding out merely if an action has taken place, the question must be posed with the *imperfective past.* In such questions the completion or result of the action is not of interest to the questioner. The *imperfective* is also used in the answer to these questions as a mere *statement of fact* that the action did (or did not) take place.

—Вы́ **чита́ли** «А́нну Каре́нину»?	*Did you ever read "Anna Karenina"?*
—Да́, **чита́л**. / Не́т, не **чита́л**.	*Yes, I read it. / No, I did not read it.*

Similarly, to ask general questions like "What did you do yesterday?" or "What went on at the meeting?", the question (and the answer) will employ the *imperfective,* since the focus of the question is on *activities engaged in,* not results.

—Что́ ты́ **де́лал** вчера́?	*What did you do yesterday?*
—Я́ **гото́вился** к экза́мену.	*I was preparing for an exam.*

Perfective Past: Was an Expected Action Completed?

The notion of "intent" or "expectation" regarding the performance of an action is important in the choice of aspect in questions. When the speaker has reason to expect that the listener was to perform a given action, s/he will ask if that action *has been accomplished.* In this case, both the question and the answer will employ the *perfective.* For example, in the following exchange the questioner knows that the listener intended to see a particular play, and therefore the perfective form is used.

—Ты́ **посмотре́л** пье́су «Ча́йка»? У тебя́, ка́жется, бы́ли биле́ты на неё.	*Did you see the play "The Seagull"? It seems to me you had tickets for it.*
—Да́, **посмотре́л**.	*Yes, I saw it.*

However, if the person asking the question has no such expectation, but instead is simply inquiring if the listener has ever seen the play, then the *imperfective* is required.

—Ты́ **смотре́л** э́ту пье́су?	*Did you see this play?*
—Да́, **смотре́л**. / Не́т, не **смотре́л**.	*Yes, I did. / No, I didn't.*

27. Complete each of the following sentences with the correct past-tense aspectual form of the verbs on the right. Determine whether the context calls for an *imperfective* denoting *process* or a *perfective* denoting *result.*

1. Мы́ це́лый го́д ________________ к жи́зни в э́том ма́леньком городке́, но та́к и не ________________. — привыка́ть/привы́кнуть
2. Я́ до́лго ________________ его́ позвони́ть е́й, но́ о́н не соглаша́лся. Но́ в конце́ концо́в я́ его́ ________________. — угова́ривать/уговори́ть
3. Она́ вчера́ ________________ экза́мен, но не ________________. Она́ пло́хо подгото́вилась. — сдава́ть/сда́ть

4. Мо́й дру́г ве́сь де́нь проводи́л на о́зере. О́н та́м ________________ ры́бу. В конце́ дня́ о́н ________________ щу́ку. ― лови́ть/пойма́ть
5. Оте́ц не мо́г пойти́ с на́ми в па́рк, потому́ что о́н ________________ докла́д. ― гото́вить/пригото́вить
6. Мо́й клю́ч куда́-то исче́з. Я́ ________________ его́, но не ________________. ― иска́ть/найти́
7. Ма́ма до́лго ________________ сы́на, но та́к и не ________________ его́. ― буди́ть/разбуди́ть

28. Complete each of the following sentences with the correct past-tense aspectual form of the verb on the right. Determine whether the action is *ongoing* or *of limited duration.*

1. Мы́ ________________ немно́го, отдохну́ли и пошли́ да́льше. ― (по)сиде́ть
2. Она́ была́ больна́ и всю́ суббо́ту ________________ до́ма. ― (по)сиде́ть
3. У́тром по́сле за́втрака они́ до́лго ________________ по го́роду. ― (по)гуля́ть
4. Я́ ________________ полчаса́ и лёг спа́ть. ― (по)рабо́тать
5. О́н ве́сь ве́чер ________________ на компью́тере. ― (по)рабо́тать
6. Я́ до́лго ________________ об э́том. Наконе́ц, я при́нял реше́ние. ― (по)ду́мать
7. Учени́к ________________ мину́тку и отве́тил на вопро́с учи́теля. ― (по)ду́мать

29. Complete each of the following sentences with the correct aspectual form of the verb on the right. Determine whether the context indicates *an action in progress* or *the beginning of an action.*

1. Когда́ де́вочка узна́ла о сме́рти ба́бушки, она́ ________________. ― (за)пла́кала
2. Де́вочка ________________ це́лый де́нь. ― (за)пла́кала
3. Мы́ попроща́лись с ни́м на платфо́рме, и о́н ________________ к ваго́ну. ― (по)шёл
4. Всё у́тро ________________ до́ждь. ― (по)шёл
5. Мы́ бы́ли в Изма́йлово на вернису́же, когда́ вдру́г ________________ си́льный до́ждь. ― (по)шёл
6. Когда́ на́м сказа́ли э́ту но́вость, мы́ ________________ от ра́дости. ― (за)пры́гали
7. Мы́ смотре́ли, как де́ти ________________ на одно́й ноге́. ― (за)пры́гали
8. Когда́ до́чь пришла́ домо́й по́здно, ма́ма ________________. ― (рас)серди́лась
9. Мы́ споко́йно гуля́ли в па́рке, когда́ вдру́г ________________ кри́к. ― (у)слы́шали
10. Когда́ мы́ сиде́ли на скаме́йке, мы́ ________________, ка́к пе́ли пти́цы. ― (у)слы́шали

30. Complete each of the following sentences with the correct past-tense aspectual form of the verbs on the right. Determine whether the context expresses *a repeated action* or *a one-time completed action.*

1. О́н вчера́ ________________ по́здно, в де́сять часо́в. ― встава́л/вста́л
   Ле́том о́н всегда́ ________________ ра́но, в се́мь часо́в.
2. Вчера́ ма́ма ________________ сы́ну дли́нное письмо́. ― писа́ла/написа́ла
   Ка́ждую неде́лю ма́ма ________________ сы́ну пи́сьма.
3. Сего́дня мы́ ________________ письмо́ от на́ших друзе́й. ― получа́ли/получи́ли
   Ра́ньше мы́ ________________ пи́сьма от ни́х ра́з в ме́сяц.
4. Она́ ________________ рабо́ту в 3 часа́ и пошла́ домо́й. ― конча́ла/ко́нчила
   Ка́ждый де́нь она́ ________________ рабо́ту в 3 часа́.
5. Вчера́ ма́ма ________________ о́чень вку́сный пиро́г. ― пекла́/испекла́
   По воскре́сеньям ма́ма ча́сто ________________ пироги́.

31. Complete each of the following sentences with the correct future-tense aspectual form of the verbs on the right. Determine whether the action will be *in progress,* will be *repeated,* or will be *a one-time completed action.*

1. На ка́ждом уро́ке я ________________ ва́м грамма́тику. — бу́ду объясня́ть / объясню́
   Я́ сейча́с ________________ ва́м ва́жное пра́вило.
2. Сего́дня я ________________ твою статью́ и отда́м её тебе́. — бу́ду чита́ть / прочита́ю
   Когда́ я бу́ду в Испа́нии, я ________________ испа́нские газе́ты.
3. О́н сказа́л, что ________________ на́м ча́сто. — бу́дет писа́ть / напи́шет
   О́н сказа́л, что ________________ письмо́ и сра́зу пошлёт.
4. Она́ обеща́ла, что ________________ и ска́жет на́м сво́й отве́т. — бу́дет звони́ть / позвони́т
   Она́ обеща́ла, что ________________ на́м ка́ждую неде́лю.
5. Сего́дня на уро́ке мы́ ________________ все́ упражне́ния. — бу́дем де́лать / сде́лаем
   Я́ не зна́ю, что́ мы́ ________________ сего́дня на уро́ке.

32. Complete each of the following sentences with the correct past-tense aspectual form of the verbs on the right. Determine whether the result of the action *is still in force* or *has been annulled.*

1. (a) Мы́ ________________ на верши́ну горы́. Бо́льше мы́ никогда́ не вернёмся в те́ живопи́сные места́. — поднима́ться/подня́ться
   (b) Мы́ ________________ на верши́ну горы́. Тепе́рь мы́ мо́жем отдохну́ть в ла́гере альпини́стов.
2. (a) Я́ ________________ тебе́ тво́й компа́кт-ди́ск, во́т о́н. — приноси́ть/принести́
   (b) Вчера́ я ________________ тебе́ тво́й компа́кт-ди́ск, но тебя́ не́ было до́ма.
3. (a) —Са́ша, ты́ вчера́ ________________ телеви́зор? — включа́ть/включи́ть
   —Да́, ________________. А что́?
   —О́н сего́дня почему́-то не рабо́тает.
   (b) —Где́ па́па?
   —О́н ________________ телеви́зор и смо́трит како́й-то фи́льм.
4. (a) —Где́ магнитофо́н? — отдава́ть/отда́ть
   —Не зна́ю. Я́ его́ ________________ в ремо́нт, но́ вчера́ я его́ принёс, и о́н до́лжен бы́ть где́-то до́ма.
   (b) —Где́ магнитофо́н?
   —Я́ его́ ________________ в ремо́нт. Его́ не́т до́ма.
5. (a) —Я́ ________________ но́вую руба́шку и пошёл на та́нцы. — надева́ть/наде́ть
   (b) —Почему́ ты́ не но́сишь свою́ но́вую руба́шку?
   —Я́ её вчера́ ________________.

33. Complete each of the following sentences with the correct past-tense aspectual form of the verbs on the right. Determine which sentences focus on *how long the action was in progress,* and which sentences are concerned with *the time needed to accomplish the action.*

1. Мы́ ________________ на мо́ре две́ неде́ли. За э́то вре́мя мы́ хорошо́ ________________. — отдыха́ть/отдохну́ть
2. А́втор не́сколько ме́сяцев ________________ материа́л для кни́ги. За э́ти ме́сяцы он ________________ отли́чный материа́л. — собира́ть/собра́ть

3. О́н о́чень до́лго __________ э́тот те́кст, но его́ сестра́ __________ тако́й же те́кст бы́стро. — переводи́ть/перевести́
4. Аспира́нт __________ диссерта́цию це́лых два́ го́да. Но́ за э́то вре́мя о́н __________ то́лько полови́ну. — писа́ть/написа́ть
5. —За ско́лько вре́мени ты́ __________ э́ту зада́чу? —Я́ её __________ всего́ за не́сколько мину́т. — реша́ть/реши́ть

34. Indicate whether the underlined verbs in each of the following sentences express actions that are *simultaneous, sequential,* or *"interrupted."*

1. Когда́ ма́ма мы́ла посу́ду, па́па отдыха́л в своём люби́мом кре́сле. __________
2. Мы́ у́жинали, когда́ позвони́л телефо́н. __________
3. Мы́ бы́стро поужи́нали и пошли́ на конце́рт. __________
4. Когда́ мы́ отдыха́ли на мо́ре, сы́н заболе́л. __________
5. Когда́ худо́жник рисова́л мо́й портре́т, я́ сиде́ла соверше́нно неподви́жно. __________
6. Когда́ худо́жник нарисова́л мо́й портре́т, о́н да́л его́ мне́. __________
7. Когда́ Ле́на сдава́ла экза́мен, она́ не́рвничала. __________
8. Когда́ Ле́на сдала́ экза́мен, она́ пошла́ с подру́гами в кафе́. __________

35. Complete each of the following sentences with the correct aspectual form of the verbs on the right. Determine from the context whether the questioner is asking merely if *an action ever took place,* or if the question implies an expectation that *an intended action was done.*

1. (a) —Ты́ __________ но́вый рома́н Аксёнова? Я́ зна́ю, что ты́ давно́ хоте́л э́то сде́лать. — чита́л/прочита́л
   —Да́, __________. Рома́н о «но́вых ру́сских».
   (b) —Тебя́ интересу́ет ру́сская литерату́ра. Ты́ __________ Васи́лия Аксёнова?
   —Да́, __________. По-мо́ему, о́н хоро́ший писа́тель.
2. (a) —Та́ня, ты́ __________ но́вые джи́нсы? Ты́ ведь собира́лась э́то сде́лать. — покупа́ла/купи́ла
   —Да́, __________. Я́ и́х уже́ надева́ла.
   (b) —Та́ня, ты́ когда́-нибудь __________ духи́ «Эсте́»?
   —Не́т, не __________. Они́ сли́шком до́рого сто́ят.
3. (a) —Ма́ша __________ тебе́ фотогра́фии свое́й сва́дьбы? — пока́зывала/показа́ла
   —Да́, __________. О́чень хоро́шие фотогра́фии.
   (b) —Ма́ша уже́ __________ фотогра́фии свое́й сва́дьбы? Она́ ведь хоте́ла, чтобы ты́ и́х посмотре́ла.

36. Complete each of the following sentences with the correct past-tense aspectual form of the underlined verb. In one context the speaker indicates that he *had no intention* of performing the action, while in the other context the speaker *has failed* to carry out an intended action.

1. —Кто́ сказа́л, что за́втра не бу́дет экза́мена?
   —Не зна́ю, я́ не __________.
2. —Ты́ поздра́вил Ми́шу с днём рожде́ния?
   —Не́т, ещё не __________.
3. —Э́то ты́ откры́л окно́?
   —Не́т, я не __________.

4. —Ктó включи́л телеви́зор?
   —Не знáю, я́ не ________________.
5. —Чтó ты́ с ни́м сдéлал! Почемý óн плáчет?
   —Я́ ничегó емý не ________________!

Aspect in the Infinitive

The uses of the imperfective and perfective aspects in the infinitive fall within the same parameters as those in the past and future tenses.

The imperfective infinitive may indicate a *continuous process* or *repeated action*.

Continuous Process

Вéчером я́ дóлжен **писáть** пи́сьма друзья́м.	*This evening I have to write letters to friends.*

Repeated Action

Моя́ подрýга проси́ла меня́ **писáть** éй чáще.	*My girlfriend asked me to write her more often.*

The perfective infinitive indicates a *result* to be achieved.

Я́ дóлжен **написáть** письмó дрýгу и срáзу послáть егó.	*I have to write a letter to a friend and send it right away.*

In general, after modal words (**хотéть** *to want,* **мóчь** *to be able,* **нáдо/нýжно** *it is necessary, one must,* **дóлжен** *one should, one is supposed to*) the choice of imperfective or perfective infinitive depends on the meaning of the verb, and what the speaker intends to communicate. If the action is *specific and occurs on one occasion only,* then the *perfective* infinitive is used, while an action that is *recurring* is expressed by an *imperfective* infinitive.

Мнé нýжно **приня́ть** аспири́н.	*I need to take a dose of aspirin.*
Мнé нýжно **принимáть** аспири́н.	*I need to take aspirin (regularly).*

Verbs Followed Only by Imperfective Infinitives

The following verbs, in either aspect, require that an accompanying infinitive be *imperfective.* Several of these verbs express the beginning, continuation, or end of an action; others refer to habitual processes or desirable/undesirable activities.

начинáть/начáть *to begin*	надоедáть/надоéсть *to be fed up with*
стáть *to begin*	привыкáть/привы́кнуть *to become accustomed*
кончáть/кóнчить *to finish*	отвыкáть/отвы́кнуть *to get out of the habit*
переставáть/перестáть *to cease*	учи́ться/научи́ться *to learn how*
бросáть/брóсить *to quit*	разучи́ться *to forget how*
продолжáть/продóлжить *to continue*	нрáвиться/понрáвиться *to like*
уставáть/устáть *to grow tired*	

Óн **нáчал вставáть** рáно.	*He has started getting up early.*
Онá **кóнчила печáтать** доклáд.	*She has finished typing the report.*
Наконéц, он **брóсил кури́ть**.	*He finally quit smoking.*
Онá **перестáла рабóтать**.	*She has stopped working.*
Я́ **устáл говори́ть** об э́том.	*I'm tired of talking about this.*
Емý **надоéло решáть** задáчи.	*He's fed up with solving problems.*
Éй **нрáвится игрáть** в тéннис.	*She likes to play tennis.*
Óн **ýчится води́ть** маши́ну.	*He is learning to drive a car.*

Verbs Followed Only by Perfective Infinitives

The following *perfective* verbs are followed only by *perfective infinitives.*

забы́ть *to forget*
успе́ть *to manage, have time*
уда́ться *to manage, succeed*

Я́ забы́л купи́ть пода́рок Са́ше. — *I forgot to buy a present for Sasha.*
Ты́ **успе́ешь посмотре́ть** Эрмита́ж? — *Will you manage to see the Hermitage?*
О́н не **успе́л поза́втракать.** — *He didn't have time to eat breakfast.*
Мне́ не **удало́сь купи́ть** биле́ты на конце́рт, все́ биле́ты бы́ли про́даны. — *I was unable to buy tickets for the concert; all the tickets were sold.*

37. For each of the following sentences, circle the imperfective or perfective infinitive, as appropriate.

1. Сего́дня профе́ссор на́чал (объясня́ть | объясни́ть) ви́ды глаго́ла.
2. Когда́ де́ти ко́нчили (обе́дать | пообе́дать), ма́ма убрала́ со стола́.
3. Я́ у́тром та́к торопи́лся, что не успе́л (за́втракать | поза́втракать).
4. Ма́ма, извини́, я́ была́ та́к занята́, что забы́ла тебе́ (звони́ть | позвони́ть).
5. О́н ко́нчил университе́т, но продолжа́л (изуча́ть | изучи́ть) ру́сский язы́к.
6. Мы́ ра́ды, что на́м удало́сь (посеща́ть | посети́ть) э́тот интере́сный го́род.
7. Ви́ка переста́ла (встреча́ться | встре́титься) с э́тим па́рнем.
8. Роди́тели уста́ли (отвеча́ть | отве́тить) на бесконе́чные вопро́сы ребёнка.
9. У кого́ ты́ та́к хорошо́ научи́лся (игра́ть | сыгра́ть) в ша́хматы?
10. Мне́ надое́ло (реша́ть | реши́ть) э́ти тру́дные зада́чи.
11. Когда́ она́ жила́ в дере́вне, она́ привы́кла (встава́ть | вста́ть) ра́но.
12. Врачи́ ему́ сове́товали бро́сить (пи́ть | вы́пить).

Negation and Imperfective Infinitives

There is a strong correlation between negation and the imperfective aspect. This was evident in the use of the negated imperfective past tense to signal the speaker's denial of involvement in an action and/or his lack of intention to carry it out. Negation is also tied to the use of the imperfective aspect in the infinitive.

Не + Imperfective Infinitives

A *negated infinitive* normally occurs in the *imperfective* aspect after verbs that express exhortation or intention to perform an action, for example, after the following verbs.

обеща́ть/пообеща́ть *to promise*
проси́ть/попроси́ть *to ask (request)*
реша́ть/реши́ть *to decide*
сове́товать/посове́товать *to advise*
угова́ривать/уговори́ть *to persuade*

Compare the aspect of the infinitives when preceded and when not preceded by the negative particle **не**.

О́н посове́товал мне́ **купи́ть** слова́рь. — *He advised me to buy a dictionary.*
О́н посове́товал мне́ **не покупа́ть** слова́рь. — *He advised me not to buy a dictionary.*

Она́ уговори́ла его́ **наде́ть** ку́ртку. — *She persuaded him to put on a jacket.*
Она́ уговори́ла его́ **не надева́ть** ку́ртку. — *She persuaded him not to put on a jacket.*

38. Complete the answer to each of the following questions, changing the aspect of the underlined verb according to the model.

MODEL —Ма́ма приготóвила обéд?
—Нéт, онá решила не ___готóвить___ обéд.

1. —Сергéй рассказáл об э́том? —Нéт, óн решил не ________________.
2. —Натáша позвони́ла своéй мáтери? —Нéт, онá реши́ла не ________________.
3. —Онá встрéтилась с э́тим пáрнем? —Нéт, онá обещáла не ________________.
4. —Óн посмотрéл э́тот фи́льм? —Нéт, мы́ посовéтовали емý не ________________.
5. —Óн постáвил маши́ну на ýлице? —Нéт, я́ уговори́л егó не ________________.
6. —Йра сказáла емý чтó случи́лось? —Нéт, мы́ проси́ли её не ________________.

Absence of Necessity (*не нáдо*) + Imperfective Infinitives

Only *imperfective* infinitives occur after modal expressions that denote lack of necessity, or inadvisability, such as **не нáдо** / **не нýжно** *it is not necessary,* **не обязáтельно** *one doesn't have to,* **не стóит** *it is not worth / it doesn't make sense.*

Compare the aspect of the infinitives in the sentences that express the necessity or advisability of doing something with those that express the *absence of necessity* to carry out those actions.

Вáм **нáдо отвéтить** на письмó. *You have to answer the letter.*
Вáм **не нáдо отвечáть** на письмó. *You do not have to answer the letter.*

Нáм **нýжно купи́ть** э́ту кни́гу. *We need to buy this book.*
Нáм **не нýжно покупáть** э́ту кни́гу. *We don't need to buy this book.*

Э́тот фи́льм **стóит посмотрéть**. *This movie is worth seeing.*
Э́тот фи́льм **не стóит смотрéть**. *This movie is not worth seeing.*

39. Complete each of the following sentences with the infinitive of the underlined verb in the appropriate aspect.

1. —Нýжно объясни́ть емý, кáк éхать к нáм.
   —Не нýжно ________________, я́ емý ужé объясни́л.
2. —Нáдо узнáть áдрес э́того магази́на.
   —Не нáдо ________________, я́ ужé узнáл.
3. —Нáдо взя́ть э́ту кни́гу в библиотéку.
   —Не нáдо ________________, я́ ужé взя́л.
4. —Нýжно вы́звать элéктрика.
   —Не нýжно ________________, я́ ужé вы́звал.
5. —Нáдо заказáть билéты на концéрт.
   —Не стóит ________________. Я́ знáю, билéты ужé распрóданы.
6. —Нáдо спроси́ть Бори́са, о чём э́та статья́?
   —Не стóит егó ________________. Óн сáм не читáл.

Нельзя́ and Aspect in the Infinitive

The modal word **нельзя́** has two potential meanings: *it is not possible* and *it is not allowed / one should not.* When **нельзя́** is followed by a *perfective* infinitive, it expresses the *impossibility* of performing the action. However, when **нельзя́** is followed by an *imperfective* infinitive, it expresses *prohibition* (*it is not allowed*).

Э́ту ба́нку икры́ **нельзя́ откры́ть**: у на́с не́т открыва́лки.	*This can of caviar cannot be opened: we don't have an opener.*
Э́ту ба́нку икры́ **нельзя́ открыва́ть**: э́то пода́рок дру́гу.	*This can of caviar is not to be opened: it is a gift for a friend.*

The modal word **мо́жно**, like **нельзя́**, has two possible interpretations relating to *possibility* and *permission,* namely, *one can* and *one may* (in questions, *can I?* and *may I?*). Compare the two answers to the following question.

	—Мо́жно включи́ть телеви́зор?	*Can I turn on the television?*
(a)	—Не́т, его́ нельзя́ включи́ть. О́н не рабо́тает.	*No, it won't turn on. It is not working.*
(b)	—Не́т, его́ нельзя́ включа́ть. Тебе́ на́до занима́ться.	*No, you may not turn on the TV. You have to study.*

40. For each of the following sentences, circle the infinitive in the correct aspect. Determine from the context whether the action is *not possible* or *not allowed / not advisable.*

1. Реце́пт врача́ нельзя́ (чита́ть | прочита́ть), о́н напи́сан неразбо́рчиво.
2. Э́то письмо́ нельзя́ (чита́ть | прочита́ть), оно́ не тебе́.
3. В аудито́риях нельзя́ (е́сть | съе́сть), э́то пра́вило университе́та.
4. Его́ нельзя́ (буди́ть | разбуди́ть), о́н та́к кре́пко спи́т.
5. Его́ нельзя́ (буди́ть | разбуди́ть), о́н бо́лен и до́лжен спа́ть.
6. Э́ту кни́гу нельзя́ (бра́ть | взя́ть), о́н её ещё чита́ет.
7. У пожа́рного кра́на нельзя́ (оставля́ть | оста́вить) маши́ну, та́м штрафу́ют.
8. На ле́кции нельзя́ (опа́здывать | опозда́ть), на́до приходи́ть во́время.
9. В общежи́тии нельзя́ (отдыха́ть | отдохну́ть), та́м о́чень шу́мно.
10. О́н говори́т с таки́м си́льным акце́нтом, что его́ нельзя́ (понима́ть | поня́ть).
11. Отсю́да нельзя́ (звони́ть | позвони́ть), зде́сь не́т телефо́на.
12. Де́тям до 14 ле́т нельзя́ (смотре́ть | посмотре́ть) э́тот фи́льм.
13. В э́том о́зере нельзя́ (лови́ть | пойма́ть) ры́бу, не разреша́ется.
14. Нельзя́ (продава́ть | прода́ть) спи́рт по воскресе́ньям, э́то зако́н шта́та.
15. Нельзя́ как сле́дует (учи́ть | вы́учить) иностра́нный язы́к, не побыва́в в стране́ языка́.

Imperatives

The imperative is used to give commands or make requests. There are three types of imperatives in Russian: a second-person imperative (*Cut* the cake, *Sit* next to me), a first-person imperative (*Let's buy* wine, *Let's write* to him), and a third-person imperative (*Let* Sasha *buy* the wine, *Let* Katya *make* dinner). Of the three types, the most commonly used is the second-person imperative.

Second-Person Imperative: Formation

The second-person imperative is formed easily from the verb's basic stem. There are two possibilities, depending on where the stress falls in the verb's conjugation: (1) If the first-person singular ending of the verb is stressed, then the stressed ending **-и́(те)** is added to the basic stem (**те** is added to the ending for the formal and/or plural *you*); (2) if the stress falls only on the stem of a verb, then no vowel is added, and the final vowel of the basic stem, if there is one, drops.

Examples of Imperative Formation

1. Stress on the first-person singular **-ý/-ió**: imperative in stressed **-и́**

INFINITIVE	BASIC STEM	FIRST-PERSON SINGULAR	IMPERATIVE
говори́ть *to speak*	говор**и-**	говорю́	говори́(те)
учи́ться *to study*	уч**и-ся**	учу́сь	учи́сь/учи́тесь
плати́ть *to pay*	плат**и-**	плачу́	плати́(те)
купи́ть *to buy*	куп**и-**	куплю́	купи́(те)
писа́ть *to write*	пис**а-**	пишу́	пиши́(те)
сказа́ть *to tell*	сказ**а**-	скажу́	скажи́(те)
ждать *to wait*	жд**а-**	жду́	жди́(те)
лежа́ть *to lie*	леж**а-**	лежу́	лежи́(те)
сиде́ть *to sit*	сид**е-**	сижу́	сиди́(те)
нести́ *to carry*	не**с-**	несу́	неси́(те)

The rules that apply when combining stems and endings in conjugation (i.e., addition and truncation) also apply in the formation of the imperative. Therefore, when the imperative vowel ending **-и** is added to a nonsuffixed consonant stem, it is a matter of simple addition (**нес-** + **и́** > **неси́**). When the vowel **-и** is added to a basic stem ending in **-и**, **-а**, or **-е**, the first of these two "likes" is truncated (e.g., **говор*и*-** + **и́** > **говори́**, **жд*а*-** + **и́** > **жди́**, **сид*е*-** + **и́** > **сиди́**). Also, if a verb undergoes a consonant alternation *throughout* the non-past, as do verbs with a stem in **-а**, then the same alternation occurs in the imperative (**писа́-**: **пи*ш*у́**, **пи́*ш*ешь** / **пи*ш*и́** and **сказа-**: **ска*ж*у́**, **ска́*ж*ешь** / **ска*ж*и́**). However, a verb that undergoes a consonant alternation in the *first-person singular only*, will *not* have that alternation in the imperative (**купи́**, **плати́**, **сиди́**).

2. Stress on the stem

Stem-stressed verbs can be divided into two main subgroups.

(a) Verbs with stem-final **-й**: No ending is added, and the imperative is identical to the shape of the basic stem. Verbs with a stem in **-а-вай**, though end-stressed in the non-past, also belong in this group, e.g., **да-вай-**: **даю́**, **даёшь**, **даю́т** / **дава́й(те)**.

INFINITIVE	BASIC STEM	IMPERATIVE
чита́ть *to read*	чит**ай-**	чита́й(те)
занима́ться *to study*	заним**ай**-ся	занима́йся/занима́йтесь
надева́ть *to put on*	наде**вай-**	надева́й(те)
расска́зывать *to tell*	расска**зывай-**	расска́зывай(те)
открыва́ть *to open* (impfv.)	откр**ывай-**	открыва́й(те)
откры́ть *to open* (pfv.)	откр**ой-**	откро́й(те)
сове́товать to advise	совет**ова-/уй-**	сове́туй(те)
дава́ть *to give* (impfv.)	**да-вай-**	дава́й(те)
вставать *to get up*	вст**а-вай-**	встава́й(те)
узнава́ть *to find out* (impfv.)	узн**а-вай-**	узнава́й(те)
узна́ть *to find out* (pfv.)	узн**ай-**	узна́й(те)
да́ть *to give* (pfv.)	(irreg.)	да́й(те)

(b) Other stem-stressed verbs: No ending is added, and if there is a stem-final suffix, it is dropped; the imperative is spelled with **-ь** (even if the preceding consonant is one that is always hard, e.g., **ре́зать** *to cut*: **ре́жь**).

INFINITIVE	BASIC STEM	IMPERATIVE
гото́вить *to prepare*	готов**и-**	гото́вь(те)
отве́тить *to answer*	ответ**и-**	отве́ть(те)
вста́ть *to get up* (pfv.)	вста**н-**	вста́нь(те)
наде́ть *to put on* (pfv.)	наде**н-**	наде́нь(те)

The vowel **-и** is never dropped after a cluster of two consonants.

ко́нчить *to finish*	конч**и-**	ко́нчи(те)
по́мнить *to remember*	помн**и-**	по́мни(те)

Irregular Second-Person Imperatives

The following verbs have imperatives that are irregular.

е́сть *to eat*	е́шь(те)	ле́чь *to lie down*	ля́г(те)
да́ть *to give*	да́й(те)	пе́ть *to sing*	по́й(те)
(по)е́хать *to go by vehicle*	поезжа́й(те)	пи́ть *to drink*	пе́й(те)

NOTE: There are five verbs of the **пи́ть** type, all of which form their imperative the same way, e.g., **би́ть/бе́й(те)** *beat,* **ви́ть/ве́й(те)** *twist,* **ли́ть/ле́й(те)** *pour,* **ши́ть/ше́й(те)** *sew.*

Aspect and the Second-Person Imperative

The choice of aspect in the imperative is generally dictated by the same contexts already enumerated for aspect use in the past and future tenses, as well as the infinitive. Imperatives can be affirmative (*Do* ...) or negated (*Do not* ...).

Affirmative Imperatives

Use of the Perfective Imperative

The primary use of the perfective aspect in affirmative commands is to request that a concrete action be performed on a single occasion. A transitive perfective verb must be used with its direct object (stated or implied), which draws attention to a result.

Запиши́те мо́й телефо́н.	*Write down my telephone number.*
Ты́ идёшь на по́чту. **Купи́** мне́ ма́рки.	*You are going to the post office. Buy me some stamps.*
Закро́йте, пожа́луйста, окно́.	*Close the window, please.*
Позвони́те мне́ в се́мь часо́в.	*Call me at seven o'clock.*

Uses of the Imperfective Imperative

The *imperfective* imperative is used in a wide range of contexts, including the following.

(a) Requests for *a repeated action* or when giving *general advice*

Пиши́ на́м ча́ще.	*Write to us more often.*
Покупа́йте о́вощи на э́том ры́нке.	*Buy vegetables at this market.*
Береги́те здоро́вье.	*Look after your health.*

(b) Requests to *modify an action in progress* (used with an adverb of manner)

Говори́те гро́мче.	*Speak louder.*
Пиши́ аккура́тнее.	*Write more carefully.*

(c) *Prompting* the addressee to *begin an action* that had already been requested (with the perfective imperative), but not yet implemented. By repeating the request with the imperfective partner of the verb, the speaker may convey a sense of *urgency* to perform the action.

—**Расскажи́**, что́ случи́лось. Что́ же ты́ молчи́шь? **Расска́зывай!** — *Tell me what happened. Why are you keeping silent? Go ahead, tell me!*

—**Возьми́** э́ти де́ньги. Они́ тебе́ бу́дут нужны́. Ну, чего́ ты́ ждёшь? **Бери́!** — *Take this money. You will need it. Well, what are you waiting for? Take it.*

(d) Imperfective imperatives are used to convey *polite invitations* in social situations. For example, a host(ess) may say the following to guests.

Входи́те. — *Come in.*
Раздева́йтесь, пожа́луйста. — *Please take off your coat.*
Сади́тесь, пожа́луйста. — *Please sit down.*
Бери́те! — *Take one/some.*

Negated Imperatives

Use of the Negated Imperfective

When requesting that an action *not* be performed, the *imperfective* imperative is normally used, even when the action is a specific one-time action. In other words, in these negated imperatives, one uses the imperfective partner of the perfective verbs that would be used in affirmative imperatives.

Закро́йте, пожа́луйста, окно́. — *Please close the window.*
Не закрыва́йте, пожа́луйста, окно́. — *Please don't close the window.*

Посмотри́те э́тот фи́льм. — *See this movie.*
Не смотри́те э́тот фи́льм. — *Don't see this movie.*

Спроси́те его́ об э́том. — *Ask him about it.*
Не спра́шивайте его́ об э́том. — *Don't ask him about it.*

Use of the Negated Perfective

The negated perfective is used only when the speaker is expressing a *warning* against an action that might be performed *inadvertently,* and with undesirable results. The sense of warning is sometimes emphasized by the words **Смотри́/Смотри́те** *See (to it you don't)* or **Осторо́жно** *Careful.* The verbs used in the negated perfective usually denote actions that have obvious negative consequences, e.g., **упа́сть** *to fall,* **обже́чься** *to burn oneself,* **простуди́ться** *to catch cold,* **опозда́ть** *to be late,* **потеря́ть** *to lose,* **забы́ть** *to forget.*

Не упади́те, зде́сь ско́льзко. — *Don't fall, it's slippery here.*
Не обожги́сь, вода́ горя́чая. — *Don't burn yourself, the water is hot.*
Смотри́, **не опозда́й.** — *See to it that you are not late.*
Осторо́жно, **не урони́** э́ту ва́зу. — *Be careful, don't drop that vase.*

41. Complete the answer to each of the following questions, telling the questioner "Alright," go ahead with the action of the underlined verb.

MODEL Мо́жно записа́ть телефо́н? —Хорошо́, запиши́те.

1. —Мо́жно тебя́ подожда́ть? —Хорошо́, ____________.
2. —Мо́жно включи́ть телеви́зор? —Хорошо́, ____________.
3. —Мо́жно нали́ть вино́? —Хорошо́, ____________.

4. —Мóжно нарéзать хлéб? —Хорошó, __________.
5. —Мóжно спéть вáм пéсню? —Хорошó, __________.
6. —Мóжно надéть гáлстук? —Хорошó, __________.
7. —Мóжно открыть окнó? —Хорошó, __________.
8. —Мóжно заплатúть за э́то? —Хорошó, __________.
9. —Мóжно вы́пить чáшку чáя? —Хорошó, __________.
10. —Мóжно танцевáть? —Хорошó, __________.
11. —Мóжно отвéтить на егó письмó? —Хорошó, __________.
12. —Мóжно приготóвить обéд? —Хорошó, __________.

42. Complete each of the following sentences with the imperative of the appropriate verb in parentheses.

(писáть/написáть)
1. —__________ áдрес. Ну, __________ аккурáтнее, а то бýдет непоня́тно.

(говорúть/сказáть)
2. —__________, кáк тáм погóда? Чтó? Чтó? __________ грóмче, вáс плóхо слы́шно.

(расскáзывать/рассказáть)
3. —__________ о поéздке. Пожáлуйста, __________ подрóбнее. Нáм ведь всё óчень интерéсно.

(читáть/прочитáть)
4. —__________ тéкст вслýх. Ну, __________ мéдленнее, чтóбы всéм бы́ло поня́тно.

43. Disagree with each of the following requests in the perfective imperative. Use the imperfective imperative of the underlined verb to request that the action not be performed (it isn't necessary).

MODEL Подождúте егó. —Нéт, не ждúте. Не нáдо.

1. —Включúте телевúзор. —Нéт, __________. Не нáдо.
2. —Покажúте емý вáшу рабóту. —Нéт, __________. Не нáдо.
3. —Переведúте э́тот тéкст. —Нéт, __________. Не нáдо.
4. —Расскажúте éй о командирóвке. —Нéт, __________. Не нáдо.
5. —Дáйте емý совéт. —Нéт, __________. Не нáдо.
6. —Узнáй об э́том. —Нéт, __________. Не нáдо.
7. —Закрóйте окнó. —Нéт, __________. Не нáдо.
8. —Съéшь ещё одúн пирожóк. —Нéт, __________. Не нáдо.

44. Object to each of the following requests to perform an action. Use the negated imperfective of the underlined verb to indicate that there is no need for the action (it has already been done).

MODEL Мы́ хотúм заплатúть за обéд. —Не платúте, я ужé заплатúл.

1. —Я́ хочý позвонúть Мúше. —__________, я́ емý ужé позвонúл.
2. —Мы́ хотúм помóчь сосéдке. —__________, я́ éй ужé помóг.
3. —Я́ хочý сказáть éй об э́том. —__________ éй. Éй ужé сказáли.
4. —Мы́ хотúм купúть ребёнку шоколáда. —__________, я́ ужé купúла.
5. —Я́ хочý приготóвить зáвтрак. —__________, И́ра ужé приготóвила.

45. Warn against performing each indicated action by using the appropriate imperative form of a verb on the right.

1. Поезд отхо́дит ро́вно в се́мь утра́. Не ____________. опа́здывай/опозда́й
2. Сего́дня бу́дет до́ждь. Не ____________ зо́нтик. забыва́й/забу́дь
3. В де́тской спи́т ребёнок. Смотри́, не ____________. буди́/разбуди́
4. Осторо́жно, не ____________ э́ту ва́зу, она́ о́чень дорога́я. роня́й/урони́
5. Не ____________ со́к, пя́тна от э́того со́ка не отмыва́ются. пролива́й/проле́й
6. Не ____________ по оши́бке мою́ су́мку. бери́те/возьми́те

First-Person Imperative

The first-person imperative is used to suggest an action that will be performed together with the speaker, e.g., *Let's go, Let's play.* This imperative is formed in one of two ways, depending on the nature of the action.

(a) **Дава́й/дава́йте** + imperfective infinitive

This form of the imperative is used when the action to be performed will be continuous or repeated. The form **дава́й** is used when addressing one person informally, while **дава́йте** is the formal and/or plural form of address.

Дава́й говори́ть на ты́.	*Let's speak using the informal "you."*
Дава́йте чита́ть то́лько по-ру́сски.	*Let's read only in Russian.*

Дава́й(те) + imperfective infinitive is also used to make a negative suggestion (*Let's not* ...). In negative suggestions, however, the first-person plural form **бу́дем** must precede the infinitive, creating the imperfective future tense.

Дава́й не бу́дем спо́рить об э́том.	*Let's not argue about this.*
Дава́й не бу́дем смотре́ть телеви́зор.	*Let's not watch television.*

To make an alternative suggestion to do something *instead,* the word **лу́чше** is used between **дава́й(те)** and the verb.

Дава́й не бу́дем рабо́тать. **Дава́й лу́чше слу́шать** но́вый компа́кт-ди́ск.	*Let's not work. Let's listen to the new CD instead.*

(b) **Дава́й(те)** + perfective first-person plural

This form of the imperative is used when the speaker is suggesting a specific, one-time action. The perfective **мы́** form of the verb is used *without* the pronoun subject.

Дава́й напи́шем письмо́.	*Let's write a letter.*
Дава́й позвони́м роди́телям.	*Let's make a call to our parents.*
Дава́й встре́тимся в два́ часа́.	*Let's meet at two o'clock.*

46. In each of the following sentences, you state that you wish to perform an action. Write a sentence to invite others to join you, using the first-person imperative of the underlined verb(s).

MODELS Я́ хочу́ <u>купи́ть</u> моро́женое. > Дава́й ку́пим моро́женое.
Я́ хочу́ <u>смотре́ть</u> телеви́зор. > Дава́й смотре́ть телеви́зор.

1. Я́ хочу́ <u>вы́пить</u> за Са́шу. ____________
2. Я́ хочу́ <u>отдохну́ть</u>. ____________
3. Я́ хочу́ <u>взя́ть</u> такси́. ____________

4. Я́ хочу́ заказа́ть ры́бу. ____________
5. Я́ хочу́ подожда́ть бра́та. ____________
6. Я́ хочу́ потанцева́ть. ____________
7. Я́ хочу́ рабо́тать у́тром. ____________
8. Я́ хочу́ погуля́ть в па́рке. ____________
9. Я́ хочу́ сиде́ть и говори́ть. ____________
10. Я́ хочу́ игра́ть в те́ннис. ____________
11. Я́ хочу́ пое́хать в Москву́. ____________
12. Я́ хочу́ съе́сть кусо́к пирога́. ____________

47. Object to each of the following invitations to join the speaker in performing an action. Use the negative first-person imperative to suggest that you and the speaker not perform the action of the underlined verb.

MODEL —Дава́й поду́маем об э́том. > —Не́т, дава́й не бу́дем ду́мать об э́том.

1. —Дава́й уберём ко́мнату. —Не́т, ____________ ко́мнату.
2. —Дава́й испечём то́рт. —Не́т, ____________ то́рт.
3. —Дава́й вы́трем посу́ду. —Не́т, ____________ посу́ду.
4. —Дава́й пообе́даем. —Не́т, ____________.

Third-Person Imperative

The third-person imperative conveys a command or request to be given to a third person or persons (*Let Petya buy* wine / *Have them call* Misha). This imperative is formed with the word **пу́сть** *let/allow* (or the more colloquial **пуска́й**). The person who is to perform the action is the grammatical subject in the *nominative* case, and the verb is perfective or imperfective, depending on the nature of the action (e.g., *single specific* action or *continuous*).

Пу́сть Ле́на **испечёт** то́рт. — *Let Lena bake a cake.*
Пу́сть Ми́ша **уберёт** ко́мнату. — *Have Misha clean up his room.*
Пу́сть де́ти **игра́ют**. — *Let the children play.*

48. Refuse to participate in each of the following actions suggested by the speaker. Suggest that someone else perform the action, using the third-person imperative.

MODEL —Дава́й напи́шем Ви́те письмо́. > —Не́т, пу́сть Серёжа напи́шет.

1. —Дава́й вы́моем посу́ду. —Не́т, ____________.
2. —Дава́й заплáтим за обе́д. —Не́т, ____________.
3. —Дава́й ся́дем ря́дом с ма́мой. —Не́т, ____________.
4. —Дава́й откро́ем буты́лку вина́. —Не́т, ____________.
5. —Дава́й споём пе́сню. —Не́т, ____________.

The Conditional

Real and Unreal Conditionals

There are two types of conditional statements: (1) *real* conditionals, i.e., those that present the action as likely to occur, and (2) *unreal* conditionals, i.e., those that present the action either as unlikely to occur (*hypothetical*) or as having failed to occur (*contrary-to-fact*).

Real Conditional

Е́сли о́н позвони́т, (то́) я́ тебе́ скажу́. — *If he calls* (*will call*), *(then) I will tell you.*

Unreal Conditional

Е́сли бы о́н позвони́л, (то́) я́ бы́ тебе́ сказа́л.	(hypothetical) *If he were to call, (then) I would tell you.*
	(contrary-to-fact) *If he had called, (then) I would have told you.*

The first sentence (the real conditional) presents the situation as likely to occur and is expressed in the *indicative mood,* i.e., it presents the condition as an objective fact. Thus, it is a fact that the condition, if met, *will have* the indicated consequence. In Russian, as in English, real conditional sentences consist of two clauses: a subordinate clause (containing the condition) usually introduced by the conjunction **е́сли** *if,* and the main clause (containing the consequence) that may be introduced by the conjunction **то́** (or **тогда́**) *then.* This word, as in English, is often omitted.

Е́сли ..., (то́) ...	*If ..., (then) ...*

Real conditionals in Russian differ from those in English in one important respect: When the verb in the *if*-clause refers to a *future* action, Russian grammar requires the verb to be in the future tense (the example above has **позвони́т** (perfective) *will call*), whereas English uses the present tense (*if he calls*).

The second sentence above (the unreal conditional) describes the situation as doubtful (or impossible) and is expressed in the *conditional mood.* Unreal conditions in Russian consist of a condition clause and a consequence clause, each of which must contain the unstressed particle **бы** + *the past-tense form* of the verb.

Condition clause	**Е́сли бы** + past-tense form of the verb
Consequence clause	**(то́)** + past-tense form of the verb + **бы**

In an unreal conditional the past tense of the verb is past in *form only,* it is *not* necessarily past in meaning. The tense form in an unreal conditional construction may, depending on context, relate to present, past, or future time. For example, in the following two sentences it is the adverbs **за́втра** *tomorrow* and **вчера́** *yesterday* that relate the time of the situation to the future (*If I were to receive ...*) and the past (*If I had received ...*), respectively.

Е́сли бы за́втра я́ **получи́л** де́ньги, я́ **бы купи́л** пле́йер.	*If I were to receive the money tomorrow, I would buy a CD player.*
Е́сли бы вчера́ я́ **получи́л** де́ньги, я́ **бы купи́л** пле́йер.	*If I had received the money yesterday, I would have bought a CD player.*

49. Combine each of the following pairs of sentences into a complex sentence introduced by a **е́сли**-clause of real condition, according to the model.

MODEL За́втра бу́дет хоро́шая пого́да. Мы́ пойдём купа́ться. >
Е́сли за́втра бу́дет хоро́шая пого́да, (то́) мы́ пойдём купа́ться.

1. За́втра бу́дет до́ждь. Мы́ бу́дем сиде́ть до́ма.
____
2. Ты́ не оде́нешься быстре́е. Мы́ опозда́ем на конце́рт.
____
3. Ты́ и́м позвони́шь. Они́ бу́дут о́чень ра́ды.
____
4. Вы́ придёте к на́м. Я́ пригото́влю ва́м вку́сный обе́д.
____
5. У меня́ бу́дет вре́мя. Я́ тебе́ помогу́.
____
6. У на́с бу́дут де́ньги. Мы́ ку́пим но́вую маши́ну.
____

50. Rewrite each of the following sentences, changing the mood from the indicative (it is a fact that the action did not occur) to the conditional mood (hypothetical or contrary-to-fact).

MODEL Óн не дáл нáм свóй áдрес, и мы́ не написáли емý. >
Éсли бы óн дáл нáм свóй áдрес, (тó) мы́ бы написáли емý.

1. Онá не пришлá, и я́ не поговори́л с нéй.
______
2. Нáши друзья́ не позвони́ли, и мы́ не пригласи́ли и́х в гóсти.
______
3. Óн не захотéл смотрéть фи́льм, и мы́ не пошли́ в кинó.
______
4. Мы́ не пригласи́ли егó, и óн не пришёл на вечери́нку.
______
5. Ты́ не проси́л меня́, и я́ не купи́л буты́лку винá.
______

51. Rewrite each of the following sentences, changing the real condition to an unreal condition.

MODEL Éсли ты приéдешь в Петербýрг, я́ покажý тебé Эрмитáж. >
Éсли бы ты́ приéхал в Петербýрг, я́ бы показáл тебé Эрмитáж.

1. Éсли фи́льм кóнчится в дéвять часóв, мы́ встрéтимся с вáми.
______
2. Éсли óн попрóсит, я́ обязáтельно помогý емý.
______
3. Éсли мы́ успéем купи́ть билéты, мы́ пойдём смотрéть концéрт.
______
4. Éсли вы́ скáжете нáм дорóгу, мы́ поéдем тудá.
______
5. Éсли óн сдéлает всé упражнéния, óн смóжет пойти́ в кинó.
______
6. Éсли у меня́ бýдет врéмя, я́ позвоню́ вáм.
______

The Subjunctive

While the conditional mood is used to express hypothetical and contrary-to-fact conditional statements, the *subjunctive* mood is used to refer to other situations that are uncertain, tentative, unlikely, hypothetical, or contrary-to-fact. In particular, the subjunctive is used to express advice, wishes, hopes, desires, requests, and commands that may or may not be (or may not have been) realized. The grammatical means for expressing the subjunctive mood, like the conditional mood, is the unstressed particle **бы** and the *past-tense form* of the verb. The subjunctive mood may also be expressed in certain subordinate clauses introduced by the conjunction **чтóбы** (**чтó** + **бы**). In the subjunctive, as in the conditional mood, the past-tense form of the verb used with **бы** or **чтóбы** does *not* necessarily signal past-tense *meaning*. The time of the situation expressed by the verb in the subjunctive mood is determined by the context.

The Subjunctive with *бы* + Past Tense

Following are the most common uses of the subjunctive mood expressed by **бы** and the past-tense form of the verb. Depending on the meaning of the verb and the context, this construction may convey mild advice, polite requests, or wishes.

Expressing Polite Advice

The particle **бы** combined with the past-tense forms of the verbs **совéтовать** *to advise* and **рекомендовáть** *to recommend* are commonly used to express polite, mild advice.

Я́ бы тебé **посовéтовал** позвони́ть éй.	*I would advise you to call her.*
Я́ бы вáм **рекомендовáл** прочитáть э́ту кни́гу.	*I would recommend that you read this book.*

The particle **бы** may be combined with verbs of other meanings, which results in nuances ranging from mild advice and recommendations to polite requests. This construction is milder than commands of the second-person imperative, and is more common in informal, colloquial style.

Вáня, **пошёл бы** ты́ купáться.	*Vanya, why don't you go for a swim.*
Свéта, **поговори́ла бы** ты́ с ни́м.	*Sveta, you ought to talk with him.*
Пáпа, **лёг бы** ты́ отдохну́ть.	*Dad, why don't you lie down and rest.*
Сóня, **помоглá бы** ты́ ему́.	*Sonya, why don't you help him!*

Expressing a Wish

The speaker may use the particle **бы** + the past tense of the verb **хотéть** *to want* to express a mild wish or desire to perform an action, e.g., **Я́ хотéл бы ...** *I would like to....* This construction is less categorical than saying **Я́ хочу́ ...** *I want....*

Я́ хотéл бы поспáть.	*I would like to take a nap.*
Онá **хотéла бы** пойти́ в кинó.	*She would like to go to a movie.*

The particle **бы** may be combined with other verbs to express a wish. This construction is used in informal, colloquial style.

Э́х, **поспáл бы** я́ часóк!	*Boy, I wish I could take an hour's nap!*
Óх, **поéл бы** я́ сейчáс чегó-нибудь!	*Boy, I could eat something right now!*
Óх, **вы́пил бы** я́ сейчáс пи́ва!	*Boy, I sure could drink some beer!*

The speaker may also use the subjunctive mood to express a wish that someone else do something, or that some situation were different.

Тóлько **бы** óн **позвони́л**!	*If only he would call (had called)!*
Éсли **бы** óн бóльше **занимáлся**!	*If only he would study (had studied) more!*
Пришлá бы онá порáньше.	*If only she could (have) come a little earlier.*
Бы́ло бы у меня́ врéмя!	*If only I had (had) the time!*
Хорошó **(бы́ло) бы** имéть маши́ну!	*It would be good to have a car.*

The Subjunctive with *чтóбы* + Past Tense

The subjunctive mood may also be used in a complex sentence with a subordinate clause introduced by the conjunction **чтóбы**. There are two types of sentences that require the subjunctive mood: (1) those in which the predicate of the main clause has the meaning of *desire, wish, advice, command,* or *necessity,* and (2) those in which the **чтóбы**-clause expresses the *purpose* of the action expressed by the verb in the main clause.

Wishes, Desires, and Commands Expressed by One Person to Another

The subjunctive mood is used in the Russian translation of English sentences of the type indicated by (b), but not those of the type indicated by sentence (a).

(a) *I want to see this movie.*
(b) ***I** want **her** to see this movie.*

In sentence (a) there is only one subject; the subject of the verb *want* is also understood to be the subject of the infinitive *to see,* that is, the person expressing the wish is the same person who is to see the movie. In sentences like (a) the English infinitive is rendered by an infinitive in Russian: **Я́ хочу́ *посмотре́ть* э́тот фи́льм**.

In sentence (b), by contrast, there are two subjects; the subject of the verb *want* is different from the subject of the infinitive *to see.* In sentences like (b), the so-called "direct object + infinitive" construction of English must be rendered in Russian by the subjunctive with **что́бы** + past-tense form of the verb. In the Russian translation of this construction, the English direct object becomes the *nominative subject* (*her* becomes **она́** *she*).

Я́ хочу́, **что́бы** она́ **посмотре́ла** э́тот фи́льм.

Following are some common verbs with the meaning of desire, wish, or command that may be used as predicates in the main clause of complex sentences of the type illustrated by sentence (b) and its Russian equivalent.

хоте́ть/захоте́ть *to want*
проси́ть/попроси́ть *to ask*
веле́ть *to order*
сказа́ть *to tell* (*someone to do something*)
тре́бовать/потре́бовать *to demand*

Жена́ **проси́ла**, **что́бы** я́ е́й **позвони́л**.	*My wife asked me to call her.*
Ма́ть **сказа́ла**, **что́бы** сы́н **убра́л** ко́мнату.	*The mother told her son to clean up his room.*
Вра́ч **веле́л**, **что́бы** о́н **лежа́л** в посте́ли.	*The doctor ordered him to stay in bed.*
Она́ **тре́бует**, **что́бы** о́н **извини́лся**.	*She is demanding that he apologize.*

A few verbs, for example, **проси́ть/попроси́ть**, **сове́товать/посове́товать**, may be followed either by an infinitive or by **что́бы** + past tense.

Она́ **попроси́ла** меня́ **позвони́ть** е́й.	*She asked me to call her.*
Она́ **попроси́ла**, **что́бы** я́ **позвони́л** е́й.	*She asked me to call her.*
Вра́ч **посове́товал** ему́ похуде́ть.	*The doctor advised him to lose weight.*
Вра́ч **посове́товал**, **что́бы** о́н **похуде́л**.	*The doctor advised him to lose weight.*

In addition to the verbs listed above, there are also modal words with the meaning of desire or necessity that may serve as the predicate in the main clause of such sentences, e.g., **жела́тельно** *it is desirable,* **ва́жно** *it is important,* **на́до/ну́жно** *it is necessary.*

Жела́тельно, **что́бы** вы́ **бы́ли** на собра́нии.	*It is desirable that you be at the meeting.*
Ва́жно, **что́бы** о́н **сда́л** экза́мен.	*It is important that he pass the exam.*
На́до, **что́бы** все́ **голосова́ли**.	*It is necessary that everyone vote.*

Subjunctive in Purpose Clauses

Analogous to the two sentence types expressing desires, wishes, and commands noted above in (a) and (b), *purpose* clauses introduced by **что́бы** have two possible forms.

1. **что́бы** + *infinitive,* when the subject of the purpose clause is the same as the subject in the main clause

Са́ша включи́л телеви́зор, **что́бы** **смотре́ть** но́вости.	*Sasha turned on the TV (in order) to watch the news.*

The conjunction **чтóбы** may be omitted, especially when it follows a verb of motion.

Онá **пошлá** на пóчту **купи́ть** мáрки. — *She went to the post office to buy stamps.*

2. **чтóбы** + *past tense* (the subjunctive mood), when the two clauses have different subjects

Сáша включи́л телеви́зор, **чтóбы** пáпа **смотрéл** нóвости. — *Sasha turned on the TV so that his dad could watch the news.*

Лéна остáвила запи́ску, **чтóбы** мы́ **знáли**, кудá онá пошлá. — *Lena left a note so that we might know where she went.*

52. Rewrite each of the following sentences, adding the particle **бы** and changing the underlined verb to the past tense, according to the model. The wish or advice you have expressed is now less categorical and more polite.

MODEL Я́ советую вáм посети́ть Рýсский музéй. > Я́ бы посовéтовал вáм посети́ть Рýсский музéй.

1. Я́ хочý читáть нóвый ромáн Пелéвина.
____
2. Я́ рекомендýю вáм сходи́ть на э́ту вы́ставку.
____
3. Я́ совéтую вáм поговори́ть с начáльником.
____
4. Чтó вы́ хоти́те посмотрéть по телеви́зору?
____
5. Какóй словáрь ты́ совéтуешь мнé купи́ть?
____

53. Rewrite each of the following sentences, removing the verb **хочý** and adding the particle **бы** and the past-tense form of the underlined verb, according to the model. The wish you have expressed is now less categorical and more conversational in style.

MODEL Я́ хочý поигрáть в тéннис. > Я́ бы поигрáл в тéннис.

1. Я́ хочý вы́пить стакáн холóдного пи́ва.
____
2. Я́ хочý поспáть немнóго.
____
3. Я́ хочý послýшать хорóшую рок-мýзыку.
____
4. Я́ хочý поéсть салáт «Столи́чный».
____
5. Я́ хочý поéхать на мóре.
____

54. Rewrite each of the following sentences, replacing the underlined imperative with a more mild, polite form of request, according to the model.

MODEL Покажи́ емý свои́ карти́ны. > Показáл бы ты́ емý свои́ карти́ны.

1. Помоги́ éй реши́ть задáчу.
____

2. Посмотри́ э́тот но́вый францу́зский фи́льм.

3. Убери́ свою́ ко́мнату.

4. Послу́шай мо́й но́вый ди́ск.

5. Поговори́ с ни́м об э́том.

55. Rewrite each of the following sentences, changing the underlined infinitive to the subjunctive construction with **чтóбы** + the past tense of the verb, according to the model.

MODEL Студе́нт попроси́л преподава́теля объясни́ть ему́ зада́чу. >
Студе́нт попроси́л преподава́теля, что́бы о́н объясни́л ему́ зада́чу.

1. Я́ посове́товал дру́гу бро́сить кури́ть.

2. Ми́ша попроси́л меня́ купи́ть ему́ газе́ту.

3. Мы́ угова́ривали дру́га пое́хать отдыха́ть на мо́ре.

4. Я́ попроси́л бра́та помо́чь мне́.

5. Учи́тель посове́товал ученика́м слу́шать внима́тельнее.

56. Complete the purpose clause of each of the following sentences, using the correct form of the verb in parentheses, i.e., either the unchanged infinitive or the past-tense form.

1. Я́ взя́л слова́рь, что́бы ________ (перевести́) поэ́му.
2. Я́ взя́л слова́рь, что́бы Бори́с ________ (перевести́) те́кст.
3. Она́ принесла́ фотогра́фии, что́бы мы́ ________ (посмотре́ть) и́х.
4. Я́ принёс докла́д, что́бы ________ (показа́ть) его́ нача́льнику.
5. О́н вста́л, что́бы ________ (поздоро́ваться) с друзья́ми.
6. О́н вста́л, что́бы же́нщина ________ (мо́чь) се́сть.

57. Translate each of the following English sentences into Russian, using the subjunctive mood.

1. It would be good to vacation in Europe.

2. It is important that you finish the report.

3. It is necessary that he answer the letter.

4. If only he would find work.

5. If only I had more time.

Transitive and Intransitive Verbs

Verbs in Russian, as in English, are either transitive or intransitive. Transitive verbs in Russian may take a direct object in the accusative case. Transitive verbs do not have any grammatical form to signal their transitivity. However, a useful diagnostic for whether a verb is transitive or not is if it can be used in a question with **Чтó?** or **Когó?**, the accusative case forms of the pronouns *What?* and *Whom?* For example, the verbs **читáть** *to read* and **слýшать** *to listen to* are transitive.

—**Чтó** ты́ **читáешь**!	*What are you reading?*
—Я́ **читáю поэ́му**.	*I'm reading a poem.*
—**Когó** ты́ **слýшаешь**!	*Whom are you listening to?*
—Я́ **слýшаю профéссора**.	*I'm listening to the professor.*

Many transitive verbs can be used intransitively, though a direct object is implied, e.g., **Óн лю́бит *читáть*** *He likes to read* (*novels, stories,* etc.).

Intransitive verbs *cannot* take a direct object, nor, therefore, can they be used in a question with the pronouns **Чтó?** or **Когó?** For example, verbs such as **спáть** *to sleep,* **идти́** *to go,* and **улыбáться** *to smile* are intransitive. Unlike transitive verbs, which have no marker indicating their transitivity, a great number of intransitive verbs do have a grammatical form that marks them as intransitive: These are verbs with the particle **-ся**.

Verbs with the Particle *-ся* (*-сь*)

All verbs with the particle **-ся** (spelled **-ся** after a consonant, **-сь** after a vowel) are intransitive, though some of them may take an object in a case other than the accusative.

боя́ться *to be afraid of, fear*	
Онá **бои́тся собáки**.	*She is afraid of the dog.* (genitive case)
занимáться *to study*	
Óн **занимáется би́знесом**.	*He is studying business.* (instrumental case)
учи́ться *to study*	
Óн **ýчится мýзыке**.	*He is studying music.* (dative case)

A few verbs that normally take an object in the genitive case (e.g., **боя́ться** *fear* and **слýшаться** *to obey*) may take the accusative in colloquial style, but only if the object denotes people, e.g., **Онá бои́тся бáбушку** *She fears her grandmother,* **Óн слýшается дя́дю Сáшу** *He obeys Uncle Sasha.*

Principal Groups of Verbs in *-ся*

A great number of Russian verbs exist in pairs of transitive verb / intransitive verb in **-ся**. This is because transitive verbs can have the particle **-ся** added to them to derive an intransitive counterpart in **-ся**. When this happens, the verb, in addition to becoming intransitive, often acquires an additional meaning. In fact, it is possible to divide verbs in **-ся** into a small number of groups according to these meanings. The following are the principal meanings associated with verbs in **-ся**.

Reflexive Meaning

Certain verbs to which **-ся** is added acquire a *reflexive* meaning, that is, the action of the verb is performed by the subject on himself. The verbs in this group typically denote physical actions that are characteristically reflexive.

мы́ть(ся)/помы́ть(ся) *to wash (oneself)*
вытирáть(ся)/вы́тереть(ся) *to dry (oneself)*
бри́ть(ся)/побри́ть(ся) *to shave (oneself)*
причёсывать(ся)/причесáть(ся) *to comb one's hair*
одевáть(ся)/одéть(ся) *to dress (oneself)*

Note the contrast in the following pairs of sentences.

Жена́ **мо́ет** посу́ду.	*The wife washes the dishes.*
Она́ **мо́ется** холо́дной водо́й.	*She washes (herself) with cold water.*
Му́ж **вытира́ет** посу́ду.	*The husband dries the dishes.*
О́н **вытира́ется** полоте́нцем.	*He is drying himself with a towel.*

Characteristically reflexive verbs normally do not occur transitively with the direct-object pronoun **себя́** *oneself.* However, transitive verbs that are not usually conceived of as reflexive may be used in a reflexive construction with **себя́**, e.g., **Она́ хорошо́ *понима́ет* себя́** *She understands herself well,* **О́н не *лю́бит* себя́** *He doesn't like himself.*

Reciprocal Meaning

Certain verbs to which **-ся** is added acquire a *reciprocal* meaning, that is, they denote actions that involve more than one subject, each performing the action on the other. The verbs in this group typically involve two participants, and the action is characteristically a mutual one. One of the participants may be expressed in the instrumental case after the preposition **с** *with.*

встреча́ть(ся)/встре́тить(ся) *to meet (each other)*
ви́деть(ся)/уви́деть(ся) *to see each other*
знако́мить(ся)/познако́мить(ся) *to meet (each other)*
обнима́ть(ся)/обня́ть(ся) *to embrace (each other)*
целова́ть(ся) /поцелова́ть(ся) *to kiss (each other)*

Compare the transitive and intransitive use of these verbs.

Я́ встре́тил его́ по́сле ле́кции.	*I met him after the lecture.*
Мы́ **встре́тились** по́сле ле́кции.	*We met (each other) after the lecture.*
Я́ о́бнял и поцелова́л её.	*I hugged and kissed her.*
Мы́ **обняли́сь и поцелова́лись.**	*We hugged and kissed (each other).*
Хо́чешь, я тебя́ **познако́млю** с не́й?	*If you want, I'll introduce you to her.*
О́н **познако́мился** с не́й в шко́ле.	*He met her in school.*

Verbs that characteristically denote reciprocal actions normally do not occur with the reciprocal pronoun **дру́г дру́га** *one another.* However, this pronoun is used to provide a reciprocal meaning to verbs that do not inherently have this meaning, e.g., **Они́ *уважа́ют* дру́г дру́га** *They respect one another.*

Verbs Denoting Emotion

Several common verbs denoting emotions and attitudes may be used transitively with an *animate* direct object. When such verbs are used intransitively with **-ся**, the animate direct object appears as the subject in the nominative case, and the noun denoting the source of the emotion appears in an oblique case, with or without a preposition.

Following are some common emotion verbs of this type.

Transitive	**Intransitive in *-ся* + Instrumental**
интересова́ть/заинтересова́ть *to interest*	интересова́ться/заинтересова́ться *to be interested in*
увлека́ть/увле́чь *to fascinate*	увлека́ться/увле́чься *to be fascinated by*

Transitive	**Intransitive in *-ся* + Dative**
ра́довать/обра́довать *to make glad*	ра́доваться/обра́доваться *to be glad for*
удивля́ть/удиви́ть *to surprise*	удивля́ться/удиви́ться *to be surprised at*

Transitive	Intransitive in -ся + Genitive
пуга́ть/испуга́ть *to frighten, scare*	пуга́ться/испуга́ться *to be frightened of*

Transitive	Intransitive in -ся (на + Accusative)
серди́ть/рассерди́ть *to anger*	серди́ться/рассерди́ться *to be angry at*
обижа́ть/оби́деть *to offend*	обижа́ться/оби́деться *to be offended by*

Transitive	Intransitive in -ся (о + Prepositional)
беспоко́ить/обеспоко́ить *to worry, bother*	беспоко́иться/обеспоко́иться *to be worried about*
волнова́ть/взволнова́ть *to worry, disturb*	волнова́ться/взволнова́ться *to be nervous about*

Compare the transitive and intransitive use of these verbs.

Меня́ **интересу́ет** му́зыка.	*Music interests me.*
Я́ **интересу́юсь** му́зыкой.	*I'm interested in music.*
На́с **удиви́ла** его́ ще́дрость.	*His generosity surprised us.*
Мы́ **удиви́лись** его́ ще́дрости.	*We were surprised at his generosity.*
Э́то **беспоко́ит** его́.	*This worries him.*
О́н **беспоко́ится** об э́том.	*He is worried about this.*

Verbs That Occur Only in *-ся*

A relatively small number of verbs occur only intransitively with the particle **-ся**, i.e., they have no transitive counterpart. Several of these also express some emotion. Some common verbs in this group include the following.

боя́ться *to be afraid of* (+ Gen.)
смея́ться *to laugh* (**над** + Instr.)
улыба́ться *to smile*
наде́яться *to hope* (**на** + Acc.)
нра́виться/понра́виться *to like* (+ Dat. of the person who "likes" and Nom. for what/who is liked)

Она́ всегда́ **смеётся** над его́ шу́тками.	*She always laughs at his jokes.*
О́н **улыба́ется** при ви́де отца́.	*He smiles when he sees his father.*
Мне́ **нра́вится** твоя́ но́вая ша́пка.	*I like your new hat.*

58. Complete each of the following sentences with the correct form of the transitive or intransitive verb on the right.

1. Ка́ждое у́тро Ва́ня ____________ в ду́ше.	мы́ть/мы́ться
2. Ка́ждую неде́лю о́н ____________ свою́ маши́ну.	мы́ть/мы́ться
3. До́чка сейча́с ____________ сама́ в ва́нне.	мы́ть/мы́ться
4. Ма́ть бы́стро ____________ и пошла́ на рабо́ту.	оде́ть/оде́ться
5. До́чка до́лго ____________ ку́клы.	одева́ть/одева́ться
6. Ма́ма о́чень тепло́ ____________ ребёнка и повела́ его́ на като́к.	оде́ть/оде́ться
7. В Сиби́ри зимо́й на́до всегда́ ____________ тепло́.	одева́ть/одева́ться
8. Де́вочка ча́сто ____________ свои́ во́лосы.	причёсывать/причёсываться
9. Де́вочка сиде́ла пе́ред зе́ркалом и ____________.	причёсывать/причёсываться
10. Сестра́ ____________ мла́дшего бра́та.	причёсывать/причёсываться

59. Complete each of the following sentences with the correct form of the transitive or intransitive verb on the right.

1.	Друзья́ до́лго не __________.	ви́деть/ви́деться
2.	О́н не __________ свою́ подру́гу уже́ три́ го́да.	ви́деть/ви́деться
3.	Я́ наде́юсь, что мы́ ско́ро __________.	увидеть/увидеться
4.	Мне́ каза́лось, что мы́ с ни́м где́-то __________.	встреча́ть/встреча́ться
5.	По доро́ге домо́й я́ __________ дру́га.	встре́тить/встре́титься
6.	Ми́ша __________ с сестро́й.	поцелова́ть/поцелова́ться
7.	До́чь __________ отца́.	поцелова́ть/поцелова́ться
8.	Оте́ц с сы́ном __________.	обня́ть/обня́ться
9.	Кто́ вас __________ с э́той де́вушкой?	познако́мить/познако́миться
10.	Мы́ __________ на заня́тиях в институ́те.	познако́мить/познако́миться

60. Complete each of the following sentences with the correct form of the appropriate verb on the right.

1.	Твоё письмо́ на́с о́чень __________.	обра́довать/обра́доваться
2.	Мы́ __________ твое́й хоро́шей но́вости.	обра́довать/обра́доваться
3.	Меня́ о́чень __________ здоро́вье отца́.	беспоко́ить/беспоко́иться
4.	О́н о́чень __________ об отце́.	беспоко́ить/беспоко́иться
5.	Каки́е писа́тели ва́с __________?	интересова́ть/интересова́ться
6.	О́н __________ ру́сскими писа́телями.	интересова́ть/интересова́ться
7.	Я́ о́чень __________, сы́н ещё не пришёл из шко́лы.	волнова́ть/волнова́ться
8.	Экономи́ческая ситуа́ция в стране́ __________ всё́х.	волнова́ть/волнова́ться
9.	Она́ __________ на него́: о́н не пришёл и не позвони́л.	серди́ть/серди́ться
10.	Его́ поведе́ние о́чень __________ жену́.	серди́ть/серди́ться
11.	На́с __________ хоро́шие отме́тки сы́на.	удиви́ть/удиви́ться
12.	Роди́тели __________ успе́хам сы́на.	удиви́ть/удиви́ться

Voice and the Particle *-ся*

Active Voice

The term *voice* refers to the relationship between the verbal action, the Agent (the conscious initiator of the action), and the Patient (the entity that undergoes the action). Normally, the Agent of the action is the grammatical subject of the sentence and in Russian is in the nominative case, while the Patient is the direct object in the accusative case. This arrangement, which presents the action as emanating from the Agent to the Patient, is called the *active* voice. Sentences presented in the active voice are transitive constructions, since the verb is followed by a direct object.

Active Voice

Nominative subject (Agent) —	Transitive verb —	Accusative direct object (Patient)
Студе́нты	организу́ют	клу́б.
The students	*are organizing*	*a club.*

Passive Voice

The active voice is not the only way to represent the relationship of the Agent and Patient to the verbal action. For example, the speaker may wish to present the action in the *passive* voice, that is, from the perspective of the object that undergoes the action (the Patient). In the passive voice the Patient is made prominent and the Agent is deemphasized. This is accomplished by removing the Agent from the subject position, and replacing it with the direct object Patient. In forming the Russian passive, two things happen when the direct object is made the grammatical subject in the nominative case: (1) The particle **-ся** is added to the (imperfective) verb, and (2) the Agent, if mentioned, is put in the instrumental case.

Passive Voice

Nominative subject (Patient) —	Intransitive verb in **-ся** —	(Instrumental Agent)
Клу́б	организу́ется	студе́нтами.
A club	*is being organized*	*by the students.*

Though the action in a passive construction is always understood to involve an Agent, the Agent may not be mentioned if his identity is either unknown or unimportant.

Програ́мма «Вре́мя» **передаётся** ка́ждый ве́чер.	*The program "Vremya" is aired every evening.*
В э́том кинотеа́тре **пока́зываются** иностра́нные фи́льмы.	*Foreign films are shown in this movie theater.*

In more informal style, the so-called "indefinite personal" construction may be used as an alternative to the passive construction with the verb in **-ся**. The indefinite personal uses a transitive verb in the third-person plural and an accusative direct object. There is no overt subject Agent, but the personal form of the verb implies an indefinite subject "they." This construction may be translated into English either in the passive voice (as above), or in the active voice, as shown below.

Програ́мму «Вре́мя» **передаю́т** ка́ждый ве́чер.	*They show the program "Vremya" every evening.*
В э́том кинотеа́тре **пока́зывают** иностра́нные фи́льмы.	*They show foreign films in this movie theater.*

Middle Voice

Another way to present the action from the perspective of the Patient is to make the direct object the subject and completely eliminate reference to an Agent. This *middle voice* construction is formed the same way as the passive, except that in the passive the Agent is only *deemphasized* and may occur in the instrumental, while in a middle construction there can be *no mention of an Agent.* Both imperfective and perfective verbs form middles in **-ся**.

Following are examples of the middle voice in which the situations involve phenomena of nature, and therefore exclude the possibility of an Agent's participation.

Со́лнце **поднима́ется**.	*The sun rises / is rising.*
Ве́тер **уси́лился**.	*The wind strengthened.*
Температу́ра **повы́силась**.	*The temperature rose.*

A middle construction may also be used when the real-world situation is one that may involve an Agent, but where the speaker chooses to present the action as occurring autonomously. The following middle sentences cannot occur with an instrumental Agent.

Две́рь **откры́лась**.	*The door opened.*
Компью́тер **отключи́лся**.	*The computer shut down.*
Маши́на **останови́лась**.	*The car stopped.*
Ле́кция **начала́сь** в де́вять часо́в.	*The lecture began at nine o'clock.*

61. Rewrite each of the following sentences, changing it from active voice to passive voice.

MODEL Экономи́сты обсужда́ют э́ти вопро́сы. > Э́ти вопро́сы обсужда́ются экономи́стами.

1. Студе́нты в э́той гру́ппе реша́ют тру́дные зада́чи.
______
2. Социо́логи в э́том институ́те прово́дят опро́с.
______
3. Тури́сты покупа́ют матрёшки.
______
4. Преподава́тели проверя́ют контро́льные рабо́ты.
______
5. У́личные торго́вцы продаю́т вся́кие ве́щи.
______

62. Rewrite each of the following sentences, changing it from the "indefinite personal" to the passive construction in **-ся**.

MODEL Лаборато́рию закрыва́ют в ше́сть часо́в. >
Лаборато́рия закрыва́ется в ше́сть часо́в.

1. На э́той ка́федре изуча́ют мето́дику преподава́ния.
______
2. В го́роде открыва́ют но́вую карти́нную галере́ю.
______
3. Сво́дку пого́ды передаю́т по Второ́й програ́мме в 21.00.
______
4. В э́том журна́ле публику́ют рабо́ту э́того а́втора впервы́е.
______
5. В Росси́и кни́ги Аку́нина чита́ют с больши́м интере́сом.
______

Verbal Government

Besides transitive verbs that may be followed by a direct object in the accusative case, there are other verbs (and prepositions) in Russian that govern, or require, one of the so-called oblique cases—dative, genitive, or instrumental—in their objects. Since the particular oblique case required by such a verb is largely unpredictable, the case-governing properties of these verbs must be memorized. For example, the verbs **звони́ть** *to ring, telephone,* **помога́ть** *to help,* and **сове́товать** *to advise* govern the dative case; **боя́ться** *to be afraid of,* **достига́ть** *to attain,* and **избега́ть** *to avoid* govern the genitive; and **владе́ть** *to command,* **по́льзоваться** *to use,* and **руководи́ть** *to direct* govern the instrumental. A more complete listing of the verbs that govern one of the oblique cases is given in Chapter 2, where each case is discussed.

Other verbs are regularly followed by a preposition that governs a particular case, for example, **ве́рить в** (+ Acc.) *to believe in,* **рассчи́тывать на** (+ Acc.) *to rely on,* **благодари́ть за** (+ Acc.) *to thank for,* **отлича́ться от** (+ Gen.) *to differ from,* **уча́ствовать в** (+ Prep.) *to participate in,* **наста́ивать на** (+ Prep.) *to insist on,* **гото́виться к** (+ Dat.) *to prepare for,* and **следи́ть за** (+ Instr.) *to keep up with, look after.* A more complete listing of verbs that are followed by a particular preposition + case is given in Chapter 3, where each of the prepositions is presented.

Verbs of Motion

Unidirectional and Multidirectional Verbs

The vast majority of Russian verbs have only one imperfective. However, there is one special group of paired unprefixed verbs denoting various types of movement (walking, driving, running, swimming, flying, taking, etc.), called the *verbs of motion,* that have *two imperfectives.*

1. The *unidirectional* (or *determinate*) imperfective normally refers to continuous motion in one direction toward a stated (or implied) goal.

Мы́ **идём** в па́рк.	*We are walking to the park.*
Мы́ **шли́** домо́й из па́рка.	*We were walking home from the park.*

2. The *multidirectional* (or *indeterminate*) imperfective has several uses. Specifically, it may be used to denote (a) motion that is random, or in more than one direction, (b) motion that is habitual (when a return trip is implied), (c) motion spoken of in general terms, and (d) round-trip motion in the past (went and returned).

(a) О́н **хо́дит** по ко́мнате.	*He walks around the room.*
(b) О́н ча́сто **хо́дит** на рабо́ту.	*He often walks to work.*
(c) На́ша де́вочка уже́ **хо́дит**.	*Our little girl already walks.*
(d) Вчера́ я **ходи́л** в библиоте́ку.	*Yesterday I went to the library.*

Among the motion verbs, some are transitive, while others are intransitive. Following are the five most important pairs of intransitive verbs of motion, listed with the unidirectional imperfective (U) preceding the multidirectional imperfective (M).

Intransitive Verbs of Motion

INFINITIVE	NON-PAST	PAST	IMPERATIVE
(1) *to walk, go on foot*			
идти́ (U)	иду́, идёшь, иду́т	шёл, шла́, шли́	иди́(те)
ходи́ть (M)	хожу́, хо́дишь, хо́дят	ходи́л, ходи́ла, ходи́ли	ходи́(те)
(2) *to ride, go by vehicle*			
е́хать (U)	е́ду, е́дешь, е́дут	е́хал, е́хала, е́хали	поезжа́й(те)
е́здить (M)	е́зжу, е́здишь, е́здят	е́здил, е́здила, е́здили	е́зди(те)
(3) *to run*			
бежа́ть (U)	бегу́, бежи́шь, бежи́т, бежи́м, бежи́те, бегу́т	бежа́л, бежа́ла, бежа́ли	беги́(те)
бе́гать (M)	бе́гаю, бе́гаешь, бе́гают	бе́гал, бе́гала, бе́гали	бе́гай(те)
(4) *to fly*			
лете́ть (U)	лечу́, лети́шь, летя́т	лете́л, лете́ла, лете́ли	лети́(те)
лета́ть (M)	лета́ю, лета́ешь, лета́ют	лета́л, лета́ла, лета́ли	лета́й(те)
(5) *to swim; to sail*			
плы́ть (U)	плыву́, плывёшь, плыву́т	плы́л, плыла́, плы́ли	плыви́(те)
пла́вать (M)	пла́ваю, пла́ваешь, пла́вают	пла́вал, пла́вала, пла́вали	пла́вай(те)

Principal Uses of Unidirectional Verbs

Following are the most important uses of the unidirectional verbs.

1. A unidirectional verb is used to denote motion in progress in one direction in the present, past, or future. A goal or destination is expressed by the preposition **в** or **на** + accusative (of nouns denoting places), or **к** + dative (of nouns denoting people). Otherwise, a goal is expressed by directional adverbs, e.g., **домóй** *home(ward),* **сюдá** *here,* **тудá** *there.*

   Кудá вы́ **идёте**, домóй? — *Where are you going, home?*
   Я́ **иду́** на лéкцию. — *I am going (walking) to a lecture.*
   Мы́ **éдем** к дру́гу. — *We are going to our friend's place.*
   Óн **éдет** в Москву́. — *He is going (traveling) to Moscow.*
   Онá **лети́т** к брáту в Пари́ж. — *She is flying to her brother's in Paris.*

   In the past and future tenses the unidirectional verb of motion is normally used to provide a background against which some other action occurs. Thus, the motion verb is in one clause of a complex sentence, while the verb in the other clause, if imperfective, denotes a simultaneous action, but if perfective, denotes one that was (will be) completed during the time the motion was (will be) in progress.

   Когдá я **летéл** в самолёте, я **читáл** детекти́в. — *When I was flying in the airplane, I was reading a detective novel.*
   Когдá мы́ **éхали** в маши́не, у нáс **кóнчился** бензи́н. — *When we were riding in the car, we ran out of gas.*
   Когдá ты́ **бу́дешь идти́** ми́мо киóска, **купи́** мнé газéту. — *When you are walking past the newsstand, buy me a newspaper.*

2. A unidirectional verb in the present tense may be used to denote an action that is intended for the near future, just as in English.

   Сегóдня вéчером я **иду́** в кинó. — *Tonight I'm going to the movies.*
   Зáвтра мы́ **éдем** на дáчу. — *Tomorrow we're going to the dacha.*

3. A unidirectional verb is used when the focus is on some circumstance or characteristic of one-way motion, e.g., the speed, manner, or means of travel.

   Письмó **шлó** к нáм недéлю. — *The letter reached us in a week.*
   Я́ **éду** на рабóту чáс. — *It takes me an hour to drive to work.*
   Óн **éхал** домóй сегóдня на метрó. — *He went home today by metro.*
   Онá **шлá** в кинотеáтр однá. — *She went to the movie theater alone.*

4. Only the unidirectional is used to indicate figurative motion in certain idiomatic expressions. The multidirectional cannot occur here, even when the motion is repeated. This is because the subject in these idioms is understood to move in only one direction.

   Кáк **лети́т** врéмя! — *How time flies!*
   Сегóдня **шёл** дóждь. — *It rained today.*
   Лéтом здéсь чáсто **иду́т** дожди́. — *It often rains here in the summer.*
   Чтó **идёт** в кинотеáтре? — *What's playing at the movie theater?*

Principal Uses of Multidirectional Verbs

Following are the most important uses of the multidirectional verbs.

1. To indicate random motion, i.e., motion in no specific direction or in several directions. The meaning of motion "around" or "about" is often expressed by the preposition **по** + dative case, but nondirected motion may also occur "in a place" expressed by **в/на** + prepositional case.

Мы́ **ходи́ли** по па́рку.	*We walked around the park.*
Са́ша ве́сь де́нь **е́здил** по го́роду.	*Sasha drove around town all day.*
Соба́ка **бе́гает** во дворе́.	*The dog is running about in the yard.*

2. To indicate motion that is repeated or habitual (implying *two* opposite directions, "there and back").

Он ка́ждый де́нь **хо́дит** в институ́т.	*Every day he goes to the institute. (He goes there and then returns.)*
Мы́ **е́здим** на да́чу по суббо́там.	*We go to the dacha on Saturdays.*

3. To indicate motion spoken of in general terms, for example, when characterizing one's ability or propensity for the action. Thus, a multidirectional verb is often used with qualitative adverbs and after verbs such as **уме́ть** *to know how,* **люби́ть** *to love, like,* **нра́виться** *to like,* and **боя́ться** *to be afraid.*

О́н не уме́ет **пла́вать**.	*He doesn't know how to swim.*
Она́ бы́стро **бе́гает**.	*She runs fast (is a fast runner).*
Моя́ жена́ бои́тся **лета́ть**.	*My wife is afraid to fly.*
Э́тот ребёнок ещё не **хо́дит**.	*This child cannot walk yet.*

4. To denote a single "round-trip" in the past. This use of the multidirectional verb implies that the subject "was" somewhere and has returned. Therefore, questions that ask where one *was* (**Где́ ты́ бы́л ...?**) can be answered with the past tense of the multidirectional verb (a round-trip was completed).

—Где́ ты́ **была́** вчера́?	*Where were you yesterday?*
—Я́ **ходи́ла** к сестре́.	*I went to my sister's (place).*
—Где́ вы́ **бы́ли** в суббо́ту?	*Where were you on Saturday?*
—Мы́ **е́здили** на да́чу.	*We went to the dacha.*

63. For each of the following sentences, circle the unidirectional or multidirectional imperfective(s), as appropriate.

1. Мы́ сейча́с (идём | хо́дим) в магази́н. Мы́ (идём | хо́дим) туда́ ча́сто.
2. Когда́ мы́ (шли́ | ходи́ли) домо́й, мы́ встре́тили ста́рого дру́га.
3. За́втра па́па (идёт | хо́дит) к врачу́. О́н (идёт | хо́дит) к врачу́ ра́з в ме́сяц.
4. Я́ сего́дня (е́ду | е́зжу) в командиро́вку в Ки́ев. Я́ туда́ ча́сто (е́ду | е́зжу).
5. —Куда́ ты́ та́к бы́стро (бежи́шь | бе́гаешь)?
   —Я́ (бегу́ | бе́гаю) на экза́мен.
6. —Ты́ (бежи́шь | бе́гаешь) на стадио́не?
   —Не́т, я́ (бегу́ | бе́гаю) в па́рке.
7. Вчера́ мы́ (шли́ | ходи́ли) в теа́тр. На́м о́чень понра́вился конце́рт.
8. Она́ не лю́бит (бежа́ть | бе́гать), она́ предпочита́ет (идти́ | ходи́ть).
9. Моя́ до́чка хорошо́ (плывёт | пла́вает), она́ (плывёт | пла́вает) ка́ждый де́нь.
10. Про́шлым ле́том мы́ (е́хали | е́здили) в о́тпуск на мо́ре.
11. Куда́ (плывёт | пла́вает) э́тот кора́бль? О́н (плывёт | пла́вает) из Та́ллина в Санкт-Петербу́рг.
12. —Где́ бы́л Са́ша на про́шлой неде́ле?
    —О́н (лете́л | лета́л) в Москву́.

13. Я́ сего́дня (лечу́ | лета́ю) в Нью-Йо́рк. А куда́ ты́ (лети́шь | лета́ешь)?
14. —Где́ ты́ бы́л вчера́?
    —Я́ (е́хал | е́здил) за го́род к сестре́.
15. Когда́ я́ (е́хал | е́здил) к сестре́, я́ ду́мал о то́м, ка́к я́ скуча́ю по не́й.
16. Каки́е фи́льмы сейча́с (иду́т | хо́дят) в кинотеа́тре «Росси́я»?
17. В э́том теа́тре ча́сто (иду́т | хо́дят) америка́нские фи́льмы.
18. Зимо́й в Москве́ ча́сто (идёт | хо́дит) сне́г.

Transitive Verbs of Motion

Following are the three most commonly used transitive verbs of motion, listed with the unidirectional followed by the multidirectional imperfective.

	INFINITIVE	NON-PAST	PAST	IMPERATIVE
(1)	*to carry (while walking)*			
	нести́ (U)	несу́, несёшь, несу́т	нёс, несла́, несли́	неси́(те)
	носи́ть (M)	ношу́, но́сишь, но́сят	носи́л, носи́ла, носи́ли	носи́(те)
(2)	*to transport, to take by vehicle*			
	везти́ (U)	везу́, везёшь, везу́т	вёз, везла́, везли́	вези́(те)
	вози́ть (M)	вожу́, во́зишь, во́зят	вози́л, вози́ла, вози́ли	вози́(те)
(3)	*to lead on foot*			
	вести́ (U)	веду́, ведёшь, веду́т	вёл, вела́, вели́	веди́(те)
	води́ть (M)	вожу́, во́дишь, во́дят	води́л, води́ла, води́ли	води́(те)

Transitive motion verbs have the same uses outlined above for intransitive motion verbs. The following examples illustrate these uses for transitive verbs of unidirectional and multidirectional motion.

Transitive Verbs of Unidirectional Motion

Я́ сейча́с **несу́** письмо́ на по́чту.	*I am taking a letter to the post office.*
Ма́ть **ведёт** до́чь в шко́лу.	*The mother is taking (walking) her daughter to school.*
Когда́ она́ **вела́** де́вочку в па́рк, пошёл до́ждь.	*When she was taking the little girl to the park, it began to rain.*
Грузови́к **везёт** фру́кты на ры́нок.	*The truck is taking fruit to the market.*

Transitive Verbs of Multidirectional Motion

Я́ всегда́ **ношу́** с собо́й фотогра́фии свои́х дете́й.	*I always carry photos of my children with me.*
Почтальо́н **но́сит** пи́сьма, газе́ты, и журна́лы.	*The mail carrier carries letters, newspapers, and magazines.*
Она́ рабо́тает ги́дом и **во́дит** тури́стов по музе́ю.	*She works as a guide and takes tourists around the museum.*
Вчера́ мы́ **вози́ли** дете́й на о́зеро.	*Yesterday we took the children to the lake (and back).*

Transitive Motion Verbs in Idiomatic Expressions

Transitive motion verbs, like intransitive motion verbs, can be used figuratively.

The multidirectional verb **носи́ть** can be used in the meaning *to wear (regularly)*.

Я́ ча́сто **ношу́** джи́нсы.	*I often wear jeans.*
Она́ **но́сит** очки́.	*She wears glasses.*

The pair **водить/вести** may take the object **машину** in the meaning *to drive a car.*

Она́ у́чится **води́ть** маши́ну.	*She is learning to drive a car.*
Кто́ **вёл** маши́ну, когда́ произошла́ ава́рия?	*Who was driving the car when the accident occurred?*

Correlating Transitive and Intransitive Motion Verbs

When transitive and intransitive motion verbs are used in the same context, they must correlate in two respects: They must both be unidirectional or multidirectional, and normally they must both express motion "on foot" or "by vehicle."

Она́ **идёт** на по́чту, **несёт** туда́ письмо́.	*She is walking to the post office, she's taking (carrying) a letter there.*
Я́ **иду́** в па́рк с соба́кой, **веду́** её гуля́ть.	*I'm going to the park with the dog, I'm taking it for a walk.*
Ги́д **е́дет** на авто́бусе с тури́стами, о́н **везёт** и́х в музе́й.	*The guide is riding the bus with tourists, he's taking them to a museum.*
Ма́ть часто **хо́дит** в па́рк и **во́дит** туда́ детей.	*The mother often walks to the park and takes the children there.*

64. Complete each of the following sentences with the correct present-tense form of the appropriate transitive verb of motion: **нести́**, **вести́**, or **везти́**.

1. По у́лице иду́т шко́льники и ________________ кни́ги.
2. По у́лице е́дут грузовики́ и ________________ фру́кты и о́вощи.
3. Де́ти иду́т из са́да и ________________ цветы́.
4. Ма́ть идёт и ________________ до́чь в шко́лу.
5. Во́т идёт почтальо́н, о́н ________________ на́м пи́сьма.
6. Авто́бусы е́дут к теа́тру, они́ ________________ зри́телей.
7. Студе́нт идёт на ле́кцию и ________________ портфе́ль.
8. Самолёт лети́т на Кари́бские острова́ и ________________ тури́стов.
9. Ребя́та иду́т из ле́са и ________________ грибы́.
10. Оте́ц е́дет домо́й из командиро́вки и ________________ де́тям пода́рки.

65. Complete each of the following sentences with the correct present- or past-tense form of the appropriate transitive verb of motion: **носи́ть/нести́**, **води́ть/вести́**, or **вози́ть/везти́**.

1. Ми́ша рабо́тает води́телем авто́буса. О́н ________________ пассажи́ров по го́роду.
2. По доро́ге е́хали маши́ны. Они́ ________________ пассажи́ров в аэропо́рт.
3. Моя́ сестра́ рабо́тает экскурсово́дом. Она́ ________________ тури́стов по музе́ю.
4. Ги́д шёл с гру́ппой тури́стов, о́н ________________ и́х в гардеро́б.
5. О́н рабо́тает носи́льщиком и ________________ бага́ж прожива́ющих в гости́нице.
6. Вот идёт почтальо́н. О́н ________________ на́м посы́лку.
7. О́н учи́лся на ку́рсах води́телей и тепе́рь о́н хорошо́ ________________ маши́ну.
8. Оле́г ________________ маши́ну, когда́ вдру́г ко́нчился бензи́н.
9. У него́ плохо́е зре́ние, поэ́тому о́н ________________ очки́.
10. Я́ ненави́жу шо́рты и никогда́ не ________________ и́х.

Prefixed Verbs of Motion

Unidirectional Verbs with the Prefix *по-*

Unidirectional imperfectives become perfective when formed with the prefix **по-**.

UNIDIRECTIONAL IMPERFECTIVE	PREFIXED PERFECTIVE
идти́	пойти́
е́хать	пое́хать
бежа́ть	побежа́ть
лете́ть	полете́ть
плы́ть	поплы́ть
нести́	понести́
везти́	повезти́
вести́	повести́

NOTE: When **по-** (or any other prefix) is added to **идти́**, the shape of the infinitive changes to **-йти**, and the shape of the root in the non-past changes from **ид-** to **йд-**: **пойду́**, **пойдёшь**, **пойду́т** (the only exception is **прийти́**: **приду́**, **придёшь**, **приду́т**).

The perfective motion verb with the prefix **по-** may express the following.

1. The onset or beginning of movement in one direction

Когда́ ко́нчился фи́льм, мы́ вста́ли и **пошли́** к вы́ходу.	*When the movie ended, we got up and began walking toward the exit.*
Де́вочка уви́дела отца́ и **побежа́ла** к нему́.	*The little girl saw her father and started running toward him.*
Когда́ на светофо́ре загоре́лся зелёный све́т, маши́на **пое́хала**.	*When the traffic light turned green, the car took off.*

2. The beginning of a new direction, or change in the speed of the movement

Снача́ла мы́ шли́ пря́мо, пото́м **пошли́** напра́во.	*First we walked straight, then we started walking to the right.*
Я́ шёл ме́дленно, пото́м посмотре́л на часы́ и **пошёл** быстре́е.	*I was walking slowly, then I looked at my watch and began to walk faster.*

3. The beginning of one-time unidirectional movement in the future. The form in **по-** may indicate an action *to occur* (in the infinitive) or one that *will begin* (in future perfective), or it may be used to indicate a suggestion by the speaker for joint action (first-person imperative).

За́втра я́ хочу́ **пойти́** в кино́.	*Tomorrow I want to go to the movies.*
Когда́ я́ ко́нчу писа́ть зада́ния, я́ **пойду́** к тебе́.	*When I finish my homework, I'll come to your place.*
Пое́дем на вы́ставку!	*Let's go to the exhibit!*

4. The beginning of movement in the past. The past-tense form in **по-** indicates that the subject *has gone* or *has set out* for some destination, but says nothing about whether or not the subject has reached the intended destination.

Ле́ны зде́сь не́т. Она́ **пошла́** домо́й.	*Lena is not here. She has gone home.*
Ва́ни не́т до́ма. О́н **пое́хал** на рабо́ту.	*Vanya is not home. He left for work.*

—Где́ Ири́на?	*Where is Irina?*
—Она́ **понесла́** ребёнка в де́тскую.	*She carried the baby to the nursery.*
—Где́ па́па?	*Where is Dad?*
—О́н **повёз** дру́га на вокза́л.	*He drove his friend to the station.*

Multidirectional Verbs with the Prefix *по-*

The prefix **по-** makes a multidirectional verb perfective and denotes that the given movement occurs *for a while,* e.g., **походи́ть** *to walk around for a while,* **поéздить** *to drive around for a while,* **побе́гать** *to run around for a while.* This meaning may be reinforced by the adverb **немно́го** *a little* or by a time expression indicating short duration.

Мы́ **походи́ли** немно́го по Арба́ту.	*We walked awhile around the Arbat.*
Они́ **поéздили** немно́го по го́роду.	*They drove awhile around the city.*
Самолёт **полета́л** не́сколько мину́т над аэропо́ртом и приземли́лся.	*The airplane flew several minutes above the airport and landed.*

66. Complete each of the following sentences with the appropriate motion verb, the unidirectional imperfective, or the same verb "perfectivized" with the prefix **по-**.

(éхала/поéхала)

1. Маши́на ________________ бы́стро, а на перекрёстке ________________ ме́дленнее.
2. Маши́на ________________ по у́лице, вдру́г сде́лала разворо́т и ________________ в другу́ю сто́рону.
3. Я́ се́ла в такси́ и ________________ в аэропо́рт.

(шли́/пошли́)

4. Они́ ________________ по у́лице, останови́лись поздоро́ваться с на́ми и ________________ да́льше.
5. Мы́ до́лго ________________ по лесно́й тропи́нке. Наконе́ц, уви́дели ре́чку и ________________ к не́й.

(плы́л/поплы́л)

6. Снача́ла Ми́ша ________________ во́льным сти́лем, а пото́м ________________ на спине́.
7. Кора́бль ________________ на за́пад, измени́л ку́рс и ________________ на восто́к.

(нёс/понёс)

8.Носи́льщик по́днял чемода́ны и ________________ и́х к такси́.
9. На́ши чемода́ны бы́ли тяжёлые, и о́н ________________ и́х с трудо́м.

67. Complete each of the following sentences with the appropriate perfective motion verb with the prefix **по-**.

(попла́вали/поплы́ли)

1. У́тки ________________ у бе́рега и ________________ в другу́ю сто́рону.

(полета́ли/полете́ли)

2. Пти́цы немно́го ________________ над на́ми, а пото́м ________________ на большо́е де́рево.

(походи́ли/пошли́)

3. Мы́ ________________ ча́с по го́роду, уста́ли и ________________ домо́й.

(побе́гали/побежа́ли)

4. Де́ти ________________ полчаса́ по па́рку, проголода́лись и ________________ домо́й обе́дать.

Directional Prefixes

Certain prefixes give verbs of motion a specific *directional* meaning. Following are some common prefixes and the basic meanings they have when used with verbs of motion.

DIRECTIONAL PREFIX	BASIC MEANING
при-	*come, arrive*
у-	*leave, depart*
в-	*into, enter into*
вы-	*out, exit*
под-	*come up to, approach*
от-	*away from*
пере-	*across*
про-	*past; through*
за-	*drop in; behind*

A new aspect pair is formed when a directional prefix is added to an unprefixed pair of unidirectional and multidirectional imperfectives. Specifically, when a unidirectional imperfective is prefixed, it becomes *perfective*; however, when a directional prefix is added to a multidirectional verb, it remains *imperfective.*

IMPERFECTIVE	PERFECTIVE	NEW MEANING
ходи́ть (multidirectional, imperfective)	идти́ (unidirectional, imperfective)	*to go* (*on foot*)
приходи́ть	прийти́	*to come, arrive*
уходи́ть	уйти́	*to leave, depart*
входи́ть	войти́	*to go into, enter*
выходи́ть	вы́йти	*to go out, exit*
подходи́ть	подойти́	*to go up to, approach*
отходи́ть	отойти́	*to go away from*
переходи́ть	перейти́	*to go across*
проходи́ть	пройти́	*to go past; to go through*
заходи́ть	зайти́	*to drop in; to go behind*

NOTE: The table above uses **ходи́ть/идти́** to illustrate the effect of adding the various prefixes to create new prefixed imperfective/perfective pairs with new meaning. These prefixes, however, can be used with any of the intransitive or transitive verbs of motion, e.g., **приноси́ть/принести́** *to bring* (*on foot*), **привози́ть/привезти́** *to bring* (*by vehicle*), **уводи́ть/увести́** *to lead away.*

Note the following modifications that result from prefixation.

- After a prefix **идти́** changes to **-йти** (**прийти́**, **уйти́**).
- The vowel **о** is inserted after prefixes ending in a consonant (**в-**, **от-**, **под-**) before **-йти** (**в-ходи́ть/во-йти́**, **от-ходи́ть/ото-йти́**, **под-ходи́ть/подо-йти́**).
- A hard sign **ъ** is inserted when the same consonantal prefixes **в-**, **от-**, **под-** are added to **е́хать** and **е́здить** (**въе́хать**, **отъе́хать**, **подъе́хать**).

- The stem of two multidirectional verbs is modified by a *directional* prefix: **éздить** changes to **-езжáть** (**подъезжáть**, **приезжáть**, **уезжáть**), and the stem of **плáвать** *to swim* changes to **-плывáть**, e.g., **переплывáть**, **уплывáть**).
- The stress on the stem of **бéгать** changes to **-бегáть** (**прибегáть**).

Aspectual Usage of Prefixed Motion Verbs

The prefixed motion verbs follow the same general guidelines for choosing the imperfective or perfective aspect of other verbs: The perfective is used primarily to denote a single completed action, while the imperfective may denote actions that are ongoing, repeated, habitual, etc.

Prefixed Imperfective and Annulled (Round-Trip) Action

One important contrast between the perfective and imperfective aspects applies uniquely to verbs expressing movement, and particularly to motion verbs: The perfective in the past tense denotes an action whose result remains "in effect," while the imperfective past tense may denote an action whose effect has been "annulled" or reversed. Such annulled actions are identical to what was characterized as the "round-trip" meaning of unprefixed multidirectional imperfectives (see page 274).

Compare the following examples.

Вчерá ко мнé **приéхал** дрýг. Сегóдня я́ тебя́ с ни́м познакóмлю.	*Yesterday my friend came to visit me. Today I'll introduce you to him.*
Вчерá ко мнé **приезжáл** дрýг. Я́ попрощáлся с ни́м ужé сегóдня ýтром.	*Yesterday my friend came to visit me. I already said good-bye to him this morning.*
К тебé **зашёл** Сергéй. Óн ждёт тебя́ на кýхне.	*Sergey has dropped by to see you. He is waiting in the kitchen.*
К тебé **заходи́л** Сергéй. Óн сказáл, что вернётся чéрез чáс.	*Sergey dropped by to see you. He said he would come back in an hour.*
Мáша **принеслá** вáм подáрок. Óн лежи́т тáм на столé.	*Masha brought you a present. It is lying there on the table.*
Мáша **приноси́ла** вáм подáрок, но не остáвила. Онá хóтела дáть егó вáм самá.	*Masha brought you a present, but didn't leave it. She wanted to give it to you in person.*

As the examples above indicate, the past tense of the prefixed imperfective may denote an action carried out in two directions: *came and left, brought and took away.* Following is a partial list of prefixed imperfective motion verbs that, in the past tense, may be used to denote an annulled (round-trip) action.

Prefixed Imperfectives Denoting Annulled Action

приходи́л	=	пришёл и ушёл
уходи́л	=	ушёл и пришёл
приезжáл	=	приéхал и уéхал
уезжáл	=	уéхал и приéхал
приноси́л	=	принёс и унёс
уноси́л	=	унёс и принёс
подходи́л	=	подошёл и отошёл
отходи́ть	=	отошёл и подошёл

68. Complete each of the following sentences with the prefixed motion verb of the correct aspect in parentheses.

1. —Мы́ вчера́ ва́м звони́ли, но ва́с не́ было до́ма.
   —Да́, мы́ ____________ (уходи́ли/ушли́) в кино́.
2. —Где́ сейча́с Ва́ня?
   —Его́ не́т. О́н ____________ (уходи́л/ушёл) к дру́гу.
3. —Приве́т, Ви́тя! Я́ тебя́ давно́ не ви́дел.
   —Я́ ____________ (уезжа́л/уе́хал) в командиро́вку в Росто́в.
4. —А где́ же Ва́ля? Я́ не ви́дел её уже́ неде́лю.
   —Она́ ____________ (уе́зжала/уе́хала) в Москву́ и прие́дет домо́й за́втра.
5. —Кто́ к тебе́ ____________ (подходи́л/подошёл) по́сле ле́кции?
   —Э́то бы́л бра́т Вале́ры.
6. —Кто́ э́то ____________ (подходи́л/подошёл) к Ко́ле? С ке́м о́н разгова́ривает?
   —Э́то его́ дру́г Ми́ша.

Verbal Adjectives (Participles)

A participle combines characteristics of both a verb and an adjective. Like verbs, a participle may be transitive or intransitive, perfective or imperfective in aspect, present or past (but not future) in tense, and in the active or passive voice. A participle governs the same case (or preposition + case) as the verb from which it is derived. On the other hand, a participle is like an adjective in that it takes adjective endings and agrees in gender, number, and case with the noun it modifies.

Participles are used primarily in the written language, especially in journalistic, academic, and scientific writing. A participle is sometimes used in place of a relative clause. For example, the English present participle *reading* in "the boy *reading* the book" is equivalent to the relative clause *who is reading* in "the boy *who is reading* the book." There are two kinds of participles in Russian: active and passive. Each kind of participle can be present or past.

Active Participles

An active participle can be used in place of a relative clause introduced by the pronoun **кото́рый** *who, which, that,* if **кото́рый** is the subject of the clause in the *nominative* case. A *present* active participle can replace a clause with **кото́рый** in the nominative case and a verb in the *present* tense, while a *past* active participle replaces such a clause with a verb in the *past* tense.

Present Active Participles

Present active participles are formed from *imperfective* verbs by adding **-ущий/-ющий** to the basic stem of a first-conjugation verb, or **-ащий/-ящий** to the stem of a second-conjugation verb. Active participles formed from verbs in **-ся** simply add **-ся** (never **-сь**) after the participle ending. The general rule for combining stems and endings (truncate the first of two "likes," add two "unlikes") applies in the formation of participles.

First conjugation	читай- + ущий	чита́ющий *who is reading*
	занимай- + ущий-ся	занима́ющийся *who is studying*
	жив- + ущий	живу́щий *who is living*
Second conjugation	говори- + ящий	говоря́щий *who is speaking*
	сиде- + ящий	сидя́щий *who/which is sitting*
	лежа- + ащий	лежа́щий *who/which is lying*

NOTE: In verbs with a basic stem in **-ова-**, this suffix alternates with **-уй-** in forming the present active participle: **рисова-/уй- + ущий > рису́ющий** *who is drawing.*

Compare the following synonymous pairs of sentences. Note that a relative clause introduced by **кото́рый** in the *nominative* case and containing a verb in the present tense, can be replaced by a present active participle.

Ма́льчик, **кото́рый чита́ет** кни́гу, мо́й сы́н. Ма́льчик, **чита́ющий** кни́гу, мо́й сы́н.	*The boy (who is) reading the book is my son.*
Де́вочка, **кото́рая сиди́т** за столо́м, моя́ до́чь. Де́вочка, **сидя́щая** за столо́м, моя́ до́чь.	*The little girl (who is) sitting at the table is my daughter.*
Па́рни, **кото́рые говоря́т** по-ру́сски, мои́ студе́нты. Па́рни, **говоря́щие** по-ру́сски, мои́ студе́нты.	*The guys (who are) speaking Russian are my students.*

69. Rewrite each of the following sentences, replacing the underlined present active participle with a relative clause introduced by **кото́рый**.

1. Де́вушка, <u>живу́щая</u> в кварти́ре 7, у́чится в МГУ.
   ____
2. Кни́ги, <u>лежа́щие</u> на столе́, не мои́.
   ____
3. Молодо́й челове́к, <u>занима́ющийся</u> маркéтингом, хо́чет нача́ть своё де́ло.
   ____
4. Профе́ссор, <u>чита́ющий</u> ле́кцию, неда́вно прие́хал из Москвы́.
   ____
5. Студе́нты, <u>реша́ющие</u> э́ту зада́чу, о́чень у́мные.
   ____

Past Active Participles

Past active participles are formed from both perfective and imperfective verbs by adding either **-ший** or **-вший** to the basic stem. Those verbs used with the particle **-ся** take a final **-ся**, never **-сь**.

- Stems ending in **д**, **т**, **г**, **к**, **б**, **п**, **р**, **с**, **з**, and **(ну)** add **-ший**.

привык(ну)- + ший	привы́кший *who got used to*
помо́г- + ший	помо́гший *who helped*
вы́рос- + ший	вы́росший *who grew up*
перевед- + ший	переве́дший *who translated*

- All other stems add **-вший**.

сиде- + вший	сиде́вший *who was sitting*
написа- + вший	написа́вший *who wrote*
роди- + вший-ся	роди́вшийся *who was born*

NOTE: Past active participles of the irregular motion verb **идти́** *to go* and its prefixed perfectives (e.g., **прийти́**, **уйти́**, **вы́йти**) are formed from the root **шед-**: **ше́дший** *who was walking,* **прише́дший** *who arrived,* **уше́дший** *who left.*

Compare the following synonymous pairs of sentences. Note that a relative clause introduced by **кото́рый** in the *nominative* case that contains a verb in the past tense, can be replaced by a past active participle.

Де́вушка, **кото́рая сиде́ла** ря́дом со мно́й, моя́ сестра́.	*The girl who was sitting next to me is my sister.*
Де́вушка, **сиде́вшая** ря́дом со мно́й, моя́ сестра́.	
Челове́к, **кото́рый принёс** журна́л, колле́га моего́ отца́.	*The person who brought the magazine is a colleague of my father.*
Челове́к, **принёсший** журна́л, колле́га моего́ отца́.	
Я́ зна́ю челове́ка, **кото́рый роди́лся** в э́том селе́.	*I know a person who was born in this village.*
Я́ зна́ю челове́ка, **роди́вшегося** в э́том селе́.	

70. Rewrite each of the following sentences, replacing the underlined past active participle with a relative clause introduced by **кото́рый**.

1. А́втор, <u>написа́вший</u> э́ту кни́гу, получи́л пре́мию.
   ____
2. Ма́льчик, <u>помо́гший</u> тебе́, мо́й мла́дший бра́т.
   ____
3. Челове́к, <u>переве́дший</u> э́ту кни́гу, отли́чный перево́дчик.
   ____
4. Я́ сего́дня познако́мился с челове́ком, <u>вы́росшим</u> в моём родно́м го́роде.
   ____
5. Учени́к, <u>уше́дший</u> ра́но с уро́ка, пло́хо себя́ чу́вствовал.
   ____

Passive Participles

A passive participle can be used in place of a relative clause introduced by the pronoun **кото́рый**, if this pronoun is in the *accusative* case. A *present* passive participle replaces the accusative of **кото́рый** and the *present-tense* verb in the clause it introduces, while a *past* passive participle replaces such a clause with a verb in the *past* tense.

Present Passive Participles

Present passive participles are formed from a limited number of *imperfective transitive* verbs. First-conjugation verbs form present passive participles by adding **-емый** to the basic stem, while second-conjugation verbs add **-имый**.

First conjugation	читай- + емый	чита́емый *which is being read*
	издавай- + емый	издава́емый *which is published*
Second conjugation	люби- + имый	люби́мый *who/which is loved*
	цени- + имый	цени́мый *who/which is valued*

NOTE: First-conjugation verbs with a basic stem in **-ова-**, alternate with **-уй-** in forming the present passive participle: **публикова-/уй-** + **емый** > **публику́емый** *that is published.*

NOTE: For many conjugation I and II verbs, this participle is equivalent to the **мы-** form of the verb + adjective endings.

Compare the following synonymous pairs of sentences. Note that a relative clause introduced by **кото́рый** in the *accusative* case and containing a verb in the present tense, can be replaced by a present passive participle. If the relative clause contains a subject/agent in the nominative case, then the corresponding participle phrase will have the agent in the instrumental case.

Пробле́ма, **кото́рую изуча́ют** специали́сты, о́чень важна́.	*The problem being studied by specialists is very important.*
Пробле́ма, **изуча́емая** специали́стами, о́чень важна́.	
Я́ получа́ю журна́л «Огонёк», **кото́рый издаю́т** в Москве́.	*I receive the magazine "Ogonyok," which is published in Moscow.*
Я́ получа́ю журна́л «Огонёк». **издава́емый** в Москве́.	

71. Rewrite each of the following sentences, replacing the underlined present passive participle with a relative clause introduced by **кото́рый**.

1. Зада́ча, решáемая студе́нтом, тру́дная.
 ____
2. Учи́тель, люби́мый все́ми, вы́шел на пе́нсию.
 ____
3. Собы́тия, опи́сываемые в э́той статье́, происходи́ли давно́.
 ____
4. Това́ры, производи́мые на э́том заво́де, высо́кого ка́чества.
 ____
5. Ве́чер, организу́емый студе́нтами, бу́дет о́чень интере́сный.
 ____

Past Passive Participles

Past passive participles are formed from perfective transitive verbs by adding one of three endings to the verb's basic stem: **-тый**, **-енный**, or **-нный**.

- After suffixed stems in **-ну-** and **-о-**, and after nonsuffixed stems in **р**, **м**, **н**, **й**, and **в**, add **-тый**.

заверну- + тый	завёрнутый *wrapped*
выпий- + тый	вы́питый *drunk*
запер- + тый	за́пертый *locked*
оден- + тый	оде́тый *dressed*

- After suffixed stems in **-и-** and after nonsuffixed stems in **б**, **д**, **г**, **к**, **п**, and **т**, add **-енный**. Verbs with a stem in **-и** undergo the same consonant alternation as in the first-person singular non-past.

с > ш	броси- + енный	бро́шенный *thrown*
п > пл	купи- + енный	ку́пленный *bought*
	получи- + енный	полу́ченный *received*
	построи- + енный	постро́енный *built*
	перевед- + енный	переведённый *translated*
	испек- + енный	испечённый *baked*

- After all other stems, add **-нный**.

написа- + нный	напи́санный *written*
прочитай- + нный	прочи́танный *read*
увиде- + нный	уви́денный *seen*
нарисова- + нный	нарисо́ванный *painted*

Compare the following pairs of synonymous sentences. Note that a relative clause introduced by **кото́рый** in the *accusative* case and containing a verb in the past tense, can be replaced by a past passive participle. If the relative clause contains a subject/agent in the nominative case, then the corresponding participle phrase will have the agent in the instrumental case.

Шампа́нское, **кото́рое купи́л** Вади́м, о́чень дорого́е.	*The champagne bought by Vadim is very expensive.*
Шампа́нское, **ку́пленное** Вади́мом, о́чень дорого́е.	
Пироги́, **кото́рые испекла́** ба́бушка, бы́ли вку́сные.	*The pies baked by Grandma were tasty.*
Пироги́, **испечённые** ба́бушкой, бы́ли вку́сные.	

72. Rewrite each of the following sentences, replacing the underlined past passive participle with a relative clause introduced by **кото́рый**.

1. Я́ чита́л интере́сную кни́гу, написанную э́тим журнали́стом.
   ____
2. В э́той кни́ге мно́го краси́вых фотогра́фий, сде́ланных а́втором.
   ____
3. Я́ ви́дел фотогра́фию портре́та, нарисо́ванного э́тим худо́жником.
   ____
4. Э́тот музе́й нахо́дится в зда́нии, постро́енном в девятна́дцатом ве́ке.
   ____
5. Я́ рассказа́л ему́ о письме́, полу́ченном на́ми вчера́.
   ____
6. В аудито́рии мы́ нашли́ забы́тую ке́м-то су́мку.
   ____

Short Past Passive Participles

Past passive participles may occur in a short form when they are used predicatively, that is, after the verb *to be*. The short-form passive participles are very common in both written and conversational Russian. They are easily formed from their long-form counterparts by dropping the attributive adjective ending (and reducing the **-нн** suffix to one **-н**). The short passive participles express gender and number, but not case.

LONG FORM		SHORT FORM
подпи́санный	*signed*	подпи́сан, подпи́сана, подпи́сано, подпи́саны
постро́енный	*built*	постро́ен, постро́ена, постро́ено, постро́ены
сде́ланный	*done*	сде́лан, сде́лана, сде́лано, сде́ланы
полу́ченный	*received*	полу́чен, полу́чена, полу́чено, полу́чены
забы́тый	*forgotten*	забы́т, забы́та, забы́то, забы́ты
за́пертый	*locked*	за́перт, заперта́, за́перто, за́перты
закры́тый	*closed*	закры́т, закры́та, закры́то, закры́ты
откры́тый	*open(ed)*	откры́т, откры́та, откры́то, откры́ты

The short participle agrees with its subject in gender and number. Tense is expressed by the past and future forms of **бы́ть**.

The short past passive participle may be used to denote the following.

(a) A completed action undergone by the subject

Докуме́нты **подпи́саны**.	*The documents have been signed.*
Окно́ бы́ло **откры́то** ке́м-то.	*The window had been opened by someone.*
За́втра магази́н бу́дет **закры́т**.	*Tomorrow the store will be closed.*
Я́ посети́л дворе́ц, кото́рый бы́л **постро́ен** в XVIII ве́ке.	*I visited a palace that was built in the 18th century.*

(b) A state of the subject

Две́рь **заперта́**.	*The door is locked.*
Окно́ **закры́то**.	*The window is closed.*
Све́т **включён**.	*The light is (turned) on.*

73. Rewrite each of the following sentences, making the subject the direct object and replacing the underlined short-form past passive participle with the third-person plural past tense of the same (subjectless) verb. The result is a synonymous sentence with passive meaning.

MODEL Э́та ва́за <u>была́ сде́лана</u> из фарфо́ра. > Э́ту ва́зу сде́лали из фарфо́ра.

1. Э́та исто́рия <u>была́ забы́та</u> давно́.
____
2. Телегра́мма <u>была́ полу́чена</u> в суббо́ту.
____
3. Вы́ставка <u>была́ откры́та</u> на про́шлой неде́ле.
____
4. Рабо́та <u>была́ сде́лана</u> хорошо́.
____
5. До́м <u>бы́л постро́ен</u> в про́шлом ве́ке.
____

Verbal Adverbs (Gerunds)

Verbal adverbs, also called gerunds, express an action accompanying the action of the main verb and performed by the same subject. Verbal adverbs combine characteristics of both verbs and adverbs. Like verbs, a verbal adverb can be imperfective or perfective, transitive or intransitive, depending on the verb from which it is derived. Similarly, it governs the same case, or preposition + case, as its underlying verb.

On the other hand, a verbal adverb is like an adverb in that it is indeclinable and modifies the verb in the main clause. It indicates, depending on context, the manner, time, reason, or condition under which the action of the main verb takes place. Found primarily in written Russian, verbal adverbs can be used in place of subordinate clauses introduced by conjunctions such as *when, since, because,* and *if.* Russian verbal adverbs have English equivalents in *-ing*. For example, the English *-ing* form in the following sentence would be translated by an (imperfective) verbal adverb: "You will strain your eyes *reading* [i.e., if you read] in bed."

Russian verbal adverbs are divided into two basic types: *imperfective* verbal adverbs (formed from imperfective verbs) and *perfective* verbal adverbs (formed from perfective verbs).

Imperfective Verbal Adverbs

An imperfective verbal adverb is formed from the verb's basic stem by adding the suffix **-а/-я**. If the verb ends in **-ся**, then a final **-сь** is added to the vowel suffix.

INFINITIVE	STEM	VERBAL ADVERB	MEANING
чита́ть	читай-	чита́я	*reading*
занима́ться	занимай-ся	занима́ясь	*studying*
име́ть	имей-	име́я	*having*
волнова́ться	волнова/уй-ся	волну́ясь	*being nervous*
боя́ться	боя-ся	боя́сь	*fearing*
встава́ть	вставай-	встава́я	*getting up*
жи́ть	жив-	живя́	*living*
идти́	ид-	идя́	*going, walking*
говори́ть	говори-	говоря́	*speaking*
смотре́ть	смотре-	смотря́	*looking*
слы́шать	слыша-	слы́ша	*hearing*

NOTE: Some verbs have no imperfective verbal adverb, for example, the irregular verbs **бежа́ть** *to run,* **е́хать** *to go by vehicle,* **е́сть** *to eat,* **мо́чь** *to be able,* **спа́ть** *to sleep.* The irregular verb **хоте́ть** *to want* has no imperfective verbal adverb (the form **хотя́** already serves as a conjunction with the meaning *although*), but the one formed from its synonym **жела́ть** *to wish* can be used in its place: **жела́я** *wishing, wanting.*

Imperfective verbal adverbs denote an attendant action that occurs simultaneously with that of the verb in the main clause. The verbal adverb by itself does not express tense; its tense coincides with the present, past, or future tense of the main verb.

О́н занима́ется, **слу́шая** му́зыку.	*He studies while listening to music.*
О́н занима́лся, **слу́шая** му́зыку.	*He studied while listening to music.*
О́н бу́дет занима́ться, **слу́шая** му́зыку.	*He will study while listening to music.*

Verbal adverbs indicate the time, reason, condition, or manner of the action expressed by the main verb. They can be used as an alternative to a subordinate clause, where these meanings are expressed explicitly by conjunctions such as **когда́** *when, while,* **пока́** *while,* **та́к как** *since, because,* **потому́ что** *because,* and **е́сли** *if.*

Чита́я те́кст, о́н подчёркивает незнако́мые слова́.	*(When) reading a text, he underlines the unfamiliar words.*
Когда́ о́н чита́ет те́кст, ...	*When he reads a text, ...*
Гуля́я по па́рку, я́ встре́тил дру́га.	*(While) walking in the park, I met a friend.*
Пока́ я́ гуля́л по па́рку, ...	*While I was walking in the park, ...*
Не **зна́я** её но́мер телефо́на, я́ не мо́г е́й позвони́ть.	*Not knowing her telephone number, I was not able to call her.*
Та́к как я́ не зна́л её но́мер телефо́на, ...	*Since I did not know her telephone number, ...*
Занима́ясь бе́гом, о́н снима́ет стре́сс.	*By running, he will reduce stress.*
Е́сли о́н занима́ется бе́гом, ...	*If he runs, ...*

74. Rewrite the underlined imperfective verbal adverb phrase in each of the following sentences, replacing it with a subordinate clause introduced by **когда́** *when, while*. Be sure to put the verb in the same tense as the verb in the main clause.

MODEL Убира́я ко́мнату, Све́та нашла́ потёрянную серёжку. > Когда́ она́ убира́ла ко́мнату, …

1. Занима́ясь аэро́бикой, она́ улучша́ет своё здоро́вье.
   ______________________, …
2. Возвраща́ясь домо́й из кинотеа́тра, друзья́ разгова́ривали о фи́льме.
   ______________________, …
3. Выходя́ из аудито́рии, студе́нты говори́ли об экза́мене.
   ______________________, …
4. Рабо́тая на компью́тере, о́н де́лает бо́льше зада́ний.
   ______________________, …
5. Живя́ в Москве́, мы́ ча́сто ходи́ли в теа́тр.
   ______________________, …

75. Rewrite the underlined verbal adverb phrase in each of the following sentences, replacing it with a subordinate clause introduced by **та́к как** *since, because*. Be sure to put the verb in the same tense as the verb in the main clause.

MODEL Боя́сь опозда́ть, о́н взя́л такси́. > Та́к как о́н боя́лся опозда́ть, …

1. Жела́я что́-нибудь съе́сть, они́ зашли́ в заку́сочную.
   ______________________, …
2. Мы́ ходи́ли по стоя́нке, наде́ясь найти́ потёрянную су́мку.
   … ______________________.
3. Не понима́я ру́сского языка́, я́ не могу́ обща́ться с ни́м.
   ______________________, …
4. Не име́я де́нег, я́ не смо́г купи́ть биле́ты.
   ______________________, …
5. Встава́я ра́но, он успева́л сде́лать бо́льше ра́зных де́л за де́нь.
   ______________________, …

76. Rewrite the underlined imperfective verbal adverb phrase in each of the following sentences, replacing it with a subordinate clause introduced by **е́сли** *if*. Be sure to put the verb in the same tense as the verb in the main clause.

MODEL Гуля́я по ча́су в де́нь, вы́ намно́го укрепи́те своё здоро́вье. > Е́сли вы́ бу́дете гуля́ть по ча́су в де́нь, …

1. Та́к волну́ясь, ты́ расшата́ешь своё здоро́вье.
   ______________________, …
2. Изуча́я иностра́нные языки́, вы́ смо́жете хорошо́ ознако́миться с ра́зными культу́рами.
   ______________________, …
3. Путеше́ствуя по ра́зным стра́нам, вы́ смо́жете расши́рить сво́й кругозо́р.
   ______________________, …
4. Занима́ясь му́зыкой, вы́ смо́жете обогати́ть себя́.
   ______________________, …

Perfective Verbal Adverbs

The perfective verbal adverb of most verbs is formed by adding the suffix **-в** to the verb's basic stem.

INFINITIVE	STEM	VERBAL ADVERB	MEANING
прочита́ть	прочитай-	прочита́в	*having read*
написа́ть	написа-	написа́в	*having written*
отве́тить	ответи-	отве́тив	*having answered*
зако́нчить	закончи-	зако́нчив	*having finished*

For perfective verbs with the particle **-ся**, add **-вшись**.

верну́ться	верну-ся	верну́вшись	*having returned*
прости́ться	прости-ся	прости́вшись	*after saying good-bye*
умы́ться	умой-ся	умы́вшись	*having washed*

Some perfective verbs that lose **-л** in the masculine past tense are found with the suffix **-ши** added to the masculine past-tense form of the verb. These forms occur in Russian literature of the 19th century, but are now considered obsolete.

INFINITIVE	MASCULINE PAST	VERBAL ADVERB	MEANING
запере́ть	за́пер	за́перши	*having locked*
помо́чь	помо́г	помо́гши	*having helped*
испе́чь	испёк	испёкши	*having baked*

Verbs that lose the suffix **-ну-** in the past tense, as well as those with a stem in **-р**, now normally form their perfective verbal adverb from the infinitive stem by adding **-в**.

запере́ть		запере́в	*having locked*
вы́тереть		вы́терев	*having wiped (dry)*
привы́кнуть		привы́кнув	*having got used to*

Some perfective verbs with a basic stem in **-з** or **-с**, as well as those in **-д** or **-т** (especially prefixed motion verbs in **-йти**), form perfective verbal adverbs with the same suffix that imperfective verbs use, i.e., with **-я**.

INFINITIVE	STEM	VERBAL ADVERB	MEANING
привезти́	привез-	привезя́	*having brought by vehicle*
принести́	принес-	принеся́	*having brought/carried*
привести́	привед-	приведя́	*having brought / led on foot*
прийти́	при-ид-	придя́	*having arrived on foot*
сойти́	со-ид	сойдя́	*having stepped off*

Perfective verbal adverbs normally denote an action that is completed prior to the action denoted by the verb in the main clause.

Поза́втракав, ма́льчик пошёл в шко́лу. — *After having breakfast, the boy set out for school.*

Perfective verbal adverb phrases may replace subordinate clauses introduced by conjunctions of time (**когда́** *when*), cause (**потому́ что** *because*), or condition (**е́сли** *if*).

Прочита́в газе́ту, о́н пошёл погуля́ть с соба́кой.	*When/After he read the newspaper, he went for a walk with the dog.*
Когда́ о́н прочита́л газе́ту, о́н пошёл погуля́ть с соба́кой.	
Почу́вствовав себя́ пло́хо, она́ ра́но ушла́ с рабо́ты.	*Not feeling well, she left work early.*
Она́ ра́но ушла́ с рабо́ты, потому́ что почу́вствовала себя́ пло́хо.	*She left work early because she didn't feel well.*
Зако́нчив рабо́ту, о́н смо́жет позвони́ть тебе́.	*If he finishes his work, he will be able to call you.*
Е́сли о́н зако́нчит рабо́ту, о́н смо́жет позвони́ть тебе́.	

77. Rewrite the underlined perfective verbal adverb phrase in each of the following sentences, replacing it with a subordinate clause introduced by **когда́** *when, after.* Be sure to put the verb in the same tense as the verb in the main clause.

MODEL Убра́в со стола́, она́ помы́ла посу́ду. > Когда́ она́ убрала́ со стола́, ...

1. Умы́вшись, о́н се́л обе́дать.
   ____, ...
2. Зако́нчив рабо́ту, она́ начала́ отдыха́ть.
   ____, ...
3. Войдя́ в ко́мнату, учи́тель сра́зу на́чал уро́к.
   ____, ...
4. Заперёв две́рь, она́ легла́ спа́ть.
   ____, ...
5. Испёкши пиро́г, ба́бушка позвала́ дете́й попро́бовать его́.
   ____, ...

Conjunctions

A conjunction is a part of speech consisting of one or more words that link or connect other words, phrases, or clauses in a sentence. There are two basic types of conjunctions: *coordinating* conjunctions and *subordinating* conjunctions.

Coordinating Conjunctions

Coordinating conjunctions link elements of equal value in a sentence. The most common coordinating conjunctions in Russian are the following.

и *and*
и́ли *or*
но *but*
а *and, but (rather), whereas*
одна́ко *but, however*
и ... и ... *both ... and ...*
ни ... ни ... *neither ... nor ...*
и́ли ... и́ли ... *either ... or ...*
как ... так и ... *not only ... but also ...*
не то́лько ... но и ... *not only ... but also ...*

Coordinating conjunctions fall into the following subgroups: copulative, disjunctive, and adversative.

The elements connected by a coordinating conjunction must be equal and parallel. That is, the connected words, phrases, or clauses must perform an identical function in the sentence, e.g., as subjects or objects of the same verb, or modifiers of the same word.

In the following examples, the conjunction **и** joins two subjects, two predicates, and two clauses, respectively.

Та́ня **и** Ма́ша хорошо́ понима́ют по-англи́йски.	*Tanya and Maria understand English well.*
Они́ говоря́т **и** чита́ют по-англи́йски.	*They speak and read English.*
Та́ня ру́сская, **и** Ма́ша ру́сская.	*Tanya is Russian and Masha is Russian.*

In the following example, the conjunction **и́ли** joins two prepositional phrases.

Куда́ мы́ пое́дем ле́том: на пля́ж **и́ли** в го́ры?	*Where shall we go in the summer, to the beach or to the mountains?*

In the following example, the conjunction **но** joins two independent clauses.

Тама́ра родила́сь в Росси́и, **но** она́ не говори́т по-ру́сски.	*Tamara was born in Russia, but she doesn't speak Russian.*

Copulative (Connective) Coordinating Conjunctions

A copulative coordinating conjunction connects two or more elements that have something in common.

и

and

Ле́том мы пое́дем на пля́ж **и** в го́ры.	*In the summer we'll go to the beach and to the mountains.*

и ... и ...

both ... and ...

More emphatic than **и** *and,* the double **и ... и ...** has one **и** before each parallel element.

Ле́том мы́ пое́дем **и** на пля́ж, **и** в го́ры.	*In the summer we'll go both to the beach and to the mountains.*

как ... так и ...

both ... as well as ...

This is a more literary, learned style used mainly in writing.

На конфере́нции обсужда́ли **как** но́вые откры́тия в фи́зике, **так и** передовы́е взгля́ды совреме́нных фило́софов.	*At the conference they discussed new discoveries in physics, as well as the advanced views of modern philosophers.*

не то́лько ..., но и ...

not only ... but also ...

This is more emphatic and bookish in style.

Учёные на́шего институ́та интересу́ются **не то́лько** эконо́микой Росси́и, **но и** ро́лью Росси́и в европе́йском о́бществе.	*The scholars of our institute are interested not only in Russia's economy but also in Russia's role in European society.*

The coordinating conjunction **а** can also be used in this copulative meaning if it is followed by the adverb **та́кже**. It conveys a more formal connotation than the usual conjunction **и**.

Профе́ссор Алексе́ева преподаёт ру́сский язы́к, **а та́кже** францу́зский язы́к.	*Professor Alekseeva teaches Russian as well as French.*

When **и** joins two complete sentences, the adverb **то́же** *also, too, likewise* is often added to the second clause.

Ма́ма пошла́ в магази́н, **и** па́па **то́же** пошёл туда́.	*Mom went to the store, and Dad went there, too.*

1. Rewrite each of the following sentences, replacing **и** with **и … и….**

MODEL Ки́ра и Ла́ра чита́ют по-ру́сски. > И Ки́ра и Ла́ра чита́ют по-ру́сски.

1. Жа́нна и Ма́ра занима́ются ру́сским языко́м.
   ____
2. Моя́ сестра́ говори́т по-ру́сски и по-испа́нски.
   ____
3. Ве́чером студе́нты смо́трят телеви́зор и слу́шают му́зыку.
   ____
4. Мы́ пригласи́ли к себе́ А́нну и Ива́на.
   ____

ни … ни …

neither … nor …

The negating particle **не** must be placed in front of the predicate (conjugated verb) of the clause.

Мы́ не ви́дели **ни** Ве́ру, **ни** Ива́на.	*We saw neither Vera nor Ivan.*
Соба́ки не́ было **ни** в до́ме, **ни** в гараже́.	*The dog was neither in the house nor in the garage.*

However, if the negated parallel elements are themselves the predicates of the sentence, each of them is preceded by **ни**, and **не** is omitted.

Больно́й **ни** ви́дит, **ни** слы́шит.	*The patient neither sees nor hears.*

2. Rewrite each of the following sentences, negating it by replacing **и … и …** with **ни … ни….** Be sure to use **не** to negate the predicate where necessary.

MODEL Мэ́ри понима́ет и по-ру́сски, и по-кита́йски. >
Мэ́ри не понима́ет ни по-ру́сски ни по-кита́йски.

1. Мари́на лю́бит и фру́кты, и о́вощи.
   ____
2. Ле́том мы́ е́здили и в го́ры, и на пля́ж.
   ____
3. Э́та де́вушка и говори́т, и чита́ет по-англи́йски.
   ____
4. Слова́ э́той пе́сни и краси́вые, и интере́сные.
   ____
5. Ве́чером я́ писа́ла и пи́сьма, и упражне́ния.
   ____

да

and

In informal conversation and in many folk sayings and idiomatic expressions, the unstressed conjunction **да** is often used to mean **и** *and*.

Поспеши́шь, **да** люде́й насмеши́шь. (PROVERB)	*Haste makes waste.* (lit., *Make haste and make people laugh.*)
Жи́ли-бы́ли стари́к **да** стару́ха.	*Once upon a time there lived an old man and an old woman.*

Disjunctive Coordinating Conjunctions

The disjunctive coordinating conjunctions present alternatives. The most common disjunctive conjunctions are **и́ли** *or* and **и́ли ... и́ли ...** *either ... or....*

и́ли

or

Кто́ приéдет сего́дня ве́чером: Никола́й **и́ли** Ната́ша?	*Who will arrive this evening, Nicholas or Natasha?*

и́ли ... и́ли ...

either ... or ...

И́ли Никола́й, **и́ли** Ната́ша приéдет сего́дня ве́чером.	*Either Nicholas or Natasha will arrive this evening.*

NOTE: The double conjunction **ли́бо ... ли́бо ...** is sometimes used in place of **и́ли ... и́ли ...**, especially in conversation. **Ли́бо** can also be used singly to replace **и́ли**.

не то ... не то ...

either ... or ...

This is used in conversational style to connote uncertainty and difficulty in specifying the exact nature of the action or thing described.

Де́ти услы́шали стра́нный зву́к— **не то** кри́к, **не то** пла́ч.	*The children heard a strange sound— either a yell or a sob.* (*Not quite one and not quite the other.*)

то ... то ...

now ... now ...

This is used to connect changing actions or states.

То о́н смо́трит в окно́, **то** о́н хо́дит по ко́мнате.	*Now he looks out the window, now he paces the room.*

3. Rewrite each of the following sentences, replacing **и** with **и́ли** and **и ... и ...** with **и́ли ... и́ли....**

MODELS Ве́чером я́ бу́ду чита́ть и отдыха́ть. > Ве́чером я́ бу́ду чита́ть и́ли отдыха́ть.
Де́ти и бе́гают, и пры́гают. > Де́ти и́ли бе́гают, и́ли пры́гают.

1. На у́жин у на́с бу́дет су́п и сала́т.
____
2. Мо́й бра́т хо́чет купи́ть чёрные джи́нсы и си́ние брю́ки.
____
3. Купи́ мне, пожа́луйста, журна́л и газе́ту.
____
4. Возьми́те и молоко́, и лимона́д.
____
5. На́ш сы́н хо́чет ста́ть и космона́втом, и президе́нтом.
____

Adversative Coordinating Conjunctions

An adversative coordinating conjunction joins elements that seem contradictory or antithetical to one another.

но

but

The thought that follows **но** interrupts, adjusts, or contradicts what is asserted in the first clause.

Героиня была́ молодо́й, **но** си́льной и хра́брой.	*The heroine was young, but (she was) strong and brave.*
Э́тот а́втор хорошо́ пи́шет, **но** никто́ не покупа́ет его́ кни́ги.	*This author writes well, but no one buys his books.*

одна́ко

but, however

This is synonymous with **но**, but must always be followed by a complete clause. It is used in more formal speaking and in writing, and emphasizes the antithesis between the two ideas more strongly than **но**.

Герои́ня была́ молодо́й, **одна́ко** она́ была́ си́льной и хра́брой.	*The heroine was young; she was, however, strong and brave.*
Вра́ч до́лго объясня́л процеду́ру, **одна́ко** для испу́ганного больно́го его́ слова́ не име́ли никако́го значе́ния.	*The doctor spent a long time explaining the procedure; however, for the frightened patient his words had no meaning.*

4. Combine each of the following pairs of sentences into one sentence, using **и** if the elements have something in common and **но** if the second element appears to contradict the first.

MODELS Вчера́ шёл си́льный до́ждь. Вчера́ бы́л си́льный ве́тер. >
Вчера́ шёл си́льный до́ждь и бы́л си́льный ве́тер.

Вчера́ шёл си́льный до́ждь. Вчера́ бы́ло о́чень тепло́. >
Вчера́ шёл си́льный до́ждь, но бы́ло о́чень тепло́.

1. Ба́бушка хорошо́ понима́ет по-англи́йски. Она́ не чита́ет по-англи́йски.
____

2. Мои́ сёстры лю́бят танцева́ть. Я не люблю́ танцева́ть.
____

3. Ве́чером мы́ переводи́ли статью́. Мы́ не ко́нчили переводи́ть её.
____

4. Вади́м поéдет на Ура́л. Его́ брат то́же поéдет туда́.
____

5. Э́то дли́нный рома́н. О́н о́чень интере́сный.
____

6. В э́том рестора́не хлéб о́чень вку́сный. Су́п то́же о́чень вку́сный.
____

The Adversative Conjunction *a*: Contrastive and Contradictory

The adversative conjunction **a** has both a *contrastive* meaning and a *contradictive* meaning. In its contrastive function it is used to join two or more *complete statements* that are juxtaposed. In this usage it is usually translated *and,* with the connotation *while, whereas.*

Ма́ша рабо́тает в институ́те, **а** её подру́га рабо́тает в библиоте́ке.	*Masha works at the institute, and her girlfriend works at the library.*
Ма́ма слу́шает ра́дио, **а** па́па смо́трит фотогра́фии.	*Mom is listening to the radio, and Dad is looking at photos.*

If both statements share the same predicate, that predicate is often omitted from the second clause and replaced with a dash.

Ты́ говори́шь бы́стро, **а** я́—ме́дленно.	*You speak quickly, and I (speak) slowly.*

In its contradictive meaning, **a** joins words, phrases, or clauses, one of which is asserted to be correct as opposed to the other, which is declared incorrect. The incorrect element is preceded by **не**. In this function **a** is translated *and* when it precedes the *negated* element, and *but (rather)* when it precedes the *positive* element.

Ма́ша рабо́тает в институ́те, **а** не в библиоте́ке.	*Masha works at the institute, (and) not at the library.*
Подру́га Ма́ши рабо́тает не в институ́те, **а** в библиоте́ке.	*Masha's girlfriend works, not at the institute, but (rather) at the library.*
В библиоте́ке рабо́тает не Ма́ша, **а** её подру́га.	*Not Masha, but (rather) her girlfriend, works at the library.*
Подру́га, **а** не Ма́ша рабо́тает в библиоте́ке.	*The girlfriend, (and) not Masha, works at the library.*

The conjunction **a** is also used in the meaning *and* to introduce follow-up questions.

—Э́то мо́й но́вый дру́г.	*This is my new friend.*
—**А** ка́к его́ зову́т?	*And what's his name?*

5. Read each of the following sentences and indicate whether the **a** is contrastive or contradictive.

	Contrastive	Contradictive
1. Моя́ ста́ршая сестра́ живёт в Бо́стоне, а я́ живу́ в Вашингто́не.	☐	☐
2. Моя́ ста́ршая сестра́ живёт не в Вашингто́не, а в Бо́стоне.	☐	☐
3. Моя́ ста́ршая сестра́ живёт в Бо́стоне, а не в Вашингто́не.	☐	☐
4. Тури́сты живу́т в гости́нице, а студе́нты—в общежи́тии.	☐	☐
5. Москва́ нахо́дится на реке́, а Оде́сса нахо́дится на мо́ре.	☐	☐
6. Оде́сса нахо́дится не на реке́, а на мо́ре.	☐	☐
7. Санкт-Петербу́рг нахо́дится не на ю́ге, а на се́вере.	☐	☐
8. Моя́ сестра́ мно́го говори́т, а мо́й бра́т ма́ло.	☐	☐
9. Мы́ реши́ли поéхать в го́ры, а не на мо́ре.	☐	☐
10. Ю́рий позвони́л мне́ не потому́, что о́н хоте́л со мно́й поговори́ть, а потому́, что ему́ нужна́ моя́ по́мощь.	☐	☐

Choosing *и, а,* or *но*

Two independent clauses can be linked together by a coordinating conjunction into one compound sentence. The differences between **и**, **а**, and **но** can be subtle and therefore require special mention. The correct conjunction depends on the type of relationship between the connected elements.

(1) When to use **и**

The conjunction **и** joins independent clauses *only* (a) when the same statement is being made about two different subjects, (b) when each clause has the same subject and the word **та́кже** *in addition* can be inserted before the information in the second clause, or (c) whenever the second clause follows logically from the first.

(a) Ма́рк лю́бит рисова́ть, **и** Ла́ра (**то́же**) лю́бит рисова́ть. — *Mark likes to draw, and Lara (also) likes to draw.*

In such a sentence the word **то́же** is often inserted after the second subject. If such a compound sentence is split into two separate sentences, the conjunction **и** takes on the meaning *also.*

Ма́рк лю́бит рисова́ть. **И** Ла́ра лю́бит рисова́ть. — *Mark likes to draw. Lara also likes to draw.*

(b) Мари́я о́чень хорошо́ танцу́ет, **и** она́ та́кже игра́ет на фле́йте. — *Maria dances very well, and, in addition, she plays the flute.*

The subject of both clauses is Maria, and the word **та́кже** *in addition* pertains to the new information in the second clause.

(c) Ма́рк лю́бит рисова́ть, **и** он хо́чет ста́ть худо́жником. — *Mark likes to draw, and he wants to become an artist.*

Пошёл до́ждь, **и** (**поэ́тому**) мы́ отмени́ли пикни́к. — *It began to rain, and (therefore) we canceled the picnic.*

In both these sentences, the second statement follows logically from the first. In such cases, the adverb **поэ́тому** *therefore* is often inserted after the **и**.

(2) When to use **а**

If the statements in each clause have a parallel structure and are different but not conflicting, the statements are in *contrast* to each other, and the conjunction **а** is normally used. It can be translated *and, whereas,* or *while,* depending on the style. Usually there is a common element in both clauses, along with at least two contrasting elements.

Ма́рк лю́бит рисова́ть, **а** Ла́ра бо́льше лю́бит чита́ть. — *Mark likes to draw, and (whereas, while) Lara prefers to read.*

Сего́дня и за́втра я́ бу́ду рабо́тать, **а** послеза́втра я́ бу́ду отдыха́ть. — *Today and tomorrow I'll work, and the day after tomorrow I'll rest.*

То́м сиде́л на дива́не, **а** я́ стоя́ла у окна́. — *Tom was sitting on the sofa, and I was standing by the window.*

In the first example the common element is the verb **лю́бит**. The subjects are not the same and they like different things. In the second example, the common element is **я́**. The adverbs of time and the activities are contrasted. In the third example, all three elements are contrasted.

(3) When to use **но**

If the information in the second independent clause appears to contradict, or is at odds with, what is asserted in the first clause, the conjunction **но** is required. If in the English translation, *however* can be used in place of *but,* **но** is usually the correct choice.

Ма́рк лю́бит рисова́ть, **но** о́н не лю́бит пока́зывать свои́ рису́нки.	*Mark likes to draw, but (however) he doesn't like to show his drawings.*

In some instances either **а** or **но** can be used, with **но** expressing the stronger opposition.

Ма́рк лю́бит рисова́ть, **а** Ла́ра не лю́бит.	*Mark likes to draw, and Lara doesn't.*
Ма́рк лю́бит рисова́ть, **но** Ла́ра не лю́бит.	*Mark likes to draw, but Lara doesn't.*

6. Complete each of the following sentences with the appropriate conjunction: **и**, **а**, or **но**.

1. Пе́рвого сентября́ начина́ется учёба в шко́ле, ________ все́ шко́льники ра́но выхо́дят из до́ма.
2. Учёба в шко́ле начина́ется в сентябре́, ________ конча́ется в ию́не.
3. Учёба в шко́ле начина́ется пе́рвого сентября́, ________ Бори́с не пойдёт на заня́тия. О́н бо́лен.
4. Я́ хочу́ сего́дня ве́чером пойти́ в кино́, ________ моя́ сестра́ хо́чет пойти́ на конце́рт.
5. Вади́м хо́чет пойти́ на футбо́льный ма́тч, ________ его́ ма́ма ему́ не разреша́ет.
6. Вчера́ мы́ е́здили за́ город, ________ на́ши друзья́ е́здили с на́ми.
7. Я́ хорошо́ понима́ю бра́та, ________ о́н хорошо́ понима́ет меня́.
8. Ле́на хорошо́ у́чится, ________ она́ о́чень хорошо́ сдаёт экза́мены.
9. О́льга мно́го занима́ется, ________ она́ пло́хо сдаёт экза́мены.
10. Оле́г хорошо́ говори́т по-англи́йски, ________ его́ жена́ хорошо́ говори́т по-францу́зски.

Subordinating Conjunctions

Subordinating conjunctions connect an independent, or main, clause with a dependent, or subordinate, clause that completes or modifies it. The subordinate clause is called "dependent" because it cannot stand on its own. The subordinating conjunction specifies the type of relationship between the main clause and the statement made in the dependent clause. The principal relationship types are temporal (*when, before, after, until*), causal (*because, since*), purposive (*in order to*), resultative (*so that*), concessive (*although, whereas*), and conditional (*if*).

As in English, most subordinate clauses may either precede or follow the main clause, depending on the preference or intention of the speaker. Following are the most frequently encountered subordinating conjunctions, categorized according to the type of relationship they indicate between the main and dependent clauses.

Temporal Conjunctions

когда́

when, whenever, as, while, after

The meaning of this conjunction depends on the aspect and tense sequence of the verbs in each clause. For example, **когда́** has the sense of *after* when the predicate of the **когда́**-clause is in the perfective aspect.

Когда́ па́па прие́хал, все́ се́ли за сто́л.	*When (After) Dad had arrived, everyone sat down at the table.*

If the action is to take place in the future, the future tense must be used in the Russian **когда́**-clause (whereas English uses the present tense).

Когда́ па́па прие́дет, все́ ся́дут за сто́л.	*When (After) Dad arrives, everyone will sit down at the table.*

The conjunction **когда́** normally has the sense of *while* or *as* when the predicate of the **когда́**-clause is in the imperfective aspect.

Когда́ па́па шёл домо́й, о́н зашёл в магази́н.	*When (While, As) Dad was walking home, he stopped off at the store.*
Когда́ Пе́тя учи́лся в институ́те, о́н жи́л в общежи́тии.	*When (While) Pete was a student at the institute, he lived in the dormitory.*

пока́

while

This refers to an ongoing action or process; therefore, the predicate of the **пока́**-clause is imperfective.

Пока́ ма́ма гото́вила обе́д, де́ти смотре́ли телеви́зор.	*While Mom was making lunch, the children watched television.*
Пока́ ребёнок спи́т, ма́ма отдыха́ет.	*While the baby sleeps, Mom rests.*

пока́ ... не

until

The predicate of the *until*-clause may be perfective future or past.

Мы́ никуда́ не пойдём, **пока́** вы́ **не** прекрати́те разгова́ривать.	*We won't go anywhere until you stop talking.*
Мы́ подожда́ли, **пока́** до́ждь **не** прекрати́лся.	*We waited until the rain stopped.*

как

when

Как can replace **когда́** in situations that express unexpectedly sudden action or change. The idea conveyed is usually *hardly, barely, no sooner than.*

Я́ едва́ вошла́ в ли́фт, **как** две́ри закры́лись.	*I had barely entered the elevator, when the doors closed.*
Не успе́ли мы́ се́сть в такси́, **как** води́тель пое́хал.	*We had hardly taken our seats in the taxi, when the driver took off.*

Many composite subordinating conjunctions are formed by joining **как** with other words to render a more specific time-related meaning.

как то́лько

as soon as

As with **когда́**, a future action in the dependent clause must be expressed in the future tense.

Я́ бу́ду де́лать дома́шнюю рабо́ту, **как то́лько** зако́нчится фи́льм.	*I will do my homework as soon as the film is over.*
Она́ обы́чно де́лает дома́шнюю рабо́ту, **как то́лько** прихо́дит домо́й.	*She usually does her homework as soon as she comes home.*

в то вре́мя как

while

The predicates of both clauses are usually imperfective.

Де́ти игра́ли во дворе́ под присмо́тром учи́тельницы, **в то вре́мя как** и́х роди́тели бы́ли на шко́льном собра́нии.	*The children were playing in the yard under a teacher's supervision, while their parents were at the school meeting.*

Many composite subordinating conjunctions are formed by combining a preposition with the demonstrative **то** in the required case, followed by the conjunction **как**.

до того́ как

before

This conjunction may be followed by a complete clause or—if the subject of both clauses is the same—an infinitive may replace the finite (conjugated) predicate.

До того́ как на́ш сы́н поступи́л в МГУ, мы́ никогда́ не е́здили в Москву́.	*Before our son entered Moscow University, we had never gone to Moscow.*
До того́ как поступи́ть в МГУ, о́н до́лжен рабо́тать го́д.	*Before entering Moscow University, he must work for a year.*

пре́жде чем

before

This conjunction is used in place of **до того́ как** whenever the *before*-clause contains a precaution or an essential prerequisite to the action of the main clause. Usually the subjects of both clauses are the same, and **пре́жде чем** is followed by an infinitive.

Пре́жде чем обвиня́ть друго́го, на́до че́стно оцени́ть свои́ со́бственные посту́пки.	*Before accusing another, one should honestly evaluate one's own actions.*

пéред тем как

(right) before

This conjunction may be followed by a finite verb or—if the subject of both clauses is the same—by an infinitive.

Пéред тем как извéстный актёр вы́шел на сцéну, зáл зати́х. — *Right before the famous actor came out on stage, the hall became quiet.*

Включи́те свéт **пéред тем как** войти́ в зáл. — *Turn on the light before entering the auditorium.*

пóсле тогó как

after

This is followed only by a finite verb.

Я́ реши́ла изучáть рýсский язы́к **пóсле тогó как** я́ побывáла в Москвé. — *I decided to study Russian after I visited Moscow.*

Пóсле тогó как ты́ вернёшься из командирóвки, позвони́ мнé. — *After you return from your business trip, phone me.*

с тех пор как

since

Прошлó двá гóда **с тех пор как** мы́ ви́делись в послéдний рáз. — *Two years have passed since the last time we saw each other.*

до тех пор, покá ... не

until

This is a more formal version of **покá ... не**.

Зри́тели стоя́ли и аплоди́ровали **до тех пор, покá** музыкáнты **не** сéли и нáчали игрáть. — *The audience stood and applauded until the musicians sat down and began playing.*

7. Combine each of the following pairs of simple sentences into a complex sentence, using the conjunction **когдá**. State whether **когдá** has the sense *while* or *after*.

MODEL Свéта писáла пи́сьма. Онá слýшала мýзыку. >
Когдá (*While*) Свéта писáла пи́сьма, онá слýшала мýзыку.

1. Друзья́ возвращáлись домóй. Они́ разговáривали обо всём.
___
2. Друзья́ вернýлись домóй. Они́ легли́ и уснýли.
___
3. Мы́ прощáлись. Мы́ крéпко обнимáлись.
___
4. Мы́ прости́лись. Я́ пошёл домóй.
___
5. Мáша смотрéла стáрые фотогрáфии. Онá вспоминáла прóшлое.
___
6. Мáша посмотрéла передáчу. Онá вы́ключила телеви́зор.
___

8. Combine each of the following pairs of simple sentences into a complex sentence beginning with a subordinate clause introduced by **после того́ как**.

MODEL Са́ша реши́л зада́чи. Пото́м о́н пошёл погуля́ть. >
После того́ как Са́ша реши́л зада́чи, о́н пошёл погуля́ть.

1. Де́ти поза́втракали. Пото́м они́ пошли́ в шко́лу.
2. Ма́ма пригото́вила обе́д. Пото́м она́ позвала́ на́с се́сть за сто́л.
3. Андре́й сда́л экза́мен. Пото́м о́н пошёл с подру́гой в кафе́.
4. Ко́нчилась телепереда́ча. Пото́м ребя́та на́чали слу́шать но́вый ди́ск.
5. Оте́ц ко́нчил писа́ть докла́д. Пото́м о́н ста́л отдыха́ть.

9. Answer each of the following questions, stating that one should perform the action *before* performing the second action in parentheses. Use the conjunction **до того́ как** or **пе́ред тем как**, as appropriate.

MODEL —Когда́ на́до чи́стить зу́бы? (ложи́ться спа́ть) >
—На́до чи́стить зу́бы пе́ред тем как ложи́ться спа́ть.

1. —Когда́ на́до зако́нчить изуча́ть ру́сский язы́к? (пое́дешь в Росси́ю)
2. —Когда́ на́до мы́ть ру́ки? (обе́дать)
3. —Когда́ на́до побри́ться? (уйти́ на рабо́ту)
4. —Когда́ на́до ко́нчить э́ту рабо́ту? (уе́хать в о́тпуск)
5. —Когда́ на́до чи́стить фру́кты? (и́х е́сть)
6. —Когда́ на́до вы́ключить све́т? (уйти́ из ко́мнаты)

10. Combine each of the following pairs of simple sentences into a complex sentence, using the conjunction **до тех пор, пока́ ... не**.

MODEL Де́ти игра́ли во дворе́. Ма́ма позвала́ и́х обе́дать. >
Де́ти игра́ли во дворе́ до тех пор, пока́ ма́ма не позвала́ и́х обе́дать.

1. Мы́ зде́сь бу́дем стоя́ть. Магази́н откро́ется.
2. Ребёнок пла́кал. Ма́ма покорми́ла его́.
3. Ви́ктор реша́л зада́чи. О́н уста́л.
4. Ребя́та загора́ли на пля́же. Ста́ло хо́лодно.
5. О́н пи́л пи́во. Он напи́лся.

11. Rewrite each of the following sentences, using the conjunction **с тех пор как** to state how much time has passed *since* the given event occurred.

MODEL Я́ бы́л в Москве́ пя́ть ле́т наза́д. >
Прошло́ пя́ть ле́т с тех пор как я́ бы́л в Москве́.

1. Па́влик купи́л маши́ну полтора́ ме́сяца наза́д.
____
2. Они́ перее́хали в но́вый до́м три́ го́да наза́д.
____
3. Ребёнок роди́лся ше́сть ме́сяцев наза́д.
____
4. Мы́ получи́ли письмо́ от Ли́и полтора́ го́да наза́д.
____

Causal Conjunctions

Causal subordinating conjunctions answer questions such as **почему́?** *why?* and **по како́й причи́не?** *for what reason?*

потому́ что

because

The subordinate clause containing **потому́ что** must always follow the main clause.

Мы́ спеши́ли, **потому́ что** опа́здывали на конце́рт.	*We were in a hurry because we were late for the concert.*

A comma is inserted between **потому́** and **что** when special emphasis is placed on the cause. An emphatic or delimiting word such as **то́лько** *only* or **и́менно** *precisely* may precede the conjunction.

Его́ взя́ли на рабо́ту то́лько **потому́, что** о́н дру́г нача́льника.	*They hired him only because he is a friend of the boss.*
Президе́нт реши́л не е́хать на конфере́нцию и́менно **потому́, что** о́н не мо́жет согласи́ться с пози́цией Европе́йского соо́бщества.	*The president decided not to go to the conference, precisely because he is unable to agree with the position of the European Community.*

та́к как

since, because

The subordinate clause containing **та́к как** may precede or follow the main clause.

Та́к как президе́нт не мо́жет согласи́ться с пози́цией ЕС, о́н реши́л не е́хать на конфере́нцию.	*Since the president is unable to agree with the position of the EC, he has decided not to go to the conference.*

благодаря́ тому́ что

because, thanks to the fact that

This conjunction usually suggests a positive circumstance and a sense of the speaker's satisfaction or appreciation. It is often used in scientific and journalistic writing.

Мы́ смогли́ зако́нчить э́ту рабо́ту **благодаря́ тому́ что** вы́ на́м помогли́.	*We were able to finish the work thanks to the fact that you helped us.*

из-за того́, что
because, on account of

This conjunction usually suggests a negative circumstance and a sense of the speaker's disapproval or dissatisfaction.

Из-за того́, что шёл до́ждь, я́рмарка не состоя́лась.	*Because it was raining, the fair did not take place.*

поско́льку
as long as, in so far as, since

Поско́льку о́н зна́ет ру́сский, пу́сть о́н де́лает э́тот перево́д.	*As long as he knows Russian, let him do this translation.*

Other causal conjunctions, found primarily in official, bookish style, include the following.

ввиду́ того́, что
in view of (the fact that)

вследствие того́, что
in consequence of (the fact that)

в си́лу того́, что
because of, on the strength of (the fact that)

12. Combine each of the following pairs of simple sentences into a complex sentence, using the conjunction **потому́ что** or **та́к как**.

MODEL Студе́нты уста́ли. Они́ занима́лись 3 часа́ без переры́ва. >
Студе́нты уста́ли, потому́ что они́ занима́лись 3 часа́ без переры́ва.

1. Пётр бы́стро реши́л э́ту тру́дную зада́чу. О́н хорошо́ зна́ет матема́тику.
____
2. Ле́на сего́дня о́чень уста́ла. Она́ не вы́спалась.
____
3. Ди́ма спеши́л. О́н опа́здывал на ле́кцию.
____
4. Серёжа пошёл в библиоте́ку. О́н до́лжен верну́ть кни́гу.
____
5. Лари́са не была́ на заня́тиях. Она́ была́ больна́.
____

13. Combine each of the following pairs of simple sentences into a complex sentence using the conjunction **благодаря́ тому́, что** or **из-за того́, что**, depending on whether the events described are positive or negative.

MODEL О́н отли́чно перево́дит. У него́ большо́й о́пыт и тала́нт. >
О́н отли́чно перево́дит благодаря́ тому́, что у него́ большо́й о́пыт и тала́нт.

1. Экску́рсия была́ отменена́. Вы́пал большо́й сне́г.
____
2. О́н выполня́ет свою́ рабо́ту в сро́к. О́н о́чень организо́ванный челове́к.
____

3. Проду́кты испо́ртились. Они́ не храни́лись в холоди́льнике.

____

4. Хоро́шие результа́ты бы́ли дости́гнуты. Бы́л применён но́вый ме́тод.

____

5. Она́ хорошо́ зако́нчила университе́т. Она́ усе́рдно рабо́тала.

____

Purposive Conjunctions

Subordinating conjunctions of purpose answer the question **заче́м?** *why? for what purpose?* They introduce clauses stating the purpose or goal of an action and the intention or desire of the subject of the main clause.

что́бы

in order to, so that, or untranslated

With most verbs of desire, intention, request, or instruction, **что́бы** is used with the past-tense form of the verb, when the main clause and the subordinate clause have different subjects. See pages 263–264.

Мы́ покра́сили до́м, **что́бы** о́н бо́льше нра́вился потенциа́льным покупа́телям.	*We painted our house so that it would be more appealing to potential buyers.*
Профессора́ на́шей ка́федры хотя́т, **что́бы** все́ студе́нты пое́хали ле́том на пра́ктику.	*The professors in our department want all the students to do field training this summer.*
Сестра́ сказа́ла, **что́бы** все́ друзья́ встре́тились у вхо́да в кинотеа́тр.	*My sister told all her friends to meet at the entrance to the movie theater.*

If, however, the subject of the purpose clause is the same as the subject of the main clause, **что́бы** is followed by an infinitive.

О́н серьёзно гото́вится к экза́менам, **что́бы** поступи́ть в шко́лу би́знеса.	*He is seriously preparing for his exams in order to enter the business school.*

Что́бы can be combined with the prepositions **для** *for* and **с** *with* and the demonstrative **то** in the required case to form more emphatic composite conjunctions.

для того́, что́бы

for the purpose of, so that

Юри́ст гро́мко и уве́ренно защища́л своего́ клие́нта, **для того́, что́бы** все́ в суде́ пове́рили в его́ невино́вность.	*The lawyer defended his client loudly and confidently, so that everyone in the courtroom would be convinced of his innocence.*

с тем, что́бы

with the purpose of, so that

за тем, что́бы

for the purpose of, so that

Subordinating Conjunctions *что* and *как*

что

that

The conjunction **что** (unstressed and always preceded by a comma) normally introduces a subordinate clause that is dependent on a main clause containing a verb meaning *say, think, know, hope, feel,* etc. Unlike English, which permits the omission of the word *that,* Russian does not normally permit the conjunction **что** to be dropped from the sentence. When reporting speech indirectly, observe the rule of reported speech and express the reported clause in the *same tense* that the speaker used in the original, direct speech.

Ла́ра сказа́ла, **что** она́ на́с встре́тит по́сле конце́рта.	*Lara said (that) she would meet us after the concert.*
Я́ зна́ю, **что** она́ ска́жет, **что** фи́льм е́й понра́вился.	*I know (that) she'll say (that) she liked the film.*
Мне́ ка́жется, **что** ма́ма почему́-то волну́ется.	*It seems to me that Mom is upset for some reason.*

In addition, **что** introduces subordinate clauses after short-form adjectives and adverbs that express states of mind, emotion, or perception.

Я́ о́чень ра́да, **что** вы́ ра́но прие́хали.	*I'm very glad that you came early.*
Ви́дно бы́ло, **что** студе́нтам ста́ло ску́чно.	*It was evident that the students had gotten bored.*

In all of the above cases, **что** is an unstressed connective word that is not part of either clause. When the word **что** functions as a subject or object in the dependent clause, it is not a conjunction, but rather a stressed pronoun, and is translated *what.*

Я́ зна́ю, **что́** она́ ска́жет. (**Что́** is the direct object of the verb **ска́жет**.)	*I know what she'll say.*
Мне́ интере́сно, **что́** её волну́ет. (**Что́** is the subject of the verb **волну́ет**.)	*I wonder what is upsetting her.*

14. Translate each of the following sentences into Russian, using the conjunction **что́бы** or **что**, or the stressed pronoun **что́**.

1. Dad said that Misha had called home.
____
2. Dad told Misha to call home.
____
3. I understand that you told the truth.
____
4. We wanted you to tell the truth.
____
5. We know what you said.
____
6. Masha turned on the television in order to watch the film.
____
7. Masha turned on the television so that we could watch the film.
____

как

untranslated

To express the idea that someone *perceives* an action occurring (e.g., *I saw him leaving, we heard them talking*), the main clause contains the verb of perception and the subordinate clause containing the action verb is normally introduced by the conjunction **как** (preceded by a comma and not translated).

Та́ня заме́тила, **как** о́н подходи́л ко мне́.	*Tanya noticed him approaching me.*
Мы́ слы́шали, **как** она́ ушла́.	*We heard her leave.*
Все́ ви́дели, **как** о́н ходи́л по ко́мнате.	*Everyone saw him pacing the room.*

Such sentences can be rendered with the conjunction **что** *that,* but then the sentence does not convey the perception of the action, but instead reports a *fact.*

Все́ ви́дели, **что** о́н ходи́л по ко́мнате.	*Everyone saw that he was pacing the room.*

15. Translate each of the following sentences into Russian, using the appropriate conjunction: **как** or **что**.

1. I saw him arrive.
   ____
2. I saw that he had arrived.
   ____
3. We heard her singing.
   ____
4. We noticed that he had left.
   ____

Resultative Conjunctions

Subordinating conjunctions of result invariably follow the main clause, and express the logical result or consequence of the situation in the main clause.

та́к что

so, so that

Я́ не о́чень хорошо́ его́ зна́ю, **та́к что** мне́ неудо́бно звони́ть ему́.	*I don't know him very well, so I feel uncomfortable calling him.*

Such a relationship can be expressed equally well by using the coordinating conjunction **и** and the adverb **поэ́тому** *therefore.*

Я́ не о́чень хорошо́ его́ зна́ю **и поэ́тому** мне́ неудо́бно звони́ть ему́.

16. Combine each of the following pairs of simple sentences into a complex sentence using the conjunction **та́к что**.

MODEL Я́ вчера́ бы́л бо́лен. Мне́ пришло́сь пропусти́ть заня́тия. >
Я́ вчера́ бы́л бо́лен, та́к что мне́ пришло́сь пропусти́ть заня́тия.

1. О́н опозда́л на авто́бус. О́н реши́л взя́ть такси́.
   ____
2. Мо́й дру́г до́лго жи́л в Ки́еве. О́н хорошо́ зна́ет э́тот го́род.
   ____

3. Э́то о́чень просто́й те́кст. Я́ его́ бы́стро перевёл.

____

4. Я́ уже́ прочита́л газе́ту. Я́ да́л её сосе́ду.

____

5. Я́ зна́л, что она́ лю́бит рок-му́зыку. Я́ пригласи́л её на рок-конце́рт.

____

Conditional Conjunctions

е́сли

if

See the discussion of real and unreal conditions in Chapter 7 (page 259). The conjunction **е́сли** expresses a condition that

(a) may occur regularly.

Е́сли пого́да хоро́шая, мы́ гуля́ем в па́рке. — *If the weather is nice, we walk in the park.*

(b) is likely to occur in the future. (When the event has yet to occur, the **е́сли**-clause must be in the future tense.)

Е́сли вы́ дади́те мне́ сво́й а́дрес, то́ я ва́м напишу́. — *If you give me your address, (then) I'll write to you.*

(c) has perhaps already occurred.

Е́сли по́езд пришёл во́время, то́ па́па сейча́с до́лжен прийти́. — *If the train arrived on time, (then) Dad should be coming home any minute now.*

е́сли ... не

unless

Я́ э́то не пойму́, **е́сли** ты́ мне́ **не** объясни́шь. — *I won't understand that unless you explain it to me.*

раз

since, now that

This is used in both conversational and literary styles. It expresses a real condition.

Раз о́н пришёл, пу́сть о́н са́м расска́жет на́м об э́том. — *Since/Now that he's come, let him tell us about this himself.*

Concessive Conjunctions

хотя́ (хоть)

although

The **хотя́**-clause may contain the particle **и**, placed for emphasis before the key word or phrase of the clause. The main clause frequently is introduced with a contradictive conjunction such as **но**.

Хотя́ о́н **и** небога́тый челове́к, он о́чень мно́го де́лает для свои́х дете́й. — *Although he is a person of moderate means, he still does quite a lot for his children.*

Хоть и трýдно емý бы́ло, óн всё-таки при́нял э́то решéние. — *Although it was difficult for him, he nevertheless made this decision.*

несмотря́ на то, что

despite the fact that

This construction is more formal than **хотя́** and **хоть**.

Несмотря́ на то, что я живý в Москвé ужé двá гóда, я́ чáсто теря́ю дорóгу. — *Despite the fact that I've been living in Moscow for two years, I often get lost.*

17. Combine each of the following pairs of simple sentences into a complex sentence with either a conditional clause introduced by **éсли** or a concessive clause introduced by **хотя́**.

MODEL Óн мнóго занимáлся. Óн плóхо сдáл экзáмен. >
Хотя́ óн мнóго занимáлся, óн плóхо сдáл экзáмен.

1. Мы́ уговáривали егó. Óн не согласи́лся.
   ____
2. Снéг пойдёт. Мы́ бýдем катáться на лы́жах.
   ____
3. Емý предложи́ли большýю зарплáту. Óн не согласи́лся на э́ту рабóту.
   ____
4. Всé устáнут. Мы́ остановим рабóту.
   ____
5. Всé устáли. Мы́ продолжáли рабóтать.
   ____

Comparative Conjunctions

как

as, the (same) way that

This expresses a similarity or comparison.

Они́ лю́бят дрýг дрýга **как** родны́е сёстры (лю́бят дрýг дрýга). — *They love each other like true sisters (love each other).*

Often the words **так же** precede **как**, making the comparison more emphatic.

Тебé нáдо относи́ться к свои́м заня́тиям **так же** серьёзно, **как** ты́ отнóсишься к мýзыке. — *You should relate to your studies as seriously as you relate to music.*

The conjunction **как** occurs regularly in similes such as the following.

бы́стрый **как** мóлния	*fast as lightning*
голóдный **как** вóлк	*hungry as a wolf*
пья́н **как** сапóжник	*drunk as a shoemaker*
свобóден **как** пти́ца	*free as a bird*

как бу́дто, бу́дто бы, как бу́дто бы, сло́вно

as though, as if

These conjunctions indicate that the similarity suggested is not the case in actual fact.

Молодо́й води́тель смотре́л на полице́йского, **как бу́дто** о́н бы́л ни в чём не винова́т.	*The young driver looked at the policeman as though he were not guilty of anything.*
Я́ по́мню то́т де́нь, когда́ родила́сь моя́ до́чь так хорошо́, **как бу́дто** э́то бы́ло то́лько вчера́.	*I remember the day my daughter was born as well as if it were only yesterday.*

18. Complete each of the following sentences with the appropriate conjunction: **как** or **как бу́дто**.

1. О́н ведёт себя́ так, ________________ обы́чно.
2. О́н ведёт себя́, ________________ ничего́ не случи́лось.
3. Пого́да была́, ________________ э́то ча́сто быва́ет в а́вгусте: жа́ркая и вла́жная.
4. Пого́да в ма́е была́ жа́ркая и вла́жная, ________________ ле́то уже́ наступи́ло.

чем

than

This conjunction introduces the second term of a comparison.

Та́ня бо́лее серьёзная студе́нтка, **чем** Ма́ша.	*Tanya is a more serious student than Masha.*
О́н бо́лее спосо́бный челове́к, **чем** я́ ду́мал.	*He is a more capable person than I thought.*

For discussion and exercises on the uses of **чем**, see Chapter 5 (page 165).

Answers to Exercises

Chapter 1

1.
1. Алабáма
2. Аризóна
3. Вермóнт
4. Индиáна
5. Колорáдо
6. Иллинóйс
7. Миннесóта
8. Монтáна
9. Небрáска
10. Невáда
11. Óрегон
12. Флори́да

2.
1. Амéрика
2. Канáда
3. Пакистáн
4. Торóнто
5. Бóстон
6. Лóндон
7. Берли́н
8. Ерева́н
9. Мадри́д
10. Панáма

3.
1. student
2. professor
3. campus
4. college
5. hamburger
6. ketchup
7. hot dog
8. compact disc
9. computer
10. printer

4.
1. привéт
2. спаси́бо
3. пáмять
4. письмó
5. телеви́зор
6. сёрфинг
7. рюкзáк
8. гóсть
9. рэ́ппер
10. дéсять

5.
1. прямóй
2. пóяс
3. едá
4. съёмка
5. плáтье
6. Татья́на
7. я́блоко
8. мáй
9. ю́мор
10. заём

6.
1. астронóм
2. парадóкс
3. таракáн
4. головá
5. мотóр
6. над дóмом
7. молокó
8. газéта
9. талáнт
10. о клáссе

7.
1. óрган
2. кóлокол
3. панорáма
4. бáня
5. ю́мор
6. мéсто
7. нóвое
8. дя́дя
9. потолóк
10. кварти́ра

8.
1. телефóн
2. мяснóй
3. вéчер
4. ресторáн
5. экóлог
6. пáмятник
7. ветеринáр
8. рекá
9. этáж
10. сейчáс

9.
1. бы́стро
2. цемéнт
3. жи́вопись
4. цыплёнок
5. ци́рк
6. женá
7. жёны
8. шикáрный
9. шестóй
10. шербéт

10.
1. щи́
2. ещё
3. считáешь
4. щекá
5. мужчи́на
6. расскáзчик
7. подпи́счик
8. исчезáть
9. и́щут
10. щёлк

11.
1. глáз
2. сбóр
3. отдéл
4. крýжка
5. круи́з
6. дрóбь
7. творóг
8. вчерá
9. абсýрд
10. к дóму

12.
1. ска-жи́-те
2. по-ни-мáй-те
3. ла-бо-ра-тó-ри-я
4. ди-рé-ктор
5. на-чáль-ник
6. сло-вáрь
7. кóм-на-та
8. рý-чка
9. ка-ран-дáш
10. у-ни-вер-си-тéт

13.
1. xerox
2. comics
3. sandwich
4. marketing
5. manager
6. know-how
7. disc player
8. fax
9. computer
10. happy end

14.
1. Agatha Christie
2. Jack London
3. Ernest Hemingway
4. Charles Dickens
5. Walt Disney
6. Richard Nixon
7. John Quincy Adams
8. Winston Churchill

Chapter 2

1.
1. neuter, hard
2. feminine, hard
3. masculine, soft
4. masculine, hard
5. feminine, soft
6. neuter, soft
7. masculine, soft
8. masculine, hard
9. neuter, soft
10. feminine, soft

2. 1. óн
2. онá
3. онó
4. óн
5. óн
6. онá
7. óн
8. онó
9. онá
10. онó

3. 1. мóй
2. моё
3. моя́
4. мóй
5. мóй
6. моя́
7. моя́
8. моя́

4. 1. óн
2. онá
3. óн
4. óн
5. онá
6. онá
7. óн
8. онá
9. óн
10. óн

5. 1. нóвый
2. написáла
3. извéстный
4. óпытный
5. большóй
6. занятá

6. 1. певи́ца
2. счастли́вец
3. америкáнка
4. канáдка
5. испáнец
6. писáтельница
7. учи́тель
8. худóжница
9. перевóдчик
10. танцóвщица
11. англичáнка
12. грузи́н
13. портни́ха
14. продавéц

7. 1. онó
2. óн
3. онó
4. онá
5. онá
6. óн
7. онá
8. óн
9. óн
10. óн
11. óн
12. онó

8. 1. Э́то газéты.
2. Э́то учéбники.
3. Э́то кни́ги.
4. Э́то крéсла.
5. Э́то рýчки.
6. Э́то тетрáди.
7. Э́то плáтья.
8. Э́то телефóны.
9. Э́то портфéли.
10. Э́то музéи.
11. Э́то лáмпы.
12. Э́то студéнты.
13. Э́то студéнтки.
14. Э́то институ́ты.
15. Э́то пля́жи.
16. Э́то плóщади.

9. 1. Гдé значки́?
2. Гдé ножи́?
3. Гдé платки́?
4. Гдé словари́?
5. Гдé сёстры?
6. Гдé отцы́?
7. Гдé звёзды?
8. Гдé ключи́?
9. Гдé óкна?
10. Гдé жёны?

10. 1. Мои́ сыновья́ учителя́.
2. Мои́ дóчери учи́тельницы.
3. Мои́ брáтья врачи́.
4. Мои́ сёстры студéнтки.
5. Мои́ друзья́ америкáнцы.

11. 1. Вóт нáши дéти.
2. Вóт нáши паспортá.
3. Вóт нáши стýлья.
4. Вóт нáши именá.
5. Вóт нáши дерéвья.

12. 1. рýсская молодёжь
2. мóдная одéжда
3. крáсные черни́ла
4. свéжая мали́на
5. желéзные пери́ла
6. чи́стая посýда
7. прия́тные духи́
8. сухи́е дровá
9. нóвые дéньги
10. весёлая детворá

13. 1. nominative
2. nominative
3. accusative
4. nominative
5. nominative
6. accusative
7. nominative
8. accusative
9. accusative
10. accusative
11. nominative
12. nominative
13. accusative
14. nominative

14. 1. журнáлы
2. компьютеры
3. пи́сьма
4. студéнтов
5. тетрáди
6. словари́
7. плáтья
8. свекрóвей

15. 1. литератýру
2. истóрию
3. брáта
4. собáку
5. преподавáтеля
6. задáние
7. рáдио
8. математи́ку
9. мáть
10. отцá

16. 1. nominative, accusative, genitive
2. nominative, genitive
3. nominative, genitive
4. nominative, accusative, genitive
5. genitive, nominative
6. accusative, genitive
7. nominative, genitive
8. nominative, genitive
9. accusative, genitive
10. nominative, genitive
11. accusative, genitive
12. nominative, genitive
13. nominative, genitive
14. accusative, genitive
15. genitive
16. nominative, genitive
17. nominative, genitive
18. accusative, genitive
19. nominative, genitive
20. nominative, genitive

17. 1. Э́то портфе́ль профе́ссора.
2. Э́то су́мка ма́мы.
3. Э́то кабине́т па́пы.
4. Э́то пода́рок го́стя.
5. Э́то пла́тье сестры́.
6. Э́то игру́шки дете́й.
7. Э́то маши́на отца́.
8. Э́то учёбники студе́нтов.
9. Э́то кварти́ра бра́тьев.
10. Э́то жёны друзе́й.
11. Э́то бра́т студе́нтки.
12. Э́то рома́н писа́теля.
13. Э́то да́ча дя́ди.
14. Э́то плато́к ба́бушки.
15. Э́то крова́ть ребёнка.

18. 1. пло́щадь Пу́шкина
2. у́лица Королёва
3. бульва́р Го́голя
4. теа́тр Мейерхо́льда
5. библиоте́ка Ге́рцена

19. 1. арти́стки
2. певца́
3. дете́й
4. ученико́в
5. враче́й

20. 1. маши́ны
2. обе́да
3. зада́ния
4. музе́я
5. литерату́ры

21. 1. но́чи
2. студе́нтки
3. мо́ря
4. ма́тери
5. люде́й
6. о́браза
7. друзе́й
8. писа́телей
9. гости́ниц
10. оши́бок

22. 1. Зде́сь не бу́дет гости́ницы.
2. Сего́дня не́т семина́ра.
3. Вчера́ в клу́бе не́ было конце́рта.
4. У меня́ сейча́с не́т вре́мени.
5. У нас вчера́ не́ было ле́кции.
6. Сего́дня в кла́ссе не́т Ви́ктора.
7. Вчера́ Серге́я не́ было до́ма.
8. За́втра не бу́дет роди́телей.
9. Сего́дня не бу́дет дождя́.
10. В ка́ссе теа́тра не́ было биле́тов.

23. 1. теа́тров
2. музе́ев
3. библиоте́ки
4. де́вушек
5. спа́льни
6. пи́сем
7. лаборато́рий
8. карандаше́й
9. ру́чек
10. челове́к

24. 1. са́хару/са́хара
2. мёду/мёда и я́блок
3. пирожко́в
4. су́пу/су́па
5. коньяку́/коньяка́
6. де́нег
7. ри́су/ри́са и овоще́й
8. фру́ктов
9. грибо́в
10. сы́ру/сы́ра и хле́ба

25. 1. Же́нщины не име́ли пра́ва го́лоса.
2. Фи́льм не произвёл впечатле́ния.
3. Она́ не ви́дела авто́буса.
4. О́н не пи́л спи́рта.
5. Студе́нт не по́нял отве́та.

26. 1. dative
2. accusative
3. dative
4. accusative
5. dative
6. accusative
7. dative
8. accusative
9. dative
10. dative

27. 1. сёстрам
2. друзья́м
3. чита́телям
4. гостя́м
5. слу́шателям
6. бра́тьям
7. матеря́м
8. дочеря́м
9. вну́кам
10. профессора́м

28. 1. сестре́
2. учи́телю
3. до́чери
4. вну́чке
5. врачу́
6. дя́де
7. го́стю
8. де́тям

29. 1. Де́тям на́до убира́ть ко́мнату.
2. Сестре́ мо́жно отдыха́ть.
3. Серёже нельзя́ гуля́ть сего́дня.
4. Пожилы́м лю́дям мо́жно входи́ть без о́череди.
5. Врачу́ на́до прописа́ть лека́рство.

30. 1. Ма́льчику не чита́ется.
2. До́чке не е́лось.
3. Певи́це не поётся.
4. Сы́ну сего́дня не игра́лось.
5. Тёте вчера́ не спало́сь.

31. 1. ме́лом
2. ру́чками
3. карандашо́м
4. ключо́м
5. платко́м
6. руко́й
7. па́льцем
8. глаза́ми
9. уша́ми
10. рука́ми

32.
1. стрелóй
2. хóром
3. грýппой
4. хлóпьями
5. ты́сячами
6. самолётом
7. тóном
8. ýлицей
9. трамвáем
10. бéрегом

33.
1. зимóй
2. вечерáми
3. нóчью
4. веснóй
5. ýтром
6. óсенью
7. днём

34.
1. журнали́стом
2. студéнтами
3. мáтерью
4. секретарём
5. тётей

35.
1. волнóй
2. гранáтой
3. вéтром
4. свéтом
5. маши́ной

36.
1. учи́телем
2. студéнткой
3. ветеринáром
4. врачóм
5. программи́стом
6. перевóдчицей
7. поэ́том
8. балери́ной
9. председáтелем
10. секретáршей
11. столи́цей
12. дуракóм
13. мáтерью
14. гéнием
15. герóем

37.
1. специали́стом
2. мéнеджером
3. Сóней
4. преподавáтелем
5. судьёй

38.
1. балéтом
2. футбóлом
3. гимнáстикой
4. красотóй
5. дóчерью
6. и́скренностью
7. кружкóм
8. кварти́рой
9. госудáрством
10. совéтами

39.
1. студéнтами
2. анги́ной
3. едóй
4. лесáми и озёрами
5. красотóй
6. шитьём

Chapter 3

1.
1. за
2. чéрез
3. в
4. чéрез
5. про
6. чéрез
7. чéрез
8. про
9. сквóзь
10. в

2.
1. по
2. по
3. с
4. по
5. о
6. с

3.
1. сýмку
2. дивáне
3. ры́нок
4. музéе
5. скамéйку
6. столé
7. шкáф
8. дáчу
9. пóлке
10. верáнде

4.
1. на
2. в
3. на
4. на
5. в
6. на
7. в
8. в
9. на
10. в
11. в
12. на
13. в
14. на
15. в

5.
1. угол
2. углóм
3. пóлку
4. скамéйку
5. кни́гой
6. крéслом
7. тýчу
8. нóсом
9. водóй
10. верáнду

6.
1. за
2. за
3. под
4. за
5. за
6. за
7. за
8. под
9. за
10. за
11. пóд
12. за

7.
1. Пóсле
2. прóтив
3. ми́мо
4. óколо
5. без
6. из-за
7. для
8. крóме
9. из-под
10. из-под
11. для
12. пóсле
13. óколо
14. из-за
15. прóтив

8.
1. до
2. из
3. с
4. от
5. у
6. из
7. от
8. из
9. от
10. из
11. у, от
12. из, с
13. до
14. с, до
15. от
16. у
17. от
18. у

9.
1. путём
2. рáди
3. свéрх
4. вмéсто
5. Ввидý
6. вне
7. врóде

10. 1. во́зле
2. вокру́г
3. вдо́ль
4. вблизи́
5. вну́трь
6. впереди́
7. внутри́
8. Ме́жду
9. Пове́рх
10. сза́ди
11. Среди́
12. Посреди́
13. напро́тив

11. 1. на, о
2. В, на
3. При
4. По
5. При
6. в
7. на, на
8. в
9. о
10. на
11. в
12. при
13. в
14. При
15. в
16. в
17. При
18. на
19. На, в
20. в

12. 1. к
2. по
3. по
4. к
5. Благодаря́
6. Вопреки́
7. к
8. Согла́сно
9. навстре́чу
10. по
11. к
12. по
13. по

13. 1. за
2. пе́ред
3. с
4. ме́жду
5. над
6. за
7. с
8. пе́ред
9. под
10. над
11. с
12. за
13. Ме́жду
14. с
15. над
16. под
17. за
18. с

Chapter 4

1. 1. ты́, Она́
2. Вы́, я́
3. вы́, Мы́
4. Они́
5. Они́
6. оно́
7. О́н

2. 1. его́
2. него́
3. него́
4. её
5. неё
6. и́х
7. ни́х
8. Его́
9. Её
10. неё
11. него́
12. на́с
13. меня́
14. тебя́
15. ва́с

3. 1. меня́
2. тебя́
3. его́
4. него́
5. неё
6. на́с
7. ва́с
8. ни́х

4. 1. о нём
2. обо мне́
3. о не́й
4. о ва́с
5. о ни́х
6. о тебе́

5. 1. Мы́ мно́го слы́шали о нём.
2. Де́ти говори́ли о ни́х.
3. О́н ча́сто ду́мает о не́й.
4. Она́ не забы́ла о нём.
5. Они́ спра́шивали о ни́х.

6. 1. ему́
2. и́м
3. е́й
4. тебе́
5. мне́

7. 1. Мы́ купи́ли ему́ велосипе́д.
2. Она́ подари́ла е́й ша́рф.
3. О́н пошёл к нему́.
4. Мы́ ча́сто ходи́ли в го́сти к ни́м.
5. О́н придёт к не́й.
6. Мы́ ча́сто ходи́ли по нему́.

8. 1. тобо́й
2. мно́й
3. ни́м
4. на́ми
5. ни́ми
6. ни́м
7. не́й
8. и́м
9. ни́ми
10. е́й

9. 1. себе́
2. собо́й
3. себе́, себя́
4. себя́
5. себя́
6. собо́й
7. собо́й
8. себе́
9. себе́
10. собо́й
11. себя́
12. себя́
13. собо́й
14. себе́
15. себя́

10. 1. дру́г с дру́гом
2. дру́г дру́га
3. дру́г дру́гу OR дру́г для дру́га
4. дру́г без дру́га
5. дру́г к дру́гу
6. дру́г на дру́га
7. дру́г за дру́га
8. дру́г на дру́га
9. дру́г от дру́га
10. дру́г к дру́гу

11. 1. ко́м
2. ке́м
3. кого́
4. Кого́
5. кого́
6. Кому́
7. кого́
8. Ке́м
9. кого́
10. кого́

12. 1. че́м 2. что́ 3. чего́ 4. Что́ 5. чего́ 6. что́ 7. что́ 8. Чего́ 9. Че́м 10. че́м

13. 1. моего́ 2. на́шими 3. твое́й 4. ва́шу 5. Чья́ 6. чьё 7. мое́й 8. чье́й 9. чьём 10. твоего́ 11. на́шем 12. твое́й

14. 1. своём, свое́й, Её 2. своему́, Его́ 3. своего́, своём 4. свои́, И́х 5. свое́й 6. Его́, свою́ 7. сво́й, Его́, своего́ 8. свое́й 9. своём 10. своя́ 11. свою́, её 12. свои́ 13. Её, свои́х 14. свое́й

15. 1. э́той, то́й 2. э́ти, те́ 3. э́том, то́м 4. э́то, то́ 5. Э́та, та́ 6. э́тим, те́м 7. Э́тот, то́т 8. э́тими, те́ми 9. э́тому, тому́ 10. э́то, то́

16. 1. то́т 2. те́ 3. те́ 4. то́т 5. то́т 6. та́

17. 1. бы́л 2. бы́ло 3. бы́ло 4. была́ 5. бы́ли 6. бы́л

18. 1. така́я 2. тако́й 3. таку́ю 4. тако́го 5. така́я 6. тако́й

19. 1. са́м 2. само́ 3. са́ми 4. саму́ 5. самого́ 6. само́й 7. сами́х 8. самому́ 9. само́й 10. само́м 11. сами́м 12. само́й 13. само́м 14. самого́

20. 1. са́мого 2. са́мой 3. са́мом 4. са́мого 5. са́мому

21. 1. Все́ 2. Всё 3. все́х 4. Все́ 5. все́м 6. все́х, все́ 7. всём 8. все́ми 9. все́х 10. все́

22.
1. Ка́к зову́т де́вушку, кото́рая прие́хала неда́вно из Новосиби́рска?
2. О́н живёт в до́ме, кото́рый нахо́дится в це́нтре го́рода.
3. Во́т иду́т ма́льчики, кото́рые у́чатся в шко́ле вме́сте с на́шим сы́ном.

23.
1. Я́ чита́л статью́, кото́рую рекомендова́л профе́ссор.
2. Ка́к называ́ется университе́т, кото́рый ты́ око́нчил?
3. Я́ зна́ю одного́ бизнесме́на, кото́рого зову́т Влади́мир Соро́кин.
4. На́ши сосе́ди нашли́ де́ньги, кото́рые ты́ потеря́л.
5. Вчера́ к на́м прие́хали друзья́, кото́рых мы́ давно́ не ви́дели.

24.
1. Я́ позвони́л дру́гу, от кото́рого я́ давно́ не получа́л письма́.
2. На́с помести́ли в све́тлую ко́мнату, о́кна кото́рой смо́трят на пля́ж.
3. О́н рабо́тает в институ́те, о́коло кото́рого стро́ят гости́ницу.
4. Ка́к фами́лия студе́нтки, роди́тели кото́рой живу́т в Росто́ве?
5. О́н подари́л е́й духи́, за́пах кото́рых е́й о́чень понра́вился.

25.
1. Ты́ чита́л кни́гу, о кото́рой я тебе́ говори́л?
2. Мы́ бы́ли на спекта́кле, в кото́ром уча́ствовала на́ша до́чь.
3. Сего́дня ко мне́ прие́дет дру́г, о кото́ром я тебе́ расска́зывал.
4. Че́рез воро́та Кремля́ прое́хал лимузи́н, в кото́ром е́хал президе́нт.
5. Та́м стро́ят общежи́тия, в кото́рых бу́дут жи́ть студе́нты.

26.
1. Они́ вы́шли из ле́са и уви́дели о́зеро, к кото́рому они́ направля́лись.
2. Как зову́т де́вушку, кото́рой я до́лжен переда́ть письмо́?
3. Во́т бе́рег, по кото́рому мы́ бе́гаем ка́ждое у́тро.
4. Вчера́ я сдава́ла экза́мен, к кото́рому я́ до́лго гото́вилась.
5. За́втра к на́м прие́дут друзья́, к кото́рым мы́ ча́сто е́здим.

27. 1. Я́ хочу́ познако́мить тебя́ с де́вушкой, с кото́рой я рабо́таю в институ́те.
2. Вдали́ мы́ уви́дели го́ры, ме́жду кото́рыми вила́сь доро́га.
3. Студе́нт подошёл к столу́, за кото́рым сиде́л экзамена́тор.
4. Мы́ подошли́ к теа́тру, пе́ред кото́рым тяну́лась дли́нная о́чередь.
5. Она́ вчера́ узна́ла результа́ты экспериме́нта, кото́рыми она́ о́чень дово́льна.

28. 1. како́й 2. како́м 3. каки́х 4. како́й 5. кака́я 6. како́м 7. каки́м 8. каки́е

29. 1. То́ 2. то́м 3. те́м 4. че́м 5. че́м 6. те́м 7. то́м 8. те́м 9. чему́ 10. тому́

30. 1. кого́ 2. кто́ 3. то́т 4. того́ 5. тому́

31. 1. кто́-нибудь, Кто́-то
2. каки́м-нибудь
3. кому́-то
4. кто́-нибудь, како́й-то
5. каки́е-нибудь, каку́ю-то
6. кому́-нибудь
7. кого́-то
8. кого́-нибудь
9. что́-нибудь
10. что́-то, како́й-то
11. че́й-нибудь
12. чью́-то

32. 1. Мне́ никто́ не нра́вится.
2. Его́ ничто́ не интересу́ет.
3. Я́ ничего́ не де́лаю.
4. Я́ ни к кому́ не иду́.
5. Я́ ни о ко́м не мечта́ю.
6. Она́ ниче́м не занима́ется.
7. О́н ни с ке́м не встре́тился.
8. Я́ ни у кого́ не была́.
9. О́н ничего́ не бои́тся.
10. Я́ ни к чему́ не гото́влюсь.
11. Они́ не согласи́лись ни на каки́е усту́пки.
12. Она́ не слу́шала ничьи́ сове́ты.
13. Меня́ никаки́е вопро́сы не интересу́ют.
14. Я́ не води́л ничью́ маши́ну.
15. Я́ ни на кого́ не наде́юсь.

33. 1. не́кого 2. не́ на что 3. не́чего 4. не́чем 5. не́кому 6. не́ с кем 7. не́ к кому 8. не́кому 9. не́ о чем 10. не́ за что

Chapter 5

1. 1. лени́вая 2. ста́рой 3. глу́пый 4. бе́лую 5. гру́стный 6. бы́строе 7. гру́бый 8. зло́бный 9. ску́чный 10. молчали́вый 11. серьёзные 12. чёрными 13. ста́рый 14. некраси́вая 15. гря́зной 16. неопря́тный

2. 1. ра́ннего, по́зднего
2. ли́шнего
3. сосе́дней
4. после́днему
5. Вече́рнюю
6. дома́шними
7. у́треннем
8. сего́дняшней
9. ве́рхнюю
10. зде́шних

3. 1. жа́ркие 2. вели́ким 3. широ́ким 4. таки́х дороги́х 5. я́ркое 6. высо́кими 7. плохи́е 8. сла́дкую 9. бли́зкими 10. до́лгой

4. 1. чужи́е 2. све́жим 3. горя́чее 4. хоро́шей 5. о́бщих 6. больши́м 7. мла́дшем 8. ры́жей 9. настоя́щей 10. рабо́чим 11. бу́дущему 12. бы́вшего

5. 1. Ча́й кре́пок.
2. Сове́т поле́зен.
3. Пробле́ма серьёзна.
4. Де́нь прекра́сен.
5. Пиджа́к коро́ток.
6. Стари́к бе́ден.
7. Слова́рь ну́жен.
8. За́работок ни́зок.
9. Зачёт лёгок.
10. Апельси́н сла́док.
11. Ребёнок умён.
12. За́л по́лон.
13. По́рции равны́.
14. Места́ свобо́дны.
15. Су́мка легка́.

6. 1. здорóвая, здорóва
2. занятóй, зáнят
3. больнáя
4. больнá
5. спокóйное, спокóйно

7. 1. малá
2. мáленькая
3. стáрые
4. стáрый, стáр
5. широкú
6. ширóкие
7. ýзкая, узкá
8. длúнные, длинны́
9. молодá, молодá
10. большóе, великó

8. 1. живáя
2. жúв
3. непрáвое
4. неправá
5. смешнóй
6. смешнó
7. ужáсны
8. ужáсный

9. 1. трýдная, труднá
2. богáт
3. довóльный, довóльна
4. достóин
5. достóйная
6. прéдан
7. прéданная
8. пóлный
9. пóлон
10. свобóдна
11. свобóдной
12. близкú
13. блúзкие
14. виновáт
15. виновáтыми
16. спосóбный, спосóбен
17. склóнен
18. склóнным
19. готóвых, готóвы
20. знакóмой, знакóмы
21. похóжи
22. похóжие
23. сильнá
24. сúльные
25. равнодýшна
26. равнодýшные
27. нормáльно
28. нормáльные
29. непонятно
30. непонятный

10. 1. Каковы́
2. Какúе
3. Такóго
4. тáк
5. Какóй
6. Таковó
7. Какóв
8. такóй
9. Кáк

11. 1. бýлочную
2. пивнóй
3. прóшлом
4. рýсской
5. больны́х
6. налúчными
7. учёного
8. морóженым
9. шампáнского
10. живóтных
11. воéнных
12. взрóслыми

12. 1. стáрого, нóвого
2. слáдкое
3. дорогóе
4. стáрое
5. зарабóтанное
6. смешнóго
7. óстренького
8. óстрого
9. горячего
10. необходúмое

13. 1. мáминой
2. пáпином
3. собáкину
4. Тáниного

14. 1. мéнее трýдную
2. бóлее интерéсного
3. бóлее дорогóй
4. вы́сшую
5. бóлее нóвых
6. бóлее серьёзных
7. стáршим
8. бóлее стáрые
9. лýчший
10. бóлее высóкую
11. мéньшей
12. бóлее молоды́е

15. 1. вы́ше
2. бóльше
3. дорóже
4. чáще
5. симпатúчнее
6. лýчше
7. вы́ше
8. лéгче
9. быстрée
10. хýже

16. 1. Россúя бóльше Китáя.
2. В Новосибúрске холоднée, чéм в Торóнто.
3. Ноябрь корóче октября.
4. Здéсь теплée в мáе, чéм в декабрé.
5. Жирáф вы́ше кенгурý.
6. Кúев дáльше Парúжа от США.
7. Нью-Йóрк мéньше Техáса.
8. Москвá старée Сáнкт-Петербýрга.
9. «Мерседéс» дорóже «Москвичá».
10. Байкáл глýбже Мичигáна.
11. Мёд слáще сóка.
12. Коньяк крéпче шампáнского.
13. Печáтать на компьютере удóбнее, чéм на пúшущей машúнке.
14. Éсть фрýкты полéзнее, чéм пúть кóка-кóлу.
15. Вóлга длиннée Днепрá.

16. Читáть по-рýсски лéгче, чéм говорѝть.
17. На дискотéке веселéе, чéм на лéкции.
18. На автóбусе éздить быстрéе, чéм на трамвáе.

17. 1. сáмое глубóкое
2. сáмая длѝнная
3. сáмых популя́рных
4. сáмом большóм
5. сáмым блѝзким

18. 1. Нью-Йорк—э́то крупнéйший морскóй пóрт.
2. В э́том ресторáне подаю́т вкуснéйшие пельмéни.
3. Сибирякѝ считáются здоровéйшими людьмѝ.
4. Горá Эверéст—э́то высочáйшая горá.
5. Владѝмир Петрóв—строжáйший учѝтель.

19. 1. мóдно
2. аккурáтно
3. верхóм
4. по-брáтски
5. по-другóму
6. по-рáзному
7. понимáюще
8. одобря́юще
9. по-китáйски
10. вслýх
11. по-человéчески
12. угрожáюще
13. по-прéжнему
14. осторóжно
15. интерéсно
16. умоля́юще
17. босикóм
18. по-дурáцки
19. раздражáюще
20. бодря́ще

20. 1. ýтром
2. давнó
3. тогдá
4. послезáвтра
5. позавчерá
6. Сначáла, потóм
7. тепéрь
8. сейчáс
9. лéтом
10. наконéц
11. Днём
12. скóро
13. веснóй
14. пóздно
15. срáзу
16. вóвремя
17. рáно, рáно

21. 1. навсегдá
2. дóлго
3. дóлго
4. давнó
5. надóлго

22. 1. всегдá
2. рéдко
3. обы́чно
4. иногдá

23. 1. ужé не
2. всё ещё
3. ужé
4. ещё не
5. ужé

24. 1. дóма
2. налéво, напрáво
3. откýда
4. внѝз
5. вездé
6. нарýжу
7. Снарýжи
8. отовсю́ду
9. навéрх
10. изнутрѝ
11. внѝз
12. назáд, вперёд
13. свéрху
14. внýтрь
15. сюдá
16. тáм, гдé
17. сзáди
18. впередѝ
19. домóй
20. слéва, спрáва

25. 1. тáк
2. óчень
3. мнóго
4. почтѝ
5. мáло
6. немнóго
7. совершéнно
8. чуть-чýть
9. совсéм
10. достáточно
11. слѝшком
12. слегкá

26. 1. кудá-нибудь
2. гдé-то
3. кáк-нибудь
4. почемý-нибудь
5. кудá-нибудь
6. кудá-нибудь
7. когдá-то
8. почемý-то
9. кáк-то
10. когдá-нибудь

27. 1. Вáм нéкуда пойтѝ сегóдня вéчером.
2. Я́ никудá не пойдý пóсле семинáра.
3. Вáм нéгде рабóтать.
4. Вы́ нигдé не бýдете рабóтать.
5. Емý нéзачем читáть э́ту кнѝгу.
6. О́н никáк не спрáвится с э́тим.

Chapter 6

1. 1. одѝн
2. однý
3. однѝ
4. однý
5. однóй
6. однóй
7. однá
8. однѝ
9. однóм
10. одногó

2. 1. двýм сыновья́м
2. трёх городáх
3. трѝдцать четы́ре студéнта, трѝдцать двá мéста
4. двýх мужчѝн, трёх жéнщин
5. двáдцать двá студéнта
6. двé библиотéки
7. четырёх километрах
8. трёх дéвушек
9. тремя́ дóчками
10. трём друзья́м

3. 1. но́вых рестора́на
2. ру́сских учёных
3. больши́е гости́ницы
4. свобо́дных ме́ста
5. иностра́нных студе́нта
6. студе́нческие столо́вые

4. 1. дву́х живы́х крокоди́лов
2. дву́м но́вым студе́нткам
3. трёх ча́йных ло́жек
4. двумя́ ру́сскими ма́льчиками
5. четырёх университе́тских общежи́тиях

5. 1. шестью́ ру́сскими тури́стами
2. се́мь тру́дных зада́ч
3. десяти́ но́вым ученика́м
4. пя́ть ча́стных университе́тов
5. двадцатью́ ста́рыми ко́шками
6. тридцати́ пяти́ хоро́шим друзья́м
7. ста́ небольши́х острова́х
8. трёхсот пяти́десяти о́пытных профессоро́в
9. двухсо́т пятна́дцати дождли́вых дне́й
10. пятисо́т сорока́ постоя́нных жи́телей

6. 1. десятью́ ты́сячами рубле́й
2. пятна́дцати ты́сяч посети́телей
3. два́дцать четы́ре ты́сячи студе́нтов
4. десяти́ ты́сячах ко́мнат
5. ста́ пяти́десяти ты́сяч до́лларов
6. двадцати́ миллио́нов сове́тских гра́ждан
7. девятьсо́т биллио́нов до́лларов

7. 1. шестьдеся́т де́вять рубле́й три́дцать три́ копе́йки
2. семна́дцать рубле́й ше́сть копе́ек
3. се́мьдесят рубле́й со́рок де́вять копе́ек
4. три́дцать три́ рубля́ во́семьдесят пя́ть копе́ек
5. во́семнадцать рубле́й се́мьдесят де́вять копе́ек

8. 1. семьсо́т со́рок два́ – но́ль но́ль – шестьдеся́т ше́сть
2. две́сти три́дцать де́вять – двена́дцать – де́сять
3. четы́реста со́рок четы́ре – во́семьдесят се́мь – но́ль де́вять
4. девятьсо́т девяно́сто три́ – но́ль три́ – три́дцать
5. пятьсо́т два́дцать оди́н – пятьдеся́т пя́ть – се́мьдесят се́мь

9. 1. пятёрку
2. деся́тку
3. деся́ток
4. шестёрку
5. семёрка
6. дво́йку

10. 1. О́бе
2. обо́их, обе́их
3. тро́е
4. дво́е
5. четверы́х
6. двои́х
7. тро́е
8. че́тверо
9. се́меро
10. семеры́х

11. 1. пе́рвом
2. второ́м
3. тре́тьей
4. пя́того
5. седьмо́м
6. девя́тую

12. 1. три́дцать втора́я глава́
2. семна́дцатый то́м
3. пятьдеся́т шесто́й ря́д
4. тре́тий кана́л OR тре́тья програ́мма
5. шестьдеся́т седьмо́й авто́бус
6. сто́ два́дцать пя́тое ме́сто

13. 1. полтора́ пирожка́
2. полторы́ мину́ты
3. полу́тора ты́сяч
4. полу́тора миллио́нах
5. полтора́ часа́

14. 1. три́ восьмы́х
2. но́ль це́лых, се́мь деся́тых OR но́ль и се́мь деся́тых
3. две́ це́лых и три́ пя́тых
4. четы́ре це́лых и одна́ восьма́я
5. одна́ четвёртая OR (одна́) че́тверть
6. две́ тре́тьих OR две́ тре́ти
7. четы́ре це́лых, пя́ть со́тых OR четы́ре и пя́ть со́тых

15. 1. но́ль два́дцать пя́ть ли́тра OR че́тверть ли́тра
2. но́ль три́дцать три́ ли́тра OR тре́ть ли́тра
3. но́ль пя́ть OR пол-ли́тра
4. но́ль се́мьдесят пя́ть ли́тра OR три́ че́тверти ли́тра
5. оди́н ли́тр
6. полкило́

16. 1. в пя́тницу
2. на бу́дущей/сле́дующей неде́ле
3. в про́шлую сре́ду
4. в э́тот/то́т ве́чер
5. весно́й
6. в ию́не
7. в э́том году́
8. в ма́рте э́того го́да
9. в декабре́ бу́дущего го́да
10. на э́той неде́ле
11. в про́шлом ме́сяце
12. днём OR во второ́й полови́не дня́
13. в бу́дущую суббо́ту
14. ле́том
15. в про́шлом ве́ке/столе́тии
16. про́шлой зимо́й

17. 1. седьмо́е ию́ня ты́сяча девятьсо́т девяно́сто восьмо́го го́да
2. шесто́го февраля́ ты́сяча девятьсо́т девяно́стого го́да
3. в ты́сяча девятьсо́т шестьдеся́т шесто́м году́
4. в восемьсо́т шестидеся́том году́ н.э.
5. с пя́того до двена́дцатого
6. два́дцать пе́рвое апре́ля
7. пя́того ию́ля две́ ты́сячи девя́того го́да
8. с пятна́дцатого сентября́

18. 1. Е́й два́дцать оди́н го́д.
2. Ему́ со́рок пя́ть ле́т.
3. Ско́лько ребёнку ме́сяцев?
4. Ско́лько ле́т ма́тери?
5. Ребёнку го́д и три́ ме́сяца.
6. Ему́ идёт шестна́дцатый го́д.
7. В како́м во́зрасте о́н у́мер?
8. О́н у́мер в (во́зрасте) се́мьдесят оди́н.

19. 1. Сейча́с се́мь часо́в утра́.
2. Сейча́с тре́тий ча́с.
3. ше́сть часо́в ве́чера
4. пятна́дцать мину́т девя́того OR четверть девя́того
5. в полови́не деся́того ве́чера OR полдеся́того ве́чера
6. в по́лночь
7. в три́ часа́ но́чи
8. без че́тверти ча́с
9. Сейча́с ча́с дня́.
10. без трёх четы́ре
11. без одно́й мину́ты де́сять
12. по́лдень

20. 1. ше́сть (часо́в) со́рок (мину́т)
2. во́семь (часо́в) три́дцать пя́ть (мину́т)
3. де́сять (часо́в) два́дцать (мину́т)
4. трина́дцать часо́в
5. пятна́дцать (часо́в) пятна́дцать (мину́т)
6. восемна́дцать (часо́в) пя́ть (мину́т)
7. два́дцать (часо́в) де́сять (мину́т)
8. два́дцать три́ (часа́) со́рок (мину́т)
9. но́ль часо́в (но́ль но́ль мину́т)
10. но́ль (часо́в) пятьдеся́т (мину́т)

Chapter 7

1. 1. слу́шает
2. собира́ю
3. реша́ет
4. за́втракаем
5. де́лаешь
6. мечта́ет
7. покупа́ет
8. игра́ет
9. обе́дают
10. вспомина́ем
11. гуля́ет
12. выступа́ет
13. отдыха́ем
14. рабо́тает
15. опа́здывает
16. занима́ется
17. чита́ю
18. обсужда́ют
19. получа́ем
20. объясня́ет
21. понима́ете
22. начина́ет
23. конча́ет
24. расска́зывает
25. спра́шивает

2. 1. бледне́ет
2. боле́ет
3. красне́ет
4. неме́ет
5. гре́ет
6. желте́ют
7. лысе́ет
8. сме́ешь
9. успе́ем
10. худе́ет
11. слабе́ет
12. робе́ешь
13. седе́ют
14. владе́ют
15. голубе́ет
16. здорове́ет
17. беле́ет
18. пусте́ют
19. пьяне́ет
20. жале́ю
21. полне́ет
22. весeléет
23. име́ете
24. реде́ют
25. богате́ют, бедне́ет

3. 1. организу́ют
2. тре́буете
3. импорти́рует
4. парку́ем
5. сове́тую
6. уча́ствует
7. ра́дуют
8. рису́ет
9. экспорти́рует
10. интересу́етесь
11. жа́луется
12. практику́ется
13. ремонти́руем
14. приватизи́рует
15. фотографи́руют
16. де́йствует
17. комбини́рует
18. реклами́рует
19. чу́вствую
20. путеше́ствуют
21. горю́ет
22. танцу́ют
23. сле́дует
24. копи́рует
25. рекоменду́ю

4. 1. тя́нет
2. па́хнет
3. отдохнём
4. га́снут
5. со́хнет
6. проснётся
7. пры́гнет
8. верну́сь
9. вы́кинет
10. вздохнём
11. ло́пнет
12. привы́кнете
13. ки́снет
14. мёрзну
15. кре́пнет

5. 1. поги́бли
2. поблёкли
3. дости́г
4. привы́кли
5. засну́л, замо́лкли
6. замёрзло
7. вздохну́ла
8. га́с
9. исче́з
10. па́хло
11. кре́пла
12. верну́лся
13. ру́хнула
14. рискну́л

6. 1. пи́шет
2. пря́чу
3. и́щет
4. ре́жут
5. ска́жете
6. ше́пчет
7. пла́чет
8. сви́щет
9. коле́блется
10. щеко́чет
11. дре́млет
12. вы́пишу
13. отка́жет
14. сы́плет

7. 1. ла́ет
2. та́ет
3. смею́сь
4. наде́емся
5. се́ет

8. 1. беру́
2. ржу́т
3. врёт
4. ждём
5. рвёт
6. лжёшь
7. зовёт
8. жрёт
9. деру́т

9. 1. передаёт
2. продаю́т
3. отстаёт
4. подаю́т
5. признаёт
6. преподаёт
7. сознаю́
8. отдаёт
9. узнаю́
10. устаёт
11. встаю́, раздаётся
12. остаётся

10. 1. ко́лет
2. бо́ремся
3. ме́лет
4. по́лют
5. по́рет

11. 1. хва́лит
2. ку́ришь
3. хожу́
4. но́сят
5. вожу́
6. говоря́т
7. у́чит
8. люблю́, ко́рмят
9. же́нится
10. ва́рит
11. плачу́
12. ло́вит, чи́щу

12. 1. зави́шу
2. те́рпит
3. лечу́, лети́шь
4. гори́т
5. храпи́т
6. свищу́
7. виси́т
8. шумя́т
9. ви́жу
10. боли́т

13. 1. стучи́т
2. слы́шу
3. молчи́т
4. держу́
5. дрожи́шь
6. кричи́шь
7. стоя́т
8. звучи́т
9. бои́тся
10. лежи́т

14. 1. хо́чет, хотя́т
2. хоти́те, хочу́
3. хоте́ла
4. бежи́шь, бегу́
5. бегу́т
6. бежи́м, хоти́м

15. 1. живём, живёт
2. плыву́, плывёт
3. слывёт

16. 1. наде́нешь
2. ста́нет
3. вста́ну
4. разде́нется
5. оде́немся

17. 1. мо́ет
2. откро́ю
3. ро́ет
4. закро́ете
5. но́ют

18. 1. шью́
2. льёт
3. вьёт
4. пьём
5. бьёт

19. 1. поёт
2. ду́ет
3. бре́ет
4. гниёт

20. 1. поймёт
2. возьму́
3. при́мет
4. отни́мет
5. займёт
6. наймём
7. начнёт
8. жмёт
9. жну́т
10. подни́мет
11. мнёт
12. сниму́

21. 1. тру́т
2. вы́тру
3. сотрёт
4. запрёт
5. отопрёт
6. умрёт

22. 1. ся́дет
2. скребёт
3. приобретёт
4. несли́
5. кладёшь
6. мёл
7. цвету́т
8. плёл
9. грёб
10. ползли́
11. ле́зла
12. трясу́т
13. спасло́
14. везла́
15. ведёт
16. упадёт

23. 1. ля́жет
2. бережёт
3. мо́жет
4. печёт
5. помо́жем
6. отвлечёт
7. стрижёт
8. обожгёт
9. течёт
10. привлечёт

24. 1. бу́дете де́лать
2. бу́дем смотре́ть
3. бу́дешь писа́ть
4. бу́ду рабо́тать
5. бу́дет изуча́ть
6. бу́дут реша́ть

25.
1. вы́пил
2. пригото́вила
3. реши́ли
4. нарисова́л
5. вы́учил
6. купи́ли
7. заплати́ла
8. отдохну́л
9. спроси́л
10. отве́тил

26.
1. собира́ет
2. запи́сывает
3. вызыва́ем
4. кладёт
5. берёт
6. говори́т
7. закрыва́ет
8. умыва́ет
9. и́щет
10. ло́вим

27.
1. привыка́ли, привы́кли
2. угова́ривал, уговори́л
3. сдава́ла, сдала́
4. лови́л, пойма́л
5. гото́вил
6. иска́л, нашёл
7. буди́ла, разбуди́ла

28.
1. посиде́ли
2. сиде́ла
3. гуля́ли
4. порабо́тал
5. рабо́тал
6. ду́мал
7. поду́мал

29.
1. запла́кала
2. пла́кала
3. пошёл
4. шёл
5. пошёл
6. запры́гали
7. пры́гали
8. рассерди́лась
9. услы́шали
10. слы́шали

30.
1. вста́л, встава́л
2. написа́ла, писа́ла
3. получи́ли, получа́ли
4. ко́нчила, конча́ла
5. испекла́, пекла́

31.
1. бу́ду объясня́ть, объясню́
2. прочита́ю, бу́ду чита́ть
3. бу́дет писа́ть, напи́шет
4. позвони́т, бу́дет звони́ть
5. сде́лаем, бу́дем де́лать

32.
1. (a) поднима́лись
   (b) подняли́сь
2. (a) принёс
   (b) приноси́л
3. (a) включа́л, включа́л
   (b) включи́л
4. (a) отдава́л
   (b) отда́л
5. (a) наде́л
   (b) надева́л

33.
1. отдыха́ли, отдохну́ли
2. собира́л, собра́л
3. переводи́л, перевела́
4. писа́л, написа́л
5. реши́л, реши́л

34.
1. simultancous
2. interrupted
3. sequential
4. interrupted
5. simultaneous
6. sequential
7. simultaneous
8. sequential

35.
1. (a) прочита́л, прочита́л
   (b) чита́л, чита́л
2. (a) купи́ла, купи́ла
   (b) покупа́ла, покупа́ла
3. (a) пока́зывала, показа́ла
   (b) показа́ла

36.
1. говори́л
2. поздра́вил
3. открыва́л
4. включа́л
5. де́лал

37.
1. объясня́ть
2. обе́дать
3. поза́втракать
4. позвони́ть
5. изуча́ть
6. посети́ть
7. встреча́ться
8. отвеча́ть
9. игра́ть
10. реша́ть
11. встава́ть
12. пи́ть

38.
1. расска́зывать
2. звони́ть
3. встреча́ться
4. смотре́ть
5. ста́вить
6. говори́ть

39.
1. объясня́ть
2. узнава́ть
3. бра́ть
4. вызыва́ть
5. зака́зывать
6. спра́шивать

40.
1. прочита́ть
2. чита́ть
3. е́сть
4. разбуди́ть
5. буди́ть
6. бра́ть
7. оставля́ть
8. опа́здывать
9. отдохну́ть
10. поня́ть
11. позвони́ть
12. смотре́ть
13. лови́ть
14. продава́ть
15. вы́учить

41.
1. подожди́
2. включи́те
3. нале́йте
4. наре́жьте
5. спо́йте
6. наде́ньте
7. откро́йте
8. заплати́те
9. вы́пейте
10. танцу́йте
11. отве́тьте
12. пригото́вьте

42.
1. Напиши́те, пиши́те
2. Скажи́те, Говори́те
3. Расскажи́те, расска́зывайте
4. Прочита́й, чита́йте

43.
1. не включа́йте
2. не пока́зывайте
3. не переводи́те
4. не расска́зывайте
5. не дава́йте
6. не узнава́йте
7. не закрыва́йте
8. не е́шьте

44.
1. Не звони́те
2. Не помога́йте
3. Не говори́те
4. Не покупа́йте
5. Не гото́вьте

45.
1. опозда́й
2. забу́дь
3. разбуди́
4. урони́
5. проле́й
6. возьми́те

46.
1. Дава́й вы́пьем за Са́шу.
2. Дава́й отдохнём.
3. Дава́й возьмём такси́.
4. Дава́й зака́жем ры́бу.
5. Дава́й подождём бра́та.
6. Дава́й потанцу́ем.
7. Дава́й рабо́тать у́тром.
8. Дава́й погуля́ем в па́рке.
9. Дава́й сиде́ть и говори́ть.
10. Дава́й игра́ть в те́ннис.
11. Дава́й пое́дем в Москву́.
12. Дава́й съеди́м кусо́к пирога́.

47.
1. дава́й не бу́дем убира́ть
2. дава́й не бу́дем пе́чь
3. дава́й не бу́дем вытира́ть
4. дава́й не бу́дем обе́дать

48. *Names may vary.*
1. пусть Ле́на вы́моет
2. пусть Па́ша запла́тит
3. пусть Та́ня ся́дет с ма́мой
4. пусть Ва́ня откро́ет
5. пусть Са́ша споёт

49.
1. Е́сли за́втра бу́дет до́ждь, мы́ бу́дем сиде́ть до́ма.
2. Е́сли ты́ не оде́нешься быстре́е, опозда́ем на конце́рт.
3. Е́сли ты́ и́м позвони́шь, они́ бу́дут о́чень ра́ды.
4. Е́сли вы́ придёте к на́м, я приготу́влю вку́сный обе́д.
5. Е́сли у меня́ бу́дет вре́мя, я тебе́ помогу́.
6. Е́сли у на́с бу́дут де́ньги, мы́ ку́пим но́вую маши́ну.

50.
1. Е́сли бы она́ пришла́, я бы поговори́л с не́й.
2. Е́сли бы на́ши друзья́ позвони́ли, мы́ бы пригласи́ли и́х в го́сти.
3. Е́сли бы о́н захоте́л смотре́ть фи́льм, мы́ пошли́ бы в кино́.
4. Е́сли бы мы́ пригласи́ли его́, о́н пришёл бы на вечери́нку.
5. Е́сли бы ты́ проси́л меня́, я бы купи́л буты́лку вина́.

51.
1. Е́сли бы фи́льм ко́нчился в де́вять часо́в, мы́ бы встре́тились с ва́ми.
2. Е́сли бы о́н попроси́л, я бы обяза́тельно помо́г ему́.
3. Е́сли бы мы́ успе́ли купи́ть биле́ты, мы́ бы пошли́ смотре́ть конце́рт.
4. Е́сли бы вы́ сказа́ли на́м доро́гу, мы́ бы пое́хали туда́.
5. Е́сли бы о́н сде́лал все́ упражне́ния, о́н смо́г бы пойти́ в кино́.
6. Е́сли бы у меня́ бы́ло вре́мя, я бы ва́м позвони́л.

52.
1. Я́ бы хоте́л чита́ть но́вый рома́н Пеле́вина.
2. Я́ бы рекомендова́л ва́м сходи́ть на э́ту вы́ставку.
3. Я́ бы сове́товал ва́м поговори́ть с нача́льником.
4. Что́ вы́ бы хоте́ли посмотре́ть по телеви́зору?
5. Како́й слова́рь ты́ бы сове́товал мне́ купи́ть?

53.
1. Я́ бы вы́пил стака́н холо́дного пи́ва.
2. Я́ бы поспа́л немно́го.
3. Я́ бы послу́шал хоро́шую рок-му́зыку.
4. Я́ бы пое́л сала́т «Столи́чный».
5. Я́ бы пое́хал на мо́ре.

54.
1. Помо́г бы ты́ е́й реши́ть зада́чу.
2. Посмотре́л бы ты́ э́тот но́вый францу́зский фи́льм.
3. Убра́л бы ты́ свою́ ко́мнату.
4. Послу́шал бы ты́ мо́й но́вый ди́ск.
5. Поговори́л бы ты́ с ни́м об э́том.

55.
1. Я́ посове́товал дру́гу, что́бы о́н бро́сил кури́ть.
2. Ми́ша попроси́л меня́, что́бы я купи́л ему́ газе́ту.
3. Мы́ уговори́ли дру́га, что́бы о́н пое́хал отдыха́ть на мо́ре.
4. Я́ попроси́л бра́та, что́бы о́н помо́г мне́.
5. Учи́тель посоветова́л ученика́м, что́бы они́ слу́шали внима́тельнее.

56.
1. перевести́
2. перевёл
3. посмотре́ли
4. показа́ть
5. поздоро́ваться
6. могла́

57.
1. Хорошо́ (бы́ло) бы отдыха́ть в Евро́пе.
2. Ва́жно, что́бы вы́ ко́нчили докла́д.
3. На́до, что́бы о́н отве́тил на письмо́.
4. То́лько бы о́н нашёл рабо́ту!
5. Бы́ло бы у меня́ бо́льше вре́мени.

58. 1. мо́ется
2. мо́ет
3. мо́ется
4. оде́лась
5. одева́ет
6. оде́ла
7. одева́ться
8. причёсывает
9. причёсывалась
10. причёсывает

59. 1. ви́делись
2. ви́дел
3. уви́димся
4. встреча́лись
5. встре́тил
6. поцелова́лся
7. поцелова́ла
8. обняли́сь
9. познако́мил
10. познако́мились

60. 1. обра́довало
2. обра́довались
3. беспоко́ит
4. беспоко́ится
5. интересу́ют
6. интересу́ется
7. волну́юсь
8. волну́ет
9. се́рдится
10. се́рдит
11. удиви́ли
12. удиви́лись

61. 1. Тру́дные зада́чи реша́ются студе́нтами в э́той гру́ппе.
2. Опро́с прово́дится социо́логами в э́том институ́те.
3. Матрёшки покупа́ются тури́стами.
4. Контро́льные рабо́ты проверя́ются преподава́телями.
5. Вся́кие ве́щи продаются у́личными торго́вцами.

62. 1. Мето́дика преподава́ния изуча́ется на э́той ка́федре.
2. Но́вая карти́нная галере́я открыва́ется в го́роде.
3. Сво́дка пого́ды передаётся по Второ́й програ́мме в 21.00.
4. Рабо́та э́того а́втора публику́ется впервы́е в э́том журна́ле.
5. В Росси́и кни́ги Аку́нина чита́ются с больши́м интере́сом.

63. 1. идём, хо́дим
2. шли́
3. идёт, хо́дит
4. е́ду, е́зжу
5. бежи́шь, бегу́
6. бе́гаешь, бе́гаю
7. ходи́ли
8. бе́гать, ходи́ть
9. пла́вает, пла́вает
10. е́здили
11. плывёт, плывёт
12. лета́л
13. лечу́, лети́шь
14. е́здил
15. е́хал
16. иду́т
17. иду́т
18. идёт

64. 1. несу́т
2. везу́т
3. несу́т
4. ведёт
5. несёт
6. везу́т
7. несёт
8. везёт
9. несу́т
10. везёт

65. 1. во́зит
2. везли́
3. во́дит
4. вёл
5. но́сит
6. несёт
7. во́дит
8. вёл
9. но́сит
10. ношу́

66. 1. е́хала, пое́хала
2. е́хала, пое́хала
3. пое́хала
4. шли́, пошли́
5. шли́, пошли́
6. плы́л, поплы́л
7. плы́л, поплы́л
8. понёс
9. нёс

67. 1. попла́вали, поплы́ли
2. полета́ли, полете́ли
3. походи́ли, пошли́
4. побе́гали, побежа́ли

68. 1. уходи́ли
2. ушёл
3. уезжа́л
4. уе́хала
5. подходи́л
6. подошёл

69. 1. Де́вушка, кото́рая живёт в кварти́ре 7, у́чится в МГУ.
2. Кни́ги, кото́рые лежа́т на столе́, не мои́.
3. Молодо́й челове́к, кото́рый занима́ется марке́тингом, хо́чет нача́ть своё де́ло.
4. Профе́ссор, кото́рый чита́ет ле́кцию, неда́вно прие́хал из Москвы́.
5. Студе́нты, кото́рые реша́ют э́ту зада́чу, о́чень у́мные.

70. 1. А́втор, кото́рый написа́л э́ту кни́гу, получи́л пре́мию.
2. Ма́льчик, кото́рый помо́г тебе́, мо́й мла́дший бра́т.
3. Челове́к, кото́рый перевёл э́ту кни́гу, отли́чный перево́дчик.
4. Я́ сего́дня познако́мился с челове́ком, кото́рый вы́рос в моём родно́м го́роде.
5. Учени́к, кото́рый ушёл ра́но с уро́ка, пло́хо себя́ чу́вствовал.

71. 1. Зада́ча, кото́рую реша́ет студе́нт, тру́дная.
2. Учи́тель, кото́рого лю́бят все́, вы́шел на пе́нсию.
3. Собы́тия, кото́рые опи́сывают в э́той статье́, происходи́ли давно́.
4. Това́ры, кото́рые произво́дят на э́том заво́де, высо́кого ка́чества.
5. Ве́чер, кото́рый организу́ют студе́нты, бу́дет о́чень интере́сный.

72. 1. Я́ чита́л интере́сную кни́гу, кото́рую написа́л э́тот журнали́ст.
2. В э́той кни́ге мно́го краси́вых фотогра́фий, кото́рые сде́лал а́втор.
3. Я́ ви́дел фотогра́фию портре́та, кото́рый написа́л э́тот худо́жник.
4. Э́тот музе́й нахо́дится в зда́нии, кото́рое постро́или в девятна́дцатом ве́ке.
5. Я́ рассказа́л ему́ о письме́, кото́рое мы́ получи́ли вчера́.
6. В аудито́рии мы́ нашли́ су́мку, кото́рую кто́-то забы́л.

73. 1. Э́ту исто́рию давно́ забы́ли.
2. Телегра́мму получи́ли в суббо́ту.
3. Вы́ставку откры́ли на про́шлой неде́ле.
4. Рабо́ту сде́лали хорошо́.
5. До́м постро́или в про́шлом ве́ке.

74. 1. Когда́ она́ занима́ется аэро́бикой, …
2. Когда́ друзья́ возвраща́лись домо́й из кинотеа́тра, …
3. Когда́ студе́нты выходи́ли из аудито́рии, …
4. Когда́ о́н рабо́тает на компью́тере, …
5. Когда́ мы́ жи́ли в Москве́, …

75. 1. Та́к как они́ хоте́ли что́-нибудь съе́сть, …
2. … та́к как наде́ялись найти́ потерянную су́мку.
3. Та́к как я́ не понима́ю ру́сского языка́, …
4. Та́к как я́ не име́л де́нег, …
5. Та́к как о́н встава́л ра́но, …

76. 1. Е́сли ты́ бу́дешь та́к волнова́ться, …
2. Е́сли вы́ бу́дете изуча́ть иностра́нные языки́, …
3. Е́сли вы́ бу́дете путеше́ствовать по ра́зным стра́нам, …
4. Е́сли вы́ бу́дете занима́ться му́зыкой, …

77. 1. Когда́ о́н умы́лся, …
2. Когда́ она́ зако́нчила рабо́ту, …
3. Когда́ учи́тель вошёл в ко́мнату, …
4. Когда́ она́ заперла́ две́рь, …
5. Когда́ ба́бушка испекла́ пиро́г, …

Chapter 8

1. 1. И Жа́нна и Ма́ра занима́ются ру́сским языко́м.
2. Моя́ сестра́ говори́т и по-ру́сски и по-испа́нски.
3. Ве́чером студе́нты и смо́трят телеви́зор и слу́шают му́зыку.
4. Мы́ пригласи́ли к себе́ и А́нну и Ива́на.

2. 1. Мари́на не лю́бит ни фру́ктов ни овоще́й.
2. Ле́том мы́ не е́здили ни в го́ры ни на пля́ж.
3. Э́та де́вушка ни говори́т ни чита́ет по-англи́йски.
4. Слова́ э́той пе́сни ни краси́вые ни интере́сные.
5. Ве́чером я́ не писа́ла ни пи́сем ни упражне́ний.

3. 1. На у́жин у на́с бу́дет су́п и́ли сала́т.
2. Мо́й бра́т хо́чет купи́ть чёрные джи́нсы и́ли си́ние брю́ки.
3. Купи́ мне́ пожа́луйста, журна́л и́ли газе́ту.
4. Возьми́те и́ли молоко́, и́ли лимона́д.
5. На́ш сы́н хо́чет ста́ть и́ли космона́втом, и́ли президе́нтом.

4. 1. Ба́бушка хорошо́ понима́ет по-англи́йски, но не чита́ет по-англи́йски.
2. Мои́ сёстры лю́бят танцева́ть, но я не люблю́ танцева́ть.
3. Ве́чером мы́ переводи́ли статью́, но не ко́нчили переводи́ть её.
4. Вади́м поéдет на Ура́л и его́ брат то́же поéдет туда́.
5. Э́то дли́нный рома́н, но о́чень интере́сный.
6. В э́том рестора́не хле́б о́чень вку́сный и су́п то́же о́чень вку́сный.

5.

1. contrastive	6. contradictive
2. contradictive	7. contradictive
3. contradictive	8. contrastive
4. contrastive	9. contradictive
5. contrastive	10. contradictive

6.

1. и	6. и
2. а (OR и)	7. и
3. но	8. и
4. а	9. но
5. но	10. а

7. 1. Когда́ (*While*) друзья́ возвраща́лись домо́й, они́ разгова́ривали обо всём.
2. Когда́ (*After*) друзья́ верну́лись домо́й, они́ легли́ и усну́ли.
3. Когда́ (*While*) мы́ проща́лись, мы́ кре́пко обнима́лись.
4. Когда́ (*After*) мы́ прости́лись, я́ пошёл домо́й.
5. Когда́ (*While*) Ма́ша смотре́ла ста́рые фотогра́фии, она́ вспомина́ла про́шлое.
6. Когда́ (*After*) Ма́ша посмотре́ла переда́чу, она́ вы́ключила телеви́зор.

8. 1. По́сле того́ как де́ти поза́втракали, они́ пошли́ в шко́лу.
2. По́сле того́ как ма́ма пригото́вила обе́д, она́ позвала́ на́с се́сть за сто́л.
3. По́сле того́ как Андре́й сда́л экза́мен, о́н пошёл с подру́гой в кафе́.
4. По́сле того́ как ко́нчилась телепереда́ча, ребя́та на́чали слу́шать но́вый ди́ск.
5. По́сле того́ как оте́ц ко́нчил писа́ть докла́д, о́н ста́л отдыха́ть.

9. 1. На́до зако́нчить ку́рс ру́сского языка́ до того́ как пое́дешь в Росси́ю.
2. На́до мы́ть ру́ки пе́ред тем как обе́дать.
3. На́до бри́ться пе́ред тем как уйти́ на рабо́ту.
4. На́до ко́нчить э́ту рабо́ту до того́ как уе́хать в о́тпуск.
5. На́до чи́стить фру́кты пе́ред тем как и́х е́сть.
6. На́до вы́ключить све́т пе́ред тем как уйти́ из ко́мнаты.

10. 1. Мы́ зде́сь бу́дем стоя́ть до тех пор, пока́ магази́н не откро́ется.
2. Ребёнок пла́кал до тех пор, пока́ ма́ма не покорми́ла его́.
3. Ви́ктор реша́л зада́чи до тех пор, пока́ о́н не уста́л.
4. Ребя́та загора́ли на пля́же до тех пор, пока́ ста́ло хо́лодно.
5. О́н пи́л пи́во до тех пор, пока́ о́н не напи́лся.

11. 1. Прошло́ полтора́ ме́сяца с тех пор как Па́влик купи́л маши́ну.
2. Прошло́ три́ го́да с тех пор как они́ перее́хали в но́вый до́м.
3. Прошло́ ше́сть ме́сяцев с тех пор как роди́лся ребёнок.
4. Прошло́ полтора́ го́да с тех пор как мы́ получи́ли письмо́ от Ли́и.

12. 1. Пётр бы́стро реши́л э́ту тру́дную зада́чу, потому́ что о́н хорошо́ зна́ет матема́тику.
2. Ле́на сего́дня о́чень уста́ла, потому́ что она́ не вы́спалась.
3. Ди́ма спеши́л, потому́ что о́н опа́здывал на ле́кцию.
4. Серёжа пошёл в библиоте́ку, та́к как о́н до́лжен верну́ть кни́гу.
5. Лари́са не была́ на заня́тиях, потому́ что она́ была́ больна́.

13. 1. Экску́рсия была́ отмснсна́ из-за того́, что вы́пал большо́й сне́г.
2. О́н выполня́ет свою́ рабо́ту в сро́к благодаря́ тому́, что о́н о́чень организо́ванный челове́к.
3. Проду́кты испо́ртились из-за того́, что они́ не храни́лись в холоди́льнике.
4. Хоро́шие результа́ты бы́ли дости́гнуты благодаря́ тому́, что бы́л применён но́вый ме́тод.
5. Она́ хорошо́ зако́нчила университе́т благодаря́ тому́, что она́ усе́рдно рабо́тала.

14. 1. Па́па сказа́л, что Ми́ша звони́л домо́й.
2. Па́па сказа́л, что́бы Ми́ша звони́л домо́й.
3. Я́ понима́ю, что ты́ сказа́л пра́вду.
4. Мы́ хоте́ли, что́бы ты́ сказа́л пра́вду.
5. Мы́ зна́ем, что́ ты́ сказа́л.
6. Ма́ша включи́ла телеви́зор, что́бы смотре́ть фи́льм.
7. Ма́ша включи́ла телеви́зор, что́бы мы́ смотре́ли фи́льм.

15. 1. Я́ ви́дел, как о́н пришёл.
2. Я́ ви́дел, что о́н пришёл.
3. Мы́ слы́шали, как она́ пе́ла.
4. Мы́ заме́тили, что о́н ушёл.

16. 1. О́н опозда́л на авто́бус, та́к что о́н реши́л взя́ть такси́.
2. Мо́й дру́г до́лго жи́л в Ки́еве, та́к что о́н хорошо́ зна́ет э́тот го́род.
3. Э́то о́чень просто́й те́кст, та́к что я́ его́ бы́стро перевёл.
4. Я́ уже́ прочита́л газе́ту, та́к что я́ да́л её сосе́ду.
5. Я́ зна́л, что она́ лю́бит рок-му́зыку, та́к что я́ пригласи́л её на рок-конце́рт.

17. 1. Хотя́ мы́ угова́ривали его́, о́н не согласи́лся.
2. Е́сли сне́г пойдёт, мы́ бу́дем ката́ться на лы́жах.
3. Хотя́ ему́ предложи́ли большу́ю зарпла́ту, о́н не согласи́лся на э́ту рабо́ту.
4. Е́сли все́ уста́нут, мы́ остано́вим рабо́ту.
5. Хотя́ все́ уста́ли, мы́ продолжа́ли рабо́тать.

18. 1. О́н ведёт себя́ та́к, как обы́чно.
2. О́н ведёт себя́, как бу́дто ничего́ не случи́лось.
3. Пого́да была́, как э́то ча́сто быва́ет в а́вгусте, жа́ркая и вла́жная.
4. Пого́да в ма́е была́ жа́ркая и вла́жная, как бу́дто ле́то уже́ наступи́ло.

Bibliography

Dictionaries

Apresyan, Yu. D. (and E. M. Mednikova for Vol. 1) (eds.). 1993–94. *Новый большой англо-русский словарь,* 3 vols. Moscow: Русский язык.

Avanesov, R. I. (ed.). 1988. *Орфоэпический словарь русского языка,* 4th ed. Moscow: Русский язык.

Chernyshev, V. I. et al. (eds.). 1950–65. *Словарь современного русского литературного языка,* 17 vols. Moscow: Академия наук СССР.

Lubensky, S. 1995. *Russian-English Dictionary of Idioms.* New York: Random House.

Ozhegov, S. I. 1968. *Словарь русского языка,* 7th ed. Moscow: Советская энциклопедия.

Wheeler, M. et al. (eds.). 2000. *The Oxford Russian Dictionary,* 3rd ed. Oxford: Oxford University Press.

Wilson, E. A. M. 1982. *The Modern Russian Dictionary for English Speakers.* Oxford and Moscow: Pergamon Press and Russky yazyk.

Grammars and Grammar Texts

Baranova, N. et al. 1985. *Russian Stage Two.* Moscow: Russky yazyk.

Bogojavlensky, M. 1981. *Russian Review Grammar.* Columbus, OH: Slavica.

Borras, F. M. and R. F. Christian. 1971. *Russian Syntax: Aspects of Modern Russian Syntax and Vocabulary,* 2nd ed. Oxford: Clarendon Press.

Davis, P. A. and D. V. Oprendek. 1997. *Making Progress in Russian,* 2nd ed., revised by A. B. Bronstein and A. I. Fleszar. New York: John Wiley & Sons.

Martin, C. and I. Sokolova. 1993. *Russian Stage Two* (American Edition). Dubuque, IA: ACTR and Kendall/Hunt.

Nakhimovsky, A. D. 1985. "An Overview of Russian Conjugation" (a grammar supplement contained in S. Paperno et al., *Intermediate Russian: The Twelve Chairs.* Columbus, OH: Slavica).

Nakhimovsky, A. D. and R. L. Leed. 1987. *Advanced Russian,* 2nd ed., revised. Columbus, OH: Slavica.

Offord, D. 1996. *Using Russian: A Guide to Contemporary Usage.* Cambridge: Cambridge University Press.

Pulkina, I. M. and E. M. Zakhava-Nekrasova. 1977. *Учебник русского языка,* 6th ed. Moscow: Русский язык.

Shvedova, N. Yu. et al. (eds.). 1980. *Русская грамматика,* 2 vols. Moscow: Наука.

Timberlake, A. 2004. *A Reference Grammar of Russian.* Cambridge: Cambridge University Press.

Townsend, C. E. 1981. *Continuing with Russian.* Columbus, OH: Slavica.

Unbegaun, B. O. 1967. *Russian Grammar.* Oxford: Clarendon Press.

Wade, T. A. 2000. *A Comprehensive Russian Grammar.* Oxford: Blackwell.

Other Works on Russian Language and Linguistics

Babby, L. H. 1993. "A Theta-Theoretic Analysis of -en- Suffixation in Russian." *Journal of Slavic Linguistics* 1, pp. 3–43.

Babby, L. H. 1994. "A Theta-Theoretic Analysis of Adversity Impersonal Sentences in Russian." In *Formal Approaches to Slavic Linguistics* 2, The MIT Meeting. Ann Arbor: Michigan Slavic Publications, pp. 25–67.

Bondarenko, B. S. 1961. *Предлоги в русском языке.* Moscow: Учпедгиз.

Brecht, R. D. and J. S. Levine. 1985. "Conditions on Voice Marking in Russian." In *Issues in Russian Morphosyntax* (UCLA Slavic Studies, Vol. 10, ed. by M. S. Flier and R. D. Brecht. Columbus, OH: Slavica, pp. 117–35).

Channon, R. 1975. "The Single-Stem Verb System Revisited." *Slavic and East European Journal* 19, pp. 112–22.

Comrie, B. 1976. *Aspect.* Cambridge: Cambridge University Press.

Gerhart, G. 1995. *The Russian's World.* 2nd ed. revised. Fort Worth: Harcourt Brace.

Gerritsen, N. 1990. *Russian Reflexive Verbs: In Search of Unity in Diversity* (Studies in Slavic and General Linguistics, Vol. 15, ed. by A. A. Barentsen et al.). Amsterdam: Rodopi.

Hamilton, W. S. 1980. *Introduction to Russian Phonology and Word Structure.* Columbus, OH: Slavica.

Hart, D. K. 1996. *Topics in the Structure of Russian.* Columbus, OH: Slavica.

Jones, C. and James S. Levine. 2002. "Russian V + *šč-* Adjectives and Adverbs." *Journal of Slavic Linguistics* 10, pp. 213–50.

Levine, J. S. and C. Jones. 1996. "Agent, Purpose, and Russian Middles." *Journal of Slavic Linguistics* 4, pp. 50–75.

Matveeva, V. M. and R. E. Nazarian. 1972. *Пособие по развитию навыков устной речи.* Leningrad: Издательство Ленинградского университета.

Muravyova, L. S. 1975. *Verbs of Motion in Russian.* Moscow: Русский язык.

Nichols, J. 1981. *Predicate Nominals: A Partial Surface Syntax of Russian* (University of California Publications in Linguistics, Vol. 97). Berkeley and Los Angeles: University of California Press.

Rassudova, O. P. 1984. *Aspectual Usage in Modern Russian.* Moscow: Русский язык.

Ryazanova-Clarke, L. and T. Wade. 1999. *The Russian Language Today.* London and New York: Routledge.

Timberlake, A. 1986. "Hierarchies in the Genitive of Negation." In *Case in Slavic,* ed. by R. D. Brecht and J. S. Levine. Columbus, OH: Slavica, pp. 338–60.

Timofeeva, G. G. 1995. *Новые английские заимствования в русском языке.* St. Petersburg: «Юна».

Index of Russian Words and Affixes

This index contains the vast majority of words that occur in *Schaum's Outline of Russian Grammar.* It is intended to provide ready access to specific Russian words and to affixes (prefixes, suffixes, and endings). Included are the major parts of speech, and all pronouns, adverbs, prepositions, and conjunctions are listed. All nouns and adjectives that appear in illustrative tables in the book, and others that are grammatically significant, are listed below in their nominative singular form. All verbs deemed to have special grammatical importance are listed, including all verbs that govern an oblique case (the dative, genitive, or instrumental), verbs that are followed by a preposition + case, verbs representative of each type of suffixed and nonsuffixed stem, and verbs that have an irregular conjugation. In addition, this index includes numerals, particles, participles, acronyms, and quantifying words.

General Index